Palgrave Studies in Economic History

Series Editor
Kent Deng, London School of Economics, London, UK

Palgrave Studies in Economic History is designed to illuminate and enrich our understanding of economies and economic phenomena of the past. The series covers a vast range of topics including financial history, labour history, development economics, commercialisation, urbanisation, industrialisation, modernisation, globalisation, and changes in world economic orders.

Jordi Catalan Vidal
Editor

Crises and Transformation in the Mediterranean World

Lessons from Catalonia

palgrave
macmillan

Editor
Jordi Catalan Vidal
University of Barcelona
Barcelona, Spain

ISSN 2662-6497 ISSN 2662-6500 (electronic)
Palgrave Studies in Economic History
ISBN 978-3-031-24501-5 ISBN 978-3-031-24502-2 (eBook)
https://doi.org/10.1007/978-3-031-24502-2

Cover credit: "Art Nouveau work in the Cemetery of the coastal town of Arenys de Mar. Picture by the editor"

This Palgrave Macmillan imprint is published by the registered company Springer Nature Switzerland AG
The registered company address is: Gewerbestrasse 11, 6330 Cham, Switzerland

To Manuel Ardit, Pere Pascual and Francesc Valls in Memoriam

Contents

List of Contributors

Manuel Ardit University of Valencia, Valencia, Spain

Jordi Catalan Vidal University of Barcelona, Barcelona, Spain; Centre d'Estudis Jordi Nadal, University of Barcelona, Barcelona, Spain

Pere Pascual i Domènech University of Barcelona, Barcelona, Spain

Josep Maria Salrach Institut d'Estudis Catalans, Barcelona, Spain

Àlex Sánchez Universtiy of Barcelona, Barcelona, Spain

Francesc Valls-Junyent Universtiy of Barcelona, Barcelona, Spain

List of Figures

List of Tables

CHAPTER 1

Introduction: The Conversion of the Mediterranean into a World Centre, Its Crises and the Formation of the Late Mediaeval Commercial Empires

Jordi Catalan Vidal

Since prehistory, men and innovations had flowed from East to West for centuries along the Mediterranean and had transformed its economies and societies. Later commercial city-states emerged on the shores of the Inner

The author is grateful for the financial support of the Ministry of Science and Innovation of the Spanish Government (MCIN/AEI/https://doi.org/10.13039/501100011033), and of the European Regional Development Fund of the European Union (ERDF) (*A way of making Europe*) through project PGC2018-093896-B-I00, "Mediterranean Capitalism? Successes and Failures of Industrial Development in Spain, 1720–2020". He also thanks to the Generalitat de

J. Catalan Vidal (✉)
University of Barcelona, Barcelona, Spain
e-mail: jordi.catalan@ub.edu

J. Catalan Vidal (ed.), *Crises and Transformation in the Mediterranean World*, Palgrave Studies in Economic History,
https://doi.org/10.1007/978-3-031-24502-2_1

Sea and reinforced this process favoured by the low sea transport costs. Several of them became maritime empires or *thalassocracies*.

The most successful Mediterranean empire was Rome, which transformed the Mare Nostrum into a remarkable world centre. The Roman legions, their ports and roads, and their currency, succeeded in creating an integrated single market, which promoted rapid growth of the basin, leading to a real golden age of exchanges and economic development between 149 BC and 164 AD.

The former interconnected system subsequently experienced several structural crises, which led to a long-term depression which did not bottom out until the eighth century. The first Carolingians endeavoured to recreate the Western Roman Empire without succeeding in a lasting manner. The Roman and Carolingian heritage was, however, decisive in the formation of the Catalan counties starting from the ninth century.

Mediterranean trade again prospered between the ninth and the thirteenth centuries, driven by the north-western part of the Mare Nostrum and especially by the dynamism of the merchant republics of northern Italy, which had a paramount role in the Commercial Revolution. Barcelona, at the forefront of the Catalan counties first, and of the Crown of Aragon subsequently, attempted to replicate the path of development of the Italian late-medieval *thalassocracies*. Valencia, much later, also tried to imitate this path. Both towns of the Crown of Aragon and a few more (such as Perpignan or Mallorca) on a smaller scale, became remarkable players in the transformation of the Mare Nostrum during the late Middle Ages.

Catalunya, and the Centre d'Estudis Jordi Nadal of the University of Barcelona, which contributed to support the publication of this chapter in several ways. Last but not least, he is very thankful to Doctor Andreu Ginés who helped with the edition and to Doctor Raimon Soler, who decisively contributed to produce Map 1.1. The possible errata are the exclusive responsibility of the author.

1.1 The Formation of a World Centre, c 9000 BC–164 AD

The Mediterranean slowly developed for several millennia before becoming an important world centre. The territories bathed by the Great Sea formed an extremely complex system, with economic, social and cultural dichotomies. Compared with primitive settlements of traditional societies and successive waves of peoples from the steppes, the Inner Sea basin witnessed the emergence of dazzling new civilizations, which acted as a driving force for change. The transfer of innovations and the exchanges between societies were frequently accompanied by destructive military conflicts and, occasionally, dramatic epidemic outbreaks.

For millennia, the sea was cheaper than land transport, greatly helping many of the inventions of the East to reach the West by way of the Mare Nostrum. Men, new products and techniques from the East, which were much more advanced at the time, spread by sea. Occasionally, seafaring towns with demographic surpluses also founded colonies, thus accelerating the changes, in interacting with the populations of the receiving territories.

The most radical transformation probably took place more than 11,000 years ago with the Neolithic Revolution, which according to some authors was a response to an early crisis of growing food scarcity within the hunting and gathering societies derived from population expansion (Bellwood, 2005; Boserup, 1965; Cipolla, 1962; Cohen, 1977; Diamond, 1997). One of its outstanding centres was the Fertile Crescent, the south-western tip of which bordered the Great Sea. The domestication of animals, such as goats, sheep and cattle, and the harvesting of cereals and legumes, favoured the transition from nomadic hunting and gathering communities to more sedentary societies of shepherds and farmers.

A pioneering site seems to have been Karavac mountains (North Euphrates), where the domestication of einkorn wheat might have taken place for the first time. Eynan, today in Upper Israel, was harvesting and milling cereals around 10,000 BC. Farther south, Jericho appeared as one of the earliest settlements surrounded by walls in 8000 BC. In Anatolia, Çatal Hüyük, with a population of about 10,000 might have been one of the largest urban settlements around 7000 BC (Abulafia, 2011; Bairoch, 1985; Bryce, 2009; Hararai, 2014; Heun et al., 1997).

Migrations from Anatolia brought cereals and lentils to Crete, where civilization developed since 7000 BC. An urban society flourished on this island, which obtained olive oil, melted bronze, manufactured ceramics, built palaces and invented the pottery's weel (Finley, 1970; Spawforth, 2018). Its maritime orientation led Thucydides to consider Minos Crete as the first *thalassokratia* (Abulafia, 2011, 2014; Mollat du Jourdin, 1993). The diffusion of these critical innovations of the Neolithic Revolution reached the western Mediterranean around 5000 BC (Diamond, 1997).

Knossos also let us an amazing heritage of clay tablets, recording ancient Greek alphabet and hierographical scripture. About half of them are related with textile production. In fact, a few Cretan urban settlements were pioneer cases of towns exporting textiles and ceramics, and exchanging them by grain imports with a great extractive empire: Egypt was its main market and supplier (Postrel, 2020).

Early cuneiform scripture in clay tablets has been dated for 4200 BC Sumerian towns. These precursor records of scripture refer to property accounts, common in Lower Mesopotamia. Such a key innovation was linked to the emergence of Uruk, a relatively large urban settlement on the banks of the Euphrates. The expansion of human settlements with a few thousand of inhabitants in the region favoured the division of labour and the emergence of no agrarian activities and linked urbanization to the development of writing and accounting.

Since 3000 BC, a few extractive empires emerged in the hinterland of the eastern Mediterranean. Their economy was based on agriculture and the surplus generated allowed them to maintain elites of warriors, priests and even artists. These societies were governed with an iron fist from a position of hereditary authority. Although a considerable part of the surplus was generated by the free peasants, these theocratic monarchies used slave labour. The most significant case in view of how long it lasted and its formidable cultural wealth was pharaonic Egypt. Among many other key legacies, the Nile empire conceived the hieroglyph scripture and the papyrus. This latter invention would become a remarkable mean of saving and transmitting information along the Mare Nostrum for centuries. However, the Egyptian economy was extremely dependent on the high variability of Nile floods and periodic drought and famine led to the reinforcement of centralizing institutions such as the temple, which imposed its strong authority on cultivators (Manning, 2018; Muhs, 2016; Vallejo, 2019; Warburton, 1997).

Moreover, other theocratic empires from antiquity with these characteristics ended up converging on the eastern Mediterranean, such as Acadians, Assyrians, Babylonians and Hittites. Acadians annexed the Sumerian towns, where the early cases of scripture and accountancy of agricultural records were discovered. The Babylonian empire used the clay tablets as means of payment, developing one of the first precedents of fiduciary money. The Hittites dominated the melting of tin, copper and iron, and are credited for the early diffusion of iron arms, tools and jewels into the Inner Sea. The Assyrian kings Sargon II and Ashurbanipal created the pioneer and most reputed library of the early Antiquity (Abulafia, 2011; Bryce, 2009; Diamond, 1997; García Morá, 2018).

Temples and palaces in Bronze Age Near East are also credited for inventing key innovations for the development of entrepreneurship since 3000 BC: not only clay tablets used as money, but also weights, measures, land-leasing, account keeping, annual reports and credit (in beer). Moreover, the most urbanized parts of these societies were forced to promote export textiles in order to pay for metals, stone and wood lacking in southern Mesopotamia (Hudson, 2010).

Together with the previous situation with considerably hierarchized societies of priests, warriors and agrarian workers with an authoritarian political centre, from the continental interior, cities arose not far away on the same shore of the sea which focused on navigation, trade and manufacturing (*thalassocracy*, following Thucydides). In around 3000 BC, Byblos may have been the biggest port of the Mare Nostrum, housing between 15,000 and 30,000 inhabitants. It participated in foreign trade with cedar wood and Egyptian papyrus. Somewhat farther south Tyre emerged, famous for the production of purple dye, obtained from the murex shellfish. Ugarit, Sidon, Arvad and Jericho can be considered other examples of cities of Canaan. The Greek tablets written in the Lineal B system used the term *phoenikios* as early as around 1300 BC. However, the diffusion of the denomination of Phoenicians, the name which the Greeks gave to some of the Canaan inhabitants, might be more recent and, quite possibly, related with the red colour of their dyes (Bairoch, 1985; Quinn, 2018; Sherratt, 2016; Woolmer, 2017).

The dualism between autocratic empires of shepherds, farmers and warriors versus federated commercial and manufacturing cities was a recurrent characteristic in the long-term development of the Mediterranean basin until the industrial revolution and, on occasions, the cross-fertilization between these two types of social and economic organization drove transformation (Mollat du Jourdin, 1993; Seabright, 2004). Another crucial innovation was undoubtedly the alphabet. The first alphabetical engravings were found in the Sinai Peninsula and appear to have been produced by Semitic workers from Egypt in around 1850 BC. The Phoenicians were pioneers in standardizing their alphabet and disseminated it throughout the Mediterranean. The Greek and the Aramean alphabet come from the Phoenician alphabet. Furthermore, the Latin alphabet comes from one of the western Greek alphabets, that of Cumae.

Greece was precisely another Mediterranean territory that was organized in the form of free cities. Argos and Athens appear to be almost as old as Byblos. There is archaeological evidence of the cultivation of vines in Greece from 4000 BC. Between 1500 and 1250 BC, Mycenae and Piros emerged as dynamic cities, exporting copper products and ceramics as far as the Canaanites harbours, Egypt and the Italian peninsula (Abulafia, 2011; Finley, 1970; Spawforth, 2018).

The Minoan towns seem to have collapsed around 1425 BC. The origins of the crisis are controversial: drought derived from changing climatic conditions such as volcano eruption and tsunamis or invasion of more violent peoples such as the Achaeans or other so-called Sea Peoples. The certain fact is that the Minoan hieroglyphic language writing was replaced by the Linear B script typical of the Greeks (Bryce, 2009; Finley, 1970; Manning, 2018; Spawforth, 2018).

Another more remarkable structural crisis might have taken place around 1270, when hungry peoples from the sea or the steppes seem to have attacked outstanding ports and inner towns of the Eastern Mediterranean Basin. Invasions of peoples such as the Philistines or even intestine wars between the Achaeans themselves, would have ended with previous centuries of progress and transformation. Mycenae, Pyros, Troy and Ugarit, among others, were destroyed. Egypt abandoned the Nile delta as an effect of the attacks by pirates and peoples from the sea. The Hittite empire collapsed and its capital Hattusa was destroyed, under the invasion of Sea Peoples (Abulafia, 2011; Akurgal, 1986; Bryce, 2009; Finley, 1970; García Morá, 2018; Spawforth, 2018). However, it must be added that there are scholars who defend that the decadence of towns such as Mycenae or Pylos was, above all, the result of the restructuring of Mediterranean exchange. Cyprus merchants outstand as exporters of bronze goods, ceramics and, even iron, and conquered the markets previously dominated by Greek towns (Sherratt, 2016).

On the other hand, Phoenicians seem to have resisted far well the pressure of the Sea Peoples and the growing competitiveness of Cyprus towns. Phoenician towns, and particularly Tyre, intensified their interest in Mediterranean West. They used the woods of Mount Lebanon for building new ships, such as the trireme. They traded with wood, jewels, glassware, precious stones and purple fabrics and contributed to diffuse to the West the accounting techniques and the commercial practices conceived in southern Mesopotamia They crossed the Pillars of Hercules several times. In their expansion towards the West, they founded cities such as Carthage and, beyond Hercules columns, Gadir. However, instead of building a centralized state, Phoenician towns organized themselves as city-states or commercial and industrial communities with rather weak links among them (Abulafia, 2011, 2014; Aubet, 1993; Bairoch, 1985; Hudson, 2010; Mollat du Jourdin, 1993; Quinn, 2018; Sherratt, 2016; Spawforth, 2018; Woolmer, 2017).

The Hellenic cities began to re-emerge from the collapse of Mycenaean civilization around 1050. Since then remarkable examples of Greek ceramics can be found both in the peninsula and the islands. The government of kings during the ninth to the eighth centuries BC was followed by aristocratic regimes, dominated by the nobility. Seafaring merchants contributed to the diffusion of Near East techniques among the Greeks (Abulafia, 2011; Finley, 1970; Hudson, 2010; Sherratt, 2016; Spawforth, 2018).

The first rebellion against the nobility took place in the seventh century in Corinth, which became a pioneering commercial centre straddling the Aegean and Ionian seas. The Corinthian *thalassokratia* stood out in shipbuilding, manufacture of ceramics and textiles, melting of bronze, and export of wine and olive oil (Abulafia, 2011).

In the same century, the citizens of Sparta formed an assembly with the right to decide on the proposals of the council of elders and the constitution granted voting rights to the Hoplites. Representative institutions appeared in Chios starting from the sixth century. Chios, like Samos, consolidated itself as an exporting centre of Greek wine. Other islands, such as Euboea, exported wood, olive oil and ceramics, as well (Abulafia, 2011). In fact, all the Hellenic towns were located less than 100 kilometres far away from the sea (Spawforth, 2018). Most of them used to export their manufactured goods and complement their food and raw material needs with imports. The expansion of commercial exchange went in hand with the development of proto-democratic institutions.

In 594 BC, Solon, in Athens, banned the debt bondage of small tenants and created the assembly of citizens (*ekklesia*), which integrated the less wealthy owners into the city's government and chose its magistrates by means of a draw. Around 508, Clistenes granted the citizen to all free adult males of the surroundings of Athens, organizing the election of representatives of the different tribes which composed the town (Anderson, 1979; Finley, 1970; Spawforth, 2018).

It should, however, be taken into account that, although the modest farmers were represented by the government of Greek cities, a large part of the surplus, which made it possible to achieve the milestones of the classical golden age in philosophy, geometry, astronomy and the fine arts, was generated by resorting to slave labour (Anderson, 1979; Finley, 1963). Moreover, although the Greek cities had an undeniable democratic basis, they were not exempt from imperialist trends. Towards the mid-fifth century BC, Athens may have already had some 35,000 inhabitants and can be considered as another *thalassokratia* (McEvedy, 2011; Mollat du Jourdin, 1993). It led an imperial system integrating around 200 cities (the league of Delos), which contributed financially to guaranteeing its defence. In 454 Athens moved the treasury of the confederation from its original site in the island of Delos to the town of Attica, making unmistakably, its imperial hegemony. But in 404 the military power of Athens was definitively stopped by a more successful collation of Greek *polis*, headed by Sparta.

An even more aggressive model was the empire built by the Macedonian disciple of Aristotle, Alexander. His military campaigns subjugated Athens itself, defeated the Persians in 333 and even reached the Indus. After his death in 323, his generals founded Hellenistic kingdoms in the Mediterranean East. As a result, Alexandria and Antioch would become remarkable actors at the Great Sea. In addition, Greece also expanded to the West in a more peaceful way, founding new commercial colonies such as Syracuse, Neapolis, Cyrene and Massalia, which became the focal points of civilization on central Mediterranean.

It was not only the alphabet or representative democracy which arose in the eastern Mediterranean and spread along its shores with the creation of western colonies by Phoenicians and Greeks. In the western part of Anatolia, by around 620 BC, there is evidence of the emergence of another decisive innovation for long-term economic development, the minting of coins (Akurgal, 1986; Spawforth, 2018). Lydia appears to have preceded China and India, minting coins in electrum, gold and silver.

The Lydians were also a people of traders, who exported slaves, wine, saffron, electrum itself (a natural alloy of gold and silver), onyx and mica. They controlled the exchange routes between the Mediterranean and the East and became a naval power on the Aegean Sea. They punished idleness and favoured child labour. Although they were governed from Sardis by hereditary monarchs with an imperialist vocation, their contact with the Ionian Greeks from Asia Minor led them to respect representative governments in cities under their control, such as Ephesus or Miletus. The latter town was, precisely, the first Greek town where a coin was struck. The Lydians likewise used tablets with monetary value, as the Babylonians. In any case, the mere invention of metal currency with the royal seal converted them into an important hub of exchange, until their king Croesus was defeated by emperor Cyrus II and his country was annexed by the Persia in 545 BC (Akurgal, 1986; Bryce, 2009; García Mora, 2018).

Thalassocracies based its power in trade, manufacturing and shipping, whereas extractive empires resorted mainly to military aggression, land conquests and forced agrarian labour. But, as we have already seen, commercial city-states were never exempt of imperialist temptations, in particular when the ambition of their generals became overwhelming (Seabright, 2004).

Another particularly successful thalassocracy was Carthage, a city-state of Phoenician origin. It developed the production of olive oil, wine, ceramics and jewelry. It built shipyards, traded with all the West Mediterranean neighbours, founded commercial enclaves and even explored the Atlantic coast of Africa. It seems that its harbour had dozens of docks. Its caravans crossed the Sahara and came back with gold and ivory. A part from minting copper coins, they used fiduciary money in form of leather bills. Carthage also created a proto-democratic political system with a senate, a supreme court integrated by one hundred judges and a government of two annually elected *sufetes*. As time went on, the thalassocracy of Punic origin, created its own empire by colonizing the West Mediterranean islands, from Malta to Ibiza, including Corsica, Sardinia and Sicily. In the latter clashed with the Greek expansion to the West. After decades of recurrent wars, Syracusians stopped the expansion of the Punics in the largest island of the Mettle Sea, defeating them in the battle of Himera (480 BC) and crippling the power of Carthage there (Aubet, 1993; Aubet & Sanmartí, 1996; Montanelli, 1957; Quinn, 2018; Spawforth, 2018).

A city with an explicit republican vocation sacked its last king in 509 BC. Rome ended up building the empire which took control of the entire Mediterranean basin and became the decisive civilizing centre of its western half. With an even greater use than that of eastern societies, the Republic progressed with slave labour, the supply of which increased as it conquered new territories, in particular since the Punic Wars. In the sixth century BC, Rome had replaced the monarchy with a political system of limited pluralism or aristocratic democracy. The owners of large estates and patrician clans controlled the Senate, which was reproduced by client co-option. Consuls and, in a second moment, tribunes were elected in assemblies by the citizens. Although the former was originally of patrician origin, the electorate was later extended to the ordinary people, the *plebs*. The republican city-state gradually annexed Italian territories as it imposed itself on Latins, Etruscans, Samnites and Greeks (Beard, 2016; De Martino, 1980; Spawforth, 2018).

Central Italy usually cast bronze pieces. Rome issued the *aes grave* for the first time around 298 BC (Sear, 1988). It was a rather heavy bronze coin, with a weight close to a Roman pound (327 gr). However, when the Republic fostered trade with the Greek towns of southern Italy it required lighter and more worthy pieces, more similar to the silver coins used in Magna Graecia, and began to mint the Roman *didrachm*, cast also in silver (De Martino, 1980).

Once the Republic began to watch the sea, it clashed with another hegemonic force, which had also emerged as a city-state and evolved into an empire: Carthage. In 241 BC, the Romans, who had annexed Magna Graecia and subjected Syracuse, ended up conquering Sardinia and Corsica and the whole of Sicily as a result of the First Punic War.

Starting in 236, Punic troops invaded southern Iberia, which was rich in underground resources, particularly silver. The Carthaginians took control of former Tartessos and founded Quart Hadasht (Cartagena) in 227. Its general Hannibal Barca, destroyed the Iberian city of Arse (Sagunt), which was an ally of Rome in 219. He planned to defeat Rome by land and marched North to the Italian peninsula, crossing the Pyrenees and the Alps until, victorious, he reached Lake Trasimeno in 217. Rome counter-attacked, sending Gnaeus Cornelius Scipio to Iberia in 218. On landing in the Greek colony of Emporion (Empúries), he began the Roman occupation of Hispania. Postponing the final attack on Rome, Hannibal came back to defend his motherland and was defeated by Publius Cornelius Scipio, later Africanus, during the Battle of Zama in 202, thus concluding the Second Punic War.

Around 212, Rome minted its first denarii (De Martino, 1980; Kay, 2014). The denarius originated as an almost pure silver coin, with a weight of about 4.5 grams and a value of 10 asses. It was strongly influenced by the drachma and its multiples, which had been produced in Neapolis and other cities of Magna Graecia. The denarius and dividers such as the sestertius became the basis of the Roman monetary system for more than five centuries and, as the legions advanced, it became the reference currencies in the whole of the Mare Nostrum. The Republic counted in asses, sestertii and denarii. The denarius was the outstanding mean of payment for big transactions in the Mediterranean, driving exchanges throughout the territories bathed by the Great Sea. Bronze and copper coins were currently used for small payments. The sestertius was also minted in silver. 4 sestertii amounted to 1 denarius. Sestertii were also used in day-to-day small transactions and they were referred as *nummus*, as well, a term of Greek origin, which was used as means of account. Republican Rome also launched gold coins, as the aureus, but these were seldom minted. Gold performed the role of store value, whereas silver and copper were the usual means of payment (Bernardi, 1970; De Martino, 1980; Kay, 2014; Temin, 2017).

The cost of the Second Punic War resulted so high that Rome was forced to partially finance it through devaluation. The contents of silver of the denarius went down from 4.5 to 3.9 grams (Bernardi, 1970; Kay, 2014). Such a change would imply a devaluation of the denarius against silver of about 14%. It can be considered as a rather moderate debasement.

With the Carthaginians weakened and Iberia occupied as far as Gadir, the Roman republic began to covet the wealthy East. The Hellenistic empire of the Seleucid Antiochus III the Great was defeated by Lucius Cornellius and Publius Cornellius Scipio at Magnesia ad Sipylum in 188, opening the door to Latin control of the former Lydia, then called Asia. Oriental treasures flew to the Tiber capital and were saved under Juno's Temple. During the first half of the second century BC, Rome experienced a tremendous inflow of bullion derived from repeated booties and sustained war indemnities that defeated rivals (Carthaginians above all) paid.

Rome became so healthy that taxes on land ownership were suppressed in the capital of the empire in 167 BC (Beard, 2016; Kay, 2014). Moreover, since the 150s BC the silver mines near Cartago Nova and other locations in Southern Hispania began to be exploited by their new masters and contributed to an additional flow of bullion which complemented reach booties, war indemnities and punitive taxes paid by the occupied territories (Kay, 2014).

The Third epilogue of the wars against Carthage led to the complete destruction of the Punic town in 149 and the sale of its survivors as slaves. Rome likewise subjected Carthage's ally, Macedonia, and converted it into a Roman province in 148. After some years, silver from Macedonian mines also contributed to finance the empire, which intensified its aggressive policy. Rome defeated Corinth in 146. After the successful military campaigns and the amazing pillage of Eastern treasures, the denarius was revalued against bronze and became worth 16 asses in 141.

Moreover, the Roman victories in the Punic and Oriental wars amazingly increased the supply of slaves and radically transformed Mediterranean agriculture. Large states based on massive use of slave labour and orientated to cereal farming and grey breeding emerged in the Italian and Iberian peninsulas, in Sicily and Northern Africa. Roman colonies flourished everywhere to reward former legionaries and increase the amount of land owned by senators. Since the mid-second century, the north-western part of the Roman empire could be considered a full slave economy (Anderson, 1979; De Martino, 1980; Espluga, 1998; Kay, 2014).

The defeat of the most dangerous rivals around the Great Sea tended to foster maritime trade to supply the Italian Peninsula, which become an enormous market, importer of slaves, grain and luxuries. In exchange, the Italian states provided wine and olive oil to the most remote places of the empire and beyond (Kay, 2014).

Attalus III, king of Pergamon and an ally of Rome, left his kingdom to the Republic in his will. Meanwhile, the Roman conquests made progress in inland Iberia and North Africa. During 117, Gallia Narbonensis was also annexed. At the end of the second century BC, Rome had already planted roots on three continents and the Mediterranean was being transformed into the Roman Sea.

Gnaeus Pompeus conquered Syria and Cyrenaica and Julius Caesar annexed Gaul and Numidia. The two former triumvirs ended up confronting each other in Hispania, with the triumph of the latter. Caesar's campaigns led him to increase the salary of his legionnaires and to pay them 225 denarii per year, although he likewise reduced the weight of the denarius to 3.9 grams (De Martino, 1980; Vagi, 1999). Devaluation was again used due to the demands of an expansive fiscal policy. However, whereas gold coins were rarely struck during the Republican period, Caesar began to mint the aureus more often, with a standard content of about 8.2 gold grams. The value of one aureus was 25 denarii. After his assassination, the new triumvirate also finished in war, with the definitive victory of Octavius against Marcus Anthony, who was defeated at Actium. The former annexed Egypt and gradually buried the Tiber Republic.

Some authors have maintained that Rome recorded an early economic and social crisis between 133 and 30 BC (Comín, 2011; Turching & Nefedov, 2009), pointing at the slight decrease of the population of the Italian Peninsula. Undoubtedly, it was a period of political turmoil with agrarian conflicts and civil wars, which led to the end of the Republic in the Octavian era. The sources record critical episodes as an agrarian crisis in 133 BC and a financial recession in 88 BC, but these lasted just a few years (Kay, 2014). Moreover, even previously to the Augustus dominium, iron men such as Pompey undertook military naval successful expeditions against piracy, and contributed to making the Inner Sea much more save for exchange and promoted trade and development (Black, 2020).

Nevertheless, the key issue is that the size of the empire was dramatically expanding and, therefore, its capacity to extract tributes and surplus to subjugated peoples. The estimations of minted silver coin, measured in denarii, suggest a multiplication by tenfolds of the denarii struck between 157 and 80 BC (Kay, 2014). Such a dramatic increase of the money supply could have produced sharp inflation. However, there is no evidence of heavy inflationist tension in this period. Therefore, as Kay suggests, the sustained increase in money supply had to promote the real expansion of output. In fact, if we use as an indicator of the performance of trade along the Great Sea, the recorded number of Mediterranean shipwrecks, commercial maritime exchanges might have tripled between the third and first centuries BC (Parker, 1992).

The revealed pattern which shows Fig. 1.1 allows us to confirm the existence of an extremely remarkable long cycle of rise and decline of Mediterranean exchange which experienced its golden age between the second century BC and the second century AD. The only significant structural crises would take place later. Moreover, though very controversial, there is no doubt that the size of the own town of Rome was rocketing. It is certain that the number of recipients of wheat rations increased from 15,000 under Julius Caesar (59 BC–44 BC) to 200,000 under Augustus (27 BC–AD 14) (McEvedy, 2011). At Augustus' time, the eternal city may have already reached between 200,000 and slightly more than one million inhabitants (Beard, 2016; Beloch, 1937–1961; Brunt, 1971; Gibbon, 1776–1778; Maddison, 2007; McEvedy, 2011; Russell, 1958).

Octavian, transmuted into *princep inter pares* and Augustus, governed throughout the whole Mare Nostrum. The High Empire was mainly financed with the treasures and properties captured from the conquered peoples and with donations from the big landowners who controlled the colonies founded all around the sea. Provinces had to transfer significant annual tributes. Sicily, Africa and Sardinia paid annual tithes on grain, which sometimes could be doubled (*altera decima*) (De Martino, 1980, Maddison, 2007). Asia and Greece used to pay in cash tributes (*stipendium*). Hispania and Macedonia transferred the metals of their

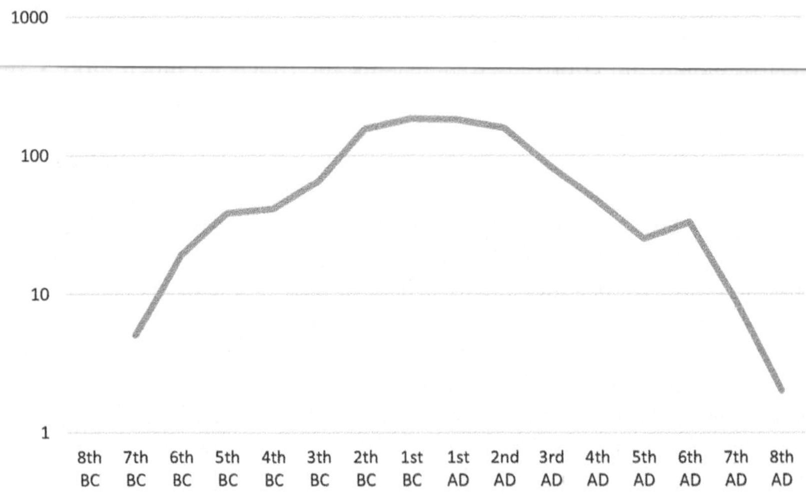

Fig. 1.1 The rise and fall of Mediterranean exchange, 7th BC–8th AD (measured with the number of shipwrecks) (*Source* Own elaboration with Parker [1992])

mines. According to classical sources, only in the mines of Carthago Nova, there were around 40,000 men working for Rome (De Martino, 1980, Kay, 2014). Additional levies taxed production (*uicesima*), inheritances (*hereditatium*), and coronation (*aurum coronarium*). Indirect levies taxed the transit of goods (*portorium*), and the freeing of slaves (*libertatis*) (Bernardi, 1970; Ripollés, 1996).

However, Nero had to bear the exceptional expense of the reconstruction of Rome, following its fire. He decided to resort to devaluation of the silver coins again: the weight of the denarius was reduced to the equivalent of 3.4 grams (a devaluation of about 12% since the defeat of Hannibal). The gold contents of the aureus also decreased from about 7.7 grams under Tiberius to around 7.3 grams under Nero (De Martino, 1980).

The empire reached one of its record dimensions at the beginning of the second century of our era, under the reign of Traianus. Roma then annexed Dacia, Arabia, Armenia and Mesopotamia. The second century AD was relatively quiet until the middle of the century, when a period of bad harvests began, which has been attributed to the end of the Roman Climatic Optimum and the beginning of a period of greater volcanic eruptions and less solar insolation. Above all, in 165, the so-called Antonine Plague began to attack the empire (Harper, 2017; Maddison, 2007).

However, between the destruction of Carthage in 149 BC and the pandemic which attacked in 165 of our era, the Mediterranean experienced three centuries of absolute Roman hegemony, converting it into a true world centre. The new order imposed by the former city-state favoured institutional homogenization and the emergence of an integrated economic system along its shores. Although the former republic, transmuted into a highly hierarchized empire, experienced intermittent wars within its borders, conflicts between its generals, the uprising of subjected nations (such as Judea) and several slave rebellions, the gradual pacification of the sea, the construction of an extensive ports and road network and the common monetary system favoured the emergence of exchanges throughout the Mare Nostrum.

The metropolis of Rome and other big cities of the basin (such as Alexandria, Antioch, Smyrna and Carthage) formed an immense market importing slaves, cereals, wine, olive oil, salted fish and meat, spices, wood, iron, lead, tin, silver, marble, silk, purple dye, linen, gems, glass, ceramics and textiles, and gradually grew as the *Pax Romana* became consolidated (De Martino, 1980; Felice, 2015; Lo Cascio, 2007; Lo

Cascio & Malanima, 2005; Maddison, 2007; Kay, 2014; Temin, 2017; Rostovtzeff, 1926). The ports and the roads equipped for the legions to pass facilitated exports of many of these goods from the far corners of the empire, which tended to specialize in accordance with their competitive advantages. Similarly, the payment of the legions and the allies favoured the dissemination of metal currency and its local minting, which in turn stimulated trade. Although the denarius and the other Roman currencies experienced the now slight trend towards depreciation initiated by Julius Caesar, actual exchanges increased, driven by a growing internal market, which would reach more than 40 million potential consumers (Beloch, 1937–1961; Brunt, 1971; Frier, 2000; Russell, 1958; Maddison, 2007; McEvedy & Jones, 1978). This market was significantly protected by import tariffs of about 25% (Bernardi, 1970).

Authorities, such as Finley, underestimated the significance of market relationships in the Antiquity (Finley, 1973). Following this path, a few more contemporary scholars insisted on denying the importance of the exchanges along the Great Sea, arguing that the movement of goods was mainly the result of taxes paid in specie to a tributary empire (Bang, 2008). On the contrary, the tremendous expansion of the minting of denarii, the growth of total population of the empire and the evolution of Mediterranean shipwrecks seem to me enough evidence to maintain that both trade and output had to significantly increase between the third and the first century BC (Felice, 2015; Hopkins, 1980; Kay, 2014; Lo Cascio, 2007; Parker, 1992; Temin, 2017). In other words, a significant transformation of the Great Sea (and even a slight growth in per capita income) took place as a result of the economic integration of the Mediterranean under Roman imperialism during the last centuries preceding our era.

In fact, the Mediterranean was so integrated in the year 92 AD that Emperor Domitian, who also slightly reduced the value of the denarius, ordered vines to be pulled up in the provinces in order to protect the large Italic estates (De Martino, 1980). The progressive expansion of the borders brought treasures, which helped to finance the Roman state, and slaves, who provided cheap labour to the *fundi* of the aristocrats.

Although the work of medium and small landowning peasants (*mediocris*) and tenants (*coloni*) was predominant in the East, in the Western Mediterranean Roman colonization made much more intensive use of slave labour under a regime of large estates. In Italy, the big patrician owners were represented in the Senate and formed the pillar of Roman aristocratic democracy, based on the establishment of client links. This limited representation model tended to be reproduced in the territories conquered, going back to the city-state origin of the imperial metropolis.

The big owners were represented on the *concilia*, provincial assemblies of notables, which elected the *flamen*, the highest provincial authority. The provincial cities also had their *ordo decurionum*, local senate or citizens' council, which met in the *curia*. The *decuriones* tended to be a hundred big owners, who held the position for life, and participated in the decisions on defence, the administration and the promotion of public works. Among other duties, the *curia* and its members, the *curiales*, were in charge of collecting and delivering to the *procurator* the direct contribution which had been assigned to each city starting from the census.

As Rome progressed a significant feature of its origins tended to consolidate, as its original tribe had its head. This *patter* had the duty of protecting its people or *gentis*. This relationship later muted to the obligation of each patrician to protect its *clients*, including juridical and financial support. In exchange, the client, which could be either a free peasant of formerly defeated territories, a plebeian *proletari*, or an emancipated slave, had to support its patron in the assembly elections and supply labour to the patron's states and works (Beard, 2016; De Martino, 1980). Such a type of patron–client links would become one of the most enduring characteristics of Mediterranean development in the very long run.

This book focuses on a coastal strip of the Iberian Peninsula, located opposite the Balearic Islands and mainly extending towards the south of the Pyrenees, although not exclusively. The islands belong also to our object of study. The external limits of the continental territory that interests us are Cartago Nova (founded by the Punic general Hasdrubal in 227 BC as Quart Hadasht) and Narbonne (created as the Roman colony of Narbo Martius in 118 BC). Until the arrival of Phoenicians, Greeks and Romans, the great majority of this part of the north-western Mediterranean had been an area very far from the most dynamic centres of civilization (Bosch i Gimpera, 1932; Maluquer de Motes, 1987; Tarradell, 1962). Moreover, our territory of analysis was rather poor in metals, as opposite to the regions further South (Roman Baetica), where the rich fields of silver, copper and sulphur had favoured to the emergence of the kingdom of Tartessos. A remarkable exception was the aluminium phosphate mines of Gavà, near the mouth of the Llobregat River, which were exploited since 3400 BC and exported output to Southern France

(Garrido, 1998). In any case, it is extremely plausible that our territories remained much poor than Southern Hispania, which according to some estimations enjoyed a higher significant income when Rome annexed them (Maddison, 2007).

Recent genetic analyses suggest that the original inheritance of hunters and gatherers who populated this part of the Mediterranean up to 5000 BC, was enriched by the chromosomes of migrants from the Anatolian Peninsula, who, probably, brought agriculture and the domestication of animals such as sheep, goat and pig (Lazuela-Fox, 2017). During the Neolithic Revolution, people were buried under stone dolmens, which have been preserved along the coast and the Pyrenees. Siles axes, ceramics and mollusc jewellery were also found close to the bones.

Later, around 2500 BC, the ancestry of Iberian people was modified by the contribution of the masculine invasions of horse-riding people from the Eurasian steppes (Lazuela-Fox, 2017). These invasions likely brought Indo-European languages to the Iberian Peninsula, in particular to their West and Central regions. More or less simultaneously, the first signs of copper culture were found. Ceramics evolved to produce bell-shaped elegant forms (Tarradell, 1962). Evidence of gold jewellery and copper knives were dated for a period comprised between 2200 and 1800 BC. By 1000 BC, the diffusion of the culture of fields of urns was remarkably consolidated, entailing the burial of ashes in this type of container. Bronze trade across the Pyrenees is already documented previously in 700 BC.

In 654 BC, the Phoenicians settled on the island of Ibiza, calling it *I busim* (Island of the Pine) and subsequently colonizing it. The Canaanites traded with the Iberians and familiarized them with key processes such as iron metallurgy, mill ceramics and vineyard growing (Aubet, 1993; Aubet & Sanmartí, 1996; Grau, 2021). Early Phoenician settlements in the continent strip opposite to Ibiza have been documented at the mouth of Segura River in Cabeçó Petit de l'Estany and La Fonteta for the late seventh century BC. The earliest presses for wine production in the Iberian Peninsula have been found in the surroundings of Denia. Not very far away, Il·lici (Elx) would become famous for its production of ceramics with stylized animals. Another indicator of the increasing wealthiness of these meridional regional elites would be the discovery of rather big sculptures, such as the Elx Dama, which belonged to the tombs found in several necropolises where the Iberian elites were buried (Asensio & Jornet, 2019; Grau, 2021).

In around 600 BC, Greeks from Phocaea departed Massalia (Marseille) and a few days later entered a bay adjacent to the Pyrenees, and decided to found the colony of Emporion (Empúries). Greeks also created another settlement on the other side of the bay, Rodhe (Roses). The interaction of the Hellenes with the native population was significant, given that there are currently Greek genetic traces in the Iberian descendants. The diffusion of olive trees and vineyards in the region is usually attributed either to Phoenicians or Greeks, but there is recent evidence which might date its origin much early. In any case, Phoenicians and Greeks contributed to integrating Iberia in the Mediterranean trade. Commercial letters written on lead were certainly found in Empúries (Sanmartí, 1996). The first coin minted in Iberia was a silver piece of about 1 gram, which was struck in Emporion around c 450 BC, following a model of Massalia (Crusafont, 1989; Ripollès, 2012). Rhodes began to mint silver drachmas of a weight of 4.7 grams, at the end of the fourth century BC. They imitated the coins produced in the Sicilian Greek colonies (Ripollès, 2012). The coins produced in Emporion and Rhodes would become the model for future pieces minted by Iberian towns.

Recent research confirms, in fact, that, before the arrival of the Romans, Hesperia was populated by a rosary of peoples who spoke, at least, five significantly differentiated languages, in addition to Punic and Greek (Ferrer & Moncunill, 2019). The most civilized, the Turdetani, settled in the south, in the basin of the River Baetis (Guadalquivir), and exploited the rich mineral deposits of former Tartessos. As it was the most favoured territory in minerals, different peoples exploited its underground resources for centuries. Epigraphy confirms that the Turdetani used to speak and write what has been called the Tartessian language (Correa & Guerra, 2019). However, variants of Phoenician and Iberian languages were also spoken in this southern area (Aubet & Sanmartí, 1996).

Between the Guadiana and the Tagus and facing the Atlantic, there were settled the Lusitanians, a rather unruly group of Celt people, dedicated to shepherding and cattle breeding. They spoke a Galic dialect with Indo-European origin. They let epigraphic legacy of their written language (Luján, 2019).

The north-west and centre of the peninsula, where woods and relatively unfertile land were predominant, was also populated by Celts (including Celt-Iberians, Vaccei, Astures and Cantabri, among others). The Celt-Iberians, which were settled in the centre of the Peninsula also let written evidence of their Indo-European language (Beltrán & Jordán, 2019).

At both sides of the West and Central Pyrenees, the Basque-Aquitaine or Euskera language was spoken. It was a relatively isolated area, with a shepherd's' population. They were poorly influenced by trade or migrations, and therefore continued using one of the most ancient languages of the Peninsula, without any Indo-European root. Unfortunately, they did not let epigraphic evidence (Orduña, 2019).

Finally, there was the area that is the concern of this research. Along the Mediterranean coast but also at both sides of the Pyrenees, there were settled the Iberians, who had their own language (two main variants), and were fragmented into different tribes such as Ceretani, Ausetani, Begistani, and Kessetani, in the North, or Contestani, Edetani, and Gimneti, in the South. Curiously, the Iberian language was not Indo-European either. In fact, it shares some words, in particular numbers, with the Euskera. Moreover, Greek was used in the corresponding colonies.

As it was already advanced, because of the influence of Phoenicians and Greeks, before the arrival of Romans, the Iberian people already grew cereals and vineyards, manufactured iron and other metals and produced ceramics with the mill. They were divided into different contending tribes, and grouped in fortified villages, build on promontories. Before the Roman invasion, Iberian tribes had already experienced a growing urban specialization and social differentiation (Asensio & Jornet, 2019; Bosch i Gimpera, 1932; Garrido, 1998; Grau, 2021; Maluquer de Motes, 1987; Tarradell, 1962). It seems that the first Iberian town which minted its own original coin was Arse (Sagunt) around c 350 BC, following the model of the Greek towns (Ripollès, 2012).

The space whose history we analyse in this book coincides, broadly speaking, with the one in which the Iberian civilization developed, which had its own alphabet, manufactured iron and ceramics and developed its own particular artistic forms. They were rapidly influenced by the Phoenicians and Greeks, with whom they traded. The latter helped to the diffusion of vineyards and olive trees. Iberian towns also imitated the minting of silver coins, which was carried out by Emporion and Rodha. In around 300 BC, Iberian mints such as Arse, Ausesken (Vic), Iltirta (Lleida) and Kese (Tarragona) minted their own silver drachma and other bronze coins. In Ibiza, the Punics made bronze shekels (of a weight of 7.2 grams) and similar pieces since mid-fourth century BC.

However, while the early Phoenician and Greek penetration in the land of the Iberians was above all commercial, much later, Carthaginians and Romans wanted to use it as a theatre to finally settle the hegemony in the Mare Nostrum and take control of its minerals. In 226, Hasdrubal signed a treaty with Rome, which delimited the area of influence of the two powers in Hispania, being divided by the River Ebro. Rome sought an alliance with the Iberian city of Arse/Saguntum, situated much further to the south of the aforementioned basin. This treaty violated the agreement with the Punics and led Hannibal to decide the already reported attack of Arse in 219, to which Rome responded with a declaration of war. The Carthaginian general subsequently headed for the Pyrenees to try to reach Italy by land. The Second Punic War contributed to a fast diffusion of the use of coins in Iberia because they were used to pay the combatants (Ripollès, 2012).

In 218, Gnaeus Cornelius Scipio Calvus disembarked in Emporion from Marseille and led the Roman offensive against the remaining Carthaginians. The Iberian cities were divided in their support for each of the contenders. Gnaeus Cornelius established his military base in Kese, the future Tarraco. From 217, he had the support of the legions of his brother Publius Cornelius Scipio. Two years later, they defeated Hasdrubal and, in 212, they evicted the Punics from Saguntum. From then on, Roman control became consolidated over the land of the Iberians, whose uprisings were not long-lasting.

In 197, Rome divided its conquests in Iberia into two provinces: Hispania Citerior and Hispania Ulterior. As Roman power became more established, colonies were founded. For the veterans of the wars with the Lusitanians, the colony of Valentia (Valencia) was created in 138. In the ager palmensis of Mallorca, a military camp established around 123 BC would become the town of Palma.

Octavian Augustus himself resided in Tarraco between 27 and 25 BC, attracted by its mild climate, and from there led the fight against the Astures. He decided to convert this city into the capital of Hispania Citerior, the biggest province of the empire. Later, under Docletian a new administrative reorganization of the empire took place and Hispania was re-divided in three provinces: Tarraconensis, Baetica and Lusitania. The former went on to be the largest province and Tarraco remained as its capital.

In 15 BC, close to the Iberian town of Barkeno, Barcino (Barcelona) was founded, a colony which for centuries was presided over by the

Temple of Augustus. Other remarkable Roman towns of this stripe of the Mare Nostrum would be Ausa, Betulo, Dertosa, Diani, Edeta, Egara, Emporiae, Eso, Gerunda, Guium, Ilerda, Il·lici, Iluro, Lucentum, Mago, Setabis and Sigarra (Mayer, 1996).

During the period between 27 and 14 BC, Rome contributed to building the backbone of the former territory of the Iberians with the construction of the Via Augusta, which had as precedent the Via Heraclea. The Via Augusta linked the metropolis of the Mare Nostrum by land with Gadir. In the Iberian space under study here, it connected Ruscino (Château-Roussillon/Perpignan) with Setabis (Xàtiva). A further two branches of the road were built during the second century, one towards the inland of the peninsula, which passed through Ilirta, and another along the coast, which crossed Il·lici (Elx) (Nolla, 1996).

The *Pax Romana* brought three centuries of increasing prosperity to Hispania Citerior. Its good sea and land communications favoured trade with the metropolis. The countryside filled up with *villae* and the sea with boats which transported amphorae of wine from Tarraco and Barcino to the Narbonensis and Aquitania (Nolla, 1996; Prevosti & Guitart eds. 2011). Wine from Baetulo and Iluro was exported as far as Carthage, Pompei and Britain (Comas, 1997; Maluquer de Motes, 1987). Setabis was known in Rome for the quality of its linen handkerchiefs. The nearby coast supplied salted fish and the garum sauce. Hams from the Iberian Ceretani (established on both sides of the Pyrenees) also achieved fame in the imperial capital (Nolla, 1996; Salrach, 1987).

Table 1.1, which has been built thanks to Angus Maddison's bets, tries to present an approximate image of the relative position of our analysed territories in terms of income and urbanization within the framework of the Mediterranean part of the Roman empire (Maddison, 2007). As it could be expected from an initially rather backward territory, Tarraconensis province must have had an income far below average, and significantly lower than Italy where senators, equites and most of the elites used to live. Tarraconensis per capita income also had to be lower than eastern Mediterranean, technically more advanced since centuries ago: Lastly, it had to be below that of the neighbour Hispania province of Baetica because its much poorer endowment of underground resources. In fact, Tarraconensis stood at the bottom part of the per capita income of Mediterranean provinces estimated by Maddison, with levels similar to Corsica, Sardinia and Sicily.

Table 1.1 Mediterranean income and urbanization under the Roman empire, c 14 AD

	Per capita income in Italy and provinces 1990 Geary-Khamis $	*c 14 AD*		*Mediterranean most populated towns Thousand inhabitants*	*c 14 AD*
1	Italia	857	1	Rome	350
2	Egypt	600	2	Alexandria	216
3	Achaea	550	3	Antioch	90
4	Asia	550	4	Smyrna	90
5	Bythia	550	5	Ephesus	51
6	Capadocia	550	6	Carthage	50
7	Cilicia	550	7	Corinth	50
8	Creta	550	8	Apamea	37
9	Cyprus	550	9	Capua	36
10	Galatia	550	10	Memphis	34
11	Judaea	550	11	Nicomedia	34
12	Lybia	550	12	Damascus	31
13	Macedonia	550	13	Athens	28
14	Syria	550	14	**Tarragona**	**27**
15	Africa	541	15	Hermopolis	24
16	Baetica	525	16	Cyzicus	24
17	Narbonensis	525	17	Pergamum	24
18	Corsica	475	18	Mytilene	23
19	Sardinia	475	19	Arsinoe	20
20	Sicilia	475	20	Cirta	20
21	**Tarraconensis**	**475**	21	Hadrumetum	20
22	Dalmatia Mauritania	450	22	Cirta	20
23	Caesarensis	450	23	Pisa	20
24	Mauritania Tingitania	450	24	Rusicade	20
25	Numidia	450	25	Tyre	20

Source Own elaboration with Russell (1958) and Maddison (2007)

Tarraco was better situated in the urbanization ranking of the main Roman towns because two remarkable reasons: on the one hand, the province of Tarraconensis was one the largest of the Empire and included much poorer territories of inner Spain than its provincial capital; on the other hand, future Tarragona was located in a central position of the Iberian Mediterranean strip, an area which, as we advanced, significantly traded with other maritime towns of North-west Mare Nostrum, in particular exporting wine and *garum*. However, taking the Mediterranean part of the as a whole, Tarraco still recorded a size slightly below average. Its size, with around 27,000 inhabitants not only could not compete with Rome but remained also very far from eastern metropoles such as Alexandria, Antioch or Smyrna.

At the beginning of the first century, Latin became widespread as the official language in Hispania. In Mediterranean Hispania, the countryside seems to have continued speaking the Iberian language until the Late Empire and in the Pyrenees the Euskera might have survived until around the tenth century (Salrach, 1987). However, from the first century on, public signs in the Iberian, Greek or Punic languages gradually disappeared. The Latin language increasingly imposed itself both in writing and speaking and it will last as the language of the Roman church for nearly two millennia. However, in the territories overlapping the maritime strip of the Tarraconensis evolved into a dialect that was used by ordinary people. One thousand years later to Rome's arrival, the inhabitants of this space began to write in this dialect, which became the Catalan language. After almost another thousand years, the natives of this Mediterranean strip continue to talk and write in this language, which derives from that of Rome, despite numerous, often unfortunate, political vicissitudes. Nowadays, the territories in question belong to different political units: the regions of Catalonia, Valencia and the Balearic Islands in Spain, and the Déparment des Pyrénées Orientales in France. These territories with a common language together are known as the Catalan Lands or Countries.

1.2 Recurrent Crises and Transformation of the Mare Nostrum, 165–800

The type of crisis on which this book focus is a prolonged fall in economic activity, associated with a significant transformation in long-term economic development. As it was seen Rome experienced agrarian crisis in c 133 BC and financial turmoil in 88 BC. Similarly, medieval agrarian societies will tend to experience persistent subsistence crises, linked to war or annual fluctuations in the harvests, which generated acute rises in prices and mortality rates (Benito ed. 2013). For their part, industrial economies will record repeated short-term cycles, such as the triennial movements linked to the accumulation of inventories, a phenomenon detected by Kitchin, or the decennial fluctuations in manufacturing production, identified by Juglar (Schumpeter, 1939). However, neither of them constitutes the main purpose of this book.

Our main interest focuses on more long-lasting down cycles such as those identified by Kondratieff and Kuznets or on structural crises and prolonged depressions, which entailed intense and profound contractions in real production and which resulted in a transformation of the model of long-term economic development (Abulafia, 2011; Campbell, 2016; Eichengreen, 2015; Freeman & Louçã, 2001; Kindleberger, 1973; Lopez & Miskimin, 1962; Maddison, 1985; Minsky, 1975; Parker, 2001; Schumpeter, 1939; Wickham, 1984).

The Low Roman Empire experienced a prolonged depression which deeply transformed it and also influenced the pattern of development of its successor states (Anderson, 1979; Bernardi, 1970; Buenacasa, 2013; De Martino, 1980; De Palol, 1996; Depeyrot, 1991; Espluga, 1998; Harper, 2017; Salrach, 1987, 1997; Wickham, 2005). Since around 165, the Mare Nostrum was subject to recurring shocks which significantly eroded the integrated economy which had emerged along the sea. Although, in the early stage, the Roman world showed a notable capacity for resilience, later, a more profound and far-reaching slump led to significant changes in the imperial system, giving rise to what is known as Late Antiquity. Moreover, recurrent migrations and invasions ended by weakening inter-Mediterranean links. Even if the Lower Empire's successor states in the West never completely abandoned economic and technical exchanges with the rest of the Great Sea and forgot the legacy of Rome either, the resulting economies became much more inward-oriented for many centuries.

As we mentioned above, between 165 and 180, the Mare Nostrum experienced a pandemic, which may have caused between 1.5 and 25 million deaths, although the most widely accepted figure is that of around 7 million. What was known as the Antonin Plague broke out dramatically in the siege of Seleucia, being transmitted by the legions to the furthest corners of the empire (McNeill & McNeill, 2003). It would appear to have been a violent transmission of smallpox (Harper, 2017; Maddison, 2007). It may have caused the death of between 2 and 33% of the empire's population (Harper, 2017). Maddison estimates the demographic lost around 17% (Maddison, 2007). We shall consider a figure of this kind as a reasonable bet. In any case, such a high loss of population must have decisively affected both the empire's military capacity and its productive activity.

With the sharp fall in the size of the workforce, whether landowning peasants, tenants or slaves, the main productive activity, the agricultural sector, had to collapse, and with it demand for land and transport services. Indeed, the evidence available indicates that the leases in kind fell, as did the actual price of land. The record about shipwrecks in the Mediterranean shows a net decreasing trend, which would indicate a significant reduction in trade by sea and increasing difficulties to supply Rome and other big cities of the basin with food (see Fig. 1.1).

The greater scarcity of labour tended to improve the living conditions of tenant farmers and free peasants. Even the slaves broadened their expectations. On the contrary, the big estates focused on the production and exporting of food suffered, on the one hand due to the fall in demand and, on the other hand, because of the increase in the price of slaves. This tended to increase because supply went down, not only due to the extraordinary mortality triggered by the pandemic but also because of the diminishing offensive capacity of the empire.

Marcus Aurelius (161–180) had to defend the Empire against the Parts who attacked the Armenian vassal state in 161, beginning a war in the East which lasted until 166. In the North, the Chatti attacked Germania Superior and the Marcomanni and the Lombards crossed the Danube. The Costoboci invaded Macedonia and Greece. During 171, Moorish troops attacked Baetica. Although Marcus repealed most of the invaders, at the moment of his death in 180, Imperial finances were depleted.

The military costs had shot up in a situation in which, due to the effect of the pandemic, revenues were falling. Marcus Aurelius had to resort to the sale of part of the imperial treasure in order to confront the fiscal crisis. Moreover, the depreciation of the denarius was used as a remarkable instrument of adjustment, its silver contents going down from the equivalent of 3.2 grams established by Nero to just around 2.4 grams under Marcus Aurelius (De Martino, 1980). On comparing the silver contents of the denarius of Marcus Aurelius with that of Nero, it appears a very significant devaluation of about 25%.

In 187 an uprising by slaves and deserters, led by Maternus, looted Hispania and Gaul. Ten years later, Clodius Albinus proclaimed itself emperor and sent the legions of Hispania and Britannia against those of Septimius Severus. The resulting Battle of Lugdunum was one of the bloodiest of all the clashes between Roman forces. The victory of Severus favoured the stabilization of the empire and gave rise to a new dynasty, which took his name.The insurrection of Albinus caused another notable rise in military expenditure during the time of Septimius Severus (193–211), who decided to double the annual salary of the average legionnaire, increasing it from 300 to 600 denarii per year (Harper, 2017). The resulting increase in public expenditure was, again and in part, financed by the debasement of the monetary standard, whose silver content went down to around 1.7 grams (De Martino, 1980). The depreciation of the denarius in the era of Septimius in relation to Marcus Aurelius period was nearly 30%.

Marcus Aurelius Antonino Caracalla (198–217) is well known for extending Roman citizenship all over the empire. But his fiscal and monetary policies followed a similar path as the previous emperors. He expanded public expenditure, approving a new increase in the salary of the legions up to 900 denarii and promoting public works, such as the monumental baths that he built in the capital of the empire (Harper, 2017). Further resources were needed to pay the *foederati* barbarians, to grant their support for the defence of the empire (De Martino, 1980). To finance such an expansive policy, he likewise resorted to monetary depreciation. The denarii minted in his mandate ended up only containing less than half silver of its weight (Sear, 1988). Moreover, in 215, he minted a new coin, the double denarius or antoninianus, with a face value of two denarii and a weight of about 5.1 grams (Harper, 2017; Sear, 1988). However, he granted it a silver content of only 1.6 times that of its predecessor. As a result, the depreciation of the main Roman monetary standard under Caracalla was not very different to that experienced under Marcus Aurelius and Septimius Severus. In fact, the devaluation of the denarius contained in the antoninianus amounted to a loss of 20% of silver in relation to the denarius minted by the latter. In addition, Caracalla also debased the aureus, whose gold content was reduced to 5.4 grams.

It should be stressed that the significant, although still reasonable, denarius' debasements by Marcus Aurelius (25%), Septimius Severus (20%) and Caracalla (20%) allowed the expansion of public expenditure and the reinforcement of the legions, whose contribution to the defence of the empire was critical. According to specialists, such as Harper, an economic and demographic recovery of the empire took place during the period of the Severan dynasty (Harper, 2017). My opinion is that, in fact, Septimius Severus and Caracalla temporarily reversed the depression trend by improving the salaries of the legions. Reasonable devaluations made possible to finance their efforts with moderate inflations.

A much more dramatic down fall began in 222, when the Goths invaded Asia Minor and the Balkans. Later in 235, emperor Alexander Severus was assassinated by its discontented army. The death of the last descendant of the dynasty gave rise to a period of prolonged internal war between generals, beginning with the so-called period of barrack emperors. A few dozen of emperors and pretenders confronted each other between 235 and 284.

In 252 a new epidemic, known as the Plague of Cyprian, reproduced the effects of its predecessor Antonine in various locations of the Mediterranean. It is believed to have been a filovirus. It's likely African, possibly Ethiopian, origins and symptoms, such as haemorrhages and the necrosis of tissues among those infected, have led it to be compared with the Ebola virus (Harper, 2017). Alexandria lost almost 60% of its inhabitants. The scarcity of labour intensified. Agricultural production again collapsed and, with it, income and prices related to the land. As Fig. 1.1 illustrates, the number of known boats sunk in the third century is 50% lower than that of the previous century, indicating a true collapse of trade along the Mare Nostrum (see Fig. 1.1).

The capacity to contain the Barbarians was considerably diminished. The Mediterranean became an insecure scenario, threatened by hordes and pirates. Visigoths and Ostrogoths invaded the Black Sea in 257. On the north-western border, the Franks looted Gaul and even attacked Tarraco in 260. Alemanni and Suevii attacked northern Italy. Imperium Galliarum temporary detached itself from Roman control. On the north-eastern strip, more than 250 cities were devastated by Goths and Herules in 267, including Athens, Corinth and Nicaea. Herules' sack of Athens led the agora to its end, after centuries of life (Spawforth, 2018). Moreover, the Moors besieged North Africa. The Sasanians advanced in the East.

The numerous emperors from the period resorted to extreme devaluations and the size and frequency of the debasements ended up destroying the monetary system based on silver and triggering unsustainable inflation. The denarii gradually disappeared from circulation, while increasingly poor antoninianii were made and used. The latter ended up being a copper coin, coated with a light surface of the silver. In 250 the antoninianus still contained one-third of silver. By the time of Gallienus (253–268) the latter coin only contained 5% of silver. If we compare the level of debasement between Caracalla and Gallienus eras, we obtain a devaluation of the denarius of about 88%. As a result, inflation became out of control, with around an 800 per increase under Gallenius (De Martino, 1980). The antoninianus had become a mere billon coin.

Gallenius ended up being murdered by his own men at Aquilea in 268. In around 271, the empire ended up splitting into three: Gallic, Roman and Palmyrene. Under Tetricus Senior (271–274), emperor of Gallia, the antoninianus only contained about 0.02 grams of silver. Imitations of the coin (and the rest of billon pieces) were usual. The prices in denarii shot up furthermore and the silver monetary system was completely destroyed. The legions began to be paid in gold. Debasement out of control fuelled extreme inflation and did little to overcome this crisis, which most of the authors considers to be total (De Martino, 1980; Harper, 2017; Spawforth, 2018).

Lucius Domitius Aurelianus (270–275) was proclaimed emperor by the legionnaires of the Danube border. He recovered Gaul for Rome and fortified the eternal city. He introduced the antoniniani containing 5% silver (the rest, bronze), giving it a face value of five denarii. He also minted copper and silver denarii, and gold aurei with a value of around 1000 denarii.

Emperor Diocletian (284–305) tried to fight inflation by approving a decree which fixed maximum prices to a large extent of goods in 301. As usually happens with price controls, such a policy failed (Depeyrot, 1991; Maddison, 2007). He also attempted to restore a monetary system inspired by the classic one of the High Empire with a silver coin, the argenteus or silver denarius, similar in weight and contents to Nero's one, and another piece, the *folis*, mainly minted in bronze, similar to the *as* (Sear, 1988). In any case, the recovery required more radical and far-reaching changes to the economic organization of the territories bathed by the Mare Nostrum. As Professor Salrach points out in our next chapter, following the path traced by authors such as Wickham, Rome's mode of production system was moving from being dominated by slavery to being based on taxation (Depeyrot, 1991; Wickham, 1984). Diocletian introduced annual budgets and reformed taxation to generate new income with the associated principles of *capitatio* and *iugatio*, which taxed men and land ownership. This was based on the creation of the imperial cadastre and the introduction of a rather efficient system of direct taxation. The higher tax revenues allowed a strengthening of the legions, bringing them to over half a million and fostering greater success in the containment of the Barbarians. The improvement in tax revenues also made it possible to again mint precious metals.

The measures taken to confront the crisis of 235–284 led to a change in the production relations in the main sector of productive activity, agriculture. The increasing scarcity of slaves led the owners of the big estates to establish tenants, *coloni*, on their properties (Bloch, 1947; Bonnassie, 1985; De Martino, 1980; Espluga, 1998; Jones, 1964; Salrach, 1987, 1997). Free peasants and tenant farmers, however, suffered more from the increase in direct tax pressure than the big owners. The senators were taxed by Constantine (306–337) with the *collatio glebalis*, a new direct tax levied on land ownership (Puech, 2011). Nevertheless, it was easier for the large landowners to defraud and even to bribe the tax collectors. As early as 332, Constantine forbade the abandonment of the farm by free tenants, creating a precedent of allegiance to the land typical of mediaeval servitude (Bernardi, 1970; De Martino, 1980). In addition, the scarcity of labour led Constantine to restrict free mobility of workers in strategical industries such as maritime transportation, mines and mills (De Martino, 1980).

The increase in tax pressure encouraged the small cultivators to join the big owners in order to pay less tax. Since 350 the landowners tended to adopt the *autopragia*, that is the faculty to collect the taxes from their coloni and peasants and to transfer them to the State (Depeyrot, 1991). Such a practice was markedly encouraged by the fact that the State required payments in gold, and this was more feasible for landowners. There is also increasing evidence of *patrocinium* agreements (Bernardi, 1970; De Martino, 1980; Salrach, 1987, 1997). The roots of feudalism began to grow during the third and fourth centuries.

The importance of these proto-estates with landowners who tended to assume former public functions is clear from the fact that Theodosius I the Great (379–395) forbade private prisons, which had been created by some notables. Theodosius himself transferred public land to private cultivators, under the *emphyteusis* regime, which represented advantageous long-term contracts for the tenants starting from 386. In any case, clientele relationships which had been a long-term feature of Roman society, took a new dimension as a way to try to deal with the crisis of the Low Empire.

Furthermore, the gradual abandonment of polytheism responded to the need of the emperors to be more closely associated with the divinity, in order to strengthen their power in a historic period in which the same was easily disputed. Aurelian began to associate himself with the sun and imposed it as the main divinity in the Roman pantheon. He proclaimed the sun to be king, Lord of the Empire, and declared himself to be its priest. Under the tetrarchy of Diocletian, the two Augusti emperors were identified with Jupiter and the two Caesars with Hercules. However, the victory of Constantine on the Milvian Bridge led to the 313 Edict of Milan and the legalization of Christianity, a religion which, also arising on the eastern side of the Mare Nostrum, had progressed rapidly in the West in the midst of the apocalyptic atmosphere of plagues, invasions and inflation of the third century.

Theodosius made Christianity the official religion of the Empire in 380 and banned pagan cults in 392. Moreover, Theodosius contributed to reduce the fiscal deficit through the confiscation of the treasures of the Pagan temples, significantly increasing its gold reserves (Depeyrot, 1991). However, the adoption of Christianity as a religion of Rome has been extremely controversial among historians. Classical scholars such as Gibbon included it among the causes of the decadence of Rome, due to the additional tensions introduced within the Empire (e.g. the conflict with the Arian) and the erosion of the up to then dominant military values (Gibbon, 1776–1778). On the other hand, more contemporary historians consider Christianism as a factor that increased the cohesion of the Low Empire and contributed to reinforce the hegemony of the Emperors. In fact, the church went from a persecuted community, still in the time of Diocletian, to hegemonic power and ruthless combatant of heterodox convictions and heretic deviations in a relatively short period of time. The conversion of Christianism in a state religion would have become a key element to deal with the crisis of the Low Empire and prepare the transition to Late Antiquity (Anderson, 1979; Wickham, 1984).

In the era of Constantine, a new monetary system gradually became consolidated based on the primacy of two metals: gold for large transactions and a store of value for the rich, and copper for daily exchanges, use by the poor and unbridled inflation (Puech, 2011). At the beginning of Constantine's reign, the coins most in circulation were the *nummus*, made from silver-plated copper and with a weight equivalent to 9 grams, and the *aureus*, a gold coin weighing 5.4 grams. At the end of his reign, the *nummus* only weighed 1 gram and, consequently, the devaluation had represented close to a drastic 90%. The prices of the basic subsistence food, wheat, which continued to be denominated in denarii, increased tenfold.

On the other hand, Constantine consolidated the trend of strengthening the role of gold in the imperial monetary system, with the creation of the *solidus* in 309 (Puech, 2011). The *solidus*, of around 4.5 grams, weighed 17% less than the *aureus*, but maintained its weight and gradually replaced the *aureus* as the main gold coin throughout the Empire. Tax payments had to be made in gold and the legions continued to be paid with this metal. Major trade and finances were likewise undertaken in gold. The rich preserved part of their assets in gold, while the poor suffered from the drastic increase in the price of subsistence food. The solidus began to be used increasingly as the unit of account (Vagi, 1999).

Finally, the partial recovery from the third-century crisis entailed a process in which the imperial power gradually abandoned the centre of the Mediterranean. First, the imperial dignity ceased to fall upon the senatorial aristocracy and the trend towards the prominence of the generals became consolidated, especially those from the provinces of the Danube. The empire ended up withdrawing towards the east. In 330, Constantine converted Byzantium, an optimal location for his defence and half way between Europe and Asia, into the new eastern capital of the empire. The growth of New Rome Constantinopolis was, moreover, driven by Theodosius's decision to divide the empire between his two sons on his death in 395. In less than a century, Constantinople went from a population of 30,000 to almost half a million, becoming the biggest Roman population in the world. For its part Rome, which may have reached one and a half million inhabitants in around 165, went down to a few hundred thousand inhabitants, after relinquishing the title of western capital first to Milan (395) and then to Ravenna (402). It was subsequently devastated by the sacking of the Visigoths of Alaric (410) and, above all, the Vandals of Genseric (455).

Seen in perspective, the decisions taken to confront the long depression of the Late Roman Empire could not have prevented the successive aggressions by Visigoths, Vandals, Burgundians, Franks or Ostrogoths, although they gave the Western part one and a half more centuries of life. Moreover, they guaranteed the survival of *Romanitas* in Byzantium for around one thousand years more (Harper, 2017). Furthermore, innovations such as attachment to the land, patronage, emphyteusis, monotheism and direct taxation connected Late Antiquity to the Middle Ages (Salrach, 1987, 1997; Wickham, 1984, 2005, 2016).

The fifth century was again a period of total crisis. However, although the last western emperor, Romulus Augustus, was deposed by the Herule Odoacer in 476, the Barbarian leaders continued to be under the influence of Rome. They frequently went from being under its orders, as allies or *federati*, to establishing their own kingdoms. They continued to apply

Roman legislation to their subjects and even promoted its compilation. The conversion of their kings to Christianity, initially in its Arian version, ratifies the persistent influence of Rome. The church acted as a counterbalance to the power of the Germanic nobility and maintained a tradition of territorial representation at the heart of the new kingdoms, with its periodic councils.

The Visigoth Athaulf (410–415), brother-in-law of the looter Alaric, was appointed *Comes Domesticus* by Emperor Priscus Attalus. He founded the Visigoth kingdom of Toulouse in 410. Subsequently, in 414, he married the daughter of Emperor Theodosius the Great and half-sister of Honorius, Galla Placidia, in Narbonne. Under pressure from general Constantius, he crossed the Pyrenees and invaded Tarraconensis, establishing his court in Barcino, where he was assassinated in 415. Constantius then allowed his men to settle in Aquitania, favouring the creation of the Visigoth kingdom of Toulouse. The reigns of Euric and Alaric II, as *federati* of Rome, strengthened the links between the two sides of the Pyrenees. Until 486, Tarraconensis came under Toulouse (Salrach, 1987).

In 507, the Franks defeated the Visigoths, putting an end to the reign of Toulouse. However, Provence, Narbonensis, Tarraconensis and Carthaginensis continued under Visigothic rule, in an alliance with the Ostrogoth Theodoric, who governed Italy. Thus, the records of the first ecclesiastical council of Tarraco in 516 date it under the reign of the latter. The Council of Carthaginensis, held in Valentia in 549, also recognized Theodoric as the monarch. Between 507 and 549, the Visigothic court resided either in Narbonne or in Barcelona, although it still looked towards Ravenna (De Palol, 1996).

The Visigoths pursued their *peregrinatio* journey south, dominating a good part of the Iberian Peninsula and installing their court in Seville, Merida and Toledo, successively. Liuva again tried to create a Mediterranean kingdom, which looked towards Narbonne, while appointing his brother Liuvigild as *Dux Hispanorum*. The former was unlucky, dying soon, but Liuvigild (569–586) was close to achieving the unification of Hispania under his sceptre, although he failed on the coasts and the mountainous territories inhabited by the Vascones. He enacted a legal code with notable Roman influence and endeavoured to close the gaps between Arians and Catholics. His son Reccared (586–601) ended up converting to Catholicism and the third ecclesiastic Council of Toledo declared Arianism to be illegal in 589. From then on, and until his last successor, Roderic (710–712), the Visigothic kings of Toledo were

Catholic. As late as 673, the *Comes* of Nimes, Hilderic, and the *Dux* of Septimania, Paulus, had tried to recreate a kingdom on both sides of the Pyrenees and obtained the support of Tarraco and Barcino, but King Wamba thwarted the attempt (De Palol, 1996).

The Catholic church of Rome, an institution of tremendous complexity and contradictions, gradually became an important link between Antiquity and the Middle Ages (Anderson, 1979; Járrega, 2013; Wickham, 1984, 2005, 2016). On the one hand, its hierarchy was gradually transformed into a formidable not very productive bureaucratic apparatus, supported by the tithe paid by the peasants and by resorting to slave labour, to which the fathers of the church did not object (Bloch, 1947; Bonnassie, 1985). On the other hand, there was an ascetic bias and, with Benedict of Nursia and his Rule, some of his followers advocated work and abstinence as forms of coming closer to God, breaking with the pejorative view that the Roman aristocrats had of them.

On analysing the records of ships sunk in the Mediterranean, trade in the Mare Nostrum again recorded a fall of almost 50% during the fifth century, a figure which confirms that this century again involved a tremendous deepening of the depression (Kay, 2014; Parker, 1992). The end of the Western Empire and the intensification of piracy took it to a level of less than 15% of what it was in the second century (see Fig. 1.1). The population of the city of Rome also experienced a sustained decline. Although without reaching the extreme of the western capital, the inhabitants of a good part of the basin abandoned cities. While trade and manufacturing collapsed and insecurity increased, they sought sustenance and protection in the countryside. As Professor Salrach stresses in Chapter 2, the municipal curia vanished. The public army tended to be substituted by private troops of Germanic origins.

Conversely, the sixth century appeared to begin with a tendency towards recovery (Duby, 2001; Harper, 2017). Emperor Justinian (527–565) was close to restoring Mediterranean unity and public jurisdiction of the emperor. In addition to maintaining the integrity of the territories of Byzantium, his generals conquered the Vandals from North Africa and expelled them from Corsica, Sardinia and the Balearics, bringing them back into the Empire. They also annexed Sicily and the Italian Peninsula as far as the Alps. In the Iberian Peninsula, they reconquered Baetica and Carthaginensis in around 544. The Emperor, from Constantinople, codified Roman law in the *Corpus iuris civilis* of 527. Looking again at the records of shipwrecks in Fig. 1.1, Mediterranean trade appears to have improved slightly during the sixth century.

However, some authors see the war costs of Justinian restoring attempt as too high (Felice, 2015). Even more significant, probably, bubonic plague appeared in 541 in the Egyptian city of Pelusium and, within a few months, the granaries of the Empire were infested with *rattus rattus*, the bite of whose fleas transmitted the bacteria *Yersinia pestis* (Harper, 2017; Maddison, 2007). Its origin appears to have been the marmots that inhabited the Central Asian plateau of Xinjiang. Volcanic explosions and excess rainfall arising from greater activity by El Niño brought the Asian rodents out of their burrows and helped to infect other species. It is an undisputed fact that the new pandemic was transmitted around the Mare Nostrum thanks to the boats which transported the black rat and its voracious fleas among their passengers. In the winter of 542, buboes already proliferated among the inhabitants of Constantinople. The estimated number of victims for what was then the capital of the empire ranges from 250,000 to 300,000 people. In 543, the epidemic reached Rome, Carthage and Arles. It was, however, especially virulent in Alexandria, Jerusalem and Antioch, whose populations were depleted. McCormick calculated that mass graves increased fivefold during the sixth century (McCormick, 2015, 2016). A contemporary Palestinian tombstone announced that a third of humanity had been eradicated by the plague (Kaldellis, 2007).

The dramatic reduction of population under Justinian resulted in a fall in prices because of a lack of demand and an increase in wages, due to the lack of labour (Harper, 2017). Moreover, the scarcity of men jeopardized Justinian military effort. As Harper, in our opinion, rightly suggests, the way of devaluation to recruit new legionaries was not as feasible as in former times when the troops were paid in silver, given the army was then paid with gold. Alternatively, he resorted to increase levies and led taxation to the highest level of the whole history of the Roman empire (Harper, 2017).

It seems that the period 530–550 was the coldest decade in two millennia. Solar irradiation changed its previous pattern and tended to diminish up to reaching a nadir during the seventh century. The decrease in solar activity was linked to the increases in volcanic activity and, probably, with the succession of different waves of plague. In fact, recurrent waves of the pandemic pest, transmitted either by flea bites or aerial contagion, were suffered by the population of the Mediterranean Basin until 749 (Harper, 2017).

In 568 another Germanic people, the Lombards, attacked the Po Plain, conquering it and establishing their capital in Pavia. The depleted offensive capacity of the Byzantine Empire could not prevent other Lombard groups from founding the duchies of Spoleto and Benevento to the south of Ancona. Byzantium continued to control the hinterland of Ravenna and the southern reaches of the peninsula. Rome resisted thanks to the election of Pope Gregory the Great, who achieved an agreement between Lombards and Byzantines (Wickham, 2016).

However, the seventh and eighth centuries were again a time of global crisis, with a general decline in the biggest cities of the basin. In 643, another people of shepherds and warriors reached the Mediterranean, possibly driven by the increasing aridity of their land of origin. For some, the true end of the Roman Empire occurred with the fall of the big metropolises of the south-eastern Mediterranean, weakened by the last waves of plague, and incapable of containing the new Arabic invaders, who brought another monotheistic cult, Islam. After the defeat of Yarmuk in 636, Emperor Heraclius ordered the withdrawal of his armies and Damascus, Jerusalem and Alexandria fell. From then on, the possessions of Byzantium were residual. The Arabs quickly imposed themselves in the East, the whole of North Africa and even Hispania and Southern Galia. These latter regions had been recently devastated by the plague. Narbonensis seems to have been quite empty because of the 693 waves. Hispania particularly suffered the 707–709 contagion (Harper, 2017).

The Muslims crossed the Pillars of Hercules in 711, conquered the Visigoths and occupied the kingdom of Toledo. Tarraconensis and Septimania tried to recreate their own kingdom, while the Arab-Berbers took over the peninsula. The latter ended up conquering Narbonne in 720. The worst record of Mediterranean trade, according to the shipwrecks found and represented in Fig. 1.1, was precisely in the eighth century (Parker, 1992). Gold continued to circulate in Al-Andalus and what remained of Byzantium, but became markedly scarce in the north-western Mediterranean (Pirenne, 1973).

Charles Martel (714–741), as leader of the Franks and Burgundians, defeated the Arabs and Berbers in the Battle of Poitiers in 732, making them retreat, and founded a new dynasty. His son, Pepin the Short

(751–768), tried to restore the *Regnum Francorum*, incorporating Septimania and Aquitania into his domains. In 754 he entered Italy, defeated the Lombards and conquered Ravenna, donating the territories to the papacy. In 759, Pepin's Franks seized Narbonne from the Muslims. One of Pepin's sons, Charlemagne (768–814), broadened his conquests and on the borders created the marches of Gothia, Friuli, Pannonia, Bavaria, Denmark and Brittany, to help to contain the Muslims, Slaves or Vikings. The territories bordering on the Pyrenees were integrated into the marquisate of Gothia. In 800, he was crowned emperor of the West by Leo III in Rome. His sovereignty ended up extending from Aachen to Pisa, from Bordeaux to Aquileia and from Bremen to Barcelona (Duby, 2001).

The Carolingian Empire has been considered the last consistent attempt to re-establish a public jurisdiction in the West, based on a series of territorial administrations under central control, the counties (Anderson, 1979; McCormick, 2001; Salrach, 1987, 1997; Wickham, 1984, 2005). They would be led by non-hereditary positions of Roman origin, the *comes* or the count and his *curia*. He would be followed by a hierarchical chain of viscounts, vicars and *vassi dominici* (vassals), who would be assigned land to administer. They would all be answerable for their decisions to the *missi dominici*, inspectors of the Emperor, and their positions would be revocable. Their alliance with the church was endorsed when the monasteries were given a role in educating the children of the imperial elites. As Professor Salrach underlines in the following chapter, the Carolingian state was halfway between the ancient world and feudalism.

Pepin minted the silver *novus denarius*, a coin with around 1.4 grams of almost pure metal, the basic unit of a new monetary system. Its multiples were the *solidus*, worth 12 *denarii*, and the *libbra*, equivalent to 20 *solidii*. Charlemagne exported this system of one *livre* (counting unit) equivalent to 240 *deniers* (circulating currency) to all the territories of Western Europe that he conquered. The first Carolingians therefore established a monetary system which was also inspired by the Roman model although, given the scarcity of metal, the *livre* (the modern pound) and the *sou* (the modern shilling) were used exclusively as counting units, and the actual circulating coins were the *deniers* (the modern pennies) (Bloch, 1954; Cipolla, 1975; Crusafont, 1996; Usher, 1943).

1.3 The Catalan Counties, Between the Roman-Carolingian Matrix and the Mediterranean Commercial Revolution, 801–1315

In 759, the Franks had entered Narbonne and occupied Roussillon. The city of Girona opened its doors to them in 785. In 801, the Frankish troops commanded by Charlemagne's son, Louis the Pious, and his cousin, William I, Count of Toulouse, conquest Barcelona. Bera I (801–820), William's son, was appointed Count of Barcelona and Marquis of Gothia, and was also count of Razès, Conflent, Girona and Besalú. His brother Gaucelm I was appointed Count of Roussillon and also ended up being Count of Perelada and Empúries. These counties, and others which subsequently joined them, such as those of Cerdanya and Urgell, experienced considerable political instability. This arose from their condition of the border lands and the raids carried out by the Emirate of Cordoba, the degree of support to the counts by the Gothic-Roman notables and the internal conflicts between Frankish families (Bolòs & Hurtado, 2009; D'Abadal, 1969–1970; Salrach, 1987, 2006, 2020).

The name of the counties which integrated the Marca Gothica, referred also as Hispanica, evocated two very long-term complementary realities. On the one hand, some derived from the denominations of old Iberian tribes settled near the Pyrenees: Cerdanya (ceretani), Osona (ausetani) and Berga (bergistani). On the other, they took the name of outstanding towns founded by Greeks (Empúries) and Romans (Rosselló, Girona, and Barcelona). The Franks expansion to the South, therefore, attempted also in this aspect to give continuity to the legacy of Antiquity and Rome, especially (Vilar, 1962).

During the era of Charlemagne, in his counties to the south of the Pyrenees, denarii were minted at least in Barcelona, Girona, Empúries and Roses, with an approximate weight of between 1.3 and 1.7 grams of almost pure silver. The Count of Barcelona and his neighbours began to count in *livres (*lliures*)*, *sous* and *deniers* (diners) like the rest of the Carolingian Empire and unlike the rest of the Iberian Peninsula. This system of counting was maintained in the future Catalonia until the mid-nineteenth century (Bloch, 1954; Cipolla, 1975; Crusafont, 1989, 1996, 2015; Feliu, 2012; Usher, 1943).

The settlement and defence of the counties taken from Muslim control were aided by institutions such as the *aprisio* and the *alou*, which ensured ownership of the land by those who cultivated it in an uninterrupted manner for 30 years. This institutional mechanism was predominant in the border lands. On the contrary, in the north-western territories, where the Muslims hardly took hold, the farms based on emphyteusis and the assignment of the peasant to the land were predominant.

The families responsible for the border counties varied until Wilfred the Hairy (878–897) succeeded in consolidating a dynasty that governed the county of Barcelona from 878 to 1410. He was also Count of Urgell, Cerdanya, Girona and Osona. His brother Miró was Count of Roussillon and Conflent. The sound Carolingian alliance with the church can be seen in the appointment of a third brother, first as Abbott of the monastery of Arles de Tec and, subsequently, as Bishop of Elne, the religious capital of Roussillon. Wilfred himself founded the monastery of Ripoll in 880, where his sons were educated. Soon later, Benedict monks, coming from Ripoll, founded the first cloister in the mountain of Montserrat (D'Abadal, 1969–1970; Salrach, 1987, 2006, 2020).

The border between the Catalan counties and Al-Andalus was fairly stable for 250 years. The frontier territories were full of castles to prevent Arab-Berber incursions but, with the passing of time, barons, vicars and lords of castles tended to demand increasing contributions to defend the peasants under their control. Another critical period occurred between 950 and 1050, as feudal violence intensified against the free peasants, who tended to be subjugated and sought a protector in exchange for transferring land and rights. The *convenientae* agreements, which recognized the commitments to military assistance and protection, proliferated during this time. The former Carolingian officials tended to become the new feudal class. This codified the value of the life of the different social strata (Bonnassie, 1990; D'Abadal, 1969–1970; Salrach, 1987, 2006, 2020).

Al-Mansur looted Barcelona in 985, even taking the bells from the cathedral. Count Borrell II (947–992) did not obtain the assistance expected from the Franks and, from 988, considered the vassalage agreement with his king, then Hugh Capet (987–996), to be broken. As early as the eleventh century, sources from Al-Andalus indicate that the King (*màlik*) of the Franks (*ifrànj*) lived in Barcelona, which should be interpreted as a sign of the de facto independence of the Catalan counties from that time. These sources also suggest that the Jews were as numerous as the Christians in the aforementioned capital (Balañá, 2002).

The Catalan courts of 1064 already referred to Ramon Berenguer I (then Count of Barcelona, Girona and Osona) and his wife Almodis, as *princepes* of the *principatus*. Circa 1115, we have another external testimony, which refers, as an early precedent, to Catalonia and to the unity of the counties led by Barcelona: in the *Liber maiolichinus de gestis pisanorum*, Henricus Pisanus describes the arrival of the sailors from Pisa in Catalania. According to Pisanus, this territory included the counties of Barcelona, Osona, Girona and Empúries (Udina, 2000).

Meanwhile, the Muslims pursued their Mediterranean adventure, invading Sicily in 827 and, subsequently, already in the Italian Peninsula, settling in Brindisi, Taranto and Bari. Arab corsairs even managed to occupy Saint Tropez between 890 and 972. Nevertheless, Muslim cities of the Mediterranean or close to its basin, such as Palermo and Cordoba, became the new centres for the transfer of eastern knowledge.

The contribution of the Muslims was notable in hydraulic techniques, perfecting the Roman irrigation systems with channels, reservoirs and waterwheels. They introduced irrigation crops such as artichokes, aubergines, apricots, oranges, cotton, rise and sugar cane, and they also harvested almonds and grenades. The secret of obtaining paper went from Baghdad (793) to Cairo (c900) and Fez (c1100) and spread in Europe through locations such as Xàtiva (1056), Toledo (1085), Amalfi (c1200) and Fabriano (1276). Codices and chess likewise began to spread among mediaeval courts and universities. The first mention of chess in European sources refers to a Catalan county: Ermengol, Count of Urgell, bequeathed his board and pieces to the Occitan abbey of Saint Gilles in 1008. Remarkable examples of the earliest textile miles in future Catalonia were located in the former Emirate of Larida (Lleida). Muslims of the *Trag al-A'là, at-* also built many hydraulic mills to obtain flour (Balañà, 2002; Barceló et al., 1996; Batet, 2001; Riera, 2005; Vernet, 1978).

The works of Avicenna and Averroes and the medical practice of Constantine the African contributed to developing the Scuola Medica Salentina, the first of its kind in Europe. Knowledge in calculus, geometry and astronomy, were also improved in the North Mediterranean thanks to the interaction with Islamic and Jewish cultures. The monk Gerbert d'Aurillac studied mathematics in the cloister of Ripoll, before moving to Islamic Cordoba and Seville. He, later in 999, became Pope Sylvester II and thanks to his studies in Al-Andalus, he contributed to the introduction of the number 0 and the decimal system in Medieval Europe. During his residence in the twelfth-century Barcelona, Abraham Bar Hiyya and Platon di Tivoli translated from the Arab into Latin, mathematical and astrological treaties such as the *Liber compos et al. itione astrolabii*. Navigation would become much more save thanks to the diffusion of such an instrument. Bar Hiyya is also considered to be the introducer of quadratic equations in Europe in his book of 1145, *Liber Embadorum*, translated with his colleague Platon (Forcano, 2021).

One thousand years ago, Muslim cities such as Cordoba, Palermo, Fez and Cairo, were home to populations of around or exceeding 100,000 inhabitants. By contrast, Rome and Athens had less than 50,000 citizens. The eternal city was still going to experience another looting in 1084 by the Normans, who had expelled the Arabs from Sicily. Other cities, such as Genoa, Pisa, Marseille, Narbonne and Barcelona, were likewise still very far from the threshold of 50,000 inhabitants.

In Western Europe, the insecurity of cities gradually favoured their abandonment and a search for protection close to the castles. Former public officials, such as counts and barons, had gradually become hereditary aristocrats. The free peasants and tenant farmers strengthened their personal links with the lords of the castles. In exchange for their protection, they accepted to provide labour services and to pay taxes in kind or in cash. The growing violence exercised in the border lands or in the internal conflicts between lords favoured the progressive subjugation of the peasant population, strengthened personal links and led to the jurisdictional domain of the nobility. The persistent looting and plundering encouraged the free peasants to seek a protector, reinforcing a trend which was visible in Rome, particularly during the Low Empire. The owners of the big estates continued, on occasions, to use slave labour, but gradually preferred the work of serfs attached to the land. The violence exercised by the lords of the castles was at the basis of the dissemination of the feudal system. Emperors, kings, dukes, counts, barons, lords of the castle and members of the military consolidated their domains, imposed new taxes and monopolies and began to exercise justice in their domains. Furthermore, they permanently competed with each other to expand their domains and extend their sovereignty to new territories of the Mediterranean (Bisson, 2009; Bonnassie, 1990; Freedman, 1993; Salrach, 1987).

The Otto dynasty enforced the rights of the Holy Roman Empire over Italy. Hugh Capet extended his domains to the farthest shores with the kingdom of Burgundy and the Gulf of Lion. In the Iberian Peninsula, the Kings of Leon and Navarre and the Count of Castile made the Caliphate of Cordoba retreat. In the Balkans, the Bulgarian Empire gradually took territory from Byzantium. The Eastern Empire continued with one foot in southern Italy and achieved the temporary conquest of Antioch, although it continued to suffer from constant pressure in the East. Despite everything Constantinople, with some 250,000 inhabitants at the dawn of the second millennium, still resisted as the main city of the Christian world.

The division of Christianity between the West and the East intensified after 1054, and continued to enhance its dualism. Moreover, the Popes of Rome revealed their increasing ambition for temporary power, entrenching themselves in the Papal States, and ideological intransigence, opposing all kinds of heretical deviations. Furthermore, the Roman Church as a whole consolidated itself as a powerful force of feudalism, thanks to the collection of tithes and taxes obtained from the land over which it exercised eminent domain.

However, the Roman Church likewise played a role in moderating the excesses of the feudal nobility. The church sometimes contributed to limiting looting, plundering and violence, which were exercised with particular intensity from castles in mountain territories not very far from the Mediterranean. It promoted initiatives such as the *Pax Dei* and *Tregua Dei*, which endeavoured to defend ecclesiastic properties and clerics from the armed aggressions of secular lords, but also women, children, peasants and even merchants. They also sought to guarantee the sanctity of religious spaces and their surroundings and to limit war to certain days of the week and months of the year. These movements took their inspiration from the legacy of *Pax Romana* and gradually took shape in councils such as those of Charroux (989), Toulouges (1027), Vic (1033), Nice (1041), Narbonne (1032), Barcelona (1064), Girona (1068), Elne (1156), Mimizan (1148) or Tarascon (1226). These initiatives to contain feudal violence were repeated in former Carolingian territories which were nostalgic for Roman peace, such as the duchies of Aquitania and Vasconia, the counties of Toulouse and Barcelona, the kingdom of Burgundy, Lombardy and even the kingdom of Leon (Bisson, 2009; Wickham, 2016).

Peasants and locals, in addition to ecclesiastics, occasionally participated in the assemblies. Sometimes, the more privileged demanded taxes in exchange for peace. The inhabitants of Vasconia and Languedoc undertook to pay the *bovaticum*, a tax in accordance with the number of oxen per household, to the Templars to guarantee order in the mid-twelfth century. Similarly, this type of tax tended to become general in the land between the Loire and the Ebro. The lords of kingdoms, duchies and counties likewise began to receive taxes in exchange for not altering the metal content of their currencies, which, like in the late Roman Empire, was a usual practice during the early Middle Ages. These periodic encounters to discuss peace and the currency, which included the participation of ecclesiastics, nobles and, sometimes, peasants, ended up transforming the old curias into courts with representation of the cities. They gave rise to Magna Cartas or constitutions. The King of Leon Alfonso IX, when he attacked Castile and Portugal, convened his *curia*, including not only nobles and ecclesiastics but also representatives of the cities, in 1188. From then on, this became a common practice of the kingdom and the body of laws enacted became the Magna Carta of Leon (Bisson, 1986; Wickham, 2016).

In Italy, Emperor Frederick Barbarossa also ratified the pacifying policy known as *Landfrieden* and tried to involve the booming northern cities in his tax demands with the respective convening of the Diet of Roncaglia in 1154 and 1158. The imperial, ecclesiastic and community representatives, meeting in the former, considered the suspension of hostilities between Lombard cities and the Emperor's demand to charge a fee for land and river transport, the minting of coins, fishing and salt production, among others. The latter announced the *Constitutio de regalibus* and the *Constitutio de pacis*, which ratified the Emperor's royalties and endeavoured to curb the military coalitions between cities. The opposition of the cities to these decisions led to the formation of the Lombard League.

Last, but not least, the church played a significant role in the mediaeval economic development of the north-western Mediterranean through monastic orders and the creation of monasteries. Benedictines, Cluniacs and Cistercians established territories, improved agricultural techniques and promoted literacy. Their *scriptorium* and libraries contributed to preserving and spreading knowledge. The number of monasteries existing in France, Italy and Iberia tripled between the tenth and thirteenth centuries, going from around 4400 to over 15,000. Even more impressive was the production of handwritten books between the two eras, which increased more than tenfold, going from less than 80,000 to over a million (Van Zanden, 2009).

Nevertheless, the violence of pillage in feudal Europe, under the aegis of the papacy, was gradually exported outside its borders until it reached the eastern Mediterranean, by means of successive crusades. In 1098, Edessa and Antioch were conquered by the Franks, giving rise to a county and a principality, respectively. Jerusalem fell in the following year, and became the capital of a new Latin kingdom. Richard I of England occupied Cyprus in 1192, which also became a crusader kingdom.

The episode which most clearly demonstrated the greed of the European feudal nobility, camouflaged by the cross, was undoubtedly the looting of Byzantium in 1204 by the Franks and Venetians, with the consequent establishment of the Latin Empire of Constantinople (Crowley, 2011; Lane, 1973). The crusader offensive also led to the creation of the kingdom of Thessaloniki, the Duchy of Athens and other Latin states in Greece, which delivered a mortal blow to the Romans of the East.

A clear improvement in trade and manufacturing, a new citizens' momentum and a certain cultural renaissance had gradually taken hold in the western Mediterranean. During the twelfth and thirteenth centuries, the cities of Languedoc and Provence experienced the development of commercial agriculture and wool drapery, the emergence of secular lyrics transmitted by troubadours and the dissemination of critical poetry and song in lenga d'òc. Marseille, Narbonne and Toulouse had more than 20,000 inhabitants in 1200. Carcassonne, Montpellier and Beziers had 10,000. Some of these cities, and other much smaller ones, saw how nobles, weavers or peasants embraced a Manichaean version of Christianity, which denied the majority of the sacraments and was known as Albigensian or Cathar heresy. Pope Innocent III (1198–1216) proclaimed a crusade against the Albigensian heresy and Philip Augustus (1180–1223) supported the invasion of the counties of Midi, which protected the cult of the *beaux hommes*. At the doors of Beziers, the papal legate, abbot Arnaud Amalric, ordered: *tuez-les tous, Dieu reconnaîtra les siens*. Simon de Montfort's host of crusaders burnt and looted important cities of Languedoc. To complete the persecution, Rome created the Inquisition in 1231, leaving it in the hands of the Dominicans (Le Roy Ladurie, 1962, 1975; Martel, 2019).

It was not only the Cathars who were persecuted. Paris and Rome also imposed restrictions on the Hebrews. In 1209 the Count of Toulouse, Raymond VI (1194–1222), was obliged to swear that he would never grant any more public positions to the Jews. An identical prohibition was imposed on his son Raymond VII (1222–1256) by the 1229 Treaty of Meaux. The 1254 Synod of Narbonne decided to oblige Hebrews to wear a sign in the form of a cross on the front of their clothes. This was a precedent for the yellow and red "wheel" which, thereafter, they would be forced to show on their cloaks (Forcano, 2014; Le Goff, 2010).

The counts of Barcelona pursued their traditional strategy of establishing their territorial base on both sides of the Pyrenees. In 1117, the forces of Ramon Berenguer III (1097–1131), who was also count of Provence, conquered the former Tarraco. His son, Ramon Berenguer IV, was betrothed to the heiress of the throne of Aragon, Peronella, in 1137, and their descendants officially held the crown of that kingdom. In 1149, Ramon Berenguer IV (1131–1162) annexed Lleida and, four years later, the last Muslim stronghold of what is now officially Catalonia, the fortress of Siurana. Although his ancestors as count of Barcelona already used the title *princeps*, Ramon Berenguer IV enjoyed referring to himself as *lo Comte e princep de Catalunya*.

The Catalan counties participated in the troubadour movement and some of its exponents, such as Guerau de Cabrera, wrote in *langue d'Oc*, very close to Catalan. The son of Ramon Berenguer IV, Alfons I the Troubadour (1162–1196), held the titles King of Aragon and Count of Barcelona, Guévaudan and Provence, among others. Catalans and the Provençal people were identified as a single nation in Jerusalem in 1187. It was usually believed that the first written evidence in Catalan, the *Homilies d'Organyà*, dates from around 1200. However, and recently, a vassalage pact signed in the county of Pallars in written Catalan has been found belonging to the eleventh century (Bonnassie, 1990; D'Abadal, 1969–1970; Fontana, 2014; Salrach, 1987; Sobrequés, 2007).

King Peter I the Catholic (1196–1213) had numerous vassals in the lands which spoke Occitan, leading him to intervene in the Battle of Muret against Simon de Monfort's crusaders, paying with his life. The defeat of the King of Aragon in 1213 against the troops of the King of France and the Pope put an end to the territorial expansion to the north and led his son, James I the Conqueror (1213–1276), to turn his attention to the *Mare Nostrum* and the Iberian south. He took Mallorca from the Muslims in 1229 and Valencia in 1249 (Furió, 2008; Ferrer i Mallol, 2011–2013; Salrach, 2006; Salrach & Duran, 1982) (Map 1.1).

Starting from 1253, James I began to appoint consuls in the main Mediterranean ports. These consuls were commercial representatives of Barcelona and other Catalan counties, with judicial duties to settle conflicts between traders. The territories with the most Catalan consuls were Languedoc, Provence, the Italian Peninsula, Sardinia and Sicily. However, they were also located in Tunis, Béjaïa, Algiers, Tripoli, Malaga, Almeria, Cartagena, Ragusa, Chios, Constantinople, Rhodes, Candia, Famagusta, Beirut, Damascus and Alexandria. From the beginning of

Map 1.1 The formation of the Crown of Aragon and the borders of the Catalan language. (*Source* Own elaboration by Raimon Soler-Becerro and Jordi Catalan)

the thirteenth century, there is evidence of the participation of Catalan merchants in the spice trade in Alexandria. In 1266, the king appointed his first consul in this Egyptian metropolis. In that same year, James I granted the city of Barcelona the privilege of appointing the commercial representative of the Crown of Aragon in the eastern ports, with the name *cónsol dels catalans*. With this decision, the monarch recognized the leading role of Barcelona in the commercial objective of the Crown of Aragon (Coulon, 2013; Cuadrada, 2001; Dufourcq, 1969; Ferrer i Mallol, 2011–2013; Smith, 1940).

The military campaigns were expensive and the count-kings collected the *bovaticum*, established tariffs *(lleudes)* and gradually reduced the content of the coins minted and in particular the silver of the Barcelona denarius (*diner*). If the *diner* minted in Barcelona in the era of Charlemagne was almost completely silver, the one made in the Barcelona mint by James I in 1222 only contained one-sixth of this metal (*diner doblenc*). This did not prevent the constant progress of the city and its commercial activity. From the time of Count Bera, when it was home to just a few thousand inhabitants, it went to greatly exceeded a population of 10,000 in the thirteenth century (Crusafont, 1996; Usher, 1943; Vilar, 1962).

In exchange for granting subsidies to the king, the city obtained from the monarch recognition of municipal autonomy comparable to that of the Italian republics. During the reign of James I, Barcelona acquired a representative council, made up of around a hundred notables, and a government of five councillors. Three citizen strata or *mans* had representation on the Consell de Cent: real-state owners and big merchants, liberal professions, and artisans. Following the conquest of Valencia, in 1258, King James was able to appreciate the Barcelona *diner* which, from then on and until the fifteenth century, was minted with one-quarter of silver (*diner de tern*). The king also promised Barcelona that he would not modify the currency law without the consent of the Consell de Cent (Crusafont, 1996; Ferrer i Mallol, 2011–2013; Usher, 1943; Vilar, 1962).

In Italy, between the years 1100 and 1340, several emerging cities led another sustained boom period, considered to be a true Commercial Revolution. Some pioneers, such as Amalfi, Pisa, Lucca, Siena, Messina, Padua, Mantua and Bologna, were important outposts in the promotion of sea and river navigation and overland trade, although they did not cross the threshold of 50,000 inhabitants. Another group did achieve this in the twelfth or thirteenth centuries: Venice, Milan, Florence, Genoa and Naples (Abulafia, 2011; Bairoch et al., 1988; De Roover, 1942; Dini, 1995; Felice, 2015; Felloni & Laura, 2004; Goldthwaite, 1980, 2009; Kocka, 2013; Lane, 1973; Lopez, 1976; Miskimin, 1975; North & Thomas, 1973; Tilly, 1990).

Although Italy was the new setting for confrontation between the Hohenstaufen Empire and the Papal States, the duality of hegemonic powers favoured a certain plurality in the Italian *comuni*, split between *gibelini* and *güelfi*. In 1159, despite the desire of Frederick Barbarossa, Milan and other neighbouring cities from northern Italy ended up joining together in the Lombard League to defend their freedom against the Germanic Emperor. In 1231 his grandson, Frederick II, finally granted the Constitutions of Melfi to the Kingdom of Sicily and gave representation to the nobility, the clergy and the cities.

Later, in addition to the traditional antagonism between the Germanic Emperor and the Pope of Rome, there were the territorial ambitions of the houses of Anjou and Aragon, which married into royal thrones of the transalpine peninsula (Abulafia, 2017). Milan evolved from an imperial territory to a republic and duchy. Palermo and Naples always maintained a considerable citizens' autonomy, whether at the heart of the Kingdom of Sicily or when exercising as rival capitals.

The three most significant cases of the capacity of the city-state to re-emerge and of the commercial momentum of Mediterranean capitalism were certainly the republics of Genoa, Florence and Venice. They can be considered the leaders of the Commercial Revolution which took place during the Late Middle Ages. After bottoming in the eighth century, Mediterranean trade began to expand, first, in a very reluctant way, and, since the tenth century with much more strength. Once more, the indicator of shipwrecks supplied by Parker has allowed us to provide global quantitative evidence of the upward trend of a new cycle of transformations in the Mare Nostrum under the lead of the new *thalassocracies* of Northern Italy (De Roover, 1942; Lane, 1973; Lopez, 1976; Parker, 1992; Abulafia, 2011, 2014). As it can be seen in Fig. 1.2, the Medieval peak of maritime exchange in the Mediterranean was reached during the thirteenth century.

Venice, Genova and Florence not only did lead the Commercial Revolution of the late Middle Ages, but also they renewed industry and finance, helped the productive forces to participate in political decision-making and again astonished the world with their thinkers, poets and artists. However, their republican regimes were never free from imperialist tendencies, internal conflicts and client relations, which emulated their predecessors from Antiquity (Abulafia, 2011; Crowley, 2011; Dini, 1995; Felice, 2015; Felloni & Laura, 2004; Goldthwaite, 1980, 2009; Kocka, 2013; Lane, 1973; Lopez, 1976; Miskimin, 1975).

The re-emergence of Mediterranean exchange may have led Genoa to double its population between the years 1000 and 1200, going from

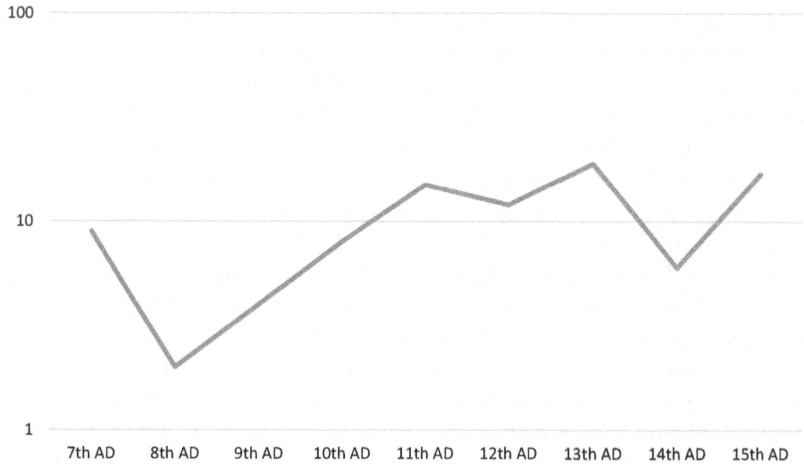

Fig. 1.2 Resilience of Mediterranean exchange during the Commercial Revolution (measured with the number of shipwrecks) (*Source* Own elaboration with Parker [1992])

around 15,000 to circa 30,000 inhabitants (Bairoch et al., 1988). In 1138, a Genoese delegation obtained permission from Emperor Conrad III for the city to be able to mint its own coin for the first time. Its mint began to strike a denarius (*denaro*) coin with a weight of around one gram, although with only 33% of silver, contrasting with the almost pure silver 1.4 grams denarii from the time of Charlemagne. Like in the majority of Mediterranean cities, the demands for public funds and for exchanges led the silver component of the denarius to be reduced, thus devaluating the currency (Cipolla, 1975).

However, the growing disbursements required by the rise of trade led the Genoese mint, in 1172, to produce a much more valuable pure silver coin, the *grosso*. Its weight was equivalent to 1.4 grams, with 11.5 twelfths of silver and a value of four denarii. Three-quarters of a century later, the needs to finance greater volumes of exchange and the accumulation of precious metals arising from the increased competitiveness of trade and of services, led the republic's mint to launch a gold coin, the *genovino d'oro*. The weight of the 1252 *genovino* was equivalent to some 3.5 grams of almost pure metal. More or less simultaneously, Florence began to mint the gold florin (Cipolla, 1975).

The Ligurian city defeated its rival Pisa in the 1284 Battle of Meloria and inherited its rights over Corsica and Sardinia, and in particular over the latter's silver mines. Likewise motivated by privileged access to spices and other goods from the East, it annexed territories of the Aegean, such as Samos, Chios, Phocaea, Lesbos, Smyrna and Lemnos and even occupied part of the Crimean Peninsula. It also operated the alum mines of Phocaea, a product with inelastic demand which was key for the wool drapery industry of the late Middle Ages, due to its use as a mordant. The Genoese thalassocracy was likewise outstanding in organizational innovations, such as shipping insurance and double-entry accounting. Its capital financed campaigns against the Muslims in Iberia and the East and they gradually became stronger over the centuries. Like other republican city-states, it combined a limited representation political system with recurrent political control by families of merchants and bankers. Genoa established one of the main commercial empires of the Mediterranean. In 1300, its metropolis already had some 100,000 inhabitants (Bairoch et al., 1988; Benvenuti, 1989; Felloni & Laura, 2004; Miskimin, 1975).

Florence was at the crossroads between the capital of the Papal States, Rome, and the Germanic Empire, on the western borders of which a new galaxy of commercial cities was formed. It was likewise half way between the Tyrrhenian and the Adriatic and, therefore, well placed to continue to trade with the Mediterranean. Its merchants imported wool from England, grain from Sicily, spices from the East and cloth from Flanders. It developed a drapery industry which employed up to 30,000 people. Its workers organized themselves in guilds, such as the *Arte della Lana*. The *güelfi*, who dominated the city, gradually split into *neri* and *bianchi*. The whites represented the financiers, merchants and artisans (*il Popolo*), while the blacks represented the local nobility (Abulafia, 2011; Dini, 1995; Felice, 2015; Goldthwaite, 1980, 2009; Kocka, 2013; Lopez, 1976; Melis, 1984; Miskimin, 1975).

During the third decade of the thirteenth century, Tuscan cities such as Siena and Pisa, which until then had minted denarii of increasingly lightweight, needed coins of a higher value to facilitate long-distance exchanges. They began to mint almost pure silver *grossi*, with a weight of 2.3 grams and a value of 12 denarii. This equivalence was intended to be equal to the theoretical value of the *solidus*.

Florence wanted to go even further and, in 1252, resumed minting in gold, launching the gold florin, with a weight of almost 3.5 grams of pure metal and a value of 240 denarii (transformed image of the *libbra*).

The *fiorinio d'oro* became the canonical model of a strong currency in the Mediterranean in the late Middle Ages, created out of the desire to emulate the Byzantine *solidus*, the Islamic gold dinar and, probably, the rival *genovino*. Indeed, the recovery of the gold trade with Africa favoured the Florentine and Genoese mints. Both cities considered the period of silver rule initiated by the Carolingians to have concluded and restored the hegemony of gold in Rome.

The government of Florence was headed by seven *priori*, representatives of the guilds, who undertook their duties on a rotating basis. In 1328, the magistrates of the local government began to be chosen at random, taking their names out of a sack which included all those who were eligible and thus evoking the democracy of Athens. Alongside traders and artisans, important banking families had emerged, such as the Bardi and Peruzzi, who financed the kings of England and Naples. Florence reached a population of around 120,000 inhabitants in 1338.

For its part, the Venetian Republic, *La Serenissima*, had a modest hinterland, but it achieved gradual control of eastern trade with its maritime enclaves, starting with the Adriatic (Trieste, Zara and Ragusa). Its traders set up in Alexandria, Constantinople and Tana, in the mouth of the Don. Caravans arrived there with silk, spices, noble metals and slaves, the subjects of *La Serenissima* re-exporting them to London and Bruges, and returning loaded with silver, tin and cloth. German merchants crossed the Alps to buy Syrian cotton, Chinese silk and Cyprus sugar in Rialto. The galleys built in the Arsenal converted it into the biggest shipyard of its time.

In 1202, while Enrico Dandolo was Doge (1192–1205), the Venetian Republic minted the *grosso, matapan* or *ducato d'argento*. This was another almost pure silver coin, equivalent in weight to 2.2 grams and with a value of 26 denarii *(piccoli)*. The employees of the Arsenal, the city's biggest industrial establishment, were paid with this *grosso* (Abulafia, 2011; Cipolla, 1975; Crowley, 2011; Felice, 2015; Kocka, 2013; Lane, 1973; Lopez, 1976; Miskimin, 1975).

In 1204, the aggression of the fourth crusade allowed Venice to annex a quarter of the Byzantine Empire. *La Serenissima* established itself in Corfu, Negroponte, the Cyclades and Crete. Its degree of control over supplies of spices, silk and metals increased significantly. The commercial empire under the banner of San Marcos ended up being the biggest of the whole of the mediaeval Mare Nostrum.

In 1284, Venice launched a new gold coin with a value of 576 denarii. The minting of the *ducato d'oro* simultaneously reflected the desire to challenge the financial hegemony of Florence and Genoa, and the consolidation of the Adriatic thalassocracy into the new centre around which the Mediterranean world gravitated for more than three centuries. Its aristocratic democracy regime, headed by the Doge, likewise evoked the ancient city-states. At the beginning of the fourteenth century, the city of Venice was home to around 110,000 inhabitants (Bairoch et al., 1988; Bloch, 1954; Cipolla, 1975; Le Goff, 2010).

The above cities and other smaller ones led the resurgence of trade or, for many, the Commercial Revolution of the Mare Nostrum during the late Middle Ages. Venice and Genoa's interest in controlling routes led them to create what must be considered the most canonical thalassocracies. Florence did not grow as much towards the sea but, after annexing manufacturing and commercial emporiums of its hinterland, such as Prato, Pistoia and Arezzo, it ended up seeking an outlet to the Tyrrhenian via Pisa or Livorno. We can therefore consider that the former city-states shared an internal drive with some of their predecessors from Antiquity, which led them to become commercial empires.

Peter II the Great (1276–1285), James's son who inherited the kingdoms of Aragon and Valencia and the Catalan counties, married Constance Hohenstaufen, a Sicilian princess. The Sicilians rose up against the Anjou in 1282 and offered the crown to Peter II, who accepted the challenge. From then on, Aragon and Sicily shared a destiny and Barcelona consolidated its Mediterranean influence. Peter's kingdoms enjoyed autonomy and were answerable to their stratified parliaments or courts. The Catalan courts evolved from the primitive assemblies of *Pax et Tregua Dei*. From when they were convened in 1283 by Peter II, the Catalan courts included representation of three strata (or *braços*): nobles, ecclesiastics and cities (or *braç reial*) (Batlle, 1988; Fontana, 2014; Salrach & Duran, 1982; Vilar, 1962).

The boom in Mediterranean trade at the end of the thirteenth century allowed coins with a high weight and value to be minted again, following the model of the Italian republics (and some locations of Provence and Languedoc). In 1284, Peter II ordered the minting of the Barcelona *gros*, with 11.5 out of 12 parts in silver and a face value of 12 *diners* and which was known as the *croat*, due to the cross on the reverse side. For this, as stipulated by his father, he had to have the approval of the city council. At the end of the thirteenth century, the county of Barcelona was already fairly similar to a crowned republic. In 1299, in exchange for new services, the monarch transferred the ***bovaticum*** tax to the Consell de Cent of Barcelona and the Catalan courts (Batlle, 1988; Crusafont, 1996; Fontana, 2014; Vilar, 1962).

In around 1300, the two main maritime cities of the Crown of Aragon were Barcelona and Valencia, with a population of between 40,000 and 50,000 inhabitants each. The city of Mallorca may have had 17,000 and Perpignan 12,000. Barcelona had become a trading and industrial emporium, with over 32 guilds documented. It exported wool cloth to Sicily, and imported large quantities of cereal from there. It also obtained cereal from its traditional sea trade with Languedoc and Provence, when the always stormy relations with the Anjou allowed this. In the ports of the French Midi, the merchants of Barcelona unloaded spices from the East, which could even reach the counties of Toulouse or Savoie (Coulon, 2013; Cuadrada, 2001; Dufourcq, 1969; Smtih, 1940).

Starting from 1326, the Crown of Aragon annexed Sardinia, after failing in its fight with Genoa for the control of Corsica. The model of exchanging cloth for cereal also tended to become consolidated between Catalonia and Sardinia. However, the most precious good obtained in Sardinia was silver, which was used to pay for the spices. The cogs, vessels and galleries of the Barcelona merchants spent the silver in Rhodes, Alexandria, Beirut and Cyprus, where they acquired pepper, ginger, cinnamon, sugar, lacquer, incense and other products with inelastic demand. In these Eastern markets, they also sold wool cloth (some home-produced, some from Flanders and France), coral, saffron and dry fruits. The traders from Barcelona ended up exporting not only the cloth manufactured in their own county but also textiles from different capitals of Catalan counties and other manufacturing locations of the crown, such as Valencia, Perpignan, Vilefranche du Conflent, Berga and Girona (Coulon, 2013; Smith, 1940).

Other preferential destinations of trade from the Catalan cities outside the territories of the Crown of Aragon were Tunis and Béjaïa, where Barcelona had had consuls since 1281. Slaves, gold and coral were purchased on the Barbary Coast and spices, cloth and iron were sold (Cuadrada, 2001; Duforcq, 1969; Smith, 1940).

In the Tyrrhenian, the preferential destinations were Genoa, despite the constant conflicts with the Ligurian republic, and the Tuscan tandem Pisa-Florence. Alum (mordant from drapery) and slaves were purchased from the Genoese, and Aragonese and Valencian wool was sold to them.

The latter was also of interest to the Florentines who, in turn, sold better-quality (and more expensive) cloth than that manufactured in Catalonia.

To summarize, Barcelona, at the head of the Catalan counties and of the Crown of Aragon, led a process of development comparable with that of the republics of northern Italy. On a political level it demonstrated imperial ambitions, which led it to annex first bordering territories and, subsequently, island possessions in the Mediterranean. However, it also created mechanisms of political representation, which included traders and artisans, and limited feudal power. In the economic sphere, it played a significant role in the Commercial Revolution headed by the cities of the northern Mediterranean. The Crown of Aragon's imperialism consequently participated in the commercial and citizens' component typical of the Mare Nostrum. Barcelona's productive dynamism was also imitated by other cities of the crown which, without reaching the same level, endeavoured to emulate it. The cases of Valencia, Mallorca and Perpignan were especially significant.

It was precisely in Perpignan where the florin was minted for the first time in the Catalan Countries by the last King of Mallorca, James III. Since its kingdom was conquest by King Peter III the Ceremonious, the latter continued minting florins. The 1346 florin minted by King Peter was a gold coin, with characteristics very similar to those of its namesake in the city of Arno: 3.5 grams of almost pure gold. Its official value change was 122 *diners*. This decision corroborates the theory that the main Catalan cities imitated and shared many characteristics of the Italian trading republics (Batlle, 1988; Coulon, 2013; Crusafont, 1996; Feliu, 2000, 2016; Fontana, 2014; Vilar, 1962).

Nevertheless, the emergence of Mediterranean trade, which occurred between the eleventh and thirteenth centuries, was severely tested during the new century. On the one hand, the early decades of the fourteenth century were a period of great famine in the western Mediterranean (Benito, 2013; Le Roy Ladurie, 1967; Vilar, 1962). On the other hand, in 1347 the black rat, its fleas and the bacteria *Y pestis* reappeared in the Mare Nostrum with renewed force. These alien passengers on the ships which sailed the seas caused the worst demographic shock in Mediterranean history in the whole of the second millennium of our era.

References

Abulafia, D. (2011). *The Great Sea*. Penguin.

Abulafia, D. (2014). Thalassocracies. In P. Horden & S. Kinoshita (Eds.), *A Companion to Mediterranean History* (pp. 139–153). Willey Blackwell.

Abulafia, D. (2017). *La guerra de los Doscientos Años. Aragón y Anjou y la lucha por el Mediterráneo*. Pasado y Presente.

Akurgal, E. (1986). *Civilisations et Sites Antiques de Turquie*. Istanbul: Haset Kitabevi.

Anderson, P. (1979). *Passages from Antiquity to Feudalism*. New Left Books.

Asensio, D., & Jornet, R. (2019). Territoris polítics i territoris ètnics a la Catalunya interior i Baix Aragó en època ibèrica. In M. C. Belarte, J. Noguera, R. Plana-Mallart, & J. Sanmartí (Eds.), Urbanization in Iberia and Mediterranean Gaul in the First Millennium BC, *Treballs d'Arqueologia de la Mediterrània Antiga*, 7, ICAC, 179–196.

Aubet, M. E. (1993). *The Phoenicians and the West: Politics, Colonies and Trade*. Cambridge University Press.

Aubet, M. E., & Sanmartí, E. (1996). La incorporació a les civitlitzacions mediterrànies. In E. Junyent (Ed.), *Història, Societat i Cultura dels Països Catalans. 1. Els temps prehistòrics fins al segle* V (pp. 220–261). Enciclopèdia Catalana.

Bairoch, P. (1985). *De Jéricho à Mexico*. Gallimard.

Bairoch, P., Batou, J., & Chèvre, P. (1988). *La Population des villes européennes, 800–1850*. Droz.

Balañá, P. (2002). *L'Islam a Catalunya (segles VIII–XII)*. Rafael Dalmau.

Bang, P. (2008). *The Roman Baazar: A Comparative Study of Trade and Markets in a Tributary Empire*. Cambridge U. P.

Barceló, M., Kirchner, H., & Navarro, C. (1996). *El agua que no duerme. Fundamentos de la arquitectura hidráulica andalusí*. Legado Andalusí.

Batet, C. (2001). Els usos feudals de l'aigua a la Vall del Corb. *Recerques, 43*, 105–128.

Batlle, C. (1988). *L'expansió baixmedieval (segles XIII–XV)*. Edicions 62.

Beard, M. (2016). *SPQR: A History of Ancient Rome*. Profile.

Beloch, J. (1937–1961). *Bevölkerungsgeschichte Italiens* (3 Vols.). De Gruyter.

Bellwood, P. (2005). *First Farmers: The Origins of Agricultural Societies*. Blackwell.

Beltrán, F., & Jordán, C. (2019). Writing and Language in Celtiberia. In J. Velaza & A. G. Sinner (Eds.), *Paleohispanic Languages and Epigraphies* (pp. 240–303). Oxford U. P.

Benito, P. (2013). De Labrousse a Sen. Modelos de causalidad y paradigmas interpretativos de las crisis alimentarias preindustriales. In P. Benito (Ed.), *Crisis alimentarias en la Edad Media. Modelos, explicaciones y representaciones* (pp. 15–32). Ed. Milenio.

Benvenuti, G. (1989). *Le Reppubliche Marinare. Amalfi, Pisa, Genova, Venezia*. Newton & Compton.
Bernardi, A. (1970). The Economic Problems of the Roman Empire. In C. M. Cipolla (Ed.), *The Economic Decadence of Empires* (pp. 27–100, Spanish edition, Alianza 1985). Methuen & Co.
Bisson, T. N. (1986). *The Medieval Crown of Aragon. A Short History*. Oxford U. P.
Bisson, T. N. (2009). *The Crisis of the Twelfth Century*. Princeton.
Black, J. (2020). *A Brief History of the Mediterranean*. Robinson.
Bloch, M. (1947). Comment et pourquoi finit l'esclavage antique. *Annales. 2on année, 1*, 30–44.
Bloch, M. (1954). *Esquisse d'une histoire monétaire de l'Europe*. Armand Colin.
Bolòs, J., & Hurtado, V. (2009). *Atles dels Comtats de Rosselló, Conflent, Vallespir i Fenollet (759–991)*. Rafael Dalmau.
Bonnassie, P. (1985). Survie et extinction du régime esclavagiste dans l'Occident du haut moyen âge (IVe–Xie s.). *Cahiers De Civilisation Médievale, XXVIII*(4), 307–343.
Bonnassie, P. (1990). *La Catalogne au tournant de l'an mil*. Albin Michel.
Bosch i Gimpera, P. (1932). *Etnologia de la Península Ibèrica*. Alpha.
Boserup, E. (1965). *The Conditions of Agricultural Growth: The Economics of Agrarian Change Under Population Pressure*. Allen & Unwin.
Brunt, P. (1971). *Italian Manpower, 225BC–AD14*. Clarendon.
Bryce, T. (2009). *The Routledge Handbook of the Peoples and Places of Ancient Western Asia*. Routledge.
Buenacasa, C. (2013). La crisi del segle III, preludi de la fi del món antic. *Butlletí de la Societat Catalana d'Estudis Històrics, XXIV*, 191–218.
Campbell, B. (2016). *The Great Transition*. Cambridge U. P.
Cipolla, C. M. (1962). *The Economic History of World Population*. Penguin.
Cipolla, C. M. (1975). *Le aventure della lira*. Il Mulino.
Cohen, C. (1977). *The Food Crisis in Prehistory: Over-Population and the Origins of Agriculture*. Yale U. P.
Comas, M. (1997). *Les marques d'àmfora*. IEC-Museu de Badalona.
Comín, F. (2011). *Historia económica mundial. De los orígenes a la actualidad*. Alianza.
Correa, J. A., & Guerra, A. (2019). The Epigraphic and Linguistic Situation in the South-East of the Iberian Peninsula. In J. Velaza & A. G. Sinner (Eds.), *Paleohispanic Languages and Epigraphies* (pp. 109–137). Oxford U. P.
Coulon, D. (2013). *Barcelona i el gran comerç d'Orient a l'edat mijtana*. Base.
Crowley, R. (2011). *City of Fortune: How Venice Won and Lost a Naval Empire*. Faber and Faber.
Crusafont, M. (1989). *Barcelona i la moneda catalana*. Caixa de Pensions.
Crusafont, M. (1996). *Història de la moneda catalana*. Crítica.

Crusafont, M. (2015). *Història de la moneda de la Corona Catalano-aragonesa medieval*. Societat d'Estudis Numismàtics, IEC.
Cuadrada, C. (2001). *La Mediterrània, cruïlla de mercaders (segles XIII–XV)*. Rafael Dalmau.
D'Abadal, R. (1969–1970). *Dels Visigots als Catalans* (2 Vols.). Edicions 62.
De Martino, F. (1980). *Storia economica di Roma antica* (2 Vols.). La Nuova Italia.
De Palol, P. (1996). La baixa romanitat i l'etapa visigòtica. In E. Junyent (Ed.), *Història, Societat i Cultura dels Països Catalans. 1. Els temps prehistòrics fins al segle V* (pp. 380–403). Enciclopèdia Catalana.
De Roover, R. (1942). The Comercial Revolution of the Thirteenth Century. *Bulletin of the Business Historical Society, XVI*, 34–39.
Depeyrot, G. (1991). *Crises et inflation entre Antiquité et Moyen Âge*. Armand Colin.
Diamond, J. (1997). *Guns, Germs and Steel: The Fates of Human Societies*. W. W. Northon.
Dini, B. (1995). *Saggi su una economia-mondo. Firenze e Italia fra Mediterraneo ed Europa (secc. XIII–XVI)*. Pacini.
Duby, G. (2001). *Atlas historique mondiale*. Larousse.
Dufourcq, C. (1969). *L'expansió catalana a la Mediterrània occidental*. Vicens Vives.
Eichengreen, B. (2015). *Hall of Mirrors*. Oxford University Press.
Espluga, X. (1998). La decadència de l'esclavisme. Un mite historiogràfic que s'esvaeix. *Butlletí de la Societat Catalana d'Estudis Històrics, IX*, 9–22.
Felice, E. (2015). *Accesa e declino*. Il Mulino.
Feliu, G. (2000). Moneda y Banca en Cataluña en el siglo XV. In A. M. Bernal (Ed.), *Dinero, moneda y crédito en la monarquía hispánica* (pp. 121–134). Marcial Pons.
Feliu, G. (2012). *Història econòmica de Catalunya*. Base.
Feliu, G. (2016). Finances, Currency and Taxation in the 14th and 15th Centuries. *Catalan Historical Review, 9*, 25–44.
Felloni, G., & Laura, G. (2004). *Genoa and the History of Finance: A Series of Firsts?* Genoa.
Ferrer, J., & Moncunill, N. (2019). Paleohispanic Writing Systems: Classification, Origin and Development. In J. Velaza & A. G. Sinner (Eds.), *Paleohispanic Languages and Epigraphies* (pp. 78–108). Oxford U. P.
Ferrer i Mallol, M. T. (Ed.) (2011–2013). *Jaume I. Commemoració del VIII centenari del naixement de Jaume I.* (2 Vols.). Institut d'Estudis Catalans.
Finley, M. I. (1963). *The Ancient Greeks*. Chatto & Windus.
Finley, M. I. (1970). *Early Greece: The Bronze and Archaic Ages*. Norton.
Finley, M. I. (1973). *The Ancient Economy*. University of California Press.

Fontana, J. (2014). *La formació d'una identitat. Una història de Catalunya*. Eumo.

Forcano, M. (2014). *Els jueus catalans*. Angle.

Forcano, M. (2021). *Tres savis jueus de la Barcelona medieval*. Rafael Dalmau.

Freedman, P. H. (1993). *Els orígens de la servitud pagesa a la Catalunya Medieval*. Eumo.

Freeman, C., & Louçã, F. (2001). *As Time Goes By*. Oxford U. P.

Frier, B. W. (2000). Demography. In A. K. Bowman, P. Garnsey & D. Rathbone (Eds.), *The high empire, AD70-190. The Cambridge ancient history* (vol. XI, pp. 787–816). Cambridge U. P.

Furió, A. (2008). *El rei conqueridor*. Bromera.

García Mora, F. (2018). *Atlas de Historia Antigua. Volumen I: El Próximo Oriente Antiguo*. Síntesis.

Garrido, C. (1998). *Arqueología de Cataluña y Baleares*. Planeta.

Gibbon, E. (1776–1788). *The History of the Decline and Fall of the Roman Empire* (6 Vols.). Strahan & Cadell.

Goldthwaite, R. A. (1980). *The Economy of Renaissance Florence*. Johns Hopkins University Press.

Goldthwaite, R. A. (2009). *The Building of Renaissance Florence: An Economic and Social History*. Johns Hopkins University Press.

Grau, I. (2021). L'àrea central d'Ibèria. *MAC, L'enigma iber* (pp. 69–81). Museu d'Arqueologia de Catalunya.

Hararai, Y. N. (2014). *Sapiens: A Brief History of Humankind*. Harvill Secker.

Harper, K. (2017). *The Fate of Rome*. Princeton.

Heun, M., Schafer-Pregl, R., Klawan, D., Castagna, R., Accerbi, M., Borghi, B., & Salamini, F. (1997). Site of Einkorn Wheat Domestication Identified by DNA Fingerprint. *Science, 278*(5341), 1312–11314.

Hopkins, K. (1980). Taxes and Trade in the Roman Empire (200BC–400AD). *Journal of Roman Studies, 70*, 101–102.

Hudson, M. (2010). Entrepreneurs: From the Near East Takeoff to the Roman Collapse. In D. Landes, J. Mokyr, & W. Baumol (Eds.), *The Invention of Enterprise* (pp. 8–39). Princeton.

Járrega, R. (2013). Crisi i canvis estructurals a la Hispània oriental entre l'Alt Imperi Romà i l'Antiquitat Tardana. *Butlletí de la Societat Catalana d'Estudis Històrics, XXIV*, 219–266.

Jones, A. H. M. (1964). *The Later Roman Empire* 284–602*: A Social, Economic and Administrative Survey* (3 Vols.). Basil Blackwell.

Kaldellis, A. (2007). The Literature of Plague and the Anxieties of Piety in Sixth-Century Bizantium. In F. Mormando & T. W. Worcester (Eds.) *Piety and Plague: From Byzantium to the Baroque* (pp. 1–22). Truman State U. P.

Kay, P. (2014). *Rome's Economic Revolution*. Oxford U. P.

Kindleberger, C. P. (1973). *The World in Depression 1929–1939*. University of California Press.
Kocka, J. (2013). *Geschichte des Kapitalismus*. Beck.
Lane, F. C. (1973). *Venice: A Maritime Republic*. Johns Hopkins University Press.
Lazuela-Fox, C. (2017). *La forja genètica d'Europa; una nova visió del passat de les poblacions humanes*. Universitat de Barcelona.
Le Goff, J. (2010). *Le Moyen Âge et l'argent*. Perrin.
Le Roy Ladurie, E. (1962). *Histoire du Languedoc*. PUF.
Le Roy Ladurie, E. (1967). *Histoire du climat depuis l'an mil*. Flammarion.
Le Roy Ladurie, E. (1975). *Montaillou, village occitan de 1294 à 1324*. Gallimard.
Lo Cascio, E. (2007). Crescita e declino. L'economia romana in prospettiva storica. *Rivista di Storia Economica, 23*(3), 269–282.
Lo Cascio, E., & Malanima, P. (2005). Cycles and Stability: Italian Population Before Demographic Transition (225 BC–AD 1900). *Rivista di Storia Economica, 21*(3), 197–232.
Lopez, R. S. (1976). *The Commercial Revolution of the Middle Ages, 950–1350*. Cambridge U. P.
Lopez, R. S., & Miskimin, H. A. (1962). The Economic Depression of the Renaissance. *Economic History Review, 2nd s., XIV*, 408–426.
Luján, E. R. (2019). Language and Writing Among the Lusitanians. In J. Velaza & A. G. Sinner (Eds.), *Paleohispanic Languages and Epigraphies* (pp. 304–334). Oxford U. P.
Maddison, A. (1985). *Two Crises: Latin America and Asia 1929–1938 and 1973–1983*. OECD.
Maddison, A. (2007). *Contours of the World Economy, 1–2030 AD: Essays in Macroeconomic History*. Oxford University Press.
Maluquer de Motes, J. (1987). *Prehistòria i edat antiga fins al segle III*. Edicions 62.
Manning, J. G. (2018). *The Open Sea*. Princeton.
Martel, P. (2019). *Histoire de l'Occitanie*. Yoran.
Mayer, M. (1996). La promoció social. In E. Junyent (Ed.), *Història, Societat i Cultura dels Països Catalans. 1. Els temps prehistòrics fins al segle V* (pp. 337–339). Enciclopèdia Catalana.
McCormick, M. (2001). *Origins of the European Economy*. Press Syndicate of the University of Cambridge.
McCormick, M. (2015). Tracking Mass Death During the Fall of Rome's Empire (I): A First Inventory of Mass Grave. *Journal of Roman Archeology, 28*, 325–357.

McCormick, M. (2016). Tracking Mass Death During the Fall of Rome's Empire (II): A First Inventory of Mass Grave. *Journal of Roman Archeology, 29*, 1004–1007.
McEvedy, C. (2011). *Cities of the Classical World*. Allen Lane.
McEvedy, C. & Jones, R. (1978). *Atlas of world population history*. Penguin.
McNeill, R., & McNeill, W. M. (2003). *The Human Web: A Bird's-Eye View of World History*. Norton.
Melis, F. (1984). *L'economia fiorentina del Rinascimento*. Le Monnier.
Minsky, H. (1975). *John Maynard Keynes*. Columbia University Press.
Miskimin, H. A. (1975). *The Economy of Early Renaissance Europe, 1300–1460*. Cambridge University Press.
Mollat du Jourdin, M. (1993). *Europe and the Sea*. Blackwell.
Montanelli, I. (1957). *Storia di Roma*. Longanesi.
Muhs, B. P. (2016). *The Ancient Egyptian Economy, 3000–30 BC*. Cambrige University Press.
Nolla, J. M. (1996). Organització i explotació del territori sota l'Imperi. In E. Junyent (Ed.), *Història, Societat i Cultura dels Països Catalans. 1. Els temps prehistòrics fins al segle V* (pp. 302–315). Enciclopèdia Catalana.
North, D., & Thomas, R. (1973). *The Rise of the Western World*. Cambridge University Press.
Orduña, E. (2019). The Vasco-Iberian Theory. In J. Velaza & A. G. Sinner (Eds.), *Paleohispanic Languages and Epigraphies* (pp. 219–239). Oxford University Press.
Parker, A. J. (1992). *Ancient Shipwrecks of the Mediterranean and the Roman Provinces*. British Archeological Reports.
Parker, G. (2001). *Europe in Crisis: 1598–1648* (2nd ed.). Blackwell.
Pirenne, H. (1973). *Mahomet et Charlemagne*. Presses Universitaires de France.
Postrel, V. (2020). *The Fabrics of Civilization: How Textiles Made the World*. Basic Books.
Prevosti, M., & Guitart, J. (Eds.) (2011). *Ager Tarraconensis 2. El poblament/ The Population (PAT 2)*. Institut Català d'Arquelogia Clàssica.
Puech, V. (2011). *Constantin*. Ellipses.
Quinn, J. (2018). *In Search of the Phoenicians*. Princeton University Press.
Riera, A. (2005). Els orígens de la manufactura tèxtil medieval a la Corona catalanoaragonesa (c. 1150–1298). In R. Narbona (Ed.), *XVIII Congrés d'Història de la Coronad'Aragó* (pp. 821–901). Universitat de València.
Ripollès, P. P. (1996). Fiscalitat i política monetària. In E. Junyent (Ed.), *Història, Societat i Cultura dels Països Catalans. 1. Els temps prehistòrics fins al segle V* (pp. 312–313). Enciclopèdia Catalana.
Ripollès, P. P. (2012). The Ancient Coinages of the Iberian Peninsula. In W. E. Metcalf (Ed.), *The Oxford Handbook of Greek and Roman Coinages* (pp. 356–374). Cambridge University Press.

Rostovtzeff, M. (1926). *Social and Economic History of the Roman Empire*. Clarendon Press.

Russell, J. C. (1958). *Late Ancient and Medieval Population*. American Philosophical Society.

Salrach, J. M. (1987). *El procés de feudalització (segles III–XII)*. Edicions 62.

Salrach, J. M. (1997). *La formación del campesinado en el Occidente antiguo y medieval*. Síntesis.

Salrach, J. M. (2006). *La formació dels Països Catalans*. UOC.

Salrach, J. M. (2020). Ramon d'Abadal i els orígens històrics de Catalunya. *Butlletí de la Societat Catalana d'Estudis Històrics, XXXI*, 63–78.

Salrach, J. M., & Duran, E. (1982). *Història dels Països Catalans. Dels orígens a 1714*. Barcelona.

Sanmartí, E. (1996). El plom grec d'Empúries. In E. Junyent (Ed.), *Història, Societat i Cultura dels Països Catalans. 1. Els temps prehistòrics fins al segle V* (pp. 226–227). Enciclopèdia Catalana.

Schumpeter, J. A. (1939). *Business Cycles: A Theoretical, Historical and Statistical Analysis of the Capitalist Process* (2 Vols.). McGraw-Hill.

Seabright, P. (2004). *The Company of Strangers: A Natural History of Economic Life*. Princeton University Press.

Sear, D. (1988). *Roman Coins and Their Values* (4th Rev.). Seaby.

Sherratt, S. (2016). *Ensayos sobre economía e ideología en el Mediterráneo antiguo*. Edicions Bellaterra.

Smith, R. S. (1940). *The Spanish Guild Merchant. A History of the Consulado, 1250–1700*. Duke University Press.

Spawforth, T. (2018). *The Story of Greece and Rome*. Yale University Press.

Tarradell, M. (1962). *Les arrels de Catalunya*. Vicens Vives.

Temin, P. (2017). *The Roman Market Economy*. Princeton.

Tilly, C. (1990). *Coercion, Capital and European States A.D. 990–1990*. Basil Blackwell.

Turching, P., & Nefedov, S. A. (2009). *Secular Cycles*. Princeton.

Udina, F. (2000). *El nom de Catalunya* (Rev.). Rafael Dalmau.

Usher, A. P. (1943). *The early history of deposit banking in Mediterranean Europe*. Harvard University Press.

Vallejo, I. (2019). *El infinito en un junco. La invención de los libros en el mundo antiguo*. Siruela.

Vagi, D. L. (1999). *Coinage and History of the Roman Empire, c. 82 BC–AD 480* (2 Vols.). Coin World.

Van Zanden, J. L. (2009). *The Long Road to the Industrial Revolution*. Brill.

Vernet, J. (1978). *La cultura hispanoárabe en Oriente y Occidente*. Ariel.

Vilar, P. (1962). *La Catalogne dans l'Espagne moderne. Recherches sur les fondaments économiques des structures nationales*. SEVPEN.

Warburton, D. (1997). *State and Temple Economy in Ancient Egypt: Fiscal Vocabulary of the New Kingdom*. Fribourg University Press.

Wickham, C. (1984). The Other Transition: From Ancient World to Feudalism. *Past & Present, 103*, 3–36.

Wickham, C. (2005). *Framing the Early Middle Ages: Europe and the Mediterranean 400–800*. Oxford University Press.

Wickham, C. (2016). *Medieval Europe*. Yale University Press.

Woolmer, M. (2017). *A Short History of the Phoenicians*. Tauris.

CHAPTER 2

Late Antiquity and Early Middle Ages: The Crisis Before the Crisis or, Again, the Transition from the Ancient System to Feudalism

Josep Maria Salrach

This article aims to provide an interpretation of the crises and changes produced in the West between the end of the Roman Empire and the twelfth century, understood as the transition from the ancient system to feudalism. It is not a question of a new examination of the celebrated debate on eleventh-century feudal change, revolution or mutation, but a personal contribution that, given its chronological and geographic framework, cannot fail to consider the fundamental elements of this debate.[1]

Institut d'Estudis Catalans.

J. M. Salrach (✉)
Institut d'Estudis Catalans, Barcelona, Spain
e-mail: josep.salrach@upf.edu

J. Catalan Vidal (ed.), *Crises and Transformation in the Mediterranean World*, Palgrave Studies in Economic History,
https://doi.org/10.1007/978-3-031-24502-2_2

Prior to the crisis of the fourteenth century, which we consider systemic and refer to as the crisis of feudalism (Bois, 2000), during Late Antiquity and the Early Middle Ages Europe suffered a series of comparatively less relevant crises. Some were temporary, relating to subsistence, and others sectoral, linked to the transition from the old system to feudalism.[2] There were many subsistence crises, linked to adverse climatic conditions, and which societies, burdened by technical weaknesses, political issues and inequalities inherent in their social systems (the ancient and the feudal), were not able to and did not know how to deal with.[3] We do not wish to address these crises here, however, but rather those that framed the transition to feudalism between Late Antiquity and the twelfth century. They were sectoral crises, in the sense that they affected sensitive, even structural, parts of the ancient system, which was transformed by them. However, with the exception, perhaps, of the crisis of the year thousand, they were not global or systemic crises, in the sense that none of them affected the system as a whole and suddenly precipitated collapse and replacement. It is for this reason that we talk about transition when taking the long-term perspective and, within this, refer to sectoral, or sometimes recurring, crises when looking at the short-term picture.

2.1 Ancient System and Crises in Roman Times

In a famous article, published over thirty years ago, Chris Wickham (1984) referred to this process as "the other transition", and defended the idea that three modes of production (MP) coexisted during Roman times: the slave, the tributary and the feudal. According to this historian, between the second century BC and the second century AD, slavery had been the dominant MP among the Romans, while taxation (territorial and personal tax: the *iugatio* and the *capitatio*) was the source of resources necessary to maintain the state apparatus and, therefore, the coercive force that guaranteed the submission of the servile masses. From the second century AD onwards, or the so-called third-century crisis, slavery declined and the roles were reversed: tributary became the dominant MP and slave the secondary or supporting MP. And while the slave MP needed the tributary MP, which guaranteed order, to survive, the inverse does not appear to have been true.[4]

The slave MP was characterized, in Roman times, by "direct exploitation" through the forced labour of the slave (all production was available to the *dominus*), who was considered a tool that could speak, due to the "concentrated" organization of production (a single decision-making centre) in large plantations (*fundi, villae*) and a strong and univocal conception of property: the *dominus* is the absolute owner of the land, the workforce and the product. The dominant weight of the model could and, in fact did, end up impregnating the medium-sized and small properties, where it was not rare to find a slave owned by the peasant working the land. The viability of the large landed property with slaves was linked to the existence of the market and, therefore, the city, which was the great beneficiary of slavery-based production. While urban demand was strong, the old (direct) kind of slavery-based production remained, although the reproduction of slave labour came up against difficulties as a result of the end of great conquests. Following the revolt of the slaves in the first century BC, this, in other words, the thinning out of the slave market, constituted the first slavery crisis. It was above all a crisis of supply, because, although slaves could reproduce on the *fundus*, or home farm, this did not guarantee the maintenance of assets, which were inevitably reduced.[5]

The tributary MP was a way of obtaining one's own, although not exclusive, surplus of large, agricultural (and mercantile) empires, whereby a social base of peasant landowners and tenants were basically the highest taxpayers. In the Roman state, this social base existed, they were the *rustici* and *coloni*, who worked their own land and others' land, and were free from everything except paying taxes (and rent on *coloni*). Of course, merchants, shopkeepers, craftsmen and, we can suppose, great landowners, all paid taxes. However, the tributary MP had been conceived and developed as the most appropriate way to drain resources from the peasant population, when they were a majority among free men. This taxation involved a complex organization of power, a State, with a decision-making centre (the court), a diverse administration for the functions (civil, military and religious administration) and a network of districts and cells applying governmental decisions on the territory and collecting taxes: this was the city. In the Roman world, these cities, understood as the urban nucleus, were political centres where the ruling class of large landowners resided, centres that drained the resources of the land through the work of slaves, taxes and rent. In this sense, the city took product from the land without giving anything or almost nothing in return. The country-city relationship was, then, unilateral and political rather than economic.[6]

The difference between slave and peasant was a substantial one. The slave was a tool that could speak; he had no legal status and belonged to an owner, as did the fruit of his labour. The peasant, on the other hand, was a citizen with rights and duties, a recognized legal status, owner of himself and, as a free man, obliged to pay taxes. The power that was at least partially sustained in this surplus of peasant labour allowed for citizens, even those most disadvantaged, like small peasants, to have rights and expectations of the governors who protected them (via the administration of justice, for example). The political concept of the commonwealth (*res publica*) was developed on the basis of this, as a result of the interaction between the citizen and the State (the powerful rulers), the politically organized reciprocal action of the given (taxation) and the received (protection). At the height of this organizational and ideological process, citizens (including peasants), often victims of shortages and famine, became accustomed to demanding solutions to food shortages from the authorities, which, in extreme situations, used tax resources to combat them. Citizens were led to think that whoever paid taxes had the right to expect not to be left to go hungry.[7]

Sometimes, doubt is cast on the difference between taxation and rent with the argument that they are similar forms of subtraction, insofar as they go from the inferior (the peasantry) to the superior (the aristocracy), for example. However, this ignores the contrast of significances and implications, even opposites, inherent in the social system. The rent was the part of the product that the non-owner peasant paid to the landowner. This was the case with the relationship between the *coloni* and the *domini*, a relationship that, in the classical Roman world, was exhausted with the act of paying the rent, and did not have the suppositions or the political-ideological implications of taxation. In any case, the *colonate*, which is this form of relationship we are referring to, can also be considered an MP, and the one that, when it became hegemonic, would be the basis of feudalism, and can therefore be called a feudal MP. While only a minority between the second century BC and second century AD, the feudal MP acquired importance from the third and fourth centuries onwards, as the city and the market declined, and with their slavery. Then the *domini*, especially those who owned large "herds" of slaves, settled many of their slaves on the land as if they were *coloni*: *servi quasi coloni*, they were called. These *casati* slaves (with house and land) resembled the *coloni*, in the sense that they worked a piece of land that had been assigned to them and they lived there, but they were legally still slaves and, as such, were the property of a master who could take whatever product he wanted from them, even their very offspring. They could not have their own family, even if they did have one.[8]

The slavery crisis, which had begun as a supply crisis in the second century when the great conquests came to an end, grew from the third or fourth century onwards due to a decline in demand in the urban market, where the production of the *fundi* was destined. This decline in demand was the result of a more widespread economic and social crisis in the Roman State, perhaps the most striking evidence of which was the decline of rural settlements throughout the West from around 350 AD and throughout the fifth century.

Among the root causes of this situation were the growing social inequality and the burden of taxation, which was becoming increasingly unbearable for the comparatively impoverished popular classes.[9] Prior to that point, fiscal burdens had served to finance an imperialistic policy that legitimized them (territorial conquests, new sources of revenue, captives), but when expansion ended and fiscal exploitation continued, or even grew and hardened (laws of *adscriptio*), it became clearer that taxation increased social differences.[10] It was then that the lower social groups became aware of the inequality and exploitation they suffered, and this awareness led to a social crisis. In several western provinces, fugitive slaves, *coloni* pursued by the tax collector and disgruntled soldiers became allies to throw themselves into the social war and loot the *villae* or *fundi* of the landlords, laying siege to the cities where the established social order was based (Sánchez León, 1996).

2.2 Successor-States: Continuities and Changes

The Germanic invasions of the fifth century exerted a powerful and complex influence on this process. The tributary MP, which must have been the hegemonic MP at the time, was severely damaged as a result. Institutionally, the Western Roman State was dismantled and the cities lost even more weight; not only demographic and economic, but also political: the municipal curia, the institution of urban government, rapidly disappeared.[11] And the public army, in the sense that it was directly financed with public taxes, had to be reinforced with private troops (the armed Germanic suites, or *comitivae*), and remunerated with lands of the fisc (benefits), rather than with resources from taxes.[12] Something similar happened with the clergy as regards remuneration. Thus, the reduction of the civil bureaucracy and the military and religious expenses incurred through taxation made taxes less necessary; taxes which, incidentally, taxpayers were reluctant to pay. Naturally, the Germanic kings and their government collaborators did not resign themselves to losing this form of revenue, however, and began to look for alternative ways to continue to collect them.[13]

Frankish, Ostrogothic and Visigothic sources from the sixth century demonstrate that taxes continued to be collected, although they also endorse the idea that this form of subtraction lost legitimacy and was not collected correctly. In Frankish Gaule, taxation was perceived as a simple source of enrichment for the monarch and a further cause of impoverishment for the poorest, who obtained no benefit from it. By contrast, in Ostrogothic Italy the weight of Roman tradition meant that during the sixth century, taxes were still considered public resources that could be mobilized to combat a subsistence crisis. It is possible that the same thing happened in Visigothic Hispania, since the Church collaborated in calculating the tax rate and applying it.[14]

In summary, the Germanic kingdoms can be considered successor States insofar as they were, in fact, the result of a pact between the Roman and Germanic aristocracies, with the mediation of the Church, which was intended to preserve the old MPs as far as possible. This started with the taxpayer, guaranteeing a certain continuity of the idea of the State and, with it, elements of the Roman legal system, which made a distinction between the public and the private. In keeping with the old tradition, it is clear that taxpayers continued to be mainly rent-paying peasants and peasant owners, though these peasant owners already in serious decline as the deterioration of the State accentuated insecurity and therefore pushed towards the search for private protectors. In any case, it is also possible that the Germanic peoples, heirs of old tribal traditions, and particularly dedicated to raising livestock, when settling in the Western Roman State reinforced the rights of property and community use of forests and pastures. If this was the case, it is possible that this Germanic influence counteracted the wearing down of the small landowner and prevented his extinction.

We have talked of the decline and partial denaturalization of the tributary MP, but what of the slave MP? It is possible that, in contrast to the decline of the third and fourth centuries, the fifth and sixth centuries saw a revival, the effect of wars caused by invasions with subsequent captures. These may in some cases have continued during the seventh century as a result of the conflicts between the Germanic kingdoms and the predatory way of life of many of the invading peoples who, arriving in the Roman or post-Roman West, made raids throughout neighbouring territories, capturing everything they found, but mostly men, women and cattle. Some of the captives, converted into slaves, were incorporated into the domestic service of the powerful and others were forced to work the land in various conditions, some directly, others indirectly exploited, without ceasing to be slaves.[15]

The vocabulary used in the texts of the sixth and seventh centuries shows the transition process taking place in European societies of the time. Firstly, very different names were designated to people who lived and worked in the countryside. The old trilogy of *servi* (slaves), *coloni* (rent-paying peasants) and *rustici* (peasant owners) survived, although masked by many other names that makes them more difficult to identify, part hybridisms of a system that was constantly moving and changing. The most revealing, however, were the names given to ways in which the labour force was exploited on large farms. The research basically reveals the existence of two opposing and well-established modes, inherited from the Roman past, on large landed property or *fundus*: the slave property, where appropriation of the surplus took place directly via a centralized command, and the property divided into *colonicas* (peasant tenures), where *coloni* and *servi casati* lived and worked, plus a hybrid and little-known mode, still embryonic, that of the classic bipartite "manorial system" (Tits-Dieuaide, 1985). On the smaller property, however, the workforce may have mostly comprised slaves.[16]

The bipartite large landed property can be defined as partially slave-based, because they had one part dedicated to direct exploitation (the *pars dominical* or demesne) and another to indirect exploitation (the *pars colonica* or peasant tenures). This we call transition hybridism. On the *pars dominical*, there were still herds of slaves (*servi*), tools of the landlords to work the land. On the *pars colonica*, peasants were more or less mixed with *casati* slaves (*servi casati*), who lived off the land, delivered part of the harvest to the *dominus* and provided services for the *pars dominical* as additional work to that done by the slaves.

With unity broken in the West, economic, social, cultural and political differences emerged and with them the different rhythms of evolution. Everywhere the public ceded to the power of the private, which is a way of saying that the *res publica* or commonwealth or those who postulated themselves as being responsible (the monarchs) backed down to private interests (of the aristocracy), even if the Church endeavoured to sacralize the kings and make them untouchable—the incarnation of an authority, they said, that did not come from below but from the up above: kings by the grace of God. In general, however, the kings' authority was weak in the Germanic kingdoms. They strove to attain the main means of power, but the fidelity of an ambitious aristocracy, desirous of offices, functions and profits, was too expensive and insecure.[17] Even the Church, the kings' principal ally, turned the Episcopal cities of Gaul into independent-style principalities,[18] while in Hispania revolts by the aristocracy and kings being deposed made the kingdom difficult to govern. When the Arabs and Berbers invaded the kingdom in 711, it seems that disunity was very strong. From time immemorial there had been a political crisis, a process of feudalization of power (atomization), which was also accompanied by a social crisis (Sayas & Garcia Moreno, 1981, pp. 348–376).[19]

When the kings of Toledo, with the help of bishops and magnates, dictated the laws contained in the *Liber Iudicum* in the seventh century they must have been overwhelmed by the situation of social crisis, otherwise it would not be possible to understand why they devoted the ninth book (*De fugitivis et refugientibus*) of this code to the problem of fugitive slaves. This was possibly the last crisis of ancient slavery. Let us recall that fugitives could be either *servi* or *servi casati*. And the differences between them were not as great as it seems. Since the days of the Late Empire, the *domini* had settled many of their *servi* on the land, thus turning them into *servi casati* or *servi quasi coloni*. One might say that their situation then improved and they even resembled the *coloni*, when in fact they were not, in either economic or legal terms: they were still slaves. Better off, if you like, but slaves nonetheless, because they were not legal entities, and had no recognized rights such as those of land ownership or rental or that of forming a family; the justice system did not protect them and they could be abused by their owners, who could take whatever they wanted from them and the fruit of their labour. We cannot say, in terms of property, that they paid rent, even as a custom. Like other slaves, they had good reason to flee. According to legislation, the *Liber* was a segregationist code.[20]

Some historians prefer to call serfs the *servi* and *mancipia* of the *Liber*. This indicates that in their opinion they held an intermediate status somewhere between the old *coloni* and the old *servi*, although it seems clear that the *coloni* of the sixth and seventh centuries were no longer the *coloni* of the Early Roman Empire. Their situation, with the laws of affiliation (*adscriptio*) and the greater dependency-protection of the owners, had worsened. There are even doubts over whether the word serf would not be better suited to the *colonus* than to the *servus* of this time. The word slave, then, still serves to mark differences and talk of evolution, although it is clear that the situations the two human groups found themselves in were coming closer together: that of the slaves was improving (*servi casati*, *servi quasi coloni*) and that of the *coloni* worsening. The impression one draws from reading the *Liber* is that the fugitive slaves found shelter in places inhabited by peasants of different status to them whom the legislators wanted to force to collaborate in the capture of the fugitives, but who in fact felt supportive of them.[21] This would appear, then, to have been a social crisis. This new crisis was surely due to the raised awareness of the lower classes, the *servi*, because they wanted to be like the *casati*, and because the *casati*, who lived as tenants, wanted to actually be tenants.[22] It was also caused by the weakness of the State apparatus aimed at maintaining social order and control over the territory, which the kings of Toledo did not seem to achieve in the final stages of the monarchy.

The Muslim invasion accelerated the process in Hispania. Those landlords who did not die in the resistance or were not exiled lost power and domains, and the slave MP became residual. References to *servi* and *mancipia* disappeared from Catalan documentation during the ninth and tenth centuries.[23]

2.3 The Carolingians: Restoration and Crisis

History was different in the kingdom of the Franks. The rise to power of the Carolingians as a result of an alliance between the Church and the aristocracy in the middle of the eighth century brought the crisis of power and political feudalization, a fundamental part of the destructuring of the ancient system, to a temporary halt. Strongly backed by the bishops, the Carolingians restored the notion of public power for a period (eighth–ninth centuries), and with it the conception and practice of a central authority bearing the prerogatives of the sovereignty (like control over the army, public lands and taxation), and guarantor of the law, peace and justice. The aristocracy lent its support in exchange for participation in the process of territorial expansion and profit; that is, to obtain government positions and the corresponding benefits.[24]

The agreement that was supposed to be implemented the day after the invasions by the Germanic and provincial Roman aristocracies to stop the destructuring of the ancient system and restore the social order (the three MPs) seems to have been renewed then in the eighth century when the Frankish aristocracy and the Church became allies to escape the crisis and restore the old structures as far as possible: to renew the Roman Empire, the ecclesiastics said. Of course, however, time had worn out the old structures and modes of production. Many specialists express doubts over the survival of the direct imposition of Roman or Roman-Germanic tradition in the Carolingian world.[25] However, in diplomas emanating from the chancery, there are terms (*functiones*, *redibitiones*, *censum publicum*, *annona publica*, *tributum*, *servitia regalia*, *servitium regis*, *pascuarium*, *mansionaticum*, *parata*) that are not exactly taken from Roman times (with the exception of the word *censum*), but that indicate different forms of public subtraction. And from judicial documentation of the period, we know, at least in Catalonia, that this was not about mere rhetoric but rather real and public modes of appropriation of the surplus (in the sense of tributes and services performed by men and communities for the authorities), which entailed the central power (together with the fiscal lands *fisci*) having to remunerate the services of agents and collaborators through full or beneficial donations.[26] Thus, something of the ancient tributary MP persisted, and, perhaps because it was already well worn, the Carolingians wanted to give it new life by instituting the tithe, a tax that seems to have been originally created to pay for the clergy, but that also benefited the lay aristocracy, which had constructed and owned the churches (Devroey, 2010).[27] This secular ownership of ecclesiastical goods and rights does not seem to have caused great conflict and violent rivalries in the Carolingian era, but rather disputes in the courts of justice, probably because the aristocracy, which hailed from both the ranks of the nobility and the Church, was one (of the same origin) and remained united around the same imperial project incarnated by the monarchy, at least for much of the ninth and tenth centuries.[28]

Just as the Carolingian reforms in one way or another led to a certain political restoration and perhaps some sort of reorganization of the fiscal system,[29] the wars of conquest in the eighth and beginning of the ninth centuries, in the times Pepin and Charlemagne, resulted in an extension of the life of the slave MP in the Frankish kingdom. Charlemagne's struggle against the Saxons, for example, seems to have ended with the capture of hundreds or even thousands of men, who were converted into slaves and distributed as such among vassals, agents and collaborators of the king, members of the high secular and ecclesiastical aristocracy, who at the same time received as a benefit or donation lands actually considered to be *ager publicus*. On the basis of this, the bipartite manorial system of the times were established, mostly on both sides of the Rhine, between the Seine and Elbe, but also in other parts of the Empire such as Italy (Toubert, 2004; Verhulst, 1990). Some of the slaves ended up on *curtis* or *pars dominicalis*, that is, the demesne (*dominicatura*) of bipartite manor or estate, where they were directly exploited for labour (Italian sources refer to them as *praebendarii*), guaranteeing the continuity of agricultural work throughout the year.[30] The other slaves, in fact probably most, were settled on tenures or tenant plots (*mansi*) in the *pars colonica*, where they coexisted alongside peasant descendents of old *coloni* and *rustici*, who had been forced, in return for the land where they lived and were fed from, to pay rents and do labour services for the demesne, as well as paying public fees. It seems logical to assume that these *casati* slaves, due to the very effect of the *casamentum* (provision with a holding: *casa*, *mansus*), multiplied and became protagonists, together with the free and dependent peasants, of the huge agrarian growth that was taking place.[31]

Depending on the place, time and circumstances, then, the Carolingian kings paid for the services of agents and collaborators by assigning them or giving them taxes or public fees (a third of the *pascuarium*, for example), public lands and part of the public workforce; so much so that in chancery diplomas it is not unusual to find those people holding administrative, military and judicial positions by a delegation of the monarch to be classified as *publicas potestates* or *personae publicae*. Anyone still doubting this view of the Carolingian State should read the capitularies granted by Charlemagne in the years of famine (763, 774, 779–780, 790, 792, 793–794, 805, 806, 807, 809 and 812) during his reign. In these, behaving like a head of state of ancient tradition, the Frankish monarch forbade cereals being taken over the borders of his empire, taxed the main food products, sold the public grain (*annona publica*) stored in his barns at half price, exhorted the members of the lay and ecclesiastical aristocracy not to let their *servi* die of hunger and commanded these powerful individuals, according to the official hierarchical scale, to keep a certain number of people hungry until the arrival of the crop, in accordance with the value of their benefices (Salrach, 2005; Verhulst, 1965).

The effectiveness of these measures can be doubted, but they are proof of the sense of responsibility that, in accordance with the ancient tradition, the superior authority held as the head of the *res publica*. It is undoubtedly, then, that with Charlemagne and his empire we witnessed a last attempt to keep the ancient system standing with its MPs. Which was the hegemonic mode? It is difficult to say, especially if we think that the bipartite manor was like a hybrid structure where slavery and feudal MPs coexisted. And this is especially true if we think that having a handful or just a couple of slaves could be or was still a form of distinction that identified the powerful and differentiated them from other mortals.[32]

Are we talking, then, of a State? Obviously, and not as reification! If historians do not have many scruples with the expression "Feudal State", why should we have them with that of the Carolingian State? We should not, and with more reason, because the Carolingian State was, in many respects, close to the ancient State; in fact, it is an imitation since Charlemagne and his collaborators tried to restore or imitate it. And it is clear that the Carolingian State was not an artificial construction, as such, alien to the society of its times: it was the fruit of the balance of forces that arose from the dynamics of the Frankish society and the societies encompassed by Frankish expansion, and the compromises between the ancient model (the Holy Roman Empire), which was normative, with a written law, Roman tradition, carried forward by the clergy, and new values (or not so new ones) such as kinship, fidelity and vassalage, more of Germanic tradition, that characterized the lay aristocracy. The result was a State halfway between the ancient world and feudalism.[33] From very early on (mid-ninth century), the members of the aristocracy who occupied important positions in the administration as royal agents or public servants and were remunerated with benefits (public goods and rights) revolted in order to accumulate more powers (*honores*) and benefits, leading to disputes among themselves and with the ecclesiastical institutions and sometimes the very monarchy itself. They did not disguise their desire to make patrimony of the monarch's delegated powers and the corresponding sources of funding. Thus, the public dissolved into the private, concepts, these of public and private, that we historians do not project onto the past from the present, but take from the narrative sources themselves and the documentation of that past. Nothing to do with anachronism, then![34]

We are not, of course, talking about a perfect State, but a transitional political era in which the researcher has been able to observe remains of the past and elements of the future. The heads of that State were considered the exclusive masters of legitimate violence, guarantors and enactors of the norms that regulated social life, and governors who maintained law and order among their peoples. In order to fulfil these functions and exercise authority, the Carolingians created a specific geography of power; that is, a network of large districts (hundreds of counties), internally divided, it would seem, into different types of smaller districts (*districtus*, *vicaria*) (Lauranson-Rosaz, 2011; Saudan, 2004),[35] and had available to them, as royal agents, the services of members of the aristocracy (counts, viscounts), who in turn counted on the collaboration of the powerful local individuals in their networks based on vassalage and fidelity. The benefits, in the sense of fiscal lands (*fisci*) and public taxation-rights, received from the monarch in recompense for these fidelities and services, circulated from top to bottom, but were generally temporary: they were linked to the exercising of public offices and functions. Of course, when a powerful individual ceased to be in office and another succeeded him, the benefits changed hands, so there were often conflicts (the powerful tended to treat benefits as if they were private goods) generally solved by the courts.[36]

The justice in the Carolingian State, at least in the Catalan counties, was public justice, which was intended to be the same for all. It is true that in the judicial documentation that has been conserved the peasants usually lost, but not always. The judges were professionals, who acted on the basis of objective evidence (testimonies and documents) and passed sentences in accordance with written law (the *Liber* and the Carolingian precepts). Taken as one, this documentation reveals an offensive by the powerful to erode the rights of the peasantry over the land, which shows that these rights did exist, and also that judges could not ignore them. However, the rights of the popular classes were not usually supported in written documents, even if there were peasants who did have some, but rather in oral testimonies, which often lost out to the written evidence provided by the powerful. Of these proofs, the most powerful were the Carolingian diplomas, whose existence demonstrates the centrality of power, a power that not only delegated judicial functions to the counts but also to bishops and abbots in their domains (privileges of immunity), and sometimes also to powerful individuals. Of course, counts, bishops and abbots appointed judges to the courts as well. The judicial system worked, then, as a chain, the first link of which was the king, and whether rightly or wrongly, the justice imparted regulated the social order. For that reason, although the landlords judged their peasants, presumably with the agreement or by the concession of the monarch (privileges of immunity), it is appropriate to speak of the public rather than seigniorial or feudal justice. Although the violence of the powerful was not alien to that society or any other, with debatable results, the courts absorbed and channelled a good part of the conflicts into some sort of solution.[37]

In the Catalan counties, many elements of ancient Roman and Roman-Gothic inheritance were preserved. This is quite noticeable in the adhesion to writing, written law and public justice. Here taxation is more than a presumption, and with it, of course, the existence of families and peasant communities free from everything except paying taxes and for public services. Of course, there were free peasants and owners, landowners and, of course, tenants, but we will never know the demographic and productive weight of any of them.[38] Trials held in all of the counties in some cases allow us to demonstrate and in others to trace or intuit the existence of individual and communal peasant properties defending themselves, but who in some way also benefitted from the wearing out of the old forms of exploitation (slavery, taxation), the processes of conquest and the appropriation and occupation of waste and derelict land for reclaiming purposes (*aprisio*) and the legal voids that the political and military changes of the Late Antiquity and the Early Middle Ages caused, to maintain or restore their status.[39] We might even speak, as Chris Wickham does for the years 400–800, of peasant MP, an expression that indicates the autonomy attained by peasants in many regions of Europe. In this sense, it must be remembered that the peasant commons were so important in some valleys of the Pyrenees that, a thousand years on, they have survived into the contemporary era (Bringué, 1995). Indeed, peasant family ownership has been so decisive in the valleys of Andorra that it alone explains its existence as a country (Viader, 2003). And all this without even mentioning the documents from the episcopal see of Vic, where peasant micro-ownership abounds.[40]

Some remnants of the old-style slavery were still noticeable, and we are not referring to judicial slavery, which is perfectly identifiable, but rather the fact that some non-judicial documents from the ninth and the beginning of the tenth centuries still referred to *servi* and *mancipia*, the word used to designate slaves of both sexes. We are referring to the *servi* who, for example, in the ninth century occupied waste and derelict land for the purposes of reclaiming it in the service of their *hispani* masters in different parts of the counties, and the *mancipia* of the Conflent, which king Charles II gave to count Sunifred of Cerdanya, in the year 843 (Abadal, 2007 [1926–1952], pp. 332–334).

2.4 The Feudal Revolution

In summary, the Carolingian world of the ninth century still seems to belong more to the ancient than to the feudal system, although it is clear that during the tenth century, the de-destructuring that we had already observed in the Germanic realms resumed and accelerated, especially in Western *Francia*. It is true that in some regions or countries, the strength of the Roman tradition favoured resistance and delayed the final fall of the system for one or two generations more, but before or after the year one thousand, the transition would culminate in the establishment of feudalism throughout Carolingian Europe.

The driving force behind the process was the secular wearing out of the old "corsets" (slavery and taxation), which allowed the social body to breathe, and the peasantry, in particular, to enter a period of growth during the eighth or ninth century.[41] We highlight the peasantry as the protagonist of growth because we believe that the individualization of production (peasant family farms) was a determining factor in the process, an individualization that took place throughout the European continent both in areas where peasant freedoms and ownership had a singular weight and on the large bipartite manors or estates, which witnessed the phenomenon of the reduction in the *pars dominical* in the benefit of the more dynamic *colonica*.[42] Growth accelerated the *casamentum* of slaves and their gradual incorporation into the ranks of the peasantry, which, in turn, led to further growth (Toubert, 2004, pp. 131–134). This also resulted in the formation of an elite group of local landowners within the peasantry, who owned good farms, elite that led the peasant communities in some areas, such as the valleys of the Pyrenees, while in others they entered the lower ranks of the nobility.[43] This growth was set to reduce the effect of chronic hunger on the peasantry, but the liberating process that this development of the productive forces entailed was soon blocked by the aristocracy, eager to seize the surplus product. Hence the origins of the feudal crisis, which are not difficult to explain.

Like the powerful Romans, who had built the Empire and then, when measuring its cost, had moved away again, precipitating its ruin, the Carolingian aristocracy also turned its back on the agreements upon which its political system had been built. These agreements, as we know, consisted of serving the monarchy which, in return, delegated the functions of the territorial government to counts, members of the aristocratic families who found the corresponding remuneration in these governmental positions. The monarchs recognized the right of lineage to obtain honours and benefits, but to avoid the dislocation of power and the counts becoming independent, they reserved the right of appointment and the allocation of the county or counties in each individual case. The right of succession was not recognized with the status of count, but families of lineage, with the networks of loyalties woven within them, desired it. In fact, they felt it was necessary because the West had entered a process of growth, the mechanisms of which remained within their reach (what was left of the tributary and slave MPs), with the obstacle of the judicial system, did not guarantee the appropriation of the surplus.

Thus, at the end of the ninth and during tenth centuries, the powerful and their faithful imposed succession in the counties. This is when territorial principalities came into being in Western *Francia*, and Carolingian royalty was stripped of its power and authority.[44] The counts, who acted as civil servants or agents (*personae publicae*), became princes, and were, in fact, granted an independent power and social control they had not previously enjoyed. It is true, that these counts were not regarded as usurpers but legitimate successors of the monarchs in the counties,[45] but it is significant that they had difficulty differentiating between the public and the private. Sometimes, they did not know whether they had a land as a fiscal or royal benefit or as an inheritance from their parents as a private asset!

Either way, this political crisis did not stop at the level of the territorial princes, the old counts, since they soon saw how their authority was questioned by the *vassi* and *fideles*: the nobles who governed the territory in the service of the princes from their castles, towns and manors. This is what Duby (1953) studied in Mâconnais, Bonnassie (1975–1976) in Catalonia, Poly (1976) in Provence, Lauranson-Rosaz (1987) in the Auvergne, Larrea (1998) in Navarra, Dolset (2004) on the Catalan borderlands and Débax (2003) in Languedoc, a general process that has its own particularities in each case. All of these lords had the same aim: to incorporate public functions and benefits, along with the castles, towns or manors where they were exercised, into their assets. And not only because of the gains that this represented but also those that might be entailed in breaking the limitations imposed by the public system of guarantees. Perhaps slightly earlier or later, and on a larger or smaller scale, depending on the place, the time of this crisis can be approximately dated between 950 and 1050.[46] Then the old districts and, in fact, the lands, hamlets, villages and towns where the public function was exercised became estates; that is, the headquarters of hereditary and autonomous or independent lordships. This process has been called dislocation of the *pagus*.[47]

The change in relationship between the powerful eventually had an effect on the whole social body. The lords did not take long to use their new powers to advance the subjection and exploitation of the peasantry, which they did by creating new dependency bonds, restricting freedom of movement, extending the tenure system (peasant family farms, centre of production, consumption, subjection and subtraction), introducing new, onerous and sometimes infamous exactions, and new customs, already considered ignominious and called *mals usos*, and maltreating the peasantry. Thus, with the old slavery system only recently or almost disappeared (and all that this entailed: liberation, peasant freedoms), the serfdom characteristic of the peasantry of feudalism was born. This was not done in a day or in a generation, but it is clear that between 950 and 1050 the lines of power that would traverse society for centuries were drawn out for the future.[48] In order to do this, the traditional judicial system, of which the counts (insomuch as the successors of the kings) were guarantors, had to be stripped of content or neutralized, at least during an initial phase. This is noticeable in Catalonia where, during the eleventh and part of the twelfth centuries, the character and function of professional judges became blurred, and justice was more seigniorial than before. The mechanics of the lawsuit, therefore, changed, trials by ordeal (in part replacing witness statements and documentary evidence) and, in many cases, private agreements and pacts among the powerful occupied the place of judicial decisions (*Le règlement*—see especially the papers by H. Débax, B. Lemesle, G. Veyssièreand J. M. Salrach). We insist on the idea of a pact among the powerful to highlight the differences in the conflicts between lords and peasants: if the latter rarely made it to court, it is not because of pacts and prior commitments, but because the powerful imposed their powers and, when it came to it, seigniorial or feudal justice resolved the issue in favour of the lords.[49]

We might say that the aristocracy turned its back on traditional public justice for two reasons. First of all, because, despite being an instrument for maintaining a social order favourable to the powerful, when the economic situation changed and growth began, this same justice system began to represent a hindrance for these powerful individuals, who wanted to increase the levels of subjugation and exploitation. And, secondly, because the lay aristocracy did not trust a traditional justice system too strongly controlled by clergymen (many judges were of the clergy), who had a monopoly over writing, the main judicial evidence. In fact, nobles generally lost to clergymen in courts (Salrach, 2013, pp. 55–61, 227–232, 236–240). Of course, all this would not have happened without the failure of the Carolingian system, within which the two aristocracies, lay and ecclesiastical, shared the same ambition, distributed the benefits of territorial, military and political expansion and depended on the same authority, the monarch, who had to moderate and arbitrate their differences. This helps us to understand why many nobles, without the opposition of the clergy, were owners of churches with the subsequent tithes and, even more so, why, with the failure of the Carolingian system and the ambitions that growth disrupted, the old alliance broke up and gave way to confrontation.

A long period of social and political crisis therefore commenced, during the course of which violence grew and spread throughout the counties, affecting the entire social body, although the nobility, especially the one comprising former county agents, guardians of the castles, was the main protagonist and ultimate winner, while the peasantry lost (Salrach, 1992). The outcome, illustrated by the *convenientiae* (conventions or agreements) and oaths of fidelity between the count of Barcelona and the country nobility, was the spread and multiplication of the castral lordship (also known as banal or jurisdictional lordship), within which a large part of the peasantry was framed to make them more firmly subjected and exploited, if only to impose new exactions on them in addition to those they already paid. The count, on the other hand, had to accept that the power of the aristocracy imposed limits on his authority, an authority founded on the feudal pact, which involved a certain distribution of the functions and rights of public power (concerning justice, the army and taxation), among those aristocrats who had previously been his officers or agents.[50]

Amidst the storm, the Church tried to preserve its presence and power in society. Unable to return to the previous Carolingian situation, it opted to try for a position of autonomous power within the new feudal world. To do this, it employed its own "weapons", which differed from those of the nobility. First of all, writing was used to delegitimize or demonize the nobility, presenting the nobleman as a violent malefactor, who was devoted to depredation and theft, with no respect for anything or anyone.[51] Thus the writings of the eleventh and twelfth centuries, with changes in language and images of violence, are the best proof of feudal change because they reveal the growing hostility of the Church towards the nobility; that is, the conflict deriving from the latter's possession of churches and tithes, in particular, and land, men and rent, in general.[52] We can never know, therefore, how much falsity and exaggeration there is in the documents of this time, but this, together with changes in the type of document (especially the deeds of the feudal pact), is sign enough of the transformations that were taking place. After writing, excommunication and sacramental humiliation were the weapons more readily used by the Church hierarchies against their enemies, although with questionable effectiveness.[53] On the other hand, the conversion of sacred spaces around churches into inviolable places, and the decrees of peace and peace and truce that sought, at least temporarily, to limit feudal violence and change customs, all under the threat of excommunication, were the best known of the Church's actions in the conflict, actions that historians contemplate from different perspectives: some see in them a defensive strategy by the institution against the nobility, if not a means (in the case of *sagreres,* sacred spaces around churches) to create spaces for its own power; while others interpret this as a protective response from the clergy to the peasantry's desire for peace (Bonnassie, 1975–1976, pp. 653–661; Farías, 1993; Farías et al., 2007).[54] However, it does not seem necessary to have to choose between one interpretation or the other, because both motivations are perfectly possible and even compatible. *Sagreres*, in addition, must also be studied within the framework of transformations in the population brought about by feudal change. We are referring, of course, to the concentration of the population, which could also in some cases be the outcome desired by the lords (to better control the workforce and extract the surplus) and, in others, an outcome not desired by the lords but by the peasants, who would thus believe that they could better escape the lords' control and domination. In this sense, the Catalan *sagrera* or *cellera*, the origin of many rural villages and towns, would have parallelisms with the Italian phenomenon of *incastellamento* (Bonnassie, 2001b; Catafau, 1998; Toubert, 1973).

Needless to say, according to mentions of *servi* and *mancipia* in the documents, rural slaves still existed in the Catalan counties at the end of the ninth and first half of the tenth centuries. As documentary references to them became scarce and even disappeared during the second half of the tenth and the first decades of the eleventh centuries, we must assume that rural slaves also disappeared, definitively becoming simple tenants, like the vast majority of peasants. And this was for many of the reasons that Toubert (2004, pp. 131–134), Bonnassie (2001a, pp. 108–132) and Bois (1989a, pp. 59–61, 158, 185–186, 198–199, 203, 252–253 and 262) have adduced. Let us briefly recall them: the influence of religion (Christian slaves), the social dynamism inherent in the agrarian growth of which the slaves themselves were protagonists, the emancipatory struggle of the slaves, the practice of *casamentum*, etc. Thus, rural slavery, through many successive crises and restorations, ended up disappearing around the year one thousand.[55]

But what of taxation? Its fate is intimately linked to that of the State, that is to say, to the notion of *res publica* and its institutionalized form, an ancient inheritance that, as we have explained, can still be traced in the Germanic kingdoms and Carolingian Empire.[56] However, this also faded out and disappeared with the fall of the Carolingian monarchy (ninth century), the creation of territorial principalities (tenth century) and the feudal revolts (circa 950–1050), when what had been the material base of public power, that is, the lands and workers of the *fisc* (*fisci, servi fiscales*) and the taxes and fiscal services of free men (*functiones, redibitiones, pascuarium, censum, servitia*) were incorporated into the patrimonies of the aristocracy as large estates or fiefs, rent charges and tributes.[57] The seigneurie was thus created or extended in a hegemonic way, a means of confiscating surplus that ended up encompassing the entire peasantry, with no, or almost no, exception.

What happened, then, to the small, free and landowner peasantry[58] (which in perhaps very distant times, when the tributary MP was predominant, had constituted the foundational base of the political system through taxation), a small peasantry that had survived but was in decline like the tributary MP itself? The Catalan documentation leaves little doubt about the existence of these peasants.[59] What was left of them disappeared around 950–1050, melting into the magma of the peasant tenures in the manorial system. This is easily explained: the right of ownership is more a concern for historians than for the protagonists of that time, the lords and peasants. It is not that it was ignored, but they were more interested in what they could take from it. It is true that during the ninth and tenth centuries, the powerful were taking what they could of the land owned by the peasantry,[60] but, it would appear, more to obtain the profit of the peasant labour than for the property itself. Those peasants who resisted and retained their property did not escape, with some exceptions, from paying land and person taxes to the authority. We say with exceptions, because in the tenth century there were still peasant communities that could prove in a trial that the land was their own, and that they had never paid taxes on it or its people, leading to the county authorities acknowledging their exemption and the land as a freehold (*alodium*).[61] These situations would have ended during the crisis of around 950–1050. And they ended because, when the peasant landowners and taxpayers were included among the estates, the lords appropriated the taxes they paid, converting them into a manorial rent, in various ways assimilating the status of these peasants with that of others. In fact, in a world where there were no peasants without a lord, it is not conceivable that free peasants and landowners could prolong their "privileged" situation indefinitely.

Thus, when we reach the beginning of the twelfth century and look back at the beginning of the ninth, we cannot avoid forming two images of society and power in these two periods, which to us seems opposed. So opposed we have the feeling that in between there must have been a cataclysm, which we can locate approximately around 950–1050.[62] But if we open our field of observation we can also say that what happened in this short time had already been brewing and, therefore, happened over a much dilated time period: that of the long transition from the ancient system to the feudal. The feudal change was, therefore, nothing more, and it is no small thing, than the final stage of the process.[63]

2.5 The Twelfth-Century Crisis

History never stops, of course. And neither do crises. The one in the eleventh century left such an unstable balance of power that it required adjustments; these, in part, would constitute the history of the twelfth-century crisis. The protagonists of this second feudal crisis were, as one would expect, the monarchy (the count or count-king in Catalonia), the nobility and the clergy, plus a new social group that had emerged from growth, the bourgeoisie.

With regard to the monarchy (let us remember that, in the Catalan case, the counts became kings due to the dynastic union with Aragon), supported by the Church and reinforced in the world of ideas by the rebirth of Roman law, it sought a way of laying the foundations of genuine government, that is, a system of power (feudal monarchy) that, by strictly respecting the authority of the lords in their estates and fiefs, placed the king above everything else, and bound the powerful more strongly to their obedience and fidelity. It was, thus, a matter of, in some way, overcoming the polyarchy of the first feudal age. As the king did not have recourse to a direct taxation system that would tax the whole of society and make him more powerful and autonomous, to achieve his aims he made as much profit as possible from indirect taxation, that is, rights over the currency, rents paid by the peasants of the royal estate and contributions from men in the royal hamlets, villages, towns and cities. At the same time, in order to advance the idea of a territorial government and make it effective, at some point a new system of territorial districts (*vegueries* and *batllies* in Catalonia) was created, in which new royal agents (*veguers* and *batlles*) enforced the king's rights over the estates and men of the lords, ensuring the presence of royal justice throughout the territory, in a difficult coexistence with the lord's justice, and maintaining the public peace and security decreed by the peace and truce assemblies, now presided over by the king. Specifically, the territorial peace dictated by the monarch in these assemblies defined the scope of his government or his claims to power in geographic terms. Some monarchs, however, tried to go further and play a kind of arbitration role in the conflicts between the nobility and the peasantry in the estates, but the strength of the nobility prevented it. In fact, frictions between the royal agents and the barons were very frequent, as were confrontations, some of them armed, between monarchs and members of the high nobility. But, as it had already happened in the eleventh century, accompanied by pacts and commitments this violence regulated the new resulting political order, that of the feudal monarchy.[64]

The outcome is also explained by the fact that the notion of *res publica* and *potestas publica*, despite being worn out during the transition and feudal change, never completely disappeared from ecclesiastical circles and the Barcelona court, where, in line with the tradition of Roman and Visigothic public law, the figure of the prince was acclaimed supreme ruler. The result was obviously not a return to the State model of the ancient world, because the system of manorial powers that had been won, or jurisdictions, prevented it. It was, rather, a political construction of feudal lordships or limited powers that, by means of pacts or interpersonal agreements, established tiered bonds of subordination or dependence that converged in the central figure of the prince. A prince who, in fact, owed his strength or authority to the agreed fidelity of his aristocracy, but who in the world of ideas aspired to be recognized as the prince, the sole holder of public authority. A power that in Roman times emanated from the status of prince (autocracy) and which, from the Early Middle Ages onwards, lay, according to the teachings of the Church, in divine will: counts and kings by the grace of God.

The new power of the prince in the feudal State in Catalonia was expressed via the creation of a new right, in accordance with the new society. Indeed, until then, the basic law regulating society had been Visigoth law (the *Liber Iudicum*), which feudal change had made obsolete, hence the need to enact new laws, which only the prince could do. The result is well known: the promulgation of the *Usatges* by the count of Barcelona (who, in doing so, invoked the power that the *Liber* awards to the prince). This was the code of Catalan feudalism, which differed from the *Liber* in many senses, but above all in the fact that the latter recognized men (the *servi*, as slaves, did not count) as being equal before the law and justice, while the *Usatges* recognized and constituted them as being unequal.[65]

The changes or adjustments that shaped the feudal State in Catalonia also inevitably affected the judicial system. While during the eleventh and early decades of the twelfth century, the counts desisted, or almost did, from presiding over trials, in the late twelfth century they reappeared when trials led by professional judges demanding written evidence and conducting lengthy interrogations became the norm. Under the influence of Roman-Canon law, the process became regularized and judges, who became more thoroughly demanding regarding the contribution of evidence, especially in cases of conflict resolution, submitted the parties to long and detailed interrogations. But justice in the feudal State no longer came from central power, as happened in the Carolingian system, which had delegated it to the lower ranks. In the feudal State, the powerful lord had diverse judicial or jurisdictional powers that did not recognize having received anything from anyone, were the fruit of formerly public powers becoming private. The plurality of jurisdictions or judicial powers observed in Catalonia in the Late Middle Ages was late proof of the dissemination of power that took place during the feudal change. These could range from the penalties that landlords could impose on their peasants for certain causes before a trial took place, to the judicial powers of the territorial lords, the barons, in their baronies, with the power or not to judge blood crimes and apply the death penalty or not. What the twelfth century appears to have added is a certain regularization or establishment of powers, possibly resulting from the conflicts and rivalries that often occurred between lords over the geographical scope and competence of each one's powers. Concepts such as high and low justice or jurisdiction, and *merum et mixtum imperium*, which we see emerging in the documentation from the thirteenth century on, must represent the commitments and norms that were dictated from the twelfth century onwards under the influence of those who knew Roman law, including judges in the service of the feudal lords.[66]

The nobility would never have managed to transform the social and political order without a military force imposing it. This combat force, which was crucial during the revolts of the eleventh century, and would be again in the twelfth century, was a combat force on horseback: the knights. It has been discussed whether they were created by the feudal lords in response to the rise of the peasant sectors, or had their roots in the Carolingian era, and were simply the children of the high nobility. The discussion is a very artificial one, however, because the two hypotheses are perfectly compatible. In any case, it seems clear that the troops of the military order grew spectacularly during the eleventh century, while the number of towers and castles also multiplied, suggesting that in addition to the traditional forces inherited from the ninth and tenth centuries there were also new troops from the popular sectors, who could only have been members of the wealthy peasantry (*milites aloders* in the words of some Catalan documents).[67]

There was always violence in the Late Antiquity and Early Middle Ages. However, that which took place around 950–1050 was singular in nature: the peasantry was the main victim, with the capturing of the fruits of growth the main goal, and the knights (*milites*), vassals of lords, the instrument. Since many of these peasants were free men prior to the year one thousand and, as such, were under the protection of the public justice system—and, therefore, the count—and many others inhabited the domains of the Church and the count, the actions of these *milites* against them were also, in fact, an attack on the authority of the counts and prelates.[68] This first phase of feudal violence was followed in the twelfth century by a second, easily identifiable in time, but diffuse in terms of content. Again, there were conflicts between monarchs and castral lords, between nobles and ecclesiastical institutions, between highs nobles and knights, and between *milites* and peasants.[69]

In the disputes between monarchs and members of the castral aristocracy, violence ended in negotiations and pacts, although sometimes the royal or county court (which could resemble an assembly of barons) had the last word. The nobility again disputed the possession of lands, men and rents, and especially churches and tithes, with the bishops and abbots. The peasants who were caught in the middle, on the Church's domains, were always the main victims, and those most sacrificed in the commitments that the confrontations sooner or later resulted in. In this struggle of unequal weapons, the Church continued to use the peace and truce assemblies to protect both themselves and the weakest (*pauperes*), but also to delimit rather than nullify the violence, which it therefore indirectly legitimized. What was new in the twelfth century was the incorporation of counts and count-kings into the presidency and assembly leadership, which they ended up calling and transforming into an instrument of government, and the attendance of the nobility at the meetings, which thus became the precedent of the *Corts* (Parliament), a fundamental institution in the feudal State in Catalonia (Bisson 1997; Gonzalvo, 1994).

Gregorian reform, which, in combating simony, sought to separate the Church from the guardianship of the laity, increased the confrontation between the Church and the nobility. Many nobles and the counts and kings themselves, who, possessing Church assets and rents, lived under the threat of excommunication, eventually handed over all their churches and tithes to the Church, while others preferred to make a pact. The "retrocession fief", which had been the means used to resolve the conflict between the count of Barcelona and the insurrectionists nobles back in the eleventh century, was, from the twelfth century onwards, the tool that in many cases ended the conflict between the nobility and the Church over the possession of tithes and churches: the nobleman, "repented of his sin of usurpation", according to the language of the documents, donated or "returned" the assets in dispute to the Church, assets that, in turn, the Church returned as a fief to the nobleman. From then on, this nobleman became a vassal of the prelate or corresponding ecclesiastical institution and incorporated the tithes and other possible ecclesiastical taxes into his income, transforming them, in fact, into feudal rent (Mallorquí, 2011; Salrach, 1999a). In this and also in other ways, using the own institutions of the feudal pact, which distributed the rent among the powerful, the great ecclesiastical institutions, all of whom possessed estates and castles, equipped themselves with their own armed forces, that is, *milites*. At the service of the clerical aristocracy, these, like all *milites*, had the mission of guaranteeing order in the places entrusted to them, as well as defending against their enemies the goods and people belonging to their lords. The prelates of the Carolingian era had also recruited men for military service and they therefore had troops when needed, but these do not seem to have been military suites like the feudal ones, in either form or content (Salrach, 2002b).

The castle lords, the main protagonists of the eleventh-century feudal revolt, also saw how the order that they had contributed so much to create was questioned by their own men during the twelfth century. We are referring to the fact that the *milites* and castle guardians (*castlans*) rose up and, in some cases, openly revolted against their own lords. They did this by overreaching their functions, abusing their power over the peasant families of the castelries, breaching the agreements on surplus distribution in their own favour, and sometimes carrying out acts of pure terrorism, the victims of which were the peasants, and indirectly the lords to whom they paid rents. The aim of these minor tyrants was to modify the feudal pacts with the lords in their favour so that they obtained the greater part of the confiscated surplus. Since this had to be done by imposing a new distribution of income and of peasant households—to remove part of the product from—, one might say that the ultimate goal was the creation of small (knights') estates within the large (barons') estates. And, indeed, the end result was this: a greater dissemination of power.[70]

In the struggles between lords and knights, those harmed most were always the peasants. This was very visible on the estates of the Barcelona counts, where *veguers* and bailiffs, failing to perform their duties, carried out acts of violence against the peasant families and communities they were supposed to be defending and keeping at a given, and therefore limited, level of submission and exploitation. The logic of this violence on the count's estates was the same as that which brought castral lords into conflict with their knights. It was a violence that sought to modify the feudal order and transform the old agents into minor lords. Despite the peasants' complaints, the counts, like the barons, do not seem to have resolved this conflict by punishing the behaviour of their men and forcing them to moderate their demands for rent. Perhaps, the subtraction of the peasantry was therefore raised so as to increase the rent of the small nobility without thereby undermining that of the lord (Bisson, 1985–1986; Bisson, 1998).

We cannot end this analysis of the twelfth-century crisis without making reference to the town and the city. Up to this point the feudal system, established after a long transition period and a short revolution, had been markedly rural in nature. However, agrarian growth, which began in the country during the eighth and ninth centuries, allowed extraordinary advances to be made in the division of labour during the second half of the tenth century and especially during the eleventh and twelfth centuries, creating a new space for economic development: the town. We are referring here to the market town born in the countryside and the one reborn away from it, the ancient city, forming a single urban community due to its nature and function. Indeed, unlike the ancient city, which was above all a political centre, the feudal town and city was an economic one, with specialized (industrial) production and exchange; that is, a market that determined the relationship between the countryside and the town or city in feudal times. This is one of the most important aspects of feudal change (Bois, 1989a, pp. 115–150; 1989b, pp. 118–125). Of course, the town and the city that were born or reborn in the tenth-eleventh century had, however, such a strong dynamism by the twelfth that its men could not be satisfied with the role the feudal order had assigned them: they wanted to be greater masters of their own destiny. Sometimes they were slow to achieve this, but in the twelfth century they were already demanding less seigniorial domination, self-government and exemptions. To this end, they would buy their freedoms—at a high price—or revolt. The result was also the creation of the boroughs, which were in fact a kind of collective lorships of the townsmen.[71]

2.6 Concluding Remarks

Thus, through the historical movement that we have described, the world was transformed and society articulated in different ways, from the ancient system to the feudal one. It was not a unidirectional movement, nor a predictable one, nor one of a single pace. To explain this, we have employed four concepts (transition, social system, mode of production and crisis) which are mental constructions, useful for grasping the historical material and studying it.[72]

With the word transition we have referred to the movement that led from one social system to another. As an expression of historical movement, we can state that men and societies always live in transition from a present to an unpredictable future. By social system we understand the structures and forms by means of which a society is articulated, with its own dynamics. And here the aim is to have a global perspective: the organization of power, social stratification, relations of production, distribution of wealth and product, culture, value system, etc. In a sense, transition and social system refer to different, if not opposite, perspectives of analysis: the analysis of transition favours an open vision of movement in the long term; whereas analysis of the social system, which seeks to identify the intrinsic characteristics of the social formations that configure it (structures and dynamics) and its internal coherence, favours a more fixed and synchronous vision. The result of the research is, in all cases, the construction of models or paradigms that express the historians' vision of the systems we analyse. Depending on the perspective (social system or transition), historical analysis tends to emphasize continuity or change. If the focus of the study is a social system, it is logical to discover complexity, a complexity that historians reduce according to their way of thinking (whichever they consider to be more determinant), in the sense of tending to favour some aspects above others. We have focused on the power and social relations of production and exploitation. Therefore, to capture the different forms in which power is organized, as well as to capture the surplus and observe hegemonies, we have employed the concept of mode of production.[73] Finally, with the word crisis, we wished to refer to strong upheavals in the evolution of societies and historical phases of change, which mark the pace of transformations in the long run (during the transition), and are generally not exempt from violence.

This is the conceptual instrument we have used, which we hope has served to make the history of a period (so often described as obscure, but which is very important for Catalan and European history) more comprehensible.

Notes

1. The debate is best summarized—meaning in the most complete and objective maner—by Christian Lauranson-Rosaz. Proof of the interest of this text is that there are editions in Spain, Poland and Italy: Lauranson-Rosaz (2000, 2001, 2002). Another brief and schematic summary of the debate from a clearly anti-mutationist position is provided by Mazel (2010).
2. The notion of social system as a set of structures with specific relationships related to exploitation or modes of production is taken from Bois (1989a, pp. 258–259).
3. On the subsistence crises of the eighth-thirteenth centuries, the main sources are taken from Curschmann (1970). For a brief study of those during the fifth-seventh centuries: Salrach (2007); and for a notably long study on those from the eighth-tenth centuries: Newfield (2013).
4. After the publication of "The other transition" (Wickham, 1984), Marxist historians such as Halil Berktay and John Haldon criticized the distinction between the ancient or tributary MP and the feudal or land MP established by Wickham, who today prefers to consider two subtypes of the

same mode of production (Wickham, 2005, p. 60). However, we consider the distinction between the tributary and feudal MPs to be fundamental, because we understand that the hegemony of one or another MP determines, as it were, the social system as a whole. The MP is essentially a way of capturing and distributing the surplus, a mode of exploiting work, which for this very reason informs or determines many other aspects of the social system, among which the organization of production itself, the structure of classes, forms of power, relations between the governors and the governed, political ideology, etc. All of this matters if we are to understand the transition and the crises that marked it.

5. For a more detailed discussion of the logic of slavery and the causes of its crisis and extinction, see Salrach (1997a).
6. These ideas regarding the ancient city, which ultimately come from Moses Finley (1973), are the starting point of Guy Bois' reflection on the role of the city in economic systems (Bois, 1989a, 1989b).
7. We have developed these ideas, based on Petrer Garnsey (1989), in Salrach (2009).
8. The process of freeing the slaves, of transforming slaves into tenants subject to servitude, that is, into serfs, is the matter of a study by Dockés (1979). Guy Bois (1989a, pp. 52–61) explains the reasons why the slaves of Late Antiquity and the Early Middle Ages were still slaves, despite being *casati*.
9. Salvian of Marseilles (fifth century) is one of the most critical authors on the tax system (1975, IV 21, IV 31, V 17, V 21 and V 28).
10. These ideas regarding the decadence and crisis of the Roman Empire come from different authors, among them, Lewit (2004) and Heather (2005). On the weight of the tax burden, and especially affecting the peasantry, and the complexity of the tax collection system, see Wickham (2005, pp. 62–72; 2009, pp. 33–36).
11. Chris Wickham (2005, pp. 591–692) is a fundamental reference on the decline of cities in the Germanic and Carolingian period in the West, with very important regional nuances.
12. We have referred to the issue on public army/private troops in Salrach (1993a). A different view in Pérez Sánchez (1989), which presents the Visigoth army as one composed of private and feudal troops. On the same problem, of a more general character and with more nuances: Wickham (2009, pp. 102–103).
13. Wickham admits that, although with many difficulties and to a notably lesser extent and irregularly, taxes continued to be collected in the Germanic kingdoms until the seventh century, and in some places until the eighth century (Wickham, 2009, pp. 103–104 and 120–121). The most renowned advocate of the continuity of the Roman fiscal system in Germanic times is Goffart (1980) and Callander ed. (1998).

14. The main Frankish and Visigoth sources, which contain news about public taxes, can be found in Salrach (1993a, pp. 119–127), and, of course, also in Durliat (1990, pp. 97–109). For Frankish Gaule: Krusch & Levison (1937–1951). For Visigoth Spain: Vives (1963, p. 54: epistle *De fisco Barcinonense a. 592*). For Ostrogothic Italy: *Cassiodori Senatoris Variae*. There are many items regarding the use of fiscal resources to fight hunger in Late Roman Empire and Ostrogothic Italy in Cracco-Ruggini (1961).
15. The reference work here is by Bonnassie (2001a).
16. This is the opinion expressed by Guy Bois based on his study on Lournand (Bois, 1989a, pp. 31–62).
17. Chris Wickham reports in detail on the Germanic monarchies of this age, their strengths and weaknesses and the differences between them (Wickham, 2009, pp. 111–129).
18. German historians speak of "episcopal republics" (Ewig, 1976–1979, Vol. 2, pp. 211–219).
19. According to R. Collins (1989, pp. 7–22), Chris Wickham does not consider that the Visigothic kingdom suffered a general crisis at the end of the seventh century; on the contrary, it was, he says, the strongest in the West (Wickham, 2009, p. 139).
20. For a more detailed explanation of our point of view on rural slavery in Late Antiquity and the Early Middle Ages, see Salrach (1997a, pp. 68–80).
21. We use the word *colonus* to remain loyal to the Roman tradition, but it does not appear in Visigothic sources (in the documents of the council of Toledo and the *Liber*) where, on the other hand, the words *servi* and *mancipia* are omnipresent (King, 1972, pp. 160–179; Thompson, 1969, pp. 267–274). Does this mean that the slave condition had been, in some way or other, extended to peasant descendents of former *coloni*? We do not know, but it is possible.
22. The survival and even resumption, according to some authors, of rural slavery in the Germanic and Carolingian period is founded on a high-quality bibliography: Fournier (1961), Rouche (1979), Bonnassie (2001a), and Verhulst (1985), especially the collaborations by C. D. Droste and D. Hägermann. Fournier and Rouche detected huge masses of slaves in Auvergne and Aquitaine, whom Rouche considers to have been mostly under direct exploitation on slavery estates. In fact, Rouche considers that rather than an ascent of the *servi* towards the *coloni*, what actually happened was a degradation in the conditions of the *coloni* towards slavery.
23. Among other documentary testimonials, there is a curious trial held in Vernet (Conflent) in 874 in which a certain Sesnan, "agent of Count Miró to investigate fiscal matters", accuses someone called Llorenç of hiding his status of *servus fiscalis* (Salrach, 2013, pp. 126–134).

24. Our point of view regarding the nature of the Carolingian political system, which we interpret as a sovereign state inspired in the Roman tradition of public power, is based on a personal reading of Carolingian narrative sources and diplomas, and hundreds of private documents from the Catalan counties (Salrach, 2013). We do not agree with the point of view expressed by J. Nelson and S. White, who do not see in Carolingian power much more than an aristocratic power (Nelson, 1986; White, 1996). Instead, we are much closer to Chris Wickham, when he says of the Carolingian system that "it was based on a clear awareness of the nature of public political power, with a hierarchy of public offices that ranged from the king to the counts and other minor officers [...]; the system was supervised by other travelling officials sent to different areas, the royal *missi*. The idea of 'the public' was inherited directly from the Roman Empire (in fact, the opposition between public and private presupposes the survival of some Roman legal concepts, although modified) [...]. What basically made this power public were two things: it organized the army and sustained courts of justice [...]. The courts emanated from royal justice; and they represented the authentic legitimation of the king as a ruler" (Wickham, 1995, p. 12).
25. Somewhere between the positions of Jean Durliat, who defends a strict survival of Roman taxation in the Carolingian age (Durliat, 1990), and that of Chris Wickham, who rejects it completely (Wickham, 1993), we find ourselves in a position that we might consider intermediate.
26. To counter the claim of unpaid taxes made by the count of Empúries in the year 913, the peasants of Vilamacolum declared that they had never paid *scubias, guaitas, calcinas, censum, functionem, tributum* and *servitium* (Salrach, 2013, p. 89). In 950, however, the peasants of the high valley of Ter were forced to recognize that they owed a third of the *pascuarium*(a tax on livestock wealth) to the bishop of Girona, a right that dated back to the donation Louis I had made to the bishops of Girona in the year 834 (Salrach, 2013, pp. 48 and 102–104). Before that, the right to receive the *pascuarium*in full, in the counties of the bishopric of Girona (those of Girona, Empúries and Besalú), formed part of the *benefitium comitalis*, hence the counts of Empúries resisted accepting the loss of a third in favour of the bishop, and in 842 the conflict between the counts and the bishop had to be resolved in a trial in which the bishop, citing Carolingian precepts, emerged victorious (Salrach, 2013, pp. 48–50).
27. Jean Durliat, who refers extensively to the tithes of the Carolingian age, maintains that they already existed in the Merovingian age, and even in the Roman times, as a tax for the clergy (Durliat, 1990, pp. 150, 239 and 246–248). The introduction of tithes in Catalonia, from the second half of the ninth century on, and the beginnings of the secular possession of tithes have been studied by Puigvert (1992).

28. The idea that the Carolingians had a political project in which moral, cultural and religious reform or correction was essential, together with the role of the Church in its conception and execution, are very much present in Wickham (2009, p. 375 and following ones).
29. The expansion of bipartite estates during Carolingian times, partially done from fiscal or public lands, could be part of this fiscal reorganization that sought to provide the empire's highest secular and religious aristocracy with economic resources (Devroey, 1986).
30. In the *curtis* in Santa Giulia abbey at Brescia there were 750 *praebendarii* (Toubert, 2004, p. 57).
31. The increase in the number of slaves and, at the same time, the determining role of their *casamentum* in the genesis and spread of bipartite estates is one of Verhulst's strong ideas, who also defends the idea that this increase was the natural effect of the population growth encouraged by the *casamentum* (Verhulst, 1990, pp. 100–101). Bonnassie refers more to slaves being taken after war (Bonnassie, 2001a, p. 116). Without denying the validity of Bonnassie's and Poly's research, who attribute the origins of growth to the free peasants and owners in Catalonia and Provence, Pierre Toubert believes that in general it was the technical innovations and elements of rationality introduced on the large estate (*casamentum*, among others) that promoted growth (Toubert, 2004, pp. 73–116).
32. Society continued to be segregationist, and the legal formulas contained on formularies, where the *servi* were what they had always been, slaves, contributed to its perpetuation (Jeannin, 2007).
33. Chris Wickham, who spared no effort to show its weaknesses, speaks of the Carolingian State as comprising the years 751–887 and that of the successor States the tenth century. He also shows very well the binding and reforming power of religious ideology in that political construction in the eighth-ninth centuries (Wickham, 2009, pp. 375–426, 427–452). We agree with Wickham when, following Claessen and Runciman, he justifies the application of the concept of State to the Germanic kingdoms and the Carolingian Empire based on five characteristics: the centrality of legitimate authority, the hierarchy of specialized agents, the notion of public power, the existence of independent and stable resources at the hands of the governors and the system of extraction and stratification of surplus based on social classes (Wickham, 2005, p. 57).
34. The concept of public (*publicus*), in the sense of what is above the private and of value, purpose or general responsibility, is very present in the documentation taken from the Carolingian chancery, where agents of authority would, as mentioned above, sometimes be classified as *personae publicae*. Even a historian of that time, Paulus Diaconus, distinguishes between *nationes* as peoples (the Germanic peoples or Barbarians) and the *res publica* as a state political construction (the Roman and the Carolingian

Empires). The concept of private is generally expressed via the adjective *proprius*, which is omnipresent, and is used in the sense of what is privately owned. Chris Wickham does not hesitate to make use of the two concepts (the absorption of the public by the private) to explain the essence of the sense of transition (Wickham, 1984), and of the crisis of the Carolingian system and the feudal revolution (Wickham, 1995).

35. *Villae* could even be both centres of nutrition and fiscal demarcations, and *mansi* units of agricultural production and fiscal subtraction (Salrach, 1997b; Salrach, 1998).
36. A very large proportion of the trials held in the Catalan counties were to this end (Salrach, 2013).
37. In this paragraph we have summarized some of the central ideas set out in our book on justice and power, which derive from the study of all or almost all judicial documents in the Catalan counties from the ninth and tenth centuries (Salrach, 2013).
38. Although the situation of the peasantry in the European West during the Germanic era and at the beginning of Carolingan was very diverse, it seems that, as general characteristics, it was based on a relative weakness of aristocratic power and an, also relative, autonomy of the rural community, a situation that gradually became the inverted (Wickham, 2005, pp. 519–588).
39. With discrepancies over proportions, C. Laliena, Ph. Sénac, E. Sarasa and J. J. Larrea consider, for example, that in the Navarran-Aragonese society of the ninth and tenth centuries there were, on the one hand, free and landowning peasants and, on the other, a ruling class with a small capacity to extract surplus (Larrea, 1998).
40. These documents which surprised Ramon d'Abadal, when he discovered the power of the ownership rights held by the small peasantry (Abadal, 1961, p. 102), have been published by Ramon Ordeig (1999).
41. We refer to peasants generically and without further precision because the division between owners and tenants has little to do with growth. The concept of property applied to the peasantry of those times has a relative value, in relation to the fees they had to pay on the land: briefly put, the fewer fees the peasant paid, the more he was owner of his land. If, due to the erosion of the tax system, the rate of subtraction tax decreased, and, on the other hand, the manorial structure did not include the entire peasantry or, at its heart, the levels of exploitation were diverse, it seems logical to defend the existence of peasant communities with a high degree of autonomy, in the sense of their disposing of the means of production and their own labour force. In this lies, it would seem to us, the last explanation of the agrarian growth of this era, with the consequent differentiation within the peasantry itself.

42. Pierre Toubert recognizes the merit of the small peasantry in the growth that took place in Catalonia, also studied by Bonnassie, and found in Poly's study of Provence, and that is because here there were not the great bipartite estates that he found and studied in Italy. In Italy, the merit of growth was, in his view, due to the landlords, who very intelligently provided the peasantry with the necessary infrastructure (mills, workshops) and the slaves with holdings, extended the *pars colonica* to the detriment of the *dominical* and encouraged exchange with the city or town, among other innovations (Toubert, 2004, pp. 37, 73–116). However, the interpretation of the causes of agricultural growth on the great Italian estates provided by Toubert seems to us to have a common denominator with those of Bonnassie and Poly in Catalonia and Provence, and that is the fact that growth in all of these countries lay in the production capacity of the small peasant family farm.
43. These local landowners seem to have been a preferential target of the judicial offensive unleashed by the aristocracy to control the land and, implicitly, men, during the ninth and tenth centuries (Salrach, 2013, pp. 73–83).
44. The classic work on this process is that by Jan Dhondt (1948). A good current summary is provided by Chris Wickham, who shows the differences between Italy, and Eastern and Western *Francia* (Wickham, 2009, pp. 427–452).
45. In 1018, in a trial over possession of the allodium of Ullastret, the prosecutor of count Hug of Empúries argued that "here the power that previously belonged to the (Carolingian) kings now belongs to count Hug" (Marqués, 1993, Doc. 77).
46. An early example of this is the revolt in the county of Besalú of the nobles against their count, whom they killed in the year 957 (Salrach, 1978).
47. The expression "dislocation of the *pagus*" comes from Jean François Lemarignier (1951). A synthetic but more complete vision of the process can be found in Lemarignier (1976, pp. 109–125). The opposite view is expressed by Dominique Barthélemy (1993, pp. 277–364).
48. Lluís To's research on the origins of the *mansus* (peasant tenure), which is linked to the serfdom of the peasantry, confirms, prolongs and completes the research by Pierre Bonnassie on this subject (To, 1993, pp. 151–177). Paul Freedman's research (1991), by contrast, linking the expansion and formalization of peasant servitude to the work carried out by notaries from the thirteenth century on, introduces a different point of view, which Gaspar Feliu (2010) reiterates and broadens in defending that the pre-feudal peasantry was neither as free nor as "landowning" as Bonnassie and we, the "mutationist" historians, in general, thought. Feliu essentially reduces feudal change to a political change (pp. 111–131). The point of view expressed by Pere Benito (2003) is, in fact, the same. Bonnassie and

To's contributions on servitude in the countries of the western Mediterranean at the round table held in Rome in October 1999 reinforced the idea that the characteristic features of servitude in Catalonia can be found in Catalan documents from the second half of the eleventh and first half of the twelfth centuries (Bonnassie, 2000; To, 2000).
49. Very little has been written on changes in the administration of justice in Catalonia in the ninth-twelfth centuries, with the exception of the thesis by Pierre Bonnassie and our book cited in Note 23. An overview can be found in Salrach (1997c).
50. Summed up here, in just a few words, is the essence of the feudal revolution, as described by Bonnassie (1975–1976).
51. Despite the exaggeration, it is clear that violence did exist, and with it the search for new forms of resolution (Weinberger, 1980).
52. The documents found in the cartulary of Sant Cugat del Vallès serve as a good laboratory for examining the language of violence used by the clergy against the nobility, which does not mean (countering the theory of violence as mere documentary revelation) that the violence of the nobility against the clergy and their people was not also very real (Salrach, 2000).
53. Abbot Oliba, for example, often used the weapon of excommunication against his enemies. At some point, he seems to have excommunicated much of the nobility of his diocese, whom he accused of usurping ecclesiastical property (Junyent, 1992, pp. 104–106, 252–254, 322–323). On the punishment of humiliation, see Patrick J. Geary (1979) and Salrach (2003).
54. The last work we know on Abbot Oliba, which discusses cultural and ideological issues and contains a very interesting analysis of various aspects of the peace assembly and truce of Toluges, the differences that opposed clergymen and nobles, and the most recent bibliographical references on the debates related to this institution, is that Stefano. M. Cingolani (2011–2013). The different views of Barthélemy, Bonnassie, Flori and Duby on the peace movements can be found in Henri Dolset (2000).
55. Juan José Larrea (2000, pp. 52–65) has provided a valuable summary on the contributions by Bonnassie and Bois and the opinions of their opponents, particularly Dominique Bathélemy, regarding the end of rural slavery and the origins of serfdom.
56. Of the Catalan documentation still existing from the ninth and tenth centuries, a reading can be made that supports the idea of there still being something similar to a tax system in the Carolingian era. However, it is impossible to know how collection worked and its effectiveness. In any case, we do not believe that the continuist vision expressed by Jean Durliat, that is to say, the continuation of the ancient or Roman system, can be applied to the Catalan case, but neither can the denialism of Chris Wickham. We have collected the evidence in Salrach (1993a, 1993b).

Having discarded the pure continuity of the Roman fiscal system, for us the problem is to determine the transformations it underwent to survive during Late Antiquity and the Early Middle Ages.

57. A reading of the documentation on the powerful in Carolingian Catalonia leads us to believe that at the base of the great patrimony of the tenth century aristocracy there were almost always lands of fiscal origin. See, for example, the property confirmation trial (around thirty *villas*) of the Ricolf magnate held in the city of Empúries in the year 959 (Salrach, 2013, pp. 174–175).
58. We will not insist on the concept of property applied to the peasantry in the year one thousand. We will only say that, at most, the peasant that could be considered best off (or the largest owner) would be the one who did not have to pay other charges than land tax, if he paid at all. And the most free, would have been free of everything except fulfilling his fiscal obligations.
59. We will not repeat here the arguments that we have many times, and for many years, presented in our work on this subject. We will only say that the renewed reading of the documentation reaffirms the same ideas.
60. This is one of the most obvious conclusions of our book (Salrach, 2013).
61. This is the case with the peasants of Vallformosa, who in a trial forced Count Borrell to recognize the land as a peasant property, that is, free from any type of tax burden (Salrach 2013, pp.110–111).
62. We have expressed this idea in a more argued way, with documentary and bibliographical references, in Salrach (2002a). If we look at the chronology of conflict and violence, perhaps we could reduce the time of change to 1020–1050/60, but it is clear that the rates of social and political change differed.
63. We express here, throughout this paragraph, our underlying agreement with Pierre Bonnassie and Guy Bois, in the sense of considering that what happened around the year one thousand, at least in certain European regions, to have been a revolution or change that led very heiristic societies, still resembling those of the ancient system, into feudalism. The discrepancy, which we also express, if one might say so, is that what happened around the year one thousand is not explained by reducing our vision to the tenth-eleventh centuries, without considering the changes that had occurred since the crisis of the Roman Empire, changes that take on clearer significance with the notion of transition. We are aware that Guy Bois would criticize this point of view, as he does with Chris Wickham's argument that "the concept of transition is in contradiction with the very strong consistency of the ancient system that he takes [Wickham, but also myself] as a starting point" (Bois, 1989a, p. 275). It is precisely this transition, we would respond, that helps us think of the resistances, adaptations and changes experienced by the system, changes that ultimately exacerbated its contradictions and weaknesses and made its fall possible.

64. For all these issues related to the twelfth century, the author of reference is Thomas N. Bisson. See a collection of his articles on France and Catalonia in Bisson (1989), and his overview of Western European issues in Bisson (2009).
65. This and the previous paragraph were inspired by the reading of the Barcelona *Usatges*, compiled at the court of the counts of Barcelona in the twelfth century (Valls, 1984). In it, the words *principes* and *potestates* (princes and powers), in reference to the counts, are ubiquitous. But the most significant of them is *Usatge 3*, in which the count invokes *Liber Iudicum* to present himself as the holder of royal power, at other times held by the kings of Toledo, to attribute himself the right to make new laws.
66. The changes in European legal culture can be seen in Manlio Bellomo (1989) and Paulo Grossi (2007). Some notes in judicial practices on Catalonia: Salrach (1997c, pp. 1039–1048).
67. We will not dwell here on the origin of the military suite, the meaning of the word *miles* and the differences between the knights of Carolingian and feudal times, subjects that have been strongly debated, with contributions by Bonnassie (2001c), Poly (1998, pp. 46–83 and 120–183), Duhamel-Amado (1995), Barthélemy (1997, pp. 173–191) and Barbero (1991). A good overview of the debate is that by Dolset (2000).
68. There has also been much debate on the nature and significance of the violence, and on the differences, if any, between the violence of the Carolingian era and the times of feudal change. The main contributions are those of Bonnassie (1975–1976, pp. 539–574), Bisson (1994), Barthélemy (1996), White (1996), Reuter (1997), and Wickham (1997).
69. We know of many of these conflicts thanks to documents of exceptional interest, the *querimoniae* (or inventories of grievances) lodged by those affected: Bisson (1998), Salrach (1999a, 1999b, see the bibliography on the *querimoniae* on p. 211, Note 20).
70. This type of conflict is especially visible in the *queremoniae* or memorials of grievances referred to in the previous note. One of the first to realize that this new conflict transformed the feudal system internally was Barthélemy (1984).
71. In Catalonia, there is only one example of a city, that of Vic, where citizens tried, in this case without success, to force the lord to accept the constitution of a citizen government against his will (Freedman, 1983, pp. 84–89).
72. When we say that the notions of the social system, mode of production and transition are "mental constructions, useful for grasping the historical material and studying it", we do not think of constructions made from nothing but from the experience of historical perception in the mind of the historian who, when identifying structures and dynamics, produce or

borrow defining global concepts to better analyse the past. We say this to express our disagreement with the theses of Elisabeth Brown (1974) and Susan Reynolds (1994), for whom the feudal system was only ever built in the minds of historians.

73. For the meaning, scope and use of the concept MP in this work, see Note 4.

References

Abadal, R. d'. (1961). *Els primers comtes catalans*. Vicens-Vives.

Abadal, R. d'. (2007). *Catalunya Carolíngia. II. Els diplomes carolingis a Catalunya* (facsimile). Institut d'Estudis Catalans. Original edition: 1926–1952.

Barbero, A. (1991). Noblesse et chevalerie en France au Moyen Âge. Une Réflexion. *Le Moyen Âge, 97*, 431–449.

Barthélemy, D. (1984). *Les Deux Âges de la seigneurie banale, Coucy (milieu XIe – milieu XIIIe siècles)*. Publications de la Sorbonne.

Barthélemy, D. (1993). *La société dans le comté de Vendôme de l'an mil au XIVe siècle*. Fayard.

Barthélemy, D. (1996). The Feudal Revolution, I. *Past and Present, 152*, 196–205.

Barthélemy, D. (1997). *La mutation de l'an mil a-t-elle eu lieu? Servage et chevalerie dans la France des Xe et XIe siècles*. Fayard.

Bellomo, M. (1989). *L'Europa del diritto commune*. Cigno Galileo Galilei.

Benito, P. (2003). *Senyoria de la terra i tinença pagesa al comtat de Barcelona, segles XI-XIII*. Centro Superior de Investigaciones Cintíficas.

Bisson, T. N. (1985–1986). The Crisis of the Catalonian Franchises (1150–1200). In J. Portella (ed.), *La formació i expansió del feudalisme català* (pp. 153–172). Girona: Estudi General.

Bisson, T. N. (1989). *Medieval France and Her Pyrenean Neighbours*. The Hambledon Press.

Bisson, T. N. (1994). The Feudal Revolution, I. *Past and Present, 142*, 6–42.

Bisson, T. N. (1997). Els orígens de les Corts catalanes. In T. N. Bisson (ed.), *L'impuls de Catalunya. L'època dels primers comtes-reis* (pp. 141–158). Eumo.

Bisson, T. N. (1998). *Tormented Voices: Power, Crisis, and Humanity in Rural Catalonia, 1140–1200*. Harvard University Press.

Bisson, T. N. (2009). *The Crisis of the Twelfth Century. Power, Lordship, and the Origins of European Government*. Princeton University Press.

Bois, G. (1989a). *La mutation de l'an mil. Lournand, village mâconnais, de l'Antiquité au féodalisme*. Fayard.

Bois, G. (1989b). Ciutat i camp en la societat preindustrial. In *L'espai viscut. Col·loqui internacional d'història local* (pp. 113–126). Diputació de València.

Bois, G. (2000). *La Grande dépression médiévale: XIVe-XVe siècles. Le précédent d'une crise systémique*. Presses Universitaires de France.
Bonnassie, P. (1975–1976). *La Catalogne du milieu du Xe à la fin du XIe siècle. Croissance et mutations d'une société* (2 Vols.). Publications de l'Université de Toulouse-Le Mirail.
Bonnassie, P. (2000). Le servage: une sous-féodalité? Le témoignage des documents catalans (fin XIe-XIIIe siècle). *Mélanges de l'École Française de Rome. Moyen Âge, 112*(2), 643–661.
Bonnassie, P. (2001a). Survie et extinction du régime esclavagiste dans l'Occident du Haut Moyen Âge (IVe-XIe s.). In P. Bonnassie (Ed.), *Les sociétés de l'an mil* (pp. 85–142). De Boeck Université.
Bonnassie, P. (2001b). Les sagreres catalanes: la concentration de l'habitat dans le "cercle de paix" des églises (XIe s.). In P. Bonnassie (Ed.), *Les sociétés de l'an mil* (pp. 285–316). De Boeck Université.
Bonnassie, P. (2001c). Les milites en pays d'Oc au XI siècle, d'après les sources hagiographiques. In P. Bonnassie (Ed.), *Les sociétés de l'an mil* (pp. 453–482). De Boeck Université.
Bringué, J. M. (1995). *Comunitats i béns comunals als Pallars Sobirà, segles XV-XVIII* (doctoral thesis). Pompeu Fabra University, Barcelona.
Brown, E. (1974). The Tyranny of a Construct: Feudalism and Historians of Medieval Europe. *American Historical Review, 79*, 1063–1088.
Callander, A. (Ed.). (1998). *After Rome's Fall: Narrators and Sources of Early Medieval History*. University of Toronto Press.
Catafau, A. (1998). *Les celleres et la naissance du village en Roussillon (Xe-XVe siècles)*. Editorial el Trabucaire, Presses Universitaires de Perpignan.
Cingolani, S. M. (2011–2013). L'abat Oliba, el poder i la paraula. *Acta Historica et Archaeologica Mediaevalia, 31*, 115–162.
Collins, R. (1989). *The Arab Conquest of Spain, 710–797*. Blackwell.
Cracco-Ruggini, L. (1961). *Economia e società nell'"Italia Annonaria". Rapporti fra agricoltura e comercio dal IV al VI secolo d. C.* A. Giuffrè.
Curschmann, F. (1970). *Hungersnöte im Mittelalter. Ein Beitrag zur deutschen Wirtschafgesschichte des 8. bis 13. Jahrhunderts*. Scientia.
Débax, H. (2003). *La féodalité languedocienne, XIe-XIIe siècles. Serments, hommages et fiefs dans le Languedoc des Trencavel*. Presses Universitaires du Mirail.
Devroey, J.-P. (1986). Réflexions sur l'économie des premiers temps carolingiens (768–877): Grands domaines et action politique entre Seine et Rhin. *Francia. Forschungen Zur Westeuropäischen Geschichte, 13*, 475–488.
Devroey, J. P. (2010). Dîme et économie des campagnes à l'époque carolingienne. In R. Viader (ed.), *La dîme dans l'Europe médiévale et moderne. Actes des XXXe Journées internationales d'histoire de l'abbaye de Flaran, 3 et 4 octobre 2008* (pp. 37–62). Presses universitaires du Mirail.

Dhondt, J. (1948). *Études sur la naissance des principautés territoriales en France (IXe-Xe siècle)*. Ghent University.

Dockés, P. (1979). *La libération médiévale*. Flammarion.

Dolset, H. (2000). En el corazón del debate sobre la feudalidad: Las clientelas militares. *Historiar, 4*, 66–83.

Dolset, H. (2004). *Frontière et pouvoir en Catalogne médiévale. L'aristocratie dans l'ouest du comté de Barcelone (début du Xe-milieu du XIIe siècle)* (doctoral thesis). University of Toulouse II-Le Mirail, Toulouse.

Duby, G. (1953). *La société aux XIe et XIIe siècles dans la région mâconnaise*. Armand Colin. Reprint 1971.

Duhamel-Amado, C. (1995). *La famille aristocratique languedocienne. Parenté et patrimoine dans les vicomtés de Béziers et d'Agde (900–1170)* (Doctoral thesis). Paris-Sorbonne University (Paris IV), Paris.

Durliat, J. (1990). *Les finances publiques de Diocletien aux Carolingiens (284–889)*. Thorbecke.

Ewig, E. (1976–1979). *Spätantikes und fränkisches Gallien*. Artemis.

Farías, V. (1993). La sagrera catalana (c. 1025-c. 1200). Características y desarrollo de un tipo de asentamiento eclesial. *Studia Historica. Historia Medieval, 11*, 81–123.

Farías, V., Marti, R., Catafau, A. (2007). *Les sagreres a la Catalunya medieval*. Associaciód'Hisòria Rural de les Comarques Gironines.

Feliu, G. (2010). *La llarga nit feudal. Mil anys de pugna entre senyors i pagesos*. Publicacions de la Universitat de València.

Finley, M. (1973). *The Ancient Economy*. University of California Press.

Fournier, G. (1961). L'esclavage en Basse-Auvergne eaux époques mérovingienne et carolingienne. *Cahiers D'histoire, 6*, 361–375.

Freedman, P. H. (1983). *The Diocese of Vic. Tradition and Regeneration in Medieval Catalonia*. Rutgers University Press.

Freedman, P. H. (1991). *The Origins of Peasant Servitude in Medieval Catalonia*. Cambridge University Press.

Garnsey, P. (1989). *Famine and Food Supply in the Graeco-Roman World: Responses to Risk and Crisis*. Cambridge University Press.

Geary, P. J. (1979). L'humiliation des saints. *Annales ESC, 1*(janvier/février), 27–42.

Goffart, W. (1980). *Barbarians and Romans, A.D. 418–584: The Techniques of Accommodation*. Princeton University Press.

Gonzalvo, G. (1994). *Les Constitucions de Pau i Treva de Catalunya (segles XI-XIII)*. Generalitat de Catalunya, Department of Justice.

Grossi, P. (2007). *L'Europa del diritto*. Roma: Laterza.

Heather, P. J. (2005). *The Fall of the Roman Empire: A New History of Rome and the Barbarians*. Oxford University Press.

Jeannin, A. (2007). *Formules et formulaires. Marculf et les praticiens du droit au premier Moyen Âge (Ve-Xe siècles)* (Doctoral thesis). Université Jean Moulin, Lyon.

Junyent, E. (1992). *Diplomatari i escrits literaris de l'abat i bisbe Oliba*. Institut d'Estudis Catalans.

King, P. D. (1972). *Law and Society in the Visigothic Kingdom*. Cambridge University Press.

Krusch, B., & Levison, W. (eds.) (1937–1951). *Gregorii Turonensis Opera. Libri historiarum X. MGH. Scriptores Rerum Merovingicarum*, 1. Hannover (reed. 1992).

Larrea, J. J. (1998). *La Navarre de IVe au XIIe siècle: Peuplement et société*. De Boeck Université.

Larrea, J. J. (2000). Esclavitud y servidumbre en el debate sobre la mutación feudal. *Historiar, 4*, 52–65.

Larrea, J. J. (2006). La condición del campesinado navarro-aragonés entre los siglos IX y XII: Una revisión crítica. *En La España Medieval, 29*, 383–409.

Lauranson-Rosaz, C. (1987). *L'Auvergne et ses marges (Velay, Gévaudan) du VIIIe au XIe siècle. La fin du monde antique?* Les Cahiers de la Haute-Loire.

Lauranson-Rosaz, C. (2000). La "mutación feudal": Una cuestión controvertida. *Historiar, 4*, 12–31.

Lauranson-Rosaz, C. (2001). Le débat sur la "mutation féodale": état de la question. In P. Urbanczyk (ed.), *Europe Around the Year 1000* (pp. 11–40). Institute of Archaeology and Ethnology, Polish Academy of Sciences.

Lauranson-Rosaz, C. (2002). Le débat sur la "mutation féodale": état de la question. *Scienza & Politica, 26*(14), 3–24.

Lauranson-Rosaz, C. (2011). À l'origine des territoires de justice: *Districtus, vicaria* et périmètres de paix. In J. Poumarède (Ed.), *Territoires et lieux de justice* (pp. 11–28). Association Française pour l'histroire de la justice.

Lemarignier, J.-F. (1951). La dislocation du *pagus* et le problème des *consuetudines* (Xe-XIe siècle). *Mélanges d'histoire du Moyen Âge dédiés à la mémoire de Louis Halphen* (pp. 401–410). Presses Universitaires de France.

Lemarignier, J.-F. (1976). *La France Médiévale: Institutions et Société*. Armand Colin.

Le règlement des conflits au Moyen Âge. XXXXIe Congrès de la SHMES (Angers, juin 2000) (2001). Publications de la Sorbonne.

Lewit, T. (2004). *Villas, Farms and the Late Roman Rural Economy: Third to Fifth Centuries AD*. Archaeopress.

Mallorquí, E. (2011). *El Llibre Verd del bisbe de Girona (1362–1371). El delme i l'estructura feudal de la diòcesi de Girona al segle XIV*. Diputació de Girona.

Marqués, J. M. (1993). *Cartoral, dit de Carlemany, del bisbe de Girona (segles IX-XIV)*. Fundació Noguera.

Mazel, F. (2010). Féodalités, 888–1180. In J. Cornette (Dir.), *Histoire de France* (Vol. 2, pp. 637–648). Belin.

Mommsen, T. (ed.). (1894). *Cassiodori Senatoris Variae. MGH. Scriptores. Auctores Antiquissimi*, 12. Hannover (reed. 1981).

Nelson, J. L. (1986). Dispute Settlement in Carolingian West Francia. In W. Davies & P. Fouracre (Eds.), *The Settlement of Disputes in Early Medieval Europe* (pp. 45–64). Cambridge University Press.

Newfield, T. P. (2013). The Contours, Frequency and Causation of Subsistence Crises in Carolingian Europe (750–950 CE). In P. Benito (ed.), *Crisis alimentarias en la Edad Media. Modelos, explicaciones y representaciones* (pp. 117–172). Milenio.

Ordeig, R. (1999). *Catalunya Carolíngia. IV. Els comtats d'Osona i Manresa.* Institut d'Estudis Catalans.

Pérez Sánchez, D. (1989). *El Ejército en la sociedad visigoda*. Ediciones Universidad de Salamanca.

Poly, J.-P. (1976). *La Provence et la société féodale, 879–1166: Contribution à l'étude des structures dites féodales dans le Midi*. Bordas.

Poly, J.-P. (1998). Dépendances cavalières. In E. Bournazel & J.-P. Poly (Eds.), *Les Féodalités* (pp. 46–83). Presses Universitaires de France.

Puigvert, X. (1992). La introducció del delme a la Marca Hispànica. *Acta Historica et Archaeologica Mediaevalia, 13*, 117–125.

Reuter, T. (1997). The Feudal Revolution, III. *Past and Present, 155*, 177–195.

Reynolds, S. (1994). *Fiefs and Vassals. The Medieval Evidence Reinterpreted.* Oxford University Press.

Rouche, M. (1979). *L'Aquitaine des Wisigoths aux Arabes, 418–781.* École des Hautes Études en Sciences Sociales.

Salrach, J. M. (1978). El comte Guifré de Besalú i la revolta de 957. Aproximació a l'estudi de la noblesa catalana de l'Alta Edat mitjana. In *II Assemblea d'estudis del Comtat de Besalú. Actes 1973* (pp. 3–36). Amics del Comtat de Besalú.

Salrach, J. M. (1992). Agressions senyorials i resistències pageses en el procés de feudalització (segles IX-XII). *Revoltes populars contra el poder de l'Estat* (pp. 11–29). Generalitat de Catalunya.

Salrach, J. M. (1993a). Del Estado romano a los reinos germánicos. En torno a las bases materiales del poder del Estado en la Antigüedad Tardía y la Alta Edad Media. In *De la Antigüedad al Medievo. Siglos IV-VIII. III Congreso de Estudios Medievales* (pp. 96–142). Fundación Sánchez Albornoz.

Salrach, J. M. (1993b). Bases materials de l'Estat a l'època carolíngia. L'exemple dels comtats catalans. In *El poder de l'Estat: evolució, força o raó. IIes Jornades de debat* (pp. 49–96). Edicions del Centre de Lectura.

Salrach, J. M. (1997a). *La formación del campesinado en el Occidente antiguo y medieval*. Síntesis.

Salrach, J. M. (1997b). Mas prefeudal i mas feudal. In J. Bolòs & J. J. Busqueta (Eds.), *Territori i Societat a l'Edat Mitjana* (pp. 13–40). Publicacions de la Universitat de Lleida.

Salrach, J. M. (1997c). Prácticas judiciales, transformación social y acción política en Cataluña (siglos IX–XIII). *Hispania, 197*, 1009–1048.

Salrach, J. M. (1998). Tres mots polèmics: *Villa*, mas i alou en època carolíngia. *Quaderns de Banyoles, 19*, 9–28.

Salrach, J. M. (1999a). Disputes i compromisos entre l'Església de Girona i la noblesa. Notes d'unes difícils relacions (segles Xi i XII). *Anuario de Estudios Medievales, 29*, 927–957.

Salrach, J. M. (1999b). Violència feudal, violència contra qui? In H. Débax (ed.), *Les sociétés meridionales à l'âge féodal (Espagne, Italie et sud de la France Xe-XIIe s.). Hommage à Pierre Bonnassie* (pp. 207–214). Centre National de Recherche Scientifique, University of Toulouse-Le Miral.

Salrach, J. M. (2000). Multa placita et contenciones: conflictos de los siglos X-XII en el Cartulario de Sant Cugat del Vallès. In J. Pérez & S. Aguadé (eds.), *Les origines de la féodalité. Hommage à Claudio Sánchez Albornoz* (pp. 197–228). Casa de Velázquez, University of Alcalá.

Salrach, J. M. (2002a). ¿Qué diferenciaba a los campesinos del siglo IX de los del siglo XII en Catalunya? In *Señores, siervos, vasallos en la Alta Edad Media. XXVIII Semana de Estudios Medievales* (pp. 309–362). Government of Navarra.

Salrach, J. M. (2002b). Recerca sobre el mot *fevum* en fonts eclesiàstiques de la Catalunya Vella (diòcesis de Girona i Barcelona). In P. Bonnassie (Ed.), *Fiefs et féodalité dans l'Europe méridionale (Italie, Frande du Midi, Péninsule ibérique) du Xe au XIIIe siècle* (pp. 397–418). Centre National de la Recherche Scientifique, University of Toulouse-Le Mirail.

Salrach, J. M. (2003). Tradicions jurídiques en l'administració de justícia a l'Edat Mitjana: el cas de l'*aliscara-harmiscara* i la humiliació penitencial. In M. Barceló, G. Feliu, A. Furió, M. Miquel & J. Sobrequés (eds.), *El feudalisme comptat i debatut. Formació i expansió del feudalisme català* (pp. 71–102). Publicacions de la Universitat de València.

Salrach, J. M. (2005). L'esprit de la *Res Publica* dans la législation de Charlemagne. In A. Dubreucq & C. Lauranson-Rosaz (Eds.), *Traditio iuris: Permanence et/ou discontinuité du droit romain durant le haut Moyen Âge* (pp. 255–269). University Jean Moulin.

Salrach, J. M. (2007). La fam a l'Europa dels regnes germànics (segles V-VII). In J. M. Delgado (ed.), *Antoni Saumell i Soler. Miscel·lània in memoriam* (pp. 69–78). Pompeu Fabra University.

Salrach, J. M. (2009). *La fam al món. Passat i present*. Eumo.

Salrach, J. M. (2013). *Justícia i poder a Catalunya abans de l'any mil*. Eumo.

Salvian of Marseilles. (1975). *Oeuvres. II. Du gouvernement de Dieu* (trans. Lagarrigue, G.). Éditions du Cerf.

Sánchez León, J. C. (1996). *Los bagaudas: rebeldes, demonios, mártires. Revueltas campesinas en Galia e Hispania durante el Bajo Imperio*. University of Jaén.

Saudan, M. (2004). *Espaces perçus, espaces vécus: géographie historique du Massif central du IXe au XIIe siècle* (Doctoral thesis). University of Paris, Paris.

Sayas, J. J., & Garcia Moreno, L. A. (1981). *Romanismo y germanismo. El despertar de los pueblos hispánicos (siglos IV-X)*. Labor.

Tits-Dieuaide, M.-J. (1985). Grands domaines, grandes et petites exploitations en Gaule mérovingienne. In A. Verhulst (Ed.), *Le grand domaine aux époques mérovingienne et carolingienne* (pp. 23–50). Publications du Centre belge d'histoire rurale.

Thompson, E. A. (1969). *The Goths in Spain*. Clarendon Press.

To, L. (1993). Le mas catalan du XIIe siècle: Genèse et évolution d'une structure d'encadrement et d'asservissement de la paysannerie. *Cahiers de Civilisation Medieval, 36*(2), 151–177.

To, L. (2000). Servitude et mobilité paysanne: les origines de la "remença" catalane (XIe-XIIe siècle). *Mélanges de l'École Française de Rome. Moyen Âge, 112*(2), 827–865.

Toubert, P. (1973). *Les structures du Latium médiéval. Le Latium méridional et la Sabine du IXe siècle à la fin du XIIe siècle*. École française de Rome.

Toubert, P. (2004). *L'Europe dans sa première croissance. De Charlemagne à l'an mil*. Fayard.

Valls Taberner, F. (1984). *Los Usatges de Barcelona*. Promociones Publicaciones Universitarias.

Verhulst, A. (1965). Karolingische Agrarpolitik. Das *Capitulare de villis* und die Hungersnöte von 792/93 und 805/6. *Zeitschrift Für Agrargeschichte Und Agrarsoziologie, 13*, 175–189.

Verhulst, A. (Ed.). (1983). *Le grand domaine aux époques mérovingienne et carolingienne. Die Grundherrschaft im frühen Mittelalter*. Rijksunivers.

Verhulst, A. (1990). Étude comparative du régime domanial classique à l'est et à l'ouest du Rhin à l'époque carolingienne. In *La croissance agricole du Haut Moyen Âge* (pp. 86–101). Centre Culturel de l'Abbaye de Flaran.

Viader, R. (2003). *L'Andorre du IXe au XIVe siècle: Montagne, féodalité et communautés*. Presses Universitaires du Mirail.

Vives, J. (1963). *Concilios visigóticos e hispanorromanos*. Centro Superior de Investigaciones Científicas.

Weinberger, S. (1980). Les conflits entre clercs et laïcs dans la Provence du XIe siècle. *Annales du Midi, 92*(148), 269–279.

White, S. D. (1996). The Feudal Revolution, II. *Past and Present, 152*, 205–223.

Wickham, C. (1984). The Other Transition: From the Ancient World to Feudalism. *Past and Present, 103*, 3–36.

Wickham, C. (1993). La chute de Rome n'aura pas lieu. *Le Moyen Âge, 99*, 107–126.

Wickham, C. (1995). El fin del Imperio Carolingio. ¿Qué tipo de crisis? In C. Wickham, H. Kamen, E. Hernández et al. (eds.), *Las crisis en la historia* (pp. 11–20). Ediciones Universidad de Salamanca.

Wickham, C. (1997). The Feudal Revolution, IV. *Past and Present, 155*, 196–208.

Wickham, C. (2005). *Farming the Early Middle Ages: Europe and the Mediterranean 400–800*. Oxford University Press.

Wickham, C. (2009). *The Inheritance of Rome: A History of Europe from 400 to 1000*. Allen Lane.

CHAPTER 3

The Great Late Medieval Depression and the Catalan Economy, 1315–1516

Jordi Catalan Vidal

After a few centuries of Commercial Revolution during the Mediaeval Warm Period, the Mediterranean experienced a triple shock at the beginning of the fourteenth century: bad harvests, generalized war and virulent

The author is grateful for the financial support of the Ministry of Science and Innovation of the Spanish Government (MCIN/AEI/10.13039/501100011033), and of the European Regional Development Fund of the European Union (ERDF) (A way of making Europe) through project PGC2018-093896-B-I00, "Mediterranean Capitalism? Successes and Failures of Industrial Development in Spain, 1720–2020." He also thanks to the Generalitat de Catalunya, and the Centre d'Estudis Jordi Nadal of the University of Barcelona, which contributed to support the publication of this chapter in several ways. A previous Spanish version of this work was published in *Revista de Historia Industrial*. The author benefited from the help and comments

J. Catalan Vidal (✉)
Centre d'Estudis Jordi Nadal, University of Barcelona, Barcelona, Spain
e-mail: jordi.catalan@ub.edu

J. Catalan Vidal (ed.), *Crises and Transformation in the Mediterranean World*, Palgrave Studies in Economic History,
https://doi.org/10.1007/978-3-031-24502-2_3

outbreaks of plague. Their combined effect reduced the population, agricultural and industrial production, trade, land rent and tax income, and increased agricultural yields, wages, debt and distribution conflicts.

However, the Mediterranean thalassocracies did not record a continuous fall during the great depression of the Middle Ages, but rather a succession of periods of recovery and subsequent crises. Catalonia and Barcelona adopted innovative measures to overcome them: an extension of political participation, the reform of taxation, new financial instruments, public banking and investment, protectionism and monetary devaluations. Thanks to these solutions, the Catalan economy was able to overcome the crises prior to 1404, showing a notable capacity for resilience. Thus, the fourteenth century in Catalonia can be overall characterized as one of growth with crises.

Nonetheless, in the fifteenth century, the dynamics of the Catalan economy fits in more with a pattern of the great depression. The costs of imperialist policy, which had already dangerously indebted the last monarchs of the house of Barcelona, rose considerably with the offensive for the kingdom of Naples, and the need to finance the campaign caused a breach among the country's institutions and classes. In spite of this, the devaluations and protectionist measures, favoured by Alfonso the Magnanimous, still generated two intense drives for recovery in the 1420s and 1450s, which again suggest the capacity for resilience of the Catalan economy.

On the other hand, the collapse during the 1462–1516 period was of another order and had grater long-lasting consequences for long-term growth. The nobility's reaction against the reformist attempts to free the serfs and the resulting civil war, between the country's institutions and the monarchy, unremittingly wrecked the Catalan commercial economy. Although it had some successes, Ferdinand the Catholic's reconstruction policy was disappointing overall. In particular, his support for an absolutist, monolithic and inquisitorial state tended to numb the recovery potential of the Catalan productive fabric. Barcelona, which until then

by Gaspar Feliu, Pere Pascual, Ricard Soto, Carolina Batet, Carles Puigferrat, and two anonymous referees. He also is in debt with Doctor Andreu Ginés who helped with the English edition. The possible errata are the exclusive responsibility of the author.

had followed the trail of Venice, Genoa and Florence, began the modern age with a decline comparable to that of Pisa, Montpellier or Thessaloniki.

3.1 The Great Depression of the Late Middle Ages in the Mediterranean

The great depression of the late Middle Ages has been considered to be a systemic crisis (Bois, 2000). The Mediterranean was subject to three interrelated shocks with profound consequences in the economic, social and political spheres. Bad harvests, wars and waves of plague contributed to converting the sea that, for a few centuries, had constituted the epicentre of the Commercial Revolution into a more erratic setting (Campbell, 2016; De Roover, 1942, 1962; Le Goff, 2010; López, 1976; Kocka, 2013).

Subsistence crises were not unknown. They existed before and after the fourteenth century all over the planet. However, since the end of the thirteenth century, the episodes of bad harvests and shortages occurred with greater frequency. The Mediaeval Climatic Optimum reached its end and the earth began to move towards a period of greater coldness. The glaciers advanced. Earthquakes occurred with greater frequency. Iceland abandoned agriculture to concentrate on fishing. In England, the cultivation of vines declined and finally disappeared. The arrival of the Little Ice Age was preceded by the Great Famine (1315–1321). In the areas close to the Alps, villages in the higher lands were abandoned (Campbell, 2016; Fagan, 2000; Fraser & Rimas, 2011; Le Roy Ladurie, 1967).

During the four decades between 1310 and 1350, subsistence crises occurred with unusual frequency in the north-western Mediterranean. Considering data series from some Italian, French and Iberian regions from this area, maximum numbers of bad harvests, shortages and famines were recorded during the 40-year period from 1310 to 1350. I have used the data from the episodes recorded by Professor Benito and we have taken into account the eleven historical regions of Tuscany, Liguria, Emilia, Lombardy, Piedmont, Provence, Languedoc, Catalonia, Valencia, Aragon and Castile (Benito, 2004). On the basis of the data compiled by the author, and referring to the interval from 1250 to 1400, there is no other moment when there have been more than five regions with over two continuous decades of famines.

The ultimate reason for the intensification of bad harvests and famines during the 1310–1350 interval is subject to controversy. One classic explanation would be that of Postan, who proposed the Malthusian crisis model (Postan, 1950): The demographic growth of the previous three centuries would have led to increasingly poor land being cultivated, reducing the size of the flocks and fertilizer, causing a fall in average yields and increasing the pressure of the population on resources. This process would have made the Mediterranean economy more vulnerable, thus eventually leading it to a great depression of a Malthusian type. One objection to this argument is that it was possible to intensify the cultivation systems, as occurred in Norfolk, Flanders or the Rhine at that time (Fig. 3.1).

We can express serious doubts about whether the more arid and mountainous lands of the Mediterranean shore could adopt the innovations of Atlantic agriculture. Nevertheless, in more recent times, there has been a preference to use the hypothesis of the end of the Mediaeval Warm Period, and the beginning of several centuries of climatic volatility as a prologue to the Little Ice Age of the modern era (Campbell, 2016; Fagan, 2000). Since the end of the thirteenth century, less rainfall, more

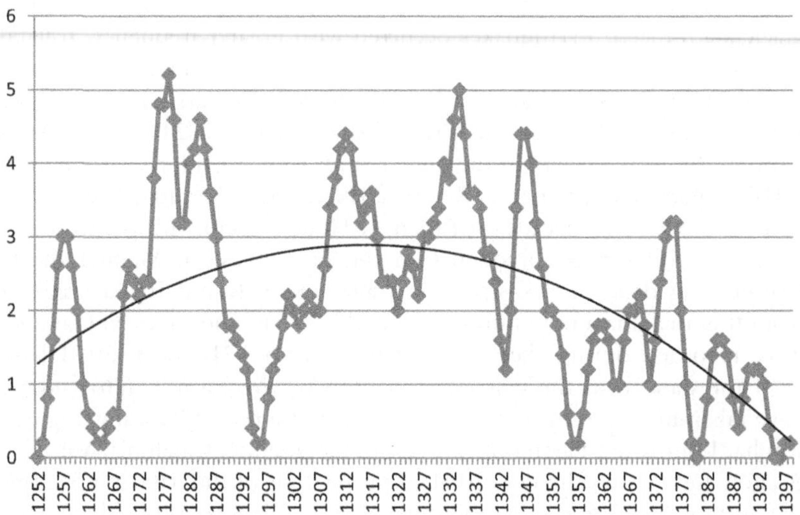

Fig. 3.1 Number of regions with famine episodes within a group of 11 North-western Mediterranean regions, 1250–1400 (five-years moving averages) (*Source* Own elaboration from data compiled by Benito [2004])

droughts and more extreme temperatures would have entailed a greater frequency of bad harvests and prolonged periods of shortages and hunger. Repeated periods of malnutrition over 40 years must have weakened the organisms of the inhabitants of the Mediterranean and left them badly prepared for when *Y. pestis* returned to the area.

Moreover, despite the climax achieved by intra-Mediterranean trade at the beginning of the 1300s, the military conflicts intensified, both in the centre and on the periphery of the Mare Nostrum (Bois, 2000; Holmes, 1975): France's Philip IV the Fair attacked Guyenne and Flanders and subsequently annexed the Franche Comté, Lyon and Champagne: Since 1282, the Anjou and Aragon fought for the control of Sicily, with a final result in favour of the latter (Abulafia, 2017). The advance of the Turks in Anatolia led Byzantium to hire mercenaries to try to contain them. Catalan Almogavar, Aragonese and Italian warriors, after having helped to consolidate Frederick of Sicily on the throne, offered their services to Emperor Andronikos II and disembarked in Constantinople in 1303. The so-called Catalan Company of the Orient obtained some victories against the Ottomans in Asia Minor (Vinas & Vinas, 2017). Then the Almogavars saw how their leader was murdered in Adrianople in 1305 by a group of Alans under the orders of the co-emperor Michael IX and broke up with Byzantium. After confronting Bulgarians and Genoese, they devastated Thrace and looted the monasteries of Mount Athos. The result was the annexation of the Duchy of Athens in 1311. The company held on to it, together with other Greek conquests, until 1387, when it was evicted by the Florentines. In 1324, the Catalan-Aragonese forces challenged the Pisans for the control of Sardinia and, in 1329, the conflict broke out between the former and Genoa.

For his part, in France, Philip VI confiscated Aquitaine in 1337, beginning a secular contention with England, known as the Hundred Years' War. During the conflict, which had devastating consequences, the policy of alliances extended the war: Whereas Castile helped France, Portugal and Aragon preferred agreements with England. In 1343, Aragon again annexed Mallorca, which, together with Roussillon, had formed a Mediterranean vassal kingdom since the death of James I.

In 1351, Byzantium, Venice and Aragon again joined forces against Genoa. The secular struggle between the Ligurian republic and Aragon has sometimes been described as the Second Hundred Years' War (Belenguer, 2015). As for the Turks, they succeeded in conquering Gallipoli in 1354, their first stronghold in Europe. Two years later, Peter the Cruel of Castile took up arms against Peter the Ceremonious of Aragon, triggering a conflict that lasted until 1375. During the 1360s, the free companies devastated Provence. At the end of the following decade, the conflict of Chioggia broke out, taking the troops of Genoa to the doors of Venice, only to be defeated in 1380. In the mid-1380s, the Anglo-Portuguese alliance defeated Castile. During the same decade, Milan tried to annex Pisa and Siena.

Once taken Gallipoli, the Ottomans advanced into Romania. In 1387, they conquered Thessaloniki and held it until 1430. In 1389, they defeated the Serbs at the battle of Kosovo and consolidated positions in the Balkans. Florence annexed Volterra in 1361 and Arezzo in 1384. Milan sold its rights over Pisa to Florence, leading to a rebellion. However, in 1406 the Pisans were subjugated by Florence. In the first decades of the fifteenth century, France was fragmented into three domains of comparable weight: English, French and Burgundian. In 1421, Milan conquered Genoa and held on to it until 1435.

The war entailed lootings and the destruction of crops, further weakening the organisms and leaving a fertile breeding ground for the tremendous mortality of the Black Death. Infantry warfare gradually imposed itself on the traditional feudal cavalry and required new state revenues beyond the income from property and services of a seigniorial nature. Furthermore, the high financial costs of the military campaigns led to confiscations, tax increases, excessive devaluations, bankruptcies and huge losses of savings (Bois, 2000; Henneman, 1971; Le Goff, 2010; Spufford, 1988).

In 1306, Philip the Fair expelled the Hebrews from his kingdom for the first time (Forcano, 2014). Many of them had made fortune in cities such as Toulouse, Narbonne and Montpellier, and were given shelter in Catalonia, Mallorca and Provence. The same king dissolved the Templars and confiscated their properties in 1308. His desire to tax and control the church led to the transfer of the Holy See to Avignon in 1309. The French monarchy likewise imposed repeated contributions on the Jewish and Lombard moneylenders between 1311 and 1321. In 1315, Louis X allowed the Hebrew population to return to France. However, a few years later, in 1322, the Jews were again expelled from France, Languedoc and Burgundy.

Meanwhile, the Florentine banking houses of the Bardi and the Peruzzi had given loans to Edward III of England and to Robert of Naples (Cipolla, 1982; Holmes, 1975; Le Goff, 2010; Miskimin, 1975; Tanzini,

2018). But the English monarch, caught in the strangle hold of his huge military spending on the continent, could not meet the requirements to service the debt contracted, leading to the fall of the Peruzzi bank in 1343 and the Bardi in 1346, likewise affected by the withdrawal of deposits. The resulting financial crisis also took with it the most important bank in Florence, the Acciaiuoli. The town of Florence also defaulted.

In Barcelona, King Peter the Ceremonious, who had financed his campaigns in the Mediterranean and in the interior of the Iberian Peninsula with sales of assets and resorting abundantly to credit, had to seek new sources of income (Belenguer, 2015). The annexation of the kingdom of Mallorca allowed him to access the contributions of the aljamas of the Balearics and Roussillon (Chismol, 2019). He also obtained gains by authorizing exchanges with infidel kingdoms, such as the North of Africa. However, none of these sources was sufficient and, as we shall see, he was forced to transfer tax sovereignty in exchange for income.

Moreover, the monarchs of the late Middle Ages financed the excessive demands of war with tremendous reductions in the metal component of their coins. Under the reign of John II of France, and just in the three-year period from 1358 to 1360, the silver coins underwent 25 alterations, with results comparable to nominal devaluations (Bois, 2000). There was another critical episode from 1418 to 1422 when the English advance forced Charles VI to retreat and gold and silver stopped circulating in France in favour of less noble coinage. Similarly, since the mid-fourteenth century and late-fifteenth century the Castilian *maravedi* lost more than 90% of its value (Feliu, 2000). Spufford talk about the plague of devaluation (Spufford, 1988).

However, the scourge that would have the deepest long-term effects was, undoubtedly, the reappearance in Europe of the bacteria *Yersinia pestis*. In 1346, the Mongols were besieging the Genoese fortress of Caffa, in the Crimean Peninsula. The Tartars threw corpses infected with bubonic plague at the besieged and, whether through this channel or more likely due to the arrival of the black rat and its strange passengers, they infected the Ligurians, whose ships travelled to the other end of the Black Sea transporting the plague. At the beginning of summer 1347, the plague reached Constantinople and, during the autumn, decimated Anatolia. In the same autumn, the Genoese ships spread the bacillus around Palermo, their own metropolis and Marseille. In March 1348, the Black Death reached Mallorca, via Sardinia, and in April, Perpignan, via Narbonne. From the Balearics, it was transmitted to Barcelona and

Valencia, where the epidemic was already detected in May 1348. The chain reaction of the epidemic meant that in Europe, from 1347 to 1534, there were 17 episodes of renewed infection (Cuadrada, 2012).

For several decades, Christian monarchies and ecclesiastic extremists used the Jews as scapegoats, especially in France. Shortly after bubonic plague reappeared in the West, the rumour spread that they were poisoning the water. As early as April 1348, about 40 Jews were burned in Toulon (Provence). In the following month, the Hebrew neighbourhood of Barcelona (*call*) was looted, as was the Jewish quarter of the Valencian town Morvedre. By 1351, over 350 incidents had been recorded throughout Europe, being considered as anti-Jewish pogroms. In the Catalan-speaking territories, a new outbreak of the plague in the 1370s triggered new lootings in the *calls* of Mallorca, Perpignan, Barcelona and Valencia. In 1386, the disturbances spread to Xàtiva's Muslim neighbourhood. Again, the pogroms against the Jewish quarters intensified in 1391 in Valencia, Mallorca, Barcelona, Girona, Lleida and Perpignan. In 1399, however, the victims were the Moors of Valencia.

Benedictow estimated the fall in population caused by the spread of the Black Death in the late Middle Ages at around 60% in Florence, and between 55 and 60% for the whole of Tuscany (Benedictow, 2004). As for Piedmont he considered it to be 52% of the total population. According to estimations by the same author, this mortality would have been 60% in both Provence and Languedoc. The author gives more drastic data for Catalonia: above 60% of mortality during the 1347–1497 period; although we consider Nadal's estimation of 53% more acceptable (Nadal, 1992). Jaldun calculated its impact on the Islamic world as of 45%. In any case, the proportions are nightmarish and, therefore, must have had a very long-lasting effect on the entire Mediterranean.

The unprecedented scale of the mortality caused by *Y. pestis* must have led to a corresponding fall in aggregate demand, dragging down both prices and quantities produced. The price series available do, indeed, show a generalized contraction in the Mediterranean world. It is more difficult to know the evolution of output, although the (more speculative) evidence confirms a major contractive shock.

In the face of the fall in demand for food and the death of peasants, the surface areas cultivated went down, barren fields appeared and woodland gained terrain. People stopped sowing on marginal land and concentrated the cultivation on higher-quality farms. The size of the flocks and the availability of fertilizer tended to increase. Yields, therefore, improved and the relative prices of agricultural products also went down.

The huge fall in manpower reduced the labour supply and caused a considerable increase in real wages throughout the Mediterranean basin, and beyond (Dyer, 2015; Holmes, 1975; North & Thomas, 1973; Phelps Brown & Hopkins, 1981). The loss of around half of the population also reduced the demand for land. This led to a decline in land rent, thus also involving a decrease in the sources of income of the owners of immovable property and, especially, of the nobility. The latter likewise tended to suffer from an erosion of the payments that they received since many of their long-term and other leaseholders ceased to exist.

Tax revenues also fell, at a time when monarchs and republics were involved in unending wars, which required great efforts by the infantry. The loss of direct income due to the death of vassals led to the creation of new indirect charges, and seigniorial tributes were replaced with state taxation. However, ordinary tax revenues were rarely sufficient and the governors resorted to huge debt and monetary devaluations (Bois, 2000; Le Goff, 2010).

The survivors who lived off their work improved their standards of living, since the prices of food went down and wages tended to rise. This may have favoured the demand for industrial and imported products, but, as there were less than half of the consumers, the effect was rather ambivalent (Miskimin, 1975). It should, moreover, be taken into account that, as already indicated, the tax requirements of the military campaigns, insensitive to the epidemic, wreaked havoc among the survivors. The military conflicts also hindered long-distance trade, having a negative impact on important cities of the basin that lived off this trade.

For instance, trade in Marseille declined from a maximum of 100, recorded in 1340, to a minimum of little more than 25, by 1410. The series is interrupted in that year but, when it is renewed, the improvement is slow and syncopated. The city was looted and burned by the Catalans in 1423. The continuing war between Provence and Aragon culminated with the destruction Marseille's fleet. Trade from Marseille only began to recover in the mid-fifteenth century with the boost in exchanges with the Orient, thanks to the trader, banker and shipowner, Jacques Coeur. Once Provence had been annexed to the kingdom of France, following the death of Charles III in 1481, Marseille became the country's main Mediterranean port, imposing itself over towns such as Narbonne, Aigües

Mortes and Montpellier (Abulafia, 2017; Baratier, 1951; Martel, 2019; Reyerson, 2005; Reynaud, 1951; Vicens, 1956).

The cities of Languedoc rose up against the increase in the tax on each household, the *fouage*, which Charles V quadrupled during the Hundred Year's War (Le Goff, 2010; Le Roy Ladurie, 1962; Martel, 2019). In Montpellier, in 1379, the ducal commissioners sent by Louis of Anjou to collect 12 francs per household were massacred by the furious population and their corpses thrown into pits. As for Montpellier, the Duke of Anjou ordered the suppression of its consulate, a fine of 600,000 francs and capital punishment for 600 inhabitants. On his deathbed, Charles V backtracked, deposing the Duke, commuting sentences and abolishing the *fouage* in 1380.

Comparable riots did, however, break out in Clermont-Lodève, Alès, Narbonne and Béziers. Furthermore, the peasant uprising of the Tuchins, which began in the mountains of Auvergne, converged on Low Languedoc from 1382 to 1383. In the dioceses of Uzès and Nimes, the rebels attacked the nobility and burned their castles. On the other hand, the repression against the tax revolt of Béziers entailed the public execution of its consuls and the hanging of a hundred accused persons, including a woman in 1382. The whole of Languedoc burned with the armed uprisings of the *menut* against the *gros* (Martel, 2019).

Although we should always take population figures with caution, the crisis of the late Middle Ages reinforced the decline of some Occitan cities. Marseille decreased from some 31,000 inhabitants in 1300, to just around 21,000 in 1400, but the recovery towards the end of the fifteenth century led it to exceed 45,000 inhabitants by 1500. On the contrary, Montpellier and Narbonne began to fall from a comparable figure of 30,000 inhabitants at the beginning of the fourteenth century, but continued to decline, recording only 6000 and 2000 inhabitants, respectively, by 1500. The path they took was very similar to that of Pisa: the maritime republic had around 38,000 inhabitants in 1300 and, in contrast, only some 10,000 people at the beginning of the fifteenth century (Bairoch et al., 1988). The destiny of Pisa was sealed by its military defeats against Genoa at Meloria in 1284 and the final defeat against Florence in 1406. The annexation of Pisa by Florence marked the unwavering decline of the former republic.

For the latter, we know the history of its main industry, wool drapery, in some detail (Dini, 1995; Melis, 1984; Miskimin, 1975). The production of cloth collapsed, diminishing from some 80,000 pieces in 1338 to only around 24,000 by 1378. The Florentine dyers, part of the so-called *popolo minuto*, began a protest movement in 1343, demanding political (*Priori*) and guild (*Arte*) representation and their segregation from the Arte della Lana, the major organization that fixed very low payments for activities such as carding or dying. Although the pioneering strike of 1345 ended with the beheading of its leader, Ciuto Brandini, the fibre carders (*ciompi*) tried again in 1378. They conducted another uprising, which led to the recognition of the three organizations, *Arte dei Ciompi, dei Farsettai* and *dei Tintori* and their access to the city government. The *ciompi* tried to confront the industrial crisis of the Tuscan capital, proposing the cancellation of the debts of the operators with the employers. They also demanded an openly protectionist policy. The subsequent repression against the movement forced its leader, Michele di Lando, into exile (Cipolla, 1982; Dini, 1995; Melis, 1984; Miskimin, 1975; Kocka, 2013).

In 1393, the Florentine wool workers demanded a prohibitive tariff on cloth imports. With the turn of century, Florentine drapery production experienced a slight improvement, reaching 30,000 pieces. However, this figure was very far from the peak of the beginning of the previous century. A series of families of merchants and bankers gradually took control of the city, finally controlling what was to be known as the oligarchic republic. They were initially the Albizi, Strozzi and Da Uzzano and, afterwards, the bankers of the Pope, the Medici (De Roover, 1962; Dini, 1995; Melis, 1984). The Medici's hegemony coincided with the most sublime moments of the Florentine Renaissance. The family of merchants-bankers had branches and aristocratic clients throughout Europe's main markets. However, their textile businesses, like Florence itself, gradually moved away from industrial mass production (wool cloth) and concentrated on luxury articles (silk fabrics). During the 1464–1465 interval, a new financial crisis affected the business of the Medici. Florence, which had some 100,000 inhabitants in 1300, had barely 55,000 by 1500 (Bairoch et al., 1988; Cipolla, 1982; De Roover, 1962; Dini, 1995; Melis, 1984).

Genoa did not fully recover from its decline in the late Middle Ages either. Trade in the Ligurian city reached its peak in 1293 (Miskimin, 1975; Zedar, 1981). During the fourteenth century, the wars against the Corsicans, Venetians and Catalans hindered trade and indebted the republic. In 1381, Genoese trade amounted only to 40% of that recorded at the peak of the thirteenth century, and the Genoese state exchanged tax revenues for credit from the local company, which, since the twelfth century, had begun to finance military expeditions. A new public debt arrangement had to be made in 1407, in favour of what became known as Società delle compere e banchi di San Giorgio. The company, subsequently known as Banco di San Giorgio, came up to collect 76 of the republic's taxes, including, most especially, those on salt, meat, olive oil, cereal, wine and iron. In 1447, the company began to control the revenues from the Cypriot city of Famagusta. In 1453, Genoa also transferred to it the collection of the duties generated by the island of Corsica. It, furthermore, disposed of the income from the Italian possessions of Sarzana, Levanto, Pieve di Teco and Ventimiglia and the Genoese colonies in Crimea. The fall of Constantinople was a decisive blow against its possessions in the Black Sea and its eastern trade. Overall, Genoese trade bottomed out by 1480, when it barely represented 30% of the 1293 level. Its population, which was close to 100,000 inhabitants in 1300, was only 58,000 by the end of the fifteenth century. Subsequently, in 1480, the beginning of the commercial transactions' recovery is observed, although, by 1520, Genoa only traded 80% of the value in pounds traded in 1293 (Bairoch et al., 1988; Miskimin, 1975; Zedar, 1981).

The Adriatic republic showed greater resilience. By 1300, Venice was the leading commercial emporium of the Mediterranean. Its arsenal did not stop growing in spite of the Black Death, whose impact was less severe than in other markets (Crowley, 2011; Lane, 1973; Malanima, 2010, 2018; Zedar, 1981). Although the constant conflicts in order to fly the flag of the Lion of Saint Mark across the length and breadth of the sea implied a considerable increase in tax pressure, the commercial gains of *La Serenissima* permitted it to mint around two million ducats a year (the majority in gold) by 1420 (more than the quantity made by France and England together). The Venetian ducats circulated in Syria, Egypt and even reached Yemen. During the fifteenth century, the Venetian ducat ousted the florin of Florence as the leading international currency (Cipolla, 1975; Le Goff, 2010).

The republic's economy had achieved a remarkable diversification, with around 16,000 artisans employed in the wool industry, 3000 in that of silk and 42,000 among sailors and those employed in naval construction. However, the greater demand for luxury goods tended to make the drapery decline in favour of silk. Its businesses in Romania were progressively threatened by the Turks. The worsening of trade in the Mediterranean led it to guarantee the supply of cereal to the metropolis, occupying the hinterland of Friuli, Treviso, Padua and Verona, annexations that it consolidated in 1454 with the Peace of Lodi. On the contrary, its possessions in Thrace and the Aegean suffered from the advance of the Ottomans. The latter, who had conquered Constantinople in 1453, massacred the republic's nationals who inhabited the Ottoman Empire in 1463. The slaughter triggered the war between Venice and the Sultanate, which lasted until 1476. The losses led La Serenissima to acquire the island of Cyprus, which guaranteed access to sugar and to alternative routes for the arrival of spices. Without experiencing setbacks like other commercial cities of the Mediterranean, the population of the Venetian metropolis in 1500 was still around 10% less than two centuries earlier. However, La Serenissima maintained its role as queen of Mediterranean trade until 1600 at least (Bairoch et al., 1988; Crowley, 2011; Lane, 1973; Malanima, 2010, 2018; Miskimin, 1975; Zedar, 1981).

3.2 Crises and Growth in Fourteenth-Century Catalonia

During the Middle Ages, growth was always volatile and the periods of recession were more common than those of net growth. Since the beginning of the fourteenth century, Catalonia shared, together with the rest of the commercial empires of the Western Mediterranean, a situation marked by a series of crises. It should, however, be underlined that the fall was not continuous in our case either. Rather, according to the figures available, it can be stated that, in the fourteenth century each of the shocks suffered was followed by vigorous periods of expansion. In the late Middle Ages, the Catalan economy showed notable resilience until 1404. Indeed, despite three successive crises, the fourteenth century had a net tendency towards the progression of development. Even in the 1420s and 1450s, Catalonia still experienced renewed drives for expansion. It was only from 1462 onwards, and as a result of the first civil war, the second peasant uprising and the unsuccessful policy of reconstruction by the Catholic King, that Catalonia sank into an unequivocal great depression. Consequently, at the beginning of the 1500s, the economic (and political) decadence of this part of the north-western Mediterranean was undeniable.

The first major crisis of the fourteenth century in Catalonia was an agricultural depression, probably linked to the end of the Medieval Climatic Optimum, which lasted from 1315 to 1336. Professor Pierre Vilar already drew attention to the shortages and famine of 1333, which the chronicles of Barcelona called *lo mal any primer* (the first awful year), noting the change of growth cycle of the Catalan economy in the Late Middle Ages (Vilar, 1962). However, thanks to the work of Benito, we know that the period of bad harvests and famine was considerably longer (Benito, 2004, 2013). This author detects three successive episodes of shortages in Catalonia, corresponding to the intervals from 1315 to 1319, 1323 to 1327 and 1333 to 1336. According to Benito's findings, if we take the period 1315–1336 as a whole, it would be a 21-year period of crisis, with 14 years of shortages and famine. During this long-lasting depressive period, the majority of the population was under nourished in 67% of the years. This represents, at least, one generation that went hungry. In the short term, the persistence of the food shortage must have affected manufacturing demand in the internal market; In the longer term, their capacity for resistance to contagious infections must have been weakened (Salrach, 1989; Sobrequés, 1971).

The second large-scale depression crisis took place during the period from 1348–1376 and was initially triggered by the arrival of bubonic plague in the Catalan Countries. The bacillus, which was transmitted by the bites of the fleas of the *rattus rattus* and also by airborne infection, encountered a population weakened by the succession of shortages and subsistence crises, which probably contributed to the terrible morbidity of the pandemic (Benedictow, 2004; Cuadrada, 2012). The economic impact of a mortality that reached, around half of the population, was already indicated in the previous section: a contraction of demand, a fall in agricultural and industrial production and an erosion of landowners' income. On the contrary, real wages and agricultural yields rose and some peasants likewise increased their income, on the basis of farming better land and possessions of deceased neighbours, whose farms had been abandoned (*masos rònecs*) (Anguera de Sojo, 1934; Feliu, 2004; Puigferrat, 2004; Vilar, 1962).

There were at least five aggravating factors in the 1348–1376 crisis. Firstly, the attacks on the Jewish quarters, also already mentioned, that targeted privileged actors in the commercial economy who controlled the credit (Cuadrada, 2012; Forcano, 2014; Vicens, 1956; Vilar, 1962). Secondly, commercial activity also fell, as a result of the spread of the pandemic throughout the Mediterranean (Coulon, 2013). Thirdly, the uprisings in Sardinia against Aragon control in 1354 and the prolonged war with Castile (1356–1375) increased the crown's financial difficulties, which had already experienced a significant loss of revenues due to the fall in the number of taxpayers (Belenguer, 2013, 2015). Fourthly, from 1359 onwards, when exchanges began to recover, there was an initial wave of bank failures, with Jaume des Vilar and Francesc Castelló as the leading figures. The latter paid for the bankruptcy with his head (Feliu, 2012, 2016b). Finally, famine dramatically reappeared in the North Mediterranean basin during the 1374–1376 interval (Benito, 2004; Furió, 2013, 2017).

The response to the 1348–1376 crisis was institutionally innovative and laid the ground for another period of formidable development of the Catalan commercial economy. In 1359, King Peter the Ceremonious accepted the permanent nature of a delegation of the Courts (*Corts*), which guaranteed the collection of taxes when the parliament was not meeting (Belenguer, 2015; Vilar, 1962). This, thus, institutionalized the Diputació del General, which had precedents in the delegations created by the courts since 1289 to collect the donations of the different estates. The Diputació (or Generalitat) would be made up of one representative from each of the three estates (*braços*): military, ecclesiastic and royal. Over three years, the Diputació del General began to collect the *dret de bolla*, a tax imposed on the production of wool cloths, both domestic and foreign, and also executed the agreements of the Courts. The Courts of Monzon also granted to the Diputació del General the right to tax imports and exports (*dret d'entrades i eixides*) in 1363. In Catalonia, consequently, the increase in tax pressure was linked to the permanent political representation from the end of the second third of the fourteenth century, a significantly early historical period. State taxation and political representation went hand in hand (Belenguer, 2015; Chismol, 2019; Sánchez Martínez, 1995, 2003; Vilar, 1962).

In the 1360s, Peter the Ceremonious, who had sold off a large part of the royal assets at the beginning of his reign, began to receive regular income from the Generalitat of Catalonia, which already exceeded the collection of other regular revenues such as the permits for navigation to infidel territories or the contributions of the aljamas (especially the Jewish populations of Perpignan and Mallorca) (Chismol, 2019). The creation of the Generalitat also stimulated the Catalan financial system, since it tended to issue debt securities (*censals* and *violaris*) in order to be able to bring forward its tax receipts. Debt is, however, always a double-edged sword and ended up being a heavy burden for development (Furió, 2013, 2017; Vilar, 1962).

In 1363, industry's depressed situation led the Courts of Monzon to ban the importing of wool cloth, to establish tariffs on the exporting of raw material and to regulate the manufacture of textiles (Belenguer, 2016; Riera, 2006). The ban was not viable, but it was substituted starting from 1365 by the approval of high tariffs on the importing of cloth. With this policy, the Catalan institutions backed tariff protectionism as a measure to support recovery.

There was also a reaction at the lowest moment of Barcelona foreign trade, reducing the metal content of the main gold coin of the Crown of Aragon. The gold content of the florin was reduced in two successive movements during 1363 and 1365, completing what had already occurred, after the first major epidemic shock, in 1349 and 1352. As a result, the gold contents of the Aragon florin went down from 3.4 grams in 1346 to 2.6 grams in 1365 (Batlle, 1988; Belenguer, 2013; Crusafont, 1989, 1996, 2015; Feliu, 2000, 2004; Usher, 1943; Vilar, 1962). This policy should be interpreted as one of the true devaluations of the *diner* (penny) and its multiples (*sou*/shilling and *lliura*/pound) in relation to gold. The official value of the florin was stabilized at 11 *sous* in 1365, that is to say, 132 *diners*, but the radical devaluation of the Barcelona diner and its multiples in relation to gold had to help to improve the foreign trade balance.

Despite the fact that a new outbreak of plague attacked the Catalan counties in 1371, on this occasion, the country's economy demonstrated a notable capacity for resilience, both on a domestic level (where wages and peasant income increased) and on an external level (with the strengthening of the spice business and exports of cloth and primary products). The 1370s were a period of rapid growth and sustained recovery. The Catalan foreign trade numbers reflected an important expansion as shown in Fig. 3.5, with the data compiled by Professor Coulon (2013). The expansion was rapid until 1381. We likewise know that, at this time, Catalan cloth (which improved its capacity of imitating Flemish cloth) gained terrain in relation to that of Languedoc and Provence. By 1378, Catalonia paid in Flanders with the leading consulates, like Florence or Venice. The shipyards of Barcelona began to expand their capacity.

Furthermore, according to the recent reconstruction by Professor Ortí, the collection of the toll paid on the entry of goods in Barcelona by outsiders (*lleuda* of Mediona) likewise experienced a rapid trend of growth in the 1360s and 1370s (Ortí, 2000, 2018). It reached its peak in 1379, as can be seen in Fig. 3.2. The overall tax revenues of the city, calculated by Broussolle, were likewise substantially higher during the decade from 1470 to 1480 than those of all the previous decades, as illustrated below (Fig. 3.4).

It should moreover be highlighted that the development of state taxation in Catalonia was so successful that the tax model spread to other territories of the crown. Thus, at the beginning of the 1380s, the ordinary royal taxation collected 50% of its indirect taxes in Catalonia, 33% in Valencia, 12% in Aragon and 5% in Mallorca (Chismol, 2019).

The last crisis of the fourteenth century took place during the period from 1381 to 1394: There was a second wave of financial crash, not unrelated to the excessive royal debt. Despite the fact that he had notably increased his tax revenues, Peter the Ceremonious appeared as an important debtor of the banking house of Pere des Caus and Andreu d'Olivella, which went bankrupt in 1381 (Carrère, 1967; Feliu, 2016b; Usher, 1943; Vicens, 1956; Vilar, 1962). Panic likewise swept away other bankers in Barcelona (Pere Pasqual), Girona (Ramon Medir) and Perpignan (Bartomeu Garcia). However, and without denying the trigger

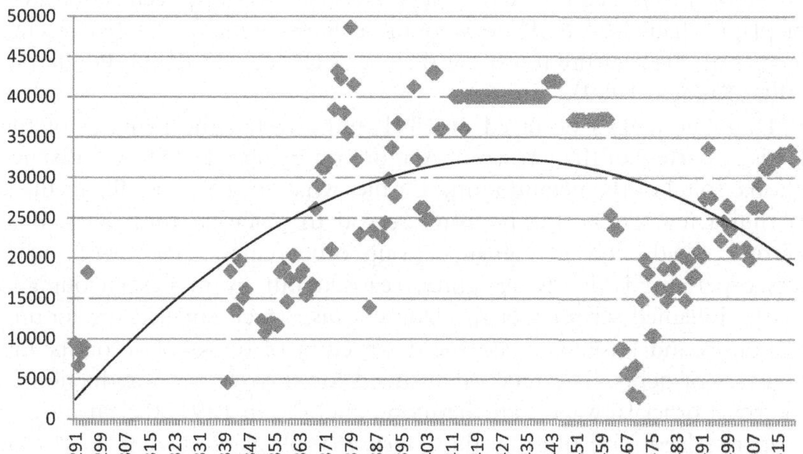

Fig. 3.2 Tax collection of the *Mediona* toll for entering goods into Barcelona, 1291–1515 (sous) (*Source* Own elaboration with data compiled by Ortí [2000, 2018])

effect of the financial crash, it should be taken into account that the very size of the banking business corroborates the degree of development achieved by early capitalism on the Mediterranean side of the Crown of Aragon. Moreover, the 1380s decline in Hamilton's Aragon price indexes confirms that the crisis was not an exclusively Catalan phenomenon, as already indicated by Professor Vicens (Hamilton, 1936; Vicens, 1956; Vilar, 1962).

As previously occurred, there were other aggravating factors. Coulon's trade series with the Levant recorded a significant contraction in the 1380s (Coulon, 2013). Moreover, Barcelona's public debt experienced a sustained rise until the end of the century (Furió, 2013, 2017; Vilar, 1962).

Two new outbreaks of plague attacked the Catalan cities from 1381 to 1387 and from 1394 to 1402. At the end of the former, in 1388, the Muslim aljama was looted in the Valencian town of Xàtiva. During the same year, there was the first official declaration of the *remensa* movement (peasants subject to personal redemption) against serfdom ("*El temps de la servitud és ja passat*", that is, time of serfdom is over) (Vicens, 1945, 1956; Vilar, 1962). Many of these peasants, who had been farming abandoned land (*masos rònecs*), wanted to maintain their control (Anguera de Sojo, 1934; Feliu, 2004; Lluch, 2010). However, recurrent waves of plague had decreased the amount of feudal rents and lords reacted increasing the pressure to exploit their serfs (Freedman, 1993; Puigferrat, 2004; Salrach, 1989).

Dramatic abuses occurred in 1391 and affected the majority of the Jewish quarters of the Crown of Aragon, on being infected by the xenophobic spiral of the neighbouring Castile, which began in Seville in June. Within a few weeks, the pogroms spread to Valencia, Inca, Barcelona, Girona, Lleida and Perpignan, among other cities. The Jewish quarters experienced bloody slaughters, carried out by masses encouraged by the inflamed sermons of the Dominicans, which entailed the looting of houses and businesses and the destruction of books of accounts and registers of debts. The rebels demanded lower taxes and a reduction in the royal officials' wages. Furthermore, and also in 1391, the burning of property deeds and titles by the *remensas* took place (Freedman, 1993; Vicens, 1945, 1956; Vilar, 1962; Wolff, 1971). The recession was not only financial: It threatened to become an unequivocal social crisis.

The subsequent responses to the intensification of the crisis combined, again institutional innovations with a clearly expansive bias. A remarkable institutional innovation was the creation of Barcelona's Taula de Canvi in 1401 (Feliu, 2004, 2016a; Usher, 1943; Vicens, 1956; Vilar, 1962). This was a pioneering example of a public bank, the first in Europe, in which the country's institutions deposited their savings and that, likewise, accepted private liabilities. There is no agreement in the assessment that economic historians have made on the contribution of the Taula de Canvi to the country's development. Vicens criticized it, arguing that it immobilized resources in unproductive uses (Vicens, 1956). On the contrary, Vilar and Feliu underlined its significant contribution to the reduction of the city's public debt, which had increased dangerously until then (Feliu, 2004, 2016a; Vilar, 1962). Taula's policy allowed debt to be gradually repaid and, indeed, Barcelona's liabilities gradually reduced until the 1460s. My opinion is also favourable for two additional reasons. The case of Barcelona was imitated by other important cities of the Crown of Aragon such as Perpignan, Valencia, Vic, Tarragona and Girona. Other more modest cities that did not have a comparable institution, which gave priority to the repayment of the debt, went bankrupt in the early 1400s. Finally, the Taula of Barcelona was significantly long-lasting, resisting until 1865, that is to say, for almost five centuries. This is an almost unqualified success for a financial institution that overcame the effects of four total wars, the Catalan Civil War (1462–1472), the Reapers' War (1640–1652), the War of the Spanish Succession (1705–1714) and the Peninsular War (1808–1814).

Other decisions that we can consider to have had an expansive fiscal bias and that may have helped to mitigate the crisis were the policy of expansion of public works with the construction of the Llotja of Barcelona between the end of the 1380s and the beginning of the 1390s and the construction of the Hospital de Sant Pau i de la Santa Creu, that began in 1401. Furthermore, in 1401, the defence of the domestic market led King Martin I the Humane to decree a ban on the Florentines, Genoese, Pisans and Venetians trading in the Crown of Aragon. The first wife of the Humane, Maria de Luna, took the side of the *remensas* and against *mals usos* (oppressive rights of the lords over this type of serfs), which she considered to have drifted away from Christian tradition. In Catalonia, protectionism began to go hand in hand with fiscal expansion, the creation of public institutions and redistributive proposals.

During the decade from 1394 to 1403, the crisis was completely overcome and there was again net growth of the Catalan economy. Foreign trade with the Levant reached its peak (Coulon, 2013). Interior trade was maintained, with fluctuations, at high levels (Ortí, 2000, 2018). The public debt of the Catalan capital went down.

3.3 The Collapse of the Catalan Economy, 1404–1516

A new recession occurred during the 1404–1417 period. What started as a moderate circumstantial contraction became a formidable major depression from which the Catalan economy of the Late Middle Ages would not recover. The beginning of this collapse was again associated with a financial crash, an important milestone being the bankruptcy of the money-changers Francesc and Manuel Gualbes, in 1404, and, subsequently, that of Jaume and Joan Massana, in 1405 (Feliu, 2016a).

The Taula de Canvi of Barcelona devaluated the change of the diner against the croat. In 1405, the exchange of the coin of nearly pure silver was fixed in 18 diners per croat, in sharp contrast with its original value of 12 diners (Feliu, 2000).

However, conflict with the Sultan of Egypt cut off the supply of spices in Alexandria. It contributed to a new fall in trade with the Levant from 1408 onwards when the greed of the Catalan merchants led to the looting of the Egyptian city (Coulon, 2013).

An additional factor aggravating the crisis included the end of the dynasty of the house of Barcelona, which had governed the county uninterruptedly for five centuries (Rovira i Virgili, 1928). Its last count-king, Martin the Humane, had lost his heir shortly before, and died without any immediate descendants in 1410. Delegates from Catalonia, Aragon and Valencia met in Caspe to choose a new monarch. Two of the three Catalans supported the Count of Urgell, the representative of a feudal family from the Principality, with deep roots in the Pyrenees and its lowlands. On the contrary, the majority of those from Aragon and Valencia voted for a representative of the leading nobility of the Crown of Castile, the house of Trastamara. They chose Ferdinand of Antequera, who was then regent of this neighbour kingdom. He ruled the Crown of Aragon from 1412 onwards.

The Count of Urgell did not accept the Compromise of Caspe, and revolted in 1413, only to be defeated. He died in prison. However, Ferdinand I was forced to make important concessions to the Catalan Courts, involving shared sovereignty (*pactisme*). His reign was short, given that he died in 1416. He was succeeded by his son, Alfonso the Magnanimous, who initially held the titles of King of Aragon and Sicily and Count of Barcelona.

Another element worsening the slump during the 1404–1417 period was the instability in the rural areas. In north-eastern Catalonia, the *remensa* conflict gained momentum again, with new burnings of deeds and crops, the excavation of graves and the planting of crosses. Thanks to the constitution approved by the Courts in 1413, the lords succeeded in banning this type of threat (Freedman, 1993; Salrach, 1989; Vicens, 1945, 1956; Vilar, 1962). However, the peasants who had been working the vacated land (*masos rònecs*) wanted to maintain their control (Anguera de Sojo, 1934; Feliu, 2004; Lluch, 2010). The farm workers surviving the different waves of plague had become progressively richer, with access to more and better land and the payment of less rent, and they opposed the vestiges of servitude that remained in the northern counties. There, between the Pyrenees and the sea, the link between the peasant and the land (*remensa*) remained, together with other feudal elements of a servile nature (*mals usos*). The commercialized and capitalist economy of Barcelona or Perpignan contrasted with a deeply rooted tough feudalism in the eastern Pyrenean valleys and adjacent mountains and plains.

Half way between the feudal rural areas and the big commercial cities of the Crown, such as Barcelona, Perpignan and, increasingly, Valencia, were the medium and small towns. As already explained, these had experienced intense processes of debt during the last decades of the fourteenth and early fifteenth centuries. The recession finally made them insolvent. Inland, Cervera suspended payments in 1411 (Verdés, 2019). The coastal Sant Feliu de Guíxols experienced a continuous contraction subsequent to 1427 (Ortí, 2018). Another inland town, Cardona, suffered from a financial collapse in 1430 and had to renegotiate its debt with its creditors (Galera, 2019). The majority were forced to create new indirect taxes to pay the debt, which significantly worsened the capacity for consumption of the medium-sized towns. Figure 3.3 presents the evolution of three taxes collected in Cardona that were levied on wine, meat and the transit of people. All three show a clearly decreasing trend from the late twenties onwards. Although, until 1459, there were successive upward movements of recovery, the collapse was unmistakable in the 1460s and 1470s. The data for Cervera, presented by Verdés, tells us a very similar story (Verdés, 2019).

Despite the depressive situation, the potential for recovery of the overall Catalan economy continued to be notable. In 1411, the Catalan

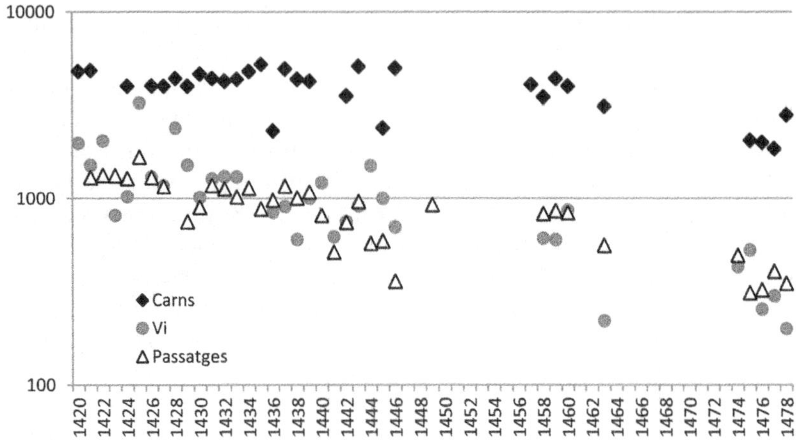

Fig. 3.3 Nondirect municipal taxes collected in the town of Cardona, 1420–1478 (sous) (*Source* Own elaboration with the data compiled by Galera [2019])

traders still paid the second-highest contributory fee in Flanders, only behind Genoa. For the merchants of Barcelona, privileged access to the markets of Sicily and Sardinia were decisive factors for productive expansion. Consequently, initially, they enthusiastically supported the intervention of Alfonso the Magnanimous to contain the new Sardinian uprising and the purchase of the rights that William III of Toulouse still maintained over the island in 1420.

Another measure that intended to win over the Catalans and allay the industrial crisis was the decision to ban the importing of wool cloth and silk textiles, in the *Havents a cor* Constitution, approved in 1422 (Batlle, 1988; Belenguer, 2019; Vilar, 1962). With this measure, the monarch from the Trastamara dynasty continued the policy of defending the national market that the house of Barcelona had begun. Here, it should be underlined that, with this proto-mercantilist attitude, a certain path dependence on Catalan development began to emerge.

Recovery seemed on the way in the 1420s, with a clear improvement in available foreign trade indicators. Coulon's and Del Treppo trade series for the Levant experiences a leap forward (without, again, reaching its peak) (Coulon, 2013; Del Treppo, 1972;—see Fig. 3.5). The overall movement of both Catalan and foreign ships leaving the port of Barcelona sets its maximum in 1428. In fact, and possibly, as a result of the foreign trade improvement the Taula de Canvi of Barcelona was able to improve the exchange of the diner in 1425, fixing the price of the croat in 15 diners (Feliu, 2000).

According to Broussolle, the collection of Barcelona taxes remained relatively high until the end of the second decade of the fifteenth century, as Table 3.4 illustrates (Brousolle, 1955). There is no continuous series of income from *periatge* (a tax on the goods transported in ships) for this century, but the collection from the 1433 to 1434 period, obtained by Smith, was much higher than that of the subsequent years (Smith, 1940; Vilar, 1962). The debt of Barcelona went down, from 387,000 *lliures* (pounds) in 1396 to 125,000 *lliures* in 1429 (Feliu, 2004). The resilience of the Catalan economy in the Late Middle Ages therefore continued to be a characteristic of its process of economic development, despite the change of dynasty.

In 1427, an earthquake caused great destruction to towns near the Pyrenees such as Olot, Puigcerdà and Amer. The foreign trade series of both Coulon and Del Treppo show a contraction in the 1430s (Coulon, 2013; Del Treppo, 1972). There was a significant fall in the movement of ships in the port of Barcelona, bottoming out in 1452. There is evidence of a decline in Catalan cloth in the Sicilian market in the face of the challenge by the Genoese, from the beginning of the 1430s. Flemish and English cloth moreover gained terrain thanks to its better price, achieved by ruralizing the activity, and gradually ruined the mass industry in the less competitive cities of the Mediterranean. Moreover, the substitution of imports encouraged by France at the end of the Hundred Years' War led to the loss by the Catalans of the market re-exporting spices to Toulouse; and Marseille, with the important support of Jacques Coeur, began to recover lost ground as a major trading port with the Orient (Reyerson, 2005; Reynaud, 1951; Vicens, 1956). The contraction of municipal taxes income as a whole collected in Barcelona (Fig. 3.4), and the fall in the collection of the *lleuda* of Mediona (Fig. 3.2), in particular, suggest a declining capacity for consumption in the Catalan capital. Finally, the advance of the Turks in the eastern Mediterranean, succeeding to subdue Byzantium in 1453, made long-distance trade even more risky and expensive.

The decline in the exports of cloth and in overall Catalan foreign trade tended to cause a fall in tax receipts from the *bolla,* the *dret d'entrades i eixides*, and the *periatge*, compromising both the finances of the Diputació del General and those of Barcelona itself. While tax revenues

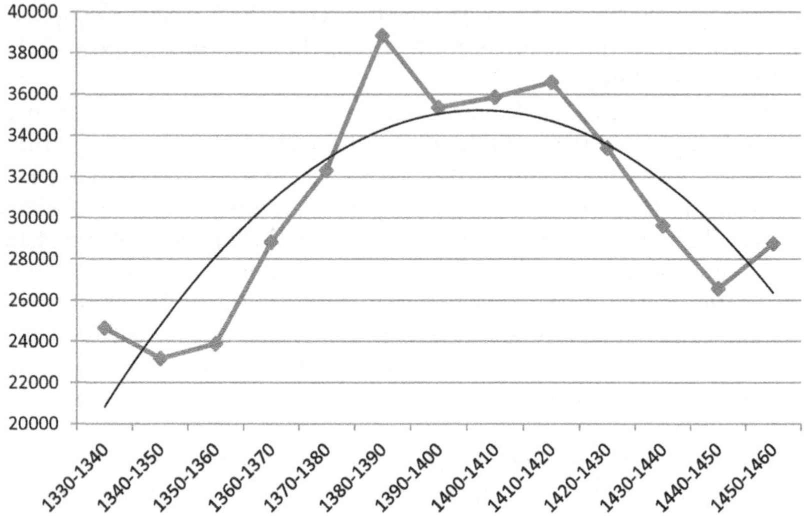

Fig. 3.4 Income collected with municipal taxes in Barcelona, 1330–1460 (lliures) (*Source* Own elaboration with the data collected by Brousolle [1955])

fell in the metropolis, the imperialist efforts of Alfonso the Magnanimous intensified (Rovira i Virgili, 1928; Vilar, 1962). In 1432, he finally abandoned the Iberian Peninsula and disembarked in Italy. In the next year, he succeeded in having Queen Joanna appoint him as heir to the throne of Naples. He confronted the majority of the Italian states, united in a league and led by Venice. Despite the fact that he was subsequently dispossessed by Joanna in a new will, Alfonso continued to fight for Naples. Defeated by the Genoese in the Battle of Ponza (1435), he had to find a ransom of 30,000 ducats in order to be released. However, far from being discouraged, in 1436 he launched a new campaign from the base of Gaeta. He finally conquered Naples and was proclaimed its king in 1442. More than a decade of conflicts left the coffers empty and huge debts. Alfonso moreover decided to establish his court in the city of Campania and, from then on, Naples became the capital of the Aragon empire, until his death in 1458 (Belenguer, 2019).

The big fortunes of Barcelona, represented on its Consell de Cent, did not support the Neapolitan campaign very enthusiastically, unlike what they had done in previous imperial offensives in the Mediterranean. On the one hand, as already explained, long-distance trade was not going through the best of times and the Italian war damaged it even more. On the other hand, the costs of the Naples adventure were considered excessive. Even so, the crisis particularly affected the artisan drapers, represented on the *ma menor* of the Consell de Cent (group mainly composed of craftsmen). The latter demanded radical measures to confront the depression, which would curb the scarcity of money. Alfonso, in exchange for authorizing the minting of additional silver coins, demanded the collection of 10,000 gold florins in 1445 (Sobrequés, 2011; Sobrequés & Sobrequés, 1973; Vicens, 1956).

The Catalan Courts celebrated in 1446 discussed, among others, the problem of the serfs of the glebe and the fall in tax collected by the Generalitat. The annual donation expected by the king from Catalonia was of 400,000 florins, which, compared with the 120,000 demanded from Valencia and the 80,000 from Aragon, proved that the former counties continued to be Alfonso's most productive possession in Iberia. The Courts decided to make the payment conditional on the presence of the king in the Principality, but the monarch never visited it again. The divide between the Catalan institutions and the house of Trastamara thus deepened.

In the absence of funds, the monarch living in Naples also gave ear to a class group that, for decades, had gradually become richer due to the abundance of land and the scarcity of labour in the Catalan countryside, the *remensas*. In 1448, he authorized the meetings of this type of serfs, with the aim of collecting 100,000 florins as a donation, in exchange for offering the abolition of the compulsory payments for abandoning the land and other degrading tributes of their servile condition (*mals usos*) (Freedman, 1993; Lluch, 2010; Sobrequés, 2011; Sobrequés & Sobrequés, 1973; Vicens, 1945, 1956). The king was willing to emancipate the peasants in exchange for funds. However, the masters of the serfs were opposed (Belenguer, 2019; Feliu, 2000, 2016b; Salrach, 1989; Vilar, 1962). The Diputació del General, controlled by important secular and ecclesiastic feudal lords, expressed its disagreement and vetoed the initiative. From then on, two blocks began to be formed that would end up confronting each other in the civil war fifteen years later.

While, in the mountains of Catalonia, 20,000 peasants joined the *remensa* union, in Barcelona, a party, which had split off from the oligarchic group that had traditionally controlled the Consell de Cent and the administration of the municipality (the Biga), was gaining influence. The new faction took the name of Busca and wanted to defend the interests of artisans and guilds, harmed and indebted by the duration of the crisis. The Busca supporters on the Consell de Cent demanded an increase in the protection of manufactured goods, with the aim of expanding demand, and a parity of the silver *croat* to be valued at 18 diners, in order to endeavour to mitigate the scarcity of money existing and ease the burden of the growing debts (Batlle, 1988; Belenguer, 2013; Vicens, 1956; Vilar, 1962). They also promoted the establishment of an organization that would group together three types of workers who opposed themselves to the Barcelona oligarchy: merchants, *artistes* (liberal professions) and manual workers. These created the Sindicat dels Tres Estaments, approved in 1452. Alfonso, eager for resources, gradually approached the Catalan working classes, both rural and urban.

Despite living in Italy, Alfonso the Magnanimous was always receptive to the demands of the popular strata of Catalonia. In 1447, he accepted the expulsion of Florentine traders from the Crown of Aragon. Two years later, he notified the Catalan institutions of his intention to favour economic recovery (*redreç*). In 1450, he gave the green light to the creation of the Estudi General of the capital of Catalonia, the origin of the University of Barcelona.

In the same direction, in 1453, Alfonso encouraged the use of local ships in Catalonia's foreign trade. That same year, he promoted a radical change at the head of the Barcelona municipality: he directly appointed councillors from the Busca to govern the city, contravening the rules of the Consell de Cent and earning the complete animosity of the Biga. Its supporters called the action a coup d'état.

The councillors of the Busca immediately opened the issue of the official exchange rate of the city's main silver coin, the Barcelona *gros* or *croat*, whose traditional official value had been 12 *diners*. While the Busca proposed a new price of 18 *diners*, the Biga supported the current value of 15 *diners*. Finally, the Busca imposed its view and the new official value of the *croat* became 18 *diners* from 1454 onwards.

Economic historians do not agree on whether or not this change should be interpreted as a devaluation. Vicens and Vilar defended that it was indeed a devaluation of the Barcelona currency, the *diner* and its multiples (*sou* and *lliura*), and a revaluation of silver (the *croat* was a coin with eleven and a half twelfths of noble metal, that is to say practically pure silver) (Vicens, 1956; Vilar, 1962). This is also Batlle's opinion (Batlle, 1988). On the contrary, the numismatic historian Crusafont rejects the hypothesis of devaluation and suggests that the new parity only reflected the adaptation of the official value of the *croat* to the relative loss of silver that had occurred with the *diner de tern*, a coin with only three-twelfths of silver and in common use, therefore having lost weight due to wear and tear (Crusafont, 1989, 1996, 2015). Crusafont's position was shared by Fontana (Fontana, 2014). My opinion, which coincides more with Vilar, Vicens and Batlle, is that it was, indeed, a devaluation of the Barcelona currency. Catalonia used and, therefore, became indebted in *diners* and their multiples, *sous* and *lliures*. From 1454 onwards, debts could be cancelled with *croats*, with less silver. As Vilar and Vicens already noted, the artisans and the monarchy were important debtors and, consequently, were behind Busca's decision.

The policy of devaluations continued in 1457, correcting the exchange rate of the main gold coin, the florin. Its parity was established as 13 *sous*, that is to say, 156 *diners*. The decision was likewise intended to curb the hoarding associated with the operation of what we now know as Gresham's law. The fact is, however, that the official exchange rate of the *diner* ended up losing value in relation to the two noble metals and, therefore, was devalued. These devaluations must have favoured cloth exports and made it cheaper to service the debt. Artisans and debtors were the winners. On the contrary, the rentiers holding debt securities and the big spice importers, who paid in gold and silver, lost out.

The other important aspect of Busca's policy was protectionism. In 1456, the municipality of Barcelona decided to reintroduce the 1422 decision to ban imports of foreign cloth (Vilar, 1962). Devaluations and protectionism were consequently the responses of the artisans' party to the deep crisis that began in 1427. The Busca had the same policy as the king, while the Biga, controlled by rentiers and big traders, continued to maintain the idea of a royal coup d'état and was preparing its revenge.

Catalonia's governor (*lloctinent general*) gradually acquired a tougher profile, as of 1454, when Alfonso gave the position to his brother John, King of Navarre. The latter, after his wife Blanche of Navarre died, married Juana Enríquez of Castile. He had one son with each wife, Charles and Ferdinand. The former was Prince of Viana and heir to Navarre and clashed with his father, John.

Alfonso again decided to turn to the serfs. In that same year, 1454, he passed an interlocutory judgement from Naples that temporarily gave freedom to the *remensas* peasants and suspended the other servile provisions (*mals usos*) (Freedman, 1976; Sobrequés, 2011; Sobrequés & Sobrequés, 1973; Vicens, 1945, 1956). John, as *lloctinent*, had to favour the acceptance of the judgement by nobles and ecclesiastics, who controlled the Diputació del General, and to confront the discontentment of the Biga and the Consell de Cent of Barcelona with the devaluation of the *diner* and the authoritarianism shown by his brother.

In the 1456 Courts, the noble and ecclesiastic arms and the representatives of the Biga in the royal arm opposed the suspension of the *remensa* and the *mals usos* and also rejected the devaluation of the currency. Finally, the Courts approved the annual allowance of 400,000 florins for Alfonso, with the condition that the interlocutory judgement and the monetary provisions were revised.

Alfonso the Magnanimous died in 1458 and his brother ascended to the throne of Aragon as John II. Meanwhile, the devaluations and the possibility of selling cloth in the Naples market took effect and the Catalan economy experienced a final period of an upward swing in the Late Middle Ages, during the period from 1454 to 1462. The arrival of long-distance ships with in the port of Barcelona suggests this (Del Treppo, 1972). The movement of trade with the Levant recorded its final local maximum in the 1450s (Fig. 3.5).

Despite the trend towards economic recovery, the social conflict between the new king, until then *lloctinent* of Catalonia, and its institutions had gradually become embittered and recorded a new conflict when Juana, the king's wife, convinced him that the son from his first marriage was conspiring against him. Consequently, John II had Charles of Viana arrested in Lleida in December 1460. The Courts, meeting in this same city, stipulated that the Generalitat and the Consell de Cent should take the necessary measures to obtain the freedom of the heir to the throne. They both agreed on the creation of the Consell del Principat of Catalonia. The new institution, controlled by feudal lords and supporters of the Biga and of the Prince of Viana, demanded the liberation of Charles by the king. John transferred his older son to Fraga, outside the Catalan borders. The Consell del Principat reacted by initiating the formation of an army and the building of a fleet. The king went a little further away, taking his prisoner to Morella, in the Kingdom of Valencia. However, in the absence of support, he set him free in February 1461. He sent Queen Juana to negotiate in Catalonia and, in June, the Surrender of Vilafranca was signed. The agreements included the separation of the executive and judicial powers, and the regulation

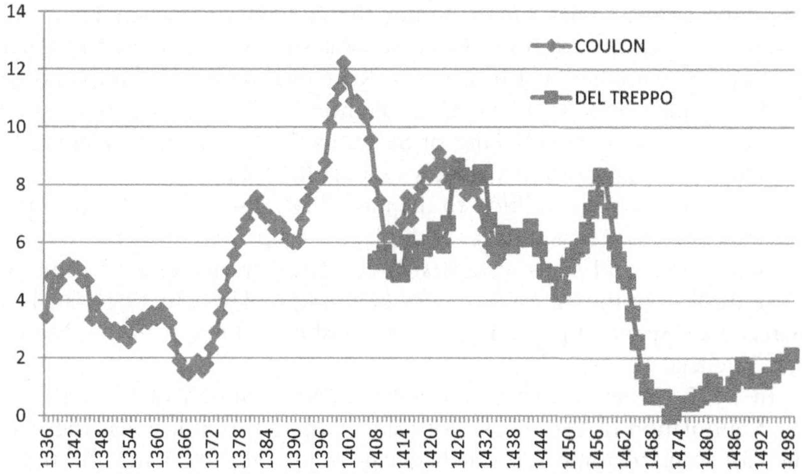

Fig. 3.5 Barcelona's haurbour long-distance foreign trade, 1336–1500 (nine-years moving averages of the number of ships) (*Source* Own elaboration with the data compiled by Del Treppo [1972] and Coulon [2013])

that the king could not enter the kingdom without the permission of the Courts (Belenguer, 2019; Sobrequés, 2011; Sobrequés & Sobrequés, 1973; Vicens, 1945, 1956).

Charles, either from illness or poisoning, died in August 1461. Meanwhile, his father approached Louis XI of France, to whom he promised the counties of Roussillon and Cerdanya, in exchange for military aid. In February 1462, the *remensas* uprisings began. A group of 600 peasants from the north-east attacked the attorney of the Baron of Santa Pau. The Consell del Principat again began to prepare an army to fight the peasants. The queen and Prince Ferdinand fled from Barcelona and moved to Girona. John II entered Catalonia without the necessary permission of the Courts and, in June, the Consell del Principat dispossessed the king and offered the crown to Henry IV of Castile. Meanwhile, the *remensa* peasants gradually occupied properties and castles of the nobility.

In his way, Catalonia rushed into a violent civil war, that lasted from 1462 to 1472, and from which it did not recover. The two blocks that clashed were, on the one hand, John II, the *remensas* and the more radical supporters of the Busca. On the other hand, there were the Consell del Principat, the Diputació del General, the Consell de Cent and the Biga.

The international allies varied during the conflict and, when Henry of Castile changed his position, the crown was successively offered to Peter of Portugal, who died in 1466, and to René of Provence, from the house of Anjou and vassal to the king of France. In 1469, John II married his son Ferdinand, already king of Sicily, to the half-sister of Henry IV, Isabella, which guaranteed Castile's support for John.

During the war, in addition to the mortality caused by the conflict and the infection from new outbreaks of plague, crops were lost, the artisans became poorer and ships were destroyed. The Barcelona's port came to a standstill. Traditional tax revenues evaporated. The Taula de Canvi of Barcelona suspended payments. Commercial capital fled to Sicily, Naples and Valencia.

In 1472 the war came to an end with the triumph of John II and the Capitulation of Pedralbes. Both sides suffered so much that the king did not want to impose a Carthaginian peace. He respected the traditional institutions of the Generalitat and Consell de Cent. He agreed to a general amnesty and the restitution of confiscated property, both castles and land and debt securities. The issue of servitude remained to be decided (Belenguer, 2019; Lluch, 2010; Sobrequés & Sobrequés, 1973; Vicens, 1945, 1956).

John II died a natural death in 1479 and was succeeded on the Crown of Aragon by the son of his marriage with Juana Enríquez. As the consort of Isabella of Castile, he had already been the sovereign of this crown since 1474. In accordance with the 1475 Concordia de Segovia, Isabella and Ferdinand agreed that they would have the same powers in their kingdoms. Four years later, they both held the crowns of Castile and Aragon and agreed to expand their domains and establish ethnic and religious uniformity in them. However, each crown maintained the majority of its own institutions.

The 1481 Catalan Courts, which continued to be controlled by the big feudal lords, blocked the agreement with the peasants, on demanding a return to the situation of servitude prior to 1455. The *remensa* discontentment led to a second uprising in 1484 led by more radical peasants, who fought not only against serfdom but also against the actual feudal system (Lluch, 2010; Salrach, 1989; Serra, 1980; Vicens, 1945, 1956). This time, the peasants fought alone and against the royal troops. They were defeated and the Catholic King imposed a heavy-handed approach to those responsible. The leader of the uprising, Pere Joan Sala, was dismembered.

The Catholic King also showed his absolutist manner in religious and political matters. In 1487 he imposed the Castilian inquisition on the Crown of Aragon, being much tougher than the local one (under the Pope's supervision). In protest, the members of the Generalitat and the city councillors refused to receive the Castilian general inquisitor when he came to Barcelona.

In 1492 Ferdinand and Isabella agreed to give the Jewish population a period of three months to convert or to abandon their kingdoms, and thus pursued an ominous path in the history of the Mediterranean, decreed by supposedly Christian monarchs (Forcano, 2014). Even the Pope, the Valencian Roderic Borgia, who was crowned with the papal tiara as Alexander VI a few months later, was somewhat less xenophobic than the Catholic monarchs, on accepting in his court some of those expelled from Aragon and Castile.

For their part, the Castilian troops took Granada in the same year, 1492. The desire to create a religiously monolithic state again became clear in 1505 when Ferdinand ordered the forced conversion of the Muslims of the former Nasrid kingdom. In 1512 Ferdinand decided to proceed to invade Navarre and to annex the Pyrenean kingdom.

In the Crown of Aragon, the Catholic King promoted the reform of the election systems in the Courts of Catalonia and the Consell de Cent of Barcelona between 1493 and 1500. The direct election of members and councillors was replaced with a system of restricted draw (*insaculació*). With these measures, he wanted to avoid the acrimonious political division, which had favoured the outbreak of the Catalan civil war.

On the contrary, Ferdinand was more condescending in social and economic matters. In 1486, he delivered the Arbitral Decision of Guadalupe, which suppressed the *remensa* condition and recognized the status of the former serfs as long-term leaseholders. That is to say that they maintained the beneficial ownership of the land cultivated in exchange for continuing to pay moderate contributions (*censos* and *tasques*) to the lords in recognition of their eminent domain. The peasants had to compensate the crown with 50,000 lliures because of their rebellion. The lords likewise received 6000 lliures for the damage suffered. The indemnities were to be collected until the end of the century (Vicens, 1945).

All in all, although in the short term the *remensas* had to pay, their struggle was not in vain because it put an end to their servile condition and they were allowed to hold on to their land, to transfer it in inheritance and even to sell and mortgage it. Although, in the short term, their burdens increased, in the long-term modern Catalonia would have a relatively well-off class of quasi-landowning peasants. Vicens, Vilar, Brenner and Freedman saw in the Decision of Guadalupe the success of the best-organized uprising against servitude in Europe (Brenner, 1978; Freedman, 1993; Vicens, 1945; Vilar, 1962). On the contrary, and more recently, Serra insisted that the uprising was against feudalism and that the final defeat of radical peasants consolidated high inequality in the Catalan rural areas (Lluch, 2010; Salrach, 1989; Serra, 1980).

In 1488 there was an additional decision on the controversial issue of the uncultivated farms, which had gradually been appropriated by the peasants (*masos rònecs*) (Anguera de Sojo, 1934; Feliu, 2004). The monarch stipulated that these farms could continue in the hands of the peasants, provided that they compensated the lords with a payment of 90 *sous* for each farm annexed and an annual rent of 3 *sous*. In the long term, this decision also favoured the peasants, especially due to the high inflation of the sixteenth century, which gradually reduced the true burden of the levy.

The monetary policy of Ferdinand II was likewise sound. It was based on two main issues: the creation of a new gold coin of high metal contents and the significant devaluation of the diner both against gold and silver. The gold piece in question was the ducat, direct imitation of the Venetian coin, which, as it has been explained above, was minted the most successful merchant nation of the fifteenth century. The ducat had already been minted in Valencia and Aragon since the time of King John II. The Barcelona's ducat was named *principat* and began its life as a consequence of the monetary reform of 1493, with a weight of around 3.5 grams of pure gold (Crusafont, 1989, 1996, 2015; Feliu, 2000, 2016b; Usher, 1943; Vicens, 1956; Vilar, 1962). Its official value was 12 croats.

The diner was remarkably devaluated in relation to silver. The parity of the croat was fixed at 24 diners, exchange rate extremely favourable to silver in relation to the previous prices of the croat. At this conversion rate, the official price of the principat or Barcelona ducat was 288 diners, a much more favourable exchange for gold than the previously applied to the florin. In short, the diner was significantly devaluated both against gold and silver. In my opinion, the policy was sound because a remarkable devaluation of the diner and its multiples was needed to stimulate the recovery of the Catalan foreign trade.

Before the death of Ferdinand II, in 1516, the economic and social measures described made possible a commencement of improvement of the Catalan economy, but without returning to the levels prior to 1462. The movement of ships which undertook long-distance trade from the port of Barcelona followed an upward trend from 1490 until the beginning of the sixteenth century, but always remained well below that prior to the civil war (Fig. 3.5) (Del Treppo, 1972). The traffic, which can be deduced from the collection of the *periatge,* was considerably lower in 1502–1503 than in 1455–1456 (Smith, 1940; Vilar, 1962). The level of revenues collected with the payment of the *lleuda* of Mediona did not recover either (Fig. 3.2) (Ortí, 2018). The number of apprenticeship contracts and the demand for slaves rapidly expanded during the 1479–1493 period, but declined afterwards and until the death of the Catholic King (Armenteros, 2012, 2015; Furió, 2002). Finally, it has been estimated that the population of Catalonia, which may have been around 224,536 inhabitants in 1497, amounted to 239,868 in 1505 (Nadal, 1992). This last figure represented barely half of the population of Catalonia in 1347. The resilience shown by the Catalan economy at the beginning of the sixteenth century was therefore weak.

3.4 Splendour and Decay of Barcelona: A Comparison from a Mediterranean Perspective

Catalan historiography has debated at length on the subjects of the decadence and the great depression of the Late Middle Ages. Romantic historiography tended to blame on the change of dynasty, with the triumph of the Trastamara in Caspe, as the origin of the decline of Catalonia (Rovira i Virgili, 1928; Soldevila, 1962). They argued, on the one hand, that their Castilian origin would have made it difficult for them to deal and negotiate with the country's institutions, such as the Courts, the Diputació del General and the Consell de Cent, whose dialogue and tendency towards *pactisme* was forged over the centuries of the reign of the house of Barcelona. Secondly, the Trastamara's imperialist vocation at the time of Alfonso the Magnanimous went beyond the purely commercial interests of Barcelona capitalism, damaging trade and making the debt unsustainable. Their constant need for resources deepened the divergence of class interests and led the country to civil war. Finally, the dynastic union with Castile converted the Crown of Aragon into an appendage of the former, with little influence in the personal ambitions of Ferdinand the Catholic and sacrificed for the sake of the project, shared with his wife Isabella, of excessive territorial expansion and absolutist intransigence.

The great masters of classic economic history, more receptive to Malthusian and Marxist interpretations, placed the origins of the depression in the fourteenth century. Vilar noted bad harvests, especially that of 1333, as the initial trigger of the depression (Vilar, 1962). He also highlighted the social consequences of the catastrophic mortality of the Black Death. In the short term, this led to the pogroms. In the longer term, it ended up accentuating the conflict between social classes in relation to the *remensa* and the *mals usos* and the control of the *masos rònecs*, pushing Catalonia towards the edge of war. In Barcelona, the confrontation of rentiers and big merchants (Biga) against debtors and artisans (Busca) was the other side of the armed conflict between urban social classes.

Vicens agreed with the above considerations to a great extent, stressing that the golden age of the Catalan economy was from the mid-thirteenth to the mid-fourteenth century. Catalonia successfully participated in the recovery of Mediterranean trade until around 1350. From then on, *an extremely long stage of depression predominated* (Vicens, 1956). In addition to the worsening of international trade, attributable to the advance of the Turks, the second half of the 1300s was depressive due to the growing debt of the monarchy and the cities, the other side of which was the immobilization of capitals generated in trade in a purely rentier activity. A clear warning about the end of the expansive wave came from the series of bank failures in 1381. An additional turn of the screw came from the announcement of the closing of Barcelona's Jewish quarter in 1391, after the dramatic attack already discussed. Feliu likewise considers that the second half of the fourteenth century was one of crisis, as a result of the impact of the Black Death, the exacerbation of the distributive conflict and the excess of both private and public debt (Feliu, 2016b).

For Vilar and Vicens, the fifteenth century was unequivocally one of great depression, despite some temporary upturns in foreign trade, and the crisis led to the civil war that, for the latter, was a true revolution. On the contrary, the last years of the reign of Ferdinand the Catholic were viewed positively by Vicens (1956). It would have been a period of recovery (*redreç*) due to measures of redistribution (Guadalupe), of reorganization of Barcelona and the Diputació del General (including the drawing of lots) and favouring industrial expansion (devaluations and protectionism).

There was no agreement among the economic historians who studied Catalan foreign trade. Carrère, who paid great attention to the situation of the drapery industry, agreed with Vicens on considering the existence of a prolonged crisis of the Barcelona economy between 1380 and 1461 (Carrère, 1967). Del Treppo, who focused his research on the fifteenth century, maintained a much more optimistic position, underlining the profits from Barcelona trade subsequent to the conquest of Naples (Del Treppo, 1972). More recently, the reconstruction of trade with the Orient, carried out by Coulon, offered a more positive panorama of the course of the fourteenth century (Coulon, 2013). I used the data from these last two authors to generate Fig. 3.5, already analyzed. Once the undeniable annual fluctuations in foreign trade have been smoothed, the resulting image shows a net expansion of the Barcelona commercial expeditions in the fourteenth century. The trend was contractive in the following century, but with significant shoots of recovery in the 20s and 50s.

Tax collection in Barcelona, studied in the pioneering work by Broussolle, likewise experienced a period of sustained progress after the decade following the arrival of the Black Death and until 1380–1390 (Brousolle, 1955). On the contrary, in the fifteenth century, the path was clearly contractive. This outcome fits in with the fall in the collection of the *dret de periatge*, presented by Smith (1940; Vilar, 1962). This is also in tune with the income from the *lleuda* of Mediona, as compiled by Ortí and represented in Fig. 3.2, which culminated in the decades between the centuries. In short, the tax sources concerning Barcelona indicate long-term expansion during the second half of the 1300s and contraction in the 1400s (Ortí, 2000, 2018). The situation of the medium and small-sized towns of Catalonia in the fifteenth century would have been comparable or worse. At the beginning of the century, numerous locations suspended payments. The series of collection of indirect taxes also show a declining trend from before the war, in towns such as Cardona, Cervera and Sant Feliu de Guíxols (Galera, 2019; Ortí, 2018; Verdés, 2019).

The above evidence does not fit in very well with revisionist theories, such as those defended by Igual and Iradiel (Igual, 2007; Iradiel, 2007). They reject both the Malthusian and the neo-Malthusian theses of authors such as Postan or Le Roy Ladurie and the Marxist theses of Bois or Vilar (Bois, 2000; Le Roy Ladurie, 1967; Postan, 1950; Vilar, 1962). They question the existence of a great depression of the Late Middle Ages, both on the European and on the Iberian levels (Prados de la Escosura, Álvarez-Nogal & Santiago Caballero, 2020). Instead, they support Epstein's thesis, who, in the face of a systemic depression, understands the Late Middle Ages situation as a succession of crises with creative destruction, as a result of the growing integration of markets (Epstein, 2000). These authors highlight the relative dynamism of the economies of Valencia and Castile in the fifteenth century. Some even deny the existence of crises in the 1400s in Spain. My opinion is that, although it is unquestionable that Valencia is a Mediterranean economy, Castile always looked more inland and toward the Atlantic. As proof we have the port of Cartagena, which, despite the growing number of journeys by Castilians and Basques uniting the ocean with the Roman sea, did not interrupt its decadence on joining Castilian sovereignty. In the year 1000, the Muslim city still had a population of some 33,000 inhabitants (Bairoch et al., 1988). In 1300, it had gone down to 5000. We do not know the population of Cartagena in 1400, but at the end of the fifteenth century it was still falling: it was down to just 4000 inhabitants.

The last exercise before concluding this work was precisely to reposition Barcelona (and Valencia) in a Mediterranean perspective. Table 3.1 endeavours to analyze the changes in hierarchy of the Mediterranean basin's cities during the centuries of the Commercial Revolution and those of the great depression of the Late Middle Ages. In order to select the cities, I took the set of 25 towns that, in around 1300, had attained a population of close to or more than 20,000 inhabitants and for which data were available for the years 1000, 1300, 1400 and 1500 (mainly, Bairoch et al., 1988). The comparison between the first two years should allow us to assess the impact of the Commercial Revolution. That of the following two centuries will help us to understand that of the great depression of the Late Middle Ages. There are significant absences, such as Alexandria, Famagusta, Candia, Messina, Tunis and several others, but I was not able to find data for these cities for the four chosen dates. Although I am aware that mediaeval population data are speculative, as we do not have censuses (with very few exceptions), I am willing to use them to conclude this work from a comparative history perspective.

If we pay attention to the vertex of the Mediterranean cities, we find three differentiated types of towns among the top 12 in our ranking. The most numerous group of the vertex consists of five capitals from the Islamic world: Palermo, Cairo, Almeria, Granada and Mallorca. Their dominant position on the urban ranking in the year 1000 is due to a

Table 3.1 Population ranking of 25 towns of the Mediterranean basin, 1000–1500 (thousands)

		1000			1300
1	Palermo	350	1	Cairo	400
2	Constantinople	300	2	Constantinople	150
3	Cairo	135	3	Granada	150
4	Venice	45	4	Venice	110
5	Thessaloniki	40	5	Genoa	100
6	Rome	35	6	Milan	100
7	Naples	30	7	Florence	95
8	Milan	30	8	Naples	60
9	Almeria	27	9	Palermo	51
10	Granada	26	10	Thessaloniki	50
11	**Mallorca**	**25**	**11**	**Barcelona**	**48**
12	Carcassonne	20	**12**	**Valencia**	**44**
13	Verona	20	13	Malaga	40
14	Malaga	17	14	Pisa	38
15	Athens	15	15	Montpellier	35
16	Genoa	15	16	Padua	35
17	**Valencia**	**15**	17	Marseille	31
18	Florence	13	18	Rome	30
19	Mantua	12	19	Mantua	30
20	Narbonne	12	20	Narbonne	30
21	Padua	10	21	Verona	30
22	Pisa	9	22	Athens	25
23	Marseille	9	23	Almeria	18
24	**Barcelona**	**5**	**24**	**Mallorca**	**17**
25	Montpellier	1	25	Carcassonne	15
		1400			1500
1	Cairo	360	1	Cairo	400
2	Granada	100	2	Constantinople	200
3	Genoa	100	3	Naples	125
4	Venice	100	4	Venice	100
5	Milan	90	5	Milan	100
6	Constantinople	75	6	Granada	70
7	Florence	55	7	Genoa	58
8	Naples	45	8	Florence	55
9	Thessaloniki	42	9	Palermo	55
10	Malaga	40	10	Rome	55
11	**Barcelona**	**38**	11	Verona	50

(continued)

Table 3.1 (continued)

12	**Valencia**	**36**	12	Marseille	45
13	Verona	35	**13**	**Valencia**	**42**
14	Athens	35	14	Malaga	42
15	Padua	34	15	Almeria	30
16	Rome	33	16	Padua	29
17	Palermo	27	17	Carcassonne	25
18	Almeria	25	18	Mantua	25
19	Mantua	25	**19**	**Barcelona**	**20**
20	Pisa	23	20	Thessaloniki	19
21	Marseille	21	**21**	**Mallorca**	**13**
22	Carcassonne	18	22	Pisa	10
23	Montpellier	17	23	Athens	10
24	**Mallorca**	**9**	24	Montpellier	6
25	Narbonne	2	25	Narbonne	5

Source Own elaboration, mainly, with the data presented in Bairoch et al. (1988)

moment of recognized splendour of Muslim civilization. The second most important group is made up of four capitals of antiquity: Constantinople, Rome, Naples and Milan. Their important position on the list can be attributed to the legacy of the major colonizing civilizations of the ancient Mediterranean. Finally, we find a small sample of commercial cities: Venice, Thessaloniki and Carcassonne. At the beginning of the second millennium of our age, Barcelona was very far from these three groups and from the threshold of 20,000 inhabitants. With a population of around 5,000, it is in penultimate position on our list.

Three centuries later, the ranking clearly shows the result of the Commercial Revolution under the lead of emerging capitalistic city-estates or Mediterranean thalassocracies (Abulafia, 2011, 2014; De Roover, 1942; Dufourcq, 1969; Kocka, 2013; Lopez, 1976; Mazzaoui, 1981; Mollat du Jordin, 1993; North & Thomas, 1973). Half of the top 12 positions of the vertex in 1300 are now occupied by cities that stood out in trade in the Late Middle Ages: Venice, Genoa, Florence, Barcelona, Thessaloniki and Valencia. The Islamic world has lost a great deal of weight in the leading positions, due to a combination of military defeats and lower commercial drive, only having two exponents on the top 12: Cairo and Granada. The participation of the big cities of antiquity has also gone down somewhat, although not as much as the Islamic world: Rome has left the vertex, but Constantinople, Milan and Naples are still there.

Barcelona did not only manage to achieve a position at the vertex. In dynamic terms, it was the city that climbed the most positions between 1000 and 1300, from 24 to 11th position, a leap of 13 places. There were comparable, although somewhat less intense, leaps in Genoa (eleven positions), Florence (eleven), Montpellier (ten) and Pisa (eight). This group, together with Venice and Barcelona, consisted of leading players in the Commercial Revolution of the Mediterranean.

At the end of the next century, as a result of recurrent waves of the Black Death contagions, all of the cities had lost significant amounts of population. The Islamic world now has another two exponents on the list of the 12 biggest cities at the vertex: Thessaloniki, in the hands of the Turks since 1387, and Malaga, an important port of the Nasrid kingdom. The capitals of antiquity resist, despite the considerable demographic loss of Constantinople, under attack by the Ottomans. The cities of the Commercial Revolution also continue to be key players on the list, with Venice, Genoa, Florence, Barcelona and Valencia.

Genoa even continued to climb positions between 1300 and 1400, reaching third or fourth place on the ranking, shared with Venice. However, Montpellier and Pisa already began to experience a significant decline, attributable to the tax revolts and military defeat. The Tuscan maritime republic lost six positions and the Languedoc city, ten. The path taken by the commercial cities consequently began to diverge in the fourteenth century. Barcelona then resisted. Despite the crises, and confirming what we have seen in the previous sections, the productive fabric of Barcelona showed significant resilience. Venice also maintained its relative position.

The weakening of the commercial cities continued in the fifteenth century, but in a more accentuated manner. Genoa fell from third/fourth to seventh position and Florence from seventh to eighth position (Lopez & Miskimin, 1962). Barcelona and Valencia disappear from the list of the top 12. Pisa and Montpellier continue to collapse. Thessaloniki, now a commercial emporium of the Islamic world, also sinks (Mazower, 2005). The exceptions are Venice, which continues as the now undisputed queen of Mediterranean trade, and Marseille, promoted as a trading port of France with the Orient. However, these two are exceptions and the trend is one of loss of weight of the commercial cities. Comparative history consequently suggests that, for cities that had been important players of the Commercial Revolution, the fifteenth century was an unequivocally depressive period.

The Islamic world offset the taking of the kingdom of Granada with the escalade of Constantinople, much later Istanbul. However, Malaga left our list of the top 12 in 1500. Three big Muslim cities remain at the peak of the urban Mediterranean: Cairo, Constantinople and, already falling quickly after the Castilian occupation, Granada.

The cities from the ancient world were revitalized with the advance in absolutism and the strengthening of the monarchies that began to be glimpsed in the fifteenth century. With the return of Rome, there are three cities from antiquity among the top 12. Milan remains in fifth position and, for the first time, Naples overtakes Venice.

The territories linked to the Crown of Aragon experienced a notable imbalance during the 1400s. Palermo (eight positions) and Naples (five positions), rise a great deal. Valencia goes down moderately (one position). The most extreme fall of the fifteenth century is that of Barcelona: eight positions, down to 19th place. It is a true collapse!

Barcelona, as already argued, was the commercial flywheel in the machinery of the Catalan economy, and the whole of Catalonia was the motor of the historical territories of the Crown of Aragon. With the flywheel and the motor damaged, the Catalan-Aragonese commercial empire tended to derail. Valencia fared better, although its situation also worsened.

In short, Genoa, Florence, Barcelona, Valencia, Thessaloniki, Pisa and Montpellier all lost relative weight in the urban Mediterranean of the 1400s. Wars, uprisings, occupations, epidemics and the dismantling of trade flows greatly damaged these former major players of the Commercial Revolution. However, if it makes sense to talk about a great depression of the Late Middle Ages anywhere, this is in Barcelona and the Catalan Countries as a whole.

The above group of cities, which played a significant role in the Commercial Revolution, were badly placed in a world in which xenophobic absolute monarchies were emerging and imposing centralization. Furthermore, from the end of the fifteenth century, the Mediterranean cities as a whole suffered from the major trade routes moving to the Atlantic (Armenteros, 2012, 2015; Epstein, 2000). The republics of Venice and Genoa resisted better, specializing in the production of luxury goods (silks, jewels, glassware) and financial services.

Barcelona and the Catalonia were less fortunate. The trend of the first decades of the fifteenth century was already one of depression, due to the excess debt, which became more acute with the campaigns of the Trastamara dynasty, but the long-distance foreign trade still responded positively to the expansive policies adopted in the 20s and 50s. In any case, the final collapse occurred with the two military conflicts (including a total war) that were, in part, also a result of the financial needs of the crown, which stressed the undeniable social unrest of Catalonia in the Late Middle Ages.

At the end of the fifteenth century, a few Catalan merchants began to participate in the Atlantic business of the sugar, many former *remensas* prospered and business insurance performed quite well, but Ferdinand the Catholic's policy of reconstruction was unable to reverse the decadence of the Catalan thalassocracy as a whole. Barcelona became an appendage of the immense possessions of the Hispanic monarchy in the sixteenth century with a rather poor performance of the large majority of its merchants and artisans, a true sleeping beauty of the Mediterranean. It woke up suddenly with the 1640 Reapers' War and, in the second half of the 1600s, began to exploit the opportunity provided by the Atlantic to promote massive trade in eau-de-vie (Valls, 2004).

3.5 Concluding Remarks

The Mediterranean experienced an intense process of economic recovery and structural change in the three centuries following the year 1000, led by a group of dynamic cities and their hinterland, which were the principal players in the Commercial Revolution and whose main exponents tended to become merchant empires or thalassocracies. At the beginning of the fourteenth century, they experienced a succession of shocks arising from a probable climate change that worsened crops, the intensification of military conflicts and the return of the Black Death. Its consequences were a collapse of the population, agricultural and industrial production and commercial flows. Furthermore, labour income and agricultural yields tended to improve, while land and tax revenues fell, entailing an exacerbation of redistributive and ethnic-religious conflicts. The capacity for recovery and resilience was, however, still high during the fourteenth century, and that tragic period did not significantly change the hierarchy of cities that had arisen over the three previous centuries of improvement in maritime exchange across the Mare Nostrum.

On the other hand, the fifteenth century was a true great depression for the majority of cities that had been the principal players of the Commercial Revolution, due to the impact of the advance of the Turks in the Orient, the contractive effect of wars, occupations and social conflicts and the rise of absolute monarchies. During the 1400s, the commercial emporiums of Genoa, Florence, Barcelona, Valencia, Thessaloniki, Pisa and Montpellier all went down on the ranking of Mediterranean cities.

If there was one place where the impact of the fifteenth century was absolutely disruptive, this was Catalonia and its capital, Barcelona. The economy of the old Catalan counties had vigorously overcome the recessions of the fourteenth century, that is the agricultural crisis of 1315–1336 and the demographic, social and financial crisis of 1348–1375 or the financial, social and foreign trade crisis of 1381–1394. It had achieved this by expanding its foreign markets, tax reforms, protectionist and devaluation measures and the creation of innovative institutions and public capacities, such as the Diputació del General and the Taula de Canvi of Barcelona.

On the contrary, from 1404 onwards, Catalonia entered a great depression from which it had not emerged in 1516. This marked its decline as an advanced Mediterranean economy. Although the protectionist measures favoured two incipient recoveries in the 20s and 50s, they did not have time to fully prosper. However, it was civil war that irrevocably wrecked the Catalan economy. The successive social and military conflicts of 1462–1472 and 1483–1485, which were fostered by the opportunism of the Trastamara dynasty, and the aggressive reaction of nobility and urban oligarchy against reform proposals, ruined the Barcelona commercial empire.

Ferdinand the Catholic's reconstruction policy proved some successes. The Catalan peasantry was strengthened by the elimination of servitude, the consolidation of a status of quasi-owner of the land and the control of the *masos rònecs*. The new devaluations of the *diner* were those required in a situation of profound deterioration of the external competitiveness of the Barcelona economy. However, the Catholic King's backing of an absolutist, monolithic and inquisitorial state tended to numb the potential for growth of the Catalan institutions.

Barcelona, which had been close to Venice, Genoa or Florence, plunged into an abyss during the fifteenth century. It joined cities such as Pisa, Montpellier and Thessaloniki. Catalonia undoubtedly experienced an unequivocal great depression in the Late Middle Ages. Valencia captured some of the benefits arising from Catalan decadence. It did not, however, improve significantly within the Mediterranean economy.

References

Abulafia, D. (2011). *The Great Sea*. Penguin.

Abulafia, D. (2014). Thalassocracies. In P. Horden & S. Kinoshita (Eds.), *A Companion to Mediterranean History* (pp. 139–153). Willey Blackwell.

Abulafia, D. (2017). *La guerra de los Doscientos Años. Aragón y Anjou y la lucha por el Mediterráneo*. Pasado y Presente.

Anguera de Sojo, O. (1934). Dret especial de la comarca de Vic. In De Sojo A. (ed.) *Conferències sobre varietats comarcals del Dret Civil Català* (pp. 237–340). Acadèmia de Jurisprudència.

Armenteros, I. (2012). *Cataluña en la era de las navegaciones. La participación catalana en la primera economía atlántica (c. 1470–1550)*. Milenio.

Armenteros, I. (2015). *L'esclavitud a la Barcelona del Renaixement (1479–1516). Un port mediterrani sota la influència del primer tràfic negrer*. Pagès.

Bairoch, P., Batou, J., & Chèvre, P. (1988). *La Population des villes européennes, 800–1850*. Droz.

Baratier, E. (1951). Le XIVe siècle (1291–1423). In G. Rambert (Ed.), *Histoire du commerce de Marseille. II* (pp. 21–316). Libraire Plon.

Batlle, C. (1988). *L'expansió baixmedieval (segles XIII-XV)*. Edicions 62.

Belenguer, E. (2013). Una aproximació a la crisis de la Baixa Edat Mitjana a Catalunya. *Butlletí de la Societat Catalana d'Estudis Històrics, 24*, 267–296.

Belenguer, E. (2015). *Vida y reinado de Pedro IV el Ceremonioso (1319–1387)*. Milenio.

Belenguer, E. (2019). *Los Trastamara*. Pasado y Presente.

Benedictow, O. J. (2004). *The Black Death, 1346–1353: The Complete History*. Boydell P.

Benito, P. (2004). Fams i caresties a la Mediterrània occidental durant la baixa edat mitjana. *Recerques, 49*, 179–193.

Benito, P. (2013). De Labrousse a Sen. Modelos de causalidad y paradigmas interpretativos de las crisis alimentarias preindustriales. In P. Benito (ed.), *Crisis alimentarias en la Edad Media. Modelos, explicaciones y representaciones* (pp. 15–32). Ed. Milenio.

Bois, G. (2000). *La grande dépression médiévale, XIVe-XVe siècles. Le précédent d'une crise systémique*. Presses Universitaires de France.

Brenner, R. (1978). Agrarian Class Structure and Economic Development in Pre-Industrial Europe. *Past & Present, 70*, 30–75.

Broussolle, J. (1955). Les impositions municipales de Barcelone de 1328 à 1462. *Estudios de Historia Moderna, 5*, 1–164.

Carrère. (1967). *Barcelone centre économique a l'époque des difficultés. 1380–1462*. Mouton.
Campbell, B. (2016). *The Great Transition*. Cambridge U. P.
Chismol, G. (2019). Una aproximació a la conjuntura econòmica de les finances reials de Pere El Cerimoniós a partir de la seua tresoreria. In L. Tudela & P. Cateura (Eds.), *La crisi baixmedieval a la Corona d'Aragó (1350–1450)* (pp. 199–212). Illa.
Cipolla, C. (1975). *Le aventure della lira*. Il Mulino.
Cipolla, C. (1982). *The Monetary Policy of Fourteenth Century Florence*. UCLA Press.
Coulon, D. (2013). *Barcelona i el gran comerç d'Orient a l'edat mitjana*. Base.
Crowley, R. (2011). *City of Fortune*. Faber and Faber.
Crusafont, M. (1989). *Barcelona i la moneda catalana*. Caixa de Pensions.
Crusafont, M. (1996). *Història de la moneda catalana*. Crítica.
Crusafont, M. (2015). *Història de la moneda de la Corona Catalano-aragonesa medieval*. Societat d'Estudis Numismàtics.
Cuadrada, C. (2012). *El llibre de la pesta*. Rafael Dalmau.
De Roover, R. (1942). The Comercial Revolution of the Thirteenth Century. *Bulletin of the Business Historical Society* XVI, 34–39.
De Roover, R. (1962). *The Rise and Decline of the Medici Bank, 1397–1494*. Harvard U. P.
Del Treppo, M. (1972). *I mercanti catalani e l'espansione della Corona d'Aragona nel secolo XV*. Arte Tipografica.
Dini, B. (1995). *Saggi su una economia-mondo. Firenze e Italia fra Mediterraneo ed Europa (secc. XIII-XVI)*. Pacini.
Dufourcq, C. (1969). *L'expansió catalana a la Mediterrània occidental*. Vicens-Vives.
Dyer, C. (2015). A Golden Age Rediscovered: Labourers' Wages in the Fiftheenth Century. In M. Allen & D. Coffman (Eds.), *Money, Prices and Wages* (pp. 180–195). Palgrave Macmillan.
Epstein, S. R. (2000). *Freedom and Growth: The Rise of States and Markets in Europe, 1350–1750*. Routledge.
Fagan, B. (2000). *The Little Ice Age*. Basic Books.
Feliu, G. (2000). Moneda y Banca en Cataluña en el siglo XV. In A. M. Bernal (Ed.), *Dinero, moneda y crédito en la monarquía hispánica* (pp. 121–134). Marcial Pons.
Feliu, G. (2004). La crisis catalana de la Baja Edad Media: Estado de la cuestión. *Hispania, 64*, 435–466.
Feliu, G. (2012). *Història econòmica de Catalunya*. Base.
Feliu, G. (2016a). *Els primers llibres de la Taula de Canvi de Barcelona* (2 vols.). Noguera.

Feliu, G. (2016b). Finances, Currency and Taxation in the 14th and 15th Centuries. *Catalan Historical Review, 9*, 25–44.

Fontana, J. (2014). *La formació d'una identitat. Una història de Catalunya*. Eumo.

Forcano, M. (2014). *Els jueus catalans*. Angle.

Fraser, E. D. G., & Rimas, A. (2011). *Empires of Food. Feast, Famines and the Rise and Fall of Civilisations*. ArrowBooks.

Freedman, P. H. (1993). *Els orígens de la servitud pagesa a la Catalunya Medieval*. Eumo.

Furió, A. (2002). Treball esclau i treball assalariat a la baixa edat mitjana Una Introducció. *Recerques, 52–53*, 7–18.

Furió, A. (2013). La primera gran depresión europea (siglos XIV-XV). In E. Llopis & J. MaluquerJ (Eds.), *España en crisis* (pp. 17–58). Pasado y Presente.

Furió, A. (2017). La gran depressió baixmedieval. Una mirada des dels Països Catalans. *Recerques, 72–73*, 45–103.

Galera, A. (2019). La crisi en el cas del comtat de Cardona segons els indicadors fiscals municipals: Evolució de les imposicions a la vila de Cardona i els seus arrendaments entre 1420 i 1478. In L. Tudela & P. Cateura (Eds.), *La crisi baixmedieval a la Corona d'Aragó (1350–1450)* (pp. 143–160). Illa.

Hamilton, E. J. (1936). *Money, Prices and Wages in Valencia, Aragon and Navarre, 1351–1500*. Harvard U. P.

Holmes, G. (1975). *Europe: Hierarchy and Revolt, 1320–1450*. John Wiley & Sons.

Henneman, J. B. (1971). *Royal Taxation in Fourteenth Century France: The Development of War Financing, 1332–1356*. Princeton.

Igual, D. (2007). ¿Crisis? ¿Qué crisis? El comercio internacional en los reinos hispánicos de la Baja Edad Media. *Edad Media. Revista de Historia, 8*, 203–223.

Iradiel, P. (2007). El segle XV: expansió i crisi en la perspectiva econòmica. In E. Belenguer & A. Furió (Eds.), *Història de la Corona d'Aragó. I. L'època medieval (1137–1479)* (pp. 305–334). Edicions 62.

Kocka, J. (2013). *Geschichte des Kapitalismus*. Beck.

Lane, F. C. (1973). *Venice: A Maritime Republic*. John Hopkins U. P.

Le Goff, J. (2010). *Le Moyen Âge et l'argent*. Perrin.

Le Roy Ladurie, E. (1962). *Histoire du Languedoc*. PUF.

Le Roy Ladurie, E. (1967). *Histoire du climat depuis l'an mil*. Flammarion.

Lluch, R. (2010). *Els remences. La senyoria de l'Almoina de Girona als segles XIV i XV*. AHRCG.

López, R. S. (1976). *The Commercial Revolution of the Middle Ages, 950–1350*. Cambridge U. P.

Lopez, R. S., & Miskimin, H. A. (1962). The Economic Depression of the Renaissance. *Economic History Review, XIV*(3), 408–426.

Malanima, P. (2010). The Long Decline of a Leading Economy: GDP in Central and Northern Italy, 1300–1913. *European Review of Economic History, 15*, 169–219.

Malanima, P. (2018). Italy in the Renaissance: A Leading Economy in the European Context, 1350–1550. *Economic History Review, 71*(1), 3–30.

Martel, P. (2019). *Histoire de l'Occitanie*. Yoran.

Mazower, M. (2005). *Salonica. City of Ghosts: Christians, Muslims and Jewish, 1450–1950*. Knopf.

Mazzaoui, M. F. (1981). *The Italian Cotton Industry in the Later Middle Ages 1100–1600*. Cambridge U. P.

Melis, F. (1984). *L'economia fiorentina del Rinascimento*. Le Monnier.

Miskimin, H. A. (1975). *The Economy of Early Renaissance Europe, 1300–1460*. Cambridge U. P.

Mollat du Jourdin, M. (1993). *Europe and the Sea*. Blackwell.

Nadal, J. (1992). *Bautismos, desposorios y entierros*. Ariel.

North, D. C., & Thomas, R. P. (1973). *The Rise of the Western World: A New Economic History*. Cambridge U. P.

Ortí, P. (2000). *Renda i fiscalitat en una ciutat medieval: Barcelona, segles XII-XIV*. CSIC.

Ortí, P. (2018). Noves dades seriades per a noves hipòtesis sobre la crisi baixmedieval a Catalunya. In J. Morelló, P. Ortí, & P. Verdés (Eds.), *Renda feudal i fiscalitat a la Catalunya baixmedieval* (pp. 463–484). CSIC.

Phelps Brown, H., & Hopkins, S. V. (1981). *A Perspective of Wages and Prices*. Methuen.

Postan, M. M. (1950). Some Economic Evidence of Declining Population in the Latter Middle Ages. *Economic History Review, 2–3*, 221–246.

Puigferrat, C. (2004). *Sant Julià de Vilatorta després de la Pesta Negra de 1348*. Patronat d'Estudis Osonencs.

Prados de la Escosura L., Álvarez-Nogal C., & Santiago-Caballero, C. (2020, March). *Growth recurring in preindustrial Spain: Half a millenium perspective*. European Historical Economics Society Working Paper, 177.

Reyerson, K. (2005). *Jacques Coeur: Entrepreneur and King's Bursar*. Logman.

Reynaud, F. (1951). *Le XIVe siècle (1423–1480)*. In G. Rambert (Ed.), *Histoire du commerce de Marseille. II* (pp. 319–727). Libraire Plon.

Riera, A. (2006). Els orígens de la manufactura tèxtil medieval a la Corona catalanoaragonesa (c. 1150–1298). In R. Narbona (Ed.), *XVIII Congrés d'Història de la Coronad'Aragó* (pp. 821–901). Universitat de València.

Rovira i Virgili, A. (1928). *Història Nacional de Catalunya. La Catalunya Nacional* (Vol. 5). Edicions Pàtria.

Salrach, J. M. (1989). *La pesta negra i els orígens del problema remensa*. Anuario de Estudios Medievales, A 24.

Sánchez Martínez, M. (1995). *El naixement de la fiscalitat d'Estat a Catalunya (segles XII-XIV)*. Eumo.
Sánchez Martínez, M. (2003). *Pagar al rey en la Corona de Aragón durante el Siglo XIV*. CSIC.
Serra, E. (1980). El règim feudal català abans i després de la sentència arbitral de Guadalupe. *Recerques, 10*, 17–32.
Smith, R. S. (1940). *The Spanish Guild Merchant. A History of the Consulado, 1250–1700*. Duke U. P.
Sobrequés, J. (1971). *La Peste Negra en la Península Ibérica*. Anuario de Estudios Medievales VII.
Sobrequés, S. (2011). *Catalunya al segle XV* (posthumous). Base.
Sobrequés, S., & Sobrequés, J. (1973). *La guerra civil catalana del segle XV* (2 vols.). Edicions 62.
Soldevila, F. (1962). *Història de Catalunya* (3 vols). Alpha.
Spufford, P. (1988). *Money and its use in Medieval Europe*. Cambridge U. P.
Tanzini, L. (2018). *1345. La bancarotta di Firenze*. Salerno.
Usher, A. P. (1943). *The Early History of Deposit Banking in Mediterranean Europe*. Harvard U. P.
Valls, F. (2004). *La Catalunya atlàntica*. Eumo.
Verdés, P. (2019). L'evolució dels ingressos fiscals del municipi de Cervera (1331–1516). Un indicador de la conjuntura econòmica?. In L. Tudela & P. Cateura (Eds.), *La crisi baixmedieval a la Corona d'Aragó (1350–1450)* (pp. 121–141). Illa.
Vicens, J. (1945). *Historia de los Remensas (en el siglo XV)*. Instituto Jerónimo Zurita.
Vicens, J. (1956). *Els Trastàmares*. Vicens Vives.
Vilar, P. (1962). *La Catalogne dans l'Espagne moderne. Recherches sur les fondaments économiques des structures nationales*. SEVPEN.
Vinas, A., & Vinas, R. (2017). *La Companyia Catalana a Orient (1303–1311)*. Rafael Dalmau.
Wolff, P. (1971). The 1391 Pogrom in Spain. Social Crisis or Not? *Past and Present* 50, 4–18.
Zedar, B. Z. (1981). *Mercanti in crisi a Genova e Venezia nel '300*. Jouvence.

CHAPTER 4

The Crisis of the Seventeenth Century in Valencia and Catalonia

Manuel Ardit

Like other terms used by historians, the crisis of the seventeenth century is a theoretical construct with an empirical basis that has given rise to endless discussions. The stimulating work by Maurice Dobb, ***Studies in the Development of Capitalism*** (1946),[1] gave rise to a controversy concerning the transition from feudalism to capitalism, which was initiated by the American economist Paul M. Sweezy in 1950 and dragged on throughout that

Manuel Ardit died in 2013.

A previous Catalan version of this article was published in the journal *Recerques*. It got the support of Fundació Bancària "la Caixa". The editor also thanks to the family and the review for the permission to publish this English version and to Doctor Andreu Ginés for his support in editing the work.

M. Ardit (✉)
University of Valencia, Valencia, Spain
e-mail: jordi.ardit@gmail.com

J. Catalan Vidal (ed.), *Crises and Transformation in the Mediterranean World*, Palgrave Studies in Economic History,
https://doi.org/10.1007/978-3-031-24502-2_4

decade and the following one, with some contributions in the 1970s.[2] In this debate the crisis of the seventeenth century was not the main theme, although it does appear in it marginally. The discussion about the "general crisis" of the seventeenth century came not long afterwards, in part a spin-off from the debate concerning the transition and in part separate. The works that Pablo Fernández-Albadalejo (1983, p. 368) considers foundational are the book by Roland Mousnier (1953) on the sixteenth and seventeenth centuries and the articles in *Past & Present* by Eric J. Hobsbawm (1954a, b) and Hugh Trevor-Roper (1959), and the main contributions to the discussion appeared in the following two decades. Upon examining the various contributions to the discussion one finds great differences in definition, explanation and chronology, as well as a heavy dependence on contemporary problems, which is also a danger inherent in the resumption of the debate at the present time. There were hardly any contributions to the discussion from the 1980s onwards, if one rules out the allusions to the subject that can be found in the Brenner debate, which in any case does not go beyond the 1980s (Aston & Philpin, 1985). It is, therefore, an old debate to which hardly any attention has been paid for many years, but which might perhaps be revived as a result of the current world economic crisis.

Be that as it may, my intention is not for this article to be included in this discussion, but to provide some empirical information and theoretical reflections on the difficulties that the Valencian and Catalan economies experienced in the seventeenth century. I use the word "crisis", with some qualifications, according to the definition given in the *Diccionari de la llengua catalana*,[3] in the second sense of the term (since the first is applied to diseases): a circumstantially difficult stage that a person, a business, an industry, a government, etc. goes through. I consider that these stages of difficulty that an economic system may go through may be connected with processes of change or rupture (one of the meanings of the ancient Greek word *κρίσις*), so that a critical economic cycle may be the result of a process of transition in which structural changes germinate.

4.1 Some Economic Indicators from Valencia and Catalonia

The economic indicators that account for the economic cycle must necessarily be temporary series, and with regard to the seventeenth century they are not exactly abundant. As the economy was essentially agrarian, series of incomes from the land will be preferable. In the Valencian Country we have the magnificent set of documents that refer to the leases of the archbishopric of Valencia's tithes, which has been studied by several authors (Ardit, 1987; Casey, 2005). I shall use the data from my series on the major tithe—or bread and wine tithe—just as they were taken from the *Llibres d'arrendaments dels delmaris de l'arquebisbat de València*, deflated with the prices of wheat in the city of Valencia. The archbishopric of the town of Valencia encompassed approximately half of the territory of the Kingdom of Valencia, so the geographical cover is good. The tithe, and most especially the leased tithe, poses many problems, as has repeatedly been pointed out, but in this case there is no alternative (Ardit, 1989; Canales, 1982). Moreover, some of the difficulties with this indicator are characteristic of its final stage, and are non-existent or of little importance in the seventeenth century. There nevertheless remains the problem of the previous four-year lease, a circumstance that makes the tithe an imperfect indicator of the situation, due to the delay between fixing the price of the lease and the phenomenon that one assumes it has to measure.

We have no extensive series of tithes for Catalonia, but there are some incomes from the land, although not many, and they do not cover as large a territory as the Valencian ones. The most interesting one is probably that of the rent of the chaplaincies of Girona Cathedral, studied by Pere Gifre (2012, pp. 91–108). This author publishes these series grouped in ten-year averages and deflated with the prices in Barcelona. Also interesting are those of seigniorial income published by Montserrat Duran (1985), also deflated by the wheat prices in Barcelona. Given their length and completeness, only the series of taxes, tithes and other seigniorial levies received by the chapter of La Seu d'Urgell are useful for our purposes, along with those of the levies leased by the Royal Domain to the viscounty of Castellbó and the castle and municipal territory of Pals.

Since Pere Gifre presents the figures of the chaplaincies of Girona Cathedral in the form of ten-year averages and index numbers calculated on the base 1691–1700 = 100, I have also had to reduce the data of the other series to ten-year averages and index numbers on the same base. The three series are remarkably similar, especially the ones from Valencia and Girona, as can be seen in Table 4.1 and Fig. 4.1.

In the first place, there is a similarity between the relative magnitudes and the secular movement. Some highs and lows coincide in all three series, especially those of the archbishopric of Valencia and Girona Cathedral, while the series of seigniorial income of La Seu d'Urgell, Castellbó

Table 4.1 Tithes and seigniorial income in Valencia and Catalonia, 1571–1700

Ten-year periods	*València*	*Girona*	*Seigniorial income*
1571–1580	98.80	86.73	101.88
1581–1590	93.06	92.37	104.07
1591–1600	97.52	94.75	88.41
1601–1610	110.50	103.22	83.22
1611–1620	96.57	87.30	78.68
1621–1630	88.35	90.87	87.68
1631–1640	82.04	98.34	88.33
1641–1650	66.49	82.42	88.71
1651–1660	82.54	–	87.04
1661–1670	87.15	77.97	83.43
1671–1680	83.35	85.15	86.97
1681–1690	92.37	101.10	91.93
1691–1700	100.00	100.00	100.00

Tithes of the archbishopric of València, chaplaincies of Girona Cathedral and seigniorial income of La Seu d'Urgell, Castellbó and Pals (Ten-year averages numbers index 1691–1700 = 100)
Source See the main text

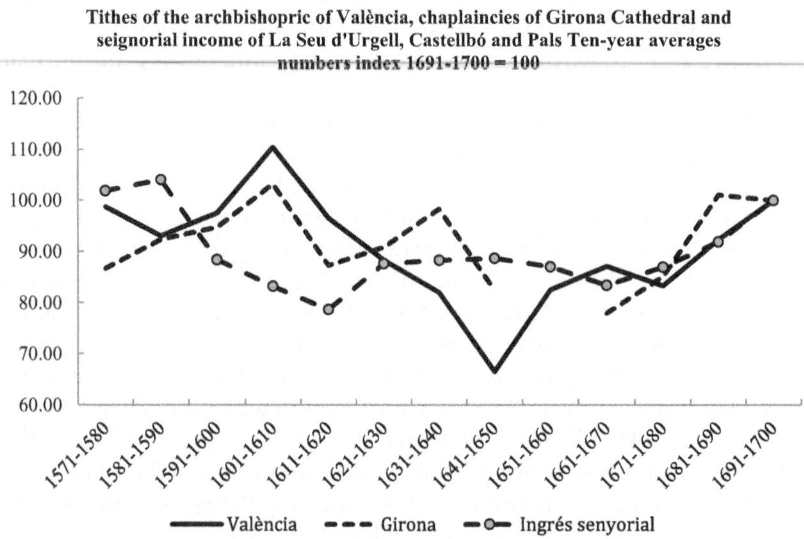

Fig. 4.1 Tithes and seigniorial income in Valencia and Catalonia, 1571–1700 (*Source* See the main text)

and Pals, which in any case is the least representative because it covers a smaller area, diverges from the path. A compact statistic, but one that does not reflect phenomena that are better detected by visual inspection, the coefficient of determination R^2 is 0.3 between the series in València and Girona, but almost zero, 0.02, between the latter and that of the seigniorial income. Other Mediterranean series, with which those I use have been compared, such as the one from Majorca or some from the interior of the Iberian Peninsula or Italy, are very different, in both the direction of the evolution and the chronology. In these cases, the coefficient of determination is zero.

Pere Gifre (2012) found the great similarity of the series from València and Girona so surprising that he noted down a reflection that in large part is the basis of this article:

> M. Ardit—he writes—has studied the leasing of the tithes of València Cathedral, comparing it to J. Casey's figures, with which it is remarkably similar for the sixteenth and seventeenth centuries. Despite the differences in the areas studied by this author, one clearly sees three stages: the growth of the sixteenth century comes to a halt with the expulsion of the Moriscos, a critical phase begins that hits rock bottom in the 1640s, and recovery begins at the start of 1700, when the levels prior to the expulsion were most likely reached. The trend, as qualified as you like, is very similar to that which can be deduced from the leasing of the chaplaincies of Girona Cathedral, with the difference that 135,000 Moriscos were expelled from the Valencian Country. Whereby one must wonder about the reasons for the trajectory of the income in Girona or qualify the impact of the expulsion of the Moriscos from Valencia. (p. 106)

I can say something about the second question posed by Pere Gifre because I have in fact made an effort to qualify the impact of the expulsion of the Moriscos from the Kingdom of Valencia, but the first one is very difficult to answer, although I shall attempt to develop some ideas on the subject in this article.

4.2 The Expulsion of the Moriscos and the Economic Crisis in Valencia

If there is one European territory in which the crisis of the seventeenth century has a cause that can hardly be doubted, it is the Kingdom of Valencia. The sudden disappearance of 135,000 inhabitants between

October and December 1609, who were slowly replaced by new settlers, must surely have had serious economic consequences. In any case the evolution of the income from the land, as it appears reflected in the series of the archbishopric of València's tithe leases, was not exactly what might have been hoped for, posing some questions that have no obvious answers. In order to analyse this phenomenon in detail it is essential to have the annual series instead of the ten-year ones I used above. In Fig. 4.2 this series of leases is reproduced, deflated with the wheat prices in the city of València and expressed in indexes on the base 1585–1599 = 100, a period that I have considered most suitable due to its stability.

The expected trajectory would have been a sudden reduction in the number of leases, if not exactly in 1610, at least between 1610 and 1613, since the tithes for the four-year period 1614–1617 were auctioned in December of that year. The fall is indeed abrupt, given that the indexes drop from 119.6 in 1609 to 97.6 in 1613, but bearing in mind that the Valencian Country had lost a third of its population, most of them working in farming, a larger drop could have been expected, much larger even. But what is most surprising is that the tithe leases continue to fall,

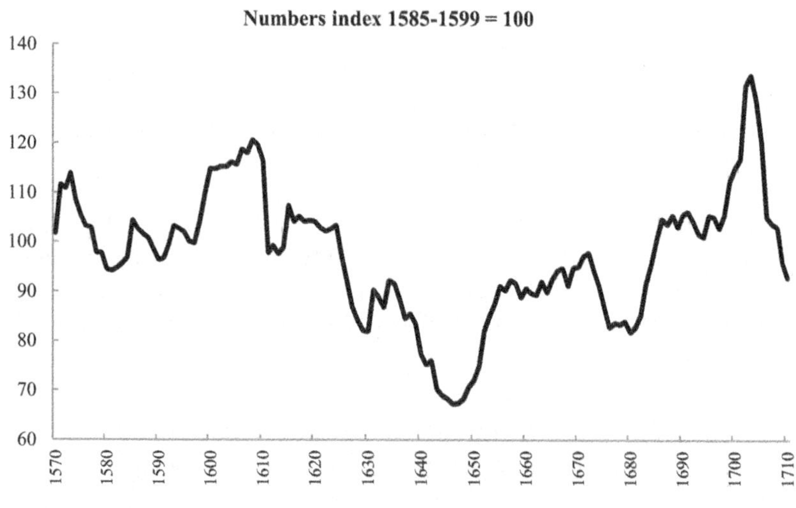

Fig. 4.2 Bread and wine tithes in the Archbishopric of Valencia (*Source* See the text)

with oscillations, until 1646–1647, when they reach the lowest indexes in the series, 67.3, before immediately beginning a recovery. This, with some inter-cycles too, would continue until the early eighteenth century, when the very negative effects of the War of the Spanish Succession, worse than those of the expulsion of the Moriscos, are observed. It is strange that with a process of resettlement and a resumption of farming that, although with great difficulty and hesitancy, was already underway in 1610, the tithes of the archbishopric of València stubbornly kept on falling until the middle of the seventeenth century. This phenomenon cannot be explained away as a consequence of the expulsion, or at least not as a direct consequence of it.

Various factors are probably responsible for this behaviour. One of them could be the financial ruin of the urban sectors that had habitually farmed tithes. They had been seriously affected by the annuities crisis—to which I shall refer later on—and they were gradually replaced by rural lessees, generally poorer, who bid less at the auctions that the archbishopric held every year. It is an unstudied phenomenon, but simple observation of the books of leases clearly shows this process, slow as it was, and which would lead, in the eighteenth century, to the absolute hegemony of rural capitalists in this business.

I do not however believe that this fact can be completely explained by this circumstance. The process of resettlement after the expulsion of the Moriscos from the Valencian Country did not consist, as Tulio Halperín-Donghi (1980, p. 267) rightly said, of the simple replacement of Morisco settlers by Christian ones. This may have been the lords' intention, but they did not succeed. The new Christian settlers came from a different cultural tradition and they introduced important structural changes to the land they occupied. One of the most important, and perhaps also one of the best recorded, was the enlargement of the surface area of the properties and the farms. The Moriscos had basically farmed irrigated smallholdings, very labour intensive and probably with high returns per unit of surface area, and had scant regard for dry-land agriculture. The new Christian agriculture corresponded to another model, with lower returns at least to begin with, larger areas, a greater use of draught animals and a considerable expansion of soil under cultivation on dry, unirrigated land. The process of extending this new agrarian model was slow and uneven, lasting for more than 300 years and culminating in the eighteenth and nineteenth centuries.

We have several witnesses to this enlargement of the size of estates and farms, despite the monarchy's recommendations for the establishment of an egalitarian rural society.[4] In the fields around Gandia this increase was very considerable and it is recorded in the short period of time from 1609 to 1630 (Bataller, 1960; La Parra, 1990, sp. p. 232; 1992). Elsewhere the changes were not as spectacular but the Christians' estates and farms were always larger than those of the Moriscos (Ardit, 2004, sp. pp. 103–116; Bernabé, 1987, pp. 61–74; Ciscar, 1997, sp. pp. 25–42; Domingo, 1983, sp. pp. 186–195). It is difficult to link this enlargement of surface areas to the decrease in tithes between 1610 and 1647, but it probably has to do with the fall in the returns per unit of surface area that I mentioned above, although it is not recorded and is simply a logical supposition.

There are also several contemporary oral accounts, most likely riddled with prejudice but repeated so often that it is hard not to believe that they were based on real phenomena. A cliché common in the Kingdom of Valencia rior to the expulsion, of which we could give different examples, was that, "ordinarily, and we have experience of it, an old Christian's house needs, to maintain it, as much as two Moriscos' houses" (Boronat, 1901, I, pp. 596–597). More explicit is the other one that said that, "the Morisco was happy with two *hanegades* of land and considered himself rich with them [...] and now the new settlers are given 15 *hanegades* of land each and they are still not happy" (Casey, 2005). These statements, confirmed by all manner of quantitative documents, as we have seen, may well have concealed a certain lack of understanding on the part of the Christians towards Muslim agriculture, which was very labour intensive. Other accounts, in this case clearly biased, stressed the Moriscos' laziness and their preference for smallholdings, easier to work, and their aversion to extensive dry-land cultivation. The Dominican Fra Jaume Bleda (2005 [1618]), wrote:

> those sad people were bad farmers and workers on dryland, and most of it lay barren in their places. They did not bother to plant either trees or vines on it, they merely went about cultivating their orchards and gardens that were irrigated, which had been divided up into small plots, and they were averse to having to work in a large wide field. They did not persevere in their work all day, as the Christians usually do, but two, three or four hours. They were naturally given to idleness and very weak because of how badly they ate and drank. (pp. 1030–1031)

Pedro Aznar Cardona (1612), from Aragon, had the same opinion of Morisco agriculture as the Valencian Bleda, saying,

> they [the Moriscos] possessed many good places but they grew hardly anything of substance in them; they only planted fig, cherry, plum and peach trees, and vines for raisins, and green vegetables, melons, and cucumbers, disregarding the important vines, fruitful olive trees and the ploughing of heavy fields. (II, fol. 34)

The changes that crops in the irrigated area underwent and the expansion of dry-land cultivation may well have been more important, but in this case we only know of one territory, the marquisate of Llombai. This estate stood on one of the marginal flanks of the Ribera Alta, and so outside the very rich areas in the centre of this *comarca*, chiefly royal domain. As an estate of the Borgia family, dukes of Gandia, the marquisate of Llombai, created in 1530 (it had previously been a barony), possesses a great deal of documentation that is part of the Osuna collection in the "Nobility" section of the Archivo Histórico Nacional, now based in Toledo. Until the year of the expulsion, it comprised four localities, Llombai, Catadau, Alfarb and Alèdua (the latter was deserted in 1609), the majority of whose population was Muslim, except for a small minority of Christians who lived in Llombai, the largest place. There is not much information about the latter, since they held their houses and lands in full or allodial ownership. Different documents of the fifteenth century, but above all numerous notebooks of rents created by the collectors of the lord's taxes in the sixteenth century and a memorial of rents from 1581, give us a precise picture of farming in the territory. Most of the crops were cereals, including wheat, but the ones characteristic of Muslim agriculture, sorghum and *panís* (millet), were more important. Only at the end of the sixteenth century, does the spread of maize from the Americas start to become obvious. It is sometimes hard to tell from sorghum because its name was the same in Arabic, *dacsa*. Also from the 1580s, one observes the spread of olives and mulberries, the latter in modest proportions. Together with the hegemonic cereals, pulses and different vegetables and fruit, forage and other perishable produce must have been grown which must have been kept for consumption by peasant families, as hardly any of it was taken to market.

The 1581 memorial of rents is no more precise but it does enable us to make an approximate quantification. The cereals are not mentioned separately by name and the size of the fields is given in whole units of surface area, Valencian *fanecades* or *hanegadas* (831 m^2) or *cafissades* (6 *fanecades*). This leads one to suspect that the surface areas are only approximate, probably by default. As for the crops, the fundamental distinction this document makes is between treeless land, called *terra campa*, and land with trees, but in this case it does state what trees were planted, very often in association. A frequent association was that of the mulberry tree with *terra campa*, where mulberries must characteristically have been grown at the edges of the fields. This obviously makes counting them difficult. This is even more difficult on dry land, since the memorial of rents hardly ever gives the surface area, using only very imprecise expressions, such as "one plot", "one small plot" and the like, and on very many occasions it specifies the number of trees planted, always close to the unit, as "one olive tree" "two carob trees", and so on. All this seems to indicate that, as some oral accounts that I reproduced above point out, the Moriscos paid very little attention to dry-land crops or that these were of little interest to those who produced the memorial of rents, which amounts to the same thing.

With these limitations it can be claimed that, on irrigated land, cereal crops were absolutely hegemonic, since *terra campa* (on which, however, pulses, green vegetables and forage could occasionally be planted) represented 86.8% of the total surface area. A long way behind, with 52%, came mulberries, very often associated with *terra campa*. The rest of the bushes or trees (vines, figs, olives and carobs) occupied only 8% (Ardit, 2004, pp. 64–71).

The Christian settlers made profound changes to this productive structure, but it is impossible to date the process precisely because the next memorial of rents in the marquisate of Llombai is from 1699. Notwithstanding this, there are clues that it began at an early date because the dukes of Gandia granted reduced *particions* (the owner's share of the tenant farmer's crops) in 1623 and 1630, with the aim of encouraging the spread of mulberry trees on irrigated land and vines on dry land.[5] By the end of the seventeenth century, according to the abovementioned memorial of rents, the agrarian structure of the marquisate of Llombai had changed greatly.

By 1699 the surface area of *terra campa* on irrigated land had fallen to 32.5%, while the mulberry trees grown exclusively in what were called "thick mulberry groves" had risen to 44.5%, and in association with other crops to 13.6%. Cereals, vines and other tree crops, chiefly olives and carobs, had been transferred en masse to dry land, which now does appear quantified (Ardit, 2004, pp. 103–116).

If these agrarian changes had been widespread in Morisco territory, something I consider very likely, they might explain, along with the factors to which I referred earlier, the peculiar movement in the tithe leases of the archbishopric of València that we have observed. Perishable produce, such as mulberry leaf, was difficult to tithe, as this was not done by *partició* but by agreement between the parties, and its spread always implied losses for the beneficiary institutions. It would be the period of the fall, 1610–1647, when these changes were put into effect, especially breaking new ground and planting on dry land, costly on mountainous terrain such as that in the Valencian Country, where adapting to the hillsides requires heavy investment; the recovery of incomes after 1648 would bear witness to the consolidation of the process.

4.3 Other Factors of the Valencian Crisis

The economic crisis of the seventeenth century in Valencia was not just agrarian, however. One of the most serious consequences of the expulsion of the Moriscos was the financial ruin of the annuities creditors and the grave difficulties suffered by their debtors, principally the nobility of Valencia. During the sixteenth century at least, the latter had obtained money by resorting to the credit market by way of a curious procedure. It was not they who underwrote the debt through an annuity but their vassals, apparently for the purpose of dealing with supply emergencies ("*per obs d'avitualllar*", as the deeds say), but it was the lords who actually received the capital from the loan. It was also the villages that paid the annuities, but in order to make it clear who the beneficiary of the loan was, the lord granted a letter of indemnity by which he declared that he was ultimately responsible for the annuity, especially its settlement or release. With the disappearance of the Moriscos in 1609, the annuity payers also disappeared and the creditors ceased to be paid. In the case of the mixed localities the surviving natural Christians could not take responsibility for the annuities because the obligation had been mutually binding and they could not cope with an obligation that had corresponded to a much larger population. Nor could the new settlers take them on because that would have hindered the resettlement, and many new settlement deeds in fact specify this, although others say nothing about the matter.

The annuities question gave rise to many problems in the courts and for a while the problem remained unresolved.

The problem of annuities is well documented in the duchy of Gandia in these early years. The annuities creditors claimed that the obligation had been inherited by the new settlers, but the latter retorted that as the previous community had disappeared so had the legal bond, since the contract had been made "*ut universi et non ut singuli*".[6] The pragmatic of 2 April 1614, completed by the "entry of the houses of the titles, barons and owners of places that due to the expulsion of the Moriscos from the kingdom of Valencia had been left empty", of 9 June 1614, provided a solution to the problem by declaring that the lords had to pay the debt, but paying 5% interest on annuities that had been habitually subscribed at 6.75% (Boronat, 1901, II, pp. 611–657). From 1622 the reduction of the interest on the annuities to 5% became widespread and not just limited to those who had been lords of Moriscos. Despite that, many of them were unable to sort out their economies, and the dukes of Gandia in particular found themselves in serious difficulty for half a century, until 1644, when they sold three estates, Torís, Albalat de la Ribera and Xella, to a more fortunate nobleman, Bertomeu Soler de Marrades, lord of Llaurí, for 106,000 Valencian pounds. With this sum they were unable to pay off the debt but they did reduce it, in agreement with the creditors, to a third of its value.[7] Other lords adopted similar strategies. The traditional solution in the Kingdom of Valencia when a noble house was close to bankruptcy consisted of placing it in a regime of *segrest i aliments* (sequestration and maintenance). From that moment on a royal sequestrator took charge of administering the estate, passing an allowance for food to the lord, which was often excessive (although insufficient from his point of view), so it was very difficult to sort out the lords' economy. Creditors were very often paid virtually nothing. The lords, who retained jurisdiction in their estates, played all kinds of tricks in order to obstruct the work of the sequestrators. Eventually, therefore, agreements between the lords and their creditors were imposed, in which reductions of the annuities below the legal 5%, releases of part of the debt and other stratagems that always harmed the annuities holders were specified (Casey, 1979).

Everyone suffered from this, and the credit market suffered a sharp contraction for much of the seventeenth century. James Casey has estimated the debt of the annuities of the lords of Valencia to have been 4,200,000 pounds, and 12,000,000, that of municipal councils and private individuals. We do not know for sure how much of these 16.2 million pounds was ever paid, but probably more than half of it. Just the annuities of this capital, estimated at the rate of 6.74%, usual before 1622, were equivalent to a quarter of the agrarian output of the Valencian Country. The 16 million of capital owed must have been far more than the GDP of Valencia at that time if it can be calculated. The situation was obviously explosive and the reduction of the interest on the annuities to 5% did nothing towards regularizing credit. The municipal bank of València, the Taula de Canvis, suspended payments three times in half a century, in 1614, 1634 and 1649 (Carreres, 1957). The collapse of the agrarian sector, as Casey (1979) writes, caused a reduction in the demand for manufactured goods and the crisis spread to all parts of the economy.[8]

As has been said above, these credit problems most likely partly explain the behaviour of tithe leases. Not because they influenced it directly but because the bankruptcy of the usual investors in annuities, who at the same time took part in the leasing of tithes, left this business in the hands of sectors with less financial clout who offered lower sums at the archbishopric's auctions. This is in any case a question that has not been studied at all.

4.4 An Explanation of the Crisis of the Seventeenth Century in Catalonia

We have seen how similarly agrarian income evolved in the Valencian Country and Catalonia, territories with a lot of things in common, but also important differences. In Catalonia, apart from the territory on the banks of the Ebro River, there was no expulsion of the Moriscos, or any of its consequences, resettlement and annuities crisis. In the Kingdom of Valencia there was no Reapers' War, but this factor could be overlooked since the crisis happened before 1640. There is only one overview of the crisis of the seventeenth century in Catalonia, by Eva Serra (1986, pp. 214–246).[9] This author provides additional information that I have not reproduced in a previous section as it is in the form of short fragmentary series. Nevertheless, they have the advantage of considerably expanding the area under observation. The archdeaconry of Barcelona's tithes on cereals and legumes fell sharply in the periods 1580–1585 and 1639–1644, and similar changes, but with a crisis that lasted longer, can be seen in the production of cereals and pulses in the barony of Sentmenat, in El Vallès Occidental (Serra, 1986, pp. 225–226). Eva Serra also recalculated Montserrat Duran's series, in this case using many more of them than I did earlier in this article, even those with important gaps. She concludes:

> feudal income, after 30, 40 or 50 years, depending on the series, of substantial and continued growth, would also begin to fall for a long period of between 20 and 30 years or between 40 and 50 years, depending on the series, and always within a period prior to 1640. (Serra, 1986, p. 228)

The author observes that the chronology of the fall in income coincides in large part with the debts of the house of Sentmenat, debts in part contingent and, I would add, structural for the nobility, but which seem to have got worse in the last decades of the sixteenth century. This observation, although limited to just one noble house, coincides with the situation that just then many aristocratic families in Valencia were experiencing, as James Casey pointed out years ago (Casey, 2005).[10] Historians in Valencia have for a long time wondered why the Valencian nobility did not take effective action against the expulsion, bearing in mind moreover that the lord of the Moriscos was at that time a Valencian aristocrat, the Marquis of Dénia and Duke of Lerma, the king's *valido* (favourite). The question still awaits a convincing answer, despite the valuable contributions made by various historians (Lomas, 2009), and in the study previously cited, Casey subtly suggested that many Valencian noblemen may have thought that the expulsion might give them the chance to rebuild their estates on more solid foundations. Eva Serra (1986) wonders:

> Could the general fall in feudal income, of 88.14% of the value of the income examined, have been an expression of changes in the structure of crops made at the expense of feudal income, the expression of an expanding peasant population that 'fragments' the farm; in other words, it establishes, changes the structure of crops and erodes feudal income? (p. 231)

The Catalan historian's suggestion is very similar to the fundamental reason that I gave above as being responsible for the fall of agrarian income in Valencia.

A few lines below Eva Serra (1986) adds that,

> it would be worthwhile wondering what role the peasants' resistance might have played in this fall in feudal income, what role the peasants' capacity and feudal incapacity could also have played in the transformations of the crop structures, and along with them very often also the new contractual developments. (p. 231)

Catalonia and the Valencian Country were territories of full ownership and of emphyteusis, a sort of quasi-ownership. Here we have the only shared characteristic that could account for the similarities observed. Perhaps the feudal incapacity that Eva Serra refers to was not as absolute as she seems to suggest. We saw above how the dukes of Gandia encouraged the spread of mulberries and vines in the marquisate of Llombai through improvements in the partitions. But where the lords could under no circumstances intervene was in the social differentiation of the peasantry. Emphyteutic useful domain was, with some limitations, ownership that could be transferred through transactions, donations and inheritances, and the lords could not interfere in the processes of concentration of ownership and of social differentiation. I have endeavoured to demonstrate that even on the hardest estates, economic growth was possible (Ardit, 2004).

4.5 Concluding Remarks

In the case of the crisis of the seventeenth century in the Valencian Country and Catalonia, we have therefore arrived at what is principally a social explanation for an economic phenomenon. The modification of the productive system, whether due to a traumatic event, the expulsion of the Moriscos from the Kingdom of Valencia, or to the dynamics of the system, as was the case in Catalonia, gave rise to a critical situation caused by these particular transformations. It was overcome in the second half of the seventeenth century and growth resumed, but there would be further critical situations in later periods that go beyond the chronological framework of this article. We might wonder, although it is a question that for the time being has no answer, what would have happened in the Valencian Country if the Moriscos had not been expelled. It is a counterfactual hypothesis that in future some historian will perhaps be able to answer with econometric reliability. For my part, and through simple intuition, I consider it highly likely that the agrarian transformations to which I have referred would have taken place anyway, but in a different context that is hard to imagine.

Notes

1. The work was translated into Spanish much later (1971).
2. In this case, the Spanish edition (Sweezy et al.) of the debate appeared in 1967, but the most complete compilation is by Rodney Hilton (1977).
3. This is the dictionary of the Institut d'Estudis Catalans, the academy that officially provides standards for the Catalan language.
4. The best-known document in this respect is the edict by Salvador Fontanet, the Royal commissioner for the resettlement of Morisco places in the kingdom of Valencia, dated 1 October 1612, in which he reviews and modifies the charters of settlement of the duchy of Gandia, the marquisate of Llombai and the county of Oliva, Arxiu del Regne de València (ARV), *Reial Justícia*, book 796, fols. 451r-456r.
5. Archivo Histórico Nacional, Nobleza (AHN, N), *Osuna*, bundle. 589, files. 2, 17 and 24.
6. AHN, N, *Osuna*, bundle. 922, 236.
7. ARV, *Reial Audiència*, Trials, 1st part, letter D, 487.
8. There is a mistake in the Catalan translation of this work, as, on page 116, it says that the reduction of the interest on the annuities at 5% was decreed in 1646. On page 95 of the English original, it says correctly that the measure was from the year 1614.
9. Much of the information and also of the reflection in this article can also be found in another book by this author (Serra, 1988). In order to avoid duplications I shall always refer to the first work that, despite being published at an earlier date, also comes from her doctoral thesis and is more specific on the subject that we are dealing with here.
10. The original article is from 1975.

References

Ardit, M. (1987). Expulsió dels moriscos i creixement agrari al País Valencià. *Afers. Fulls de Recerca i Pensament, 5–6*, 273–316.

Ardit, M. (1989). Recaudación y fraude decimal en el siglo XVIII valenciano. In *Estructuras económicas y reformismo ilustrado en la España del siglo XVIII* (pp. 391–410). Ministry of Agriculture, Fishing and Food [MAFF].

Ardit, M. (2004). *Creixement econòmic i conflicte social: la foia de Llombai entre els segles XIII i XIX*. Afers.

Aston, T. H., & Philpin, C. H. E. (Eds.). (1985). *The Brenner Debate: Agrarian Class Structure and Economic Development in Pre-industrial Europe*. Cambridge University Press.

Aznar, P. (1612). *Expulsión justificada de los moriscos españoles y suma de las excelencias christianas de nuestro rey don Felipe III, deste nombre*. Pedro Cabarte.

Bataller, A. (1960). La expulsión de los moriscos: su repercusión en la propiedad y la población en la zona de los riegos del Vernisa. *Saitabi, X*, 81–100.

Bernabé, D. (1987). La Vega Baja del Segura en vísperas de la expulsión de los moriscos: estructura de la propiedad de la tierra. In *Estructuras y regímenes de tenencia de la tierra en España*. MAFF.

Bleda, B. (2001). *Crónica de los moros de España* (facsimile). Biblioteca Valenciana, València City Council, University of València. Original edition: (1618). Felip Mey.

Boronat, P. (1901). *Los moriscos españoles y su expulsión. Estudio histórico-crítico*. Francisco Vives Mora.

Canales, E. (1982). Los diezmos en su etapa final. In G. Anes (Ed), *La economía española al final del Antiguo Régimen. I. Agricultura* (pp. 103–187). Alianza.

Carreres, S. (1957). *La Taula de Cambis* [sic] *de Valencia, 1408–1719*. Valencia City Council.

Casey, J. (1979). *The Kingdom of Valencia in the Seventeenth Century*. CUP.

Casey, J. (2005). *La terra i els homes. El País Valencià a l'època dels Àustria*. Afers.

Císcar, E. (1997). *La Valldigna, siglos XVI y XVII. Cambio y continuidad en el campo valenciano*. Diputació de València.

Crisi. (n.d.). *Diccionari de la llengua catalana. Segona edició*. http://mdlc.iec.cat. Accessed 13 February 2019.

Dobb, M. (1946). *Studies in the Development of Capitalism*. George Routledge & Sons. Spanish edition: Dobb, M. (1971). *Estudios sobre el desarrollo del capitalismo*. Siglo XXI.

Domingo, C. (1983). *La Plana de Castellón. Formación de un paisaje agrario mediterráneo*. Caixa d'Estalvis i Mont de Pietat.

Duran, M. (1985). L'evolució de l'ingrés senyorial a Catalunya (1500–1799). *Recerques, 17*, 7–42.

Fernández-Albaladejo, P. (1983). Veinticinco años de debate sobre la crisis del siglo XVII. In T. Aston (Comp.), *Crisis en Europa, 1560–1660* (pp. 368–386). Alianza.

Gifre, P. (2012). *Els senyors útils i propietaris de mas. La formació històrica d'un grup social pagès (vegueria de Girona, 1486–1730)*. Fundació Noguera.
Halperín-Donghi, T. (1980). *Un conflicto nacional. Moriscos y cristianos viejos en Valencia*. Institució Alfons el Magnànim.
Hilton, R. (Ed.). (1977). *La transición del feudalismo al capitalismo*. Crítica. English edition: Hilton, R. (ed.) (1976). *The Transition from Feudalism to Capitalism*. Verso.
Hobsbawm, E.J. (1954a). The General Crisis of the European Economy in the 17th Century. *Past & Present*, *5*(I), 33–53.
Hobsbawm, E.J. (1954b). The Crisis of the 17th Century-II. *Past & Present*, *6*(I), 44–65.
La Parra, S. (1990). *El ducado de Gandía en el siglo XVII: la ruptura de una convivencia tras 1609* [Doctoral Thesis]. Universitat deValència.
La Parra, S. (1992). *Los Borja y los moriscos (repobladores y "terratenientes" en la huerta de Gandía tras la expulsión de 1609)*. Edicions Alfons el Magnànim.
Lomas, M. (2009). Innata fidelitat i notable desconsol. La integració de la noblesa valenciana en el procés d'expulsió dels moriscos. *Afers. Fulls de Recerca i Pensament*, *62–63*, 127–150.
Mousnier, R. (1953). *Les XVIe et XVIIe siècles: La grande mutation intellectuelle de l'humanité: l'avènement de la science moderne et l'expansion de l'Europe*. Presses Universitaires de France.
Serra, E. (1986). Per una cronologia i interpretació de la crisi del segle XVII. In E. Serra, R. Garrabou, N. Sales, P. Ruiz, E. Vicedo, E. Tello, L. Ferrer, et al. (Eds.), *Terra, treball i propietat. Classes agràries i règim senyorial als Països Catalans* (pp. 214–246). Crítica.
Serra, E. (1988). *Pagesos i senyors a la Catalunya del segle XVII. Baronia de Sentmenat, 1590–1729*. Crítica.
Trevor-Roper, H. R. (1959). The General Crisis of the 17th Century. *Past & Present*, *16*(I), 31–64.

CHAPTER 5

Crises in Catalonia at a Time of Growth and Transition, 1680–1840

Àlex Sánchez and Francesc Valls-Junyent

In 1840, the physiognomy of the Catalan economy had changed significantly if we compare it with what it was like one and a half centuries earlier, at the end of the seventeenth century. Three main changes

Francesc Valls-Junyent died in 2017.

This article has been published thanks to the support of the HAR2015-64769-P and PGC2018-093896-B-I00 research projects, funded respectively by the Spanish Ministry of the Economy (MINECO) and the Ministry of Science and Innovation (MCIN/AEI/10.13039/501100011033). Both projects also received the financial support of the European Regional Development Fund (ERDF, *A way of making Europe*). The authors stress their gratitude to Professor Llorenç Ferrer Alós for making available the copious demographic information

À. Sánchez (✉) · F. Valls-Junyent
Universtiy of Barcelona, Barcelona, Spain
e-mail: alex.sanchez@ub.edu

J. Catalan Vidal (ed.), *Crises and Transformation in the Mediterranean World*, Palgrave Studies in Economic History,
https://doi.org/10.1007/978-3-031-24502-2_5

occurred over this period. Firstly, part of the population, which is difficult to specify in quantitative terms, but which was undoubtedly by no means negligible, had gone from producing for self-consumption or to supply local and regional markets, to producing to sell in increasingly remote markets. Secondly, there had been an important transfer of productive resources from the agricultural sector to activities of a manufacturing type, promoting the beginning of an industrialization process which entailed a change in "the principle of the mode of production" (Vilar, 1964–1968, III). Thirdly, such an economic dynamics led to the collapse of a particular model of social organization, that of the Ancient Regime, and to its replacement by a new model which began with the triumph of the liberal revolution (Fontana, 2014, pp. 225–292).

This general outline of the economic and social evolution of Catalonia between the end of the seventeenth century and the mid-nineteenth century should be borne in mind if we want to understand the causes, nature and consequences of the crises which affected its inhabitants during this period. In this chapter, we aim, in the first place, to identify the episodes of depression during the century and a half which goes from 1680 to 1840. And, secondly, after identifying the crises which affected a generally upward economic trend over this long period, we will endeavour to discover the causes and establish the consequences, while analysing the specific characteristics of each of them.

In order to attain the first of the objectives indicated, that is the identification of the periods of crisis or depression, we consulted sources of a demographic nature. These are the only ones which, for that period, permit a quantitative, continuous and homogeneous approach. We do not intend to perform a demographic study. We simply propose to use the demographic variables as an indirect—although, in our opinion, also very reliable–indicator of economic performance and crises.

---

that he collected over recent years, and to the Generalitat de Catalunya, the Fundació Bancària "la Caixa" and the Centre d'Estudis Jordi Nadal (Universitat de Barcelona) for further support. They are also in debt with the journal *Recerques*, where a previous Catalan version of this work was published for the first time and with Doctor Andreu Ginés for help in editing the English text. The editor thanks very much Lourdes Ribas, Marta Valls and Laura Valls to permit the publication of the English version. Very unfortunately, Francesc Valls died in 2017 without being able to see published the present work.

5.1 Crises in a Phase of Secular Growth

It may sound like a contradiction in terms to talk about crises and depressions in relation to a period which has widely been considered by historiography as one of growth and expansion. It is, however, also true that the growth experienced by the Catalan economy from the end of the seventeenth century was affected by one-off crises and by true depressions which, as we will argue below, sometimes even threatened it. At the same time, on some occasions, it was only possible to overcome these recessionary situations by varying the course of the economy in a more or less substantial manner and, even, by accepting very significant changes in the social order.

The expansive dynamics of the Catalan economy is very clear when we observe the country's demographic course, whether based on the overall population figures, as P. Vilar did—whose calculations were recently revised by Ferrer (2007, pp. 17–68)—, or by adopting an analysis of the situation through the compilation of parish data, just as we propose in this article. The series corresponding to the people baptized in a sample of 42 parishes,[1] with which Fig. 5.1 was created, leaves no doubt about the upward trend experienced by Catalan demography between the end of the seventeenth and the beginning of the nineteenth century. However, at the same time, this same curve shows several turning points which prove that the growth was not linear and, therefore, did not lack setbacks.

With the aim of being able to better specify the critical moments when the period's underlying upward trend was compromised, we calculated natural growth for this same sample of 42 parishes, that is to say, the difference between those born (baptisms) and deceased (burials). Having made this calculation, we estimated the percentage over births represented by the balance or difference between births and deceases for each of the 42 parishes of the sample, in each of the 160 years taken into consideration. The average for this percentage in the 42 parishes for each of the years is represented in Fig. 5.2. This curve, reflecting the combination of reductions in the number of births with sudden increases in deaths, allows us to determine with great accuracy the critical situations which affected the evolution of the population.

Using this same information, we endeavoured to indicate the territorial scope of these crises. We therefore prepared an indicator consisting of calculating the annual percentage of parishes from our sample in which

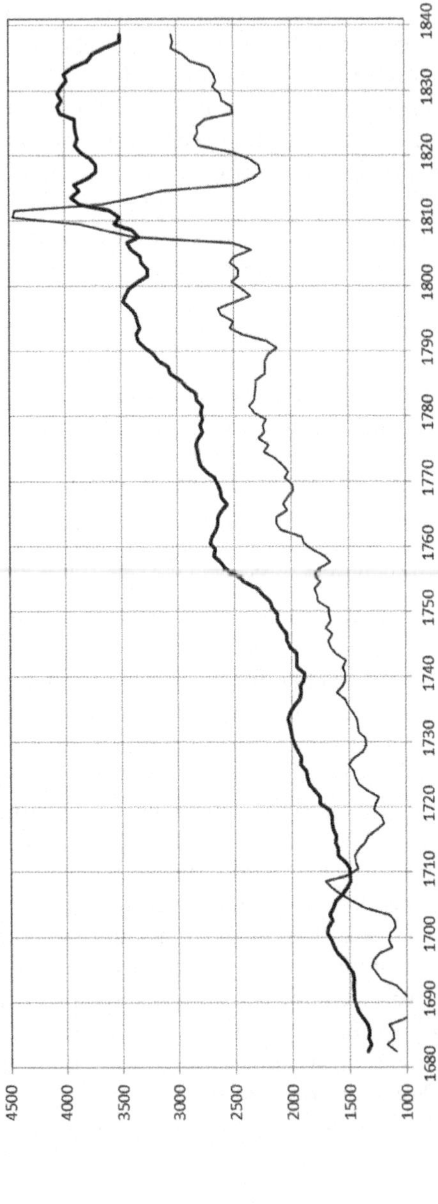

Fig. 5.1 Evolution of births and deaths in 42 Catalan parishes (moving averages of five years of the absolute figures), 1682–1838 (*Source* See the main text)

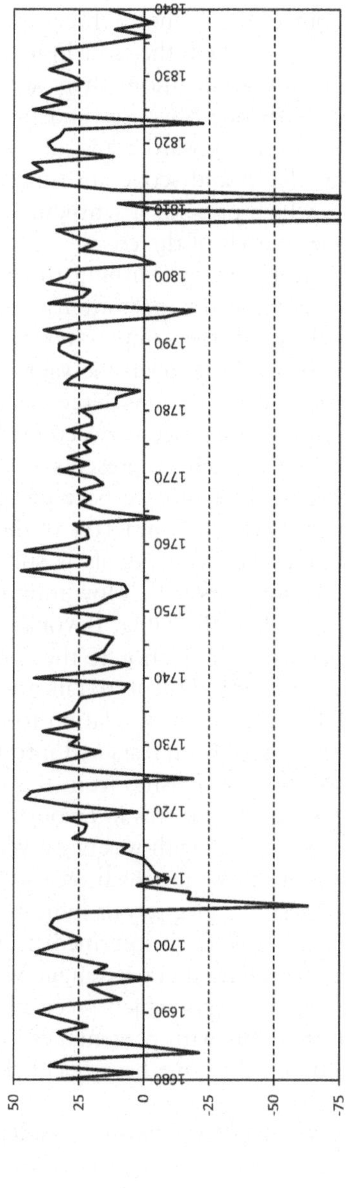

Fig. 5.2 Difference between baptisms and deaths in a sample of 42 Catalan parishes, 1680–1840 (average % represented by the difference between births and deaths out of the total births in each parish) (*Source* See the main text)

the number of deaths exceeded that of births. This proportion is reflected in Fig. 5.3.

Starting from the combination of these three indicators on the behaviour of demography, we reached the conclusion that, over the period of 160 years taken into consideration, there were a total of 16 critical moments (including both one-off crises and deeper and longer recessions) which jolted the overall upward trend of the Principality of Catalonia. Their chronology, depth and scope are summarized with the data contained in Table 5.1, which presents a synthetic indicator both of the intensity and of the scope of each of the crises.

We have obtained this indicator by establishing three levels of intensity of the crises. We have considered the most intense to be those which present a clearly negative balance in the sample average between births and deaths, therefore below 0. We have given the value 3 to those years which present this characteristic. We have considered the crises of average intensity to be those in which the difference between births and deaths is in favour of births but by very little. This represents a percentage which on average goes from 0 to 5. In the table, we have given the value 2 to these years. Although positive, between 5 and 10% of the average difference between births and burials between burials is still very small and we have considered that these are years with a low intensity of crisis. We have thus given them the value 1 in the table. Beyond the threshold of 10% positive that we have established in relation to the difference between births and deaths, we consider that it is difficult to talk about critical years.

We have proceeded in a similar manner in relation to the scope of the crises. All the years of the series have been classified into three categories in accordance with the proportion of parishes from the sample in which the difference between births and deaths was in favour of deaths in each of the years. In other words, natural growth was negative. The years with a more general scope of crisis are those in which over 40% of the sample series are negative. The value that we give to our indicator is the highest, a 3. The years in which the crisis is of an intermediate scope are those in which the series give negative values in a percentage which varies from 35 to 40% of cases. These are the years which received a value of 2 in our classification. Finally, in the years with percentages of parishes with a negative balance between 30 and 35%, we have decided to give them a value of just 1.

The sum of the two scores gives us a synthetic indicator between 1 and 6 which allows us to group the critical years of our series into the

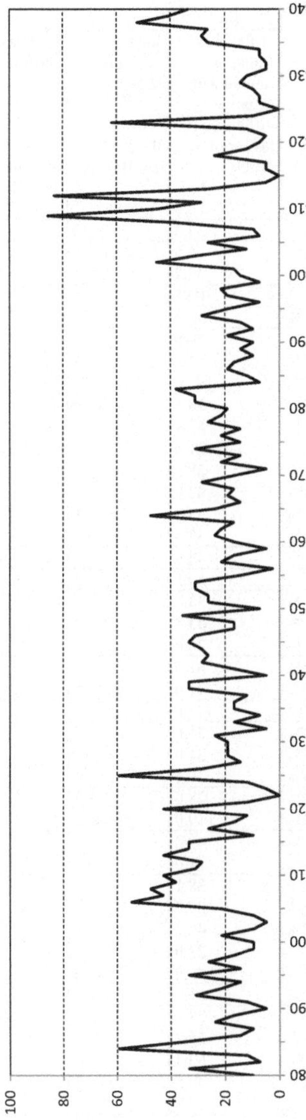

Fig. 5.3 Parishes in which the deaths exceeded the baptisms, 1680–1840 (% over a sample of 42 Catalan parishes) (*Source* See the main text)

Table 5.1 Identification and measurement of the intensity of the periods of crisis between 1680 and 1840

Crisis		(a) Difference births and deaths in % out of the total births (average of 42 parishes)	(b) % Parishes from the sample with negative difference (in favour of deaths)	(c) Intensity according to (a) < 0 = 3 0 – 5 = 2 5 – 10 = 1	(d) Intensity according to (b) >40=3 35 – 40=2 30 – 35=1	c + d
1	1681	2.6%	33.3	2	1	3
2	1684	-21.3%	59.5	3	3	6
	1685	-1.3%	35.7	3	2	5
3	1692	8.6	30.95	1	1	2
4	1695	-3.2%	33.3	3	1	4
5	1706	-63.0%	54.8	3	3	6
	1707	-16.9%	42.9	3	3	6
	1708	-17.9%	47.6	3	3	6
	1709	2.8%	38.1	2	2	4
	1710	-9.7%	42.9	3	3	6
	1711	-4.1%	31.0	3	1	4
	1712	-2.2%	28.6	3		3
	1713	0.4%	42.9	3	3	6
	1714	9.0%	33.3	1	1	2
	1715	5.7%	33.3	1	1	2
6	1720	2.5%	42.9	2	3	5
7	1725	-19.1%	59.5	3	3	6
8	1738	7.8%	33.3	1	1	2
	1739	5.5%	33.3	2	1	3
	1742	5.6%	28.6	2		2
9	1753	6.2%	31.0	1	1	2
	1754	7.8%	31.0	1	1	2
10	1764	-5.8%	47.6	3	3	6
11	1781	10.8%	31.0		1	1
	1782	10.7%	31.0		1	1
	1783	1.6%	38.1	2	2	4
12	1794	-7.9%	28.6	3		3
	1795	-19.4%	19.0	3		3
13	1802	-4.0%	45.2	3	3	6
	1803	3.4%	31.0	1	1	2
14	1808	8.2%	38.1	1	3	4
	1809	-153.4%	85.7	3	3	6
	1810	-7.5%	45.2	3	3	6
	1811	10.2%	28.6	1		1
	1812	-87.6%	83.3	3	3	6
15	1823	-22.6%	61.9	3	3	6
16	1836	-2.4%	28.6	3	0	3
	1837	11.4%	26.2			
	1838	-3.5%	52.4	3	3	6
	1839	4.8%	40.5	2	2	4
	1840	13.4%	33.3		1	1

Source Own elaboration with the sources quoted in the main text

16 episodes which appear in this table and which will serve as a guide in our presentation. However, before undertaking a more detailed analysis of the causes and consequences of each of these crises starting from this table, we would like to make a few general considerations.

First of all, Table 5.1 clearly shows that during the period which goes from the end of the seventeenth century to the end of the First Carlist War, there were two major catastrophes which swept through the country. The first one corresponds to the years of the War of the Spanish Succession and the second one to those of the Peninsular War. Both phases of recession stand out for their duration, their depth and their scope. If we add to this the fact that, in the light of our indicators, one of the moments which also shows very negative results is that of the years of the First Carlist War, we can state that war situations appear to trigger the stages with the most serious difficulties.

Furthermore, the data contained in Table 5.1 allows us, once again, to confirm the overall positive nature of the course of the eighteenth century. In the years which go from the end of the War of the Spanish Succession to the beginning of the Napoleonic occupation, the crises detected were more of a one-off nature, not too profound and with a very limited scope on a territorial level. It is only starting from the last years of the eighteenth century that we can begin to glimpse a change of trend both in relation to the increase in the frequency of critical episodes and to their intensity. This change of tendency occurred on the eve of one of the two major catastrophes indicated above, the one experienced starting from 1808.

5.2 The Crises That Affected the Phoenix Just When It Was Trying to Take Off

The Catalan historiography which has dealt with the period which goes from the Treaty of the Pyrenees to the beginning of the conflict concerning the succession of the Spanish monarchy has tended to emphasize what has commonly been called the "turnaround" of the end of the seventeenth century.[2] The use of this term is intended to demonstrate a change of tendency in the evolution of the Principality's economy which involved overcoming the phase of the depression which, starting at the end of the century, had reached its climax coinciding with the Reapers' War (Serra, 1986, 2013).

Three elements characterized this turnaround in the last decades of the seventeenth century. In the first place, we have a positive evolution in agricultural production which was demonstrated by indirect indicators, such as the evolution of manorial income (Duran, 1985).

Secondly, a greater dynamism of manufacturing activities is observed. In this respect, the decentralized nature of the recovery stands out, due to the dynamism and growing dissemination of activities such as textiles in rural areas (Dantí, 2012, pp. 58–59). And thirdly, in a clearer manner than in agriculture and industry, trade also showed signs of recovery (Fontana, 1955).

The curve of baptisms that we present in Fig. 5.1 endorses the theory of the recovery of the late seventeenth century. If we position the base 100 of the index at the average from 1681 to 1685, we find that in the five-year period from 1701 to 1705—prior to when Catalonia entered the Spanish conflict of succession as a result of signing the Pact of Genoa (20 June 1705)—, the index of baptisms reached the 128 level. This was a positive balance in the demographic field, very symptomatic of an equally upward evolution in overall terms, enough to be sufficiently perceived by peers. We should recall that emblematic and representative characters from this economic moment, such as Narcís Feliu de la Penya and Martí de Piles, did not hesitate to resort to the mythological symbol of the Phoenix when referring to the situation of the country, as they did in their well-known work of 1683 (Feliu de la Penya & de Piles, 1983).

However, such an upward dynamics experienced various setbacks, some of them major. The “turnaround” was not linear and was not of a general scope. In 1681, in a third of the parishes from our sample, deaths exceeded births. Consequently, the average increase between the two variables scarcely exceeded 2% of baptisms.

The downward dynamics of births starting from that date makes us think that this one-off crisis of 1681 was no more than the prelude to a broader and deeper crisis, the one which occurred in 1684 and 1685, in the first of which, in more than half of the 42 parishes from our sample, burials exceeded baptisms and the size of the deficit of births in relation to deaths on average exceeded 21%. This is a crisis of a really important size. It is a critical episode in demographic terms, which Nadal and Giralt (1960, pp. 44–45) attributed, in their classic work, rather than to factors of an epidemic type, to the very general famines in Catalonia due both to the bad harvests caused by the invasion of locusts and to the difficulties to supply the country with wheat through imports. Another causal element of this demographic crisis which should not be underestimated was the resumption in 1684 of the war with France by the Spanish monarchy, which "is a very harmful situation for this province having continuous billeting for this [...] in addition to the fact that there is nowhere in Catalonia which has not served his Majesty with soldiers" (Espino, 1999, p. 64). As various authors have revealed, it was precisely the state of war and all the inconveniences arising from it for the population (billeting and levying) which triggered the revolt of the *Gorretes* from 1687 to 1688 (Albareda, 1988, 1991; Dantí, 1979, 1990; Espino, 1999; Ferrer, 1981; Kamen, 1979).

The problems did not disappear when this setback was overcome, given that our indicators again point towards new difficulties in the 1690s. It is quite possible that one-off crises, such as those of 1692 and 1695, simply reflect the difficulties arising once again from bad harvests, mainly as a result of the locust plague which attacked the countryside between 1686 and 1688 (Català, 1987) and, above all, of the repeated problems due to the military occupation of part of the country on the occasion of the war between the Spanish and the French monarchy. This had recommenced in 1689 with the outbreak of the Nine Years' War, a situation which, therefore, lasted until 1697. During those years, it was not just the border regions with France which suffered from the negative consequences but even also the capital, Barcelona, had to withstand them as a result of the siege to which it was subjected by the troops of Louis XIV (Albareda, 1995; Espino, 1999). As a chronicler of the time said, between 1689 and 1697, Catalonia "had been the centre of such a long war, and had suffered from the devastation of its campaigns, the burden of extensive billeting, the ruin of cities, the looting of towns and the payment of increasing sums in contributions, inseparable effects of the war. [...] These excessive expenses had weakened the strengths of the natives and exhausted the inhabitants" (Torras Ribé, 1999, p. 30).

In this context of war, as tended to be usual, infections soon began to proliferate and epidemics to spread, such as that which in 1695 caused "the death of many people everywhere" (Simón, 1993, p. 37).

This was not a localized phenomenon, but rather a very general one, as Nadal and Giralt (1960, pp. 44–45) already suggested many years ago, using a sample of parochial series which was much more restricted than ours.

In short, although this combination of bad harvests, war and epidemics does not question the economic recovery of the Principality seen in the long term, they do make it necessary to better specify its contours in sectorial, geographic and especially social terms. On the sectorial level, it appears to be obvious that, just as the agricultural sector and more generically the rural world were the hardest hit by the crises, it was big business which suffered from them the least. The international conflicts which left France in a situation of isolation favoured Catalan exports of wine and, above all, eau-de-vie, as indicated years ago by Jaume Torras Elias (1996). The big traders involved in this export trade also tended to be the same who benefited from the situation of "constant war" (Albareda, 1993, pp. 36–37) in which the country was submerged in those last decades of the seventeenth century, as shown by the works of I. Lobato (1995) and A. Espino (1999) and on the participation of the commercial haute bourgeoisie of Barcelona in the supplies for the troops.

On a territorial level, it is clear that the place which, according to all indications, participated most actively in that turnaround was Camp de Tarragona. The early focus on winegrowing in its agriculture placed this region at the epicentre of the recovery which revolved around eau-de-vie exports, an industry which at that time already had its capital in the town of Reus. On the other hand, it should not be forgotten that this is a region which, to a large extent, stayed on the sidelines of that situation of permanent war which so much harmed the whole of that sector of the country to the north of Barcelona, most especially the regions closest to the French border.

Finally, as we indicated above, the effects of the crises were very different for each of the social strata. In certain sectors of the rural world, these critical situations entailed both individual and collective debt (Casas, 2015). In certain cases, the accumulation of debt became irreversible, triggering processes of concentration of ownership which accelerated the process of internal social differentiation of the peasants which had already begun previously, in part as a result of demographic growth (Serra, 1988, pp. 342–400). On the other hand, the crises offered speculative opportunities to commercial elites who participated in the lucrative business of leasing seigneurial rights, who became major players in the Atlantic repositioning of foreign trade through wine exports, and who also participated in the profit arising from the business of war, or acted as lenders to individuals and public institutions. However, such a dynamics was not strong enough to remove this commercial elite from the siren calls of ennoblement which, in the context of an Ancien Régime society such as Catalonia at the end of the seventeenth century, not only permitted access to the receipt of feudal income but also constituted the decisive step in any process of social improvement (Lobato, 1994, pp. 20–23).

Catalan society still formed part of the Ancien Régime and, consequently, the crises which hampered the flight of the Phoenix responded fully to the parameters of this type of society.

5.3 The Catastrophe of the War of the Spanish Succession and its Consequences

In traditional societies, the appearance of comets and meteorites was interpreted as a bad omen. The heavens showed their discontent with humanity by sending one of these signs, which announced the punishment which would inexorably follow on. However, when, on the evening of Christmas Day in 1704, a meteorite was seen and heard in Catalonia, no one could really imagine the seriousness of the events which were approaching. The curve represented in Fig. 5.2 clearly demonstrates that the years of the War of the Spanish Succession and the immediate post-war period represented one of the deepest and most persistent crises of the 160-year period taken into consideration in this chapter. Only the years of the Napoleonic occupation represented a still more intense and general crisis, although it was not as persistent as the one just one century earlier.

In relation to baptisms, Fig. 5.1 shows that there was a clear stagnation between 1700 and 1720. The 1699 levels took 22 years to be exceeded, proving the persistent nature of a crisis which clearly went beyond the chronological limits of the War of the Spanish Succession, the tough post-war years thus obviously hindering recovery. As for mortality, the acute figures for 1706 and 1707 should be underlined, in addition to the important crises from 1720 to 1721 and from 1724 to 1726. It is clear that these last two crises of mortality are related to episodes of an epidemic type, as we will see later, but it is difficult not to relate the high incidence of these epidemics to the harshness of the post-war years. Overall, the gap left in the natural growth curve by the joint action of the severe and persistent fall in births and the repeated peaks in mortality, took a long time to be filled. It was not until the end of the 20s that the positive natural increase achieved levels comparable to those of the pre-war decade, although at certain times, such as 1725, they again fell below 0, or came very close to this value, as in 1720.

Having made these considerations, we shall now address two questions. The first concerns the size of the disaster, and second, the persistence of the crisis and the difficulties to recover the rates of growth of the years of peace and economic boom which went from the end of the Nine Years' War in 1697 until the shift in support for Austria in 1705 and the full entry of Catalonia in the conflict of succession in the following year.

The only explanation for the intensity of the crisis from 1706 to 1707 is the constant movements of troops in the territory arising from the military operations undertaken starting from the autumn of 1705, when the allies succeeded in taking control of Barcelona and the Archduke of Austria was able to disembark towards the end of October. From then on, both armies carried out various offensives and counter-offensives that represented important troop movements, which affected a large part of Catalan territory (Torras Ribé, 1999). Overall, this converted Catalonia into a country devastated by armies that undertook uncontrollable actions in extensive areas of the territory, which led to absolutely indiscriminate lootings, requisitions, rape and murder.

In relation to the second of the issues raised, that of the persistence of the crisis subsequent to the end of the conflict, the main cause should be sought in the systematic repression to which the country was subject starting on the day after 11 September 1714, by means of an obsessive militarization of the territory (Torras Ribé, 2005). It is in this context of repression that we should interpret the introduction of the new cadastre tax, in so far as its collection was used to maintain the occupying army and to finance the construction of the military buildings necessary to make this military occupation more efficient.

The cadastre represented an extreme effort in tax terms in its early years and had a negative effect on the (especially peasant) economies, already depleted after the war (Mercader, 1955, 1968, pp. 149–194).[3] In this respect, the cadastre should above all be interpreted as the instrument which allowed a considerable transfer of resources from mainly peasant economies to other sectors of the urban population whose activities, as indicated by M. Arranz and R. Grau (1991), were, on the contrary, revitalized in the post-war years due to the positive stimuli arising from the demand generated by this numerous occupying army.[4]

Furthermore, as recently pointed out by J. M. Delgado (2014, pp. 152–153), it should be taken into account that the introduction of an annual monetary tax constituted, for a significant number of Catalans, a "stimulus to increase the productivity of their work, to obtain more income". In this respect, the new cadastral contribution could encourage the clearing of cultivated land considered as marginal until then in order to plant vineyards with the aim of having a marketable product in order to obtain the money necessary to pay the new contribution. This would therefore be a case similar to that which, some years ago, A. Bhaduri (1983) classified as forced commercialization, as a result of the punitive nature of the sudden increase in the tax burden represented by the introduction of the cadastre. Therefore, the considerably negative overall balance of these years should not make us lose sight of the fact that the effects of the long post-war period were very unequal both on a territorial and a social level. In short, the effects of some of the measures taken by the victors of the war were able, in the medium and long term, to stimulate and activate the growth of the Catalan economy while, in the short term, on the other hand, they had a clearly recessionary effect.

Finally, on explaining the persistence of the crisis beyond the strict end of the year, we should not forget the context of insecurity arising from the resurgence of insurrection in those sectors of the territory more affected by the repression and the tax demands of the occupying army (Vilar, 1964–1968, II. pp. 452–453).

The chronological event which marks the effective end of this period of difficulties is that of 1725, the date when the peace treaty was signed between Philip V and Charles of Austria (Albareda, 2010, pp. 460–475) and also corresponding to the last major episode of catastrophic mortality within this critical cycle linked to the War of the Spanish Succession and its post-war period. We can therefore conclude with the words of P. Vilar that although, in political terms, the eighteenth century began with the 1714 defeat or with the implementation of the Decree of Nueva Planta in 1716, "economically, the new stage did not really begin until after 1720 or even 1725 when the last consequences of the internal and external conflict disappeared" (Vilar, 1964–1968, II. p. 456).

5.4 The Crisis of 1765—When the Shadow of Malthus Loomed Over the Catalan Economy

Having overcome the 1727 crisis, our demographic curves do not give any signs of important setbacks until the middle of the 1760s. It is true that the baptisms curve shows a slight fall in the 1730s which bottoms out at the end of this decade coinciding with certain momentary upturns in mortality in certain parishes of the sample. There is, however, every reason to believe that this inflection in the rate of demographic growth is much more related to the fact that it was in those years that the generations decimated by the War of the Spanish Succession reached adult age (and therefore that of procreation) rather than to the appearance of serious problems not of a strictly demographic nature.

Starting from the early 1740s, the increase in baptisms in our sample of 42 parishes resumed strongly and accelerated during the 1750s. Between the low point of 1738 and the maximum of 1758, the annual average rate of growth achieved a level which we can only describe as impressive: 2.18%. This impulse lasted until the mid-1760s, when the expansive dynamics was cut short, revealing not just short-term difficulties but also the structural limits of the extensive growth characteristic of the societies of the Ancien Régime. The fact that the fall in baptisms (births) coincided with the intense upturn in mortality, which occurred in 1764, warns us that this may be a phenomenon with too great a scope and intensity to be explained by exclusively demographic factors.

Pierre Vilar was the first to suggest the possibility that, precisely between 1763 and 1774, a situation of at least relative "over-population" was beginning to appear in Catalonia (Vilar, 1964–1968, III. pp. 126–127). The subsequent works on the crisis of the mid-1760s, by J. M. Puigvert (1985) and A. Simon, have confirmed Vilar's interpretation on exposing the mixed character of this crisis due to the combination "of an epidemic factor [...] with the effects of a food crisis", which revealed "population-resources imbalances from which the Principality did not escape despite the agricultural transformations initiated in some Catalan regions" (Simon, 1995).[5]

Two elements reinforce this interpretative outline of the difficulties of a Malthusian type which loomed over the Catalan economy at the beginning of the second third of the eighteenth century: firstly, the downward evolution in real wages and, secondly, the changes in relative prices.

In relation to wage evolution, we have tried to summarize the data available in Fig. 5.4. The downward trend in real wages (expressed in terms of wheat) is very clear until the beginning of the 1770s, a fall which corresponds very clearly with the positive evolution in demography described above. The situation of relative demographic excess was pathetically revealed at the time of the 1763–1764 crisis, when the masses of starving peasants, underemployed in the countryside, moved to the urban centres, mainly Barcelona, as narrated by contemporary chroniclers. The parish priest of Riudellots de la Selva, in the midst of the 1764 subsistence crisis, observed (probably exaggerating the figures somewhat) that "the poor who regularly go to Girona on the three days of alms at present are more than ten thousand, and in Barcelona the poor outsiders who have gone there are more than fifteen thousand and there the step has therefore been taken to give stew or soup in different parts of the city, and in others alms of bread". The term "poor" to refer to that multitude of people from the countryside who, not without certain disorientation, came to the cities attracted by the measures taken by the authorities to try to contain "the general famine and disease" (Puigvert, 1985, p. 72), demonstrates the structural character that poverty was taking in more or less broad sectors of the rural population in those central years of the eighteenth century.

In relation to the second question mentioned, the changes in relative prices, it is only necessary to compare the evolution of the price of a basic food product such as wheat, with that of wine, a product which had become characteristic of commercial agriculture and of Catalan exports. Both in Catalunya *dins l'Espanya moderna*, and in a previously published work, Vilar already demonstrated how it was precisely starting from 1754 that wheat prices took the lead over those of wine. In that year, for the

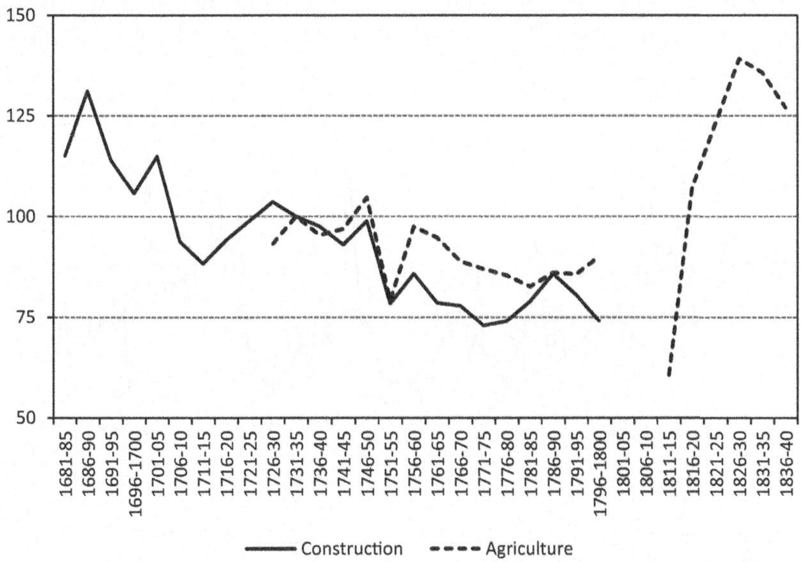

Fig. 5.4 Evolution of agricultural and of construction wages, 1682–1838 (Five-year average index numbers 1731–1735 = 100) (*Sources* Garrabou et al. [1999, pp. 422–460] and Feliu [1991, pp. 71–129]) (*Source* See the main text)

first time since 1690, the sum obtained from the sale of a *càrrega* of wine was not sufficient to buy a *quartera* of wheat. From then until the beginning of the nineteenth century when Vilar ends his analysis, the prices of wine never again succeeded in reaching those of wheat (Vilar, 1964, pp. 301–324; 1964–1968, III, pp. 430–434). Using Vilar's methodology, but with figures much more refined than his, it was recently possible for us to extend his exercise until much later (Fig. 5.5).

The deterioration of the terms of exchange of wine during the third quarter of the eighteenth century can be clearly seen in Fig. 5.5, and it was therefore necessary to await the stage subsequent to the Peninsular War in order to see a significant improvement in the same, although the trend was likewise downwards. This phenomenon should also be directly related to the situation of growing tension between the population and resources which was outlined starting from the central years of the eighteenth century.

In any case, the shadow of Malthus which had begun to be cast on the contours, especially in the rural world, of the Catalan economy, soon disappeared. The threat of a collapse of the upward dynamics, which the nature of the 1763–1764 crisis seemed to announce, did not materialize.

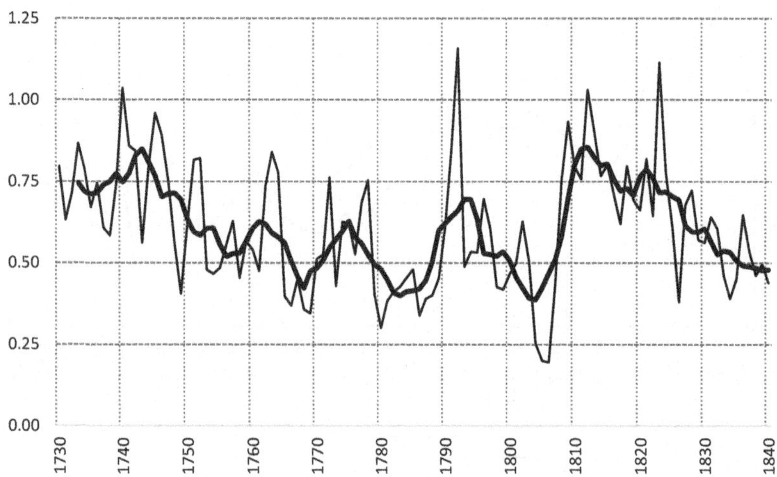

Fig. 5.5 Relative prices of wine. Hl of wheat purchased with one Hl of wine (annual values and moving averages for 7 years) (*Source* Colomé et al. [2013])

The strengthening of changes of a qualitative type that had already begun to be tested in the preceding decades made it possible to escape from the Malthusian trap, at least for the moment. In this respect, as far as agriculture is concerned, despite the deterioration in the terms of trade of wine, the intensification of the winegrowing specialization process in a broad sector of the country can be understood as a Boserupian-type emergence from this situation of growing tension between the population and the land available in so far as winegrowing, as is well-known, represents a more intensive use of this factor which had become scarce in relative terms (Boserup, 1965).[6] It should be recalled that it was in these last decades of the eighteenth century when the process of winegrowing clearings became unusually strong, regulated by the *rabassa morta* contract in a very broad sector of the Catalan pre-coastal area, making it possible to sustain increasingly high population densities in these locations (Colomé et al., 2010; Moreno, 1995; Valls-Junyent, 1997).

In addition to the intensification of the winegrowing orientation of agriculture in certain regions, the difficulties of the 1760s occurred in a period during which, as we will see below, the expansion of the manufacturing industry contributed both to mitigating the under-employment that was taking place in the rural world and also to giving work to those rural masses, which, at especially critical times, moved to the cities attracted by a better-organized welfare network (Carbonell, 1997).

In the case of the main traditional manufacturing industry of the country, drapery, Montserrat Duran has shown us how, in one of the main drapery centres of the country, Igualada, production increased in a sustained manner between 1740 and 1800, after which it began to fall quickly, mainly as a result of competition from the new cotton industry (Duran, 2012, pp. 41–45).

In other works, we have already explained the origins of cotton manufacturing, which was to become the symbol of Catalan industrialization (Grau & López, 1974; Sánchez, 1989b; Thomson, 1994).[7] Now we would just like to draw attention to the role that it played with a view to acting as a lifeline for an economy restricted by the limits arising from the considerable dependence on a traditional agriculture with substantial restrictions to manage to increase its levels of productivity. The fact is that, starting from 1760, the manufacture of printed calicoes took off in earnest, and its growth helped to stop, in the short term, the fall in real wages and to promote, in the medium and long term, a successful process of industrialization which had then already become irreversible.

5.5 "War with Everyone, and Peace with England"—The Crises of the End of the Century

The in-depth agricultural transformations (especially as regards specialization in the vine which "in the eyes of contemporaries is obviously the crop which characterized and symbolized the drive of the century") (Vilar, 1964–1968, III, p. 224) and an increase in the weight of manufacturing and industrial activities in the Catalan economy during the last third of the eighteenth century, at the same time as allowing it to escape from the Malthusian trap, also made the nature of the crises begin to change significantly and irreversibly.

The growing market orientation of the Catalan economy and especially the dependence on increasingly distant markets, access to which could be subject to numerous imponderables and contingencies, meant that the crises which broke out at the end of the century had significantly different causes and characteristics to those of the preceding stage. It is true that war again became a major crisis factor in the territory closest to the French border during the War of the Pyrenees (1793–1795), as already occurred at the end of the seventeenth century. However, the crises of the last two decades of the eighteenth and the first years of the nineteenth century revealed that very distant conflicts or those which took place in the oceans could have negative effects on the economy and on the population's standard of living as when an unbridled Mars devastated its own territory. A distant conflict such as the War of the Thirteen Colonies or the maritime disputes between France and England, in which the Spanish monarchy became involved, following the French, entailed the blocking of ports which obstructed the circuits through which imported goods flowed into the country or, on the contrary, through which the exports were channelled, on which an increasingly significant number of Catalan families depended.

As observed in Table 5.1, during the years 1781 and 1782, although in overall terms births exceeded burials, in over 30% of the towns in our sample there were, on the contrary, more burials than births. In 1783, there was no longer any doubt about the negative effect on the demography. In over 38% of towns, deaths exceeded baptisms. We can see the importance of this demographic crisis if we bear in mind that, with the exception of the year 1765, it is necessary to go back to 1725, at the end of the War of the Spanish Succession post-war period, to find a higher figure.

One of the causes of the demographic setbacks from 1781 to 1783 was a well-known epidemic that affected various locations of the Iberian Peninsula during those years.[8] However, beyond this circumstance, it is difficult for us not to relate the negative behaviour of demography during these early years of the 1780s to a whole series of problems of another kind to a large extent arising from Spanish participation in the war of independence of the Thirteen Colonies. Although it was not the first time that the disastrous consequences of the obstacles for the normal operation of Catalan foreign trade represented by maritime war were experienced, the effects were now more important given the growing export–import commercial orientation of the Catalan economy.

The pattern of this crisis—which we will see repeatedly without many variations in the crises at the turn of the century—is very simple. Firstly, the problems of navigation caused difficulties in the supply of foreign cereals, on which Catalonia increasingly depended as a result of its demographic growth and of the mounting winegrowing orientation of agriculture in increasingly broad sectors of the country. In the context of import difficulties, any bad harvest in the country's inland wheat-growing regions led to difficulties of supply, especially in Barcelona, although also in those regions which had a different productive orientation. Wheat prices, thus, shot up in Barcelona in 1782 (Fig. 5.6).

Secondly, the difficulties for transoceanic trade arising from the context of war stopped wine and eau-de-vie exports both to the markets of Northern Europe and also to the colonial market, which precisely at that time was acquiring an increasingly significant weight (Valls-Junyent, 2003, pp. 201–210). In this respect, the various testimonies collected by Voltes on the situation of collapse of the Catalan winemaking market during the first two years of the 1780s are very explicit. On 12 July 1780, a Barcelona trader expressed his concern to one of his correspondents because "the wine harvest throughout the Principality is very good, as has not been seen in many years, and we do not know where to place it; if these wars last it will be necessary to throw out the old wine to bring in the new, as has already occurred sometimes in this province, which on not being able to sell it at any price, they gave it as alms to the poor" (Voltes, 1961, p. 88). This impression is clearly confirmed by the evolution of wine prices (Fig. 5.6) which, precisely in 1780, reached their lowest point in a critical "intercycle" which, according to Vilar (1964–1968, III, pp. 420–438) and Labrousse (1944), we know also affected—even more severely—French winegrowing.

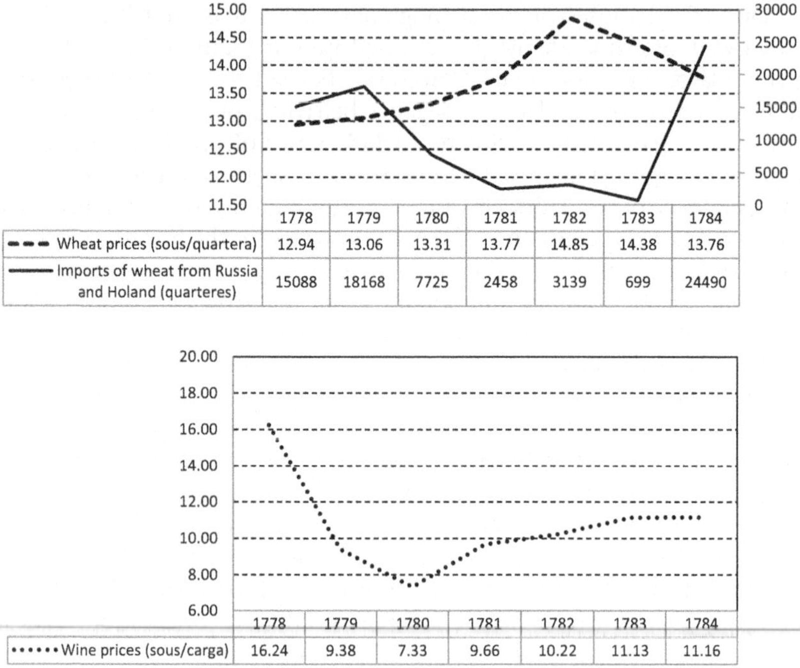

	1778	1779	1780	1781	1782	1783	1784
Wheat prices (sous/quartera)	12.94	13.06	13.31	13.77	14.85	14.38	13.76
Imports of wheat from Russia and Holand (quarteres)	15088	18168	7725	2458	3139	699	24490

	1778	1779	1780	1781	1782	1783	1784
Wine prices (sous/carga)	16.24	9.38	7.33	9.66	10.22	11.13	11.16

Fig. 5.6 Wheat imports, wheat prices and wine prices in Barcelona, 1778–1784 (*Source* Imports according to the data published by Voltes [1961, pp. 77 and 83]; prices according to Vilar [1964–1968, III, p. 431])

Thirdly and finally, however, these crises took on a more general nature, with a fall in consumption, which negatively affected those activities focused on the internal market, as a textile trader declared to one of the French suppliers of his shop:

> Si cette guerre continue nous serons entièrement en état de fermer nos magasins pour les avoir pleins de marchandises et le consome est fort peu, à cause de la misère qui regne par ce pahis pour être le commerce tout paré. Le bon Dieu veuille nous donner la consolation. (Voltes, 1961, p. 60)

The problems which were revealed in the context of the American War of Independence reappeared in an even clearer manner during the wars with England from 1796 to 1801 and, above all, from 1804 to 1807. In the midst of all this, there were, however, three critical episodes which we would like to mention in this analysis of the crises of this transitional phase: the 1787 commercial crisis, the 1789 subsistence crisis and the 1793–1795 crisis arising from the War of the Pyrenees.

The first of these three situations meant that, for the first time, the effects were categorically felt, especially in Barcelona, of a commercial crisis arising from the saturation of the colonial market, which had been favoured by the extraordinary expansion achieved by the trade towards Spanish America after 1783 when, after peace had been signed putting an end to the War of the Thirteen Colonies, the effects of the Free Trade declared in 1778 were fully expressed. The description of the 1787 crisis made at the time by J. M. Delgado fully shows the effects that it had on the level of both commercial and industrial companies (printed calico and painted linen factories which were mainly devoted to printing imported fabrics to be re-exported to America), which participated in this short exceptional moment which went from 1783 to 1787 (Delgado, 1982).[9] It is worth indicating, however, that the crisis was short and the recovery of activity took place very soon, with an unusual intensity which was maintained until the years of the War of the Pyrenees.

The second one is that of the 1789 disturbances, a subsistence crisis which led to a situation of considerable social tension but which, as shown in our series, did not have demographic consequences. Although the classic works on the subject focused on the events which occurred in Barcelona, more recent studies, such as those by M. Renom, have the great value of revealing the very general nature of the disorders (Castells, 1970; Moreu-Rey, 1967; Renom, 2012). According to the interpretation of J. Fontana (1998, pp. 123–126), it was a "disturbance characteristic of the system" (of the old system) which, far from announcing the end, "fully belongs to it and demonstrates its robustness". The fact that, with just two years' difference, two very characteristic episodes coincided, one of the new type of crisis (that of 1787) and the other of the old type of crisis (1789), is very symptomatic of this transitional character of those final years of the eighteenth century.

However, our data show that the specific difficulties of 1787 and 1789 never hindered the considerably upward dynamics experienced by demography (and also by the economy as a whole, we could add) between 1784 and 1793. Between these two dates, the births in our sample of parishes increased at an annual rate of 1.64%, one of the most intense rates of the whole century. Nevertheless, the positive tendency of the number of births in our sample of towns collapsed in the following two years, 1794 and 1795. At the same time, mortality shot up, taking natural growth to negative figures which exceeded those of the 1764 crisis. This critical episode corresponds to the consequences of the War of the Pyrenees, the effects of which were felt very intensely in the regions of the north of Catalonia, where a considerable part of the military operations were carried out, due to the proximity of the French border. It is true that the indirect negative effects of this war affected the whole country, but it is likewise true that the epicentre was very clearly in the northern regions which were those which experienced the greatest rigours: the destruction and burning of houses, theft of livestock and the destruction of crops, indiscriminate felling of woodland and damage to churches and the theft of holy objects, among many other vexations. The seriousness of the situation in Empordà caused the abandonment of some villages and a considerable demographic decline throughout the region (Roura, 1993, p. 240).

Overall, this recalls extraordinarily what occurred in the last years of the seventeenth century on the occasion of the Nine Years' War and simply predicted what would happen 15 years later, during the Peninsular War, the disastrous consequences of which, on that occasion, were not limited to a specific territorial sphere but rather affected practically the entire country. It should be added that this conflict also had serious physical consequences due to the extraordinary resources that had to be mobilized to bear its cost. These difficulties were in addition to the treasury problems that the monarchy had endured since the war of 1779–1783 and positions us in the antechamber of "bankruptcy of the absolute monarchy" (Fontana, 1971).

However, before analyzing the consequences of the Napoleonic occupation from 1808 to 1814, we should stop to address the extraordinarily critical situation arising from the effects of the two wars with England which took place almost continuously between 1786 and 1808. The hostilities only stopped in the three years of 1802, 1803 and 1804, but it was just in these years when for a moment it appeared that everything could return to normality, that one of the most intense demographic crises of the whole period analysed in this study broke out. Again, the demographic indicator appears to faithfully translate the accumulation of difficulties and hardships experienced during these years at the turn of the eighteenth to the nineteenth century.

We have already outlined the broad lines of the interpretative framework of these crises by referring to the years of the War of the Thirteen Colonies. It is now worth remarking the unusual intensity with which many of the phenomena described manifested themselves in those years at the turn of the century. Table 5.2 shows some indicators which can help us to understand the size of the calamity.

The signing of the Second Treaty of San Ildefonso in August 1796 between France and Spain opened the path for the beginning of a new conflict with England. Just one year later, the English had succeeded in blocking Spanish ports and, at the end of 1798, they had reoccupied Minorca and Trinidad. The immediate consequence of the conflict was a dramatic fall in colonial trade and a drastic reduction of North Atlantic trade, which was reduced to the traffic which permitted the presence of some vessels with neutral (especially Scandinavian) flags. The data from Table 5.2 is conclusive. The 58 shipments to the American colonies of 1796 were reduced to 9 in 1797. Moreover, although in the following years, there was a certain recovery, this did not even manage to increase the figure to half what it was during the years of peace.

The effects of the collapse in maritime trade had important consequences for export-oriented agriculture and for manufacturing activities. As can be seen in Table 5.2, eau-de-vie prices in the reference market of Reus collapsed between 1798 and 1800, being positioned between 30 and 40% below the level of 1796. As for manufacturing, the sectors most directly harmed were those which worked predominantly for the colonial market. This was the case of the Barcelona-painted linen factories, the paralysis of which was almost complete during those years. Other industrial sectors less dependent on colonial trade and more oriented towards the internal market also ended up being altered by the fall in demand that arose from the situation of depression, which affected various branches of activity. One indication of the size of the crisis in the printed calico and painted linen industry can be seen in the fall in corporate investment, a sector whose difficulties were multiplied in those years of the turn of the century not just due to problems of access to their markets but also due to the scarcity of raw cotton on the Barcelona market which the interruption of colonial trade caused (Sánchez & Valls-Junyent, 2015a). In this context, there were numerous bankruptcies, unemployment, poverty and related social problems that began to become a cause of concern for the authorities (Delgado, 1982).

Table 5.2 The crises from 1796 to 1801 and 1804 to 1807. Behaviour of some indicators

	Price of wheat in Tàrrega Lliures/ quartera	*Price of eau-de-vie in Reus* Lliures/carga	*Corporate investment in the cotton industry* Lliures	*American trade* *No. of shipments*	*Price of wheat in Tàrrega* *1796 = 100*	*Price of eau-de-vie in Reus* *1796 = 100*	*Corporate investment in the cotton industry* *1796 = 100*	*American trade* *1796 = 100*
1795	10.30	32.11	16,020	48	107	81	43	83
1796	9.65	39.64	37,380	58	100	100	100	100
1797	7.48	44.25	156,091	9	78	112	418	16
1798	7.64	23.84	24,030	21	79	60	64	36
1799	8.60	27.05	54,468	17	89	68	146	29
1800	6.55	25.06	7423	20	68	63	20	34
1801	6.52	49.13	0	14	68	124	0	24
1802	10.51	37.09	652,038	74	109	94	1744	128
1803	8.79	27.52	32,040	62	91	69	86	107
1804	8.58	20.87	427,200	64	89	53	1143	110
1805	9.40	21.02	26,700	21	97	53	71	36
1806	7.97	21.86	6098	8	83	55	16	14
1807	7.25	39.73	1602	8	75	100	4	14
1808	7.35	43.40	0	15	76	109	0	26

Sources Price of wheat, according to Garrabou (1970); price of eau-de-vie, according to Torras Elías (1976a); corporate investment, compiled by authors according to the articles of association of companies; number of shipments of American trade obtained from Delgado (1981)

The industrial crisis arising from the maritime blockade and from the paralysis of business affected especially Barcelona, but other towns which had experienced an important development of manufacturing activities, such as Sabadell, Igualada, Manresa and Olot, were not spared (Bosch, 2003, pp. 332, 341, 347 and 382; Jordà, 1975, pp. 51–57; Sarret, 1922, pp. 11–12; Torras Ribé, 1974).

The news of the negotiations of a peace treaty in October 1801 radically changed this panorama all around the country. In actual fact, the peace treaty still took some months to come (it was signed in Amiens in March 1802), but it opened the path for a substantially expansive situation, which unfortunately did not last long. In August 1804, a Barcelona trader wrote to an American correspondent that "we are faced with the disappointment of rumours of war, which is considered to be certain in relation to a division of English warships which have taken our fleet of four frigates coming from Lima with 10 million pesos and with this news all trade is disturbed, bringing its circulation to a standstill". In October, England again declared war against Spain, leading another Barcelona trader to make the following comment: "The tranquillity has already ended and we have another war with Great Britain... My friend, we'll have to make the best of a bad situation" (Delgado, 1982, p. 156).

Just like the 1779–1783 situation, in the context of the two crises which occurred during the years from 1796 to 1807, with only a short period of normality from 1802 to 1804, any contingency concerning the cereal harvest severely compromised the supply of the Principality, due to the fact that the import supply channels were obstructed by the maritime blockade. This was the case of the 1801 harvest, the insufficiency of which meant that there was a shortage in a large part of the Principality, as shown by the evolution in wheat prices in the markets of Tàrrega, Lleida and Barcelona.[10] The scarcity triggered a serious subsistence crisis in the winter of 1801–1802, especially in rural areas where it was more difficult to feel the positive effects of preliminary peace with England.

Overall, this allows us to understand perfectly the behaviour of the main demographic variables which we have decided to use as guidance on the recessions during the long period of time taken into consideration in this work. On the one hand, the curve of baptisms of our sample of parishes records a very significant decline of more than 25% from the maximum of 1798 to the minimum of 1800, remaining at this low level until 1804. On the other hand, mortality shot up in 1802 due to a typical mixed-type mortality crisis which just captured the effects of the above-mentioned subsistence crisis of that year and more generically all the negative effects of the depression caused by the war with England.

5.6 The Calamity of the Peninsular War

As predicted by the above-mentioned Barcelona trader, the tranquillity did not last long and the "bad situation" recommenced in the autumn of 1804, when the English fleet redoubled the corsair pressure on the Spanish merchant navy which wanted to cross the Atlantic. On that occasion, the stoppage of all economic activity related to foreign and, especially, colonial trade was even more radical than during the previous conflict from 1796 to 1802, as the data for these years, contained in Table 5.2, shows. At the end of 1804, the situation in the city of Barcelona was so desperate, due to the almost complete lack of activity in the factories, that it led to a considerable degradation of living conditions which, in turn, caused an increase in social delinquency to the extent that there were people who did not rule out the appearance of riots and, even, the outbreak of an uprising (Delgado, 1982, pp. 157–160).

The defeat at Trafalgar and the arrival in Barcelona of the news of the capture of the city of Buenos Aires by the English, in June 1806, unleashed all kinds of fears in the capital of the Principality. One very significant trader said:

> In this [Barcelona], with the disastrous news which is spreading about the taking of Buenos Aires by the English [...] everything is upset because all the trade with this news is overwhelmed as are [...] the factories, and I do not doubt that within a few days, if this is shown to be true, they will dismiss half of the operators and, if it comes to the crunch, we will not be safe in our houses. (Delgado, 1982, p. 159)

Things could, however, become worse and, indeed, they did. In October 1807, Spain was again forced to side with France in order to confront the pressure of the English on its trade and, especially, on the American colonies. This new rapprochement with France opened the path for the arrival of Napoleon's troops in the Iberian Peninsula.

The dreadful behaviour of demography that we observed starting from that date and during the years of the Peninsular War is the result of the accumulation of economic calamities which occurred in the years prior to the conflict and which the war itself only brought to a climax. It was, indeed, at the beginning of the war, in the context of a terrible economic crisis and as a result of the power vacuum caused by the transfer of the royal family to Bayonne, that the social outbreak predicted by the Barcelona trader in the letter that we transcribed above came off. When the disconcerted authorities of towns such as Manresa and Igualada did not know how to react in the face of the imminent arrival of the French, the people rioted, beginning a process which completely swept away the old established social order.[11]

The final crisis of the Ancien Régime, which led to the collapse of this system, had only just started in June 1808 and, as the conflict gradually spread, it progressed inexorably. In this context, one significant moment was the one that was experienced after the approval in August 1811 in the Courts of Cadiz of the decrees which declared the feudal regime to be abolished (Hernández, 1999). The effects of the approval of these legislative measures were immediate. In Orpí, near Igualada, the last appointment of a bailiff by the jurisdictional lord dates precisely from the previous year, 1810. In this village, during the Napoleonic occupation, the previous conflicts between the lord and his vassals began an escalation which led to the final crisis of the system (Torras Ribé, 1978).

We can observe the same in other locations. In Arenys de Mar a conflict broke out between the people and the Duke of Medinaceli (Gelabertó, 1991, pp. 35–38). In the jurisdiction of Tortosa, important jurisdictional lords, such as the Order of Saint John of Jerusalem, again the Duke of Medinaceli and the crown itself as the jurisdictional lord of some villages, experienced the indiscipline and insubordination of their vassals when it came to paying rent, a situation which was aggravated as a result of the loss by these lords of the prerogative to appoint officers, such as the bailiff, which traditionally allowed them to maintain an iron grip over their domains (Vinaixa, 1998, pp. 24–31). In short, these were the first steps in a long and very complex process, given that it was not just a question of demolishing the old building constructed by the rights which allowed the old aristocratic class to appropriate part of the surplus of the peasants, but rather, at the same time, it was necessary to build a new one to guarantee the rights of a new emerging owning class which, as revealed for the region of Girona by the works of R. Congost (1990, 1997), could replace the recipients of feudal rent as exploiters of the work of others.

During the almost six years which the Napoleonic occupation and the combats to achieve the liberation of Catalonia lasted, the economic and social situation collapsed to such an extent that, according to our demographic variables of reference, we can solidly state that the worst of the crises experienced in the 160 years taken into consideration took place. The size of the demographic crises of 1809 and 1812 cannot be compared with any of the others that we have studied, both in view of their intensity and of their absolutely general character. Only the years of the War of the Spanish Succession also had a very negative behaviour, but under no circumstance did the crisis of the beginning of the eighteenth century have a scope and intensity comparable with what occurred during the Napoleonic occupation.

As we have said, within the six years of the war as a whole, it is necessary to highlight especially dramatic episodes those corresponding to the years 1809 and 1812. The former was baptized by contemporaries as "the year of the diseases".[12] In that year, 85% of the parishes from our sample present a negative demographic balance. On average, burials exceeded baptisms by 153%! In the worst moments of the War of the Spanish Succession, this figure reached 63%. There can be no doubt that this demographic crisis can be described as "a true hecatomb".[13] Such a negative balance is explained by the virulence and the extension reached by a crisis of mortality of a mixed nature which, we should insist, does not just contain the first negative consequences of the war, which in actual fact had just begun, but rather arises directly from the persistence of a critical economic situation during the years prior to the Napoleonic invasion.

Numerous testimonies could be provided here on the seriousness of the 1809 crisis. From among all those available, possibly the most striking and conclusive is the one by that parish priest of Vallmoll who declare that there was overbooking in the old cemetery of the village because of the pestilence (Güell, 2013, p. 198). Moreover, if 1809 was "the year of the diseases", 1812 was "commonly called the year of hunger" (Puigjaner, 1881). The majority of contemporary testimonies insist on underlining the seriousness of the situation of food shortage which was suffered all over the country. Cereals were scarce and, above all, expensive. Indeed, all the prices had shot up in an inflationary context arising from a completely broken economy as a consequence of the French military occupation and of the insistent pressure of the guerilla which combated it intermittently but ceaselessly.

Economic activity was at a complete standstill in manufacturing centres such as Sabadell, due to the lack of raw materials, workers (who had been mobilized) and also due to the difficulties to access the markets. One distinguished industrialist from Sabadell complained about the transformation that the Vallès region underwent due to the war "what previously was a handful of gold due to the great work of the factories and the fields, is now the most miserable Country" (Benaul, 1993, pp. 14–15). In Barcelona, the majority of printed calico factories, although they endeavoured to maintain a certain activity during the early years of the conflict, towards the end of 1810 were forced to close their doors almost definitively, at least until the end of the conflict. Many manufacturers fled the city and those who, like Erasme de Gònima, chose to stay in order to thus try to prevent their factories from suffering from greater ills, were obliged to pay considerable quantities of money to the French occupiers.[14]

Catalan foreign trade and, more specifically, exports, were also practically at a standstill after the fall of Tarragona in June 1811. The assault of the city, led by Marshall Suchet, was one of the war's most bloodthirsty episodes. The entire civil population which remained in the city during the siege was assassinated and, once the city was captured, the authorities of the neighbouring towns were obliged to pass through the streets of the city covered with decomposing corpses. Until the siege, Tarragona had been a refuge for a large number of important Barcelona traders who, in so far as possible, endeavoured to maintain their activity, at least in a testimonial manner. In June 1811, the fall of Tarragona meant also the fall of the last redoubt of Catalan trade in the Peninsula. With the city in French hands, some traders set up in Palma de Mallorca and from the Island of Calm tried to continue their operations (Sánchez, 2010, p. 406).

In these circumstances, cereal imports became simply impossible and the cereal of the 1811 harvest was completely insufficient to guarantee the subsistence of the peasants themselves, if they were lucky and it was not confiscated by the troops from one or the other side who were moving up and down the territory. The commercial paralysis also affected the main export item, wine and eau-de-vie, which confronted a serious new development as a result of the incorporation of Catalonia in the French empire: competition from the wine production of Roussillon (Térmens & Valls-Junyent, 1987, p. 149).

The consequence of all this was the terrible famine of 1812. There are numerous testimonies of contemporaries who bear witness to the food shortage. In Valls, "the bread that they kneaded in individual houses had to be guarded by armed forces on being taken to and from the ovens of the town, in order to avoid it being stolen by the hungry crowds" (Puigjaner, 1881). In Alcover, "the neighbours are living in extreme poverty and many survive on alms. Almost all have lost their crops with so many troops passing through and [...] the other day others died, I think from hunger" (Güell, 2013, p. 212). In Subirats, "In the first days of the month of January 1812 wheat began to be lacking on the land and rose to exorbitant prices [...]; this lasted until the harvest of July 1812. During these six months, there was famine in Catalonia [...] There was an infinite number of poor who asked for charity. They had hunger and misery displayed on their face, weakness, paleness, the yellow colour appearing as the living image of death" (Colomé & Soler, 1997, p. 190). Even the French prefect of Boques de l'Ebre agreed with the above testimonies and was conclusive when he stated that "vers la fin de 1811 et dans les premiers jours de 1812, une infinité de malhereux sont morts de faim dans les campagnes" (Rovira, 1987, p. 51).

This episode left an indelible mark on the memory of the population who experienced it. After many years, the Peninsular War was still remembered thanks to the epic nature of certain (sometimes considerably mythicized) episodes, but also as one of the most dramatic moments experienced by the country. The demographic indicators that we have used in these pages, on positioning this episode as the most critical of the long period taken into consideration, fully subscribe to and confirm the most sinister judgements, opinions and descriptions of contemporaries.

5.7 The Crises of the Years of Collapse of the Ancien Régime and of the Liberal Revolution

After the end of the Peninsular War, a period began which, in social terms, witnessed the final collapse of the Ancien Régime as a result of the liberal revolution. However, on an economic level, the 25 years subsequent to the war were characterized by substantial deflation. The reversal of the upward tendency of prices which characterized the last decades of the eighteenth century was not an exclusively Catalan or peninsular phenomenon. It affected the European continent as a whole, more or less intensely in each country depending on the factors which in each case aggravated the downward trend of prices.

In Spain, among the factors which explain this significant change in the trend of prices, historiography has insisted on the role played by the factors of a monetary nature, arising from the reduction in the money supply due to the loss of the American continental colonies—and the consequent reduction in the arrival of silver—and from the important deficit in the current account balance which led to significant cash outflows (Sardà, 1948).[15] However, in 1978, in a pioneering work, J. Fontana (1978) put on the table the complexity presented by this phenomenon and the multiplicity of factors to be taken into consideration in order to understand it correctly, given that this was behind the explanation of the final collapse of the feudal system and of the discontent of the peasants in regions such as Catalonia, as we will see below. Thanks to the contribution by P. Nogués (2015), we now also know that Catalan deflation was not more intense and did not last longer than in other countries.

With a background of deflation, the Catalan economy had to undertake a profound restructuring in order to adapt to the succession of numerous changes that, both on Spanish and international levels, occurred from the final stages of the eighteenth to the early years of the nineteenth century. The readjustment and the adaptation to the new global state of affairs took place progressively during the quarter of a century following the Napoleonic occupation. According to a recently published work, four points summarize the changes which occurred between 1815 and 1840 (Catalan & Sánchez, 2013, pp. 89–93).

a. The loss of the American continental colonies forced a rearrangement of colonial trade which was obliged to withdraw to the Antilles. It was in relation to this change in the areas in which Catalan trade operated in the New Continent, that there was a recovery in this fundamental traffic in the second half of the 1820s. Thus, if in the best years of the eighteenth century (those from 1784 to 1796), the Catalans were capable of sending up to an annual average of 78 vessels to the American colonies, between 1828 and 1833 they had already achieved the significant figure of 125 vessels. This evolution culminated in the central years of the nineteenth century, when practically every day of the year a vessel set sail for the American continent from the port of Barcelona (Valls-Junyent, 2003, pp. 401–406).
b. The collapse of eau-de-vie exports to the north of Europe forced a profound reconversion of the most dynamic sector of the country's agriculture. It was now forced to focus on the production of wine, which had an increasing outlet in the Antillean markets. A large part

of the vessels mentioned in the above point are headed for these markets loaded with wine. The increase in American imports of raw cotton, a raw material with growing demand due to the expansion of the cotton industry, played a fundamental role in the coordination of this new export trend (Fradera, 1987).

c. The procurement of cereals in the productive areas of the peninsular interior in replacement of the traditional imports. It was essential to guarantee the supply of cereals in order to maintain and intensify the winegrowing orientation of the agriculture of increasingly broad sectors of the country, and, therefore, to maintain a type of agricultural activity with a much higher profitability per unit area, which it was impossible to attain with cereals (Colomé & Valls-Junyent, 1994).

   On the other hand, the ban on importing cereals that began in 1820 allowed a better organization of Catalan trade with the interior of the peninsula, based on the exchange of cereals-manufactured products (mainly textiles) (Fradera, 1984).

d. The maintenance of the commitment to the industry as a strategic sector due to the formulation of a project that P. Pascual described precisely as "industrialist", and that was based on two elements: the internal Spanish market—safeguarded by an important customs protection since the approval of the 1820 tariff,—and mechanization –with the aim of reducing costs and prices in order to reach a greater number of consumers (Pascual, 1990; Pascual & Sudrià, 2013). This decisive commitment to industry and to the internal market is well-known in the case of the wool industry thanks to the contributions of J. M. Benaul (1993). This author considers that, in relation to the wool district of Vallès, "the destruction caused by the war should not be overestimated". The demographic losses and the consequent scarcity of labour may have been an incentive for mechanization. The loss of the American colonies did not affect the demand of companies traditionally focused on the internal market. According to Benaul (1991, p. 816), in 1824, the Sabadell-Terrassa district had already reached the production levels of 1794. Although the recovery was fast in the case of an industry such as wool, which had always been geared towards the internal market, it would also appear that the cotton industry did not take long to complete a deep reconversion which involved completely abandoning the painting (finishing) of imported linen to be sent to the colonial market, while focusing on strictly cotton production for the Spanish market (Sánchez, 1989b, 2000, 2010). The limit of almost 1300 tonnes of raw cotton imported in the best years of the 1790s had been greatly exceeded by 1819, when our sources indicate arrivals in the port of Barcelona of close to 2000 tonnes (Sánchez & Valls-Junyent, 2015a). Since 1830, this recovery was based on an intensification of the mechanization process (especially spinning) which represented substantial investment. This mechanization, on taking place in a period of relative scarcity of labour and of increase in real wages, confirmed that the Catalan case adapted to the explanatory parameters of the dissemination of the new textile technologies that R. Allen (2009) applied to his reinterpretation of the origin of the British Industrial Revolution, as also suggested in some interesting recent research by J. Martínez and M. Prat (2016), in relation to when the first spinning machines were adopted.

Overall, this profound rearrangement experienced by the Catalan economy and society during the quarter of a century subsequent to the Peninsular War resulted in the previous territorial balance being broken and caused considerable social tension, which led to substantial unrest. On a territorial level, those areas in which it was difficult to adapt to changes of the size of those proposed supported an unyielding defence of the traditional social order proposed by, at first, the realist movements, and, subsequently, the Carlists. In social terms, the triumph of industrialization, at the same time as supporting the most dynamic sectors which promoted it (the commercial and industrial bourgeoisie), represented the appearance of a (fundamentally urban) proletariat, which began to openly reveal the contradictions of the bourgeois liberal order and to demand social justice and more democracy. The unrest arising from these social tensions is the principal element to take into account on explaining the two main critical moments indicated by the demographic curves that we have reconstructed.

The first episode corresponds to 1823 and, although a very short crisis—only that year presents extremely bad demographic behaviour—, we should not lose sight of the fact that it was an intense and very general crisis. Our indicators position the second one in the mid-1830s, coinciding with the most acute phase of the First Carlist War and with the culmination of the social unrest linked to the liberal revolution.

The 1823 demographic crisis simply revealed a whole series of problems and difficulties which broke out in the context of considerable political instability following Riego's uprising in 1820 and the restoration of the 1812 Constitution (Ardit, 1977; Arnabat, 1991; Gutiérrez, 1987; Torras Elias, 1976b). Indeed, two years earlier, in 1821, a yellow fever epidemic had already attacked a whole series of towns, including the capital itself.[16] It is quite possible that the general nature of the crisis of mortality indicated by our sources for 1823 was just the direct consequence of the spread of that epidemic in the country, favoured by circumstances such as the extremely bad harvests recorded in 1821 and 1822 due to the drought, but also to the growing difficulties of peasant economies for which deflation made the increase in fiscal pressure by a bankrupt state, especially burdensome (Fontana, 1978, 2003; Pascual, 1980; Torras Elias, 1976b). This context explains the attack on the last vestiges of the feudal system and the irreparable collapse of manorial income at the same time as the triggering of the proto-Carlist realist uprisings which took place from the spring of 1822 and which converted the country into the setting for a civil war (Ardit, 1977; Arnabat, 1991).

Apart from this serious one-off crisis in 1823, our demographic indicator does not show any other dramatic moment until the 1830s, when all kinds of difficulties arising from the civil war began to become apparent, but also from the substantial urban social unrest associated with the development of the liberal revolution. The demographic balance of our sample of parishes was always positive for the decade from 1824 to 1833. The new pre-Carlist revolt of 1827 (the War of the Aggrieved) did not leave any perceptible sign in the demographic behaviour. It was precisely two years earlier, in 1825, when our curve of baptisms achieved its maximum level. From then on, there was a downward trend which quite possibly did not have anything to do with a change in economic situation but rather with profound modifications in the patterns of reproductive behaviour of the Catalans related to the process of demographic transition (Benavente, 1980). This behaviour of natality should be taken into account considering the intensity of the demographic crisis of the years of the Carlist war. The negative balances of the years 1836 and 1838 in an important number of towns from the sample can be explained in part by this substantial downward evolution in the number of baptisms which had begun considerably earlier, at least since the second half of the 1820s. Given this downward trend in births, any upturn in mortality could have a much more intense negative impact on the demographic balance.

With this, we do not want to diminish the importance of the size of the crisis of the second half of the 1830s, which clearly responds to a very specific type of crisis, defined recently by R. Vallejo (2013) as a "catastrophe of war" in which the war is simply the exercising of political violence or the prolongation of politics by other means. It was during these years from 1836 to 1838 that a large part of the Catalan territory (only with the exception of a narrow band close to the coast) cruelly suffered from the disastrous effects of such a specific type of war like the First Carlist War. According to Vallejo, we could call this war one of "low intensity" and which very often carried out inseparable actions which we could describe as strictly military and others more characteristic of actions of delinquency and banditry (Anguera, 1995; Mundet, 1990; Santirso, 2011; Sauch, 2004). Looting, burning, murder and kidnapping were a commonplace in the interior, where the Carlist side could be found, while almost simultaneously, in those same years in the city of Barcelona and in other urban centres considered as bastions of the liberals, the social tensions took the form of "disturbances" (Ollé, 1993). All this formed part of the convulsions characteristic of the final moments of the Ancien Régime and of the strengthening of the new regime. The setbacks indicated by our demographic curves during those years simply respond to these tensions.

5.8 Concluding Remarks

The period of more than one and a half centuries which goes from the publication of the *Fènix de Catalunya* to the end of the First Carlist War has been characterized as a stage of strong economic growth. Notwithstanding this, the expansion was, at times, compromised by crises of varying intensity. Using as an indicator the series of baptisms and burials from a sample of 42 Catalan parishes, we have tried to identify the most critical moments over these almost 160 years. In total, we identified 16 crises which, overall, cover 41 years.

The overview obtained allows us to state that the most serious crises suffered during this long century and a half are related to armed conflicts. The crisis arising from the Napoleonic occupation and from the war to which it gave rise stands out above any other. The absolutely devastating effects of the 1809 epidemic and the 1812 famine left a brutal mark on the demographic curves that we have reconstructed. The crisis arising from the War of the Spanish Succession is in second position as regards the depth and seriousness attained. Especially striking is the persistence of the depression during the post-war years, undoubtedly due to the draconian conditions imposed by the Bourbon military occupation and uncontrolled repression. If we moreover add that one of the most critical episodes of the long period analysed occurred between 1836 and 1840, coinciding with the First Carlist War, we can conclude that armed conflicts are the main explanation for the most critical situations (Vallejo, 2013).

The study of the episodes of crisis contained in the preceding pages also leads us to conclude that crises, as an economic and social phenomenon, showed a changing character during the period between 1680 and 1840. This is because, in that period, the first significant steps were taken in the transition from an economy clearly geared towards self-consumption (fundamentally producing articles with only value in use) and with very limited external exchanges, to an economy destined to produce goods with exchange value, increasingly dependent on distant markets and, therefore, subject to the vicissitudes of international trade. If we first add to the crises caused by war those arising from famines and epidemics, the panorama that this offers us is one of a world in which, according to the outline traced by J. A. Schumpeter in his classic book on economic cycles, the factors which he calls "external" to the economic sphere were predominant on triggering catastrophes (Schumpeter, 1939). This would therefore be one of the phenomena of an apocalyptic nature that befell a pre-industrial type of society characterized by a weak degree of commercial development.

This approach has now been widely reviewed by mediaevalist and modernist historians who, from different points of view (especially from a Marxist and neo-Malthusian perspective), have endeavoured to "internalize" this "external" character of the factors triggering the most serious pre-industrial crises (Benito, 2013). However, this is not the central issue of a research such as ours, through which we have detected a clear breaking point in the 1760s and 1770s in relation to the previous dynamics. We confirmed that, in the mid-1760s, the long shadow of a Malthusian-type crisis was hanging over the Catalan economy. Subsistence crises such as that of 1764 would appear to endorse this idea.

However, the Catalan economy was able to escape from the Malthusian trap by expanding the transformations which it had already begun to undertake in two aspects. On the one hand, the specialization in wine-growing was accentuated, representing the main line of modernization of agriculture in a context of a Mediterranean world that would find it difficult to implement the new production techniques which, at the time, were revolutionizing North Atlantic agriculture. The wine industry provided a product with exchange value, which could be used to obtain the food resources that a rapidly growing population required. In this case, this was obviously achieved by strengthening the link with the market, which was to guarantee a paid outlet for the product of the vine, whether as wine or as eau-de-vie, and which, in turn, was to provide the food that it desisted from producing in order to increase the specialization in winegrowing.

On the other hand, both traditional (drapery) and modern (printed calico) manufacturing industries achieved unusual development in the last third of the eighteenth century. The labour opportunities that were offered, either through domestic work or in the new factories, made it possible to stop the decline in real wages which can be observed from the 1760s. With this trend reversed, when real wages rose significantly after the Peninsular War, the intensification of the process of mechanization in the industry became inevitable. In short, what we would like to remark is the fact that these dynamics represented a strengthening of the links with the market for broad sectors of the Catalan population, either by selling the surplus agricultural production or by marketing all or part of the labour force.

This is why the crises at the end of the eighteenth century were of a very different nature to those of the middle of the century. The struggles of the main European powers for continental, maritime and colonial hegemony had effects on the economy of the Principality that would have been unimaginable for the Catalans of two or three generations before. The repetition of this type of problems during the last years of the eighteenth and the first years of the nineteenth century triggered a situation of social crisis which began to be revealed in the context of the Peninsular War, which led to the final collapse of the Ancien Régime. We would like to underline that the crises subsequent to the Peninsular War, in the years of the Liberal Triennium and during the Carlist civil war, played a major role in the social convulsions arising from such momentous changes as these. Despite these setbacks revealed by our curves of baptisms and deaths, the final triumph of liberalism and of capitalist industrialization was achieved during those years (Fontana, 2003).

Notes

1. The series of baptisms and deceases used correspond to the populations indicated, together with the origin of the data: Mediona, St. Quintí de Mediona, la Geltrú, Gelida, Vilafranca del Penedès, St. Llorenç d'Hortons, Vilanova and Pacs come from Muñoz (1990); St. Pere de Riudebitlles, in Torrents (1995); Tiana-Montgat, Aguilar de Segarra, Calders, Rajadell, Sta. Ma. d'Oló, Balsareny and Casserres were kindly provided by Llorenç Ferrer Alós; Sentmenat and Maldà were supplied to us by Enric Tello (we have accepted the statistical corrections introduced by Enric Tello himself); Pierola comes from the own count carried out in the corresponding sacramental books, deposited at the Arxiu Diocesà de Barcelona; El Vendrell, for the period from 1680 to 1800, the data was obtained from Caralt (1986), for the period from 1801 to 1840, we made use of the count by Feliu Villaró (2010); Barberà de la Conca, according to the count published by Juliano (1985, pp. 47–114); Cabanes, Castelló d'Empúries, l'Escala, Navata and Roses, we took the data from Planas (1985); Torrelles de Llobregat and Sant Just Desvern were kindly supplied to us by J. Nadal; Xerta, according to data from Fabregat Galcerà (2002); Botarell, Bràfim, Catllar, Garidells, Pobla de Montornés, Cornudella, Poboleda and Ulldemolins, Andreu (1995); Llavaneres, Estadística parroquial de 1509 a 1955 y contribución al estudio de la demografia comarcal. (1956, 16 September). *Hoja Parroquial, 38*. This information had already been used by Vilar (1964–1968, III, pp. 82 and 121); Lleida, Camps Clemente and Camps Surroca (1983), and Pifarré (1998); Igualada, own count for the period 1680–1800 and for the rest of the years the information comes from Castellà (1901); Mataró has the doctoral thesis by Ros (2004); Vila-Rodona, for the period from 1680 to 1799, we have the count made by Comas (1986) and for the period from 1800 to 1840 Santesmases (1984, pp. 77–80 and 81–84).

   The selection of parishes was undertaken based on criteria of continuity of the series, territorial coverage, and quality of the information. In relation to the latter, we rejected those parishes in which the data for burials clearly presented an under-registration of the deaths of "albats" (children who died before having the use of reason).
2. The title that Pierre Vilar gave to the chapter dedicated to this period in *Catalunya dins l'Espanya moderna* is very significant: "1660–1705: segon redreçament català. Renovació de l'esperit d'iniciativa", that can be translated as: 1660–1705: Second Catalan Turnaround. Renewal of the Spirit of Initiative (Vilar, 1964–1968, II, pp. 373–411).
3. Subsequent studies have reinforced the theory of a country subjected to an impossible tax regime in the post-war context. In this respect, see Delgado (1987, pp. 25–40) and Delgado (2015, pp. 373–384).

4. We find a positive view of the cadastre in a recently published work: Tortella (2014); and also in the summary by Canal (2015, p. 109).
5. There is abundant news on the intensity of the famine, prior to the outbreak of the crisis in mortality strictly speaking. In the correspondence of the very significant Barcelona trading house of Alegre i Gibert it is said that "the news of the lack of food supplies is regrettable, much more inland and not along the coast, so that swarms of people are going and offering to work in many places just for subsistence". Biblioteca de Catalunya, Arxiu, Fons Alegre, reg. 383 (letter addressed to Solivera of Cadiz of 18.2.1764), transcribed by Simon (1995, p. 97).
6. The approach of the Danish economist is presented as an alternative to the pessimistic English cleric T.R. Malthus (1798).
7. You will find a recent panorama of the cotton sector during the eighteenth century in *Barcelona. Quaderns d'Història,* 2011, a case study with the title *La indústria de les indianes a Barcelona, 1730–1850*, coordinated by Àlex Sánchez, Sánchez (2011).
8. As was acknowledged in a preliminary warning in the publication of the results of the 1787 Floridablanca census: "It should be noted that this enquiry was undertaken after three years of an almost general epidemic of tertian and putrid fevers, especially in the two Castiles, the Kingdom of Aragon, and the Principality of Catalonia, which resulted in a considerable reduction in inhabitants". *Censo español executado de órden del rey comunicada por el excelentísimo señor conde de Floridablanca primer secretario de estado y del despacho en el año 1787*, Imp. Real, s.a., "Advertencia". See, on the effects of this epidemic in the specific case of Solsona, Planes (1986).
9. On the speculative character of the activity of many printed calico factories, see, by the same author, Delgado (1993). See also, Sánchez (1992) and Nadal (1991).
10. For Tàrrega, see table 5.2. On the behaviour of Lleida's market prices, see Vicedo (2008); and for Barcelona, Vilar (1964–1968, III, pp. 377–391).
11. On the events of June 1808 in some Catalan locations, see, for the case of the burning of the French stamped paper in Manresa, the classic work by Sarret (1922, pp. 21–28). In relation to Igualada, see Mercader (1950, pp. 87–100).
12. According to the expression by the priest of Torredembarra, Mn. Marià Miró, compiled by Güell (2013, p. 35).
13. Benaul (1993, p. 11) indicates that in Terrassa the 1809 mortality eliminated 21% of the total population.
14. Once the war had finished, Gònima lamented about everything he had had to suffer during the six years the city was occupied by the "wicked French", to whom the payments "of so many hundreds of *duros*", under

the threat of "the Ciudadela or Montjuich", he considered had ruined him (Sánchez, 2010, pp. 401–407).

15. More recently, the subject has been addressed by Pascual and Sudrià (1992).
16. Having reached Barcelona, apparently brought by two ships from Havana, it caused an almost complete standstill of economic activity, leaving without work a large number of workers who, in September, rioted and went to the Plaça de St. Jaume shouting: "We are hungry! We want bread!" (Arnabat, 2001, pp. 195–196; Fradera, 1997, p. 87).

References

Albareda, J. (1988). Els dirigents de la revolta pagesa de 1687–1689: De barretines a botiflers. *Recerques, 20*, 151–170.

Albareda, J. (1991). Catalunya a finals del segle XVII: la continuïtat de la revolta. In E. Serra (Ed.), *La revolució catalana de 1640* (pp. 291–317). Crítica.

Albareda, J. (1993). *Els Catalans i Felip V*. Editorial Vicens Vives.

Albareda, J. (1995). L'impacte de la guerra dels Nou Anys a Catalunya. L'ocupació francesa de 1697. *Afers, 20*, 29–46.

Albareda, J. (2010). *La guerra de Sucesión de España (1700–1714)*. Crítica.

Allen, R. (2009). *The British Industrial Revolution in Global Perspective*. Cambridge University Press.

Andreu, J. (1995). *El Camp de Tarragona i el Priorat durant els segles XVIII i XIX: les bases demogràfiques, agràries i comercials de l'expansió setcentista* (Doctoral Thesis). Universitat Autònoma de Barcelona

Anguera, P. (1995). *Déu, Rei i Fam. El primer carlisme a Catalunya*. Publicacions de l'Abadia de Montserrat.

Ardit, M. (1977). *Revolución liberal y revuelta campesina*. Ariel.

Arnabat, R. (1991). *Els aixecaments reialistes i el Trienni Liberal (1820–1823). El cas del Penedès i l'Anoia*. Rafael Dalmau Editor.

Arnabat, R. (2001). *La revolució de 1820 i el Trieni Liberal a Catalunya*. Eumo.

Arranz, M., & Grau, R. (1991). L'economia urbana de Barcelona i la Guerra de Successió. *Recerques, 24*, 115–142.

Benaul, J. M. (1991). *La indústria textil llanera a Catalunya, 1750–1870. El procés d'industrialització al districte industrial de Sabadell-Terrassa* (Doctoral Thesis). Universitat Autònoma de Barcelona.

Benaul, J. M. (1993). *Guerra i canvi econòmic. L'impacte de la guerra del Francès en la indústria tèxtil llanera de Sabadell i Terrassa, 1808–1814*. Fundació Bosch i Cardellach.

Benavente, J. (1980). La minva de la fecunditat a Catalunya. In J. Nadal, J. Maluquer de Motes, C. Sudrià, & F. Cabana (Eds.), *Història Econòmica de la Catalunya Contemporània, s. XIX, Població i agricultura* (pp. 79–119). Enciclopèdia Catalana.

Benito, P. (2013). De Labrousse a Sen. Modelos de causalidad y paradigmas interpretativos de las crisis alimentarias preindustriales. In P. Benito Monclús (Ed.), *Crisis alimentarias en la Edad Media. Modelos, explicaciones y representaciones* (pp. 15–32). Ed. Milenio.

Bhaduri, A. (1983). *The Economic Structure of Backward Agriculture*. Academic Press.

Bosch, A. (2003). *Memòria de las cosas notables de la vila de Sabadell comensat en desembre de 1787* (edition prepared by J. Alsina & M. Forrellad). Editorial Mediterrània.

Boserup, E. (1965). *The Conditions of Agricultural Growth: The Economics of Agrarian Change under Population Pressure*. Allen & Unwin.

Camps Clemente, M., & Camps Surroca, M. (1983). *Aspectes sanitaris de l'arxiu de Sant Joan en Lleida: segle XVII* (Doctoral Thesis). Universitat de Barcelona.

Canal, J. (2015). *Historia mínima de Cataluña*. Turner.

Caralt, S. (1986). *Evolució demogràfica del Vendrell: segles XVI-XIX* (Doctoral Thesis). Universitat Autònoma de Barcelona.

Carbonell, M. (1997). *Sobreviure a Barcelona. Dones, pobresa i assistència al segle XVIII*. Eumo.

Casas, J. (2015). *La hisenda municipal catalana. De la baixa edat mitjana a la revolució liberal (segles XIII-XIX)*. Pagès Editors.

Castells, I. (1970). Els rebomboris del pa de 1789 a Barcelona. *Recerques, 1*, 51–81.

Català Roca, P. (1987). *La plaga de la llagosta a Catalunya (1686–1688)*. Rafael Dalmau.

Catalan, J., & Sánchez, A. (2013). Cinco cisnes negros. Grandes depresiones en la industrialización moderna y contemporánea, 1500–2012. In F. Comín, & M. Hernández, (Eds.), *Crisis económicas en España. 1300–2012. Lecciones de la historia* (pp. 83–112). Alianza Editorial.

Colomé, J., & Soler, R. (Eds.) (1997). *Els mons d'Isidre Mata del Racó. Notes d'un propietari pagès al Penedès de la fi de l'Antic Règim*. Ajuntament de Sant Sadurní d'Anoia.

Colomé, J., & Valls-Junyent, F. (1994). La viticultura catalana durant la primera meitat del segle XIX. Notes per a una reflexió. *Recerques, 30*, 47–68 Ed. 62.

Colomé, J., Cucurella, M., & Valls-Junyent, F. (2010). Poblament i despoblament a la Catalunya vitícola (1760–1910). *Butlletí de la Societat Catalana d'Estudis Històrics, 21*, 137–155.

Colomé, J., Planas, J., Garcia, R., & Valls-Junyent, F. (2013). Les cicles de l'économie viticole en Catalogne. L'évolution du prix du vin entre 1680 et 1935. *Annales du Midi. Revue de la France Méridionale, 281*, 29–55.

Comas, J. (1986). *Demografia i Societat Rural a Vila-Rodona durant l'Antic Règim (segles XVI-XVIII)* (Bachelor's Thesis). Universitat de Barcelona.

Congost, R. (1990). *Els propietaris i els altres*. Eumo.

Congost, R. (1997). De pagesos a hisendats. Reflexions sobre l'anàlisi de grups socials dominants. La regió de Girona (1780–1840). *Recerques, 35*, 51–72.

Congost, R. (2000). *Els darrers senyors de Cervià de Ter. Investigacions sobre el caràcter mutant de la propietat (segles XVII-XX)*. Universitat de Girona-Biblioteca d'Història Rural.

Dantí, J. (1979). La revolta dels Gorretes a Catalunya (1687–1689). *Estudis d'Història Agrària, 3*, 79–100.

Dantí, J. (1990). *Aixecaments populars als Països Catalans (1687–1693)*. Curial.

Dantí, J. (2012). Catalunya entre el redreç i la revolta: Afebliment i diferenciciació social. *Manuscrits, 30*, 55–76.

Delgado, J. M. (1981). *Catalunya y el sistema de libre comercio (1778–1818)* (Doctoral Thesis). Universitat de Barcelona.

Delgado, J. M. (1982). El impacto de las crisis coloniales en la economía catalana (1787–1807). In J. Fontana (Ed.), *La economía española al final del Antiguo Régimen. III. Comercio y colonias* (pp. 102–118). Alianza Editorial.

Delgado, J. M. (1987). Presión fiscal y asignación de recursos en la monarquía borbónica. *Manuscrits, 4–5*, 25–40.

Delgado, J. M. (1993). "El algodón engaña". Algunas reflexiones en torno al papel de la demanda americana en el desarrollo de la indianería catalana. *Manuscrits, 11*, 61–83.

Delgado, J. M. (2014). L'economia del set-cents: Desfeta, represa i crisi. In J. Albareda (Ed.), *Catalunya, nació d'Europa 1714–2014, I* (pp. 152–153). Enciclopèdia Catalana.

Delgado, J. M. (2015). Después de Utrecht. El impacto de la nueva fiscalidad borbónica sobre la economía y la Sociedad catalanes del siglo XVIII. In J. Albareda & A. Alcoberro, (Eds.). *Els tractats d'Utrecht. Clarors i foscors de la pau. La resistència dels Catalans* (pp. 373–384). Institut Universitari d'Història Jaume Vicens Vives-Museu d'Història de Catalunya.

Duran, M. (1985). L'evolució de l'ingrés senyorial a Catalunya (1500–1799). *Recerques, 17*, 7–42.

Duran, M. (2012). *Llibre de la confraria y ofici de parayres de la vila de Igualada*. Fundació Noguera.

Espino, A. (1999). *Catalunya durante el reinado de Carlos II. Política y guerra en la frontera catalana, 1679–1697*. Universitat Autònoma de Barcelona.

Fabregat Galcerà, E. (2002). *L'evolució demogràfica del Baix Ebre i Montsià (1701–1900)* (Doctoral Thesis). Universitat Autònoma de Barcelona.

Feliu de la Penya, N., & Piles, M. (1983). *Fénix de Catalunya*. Generalitat de Catalunya. Original edition: (1683). Imp. de Rafael Figueró.

Feliu Villaró, F. (2010). *Anàlisi de la mortalitat segons els arxius parroquials del Vendrell del segle XIX (1801–1900)* (Doctoral Thesis). Universitat Rovira i Virgili.
Feliu, G. (1991). *Precios y salarios en la Cataluña moderna*. Banco de España.
Ferrer, L. (1981). L'Avalot de les Faves a Manresa. Un moment de la revolta de la terra a Catalunya el 1688. *Recerques, 11*, 125–135.
Ferrer, L. (2007). Una revisió del creixement demogràfic de Catalunya en el segle XVIII a partir dels registres parroquials. *Estudis d'Història Agrària, 20*, 17–68.
Fontana, J. (1955). Sobre el comercio exterior de Barcelona en la segunda mitad del siglo del siglo XVII. *Estudios de Historia Moderna, 5*, 198–219.
Fontana, J. (1971). *La quiebra de la monarquía absoluta (1814–1820). La crisis del Antiguo Régimen en España*. Ariel.
Fontana, J. (1978). La crisis agraria de comienzos del siglo XIX y sus repercusiones en España. *Hacienda Pública Española, 55*, 177–190.
Fontana, J. (1998). *La fi de l'Antic Règim i la industrialització (1787–1868)*. Ed. 62.
Fontana, J. (2003). *La revolució liberal a Catalunya*. Pagès Editors-Eumo.
Fontana, J. (2014). *La formació d'una identitat. Una història de Catalunya*. Eumo.
Fradera, J. M. (1984). El comercio de cereales y la prohibición de 1820 (el caso del mercado catalán). *Agricultura y Sociedad, 30*, 137–168.
Fradera, J. M. (1987). *Industria i mercat: Les bases comercials de la industria catalana moderna (1814–1845)*. Crítica.
Fradera, J. M. (1997). La febre groga del 1821 a Barcelona. In B. de Riquer (Ed.), *Història Política, Societat i Cultura dels Països Catalans, VI*. Enciclopèdia Catalana.
Garrabou, R. (1970). Sobre la formació del mercat català en el segle XVIII. Una primera aproximació a base dels preus dels grans a Tarrega (1732–1811). *Recerques, 1*, 83–121.
Garrabou, R., Tello, E., & Roca, A. (1999). Preus del blat i salaris agrícoles a Catalunya (1720–1936). In A. Carreras, P. Pascual, D. Reher, & C. Sudrià (Eds.), *Jordi Nadal: La industrialització i el desenvolupament economic d'Espanya, I* (pp. 422–460). Universitat de Barcelona.
Gelabertó, J. C. (1991). *Revolució liberal i guerra civil a la Marina de la Selva*. Caixa d'Estalvis Laietana.
Grau, R., & López, M. (1974). Empresari i capitalista a la manufactura catalana del segle XVIII. Introducció a l'estudi de les fabriques d'indianes. *Recerques, 4*, 19–57.
Güell, M. (2013). La guerra del Francès al Camp de Tarragona (1808–1814). El patiment de la societat civil. In R. Arnabat Mata (Ed.), *La guerra del Francès 200 anys després* (pp. 27–41). URV.

Gutiérrez, M. (1987). El trienni constitucional a la comarca de l'Anoia (1820–1823). *Miscellanea Aqualatensia, 4*, 153–180.
Hernández, F. J. (1999). *La abolición de los señoríos en España, 1811–1837*. Ed. Biblioteca Nueva.
Jordà, R. (1975). *La Guerra Gran vista des d'Olot (1793–1795)*. Rafael Dalmau Editor.
Juliano, D. (1985). Evolució demogràfica a Barberà de la Conca. *Aplec De Treballs, 7*, 47–114.
Kamen, H. (1979). Una insurrecció oblidada del segle XVII: l'alçament dels camperols catalans de l'any 1688. *Recerques, 9*, 11–28.
Labrousse, E. (1944). *La crise de l'économie française à la fin de l'ancien régime et au début de la Révolution*. Presses Universitaires de France.
Lobato, I. (1994). Activitat econòmica i actitud política de la burgesia mercantil barcelonina al final del segle XVII. La Família Dalmases. *L'avenç, 184*, 20–23.
Lobato, I. (1995). *Compañías y negocios en la Cataluña preindustrial*. Secretariado de Publicaciones.
Malthus, T. R. (1798). *An Essay on the Principle of Population*. J. Johnson.
Martinez, J., & Prat, M. (2016). Wages, Prices, and Technology in Early Catalan Industrialization. *Economic History Review, 69*(2), 548–574.
Mercader, J. (1950). ¿La Junta igualadina de 1808–1809, gobierno faccioso? *Miscellanea Aqualatensia, 1*, 87–100.
Mercader, J. (1955). Una visión pesimista de la economía catalana después de la guerra de Sucesión. *Estudios de Historia Moderna, 5*, 411–419.
Mercader, J. (1968). *Felip V i Catalunya*. Edicions 62.
Moreno, B. (1995). *La contractació agrària a l'Alt Penedès durant el segle xviii. El contracte de rabassa morta i l'expansió de la vinya*. Fundació Noguera.
Moreu-Rey, R. (1967). *Revolució a Barcelona el 1789*. Institut d'Estudis Catalans.
Mundet, J. M. (1990). *La primera guerra carlina a Catalunya*. Publicacions de l'Abadia de Montserrat.
Muñoz, F. (1990). *Creixement demogràfic. Mortalitat i nupcialitat al Penedès (segles XVII-XIX)* (Doctoral Thesis). Universitat Autònoma de Barcelona.
Nadal, J. (1991). Sobre l'entitat de la indianeria barcelonina del set-cents. Nota suggerida per la lectura d'un article d'Alexandre Sánchez. *Recerques, 24*, 181–185.
Nadal, J., & Giralt, E. (1960). *La population catalane de 1553 à 1717. L'immigration française et les autres facteurs de son développement*. SEVPEN.
Nogués, P. (2015). Análisis de la deflación española de la primera mitad del siglo XIX: Una comparación internacional. *Revista de Historia Económica, 23*(2), 371–405.
Ollé, J. M. (1993). *Les bullangues de Barcelona durant la primera guerra carlina (1835–1837)*. Edicions el Mèdol.

Pascual, P. (1980). Carlisme i societat rural, la Guerra dels Set Anys a la Conca d'Òdena. *Recerques, 10*, 51–91.

Pascual, P. (1990). *Agricultura i industrialització a la Catalunya del segle XIX. Formació i desestructuració d'un sistema economic*. Crítica.

Pascual, P., & Sudrià, C. (1992). Quiebra colonial y ajuste monetario en España. *Estudis d'Història Econòmica, 2*, 125–141.

Pascual, P., & Sudrià, C. (2013). Els catalans i l'economia. In J. Albareda, *Catalunya, nació d'Europa. 1714–2014. II* (pp. 29–93). Enciclopèdia Catalana.

Pifarré, F. (1998). *Aspectes sanitaris de l'arxiu parroquial de Sant Joan de Lleida, segles XVIII i XIX* (Doctoral Thesis). Universitat de Lleida.

Planas, M. (1985). *La Població de l'Alt Empordà al règim demogràfic antic* (Bachelor's Thesis). Universitat Autònoma de Barcelona.

Planes, R. (1986). Una crisis de mortalidad en el XVIII: Incidencia de las «fiebres pútridas» de 1783 en Solsona. *Cardener, 3*, 111–122.

Puigjaner, F. (1881). *Historia de la villa de Valls desde su fundación hasta nuestros días*. Imp. de Fco. Pellisser.

Puigvert, J. M. (1985). Misèries de l'any 1764: Narració d'una crisi alimentària d'Antic Règim per un clergue de la comarca de la Selva. *Manuscrits, 1*, 63–78.

Renom, M. (2012). La carestía de 1789 a Catalunya. Disfuncions mercantils, protestes veïnals i acció governamental. In G. Dorel-Ferré (Ed.), *Comme une étoffe déchirée. Les Catalognes avant et après le traité des Pyrénées* (pp. 65–80). Editions Trabucaire.

Ros, C. (2004). *Les estratègies familiars i la mobilitat social dels menestrals a Catalunya: segles XVII-XIX. El cas de Mataró* (Doctoral Thesis). Universitat Pompeu Fabra.

Roura, L. (1993). *Guerra Gran a la ratlla de França*. Curial.

Rovira, S. J. (1987). *La Guerra del francès a Altafulla: 175è aniversari de la batalla d'Altafulla*. Centre d'Estudis d'Altafulla.

Sánchez, A. (1989a). L'estructura comercial d'una fàbrica d'indianes barcelonina: Joan Rull i Cia (1790–1821). *Recerques, 22*, 9–24.

Sánchez, A. (1989b). La era de la manufactura algodonera en Barcelona, 1736–1839. *Estudios de Historia Social, 48–49*, 65–114.

Sánchez, A. (1992). La indianería catalana: ¿Mito o realidad? *Revista de Historia Industrial, 1*, 213–232.

Sánchez, A. (2000). Crisis económica y respuesta empresarial. Los inicios del sistema fabril en la industria algodonera catalana, 1797–1839. *Revista de Historia Económica, 3*, 485–524.

Sánchez, A. (2010). Guerra e industria. Consecuencias de la guerra de la independencia en la industria manufacturera Española. In E. de la Parra (Ed.), *La guerra de Napoleón en España. Reacciones, imágenes, consecuencias* (pp. 401–407). Publicacions de la Universitat d'Alacant-Casa de Velázquez.

Sánchez, A. (Ed.). (2011). *Barcelona. Quaderns d'Història, 17. La indústria de les indianes a Barcelona, 1730–1850*. Arxiu Històric.
Sánchez, A., & Valls-Junyent, F. (2015a). El mercado del algodón en Barcelona durante la crisis del Antiguo Régimen, 1790–1840. *Revista de Historia Industrial, 58*, 59–90.
Sánchez, A., & Valls-Junyent, F. (2015b). L'altre pa de la indústria. La procedència del cotó descarregat al port de Barcelona, 1790–1840. *Barcelona. Quaderns d'Història, 22*, 87–110.
Santesmases, J. (1984). *El segle XIX a Vila-Rodona*. Institut d'Estudis Vallencs.
Santirso, M. (2011). *Revolució liberal i guerra civil a Catalunya*. Pagès Editors.
Sardà, J. (1948). *La política monetaria y las fluctuaciones de la economía española en el siglo XIX*. CSIC.
Sarret, J. (1922). *Manresa en la Guerra de la Independencia. 1808–1814*. Imp. San José.
Sauch, G. (2004). *Guerrillers i bàndols civils entre l'Ebre i el Maestrat: La formació d'un país carlista (1808–1844)*. Publicacions de l'Abadia de Montserrat.
Schumpeter, J. A. (1939). *Business Cycles: A Theoretical, Historical, and Statistical Analysis of the Capitalist Process* (2 vols.). McGraw Hill.
Serra, E. (1986). Per una cronología i interpretació de la crisi del segle XVII. In E. Serra, R. Garrabou, N. Sales, P. Ruiz, E. Vicedo, E. Tello, L. Ferrer, et al. *Terra, treball i propietat. Classes agràries i règim senyorial als Països Catalans* (pp. 214–246). Crítica.
Serra, E. (1988). *Pagesos i senyors a la Catalunya del segle XVII*. Crítica.
Serra, E. (2013). La crisi del segle XVII a Catalunya. *Butlletí de la Societat Catalana d'Estudis Històrics, 24*, 297–315.
Simón, A. (1993). *Pagesos, capellans i industrials de la Marina de la Selva*. Curial.
Simón, A. (1995). Barcelona i Catalunya durant la crisi de subsistències de 1763–1764. *Barcelona. Quaderns D'història, 1*, 95–106.
Térmens, J., & Valls-Junyent, F. (1987). La guerra del francés en un poble de la comarca de l'Anoia. "Notas" del Dr. Pere Solanllonch, rector de Pierola. *Miscel·lània Aqualatensia, 4*, 111–152.
Thomson, J. (1994). *Els orígens de la industrialització a Catalunya. El cotó a Barcelona 1728–1832*. Ed. 62.
Torras Elias, J. (1976a). Aguardiente y crisis rural (Sobre la coyuntura vitícola, 1793–1832). *Investigaciones Económicas, 1*, 45–67.
Torras Elias, J. (1976b). *Liberalismo y rebeldía campesina, 1820–1823*. Ariel.
Torras Elias, J. (1996). Productes vitícoles i integració mercantil a Europa, segles XV–XVIII. *Estudis d'Història Econòmica, 14*, 23–33.
Torras Ribé, J. M. (1974). Trajectòria d'un procés d'industrialització frustrate. *Miscellanea Aqualatensia, 2*, 169–170.

Torras Ribé, J. M. (1978). El senyoriu d'Orpí. Impacte de la primera llei abolicionista (1811) sobre les relacions entre senyors i vassals. *Estudios Històricos y Documentos de los Archivos de Protocolos, 6*, 327–347.
Torras Ribé, J. M. (1999). *La guerra de Successió i els setges de Barcelona (1697–1714)*. Rafael Dalmau Editor.
Torras Ribé, J. M. (2005). *Felip V contra Catalunya*. Rafael Dalmau Editor.
Torrents, A. (1995). *Transformacions demogràfiques en un municipi industrial català: San Pere de Riudebitlles, 1608–1935* (Doctoral Thesis). Barcelona: Universitat de Barcelona.
Tortella, G. (2014). La renovación económica y social de los Borbones: la política económica de España en el siglo XVIII. In M. Morales Moya (Ed.), *1714. Cataluña en la España del siglo XVIII* (pp. 263–291). Cátedra.
Vallejo, R. (2013). Las catastróficas secuelas de las guerras en los siglos XIX y XX. In F. Comín & M. Hernández (Eds.), *Crisis económicas en España. 1300–2012. Lecciones de la historia* (pp. 253–277). Alianza Editorial.
Valls-Junyent, F. (1997). Contractació a rabassa morta i conjuntura vitícola a Catalunya. 1720–1850. *Estudis Històrics i Documents dels Arxius de Protocols, 15*, 299–334.
Valls-Junyent, F. (2003). *La Catalunya atlàntica*. Eumo.
Vicedo, E. (2008). Mercado y precios. El Almudí de Lérida, 1700–1833. *Historia Agraria, 45*, 41–79.
Vilar, P. (1964). *Crecimiento y desarrollo. Economia e historia reflexiones sobre el caso espanyol*. Ariel.
Vilar, P. (1964–1968). *Catalunya dins l'Espanya moderna*. Ed. 62.
Vinaixa, J. R. (1998). *La postguerra del Francès i la revolta reialista de 1822 a l'Ebre*. Columna.
Voltes, P. (1961). Repercusiones económicas de la intervención española en la guerra de Independencia de los Estados Unidos. *Hispania, 81*, 49–150.

CHAPTER 6

Economic and Financial Crises in Catalonia (1840–1914)

Pere Pascual i Domènech

Financial crises are caused by a growing divergence between the behaviour of basic economic variables and the expectations of investors and consumers. The aforementioned variables consist of the size of savings and the volume of demand driven by the changes experienced in prices,

Pere Pascual i Domènech died in 2023.

The author was grateful for the financial support of the Ministry of Economy and Competitiveness of the Spanish Government (MINECO), the Ministry of Science and Innovation (MCIN/AEI/ 10.13039/501100011033), and of the European Regional Development Fund of the European Union (ERDF) (*A way of making Europe*) through projects HAR2015-64769-P, "Industrial Crisis and Productive Recovery in the History of Spain, 1686–2018" and PGC2018-093896-B-I00, "Mediterranean Capitalism? Successes and Failures of Industrial

P. Pascual i Domènech (✉)
University of Barcelona, Barcelona, Spain
e-mail: jordi.catalan@ub.edu

J. Catalan Vidal (ed.), *Crises and Transformation in the Mediterranean World*, Palgrave Studies in Economic History,
https://doi.org/10.1007/978-3-031-24502-2_6

salaries and the interest rate. This divergence gives rise to an overinvestment in a certain asset—often related to innovation, as was, in the past, the case of railways—, fed by the expansion of credit and which, in the end, does not offer the expected performance for investors. The speculative bubble bursts when investors (or buyers), burdened with debt, begin to have doubts about the viability of their expectations and begin a hasty sale of assets. The collapse of stock market prices leads to increasing default. The increase in default causes the liquidity of banks to collapse. This situation deteriorates even more if the banks have accumulated assets in their portfolio for speculative purposes. In these circumstances, an increase in the interest rate worsens the situation of the banks and of the debtors. The need for liquid funds, an increasingly depressive situation and the distrust of depositors in the solvency of financial institutions lead to a withdrawal of deposits, which can instigate a succession of bank failures. The complete collapse of demand finally provokes the failure of the market, panic and a crash. In these critical situations, there are external and internal factors which can mitigate or hasten (and intensify) their scope, such as the direction of international capital movements and the exchange rate, monetary and fiscal policies applied, etc.[1]

The classical interpretation of financial crises that we have just indicated begins from the hypothesis that markets have an intrinsic propensity for instability. The above-mentioned interpretation has been questioned (but not refuted) by monetarists, who see the depression provoked by mistakes in *ex post* rather than *ex ante* monetary policy in the crisis (Friedman & Schwartz, 1993, pp. 299–419). The available literature in this respect has focused most significantly on the analysis of the causes and of the consequences of the 1930s "Great Depression",[2] which took place in a very different economic, monetary and financial context to the one existing in Catalonia and Europe in the mid-nineteenth century.[3] Therefore, if the comparative analyses are based on specific issues of monetary or fiscal policy, they are not very illustrative. However, we have overwhelming

Development in Spain, 1720–2020". He also thanked Generalitat de Catalunya, Fundació Bancària "La Caixa", the Centre d'Estudis Jordi Nadal of the University of Barcelona and the journal *Recerques*, where a previous version of this work was originally published in Catalan. Andreu Ginés helped with the revision of the English version.

historical evidence that the financial markets have been subject to a succession of speculative "bubbles" (manias), panic attacks and crashes, from the beginning of capitalism to the present day. The 2008 crisis, which arose from the property and mortgage "bubble", demonstrates this very well.

The purpose of this study is to describe the economic and financial crises suffered by the Catalan economy within the years 1840 and 1914. This time segment cannot be considered to be homogeneous, because since 1882 a series of structural changes were recorded which determined the fact that the future crises took place in a very different way to those in the nineteenth century. Firstly, there was a monetary system change, given that it went from a system based on the money with an intrinsic value to another fully fiduciary system. Secondly, the formation of the world wheat market and the trade policy adopted in 1891 represented the complete disappearance of the subsistence crises, which, until then, had led to sudden imbalances in the external sector. Thirdly, as a result of the agricultural crisis at the end of the nineteenth century and of the colonial crisis which culminated with the 1898 "disaster", there was a profound transformation in the system of external trade relations. The study of the crises occurring over these years has therefore been segmented into two periods: the one between 1840 and 1882 and the one from 1883 to 1914.

6.1 The Economic and Financial Crises of the Nineteenth Century

In order to understand the imbalances experienced by the Catalan economy during the 1840–1882 period, it is necessary to specify the characteristics of the system of external trade relations on which the beginning of industrialization was based on. The prohibitionist trade policy—introduced as a result of the enactment of the 1820 tariff—contributed decisively to its organization. The ban on importing cereals and flour meant that—in a context of increasing repression of contraband—the trade relations between Catalonia and Spain were based on exchanging grain and flour and textiles, leading to a considerable expansion in the surface area devoted to the cultivation of cereals in the whole of Spain. The increase in the marketing of textiles—as a result of the progressive integration of the Spanish internal market—made it possible for the Catalan cotton market to embark on a rapid process of mechanization (Fradera, 1987, pp. 230–297; Fontana, 1967; Garrabou & Sanz, 1985, pp. 13–67; Nadal, 1975, pp. 189–212).

The tariff policy concerning raw cotton imports monopolized a good part of the parliamentary debate on the new trade policy which was approved in 1820. This element was of decisive importance in shaping the new system of Catalan external trade relations. The collapse in eau-de-vie exports led, as is well-known, to a profound crisis in the Catalan wine sector (Torras, 1976; Valls, 2004, pp. 288–313). The following played a significant role in the recovery and the renewed expansion of the Catalan wine industry: in the first place, it was possible to keep—in the midst of the colonial defeat—sovereignty over Cuba and Puerto Rico and, secondly, the introduction of a sophisticated tariff policy on raw cotton imports, geared towards the counterpart for overseas wine exports. Most of the import of this fibre was from the plantations of the south of the United States (Pascual, 1990, pp. 170–199). The channelling of this link gave rise to a sort of virtuous circle. The expansion of the cotton industry implied a sustained increase in demand for raw cotton; the increase in imports of this fibre made it possible to export an increasing quantity of wine—on having guaranteed return freight—with reduced transport charges and, therefore, at competitive prices on the American continent; and the expansion of wine exports made it possible to overcome the crisis caused by the collapse of the eau-de-vie markets, and favoured a renewed increase in the winegrowing surface area and in wine prices.

During the second third of the nineteenth century, the new American trade organized on this basis recorded a great expansion and reached levels much higher than the best moments previous to the beginning of the disintegration of the Spanish-American colonial empire (Valls, 2004, pp. 401–406). The trade was based on importing raw cotton and exporting wine (and also eau-de-vie), which was marketed in Cuba and Puerto Rico and also, to a lesser extent, in Río de la Plata, Brazil, etc. Wine and eau-de-vie were the main export products, but they were completed with the despatch of shipments of manufactured products (shoes and tanned leather, paper, soap, textiles, etc.) and other agricultural products: ordinary olive oil, flour, nuts, rice, etc. On the return journeys, apart from raw cotton, there were imports of colonial products (sugar, cocoa, coffee, etc.), fur, colourants, wood, etc. At the same time, the beginning of the process of industrialization required a sustained increase in imports from various European countries: from Great Britain, semi-manufactured products, machinery, coal, etc.; from France, chemical products and a wide variety of manufactured articles; from the Nordic countries, cod, wood, etc.; from Italy, staves and charcoal, etc. (Fradera, 1987, pp. 263–275; Pascual, 1990, pp. 179–183). In the medium and long term, these imports were characterized by a very high-income elasticity, without the Catalan economy being in a position to generate many exports to the supplying countries. This situation determined that the surpluses obtained in the trading and financial relations of Catalonia with the rest of Spain and overseas had to be used to finance the increasing deficit of the balance with European countries.

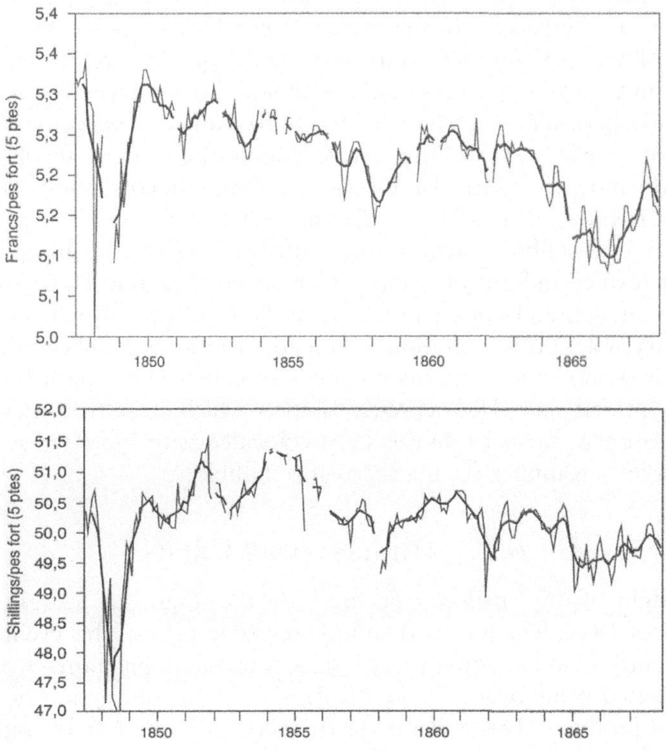

Fig. 6.1 Evolution of the exchange rate, on the Barcelona market, of bills of exchange to be cashed in Paris and London (*Source* see Table 6.8)

The economic and financial crises of Catalonia in the nineteenth century were closely related to imbalances in the system of external trade relations—which, in general, we have just specified—, which could be determined by various causes. Firstly, by the agricultural crises—we should not forget that Spain, in the nineteenth century, was an eminently agrarian country with agriculture devoted to cereal production—which involved periodic collapses of production due to adverse climatological circumstances. The decline in cereal production entailed a decline in demand for consumer goods by farmers—especially textiles—and caused a sales crisis that had negative repercussions on the activity of the Catalan textile industry. The fall in industrial activity had a negative effect on the trade balance between Catalonia and the rest of Spain, on American trade and, in short, on the balance of the overall external sector. Secondly, external causes of an unforeseeable nature, such as the disturbance caused by the American Civil War—as a result of the abolition of slavery which prevailed in the southern states—, which led to the blocking of raw cotton exports, a lack of supplies for the European, including the Catalan, textile industries, which depended to a large extent on American cotton imports. This episode is known as the "cotton famine", characterized by a huge rise in the price of this fibre which, in turn, entailed a collapse in the consumption of textiles and an imbalance in the external sector. These ruptures implied sudden and considerable net outflows of cash which, while the monetary system based on money with an intrinsic value subsisted, led to successive contractions of money supply, accompanied by upward tensions on the interest rate. The depressive impact which arose from this could even cause true financial disasters if it coincided with situations in which the market was immersed in a speculative bubble.

6.2 The 1847–1848 Crisis

The origin of this crisis can be found in the disastrous Spanish cereal harvest of 1847, which caused an intense rise in prices. This event led to a generalized famine among many sectors of the population—which, in turn, caused many deaths—and a collapse in the consumption of manufactured products. This effect is clearly reflected in the Catalan industrial production index, which in 1848 experienced a 6.09% fall compared with the previous year (Carreras, 1990, pp. 56–57; Maluquer de Motes, 1994). What differentiates this crisis from the previous ones is that it affected the financial sector. The Royal Decree of 1 May 1844 authorized the establishment of Banco de Barcelona—after a period of two years of negotiations—, which was granted an issuing monopoly on this market. The aim of the institution was to attract temporarily dormant funds in current accounts and deposits and to offer credit with good conditions—trying to reduce the interest rate—by discounting bills and mortgage loans on transferable securities and goods and by providing a service of drawing funds in other markets (Blasco & Sudrià, 2009, pp. 45–59). There were relatively few beneficiaries of the credit supply generated by the bank: the clients were limited by strict criteria of solvency which, moreover, fixed the volume of credit that each client could enjoy (Blasco & Sudrià, 2009, pp. 164–172). The rule which governed the management of the institution was that of acting with extreme prudence. The fact that the bank had been awarded the privilege of issuing meant that the notes that it bought into circulation—despite the fact that, as was typical for the issuing banks of the nineteenth century, they were only accepted as a means of payment within the same market—played an important role in financing its credit activity.

Table 6.1 Evolution of Banco de Barcelona's balance of current accounts and deposits, notes in circulation, investment portfolio and cash in hand, 1846–1849 (thousands of pesetas)

	Liabilities		*Assets*	
	Current and deposit accounts	*Notes in circulation*	*Investment portfolio (loans and discounting)*	*Cash in hand*
2nd half of 1846	4872.86	4880.55	8719.60	3000.57
1st half of 1847	4692.12	5635.30	9803.14	2631.83
2nd half of 1847	3580.47	7310.35	10732.80	2956.23
1st half of 1848	2015.37	3671.40	6420.91	1823.70
2nd half of 1848	1865.98	5365.10	5823.30	3065.54
1st half of 1849	3770.11	4432.15	4799.98	4842.45
2nd half of 1849	5434.48	3306.40	5325.02	4565.71

Source Blasco and Sudrià (2009, pp. 502–503)

The 1847–1848 agrarian crisis brought Banco de Barcelona close to bankruptcy. In this context, the current accounts and deposits balance began an intense decline in 1847, which intensified during the first half of 1848, undoubtedly due to the growing lack of liquidity of traders, industrialists, etc. Meanwhile, in 1847, the bank's management implemented an anti-cyclic policy: it increased the credit supply and, consequently, the volume of notes in circulation. At the same time, the exchange rate of the bills to be cashed in London and Paris recorded an acute rise, suggesting that there was an imbalance in the external sector which caused more or less considerable net outflows of cash (see Fig. 6.1 and Table 6.8). The reduction in currency with intrinsic value in circulation meant that traders, industrialists, etc. had a surplus of notes and a scarcity of cash to make their payments. This imbalance caused a crowding-out effect on the fiduciary currency, because the holders of notes increased their conversion demands. Due to this process, in the first half of 1848 the volume of the bank's notes in circulation experienced an intense decline and the balance of cash in hand existing fell at the same time (see Table 6.1). The growing lack of liquidity led the bank to suddenly restrict the credit supply—notably reducing the volume of the portfolio of loans—, which undoubtedly had an upward impact on the interest rate, given that the demand for credit from traders, industrialists, etc. remained, or even tended to increase due to the effect of the circumstantial situation of collapse in the settlements of contracts, of drafts and of all kinds of transactions.

The situation became even worse with the alarm caused by the outbreak of the revolution in France in February 1848. The bank's leadership succeeded in avoiding the suspension of payments by demanding from the shareholders the payment (from April onwards) of a capital call with desperate conditions, which meant that the paid-up capital was positioned at 62.5% (Blasco & Sudrià, 2009, pp. 201–220). The normalization of agricultural production permitted the recovery of demand and of industrial activity from the second half of 1848, in addition to the correction of the imbalance in the external sector. The increase in liquidity on the market became clear with the rise of the bank's current accounts and deposits balance during 1849. However, the institution's leaders were alarmed as a result of this crisis, because they put extreme limits on the granting of credit: the portfolio continued to go down in 1849 as did, at the same time, the volume of notes in circulation. Meanwhile, the balance of cash in hand to guarantee the convertibility of the notes experienced a notable increase. This flow made it possible, in 1848–1849, to perform various capital reimbursements, meaning that the paid-up capital fell to 25% of the nominal capital.

To avoid risks, the bank's management chose to limit its sphere of business. This was restricted even more when the government—to try to avoid another crisis like the one which had just been experienced—stipulated (in the Law of 4 May 1849) that the notes in circulation could not exceed the size of the paid-up capital when the previous limit was the nominal capital. The bank accepted this limitation. Between 1850 and 1854, the paid-up capital remained stable and it renounced the idea of increasing money supply. It thus adopted a markedly deflationary policy. However, the fact that it operated without competition in the market during this period meant that the balance of current accounts and deposits recorded a sustained and notable increase, which more than offset the reduction of notes in circulation and allowed the bank to maintain an expanding credit supply (Blasco & Sudrià, 2009, pp. 121–144, 229–255).

6.3 The 1857–1859 Crisis

The origin of this crisis was also related to a subsistence crisis. The extremely poor cereal harvest of 1856—which occurred after years of increasing exports of grain and of flour, thanks to the exceptional situation created by the Crimean War—led to a substantial increase in prices and a serious food situation, which forced the government to temporarily lift the ban on importing cereals. Very considerable imports of cereals and of flour were undertaken between 1856 and 1859 with a view to curbing the increase in prices and helping to meet internal demand (Sánchez-Albornoz, 1977, pp. 27–67). As usual, the collapse in cereal production had depressive effects on the demand for manufactured products and on the activity of the Catalan textile industry. In short, this crisis would have had similar effects to that of 1847–1948 had it not occurred in a different context, which eventually contributed to its intensification and extension.

As regards the change of context, it should first be taken into account that the financial sector of Barcelona was immersed, in those moments, in a process of notable expansion and diversification. The establishment of Caja Barcelonesa de Giros, Descuentos, Préstamos y Cuentas Corrientes had been authorized in 1855, and that of Caja Catalana Mercantil e Industrial in 1856. In this last year—following the passing of the

Issuing Banks and Building Society laws of 28 January 1856—the establishment of three building societies was formalized: Catalana General de Crédito, Crédito Mobiliario Barcelonés and Unión Comercial (Tortella, 1973, pp. 51–63, 80–88). The expansion and diversification of the banking system were followed by a huge increase in money supply—which destroyed the theoretical issuing monopoly of Banco de Barcelona—consisting of monetary assets with different levels of liquidity: bank notes were joined by payment orders and recorded cashier's cheques (private notes) which were put into circulation by the discounting banks, which were also convertible on demand, and short-term redeemable bonds and also recorded cashier's cheques issued by the building societies (Pascual & Sudrià, 2008, pp. 48–64). All of these monetary instruments were accepted on the market as a means of payment and circulated without limitations, meaning that, as from 1856, in Barcelona, there was a true free banking system. Furthermore, since 1852 there were the notes brought into circulation throughout Catalonia as a result of the withdrawal of the Catalan small change, which had compulsory acceptance of up to 10% of the value of all payments and which was not convertible, although there was a commitment that this fiduciary money would be redeemed (on an unspecified date) with public funds (see Table 6.2) (Pascual, 2007, pp. 184–195). In short, this sudden and substantial increase of very diversified fiduciary money supply contributed to allowing part of the currency with intrinsic value (gold or silver) to be released from the internal medium of exchange function and to limiting the increase in the interest rate although, on the other hand, it represented the establishment of a financial system much more prone to instability in situations of persistent imbalance of the external sector.

On the other hand, a huge increase in investment was recorded due to the simultaneous construction of the main lines of the Catalan railway network—the railway from Barcelona to Zaragoza (365 km) and from Mataró and from Granollers to Girona (116.5 km) (Pascual, 1999, pp. 161–234)—and of other public works (such as Urgell canal) which meant that the concessionary companies accepted huge repayment commitments during the decade from 1853 to 1862. In all cases, they were works which, once started, could not be stopped, since this would have represented huge amounts of capital being unproductive and would have caused the failure of the companies which had accepted them. Therefore, demand for capital experienced a true boom precisely at a time when the country's economy was entering a phase dominated by

Table 6.2 Size of fiduciary currency issued at the end of 1858 by the financial institutions of Barcelona and by the Junta de Moneda de Cataluña (pesetas)

	Pesetas	*Pesetas*	%
Banco de Barcelona:		10,621,375	32.56
– Notes issued	10,621,375		
Building societies and discounting banks:		13,303,155	40.78
– Bonds and payment orders	10,121,250		
– Cash cheques	3,181,905		
Junta de Moneda de Catalunya:		8,695,615	26.65
– Notes redemption small change	8,695,615		
Total		32,620,145	100.00

Sources Archivo Histórico Nacional (AHN), collection Hacienda, lligall 429/1 and Arxiu de la Diputació de Barcelona (ADB), lligall 183, Actas de la Excma. Junta de Moneda de Cataluña

depressive tensions (Pascual, 1990, pp. 225–265; Sudrià, 1994; Sudrià & Pascual, 1999). The textile industry was negatively affected by the weakness of internal demand as a result of the subsistence crisis of 1856 (Carreras, 1990, pp. 56–57; Maluquer de Motes, 1994) and winegrowing went through difficult times due to the *oidium* disease, which caused a decline in wine production and a sudden increase in wine prices (Giralt, 1990, pp. 227–230). This situation undoubtedly tended to depress the size of saving generated by the productive system and contributed to unbalancing the financial market.

The combination of the aforementioned depressive tensions and the almost uncontrolled increase in the demand for capital from public works companies led to the collapse of the price of variable-rate securities on the Barcelona stock market (see Table 6.6) (Castañeda & Tafunell, 2001, pp. 288–290, 300; Fontana, 1961). However, the collapse of the price of railway securities was also closely related—despite the fact that the shareholders, as had occurred in France, began to charge a fixed interest rate (in this case 6%) during the line construction period—to the growing mistrust generated in relation to the expectations of the railways by the scarce income offered by the short lines brought into operation between 1854 and 1857: the railways from Barcelona to Granollers and to Martorell and the first section of the line from Zaragoza, from Montcada to Sabadell (Pascual, 1999, pp. 125–130). The price of the shares in the railway companies was well below the capital paid-up, making it unfeasible to continue to place variable-rate securities, given that the legislation required the share capital to be fully paid-up. Meanwhile, many shareholders—choked by commitments to accept capital calls that they were incapable of fulfilling—were dispossessed of their shares, given that the companies declared thousands of shares to have expired due to lack of payment (Pascual, 1999, pp. 211–224). The critical situation faced by public works companies as from 1857 was solved by using a new financial product: bonds. These were fixed-income securities—inspired by Treasury bonds—which helped to hugely expand the Barcelona capital market. This financial instrument attracted a substantial quantity of saving to the financial market—in the hands of rentiers, small savers...—which would never have invested in variable-rate securities or in public debt (Pascual, 1990, pp. 251–255). The rejection of the former was due to the uncertainty concerning their expectations of profitability and, as regards debt, due to the mistrust—justified by the long suspension of payments, the debt "repudiations", the "arrangements", etc.—concerning the solvency of the state (Comín, 1996; Fontana, 1980, pp. 31–52). On the other hand, bonds offered them a known profitability—which was often very high, on being negotiated with huge damages—and, at least apparently, they were a very safe value, given that they were granted a double mortgage guarantee: on the gross profit in relation to the payment of interest and on the capital of the issuing companies in relation to their repayment.

In short, during the period from 1858 to 1859, the railway companies and other companies achieved huge quantities of capital by issuing large loans in a rather depressed context characterized—according to the exchange rate of bills to be cashed in London or Paris—by a growing imbalance in the external sector, arising in part from the considerable imports of cereals that it was necessary to make during these years due to the collapse in Spanish production (see Fig. 6.1 and Table 6.8) (Sudrià & Pascual, 1999, pp. 130–139). The investment boom meant that there was a growing divorce between the increase in the demands for capital—which implied that the financial market was subject to huge pressure—and the size of the savings available. Meanwhile, money supply increased on the basis of a substantial rise in the fiduciary currency in circulation (bank notes, payment orders, recorded cashier's cheques, short-term bonds...), at the same time as the volume of currency with intrinsic value in circulation possibly went down due to the effect of the imbalance in the external sector. This process of replacing money with an intrinsic value with fiduciary money—in the context of this monetary system—had a limit. This limit was imposed by the balance that had to exist between the volumes of currency with intrinsic value and of fiduciary money in the free cash in the hands of traders, industrialists, etc., given that although they could make many of their payments in the market with fiduciary money, it was essential for them to have smooth access to the currency with intrinsic value to make other payments.

The imbalance finally occurred in the spring of 1859, when the surplus fiduciary currency and the scarcity of cash led to a rush of requests to convert all kinds of monetary assets: bank notes, payment orders, *talons*, bonds, etc. The Barcelona banks, discounting banks and building societies experienced a drastic reduction in the fiduciary currency which they had in circulation and an intense decline in the balances of current accounts (see Table 6.3). At the same time, the aggravation of the fall in the price of stock market securities hindered the smooth sale of portfolios—without suffering from losses—in order to obtain liquidity and meant that it was not feasible to execute the guarantees (securities deposited) of bad debts without contributing to worsening the situation of the market in a dangerous fashion. The strategy of the Barcelona banks was the usual one in these cases: to restrict credit supply in order to try to increase the cash on hand available so as to meet the requests for convertibility. The contraction of money and credit supply entailed a sudden increase in the interest rate, which contributed to deteriorating the financial situation of the market and the lack of liquidity of traders, industrialists, stock market speculators, etc. In this situation, all the financial institutions of Barcelona experienced critical moments, above all the building societies due to having accumulated large quantities of variable and fixed-income securities in their portfolios, which it was impossible to trade without making a loss. The company Catalana General de Crédito avoided suspension of payments by requesting from its shareholders—as Banco de Barcelona had done in 1848—the payment of a capital call of 10%, which was fulfilled painfully amid the anger of the shareholders (Pascual, 1990, p. 255). On the other hand, another building society, Unión Comercial, with less accredited solvency, was not able to undertake an operation of this kind, suspended payments and was liquidated (Tortella, 1973, pp. 86–88).

The financial situation of the market improved in the following months. The recovery of wheat production made it possible to manage without the massive imports of cereals and helped to recover the balance of the external sector. The negotiations carried out by the railway companies and some building societies made it possible to sell, in Paris, thousands of shares in the company Ferrocarril de Barcelona a Zaragoza,

Table 6.3 Transformation of the money supply generated by Barcelona banks between April and August 1859 (pesetas) (*)

	(1) *30-IV-1859*	(2) *31-VIII-1859*	*2·100/1*
1. Cash in the hands of the public			
1.1 Bearer banknotes	9,783,900.0	8,828,800.0	90.23
1.2 Recorded cashier's cheques	2,053,830.0	973,300.5	47.38
1.3 Nominative payment orders	6,439,125.0	5,353,250.0	83.13
1.4 Bearer bonds	4,404,150.0	3,128,200.0	71.02
1.5 Notes-small change	8,695,615.0	8,695,615.0	100.00
Total cash in the hands of the public	**31,376,620.0**	**26,979,165.5**	**85.98**
2. Deposits and current accounts			
2.1 Current accounts (**)	23,353,168.5	18,812,722.0	80.55
2.2 Deposits	840,287.5	1,941,117.0	231.00
Total current accounts and deposits	**24,193,456.0**	**20,753,839.0**	**85.78**
Total (1 + 2)	**55,570,076.0**	**47,733,004.5**	**85.89**
3. Cash on hand			
3.1 Cash (currency in Au and Ag)	12,049,581.0	14,339,743.0	119.00
3.2 Means of payment issued by other institutions (***)	3,938,460.0	2,812,226.5	71.40
3.3 Notes-small change	1,810,175.0	1,704,025.0	94.13
Total cash on hand	**17,798,216.0**	**18,855,994.5**	**105.94**
Net money supply [(1 + 2) −3]	**37,771,860.0**	**28,877,010.0**	**76.45**

*These figures are the result of adding the assets and the monetary assets and liabilities of all Barcelona banking institutions: Banco de Barcelona, Caja Barcelonesa, Caja Catalana, Crédito Mobiliario Barcelonés, Catalana General de Crédito and Unión Comercial

**We were not able to find the balance for the end of April 1859 for the current accounts deposited with Unió Comercial, a defect which obliged us to use the balance in this establishment at the end of May of that year

***The aforementioned data refer to the total monetary assets of other banking institutions which each establishment had on hand, deducting, in all cases, the inactive notes, bonds, payment orders, etc. issued by each of these institutions

Source Pascual and Sudrià (2008, p. 68)

which allowed the company Catalana General de Crédito and a considerable number of shareholders of that company to recover liquidity, at the same time as the entry of cash which this operation represented helped to normalize the circulation of money, re-establishing the balance between money with an intrinsic value and fiduciary currency (Pascual, 1999, pp. 186–187; Tortella, 1973, p. 147). The renewed increase in money supply enabled the interest rate to gradually become more moderate and the financial situation of the market to become normal again.

The financial depression of 1857–1859 was overcome without reaching disaster, although it left a legacy that played an important role in the financial collapse which was recorded in 1866. In this situation, the railway companies succeeded in mobilizing the resources necessary to avoid the cessation of the works, but at the expense of jeopardizing their financial viability in the immediate future. The capital increased on the basis of issuing loans negotiated with substantial damages—which implied the payment of very high effective interest—and with extremely short repayment periods due to the demands of the investors who subscribed to these securities. This process meant that the capital bonds of the railway companies—in the face of the permissiveness of the governments, which repeatedly increased their ceiling—reached proportions that were difficult to sustain. The size of the financial burdens and of the repayment commitments meant that they would be difficult to sustain—even if the results obtained from operating the lines had fulfilled the most optimistic forecasts—, and that the viability of some of the companies would only be guaranteed if the conversion of the loans was obtained once the line was in operation (Pascual, 1999, pp. 257–262).

6.4 The 1860s Crisis and the 1866 Crash

The recovery of financial stability and the renewal of economic growth after the 1859 crisis did not last long. Another external event took the Catalan economy to another depressive situation. As a result of the abolition of slavery the American Civil War implied, as is well-known, the suspension of raw cotton exports, a lack of supplies on the European (and Catalan) market for this raw material and a huge rise in its prices. The cotton industrialists had to pass on the increase in the prices of cotton to those of the textiles and this caused—we have to infer that demand for textiles was, at that time, very elastic in relation to prices—a collapse in consumption, a decline in production and a substantial increase in unemployment in the Catalan cotton industry (Izard, 1973, pp. 51–52; Nadal, 1975, pp. 204–207). This event had a negative effect on overseas trade—while desperate attempts were made to obtain cotton of other origins—, at the same time as the imbalance returned to the external sector.[4] The exchange rate in Barcelona for bills to be cashed in London and Paris indicates this (see Fig. 6.1 and Table 6.8), which implies, as always, more or less considerable net outflows of money with an intrinsic value, which contributed to undermining the stability of the financial system.

A second factor to take into account is that the Spanish Treasury entered a new phase of out of control increase in the budget deficit. To finance it, the government was forced to exercise increasing pressure on all the financial markets. This occurred through two channels in the Barcelona market: on the one hand, through the trading of public debt—there are indications that the volume in circulation experienced a notable increase—and, in particular, through the branch of Caja General de Depósitos which, by offering excessively high interest rates, succeeded in attracting a huge quantity of cash (Navas & Sudrià, 2007, pp. 46–57; Pascual, 1990, pp. 281–283). The action of the state thus represented a crowding-out effect, on absorbing a growing proportion of the savings available to the detriment of the financing needs of the private sector.

A third element to consider is that in this increasingly depressive situation—which the state helped to worsen with its growing demands for capital—, investment experienced another upward tendency. Investment in the railway sector recorded a further increase when the construction of the line from Barcelona to Tarragona was completed and were started those of the sections from Girona to the border of the lines from Barcelona to France, of the railway from Granollers to Sant Joan de les Abadesses and of the branch from Igualada to Sant Sadurní (Pascual, 1990, pp. 285–340). At the same time, some non-Catalan railway companies (Ferrocarriles de Almansa a Valencia y Tarragona, Ferrocarril de Córdoba a Málaga and Ferrocarriles de Medina a Zamora y de Orense a Vigo) traded, between 1861 and 1864, thousands of bonds on the Barcelona stock exchange, and this represented the realization of very considerable capital (Pascual, 1990, pp. 283–286). In this context, there was a new wave of creation of financial institutions: the companies Crédito Mercantil (1863), Crédito y Fomento de Barcelona (1864), Sociedad de Crédito "El Comercio" (1865), etc. (Pascual, 1990, pp. 292–303); unincorporated discounting banks, Crédito Mutuo Fabril y Mercantil

(Caja Vilumara), Caja Mutua (Castellà, Manté, Monner y Cia.), etc. and new issuing banks from outside the capital, Banco de Reus and Banco de Tarragona (Blasco & Sudrià, 2009, pp. 281–284; Sánchez-Albornoz, 1977, pp. 144–147).

In addition to the above, a fourth factor arises from the fact that the results obtained by the railways brought into operation did not meet expectations (see Table 6.4). The operating ratios were not disastrous, but their output per unit of length operated was lower than expected. The gross profit obtained by the companies of Zaragoza (as from 1864) and Tarragona (as from 1866) lines did not reach the level necessary to cover the payment of the interest and the commitments to repay the loans, which led these companies to suspend payments (Pascual, 1999, pp. 248, 264). The company Ferrocarril de Barcelona a Zaragoza tried to avoid this through a progressive conversion of its loans. It was a question of trading small issues of bonds redeemable in the long term and with the result of these issues repaying the previous loans redeemable in the short term which moreover had a very high real interest on having been traded with considerable damages during the 1858–1859 period. Obviously, this operation could only succeed if the price of the bonds kept pace, which in the end was not feasible (Pascual, 1999, pp. 265–269).

In this context, starting from 1864, the increasingly depressive situation hastened the decline of all stock market securities and, with extreme intensity, railway company shares (see Table 6.5). Their holders became convinced that many years would have to pass before they would collect any dividend, if indeed they would at all. The situation became truly critical when the mistrust towards the expectations of the railways also caused the collapse of the price of the bonds issued by the railway companies (Castañeda & Tafunell, 2001, pp. 288–290, 300; Pascual, 1999, pp. 123–127, 261–262). The process of conversion of the loans started by the company Ferrocarril de Barcelona a Zaragoza had to be suspended due to the impossibility of carrying it out at acceptable costs, and the suspension of payments became inevitable. In January 1866, this company suspended the fulfilment of its repayment and interest payment commitments accredited by the loans, and the company Ferrocarriles de Tarragona a Martorell y Barcelona did the same... At the same time, the share price of railway companies sank to unimaginable levels, and the same occurred with the bonds traded by these companies.

The failure of the railway companies meant that the crisis affected, once and for all, the financial sector. The scenario is well-known. During 1865,

Table 6.4 Evolution of the profitability represented by the gross profit obtained from the operation of the lines of the Catalan railway network (1849–1865) (in percentages)

	Mataró line	(*)	*Granollers line*	*Martorell line*	*Zaragoza line*
1849	10.80				
1850	9.25				
1851	8.48				
1852	7.53				
1853	7.83				
1854	7.62		1.65	0.31	
1855	7.11		1.61	2.85	1.84
1856	7.44		2.46	3.77	2.05
1857	7.34		2.43	4.04	1.54
1858	8.47		2.68	4.01	1.91
1859	7.77		3.14	3.31	2.34
1860	5.33		2.16	3.31	1.57
1861	3.98		1.73	3.06	2.20
1862		3.93		2.84	1.82
1863		2.91		2.93	2.73
1864		3.35		2.42	2.82
1865		3.37		1.77	2.85

*As from 1862, the profitability refers to the operation of the coast (Mataró) and inland (Granollers) lines to Girona as a result of the merger of the former companies Ferrocarril de Barcelona a Arenys de Mar y Girona and Ferrocarril de Barcelona a Granollers y Girona
Source Pascual (1999, p. 126)

the tensions arising from the depressive situation of the real economy, the pressures of the Treasury to attract the available savings in the market and the deflationary effects arising from the imbalance of the external sector all became more acute. The financial system was thus again overwhelmed by the decline in bank current accounts and deposits and by the contraction in the volume of fiduciary currency in circulation. The availability of cash to sustain the tendency to regression of external liabilities contrasted with the increasing impossibility to realize the investment portfolio in order to acquire liquidity due to the effect of the increase in bad debts and the impossibility to trade—because of the collapse in prices—in negotiable securities without recording more or less considerable losses. The contraction of money and credit supply had an increasing upward effect on the interest rate, which contributed to worsening the situation

Table 6.5 Evolution of the share prices of railway companies and of the mixed index of variable-income securities on Barcelona stock market, 1850–1889 (Numbers Index 1850 = 100)

	Railway index	*Mixed index*		*Railway index*	*Mixed index*
1850	100.0	100.0	1870	23.6	35.6
1851	107.8	112.6	1871	32.2	46.7
1852	108.6	122.3	1872	50.2	58.1
1853	92.3	116.1	1873	40.3	50.7
1854	89.0	113.4	1874	43.6	52.7
1855	77.1	107.6	1875	52.0	63.5
1856	93.3	120.7	1876	57.4	67.3
1857	88.0	112.8	1877	58.0	66.9
1858	70.4	76.0	1878	86.6	80.7
1859	69.2	67.4	1879	105.2	88.9
1860	85.4	85.9	1880	203.0	143.4
1861	81.6	88.7	1881	224.7	167.6
1862	74.3	83.8	1882	171.1	125.6
1863	69.7	80.1	1883	140.0	96.8
1864	53.1	68.4	1884	136.3	96.1
1865	24.5	49.1	1885	108.7	83.7
1866	12.9	34.6	1886	108.7	84.3
1867	12.9	32.2	1887	99.7	78.9
1868	11.9	30.3	1888	115.7	87.4
1869	14.9	30.6	1889	101.2	84.6

Source Castañeda and Tafunell (2001, p. 300)

of traders, industrialists, etc., making the depressive tensions more acute and intensifying the collapse of prices on the financial market. Under these circumstances, at any moment there could be a banking suspension of payments which could generate panic and an unprecedented financial disaster. The crash finally took place in May 1866.

The suspension of payments of Crédito Mobiliario Barcelonés took place on a Saturday and caused panic on the market. It was obvious that, when banking institutions opened on the following Monday, a flood of current account holders, depositors, and holders of all kinds of monetary assets would run at the commercial banks, savings banks and building societies demanding repayment or conversion into cash, as did indeed occur. By mid-morning, savings banks and building societies had to close due to the impossibility of dealing with the size of the requests for reimbursement. Catalan members of parliament desperately negotiated with the government and, finally, the latter stipulated that the captain general of Catalonia should proclaim a sort of financial state of emergency and decree the temporary (in principle, for 12 days) suspension of the convertibility of notes and other monetary assets and the limitation of the availability of the funds existing in current accounts and deposits to 500 *reales* per person (Sànchez-Albornoz, 1977, p. 151; Navas & Sudrià, 2007, pp. 57–61). This provision served to avoid the total collapse of the banking system and helped to buy time while waiting for the general mood to calm down. The lifting of the suspension of convertibility and of the repayment of funds was carried out progressively over the subsequent weeks. Meanwhile, in order to obtain liquidity, a large part of the financial institutions of Barcelona stipulated the collection of capital calls, although this had contradictory effects: it contributed to strengthening the financial situation of Banco de Barcelona but worsened the decline of other insti tutions, such as Caja Barcelonesa. Its shares came to be valued "with the loss of everything disbursed and even adding 2 and 3% to that, so that the new holder undertook to pay the dividend that this company requested from its shareholders..." (Pascual, 1990, pp. 301–302). On those days, the conversations between the leaders of Banco de Barcelona and those of the savings banks resulted in an agreement: the former would be in charge—in exchange for receiving duly endorsed bills in rediscounting—of withdrawing from circulation the payment orders and the recorded cashier's cheques that the latter had in circulation. Over the following weeks, savings banks and building societies assessed—depending on the situation of their portfolios—whether to decide to reopen the institutions or to liquidate. The majority chose to liquidate. This is the case of the building societies Crédito Mobiliario Barcelonés, Crédito y Fomento de Barcelona and Sociedad de Crédito "El Comercio" and also of the savings banks Catalana Mercantil e Industrial and Barcelonesa de Giros y Descuentos. The liquidation processes were long: some of these institutions managed to amortize their liabilities and even repay part of the capital to their shareholders, but others (such as the Barcelonesa) were not able to service the whole of the debt (Navas & Sudrià, 2007, pp. 63–70).

The consequences of the disaster could not have been more devastating. Only three financial institutions survived: Banco de Barcelona and two building societies, Crédito Mercantil and Catalana General de Crédito. However, the latter was obliged to improve its portfolio, adjusting the valuation of its assets to market prices, which meant that, on making the adjustment to its income statement, it had to close with a 41.7% reduction of the capital paid-up (Pascual, 1990, pp. 302–303). The position of Banco de Barcelona was reinforced since it achieved a de facto issuing monopoly recognized de jure. The withdrawal from circulation of the payment orders, *talons* and short-term bonds represented the end of Barcelona's free banking experience, which had lasted ten years. The normalization of the raw cotton supply allowed a return to normal production conditions in the cotton industry. However, in 1867, there was a new subsistence crisis (Sánchez-Albornoz, 1975, pp. 35–39). The increase in the prices of bread made it necessary to decree another temporary lifting of the ban on importing cereals, which gave rise to another collapse in demand for manufactured products (and textiles), and, overall, probably led to a new situation of imbalance of the external sector. The net outflows of money undoubtedly had a more or less intense deflationary impact, worsened by the fact that Banco de Barcelona developed, during the period between 1867 and 1873, a markedly restrictive monetary policy (Blasco & Sudrià, 2009, pp. 443–444).

6.5 The "Gold Rush" Bubble

The Catalan economy experienced notable growth in the 1870s. Industrial production again increased at high rates—despite the political instability of the 1868–1875 period and of the episode of the Third Carlist War—(Carreras, 1990, pp. 56–57; Maluquer de Motes, 1994, pp. 45–70) and, at the same time, Catalan wine production entered its golden age with the start of the boom in wine exports to France as a result of the ravages of phylloxera (Giralt, 1990, pp. 230–235; Pujol, 1984, pp. 58–66). The intensification of economic growth enabled the recovery of gross capital formation. Meanwhile, in 1874 the issuing monopoly was awarded to the Banco of España—the insolvency of the public Treasury obliged the state, which needed credit, to fund itself through the monetization of the deficit—(Anes, 1974, pp. 125–157; Tortella, 1970, pp. 285–287), which meant that Banco de Barcelona lost the privilege and was reduced to being a simple commercial bank. The Banco de España immediately opened a branch in Barcelona, which implemented, for some years, a very expansive monetary and credit policy (Castañeda, 2001b, pp. 135–138; Tafunell, 1991, pp. 385–388). As from 1875, the pacification of the country led to another boom being recorded in railway investment, allowing the completion of the construction—at a standstill since the 1866 crisis—of the basic railway network.

In this period, the section from Girona to the border of the French line was completed, the connection (with the trench all along Carrer Aragó) of the Barcelona stations was built; the construction of the lines from Granollers to Sant Joan de les Abadesses and from Tarragona to Lleida was completed; and the construction of the new line from Valls to Vilanova and Barcelona began—with a branch line from Roda de Berà to Reus—, which completed the Catalan railway "eight" with the centre in Barcelona (Pascual, 1999, pp. 353–426). At the same time, the business holding company was formed, focused on Barcelona and promoted by Antonio López, the first Marquis of Comillas, built by Banco Hispano-Colonial, Compañía Trasatlántica, Compañía de Tabacos de Filipinas, etc. (Rodrigo, 2000, passim). It suddenly burst

This situation of growing financial euphoria culminated with the speculative bubble of the "gold rush" (1880–1881), which was characterized by the establishment of numerous banks in Barcelona and in various Catalan towns which were important industrial or agricultural centres (Tafunell, 1991, pp. 393–394; Tedde, 1974, pp. 276–278). The bubble was fed by the expansion of credit supply which increased as a result of the abundant liquidity provided by the Banco de España's branch, which Banco de Barcelona had never before offered (see Table 6.6). It suddenly burst in January 1882 when the contraction of the current of credit which had generated it caused the collapse of share prices (Castañeda, 2001b,

Table 6.6 Evolution of notes in circulation, current accounts, deposits, bills of exchange and loans from closing balance sheets of the Banco de España's branch in Barcelona, 1875–1882 (millions of pesetas)

	Liabilities			*Assets*	
	Notes in circulation	*Current accounts*	*Deposits*	*Bills of exchange*	*Loans*
1875	15.0	2.0	0.6	1.7	20.0
1876	20.3	1.4	0.5	2.1	21.2
1877	20.2	1.8	1.0	2.3	19.1
1878	28.5	2.6	1.5	2.8	25.9
1870	38.9	5.0	2.1	2.8	23.5
1880	58.4	4.9	2.4	4.5	43.7
1881	98.2	18.6	4.2	4.0	70.1
1882	52.9	7.6	4.6	9.0	37.6

Source Tortella (1974a, Table Dt V-5)

pp. 136–137; Castañeda & Tafunell, 2001, pp. 288–291). On this occasion, prices fell to the 1878 level, which implied a substantial difference in relation to the 1857–1859 and 1864–1866 crises. On those previous occasions, prices declined well below the initial level. In subsequent years, the country found itself in a depressive situation. The growth in industrial production slowed down under the depressive effects generated by the agricultural crisis with its dual wheat and wine aspects (Carreras, 1990, pp. 56–57; Garrabou, 1975, pp. 163–216; Giralt, 1990, pp. 235–244; Maluquer de Motes, 1994, pp. 45–70). In this situation, the majority of banks created during the "gold rush" gradually disappeared (Cabana, 1999, pp. 749–760; Tedde, 1974, pp. 272, 278–297). In short, although the speculative bubble of the "gold rush" remained in popular memory as an example of the nineteenth century crises of liberal capitalism—maybe as a result of the literary portrait offered by Narcís Oller—, for the reasons set forth it cannot be considered to be systemic like the previous ones, apart from the fact that the bursting of the bubble did not at all represent the financial disaster which arose from the 1866 crisis.

6.6 The Systemic Transformations of the End of the Nineteenth Century: Fiscal Crisis and New Monetary System

The model on which the Catalan (and Spanish) economy had been based was profoundly altered by various causes during the last two decades of the nineteenth century. Firstly, due to the transformation experienced by the monetary system—as a result of the new insolvency experienced by the Spanish Treasury—, which represented the disappearance of money supply contractions caused by the effect of external sector imbalances. Secondly, due to the protectionist shift determined by the wheat crisis, which also ended up as an instrument to mitigate the agricultural crises' impact.

The new crisis of the Spanish Treasury triggered during the 1860s became worse as a result of the failure of the governments of the regime arising from the Glorious Revolution of 1868 to undertake a fiscal reform in the short term. The collapse of income arising from the abolition of the unpopular tax on consumption coexisted with an expansion of public expenditure (Costas, 1988, pp. 25, 70–77, 121–123). The deficits were financed by means of successive external loans, obtained in exchange for favours, or from the sale or lease of public assets (Martín Niño, 1972, pp. 70–94; Nadal, 1975, pp. 87–121). Once these resources were exhausted, the suspension of payments was unavoidable. In this context, the subsistence of the state apparatus required the abandonment of the system of various banks of issue established by the law of 1856. The Decree of 19 March 1874 awarded the issuing monopoly to the Banco de España, and from then on the budget deficit was basically financed through credits from the Banco de España and, therefore, through their monetization (Anes, 1974, pp. 125–134; Tortella, 1970, pp. 285–293).

At the same time, there was a crisis of bimetallic monetary systems. These systems had the advantage of limiting the scope of deflationary tensions arising from external sector imbalances and the inconvenience that they were unstable due to the variations in the relative prices of gold and silver and, therefore, in the bimetallic ratio, which determined that, due to the effect of Gresham's law, the circulation of one or the other metal would gradually disappear. The British had adopted the gold standard in 1816, and the silver currency was reduced to the condition of a nominal currency as small change. However, France resisted acceptance of the gold standard. In 1865, it promoted the formation of the Latin Monetary Union—which was joined by Belgium, Switzerland, Italy and Greece—based on the agreement to: maintain the bimetallic system; establish a bimetallic ratio of 1/15.5—adjusted to the differences in market prices of gold and of silver– and to establish a maximum limit for the per capita issue of silver currency. The Spanish monetary reform promoted by Laureà Figuerola and approved by the Decree of 19 October 1868 has been considered to be a decision aimed at preparing Spain to join the Monetary Union, which, however, was never formalized. This reform meant that the peseta became the unit of the system and the adoption of the bimetallic ratio of 1/15.5 (Sardá, 1970, pp. 151–156). The collapse of the price of silver from the 1870s made it unviable to maintain bimetallic systems. The rupture of the bimetallic ratio meant that, due to Gresham's law, gold coins disappeared from circulation. In principle, in order to endeavour to maintain the system, the countries involved in the Monetary Union increased the issue of gold currency—Spain did the same—, but, in the end, faced with the intensification of silver's price fall, they decided to desist. In 1878, they agreed to suspend silver minting and the international system of economic relations became based on the gold standard. The silver currency was reduced everywhere to a nominal currency to be used as a medium of exchange in internal transactions (Jiménez, 2000, p. 39).

Spain did not follow this pattern. In 1883, the management of the Banco de España decided to suspend the convertibility of its notes into gold currency—although, it would appear that it maintained it in a very restrictive manner until the beginning of the 1890s—to avoid being left without gold reserves (Tortella, 1974b, p. 480). The fact that it was a private bank meant that the government remained completely outside such a transcendental question. What it did was to stipulate that the Treasury should limit the minting of gold coins, which fell to levels of scarce consideration (Sardá, 1970, p. 200), at the same time as—under the pressure arising from the collapse in the price of silver–gold coins disappeared from circulation during the following decade. Therefore, during the 1880s, the Spanish monetary system was completely heterodox. In theory, it continued to be a bimetallic system, but, in practice, it became de facto a fiduciary system, despite the circulation of the Banco de España's notes coexisting with silver currency (Martín Aceña, 1989, 1993, pp. 140–145; Tortella, 1974b, pp. 457–534).[5] The collapse in the price of silver, in relation to that of gold and to the general price index, converted the silver currency into "nominal" (that is to say fiduciary) due to the huge difference between the theoretical nominal value that was attributed to it and the market price of the metal that it contains[6] At the same time, the gap left by the disappearance of the gold currency was offset by a huge increase in fiduciary circulation in the last quarter of the nineteenth century.[7]

There has been considerable speculation on this decline and, above all, regret has been expressed that Spain did not join the gold standard. The reason for this appears to be clear: it was not in a position to do so. During those years, the country had a chronic budget deficit, which did not arise from the fact that public expenditure was excessive—on the contrary, it appears that it grew below GDP—, but rather from the fact that the Treasury collected little (Comín, 1996, p. 38). As already indicated, the deficit was not financed in an orthodox manner—by attracting saving through the trading of public debt—but rather the Spanish state, totally lacking in internal and external credit, after so many suspensions of payments and so many "arrangements", had to finance itself with credits from the Banco de España which, in turn, financed this credit supply by increasing money supply. Therefore, the issuing bank only had room to manoeuvre in order to implement a more or less expansive monetary policy—in actual fact, it maintained it at the minimum possible levels—, but under no circumstance was a deflationary policy. In short, the existence of a structural budget deficit (and the way in which it was financed) made it completely unviable to correct the balance of payment imbalances via prices—as required by the orthodoxy of the gold standard—, that is to say through contractions of money supply and of deflationary tensions. Whatever the case, the fact that Spain was not linked to the gold standard and that it adopted a fiduciary monetary system meant that the correction of the external sector imbalance was not carried out via prices, but rather through the depreciation of the peseta exchange rate, which had the same effect: it limited the increase in imports and promoted exports.[8]

6.7 The Wheat Crisis and the Disappearance of Subsistence Crises

Another substantial change in the operating pattern of the economic system arose from the so-called agricultural crisis at the end of the nineteenth century. It is very well-known that—as from the mid-1870s—cheap overseas cereals overcame the tariff protection of European, due to the chain effect of various causes: the substantial decline in transoceanic freight rates, as a result of the replacement of sail ships with steamships; the construction of railways, which permitted cheap transport of the wheat produced in the North American "prairies" and the Argentinian "pampas" to the shipping ports on their respective east coasts; the development of highly mechanized agriculture in the United States and in other American countries with very high productivity in relation to those of the old continent, etc. The growing imports of American and Russian wheat broke the balance of the intra-European market and, everywhere in Western Europe, implied a considerable decline in the prices of this cereal; a drastic reduction in the area cultivated; a collapse in land rent and an intense contraction of the agricultural working population (Garrabou, 1975, pp. 165–181; Garrabou & Sanz, 1985, pp. 139–182).

From 1830s, the Catalan market had received a very high proportion of the cereal surpluses marketed by Spanish agriculture. The Catalan cereal and flour deficit was, to a large extent, concentrated in the Barcelona Plain, where a large part of Catalan industry was located. In this situation, the Catalan capital's port played a leading role in importing foreign cereals. The scope of the crisis and of the confusion represented by the trading relations between Catalonia and Spain can be seen in the alterations recorded by cereal and flour traffic—by railway, cabotage and foreign trade—which converged on Barcelona. In this respect, it should be indicated that from 1869—the year in which prohibition was replaced with a protective tariff—, the supply of the Barcelona Plain continued to be carried out on the basis of considerable arrivals of cereals and of flour from inland Spain both by railway and by cabotage, although the net imports of foreign wheat experienced a marked upward trend from 1875 onwards. The boom in foreign cereal imports began in 1882 and gradually increased until the end of the century. Over these years, foreign wheat not only covered all the consumption needs of the population of the Barcelona Plain but also there was an increase in the shipment of cereals and of flour—obtained from foreign wheat by the then flourishing Barcelona flour industry—from the railway stations and from the Port of Barcelona (by cabotage) towards the rest of Catalonia and Spain (Pascual, 1990, pp. 130–150).

The uncontrolled increase in cereal imports, coupled with the beginning of the collapse in prices, represented ruin for farmers and the start of a decline in cultivated surface area. The Spanish Congress began to compile exhaustive parliamentary information—published under the title *La crisis agrícola y pecuaria* [The Agricultural and Livestock Crisis]—, and the Conservative party, given the seriousness of the situation, opted for a shift towards a generalized intensification of tariff protection. This shift took place with the enactment of the 1891 tariff, which not only aimed to increase protection for cereal agriculture but also had a much more general scope and increased the levels of protection of the overall Spanish economy (Serrano, 1987, pp. 123–163, 202–214). This change in commercial policy was seen as the start of the "nationalist route" of Spanish capitalism.

The 1891 protectionist shift created a marked distancing between internal and international wheat prices, this being explained by the incidence of the tariff and monetary protection arising from the fall of the peseta exchange rate. The fact that the United Kingdom maintained a fixed exchange rate and had decisively supported free trade in the face of the agricultural crisis meant that English prices corresponded to the prices on the international market. The comparison of Spanish and British prices demonstrates that total protection increased greatly during the decade from 1891 to 1900 and remained at very high levels between 1901 and 1915. Spanish wheat prices evolved by around 38% above English prices (Grupo de Estudios de Historia Rural, 1980, pp. 93–100; Pascual,

2000, p. 155). Tariff protection was the main element of the protection system that contributed, firstly, to sustaining internal prices—while British prices and those of the international market collapsed—and, then, to maintain the differential between internal and foreign prices. The tariff also became an instrument to stabilize internal wheat (and cereal) prices because, in the face of a bad harvest, protection was reduced, favouring an increase in imports and preventing upward tension in autochthonous prices. In the opposite case, the tariff was increased, imports were limited and an excessive fall in prices was avoided. This mechanism worked with great regularity. Imports periodically experienced great progressions—above all in 1905, avoiding an agricultural crisis—although between 1891 and 1915 they only represented 6.86% of apparent gross consumption of wheat and of flour from this cereal (Pascual, 2000, pp. 158–159). However, the impact of these imports on the establishment of internal wheat prices was very considerable, because they achieved a relatively much higher size in relation to the production of wheat marketed, as a result of deducting from apparent consumption the grain used for sowing and self-consumption by the workforce employed on the farms. This policy permitted renewed growth in cereal production, obtained in part through extensive farming, that is to say by increasing the area cultivated (Flores de Lemus, 1976, pp. 471–485; Grupo de Estudios de Historia Rural, 1983, p. 214), and contributed to delaying the pace of modernization of Spanish agriculture. On the downside of this policy, we have the fact that protection contributed to increasing the cost of living—as prohibition did in the nineteenth century—, and entailed a considerable transfer of income from the consumers to the producers of wheat. On the plus side, it contributed to stabilizing wheat prices and prevented the intense price rises—arising from the subsistence crises of the second third of the nineteenth century—which, as we have seen, had very depressive effects on internal demand and on industrial activity, affected the balance of the external sector and represented contractions in money supply, which meant that these crises were transferred to the financial sector.

6.8 The Catalan Economy Overwhelmed by the Restriction of Bank Credit, 1883–1914

American trade—which was one of the foundations of the system of external trade relations of Catalonia in the nineteenth century– fell into crisis during the last third of the century. There were various causes: the need to abolish slavery and the emergence of a pro-independence movement in Cuba; the crisis of the Greater Antilles sugar economy, faced with growing competition from beet sugar; the problems of adaptation of the shipping industry to the situation created by the abolition of differential flag duties, etc. This situation led to the insolvency of Barcelona trading houses, which had coordinated the overseas trade, and triggered a shipping crisis which meant that the country's external trade—which during the second third of the nineteenth century had, to a large extent, been carried out in vessels with an autochthonous flag–, was now mainly carried out in vessels with a foreign flag (Pascual, 1991, pp. 321–332). Meanwhile, the parallel between the expansion of raw cotton imports and wine exports stopped existing due to the stagnation of wine shipments overseas as a result of the crisis of the Cuban economy.[9] Even so, in principle this did not negatively affect the Catalan wine industry because, at the same time, there was an export boom of wines to France when phylloxera destroyed French vines. Furthermore, under the impetus of French demand, the winegrowing area continued to increase, and wine prices reached their highest levels. This was an ephemeral situation which ended when French wine production recovered after replanting with American vines, and the French market was closed to Catalan and Spanish exports. In the last decade of the century, phylloxera destroyed the country's vines, at the same time as the collapse in wine exports led to a decline in its prices (Pujol, 1984, pp. 61–73). The Cuban problem worsened and the second uprising against Spanish colonial control broke out. The repression of the revolt offered the United States the opportunity to intervene in the conflict, and the Spanish-American War of 1898 resulted in a naval disaster which sealed the loss of sovereignty over Cuba, Puerto Rico and the Philippines. The overseas trading relations of Catalonia, which were already considerably damaged, collapsed even more as a result of this defeat.

The changes that we have just indicated modified the operating model of the Catalan economy, which became much more dependent on the Spanish internal market. At that time, Spain continued to be an eminently agricultural country—agriculture still employed a very high share of the working population and contributed a very considerable proportion of gross domestic product—and, therefore, internal demand was highly influenced by the ups and downs of agricultural production and by the purchasing power of the Spanish peasants. The effects of this influence began to be seen when the agricultural crisis—regarding both cereals and wine—at the end of the nineteenth century led to the collapse of internal demand. The impact on Catalan industrial production was intensified by the fact that its industry was fully geared towards the production of consumer goods.[10] In this context, between 1885 and 1900, the textile industry maintained modest growth thanks to the increasing exports of textiles to the Cuban and Puerto Rican markets, arising from the enactment, in 1882, of the Law on Trading Relations with the Antilles, which established that the tariffs between Spain and the aforementioned islands would gradually be reduced and disappear during the following decade (Sudrià, 1983, pp. 371–376).[11] The possibility of continuing to enforce the colonial agreement was aborted with the loss of the colonies and then the weakness of internal demand led this industry to a permanent situation of overproduction. The subsequent attempt to promote exports through the "cartel" organized in 1907 by the Mutua de Fabricantes de Tejidos de Algodón—taking advantage of the high tariff protection to increase the internal price in order to finance textile exports with dumping—ended up, in a couple of years, with by no means satisfactory results (Sudrià, 1983, pp. 376–380).

During this period, while the "mature" (textile) industries tended towards stagnation due to problems of demand, the intensification of tariff protection favoured a process of substitution of imports, which enabled Catalan industrial production to begin growth through diversification. This process is related to the dissemination of the electrification and motorization processes, which characterized the so-called Second Industrial Revolution. The new technologies contributed to developing new industries: the electric and electric material, automotive, electrochemical, organic chemistry, and cement industries, among others. In the following decades, this transformation represented a very profound change in the country's industrial structure (Nadal et al., 2012, pp. 125–159).

The shift to slow (and unbalanced) industrial growth coincided with the marked and sustained contraction experienced by the Barcelona banking sector and with the intense restriction of credit supply which

Table 6.7 Barcelona's financial system behaviour, 1883–1909

a *Evolution of the capital liabilities and reserves accounts and current accounts and deposits and of the cash assets and portfolio, loans and discounts of the Barcelona banking institutions, 1883–1909 (annual averages, in millions of pesetas) (*)*

	(1) Capital and reserves	*(2) Current accounts and deposits*	*(1 + 2) Total resources*	*Index*	*2/1*	*(3) Cash*	*(4) Portfolio, loans and discounts*	*Index*	*3/2*
1883–1884	163.6	65.9	229.4	100.0	0.4	42.1	195.4	100.0	0.6
1885–1899	133.4	77.2	210.6	91.8	0.6	62.0	158.4	81.1	0.8
1890–1894	109.9	65.0	175.0	76.3	0.6	54.9	123.1	63.0	0.8
1895–1899	87.8	100.7	188.5	82.2	1.1	98.0	97.4	49.8	1.0
1900–1904	65.5	84.1	149.6	65.2	1.3	74.2	73.0	37.4	0.9
1905–1909	58.5	56.1	114.6	49.9	1.0	30.3	80.0	40.9	0.5

b *Evolution of the balance of the liabilities account, current accounts and deposits and of the cash assets and portfolio and loans of the Banco de España's branch in Barcelona (annual averages, in millions of pesetas)*

	(1) Current accounts and deposits	*Index*	*(2) Cash*	*(3) Portfolio and loans*	*Index*	*3/1*
1883–1884	19.0	100.0	20.7	29.5	100.0	1.6
1885–1889	35.7	187.9	31.1	30.9	104.9	0.9
1890–1894	44.2	232.8	40.6	19.1	64.9	0.4
1895–1899	71.7	377.3	46.2	9.7	32.8	0.1
1900–1904	87.4	459.9	86.7	28.7	97.5	0.3
1905–1909	64.2	338.0	123.2	48.2	163.5	0.7

accompanied it. Numerous banks were wound up, and some of those remaining reduced their expenses. The added volume of their portfolio of investment and of loans and discounts declined intensely. Meanwhile, the banks accumulated a large quantity of dormant resources in cash—the ratio between the cash balance and that of external resources was around 1 at the end of the nineteenth century—and the surplus liquidity, possibly caused by the return of capital as a result of the colonial defeat, was eliminated on reducing the paid-up capital. The Banco de España's branch in Barcelona, dispossessed of the autonomous capacity to issue notes—which it did have between 1875 and 1883—, was obliged to help to finance the growing public deficit. Instead of providing liquidity, between 1883 and 1900, it contributed to accentuating the restrictions in credit supply by, on the one hand, intensely attracting current account resources and, on the other hand, drastically reducing the credit granted to the private sector (see Table 6.7). The decline experienced by Barcelona banks over these years has been interpreted as the effect of a problem of demand for credit—due to a lack of bankable material—by industrialists, traders, etc. It would, however, appear to have arisen from the combination of the uncertainties caused by not being able to have the support of an issuing bank and from a process of growing sclerosis of a financial system immersed in archaic practices and terrified by events to the extent of sacrificing business opportunities to avoid taking any kind of risk. Everything seems to indicate that, over these years, there was unsatisfied demand for credit on the market. There are several signs of this, such as the fact that the Banco de España's branch cornered a growing share of the commercial credit market on being freed—as from 1900, when a budget balance was achieved—from helping to finance the public deficit; that one of the new banks in Madrid, Banco Hispano-Americano, took advantage of the situation to open a branch in Barcelona; that various foreign banks—with a business model geared towards providing credit to traders and importing industrialists—also opened branches in the city (Cabana, 1978, pp. 87–110). Whatever the case, it is obvious that the fact that the autochthonous banks accumulated dormant resources and limited the credit supply to unconceivably low levels became a burden for the development of big companies—this is the case of the large electrical industry which depended on investments of foreign capital in the face of the inhibition of the autochthonous banks—, for investment and the economic growth of the country. In this respect, Edouard Escarra pointed out (in 1908) that Catalonia "is not lacking in banks, although they participate in industrial development in a fairly restricted manner: they give minimum discounts, and give advances as little as possible. Thus, neither credit for production nor credit for circulation are seriously organized and therefore they cease to contribute to economic progress..." (Escarra, 1970, pp. 142–143). It is, however, also true that, during those years, this withdrawal completely destroyed the possibility of any kind of speculative bubble emerging, which could trigger a financial crisis. At the same time, the new monetary system and the new commercial policy guaranteed that no imbalance in the external sector would represent deflationary tensions, which had been one of the recurrent causes of the financial crises of nineteenth-century Barcelona.

6.9 Concluding Remarks

The economic and financial crises of the nineteenth century were inevitable—those described are good examples of this—, because the imbalances in the external sector and the contraction of the money supply (with all the corollaries which arose from this) could not be mitigated through the devaluation of the exchange rate. The basis of the monetary system was the currency with an intrinsic value, which implied the existence of a fixed exchange rate and, therefore, the correction of the imbalances in the balance of payments was undertaken according to the mechanism described by David Hume, that is to say by means of more or less intense deflationary processes (Hume, 1741, pp. 106–114). This mechanism subsequently served as the basis for the introduction of the gold standard. However, the collection of the external sector imbalance was not automatic because, despite the contraction in money supply, prices presented notable downward rigidity, representing persistent depressive effects. Another problem which prevented the crises from being mitigated or counteracted was the non-existence of a central bank with the capacity to act as a last resort lender, to provide the banking system with liquidity in order to avoid the collapse of credit and the unhindered rise in the interest rate and the non-existence of fiscal policies geared towards curbing drifts towards depression. The availability of a bank capable of fulfilling these functions required the introduction of the forced fiduciary currency. This was obviously not the case of the financial system of Barcelona in the period between 1840 and 1865 when, in practice, a true "free banking" system prevail.[12] Both the local bank and the building societies and discounting banks put different types of fiduciary money into circulation, and all the financial establishments had to guarantee the convertibility onsight or on the maturity of this money if they wanted to avoid insolvency.

The multifaceted crisis of the end of the nineteenth century meant that Spain adopted de facto a fiduciary monetary system which, being much more flexible, markedly attenuated the impact of the circumstantial external sector imbalances on the stability of the financial system. At the same time, the country was drawn towards a more closed economy that was more dependent on the Spanish market, with the particularity that the protection granted to the cereal sector provided the prices of wheat with stability and prevented the disturbing effects of former agricultural crises. Meanwhile, the drastic reduction in credit supply by the Barcelona banks became a safety net against any kind of speculative bubble which could lead to a financial crisis, although at the expense of limiting investment and of intensifying the effect of the depressive shocks experienced by the economic system during this period. However, the transition towards the monetary and financial system which was successful in the West during the second half of the nineteenth century was at a halfway stage. The Banco de España was—despite having the issuing monopoly—a private bank and was not responsible for providing the economic system with liquidity and, even less, for acting as a last resort lender. In short, it was not obliged to counteract restrictions in banking credit, which had intense depressive effects—as occurred in Barcelona during the period from 1883 to 1914—; or to deploy preventive policies to curb possible speculative bubbles; or to develop anti-cyclic policies, providing the financial sector with liquidity at critical moments. This was, therefore, an economic and financial context very far from the one that we have today. At present—with a very different monetary system from the one that existed in the mid-nineteenth century—, the public authorities have instruments to neutralize the depressive effects of crises through the action of the central banks as last resort lenders and through the deployment of the appropriate exchange rate, fiscal and monetary policies. It is, however, obviously one thing to have the instruments and another to use them adequately.

Appendix

See Table 6.8.

Table 6.8 Exchange rate evolution in Barcelona of the bills to be cashed in Paris and in London in Francs and in Pounds Sterling, 1847–1867

Year	*Month*	*Paris Francs/duro*	*London Shillings/ duro*	*Year*	*Month*	*Paris Francs/duro*	*London Shillings/ duro*	*Year*	*Month*	*Paris Francs/duro*	*London Shillings/ duro*
1847	4	5.32	50.35		4	5.28	51.29		4	5.23	50.22
	5	5.31	49.99		5	5.28	51.27		5	5.23	50.19
	6	5.32	50.35		6	5.25	51.25		6	5.23	50.29
	7	5.32	50.56		7		51.09		7	5.27	50.37
	8	5.34	50.68		8				8	5.22	50.07
	9	5.29	50.35		9				9	5.22	48.89
	10	5.29	49.79		10	5.25	51.19		10	5.22	49.65
	11	5.28	49.43		11	5.27	51.22		11	5.19	49.65
	12	4.99	49.00		12	5.27	51.23		12	5.19	49.55
1848	1	5.24	47.14	1855	1		51.25	1862	1		49.67
	2	5.21	48.59		2	5.25	51.00		2	5.19	49.69
	3	5.25	49.22		3	5.24	50.00		3	5.23	50.05
	4		47.25		4	5.24			4	5.25	50.28
	5		47.13		5	5.25	50.62		5	5.26	50.43
	6		47.00		6	5.25			6	5.26	50.49
	7		47.00		7	5.24	50.85		7	5.23	50.05
	8	5.09	48.75		8	5.24	50.87				
	9	5.14	49.25		9	5.24	50.55		8	5.22	49.89
	10	5.11	49.81		10	5.26	50.69		9	5.21	49.89
	11	5.22	49.66		11	5.26			10	5.24	50.13
	12	5.16	49.25		12	5.26	50.59		11	5.23	50.19
1849	1	5.19	50.00	1856	1	5.25			12	5.23	50.29
	2	5.24	50.25		2	5.25	50.29	1963	1	5.23	50.35

(continued)

Table 6.8 (continued)

Year	*Month*	*Paris Francs/duro*	*London Shillings/ duro*	*Year*	*Month*	*Paris Francs/duro*	*London Shillings/ duro*	*Year*	*Month*	*Paris Francs/duro*	*London Shillings/ duro*
	3	5.24	50.09		3	5.25	50.27		2	5.24	50.27
	4	5.26	50.19		4	5.25	50.25		3	5.23	50.35
	5	5.29	50.63		5		50.22		4	5.23	50.35
	6	5.29	50.55		6	5.23	50.12		5	5.23	50.29
	7	5.29	50.49		7	5.24	50.12		6	5.23	50.35
	8	5.31	50.53		8	5.23	50.22		7	5.23	50.29
	9	5.33	50.58		9	5.24	50.17		8	5.22	50.23
	10	5.33	50.33		10	5.19	50.15		9	5.21	50.03
	11	5.32	50.45		11	5.17	49.79		10	5.21	50.05
	12	5.31	50.09		12	5.19	50.17		11	5.19	50.05
1850	1	5.29	50.05	1857	1	5.22	50.24		12	5.19	50.05
	2	5.29	50.28		2	5.23	50.37	1864	1	5.17	49.85
	3	5.29	50.18		3	5.24	50.39		2	5.16	49.69
	4	5.31	50.23		4	5.24	50.52		3	5.17	50.00
	5	5.29	50.09		5	5.24	50.49		4	5.21	50.29
	6	5.27	50.05		6	5.23	50.22		5	5.21	50.35
	7	5.27	50.05		7	5.22	50.09		6	5.19	50.45
	8	5.28	50.79		8	5.21	50.07		7	5.19	50.35
	9	5.29	50.48		9	5.21	50.15		8	5.19	50.15
	10	5.28	50.35		10	5.19			9	5.15	49.79
	11		50.33		11	5.17			10	5.15	49.78
	12	5.24	50.29		12	5.14	49.29		11		49.00

Year	*Month*	*Paris Francs/duro*	*London Shillings/duro*	*Year*	*Month*	*Paris Francs/duro*	*London Shillings/duro*	*Year*	*Month*	*Paris Francs/duro*	*London Shillings/duro*
1851	1	5.26	50.65	1858	1	5.16	49.49		12	5.07	49.13
	2	5.22	50.59		2	5.16	49.39	1865	1	5.11	49.55
	3	5.25	50.58		3	5.17	49.85		2	5.12	49.49
	4	5.28	51.00		4	5.18	50.12		3	5.12	49.49
	5	5.26	51.00		5	5.18	50.02		4	5.16	49.79
	6	5.27	51.15		6	5.19	50.12		5	5.16	49.35
	7	5.27	51.28		7	5.19	50.27		6	5.12	49.43
	8	5.27	51.28		8	5.19	50.09		7	5.09	49.15
	9	5.28	51.49		9	5.19	50.05		8	5.11	49.34
	10	5.28	50.65		10	5.23	50.15		9	5.13	49.75
	11	5.27	50.53		11	5.22	50.19		10	5.15	49.88
	12	5.29			12	5.22	50.19		11	5.11	49.63
1852	1	5.29	50.79	1859	1	5.22	50.25		12	5.09	49.49
	2	5.29	50.78		2	5.22	50.19	1866	1	5.09	49.48
	3	5.31	50.58		3	5.22	50.15		2	5.09	49.35
	4	5.29	50.43		4		50.25		3	5.08	49.13
	5	5.29	50.29		5		50.19		4	5.11	49.33
	6				6	5.19	50.29		5	5.13	49.69
	7	5.27	50.18		7	5.23	50.59		6	5.09	49.95
	8	5.28	50.38		8	5.26	50.49		7	5.09	50.09
	9	5.27	50.43		9	5.25	50.52		8	5.09	49.67
	10	5.26	50.26		10	5.26	50.52		9	5.11	49.45

(continued)

Table 6.8 (continued)

Year	*Month*	*Paris Francs/duro*	*London Shillings/ duro*	*Year*	*Month*	*Paris Francs/duro*	*London Shillings/ duro*	*Year*	*Month*	*Paris Francs/duro*	*London Shillings/ duro*
	11	5.27	50.45		11	5.24	50.49		10	5.16	49.89
	12	5.29	50.63		12	5.24	50.49		11	5.16	49.77
1853	1	5.25	50.81	1860	1	5.24	50.59		12	5.14	49.59
	2	5.24	50.62		2		50.33	1867	1	5.13	49.59
	3	5.24	50.59		3		50.37		2	5.13	49.57
	4	5.24	50.68		4	5.23	50.29		3	5.14	49.55
	5	5.22	50.57		5	5.24	50.47		4	5.15	49.79
	6	5.22	50.69		6	5.24	50.52		5	5.17	49.85
	7	5.24	50.85		7	5.25	50.55		6	5.19	50.09
	8	5.25	50.89		8	5.26	50.65		7	5.22	50.13
	9	5.26	51.07		9	5.26	50.65		8	5.21	50.09
	10	5.28	51.29		10	5.26	50.66		9	5.19	49.85
	11				11	5.26	50.65		10	5.16	49.75
	12	5.27	51.32		12	5.25	50.59		11	5.16	49.69
1854	1	5.28	51.35	1861	1	5.23	50.15		12	5.15	49.57
	2				2	5.23	50.25				
	3	5.27	51.27		3	5.22	50.29				

Source Arxiu Nacional de Catalunya, collection Corredors Reials de Canvi de Barcelona, books *Registro de cotizaciones*

Notes

1. In relation to the origin and development of financial crises, see the essays by Kindleberger (1978, 1988). See also Sudrià (2010, pp. 161–166) for a summary on the causal interpretations of these crises provided by the existing literature.
2. See Eichengreen (1995, pp. 222–286), who sees the causes which led to the great depression in external debt and in the insistence on maintaining the gold standard. The comparative study by Temin (1989, pp. 89–137), on the (positive and negative) effects of the economic policies developed by the United States and other countries during the 1930s to endeavour to emerge from the depression, is interesting.
3. In this respect, it is well worth consulting the text of the recent presentation by Temin (2012), which compares, in a schematic manner, the great depression of the 1930s and the 2008 crisis. He lists the parallels between the two: an action burdened by the weight of ideological nostalgia which does not duly appreciate economic changes; a deficient calculation of the risks; excess credit, etc. In his analysis, he repeatedly points out that the economic changes that were experienced between the interwar period and the present day are not sufficiently taken into account and that the instruments of economic policy available to confront them are underestimat In order to illustrate this, he invokes the ironic phrase by Marx that history repeats itself "the first as tragedy, then as farce".
4. The series published by Maluquer de Motes (1974, pp. 356–357), reveals a very intense decline in Spanish exports to Cuba and Puerto Rico during the five-year period of 1865–1869.
5. However, as revealed by Castañeda (2001a, pp. 335–339), the Banco de España continued to exchange its notes for gold currency, between 1884 and 1892, in what would appear to be a very restrictive manner. On the other hand, the Spanish Treasury (Sardá, 1970, pp. 333–335) continued to mint gold coins between 1884 and 1904 in quantities of scarce consideration.
6. The price of an ounce of silver went, on the London market, from 60.40 pence during the three-year period from 1870 to 1872, to 27.64 in the period from 1897 to 1899, and the exchange rate at market prices between gold and silver from 15.59 to 34.53 (Department of Commerce and Labor, 1905, p. 57). In the first quarter of the twentieth century, the market price of silver did not recover, and the exchange rate between gold and silver even tended to increase slightly (Department of Commerce and Labor, 1926, p. 724).
7. The gold currency in circulation went from an annual average of 947.2 million pesetas to just 34.6 million between the five-year periods 1875–1879 and 1895–1899, and the fiduciary currency, from an average of

162.2 million pesetas during the first five-year period to 1238.6 in the second. Meanwhile, the spectacular increase in notes in the hands of the public contributed, to a large extent, to the Banco de España increasing credits to the state by 1363 million pesetas during this period (Martín Aceña, 1989, pp. 374–384). On the important role that the network of branches of the Banco de España played in the dissemination of the fiduciary currency in the last quarter of the nineteenth century, see Castañeda (2001b, pp. 36–99).

8. On the relations between budget deficit, money supply, prices and exchange rate, see Comisión del Patrón Oro (1987).
9. According to the data provided by Maluquer de Motes (1974, pp. 354–355), the volume of Spanish colonial trade remained stagnant—with downward variations—between 1864 and the second half of the 1880s.
10. Nadal (1992, pp. 152–154) indicates that, in 1900, the textile industry still contributed 56.7% of Catalan industrial product.
11. In relation to the substantial expansion registered by Spanish colonial trade as a result of this provision, see Maluquer de Motes (1974, pp. 354–355).
12. See White (1995) on the dynamics of operation and the debate generated by the "free banking" system which prevailed in Scotland during the first half of the nineteenth century.

References

Anes, R. (1974). El Banco de España (1874–1914). Un banco nacional. In G. Tortella (Ed.), *La banca española en la Restauración. I. Política i finanzas* (pp. 107–215). Banco de España.

Blasco, Y., & Sudrià, C. (2009). *El Banc de Barcelona (1844–1874). Història d'un banc d'emissió*. Generalitat de Catalunya.

Cabana, F. (1978). *Història del Banc de Barcelona (1844–1920)*. Edicions 62.

Cabana, F. (1999). Els bancs de la febre d'or (1881). Un esbós de balanç. In A. Carreras, P. Pascual, D. Reher, & C. Sudrià (Eds.), *Doctor Jordi Nadal. Industrialització i desenvolupament econòmic d'Espanya* (pp. 749–760). Vol. I. Publicacions de la Universitat de Barcelona.

Carreras, A. (1990). *Industrialización española: Estudios de historia cuantitativa*. Espasa Calpe.

Castañeda, L. (2001a). *Esplendor y ocaso del mercado de letras de cambio en la Barcelona del siglo XIX (Doctoral Thesis)*. European University Institute.

Castañeda, L. (2001b). *El Banco de España (1874–1900). La red de sucursales y los nuevos servicios financieros*. Banco de España.

Castañeda, L., & Tafunell, X. (2001). La bolsa de Barcelona entre1849 y 1913: un nuevo índice. In C. Sudrià & D. A. Tirado (Eds.), *Peseta y protección. Comercio exterior, moneda y crecimiento económico en la España de la restauración* (pp. 281–301). Edicions Universitat de Barcelona.

Comín, F. (1996). *Historia de la Hacienda pública. II. España (1808–1995)*. Crítica.

Comisión del Patrón Oro. (1987). Informe de la Comisión sobre el Patrón Oro. In Comisión del Patrón Oro, & L. Olariaga, *El patrón oro, la peseta y la economía española (1900–36)* (pp. 9–85). Orbis.

Costas, A. (1988). *Apogeo del liberalismo en "La Gloriosa". La reforma económica en el Sexenio liberal (1868–1874)*. Siglo XXI.

Department of Commerce and Labor. (1905). *Statistical Abstract of the United States. 1904*. Government Printing Office.

Department of Commerce and Labor. (1926). *Statistical Abstract of the United States. 1925*. Government Printing Office.

Eichengreen, B. (1995). *Golden Fetters: The Gold Standard and the Great Depression, 1919–1939*. Oxford U.P.

Escarra, E. (1970). *El desarrollo industrial de Cataluña (1900–1908)*. Barcelona: Grijalbo. Original French edition: E. Escarra (1908), *Le Développement industriel de la Catalogne*. Arthur Rousseau.

Flores de Lemus, A. (1976). Sobre la dirección fundamental de la producción rural española. *Hacienda Pública Española*, *42–43*, 471–485. First edition: (1926). Madrid.

Fontana, J. (1961). La vieja Bolsa de Barcelona (1851–1914). In *Documentos y estudios. VIII. La Bolsa de Barcelona de 1851 a 1930: líneas generales de su evolución* (pp. 15–69). Ajuntament de Barcelona.

Fontana, J. (1967). La primera etapa de la formació del mercat nacional a Espanya. In J. Maluquer de Motes (Ed.), *Homenaje a Jaime Vicens Vives* (pp. 143–161). Vol. II. Universitat de Barcelona.

Fontana, J. (1980). *La Hacienda en la historia de España, 1700–1931*. Instituto de Estudios Fiscales.

Fradera, J. M. (1987). *Indústria i mercat. Les bases comercials de la indústria catalana moderna (1814–1845)*. Crítica.

Friedman, M., & Schwartz, A.J. (1993). *A Monetary History of the United States, 1867–1960*. Princeton: Princeton U.P. First edition: (1963). Princeton U.P.

Garrabou, R. (1975). La crisi agrària espanyola de finals del segle XIX: Una etapa en el desenvolupament del capitalisme. *Recerques*, *5*, 163–216.

Garrabou, R., & Sanz, J. (1985). La agricultura española durante el siglo XIX: ¿inmovilismo o cambio? In R. Garrabou & J. Sanz (Eds.), *Historia agraria de la España contemporánea. 2. Expansión y crisis (1850–1900)* (pp. 7–191). Crítica.

Giralt, E. (1990). L'agricultura: Tradició i innovació en l'agricultura del segle XIX. In J. Nadal, J. Maluquer de Motes, C. Sudrià, F. Cabana (Eds.), *Història econòmica de la Catalunya contemporània. 2. Agricultura i població* (pp. 123–305). Enciclopèdia Catalana.

Grupo de Estudios de Historia Rural. (1980). *Los precios del trigo i de la cebada en España, 1891–1907*. Banco de España.

Grupo de Estudios de Historia Rural. (1983). Notas sobre la producción agraria española, 1893–1931. *Revista de Historia Económica, 2*, 185–252.

Hume, D. (1741). *Essays, Moral and Political*. A. Kincaid.

Izard, M. (1973). *Industrialización y obrerismo. Las Tres Clases de Vapor, 1869–1913*. Ariel.

Jiménez, J. C. (2000). El naixement d'una moneda. In J.L. García Delgado & J. M. Serrano (Eds.), *Del ral a l'euro. Una història de la pesseta* (pp. 28–44). La Caixa.

Kindleberger, C. P. (1978). *Manias, Panics, and Crashes: A History of Financial Crises*. Macmillan.

Kindleberger, C. P. (1988). *The International Economic Order: Essays on Financial Crisis and International Public Goods*. Wheatsheaf.

Maluquer de Motes, J. (1974). El mercado colonial antillano en el siglo XIX. In J. Nadal & G. Tortella (Eds.), *Agricultura, comercio colonial y crecimiento económico en la España contemporánea* (pp. 322–367). Ariel.

Maluquer de Motes, J. (1994). El índice de la producción industrial de Cataluña. Una Nueva Estimación, *Revista de Historia Industrial, 5*, 45–70.

Martín Aceña, P. (1989). Sistema financiero. In A. Carreras (Ed.), *Estadísticas históricas de España. Siglos XIX–XX* (pp. 363–394). Fundación Banco Exterior.

Martín Aceña, P. (1993). Spain During the Classical Gold Standard Years, 1880–1914. In M. D. Bordo & F. Capie (Eds.), *Monetary Regimes in Transition* (pp. 135–172). Cambridge U.P.

Martín Niño, J. (1972). *La Hacienda española y la Revolución de 1868*. Instituto de Estudios Fiscales/Ministerio de Hacienda.

Nadal, J. (1975). *El fracaso de la revolución industrial en España, 1814–1913*. Ariel.

Nadal, J. (1992). Cataluña la fábrica de España. La formación de la industria moderna en Cataluña. In J. Nadal (Ed.). *Moler, tejer y fundir. Estudios de historia industrial* (pp. 84–154). Ariel.

Nadal, J., Benaul, J. M., & Sudrià, C. (2012). La formació d'una societat plenament industrial, 1833–1935. In J. Nadal, J. M. Benaul, & C. Sudrià (Eds.), *Atles de la industrialització de Catalunya, 1750–2010* (pp. 55–177). Vicens Vives.

Navas, M., & Sudrià, C. (2007). La crisi financera de 1866 a Catalunya: Una revisió. *Recerques, 55*, 35–72.

Pascual, P. (1990). *Agricultura i industrialització a la Catalunya del segle XIX. Formació i desestructuració d'un sistema econòmic*. Crítica.
Pascual, P. (1991). La modernització dels mitjans de transport a la Catalunya del segle XIX. In J. Nadal, J. Maluquer de Motes, C. Sudrià, F. Cabana (Eds.), *Història econòmica de la Catalunya contemporània. 3. Indústria, transport i finances* (pp. 233–335). Enciclopèdia Catalana.
Pascual, P. (1999). *Los caminos de la era industrial. La construcción y financiación de la Red Catalana de ferrocarriles (1843–1898)*. Edicions de la Universitat de Barcelona and Fundación de los Ferrocarriles Españoles.
Pascual, P. (2000). *Els Torelló. Una família igualadina d'advocats i propietaris. 2. Un estudi sobre la crisi de l'agricultura tradicional (1841–1930)*. Fundació Salvador Vives Casajuana.
Pascual, P. (2007). La Diputació i la construcció de la xarxa catalana de carreteres: 1840–1868. In B. de Riquer (Ed.), *Història de la Diputació de Barcelona, 1812–2005* (pp. 153–211). Vol. I. Diputació de Barcelona.
Pascual, P., & Sudrià, C. (2008). Industrialización, desarrollo financiero y oferta monetaria en Barcelona a mediados del siglo XIX. *Investigaciones de Historia Económica, 12*, 45–74.
Pujol, J. (1984). Les crisis de malvenda del sector vitivinícola català entre el 1892 i el 1935. *Recerques, 15*, 57–78.
Rodrigo, M. (2000). *Los marqueses de Comillas, 1817–1925. Antonio y Caudio López*. Lid.
Sánchez-Albornoz, N. (1975). *Los precios agrícolas durante la segunda mitad del siglo XIX. Vol. I. Trigo y cebada*. Banco de España.
Sánchez-Albornoz, N. (1977). *España hace un siglo: Una economía dual*. Alianza Editorial.
Sardá, J. (1970). *La política monetaria y las fluctuaciones de la economía española en el siglo XIX*. Ariel.
Serrano, J. M. (1987). *El viraje proteccionista en la Restauración. La política comercial española, 1875–1895*. Siglo XXI.
Sudrià, C. (1983). La exportación en el desarrollo de la industria algodonera española, 1875–1920. *Revista de Historia Económica, 2*, 369–386.
Sudrià, C. (1994). Capitalistes i fabricants. El finançament de la industrialització catalana (1815–1866). *Butlletí de la Societat Catalana d'Estudis Històrics, 5*, 29–40.
Sudrià, C. (2010). Pasado y presente en el análisis de las crisis económicas: algunas reflexiones sobre la dinámica de los mercados y el manejo de la política fiscal. In A. Costas (Ed.), *La crisis de2008. De la economía a la política y más allá. Mediterráneo Económico, 18* (pp. 161–166). Fundación Cajamar.
Sudrià, C., & Pascual, P. (1999). Financing Railway Mania: Capital Formation and the Demand for Money in Catalonia, 1840–66. *Financial History Review, 6*(2), 127–145.

Tafunell, X. (1991). Banca i mercat de capitals, 1866–1914. In J. Nadal, J. Maluquer de Motes, & C. Sudrià, F. Cabana (Eds.), *Història Econòmica de la Catalunya Contemporània. S. XIX. Indústria, transports i finances* (pp. 379–421). Enciclopèdia Catalana.

Tedde, P. (1974), La banca privada española durante la Restauración (1874–1914). In G. Tortella (Ed.), *La banca española en la Restauración. I. Política i finanzas* (pp. 217–455). Banco de España.

Temin, P. (1989). *Lessons from the Great Depression.* MIT Press.

Temin, P. (2012). The Great Recession in Historical Perspective. Lecture. Fundación Ramón Areces. https://www.fundacionareces.es/fundacionareces/en/events/the-great-recession-in-historical-perspective.html. Accessed 10 Aug 2019.

Tortella, G. (1970). El Banco de España entre 1829–1929. La formación de un banco central. In F. Ruiz Martín & A. Moreno (Eds.), *El Banco de España. Una historia económica* (pp. 261–313). Banco de España.

Tortella, G. (1973). *Los orígenes del capitalismo en España: Banca, industria y ferrocarriles en el siglo XX*. Tecnos.

Tortella, G. (Ed.). (1974a). *La banca española en la Restauración. II. Datos para una historia económica*. Banco de España.

Tortella, G. (1974b). Las magnitudes monetarias y sus determinantes. In G. Tortella (Ed.), *La banca española en la Restauración. I. Política i finanzas* (pp. 457–521). Banco de España.

Torras, J. (1976). Aguardiente y crisis rural (Sobre coyuntura vitícola, 1793–1832). *Investigaciones Económicas, 1*, 45–67.

Valls, F. (2004). *La Catalunya atlàntica. Aiguardent i teixits a l'arrencada industrial catalana*. Eumo.

White, L. H. (1995). *Free Banking in Britain: Theory, Experience and Debate, 1800–1845*. The Institute of Economic Affairs.

CHAPTER 7

Depressions of the Catalan Economy During the Rise and Decline of the Second Industrial Revolution, 1914–2016

Jordi Catalan Vidal

This chapter aims to analyse the causes, buffers and consequences of the great depressions experienced by Catalonia in the 100-year period between the outbreak of the Great War and the crisis of the euro. The interval can be considered as that of the emergence and decline of the

The author is grateful for the financial support of the Ministry of Economy and Competitiveness of the Spanish Government (MINECO), the Ministry of Science and Innovation (MCIN/AEI/https://doi.org/10.13039/501100011033), and of the European Regional Development Fund of the European Union (ERDF) (*A way of making Europe*) through projects HAR2015-64769-P, "Industrial Crisis and Productive Recovery in the History of Spain, 1686–2018" and PGC2018-093896-B-I00, "Mediterranean Capitalism? Successes and

J. Catalan Vidal (✉)
University of Barcelona, Barcelona, Spain
e-mail: jordi.catalan@ub.edu

J. Catalan Vidal (ed.), *Crises and Transformation in the Mediterranean World*, Palgrave Studies in Economic History,
https://doi.org/10.1007/978-3-031-24502-2_7

Second Industrial Revolution. Despite the fact that it was already under way in 1914, this technological revolution had not yet driven the macroeconomic changes which, with the dissemination of processes such as high-voltage electric power, the construction of vehicles with the internal combustion engine and the synthesis of organic chemical compounds, ended up transforming the set of previously existing productive branches. At the beginning of the period studied, a typical activity from the First Industrial Revolution, the textile industry, still overwhelmingly dominated the productive system of Catalonia. At the end of this period, the information processing and transmission technologies are reshaping the country's productive assets into an authentic Third Technological Revolution.

The definition of great depression in this article is a prolonged period of crisis, during which production and consumption per inhabitant remain below the previously achieved historical maximum. In other words, a great depression is a long-lasting interval of underuse of the productive capacity and of the workforce available. Three indicators seemed to be appropriate to measure the evolution of the production and consumption capacity of Catalonia during the era of the Second Industrial Revolution : GDP, industrial product and registration of passenger cars. All three present problems as a measurement of wellbeing, which I shall not address here due to lack of space. They do, however, appear to be acceptable instruments to endeavour to measure the duration of the great crises of an industrial economy, such as the Catalan economy, during the long century of the rise and decline of the Second Industrial Revolution.

The longest series that we have is that of the industrial product. It is available from the beginning of the period in question thanks to the work of pioneers such as Albert Carreras (1985), Jordi Maluquer de Motes

Failures of Industrial Development in Spain, 1720–2020". He also thanks to the Generalitat de Catalunya, the Obra Social "la Caixa" and the Centre d'Estudis Jordi Nadal of the University of Barcelona, which also contributed to support the publication of this chapter in several ways. Moreover, the author expresses his gratitude to the journal *Recerques*, where a previous version of this work was published in Catalan language (volume 72–73, 2107). Last but not least, I am very grateful to Doctor Andreu Ginés who helped me with the English revision. The possible errata are the exclusive responsibility of the author.

(1994) and Antonio Parejo (2004, 2005). It is an extremely useful instrument to identify depressions, although it is limited to industrial activity (without construction) and may underestimate growth at times of rapid changes in the composition and prices of the productive branches. One failing of the indicator in the Catalan case is that its evolution is overly determined by the behaviour of raw cotton imports. The GDP data allow us to offset the above limitations since they offer us an indicator of the overall paid economic activity. We do not, however, have GDP figures from before 1930 and, from then until 1955, we only have the five-yearly estimates of Julio Alcaide (2003). The registration of passenger cars is a consumer indicator which is available from 1927, when it represented above all the purchasing power of the elites (Catalan, 2012f). However, as the Second Industrial Revolution spread, it becomes a better indicator of how the crises affected the consumer expectations of the majority of society. Another advantage of this indicator is that of being available annually from the above-mentioned date. For the previous years, we have the registration of automobiles (that is to say including motorcycles and industrial vehicles) from 1920.

The evolution of the aforementioned indicators, analysed in per capita terms, allows us to envisage the existence of four great depressions of economic activity in Catalonia between 1914 and 2016. The first began at the end of World War One and was not fully overcome until the coup by General Miguel Primo de Rivera.[1] The second began in 1929, including the Republican years, the Civil War and the early years of the Franco (*First Francoism*) regime and continued until the mid-1950s (*Second Francoism*). The third one broke out during the late Franco regime (*Late Francoism*) and lasted until the year Spain joined the European Economic Community. The last one includes the Great Recession, which began in 2007 and continued with the crisis of the euro, which transformed the slump into another great depression in the countries of Mediterranean capitalism. The following sections analyse them from a comparative perspective.

7.1 The Slump of the End of the Great War, 1919–1923

The exceptional stimuli created by the outbreak of the Great War in a neutral, relatively developed country, are at the origin of the first great crisis of the Catalan economy during the twentieth century. The global conflict created opportunities to export out of the blue for branches with intense specialization in the Catalan Countries, such as cotton fabrics, wool textiles, footwear and some foodstuffs (Calvo, 1988; Carreras, 1985; Deu, 1988, 1990; Fontana & Nadal, 1976; Manera, 2002; Miranda, 1992, 1998; Ramon Muñoz, 2003, 2010; Soler, 1984). It also favoured the substitution of imports in activities such as the obtention of energy, chemical and pharmaceutical production, the construction of machinery and motors, the manufacture of electric material, obtaining steel and producing cava (Calvo, 1988; Carreras & Yáñez, 1992; Deu, 2005; Fàbrega, 2009; Nadal, 1985; Nadal & Tafunell, 1992; Nadal et al., 1988; 2012; Puig, 2003; Riba, 2003; Roldán & García Delgado, 1973; Sudrià, 1990; Valls, 2003, 2011).

The scarcity of coal favoured the use of the hydraulic resources of the Pyrenees and accelerated the country's electrification process, with growing importance for the Barcelona Traction group (Calvo & Sagnes, 1995; Sudrià, 1987a, 1987b). Use of the country's limited mining resources likewise received a boost: lignite mining increased in Bergadà and Calaf; prospecting intensified in Bages, with the aim of exploiting the salt deposits; and Solvay took the first steps to mine potassium chloride from the subsoil of Súria (Fàbrega, 2009; Riba, 2003). Shipping was also promoted by the increase in freight during the international conflict, favouring the recovery of sailing.

Figure 7.1 shows us the impact of the war on the two most important production sectors of Catalan industry in 1913: the cotton and wool textile branches (Fontana, 1953). Both cotton and wool, which had become progressively more mature at the end of the nineteenth century, experienced a transitory revival during the years of the war thanks to manufacturing exports. Exports of cotton products doubled in weight during the five-year period from 1914 to 1918, in relation to that of 1909–1913. The impact of the world war was even more important for wool: the weight of wool product exports increased 30-fold (Deu, 1990).

The new export opportunities in the above sectors and others such as footwear and olive oil, generated extraordinary benefits in the hands of industrialists. Consequently, deposits in Catalan banks almost tripled in the five years of the war, while during the five-year period prior to the conflict, they only increased by 25% (Nadal & Sudrià, 1981; Nadal et al., 2012).

According to the behaviour of per capita industrial product, the moment of greatest euphoria during the war was in 1915. At that time,

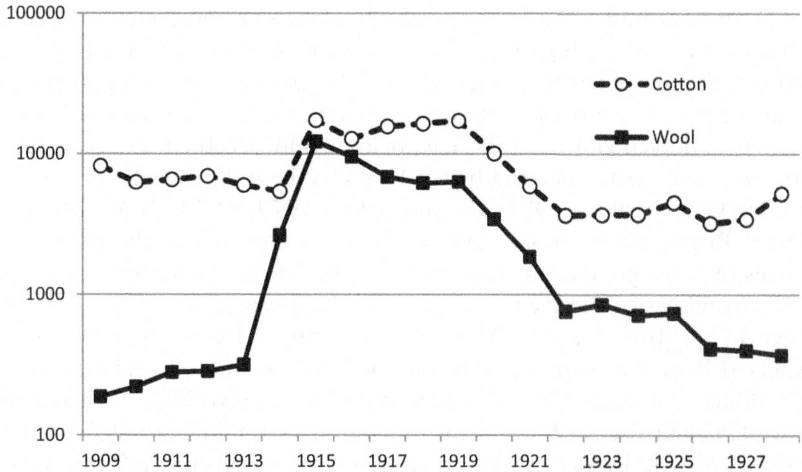

Fig. 7.1 Spanish cotton and wool fabrics exports, 1909–1928 (tonnes) (*Source* Own elaboration with Dirección General de Aduanas, *Estadística del Comercio Exterior de España*, several years. Compiled by J. M. Fontana [1953, pp. 190–199])

raw cotton imports achieved a volume two-thirds higher than that of 1913. Starting from 1916, industrial production began to recede and, following a pause during 1918, experienced a significant contraction during 1919. In view of its size, represented the transformation of the crisis into a genuine depression.

Although at the beginning of the post-war crisis, there was a progressive depletion of the exceptional conditions generated by the conflict, the recession at the end of the war became a great depression due to the confluence of three additional factors. The first involved the speculative excesses which occurred during the conflict itself and the initial post-war years. The second aggravating factor of the crisis was the loss of the purchasing power of salaries during the initial phase of the war, which led to a huge social conflict, encouraged by the struggle for the 48-hour week, and the relative intransigence of employers and those responsible for public order. Finally, the depression was fed by the adoption of a restrictive monetary policy in the United Kingdom starting from the end of 1919, followed by important countries such as the United States and France.

During the initial phase of the war, a fundamental component of speculation arose with the hoarding of raw materials, stimulated by their soaring prices and the generous credit granted by banks when using them as a guarantee. The hoarding spread to goods such as raw cotton, wool, leather and even colonial products, being gladly accepted as a guarantee for succulent credits granted by the banks to the industrialists (Beltran & Sardá, 1933; Blasco, 2007; Cabana, 1965, 1972, 1978, 2007; Muñoz, 1988; Royes, 1999; Sudrià, 2007, 2013b). Subsequently, the fall in the prices of these goods and, consequently, the erosion of a decisive part of the guarantees of the credits granted, gradually created a growing inbalance in the banks' assets. The collapse of the price of wool especially affected Banco de Tarrasa, at the end of 1919, was the second biggest in Catalonia. The excessive credits against guarantees involving raw materials also damaged the profitability of the country's leading financial institution, Banco de Barcelona. The latter moreover stands out in those years for a lack of transparency in its management, an audacious policy of taking over smaller institutions (Caja Vilumara, Banco de Préstamos y Descuentos and Crédito Mercantil) and, above all, for concentrating a large quantity of resources in foreign currency, especially German marks. The decision to invest a remarkable amount of the asset in marks, betting for the future appreciation of the German currency, resulted in fatal for what had been the country's main financial institution since 1844. Furthermore, the profitability of Banco de Barcelona was not helped by the doubtful credits granted to an Uruguayan group, which turned out to be insolvent. Not even Francesc Cambó, who acted as the bank's lawyer, was able to save it. Both the first and the second bank of Catalonia ended up closing (Beltran & Sardá, 1933; Blasco, 2007; Blasco-Martel & Sudrià, 2016; Cabana, 1965, 1972, 1978, 2007; Muñoz, 1988; Royes, 1999; Sudrià, 2007, 2013b). Consequently, deposits in Catalan banks receded between 1919 and 1924, and credit for industry diminished (Nadal et al., 2012).

The high war-induced inflation did not bring with it a corresponding increase in nominal salaries during the first years of the war, with the consequent fall in purchasing power of workers' income (Deu, 1988; Enrech, 2005; Fontana & Nadal, 1976; Gabriel, 1988; Maluquer de Motes, 1987, 1989, 2005; Maluquer de Motes & Llonch, 2005; Soto, 1989; Vilar, 2009). Real wages in the textile industry, estimated by Maluquer de Motes (1989), seemed to suggest a drop in the purchasing power of workers of around 11% between 1914 and 1916. In activities which did not experience so much prosperity during the war, the fall in purchasing power of wages must have been even greater. In the case of Sabadell, the real salaries of mechanical engineering workers, presented by Deu (2005), recorded a 9% fall over the same dates (Fig. 7.2). The erosion of real salaries during the early years of the Great War is confirmed by the value of deposits in savings banks, an important placement for the scarce savings of workers at the time. Unlike what occurred with the banks, the real value of deposits in savings banks was lower during 1916 than before the war (Fig. 7.2).

As a result of the growing impoverishment of workers, we can detect an increase in labour conflicts starting from 1916, at which time the main Spanish unions, Confederación Nacional de Trabajadores (CNT) and Unión General de Trabajadores (UGT), agreed to act in coordination to confront the rise in the cost of living. During 1917, the two unions called a revolutionary general strike, in a context heated by the demands of the military *juntas de defensa*, the autonomist proposals of the Assembly of Parliamentarians and the revolutionary successes in Russia

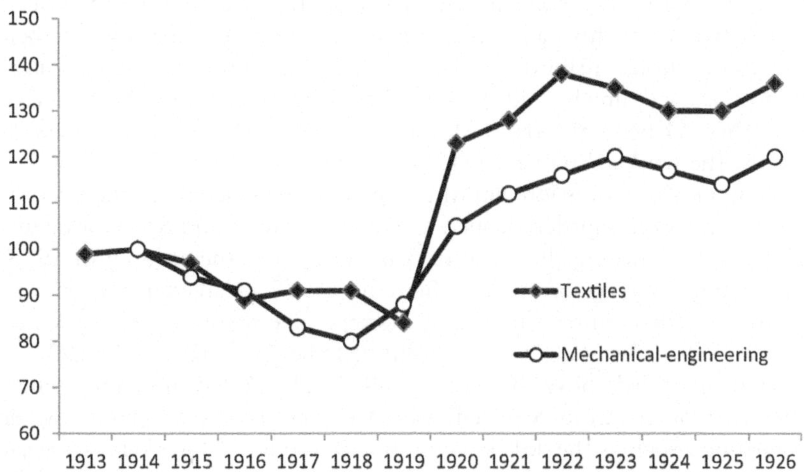

Fig. 7.2 Real wages of the textile and mechanical engineering workers in Catalonia 1913–1926 (Index Numbers 1914 = 100) (*Notes* The textile industry indices include wool and cotton. Those of metal engineering are for the workers of Sabadell. *Sources* Own elaboration with Maluquer de Motes [1987, p. 507] and Deu [2005, p. 86])

(Abelló & Gabriel, 1995; Ardit et al., 1980; Balcells, 1977; Massana, 1981; Risques et al., 1995; Termes, 1987).

During 1918, the Workers' Congress of Sants decided to replace the diverse crafs unions with a single industrial union. At the beginning of February 1919, Barcelona Traction, Light and Power (La Canadenca) dismissed several employees for defending their trade union rights and, in response, the workers' strike in the main electricity company brought Barcelona to a standstill. The stoppages out of solidarity spread quickly to the water, gas, railway, graphic arts and other branches. The country's capital was immobilized for around 40 days. Despite the declaration of a state of war, the conflict ended with those dismissed being reinstated, significant salary increases, the agreement to pay wages in the event of an accident and recognition of the 48-hour working week (Maluquer de Motes & Llonch, 2005).

The employers reacted to the workers' mobilization by supporting the resurrection of the Sometent (right-win armed militia), the creation of "free" unions and some "lock-outs". Numerous assaults on workers and industrialists turned the streets of Barcelona into a sea of blood during the early 1920s. The conflicts were particularly acute between the skilled textile workers, who had suffered from a severe deterioration of their living conditions arising from the growing mechanization and feminization of work (Enrech, 2005). With the change of decade, the new civil Governor, General Severiano Martínez Anido, toughened the repression against the workers' movement.

Neither the repression nor the violence (in which important workers' leaders were murdered, such as Francesc Layret and Salvador Seguí) succeeded in curbing the spiral of demands before the autumn of 1923. The struggle was to spread the achievements of La Canadenca workers to the rest of the country's industrial workers. The textile workers attained increases in daily wages which positioned their real salaries in 1923 at around one-third above the levels of 1913. The skilled mechanical engineering workers from Sabadell, who were employed in much smaller companies, such as the Tallers Gregori with around 20 workers, achieved much more modest, but significant increases. In the year of the Primo de Rivera coup d'état, they were paid 20% more in real terms than in 1914 (Deu, 2005).

Real wages experienced a sudden and marked increase during the period 1919–1922, when the post-war recession intensified. Despite the fact that, in some activities, the salary rise could favour demand, its timing coincided with the decline in exports and the financial crisis. In the short term, it contributed to eroding the profitability of industrial activity and to curbing investment, at times when the credit market was closed. As we will see, this occurred in the framework of an international tightening of macroeconomic policies.

Over the first months of 1919, the United States, the United Kingdom and Japan recorded a speculative boom, favoured by the suppression of the controls during the war and the positive expectations of the employers. However, during the month of October, the Bank of England increased its rate of discount in order to expand its gold reserves, with a view to re-establishing the convertibility of the pound. Consequently, the United States Federal Reserve and the Bank of France lost foreign reserves and responded by increasing their reference rates. The increase in the rates of the main economies of the time caused a new tendency towards depression at the end of the war. Furthermore, the governments of the three states planned a reduction of their public deficits for 1920. The price of silk sank in Japan at the beginning of the year and the New York stock exchange recorded a sudden contraction in the month of March. The Bank of England again raised its discount rates during the month of April and caused a toughening of the recession. At the end of the 1920s, the textile, steel and mechanical engineering of the United Kingdom collapsed and the approval of salary cuts made the fall in demand even worse. Shares listed on the Tokyo stock exchange lost 75% of their value in six months. France suffered from a considerable decline in its industrial activity. The United States experienced tremendous deflation and the unemployment rate shot up to 19% (Allen, 1946; Aldcroft, 1977; Eichengreen, 1995, 2004; Friedman & Schwartz, 1963; Glynn & Booth, 1992; James, 2001, 2009; Kindleberger, 1978; Lewis, 1949; Sauvy & Hirsch, 1984).

The consensus in favour of very restrictive monetary and fiscal policies in the United Kingdom, the United States and France entailed an intense international recession in 1920 and 1921. The depression affected Catalonia through several channels and, especially, through foreign trade and the stock market. Thus, the physical volume of cotton manufacture exports dropped by over 40% in 1920. The woolen fabrics industry declined by 46% compared with the previous year. The collapse of foreign trade caused the price of raw materials to drop and, with it, the guarantees of a large part of the bank credit. For its part, the Barcelona stock exchange, which declined intensely from the end of 1919, accentuated its downward trend. The suspension of payments was announced by a railway company based in Barcelona, Ferrocarril de Valladolid a Medina de Rioseco, and linked to the city's financial interests. In the last quarter of 1920, there were successive withdrawals of deposits from Banco de Tarrasa and from Banco de Barcelona. Word spread that the Banco de España was helping several of the city's institutions. At Christmas, the Governing Board of Banco de Barcelona decided to suspend payments.[2]

Considerable quantitative and some qualitative evidence points at 1921 as the worst moment of the crisis.[3] Per capita industrial product dropped by 20% in relation to the 1916 level. According to Hortalà's index, the real decline in share prices on Barcelona Stock Exchange in that year was approximately 13% compared with the previous year (Cuevas, 2013; Hortalà, 2007). The data for the registration of automobiles in Catalonia recorded an even more acute fall of 41%!

Whatever the case, during the depression itself, there were mechanisms that acted as a buffer against the crisis. Four were significant in Catalonia: fiscal expansion, tariff protection, depreciation of the peseta and the dissemination of the Second Industrial Revolution.

First, the tendency towards fiscal expansion during the period arose from the budgetary policy of the Spanish government and from the impulse of the Mancomunitat of Catalonia. Spain's budget balance was negative for each of the years between 1916 and 1922. On average, the seven years mentioned closed with a deficit of around 3.5% of Spanish GDP, a rate much higher than the typical imbalances of the nineteenth century.[4]

What is more, in 1914 Mancomunitat de Catalunya was created, as a first experience of Devolution since 1714, allowing the Catalan provinces to share some competences. This first experience in regional decentralization was led by Presidents Enric Prat de la Riba (1914–1917) and Josep Puig i Cadafalch (1918–1923), leaders of Catalan autonomism. Despite not having a huge budget, the Mancomunitat also acted as a public agent offsetting the crisis, with its policy of providing education facilities, promoting telephony and the railways and, above all, road construction (Balcells, 2014; Balcells et al., 1996; Casassas & Roig, 1995; Roca, 1979). For this last channel, it favoured the diffusion of automobiles, an activity with great externalities on the industrialization process (Fig. 7.3).

Second, as European production returned to the Spanish market through imports, pressure gradually grew in favour of reviewing tariff

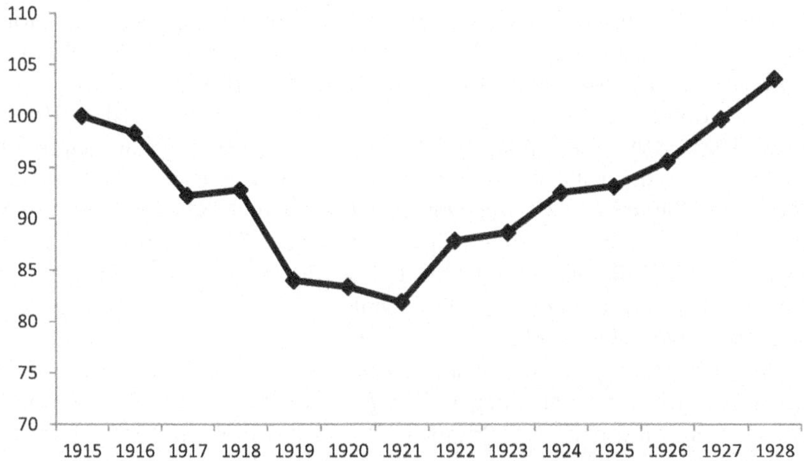

Fig. 7.3 Per capita industrial product of Catalonia, 1915–1928 (Numbers Index 1915 = 100) (*Source* Compiled by the author based on the industrial production index of Parejo [2005, pp. 135–136] and the population of Alcaide [2007, pp. 59–95])

duties, which were badly adjusted as a result of the high wartime inflation. Following a previous temporary increase in duties, in 1921 the provisional tariff of Argüelles was approved. Afterwards, Cambó, during a short stay as the head of the Ministry of Finance, prepared a subsequent revision of duties, which entailed the approval of a new tariff in 1922 (Serrano, 1986). The increases in tariff duties favoured a recovery in productive branches such as clothing and footwear, paper and metal processing industries.

Third, although the peseta had appreciated during the Great War thanks to the exceptional results from foreign trade, when, in the post-war period, difficulties began again, the Spanish currency registered a substantial foreign depreciation. The pound went from representing 19.9 pesetas in 1918 to 31.8 pesetas in 1923.[5] That is to say that, in relation to the level of five years previously, the value of the peseta against the pound sterling declined by around 37%. The formidable depreciation contributed to curbing imports and encouraging exports, acting as one of the most significant buffers of the depression.

Finally, the forces which contributed to mitigating the depression included the renewed impulse of the Second Industrial Revolution, reflected in the promotion of electrification, motorization and the rapid progression of certain metallurgical and chemical branches (Calvo, 1988; Deu, 1988, 1990; Miranda, 1992; Nadal et al., 2012). The weight of electricity in the total consumption of commercial energy in Sabadell increased from 63% in 1916 to 96% in 1924 (Deu, 1988, 1990). Production of sulphuric acid by the company Cros went from 61,000 tonnes in 1915 to 165,000 tonnes in 1925. The annual registration of passenger cars in relation to the population of Catalonia may have doubled between these two dates (Fig. 7.4).

As with other great depressions, there were deep long-term consequences of the crisis which began during the Great War. In relation to the strictly political aspect, the Primo de Rivera dictatorship can be considered as a result of the intensity attained by the depression. There were, however, economic consequences of the crisis which lasted much longer

Fig. 7.4 Registration of passenger cars for Catalonia per 10,000 inhabitants, 1913–1924 (*Notes and Sources* I have estimated the registration of passenger cars for Catalonia based on the figures for Barcelona [*Anuario Estadístico de la ciudad de Barcelona* 1917] and that of automobiles for Catalonia [*Butlletí Mensual d'Estadística*]. I have estimated the population based on Alcaide [2007], pp. 59–95)

than the Primo dictatorship, in particular the adoption of a more interventionist role by the state in the economy. This new trend, which was also European, is clear, especially, in the regulation of the labour and capital markets and in the promotion of public works (Ben-Ami, 1983; Otaegui, 1986; Prat & Molina 2014; Velarde, 1968). Finally, despite the political dictatorship, we can consider that the emergence from the crisis was favourable for the economic interests of the workers who, in practice, maintained the achievements obtained from the struggles of the end of the 1910s and beginning of the 1920s.

The Spanish government's desire for greater public intervention in the regulation of the labour market reached a significant milestone with the October 1919 decree, which established the Labour Commission of Catalonia (Palacio, 1986). Further action was taken in May 1920, with the decision to create the Ministry of Labour. Although the aforementioned Ministry integrated previously existing bodies, such as the Institute for Social Reform and the National Welfare Institute, its establishment can be interpreted as a reinforcement of the commitment to offer a political response to the workers' mobilization of the time and the intensity of the crisis. In October 1922, the Spanish government passed a new decree regulating the creation of joint committees. Finally, in February 1923, it created the Delegation of the Ministry of Labour for Catalonia and the Balearic Islands.

The 1917 Law on the Protection of National Industry, promoted by Santiago Alba, led to the creation of the Banco de Crédito Industrial, which came into operation in 1921 (Tortella & Jiménez, 1986). When, also in 1921, Cambó returned to the Spanish government as Finance Minister, the regionalist politician declared his concern to avoid future insolvency such as that of Banco de Barcelona, an institution for which he had acted as an adviser (Cabana, 1965; Martín Aceña, 2000; Tortella, 1994; Tortella & Palafox, 1982). In addition to the tariff, he prepared the Banking Law which institutionalized certain recent practices of monetary policy in order to help future financial agents with problems. This consolidated the practice of rediscounting bills by the Banco de España, with preferential rates for the banks which formed part of the Superior Banking Council. It also helped them to obtain automatic credit against collaterals of public funds. In promoting the creation of this council, it was conceived as a corporate body with regional representation, where policies regulating the banking business would be agreed upon.

In October 1922, the civil Governor General Martínez Anido was dismissed, but the social violence continued to bring blood to the streets of Barcelona. In the spring of 1923, Salvador Seguí was assassinated and the CNT called a transport strike. In September, the Captain General of Catalonia, Miguel Primo de Rivera, led an uprising with the approval of King Alfonso XIII. The coup was welcomed by Catalan institutions such as Foment del Treball and the chambers of commerce. In November, the representatives of the seven main Spanish banks met the dictator and asked him to set up a programme of public works, financed with the issue of 5 billion in public debt, in order to revive activity. This request was immediately supported by the Federation of National Industries, which brought together Catalan and Basque industrial interests. The latter, in addition to suggesting measures to subsequently regulate the entry of imports, pointed out the need to build roads and modernize the railways. Primo de Rivera took up the gauntlet and prioritized improving road surfaces and the electrification of railways, thus favouring the recovery. This policy gave continuity to what had already been attempted, although ephemerally, by politicians such as Santiago Alba and even Cambó, when he was Public Works Minister in 1918.

The Primo de Rivera dictatorship represented the loss of the workers' political and trade union rights and the dissolution of the Mancomunitat of Catalonia. The repression was not, however, intense or decisive enough to significantly overturn the economic victories achieved by the workers during the period from 1917 to 1923. As shown in Fig. 7.2, under the dictatorship real textile salaries remained 30% above the level of 1913. Skilled metallurgical workers from Sabadell maintained the real salaries 14% higher than those before the war. In terms of real income, the emergence from the post-war depression was favourable for the workers, due to the great previous political and trade union mobilization.

7.2 The Great Depression of the Twentieth Century, 1929–1955

The most long-lasting depression of the twentieth century was triggered by the New York stock exchange crash, after some years of speculative excesses (Aldcroft, 1977, 1997; Bernanke, 2013; Eichengreen, 1995, 2015; Galbraith, 1954; James, 2001, 2009; Kindleberger, 1973, 1978 Lewis, 1949; Minsky, 1975, 1977; Temin, 1989). Between 1926 and

1929, share prices had doubled, stimulated by easy credit and overoptimistic bullish expectations. However, at the end of October of that last year, share prices experienced sudden drops, bringing losses to the most risky traders. A significant number of them, who had abused of overborrowing in previous years, began to have problems to repay their loans and consequently endangered the balance sheets of the banks which had financed them. Credit collapsed. Investment became depressed due to the losses incurred, the restriction of credit and the sudden change in expectations. Imports from the United States receded. Worldwide prices for primary products, which were already on a regressive path at the end of the 1920s, sank. Furthermore, the approval of the Hawley Smoot tariff in 1930 reinforced the tendency towards the contraction of American imports.

Important European countries also restricted their primary imports. In 1930, France passed the Barthe law, which forbade foreign ordinary wines from being able to be mixed with French wines (Marseille, 1984; Palafox, 1991; Sáenz de Buruaga, 1961). The high alcohol content of many wines from southern Europe had made them suitable, until then, to be used in the *coupage* of French wines. A large part of the wine which was exported wholesale from Catalonia was used for this purpose. The ban, undertaken to favour producers from the Midi and from colonial Algeria, had a very negative effect on Catalan ordinary wine exports. Consequently, the periodic crisis of selling off wine surpluses returned with strength and contributed to worsening the *rabassaire* (vine-tenants) conflict during the Second Republic, which had been proclaimed in April 1931 (Planas & Valls, 2011; Pujol, 1984, 1989a). Indeed, Catalan ordinary wine exports fell from 1.3 million hectolitres during the period from 1926–1930 to just 700,000 from 1931 to 1935, a dramatic decline of approximately 46% in volume (Pujol, 1984). The drop in exports made prices collapse and impoverished the peasants in a large part of central and southern Catalonia, where vineyards represented the main agricultural activity.

The countries of the Commonwealth met in the Ottawa Conference, held in May 1932 (Hernández Andreu, 1986; Palafox, 1991). The resolutions of the meeting increased the duties paid on goods from third-party countries entering the United Kingdom and other countries under the area of influence of the pound sterling. The measure especially harmed the exporters of nuts, potatoes, citrus fruit and corks. The erosion of food exports especially harmed the south of Catalonia, while the barriers placed on cork had a negative influence on exports from Empordà, Gironès and Selva, northern Catalan counties.

The fall in the relative prices of primary products and contraction of world trade also caused a deep depression in the countries of America which, with Argentina at the head, were important importers of olive oil. The erosion of the income of American countries considerably harmed the sales of olive oil from the Catalan counties of Baix Ebre, Baix Camp and Garrigues. Olive oil exports through Catalan customs declined from 28,000 tonnes in 1930 to just 13,000 tonnes in 1935 (Ramon Muñoz, 2011). The decline between these two dates was, therefore, more than 50%.

The reduction in exports of primary and agro-food products impoverished the Catalan regions more geared towards the foreign market. Furthermore, the contraction of international trade had a negative effect on shipping companies and shipbuilding. Although these activities were relatively unimportant in Catalonia, one of the country's big capital equipment construction companies, La Maquinista Terrestre y Marítima (LMTYM), had built diesel engines for shipping since 1932 and could not avoid recording huge losses (Balcells, 1971; Catalan, 1989b; LMTYM, 1980; Palafox, 1991).

LMTYM, a pioneering metal and mechanical construction company, was also considerably harmed by the suspension of the railway programme of the Primo de Rivera dictatorship, starting from 1930. La Maquinista, which had built some 245 steam locomotives during 1924–1929, only produced 45 during the period 1930–1935. Moreover, the weak investment in roads throughout the years of the Second Republic likewise contributed to the deep crisis experienced by companies which manufactured intermediate goods (Palafox, 1991).

A second experiment in Devolution took place since April 1931, when the Spanish republican government and insurrectional Catalan President, Francesc Macià, agreed on the reestablishment of a new regional government, under the name of the medieval institution which used to control the king, the Generalitat de Catalunya. However, responsibility for public works was not transferred to the Generalitat until 1935, when the new legitim President, Lluís Companys, and his regional government, were already imprisoned because of the attempt to create a Federal State in October 1934. As a result, public works were paralyzed at the same time that a significant decline in residential construction took place. The number of home building permits requested from Barcelona City Council collapsed by 48% between 1931 and 1933 (Balcells, 1971).[6] Production of artificial cement in Catalonia declined from 498 tonnes in 1929 to just 302 tonnes in 1934. In the following year, both the number of permits and the production of cement began to expand, although they still remained far below the level at the beginning of the decade.

In the United States, there was an initial round of bank failures starting from October 1930. Then, in March 1931, there was a second wave of bank crises. However, the Federal Reserve moreover opted for a restrictive monetary policy at the end of the summer The Republican president, Herbert Hoover, furthermore decided to increase tax and rejected the proposals of creating an unemployment benefit and of compensating war veterans. The tightening of fiscal and monetary policies ended up causing the loss of one-third of per capita GDP in the United States, favouring the victory of the Democratic Party, led by Franklin Roosevelt. In the midst of a severe third banking crisis, which ended up affecting around 6000 financial institutions, Roosevelt abandoned the gold standard in April 1933 and the United States began to recover (Bernanke, 2013; Eichengreen, 1995, 2015; Eichengreen & O'Rourke, 2009; Friedman & Schwartz, 1963, 2008;[7] James, 2009; Lewis, 1949; Temin, 1989).

The speculative excesses also profoundly affected the financial institutions on the other side of the Atlantic and, especially, in central Europe. In Austria, Creditanstalt collapsed in May 1931. In the neighbouring Germany, the Chancellor Heinrich Brüning was unable to avoid the spread of the banking crisis, despite choosing to cut civil service salaries, reduce unemployment benefits and increase indirect taxation. The soaring unemployment rate, which reached six million people, paved the way for Hitler's triumph. The latter also broke with the gold standard rules, although he preferred exchange control to devaluation. He moreover promoted a rapid recovery based on significant expansion of public expenditure on infrastructures, motorization and rearmament (Barkai, 1988; Engelhard, 2012; James, 1986; Kindleberger, 1973; Lewis, 1949; Noakes & Pridham, 1984; Overy, 1982, 1994; Scherner, 2010; Temin, 1989, 1990; Tooze, 2007).

In Catalonia, the banking crisis of the early 1930s was much less severe than in central Europe and the United States or even the local crisis at the beginning of the 1920s (Balcells, 2013; Fontana & Nadal, 1976). It did, however, put an end to Banco de Cataluña and its subsidiaries, Banco de Reus and Banco de Tortosa. The Recasens brothers' group, which had the Republican politician Pere Corominas as its company secretary, had grown quickly in the last decade, being associated with certain investment operations promoted by the Primo de Rivera dictatorship, mainly banks and oil: Banco de Crédito Local, Banco Exterior, CAMPSA and CEPSA. It also speculated significantly with foreign exchange, its corresponding account exceeding 37 million pesetas at the time of its insolvency in July 1931. The suspension of payments of Banco de Cataluña has been attributed by Francesc Cabana, following the interpretations of Andreu Abelló or of Corominas himself, to the withdrawal of the CAMPSA deposit from the institution. This would have been ordered by the Finance Minister of the provisional government of the Second Republic, Indalecio Prieto. The deposit amounted to some 16 million pesetas, out of a total of 110 million pesetas of third-party deposits in the bank. According to Cabana, the money went straight to deposits in Banco de Vizcaya and Banco de Bilbao (Cabana, 1972, 2000).

The collapse of agricultural income in the exporting regions and the decline of construction and of the investment goods industries explain the majority of the depressive tendency shown by the product estimates available (Catalan & Sánchez 2013). If we believe the estimates of Julio Alcaide (2003), per capita GDP in Catalonia dropped by almost 5% between 1930 and 1935. In any case, it should be underlined that, despite being a crisis situation, the fall was moderate, given the international context of the time. For example, in 1935, France, which persisted in remaining in the block of countries which rejected devaluation, recorded a per capita GDP 15% lower than that of 1913. The United States, despite Roosevelt adopting expansive policies, still had a per capita GDP 12% below the level of five years previously. In 1935 smaller countries, such as Holland and Austria, had per capita GDP 13% and 21%, respectively, below that of 1929.[8]

However, despite the relatively gentle depression in Catalonia, in 1935 the country had not yet emerged from the crisis. This is not only suggested by per capita GDP estimates, which it is shown in Fig. 7.5. Other indicators, such as registration of automobiles, Barcelona City Council building permits, coal arriving in the port of Barcelona and artificial cement production corroborate the fact that the Catalan economy still had a large part of its productive capacity underused.

If the financial speculation at the end of the 1920s and the closing of the international markets at the beginning of the 1930s were the main causes of the crisis and were of an exogenous nature, the contradictions of the monetary and budgetary policy of the Spanish governments acted

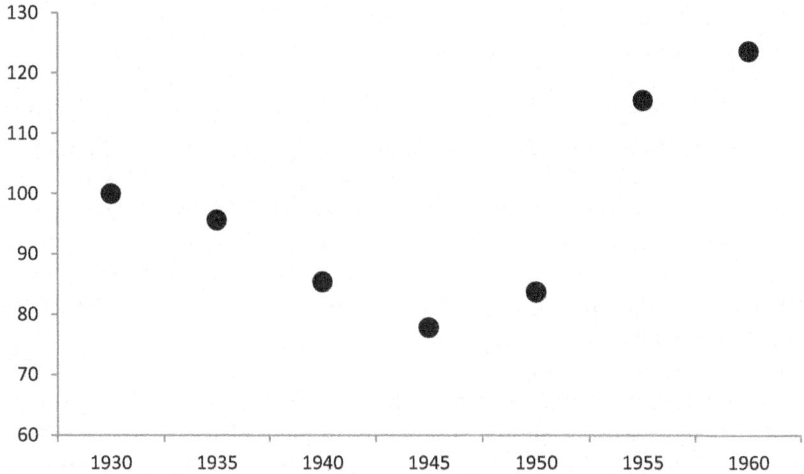

Fig. 7.5 Per capita real GDP of Catalonia, 1930–1960 (Numbers Index 1930 = 100) (*Source* Own elaboration with Alcaide [2003, p. 106])

against recovery (Sardá, 1987). Before the Republican period, Primo de Rivera's Finance Minister, José Calvo Sotelo, decided to present a restrictive budget for 1930, entailing significant cuts to construction programmes and the modernization of roads and railways (Calvo Sotelo, 1931; Comín, 1987; García Delgado, 1980; Palafox, 1976, 1991). The Banco de España increased the discount rates of commercial bills. Both measures were mistaken at a time of considerable contraction of international demand. They can fundamentally be explained by the desire to avoid a further decline in the exchange of the peseta. However, it went from an exchange rate of 33.17 pesetas to the pound in 1929 to 41.97 pesetas in the following year. Both Calvo Sotelo and Primo ended up resigning.

Another firm defender of the external value of the peseta was the Finance Minister of the first government of the Republic, Indalecio Prieto, again unsuccessfully, since speculators caused a fall in its exchange rate to an average of 47.64 pesetas per pound in 1931. His decision to withdraw the CAMPSA deposit from Banco de Cataluña and to favour the collapse of the group is not worthy of praise either. Furthermore, in

1931, the Banco de España again raised the discount rate, intensifying the restrictive monetary policy stance.

The arrival of Jaume Carner at the Ministry of Finances, in the Republican-Socialist government which arose from the December 1931 election, led to a more expansive trend in budgetary policy, closing 1932 with a deficit of 0.65% of GDP, contrasting with the surplus of 1930 (Comín, 1989).[9] Monetary policy also contributed to mitigating the depression, as the discount rate of the Banco de España went down (Balcells, 2013; Comín, 2013b; Comín & Martín Aceña, 1984; Tedde, 1984). On the contrary, the exchange rate of the peseta broke with its previous downward path and, as a result of Great Britain abandoning the gold standard in the previous year, it appreciated against the pound sterling. In 1932, the exchange rate with the pound returned to an average of 43.70 pesetas. In a similar way to the franc and the currencies from the rest of the gold block countries, the peseta became more expensive in relation to the British currency after 1931. This hindered the recovery of export volumes to the pound-sterling area. Furthermore, when Roosevelt, in spring 1933, decided to devalue the dollar, the peseta also appreciated against the United States currency. It went from 12.11 pesetas per dollar in 1932 to just 7.35 pesetas per dollar in 1935. The appreciation of the external value of the peseta curbed the recovery of export volumes and can be considered as a significant cause of why neither Catalonia nor Spain had emerged from the depression in the mid-1930s.

Moreover, the November 1933 election paved the way for centre-right governments. The discount rates continued to go down, but Joaquín Chapaprieta, Finance Minister from May 1935 and head of the government from September, again considerably restricted the budget during this year, taking the deficit from around 1.61–0.85% of GDP (Comín, 1989, 2013b). Opting for a budget adjustment, Chapaprieta subsequently delayed the recovery under way.

Nevertheless, in the Catalan case, we can consider that, like many other industrial economies of the time, the depression had bottomed out during the three-year period from 1931 to 1933. In subsequent years, there was a gradual recovery in registrations of passenger cars, coal imports in Barcelona port, artificial cement production and applications for home building permits from the City Council. The stock market index on the Barcelona stock exchange and the volume of exchange bills cleared by the Clearing House also bottomed out in 1933 and gradually improved in 1934 and 1935.[10] Besides, the estimations of per capita industrial product suggest that, in 1935, it was the highest of the whole period from 1929 to 1935 (Fig. 7.6). Indeed, the compensatory elements of the crisis of the 1930s in Catalonia include the good behaviour of the consumer goods industries and of the production of certain intermediary goods, such as superphosphates and potash (Balcells, 2013; Fontana & Nadal, 1976).

The favourable evolution of the consumer goods industries in Catalonia in the 1930s can be explained by the fact that the Republican period was a time of relatively high wages and good harvests in cereal-producing Spain. Both these factors contributed to maintaining demand for consumer goods and fertilizer, produced in Catalonia, at relatively high levels. Although some branches, such as cork dealers and food exporters, experienced difficult times, in general, the trend of the consumer goods industry was one of prosperity. Moreover, the dynamism of salaries prevented the country, and also Spain, from suffering from a deflationary trend comparable to that of other economies (Catalan & Sánchez, 2013; Fontana & Nadal, 1976). The lack of deflation prevented one of the mechanisms tarnishing international expectations from coming into operation, given that in countries with a fall in average prices investment plans tended to be postponed.

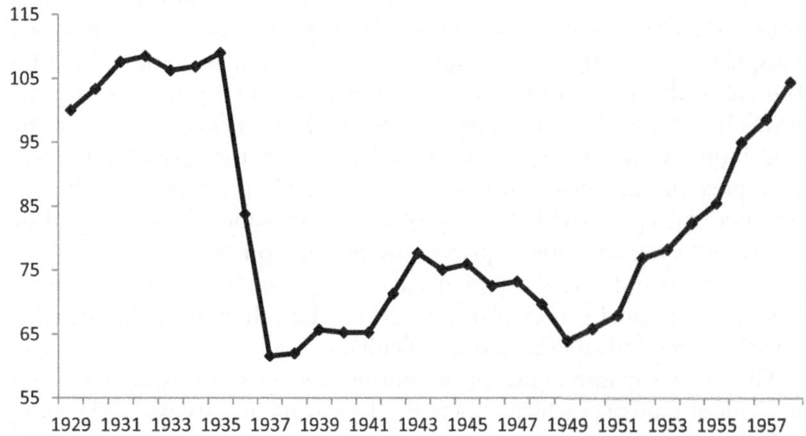

Fig. 7.6 Per capita industrial product of Catalonia, 1929–1957 (Numbers Index 1929 = 100) (*Source* Compiled by the author based on the industrial production index of Parejo [2005, pp. 135–136], the population of Alcaide [2007, pp. 59–95] and of Fundación BBV [1999, pp. 284–285])

On the contrary, the attempted coup d'état in July 1936 and the outbreak of the Civil War and revolution did have an unequivocally depressive impact on industrial activity in Catalonia. The Generalitat made a great effort to restructure the Catalan economy, through the War Industry Commission. It also endeavoured to redirect the revolutionary process by passing the Collectivization and Workers' Control of Industry Decree. It was not, however, able to avoid the loss of markets for industry and the growing bottlenecks in the supply of raw materials, energy and food (Bernecker, 1978; Bonamusa, 2004; Bricall, 1970, 1979, 1985, 2008; Castells, 1993; Catalan, 2006a, 2006b, 2008; Fàbrega, 2009; Lo Cascio, 2013; De Madariaga, 2004, 2008; Pérez Baró, 1970; Tarradellas, 2007).

The textile industry suffered from the progressive loss of markets, as the rebellious armies advanced and the proportion of the population in Republican Spain went down. The decline was clear from November 1936 and, in December 1937 only 24% of the average of the first half of the previous year was manufactured.[11] The chemical industry had a slightly more favourable path, since some of its specialities were encouraged by wartime demand but, even so, at the end of 1937 it only produced 37% of the output of the first half of 1936.

In addition to the continuous loss of markets, both industries suffered from difficulties to access imported raw materials, such as cotton and phosphates, and those from Nationalist Spain, such as wool and pyrites. The fall in the arrival of wheat and other agricultural products from the territories occupied by the rebel armies also had a negative effect on the food industry. Many specialities were harmed by the growing difficulty to import oil and coal, although the country's production of lignites increased. When, at the beginning of 1938, the Nationalists occupied the Pallars and Noguera power plants, the production of the textile, chemical and food industries experienced a new blow. The bombing of the Sant Adrià thermal power plant, which left Barcelona in darkness, made industrial production even more difficult.

The only expansive exception during the war was the metal and mechanical industry, which experienced growing activity until the spring of 1937, thanks to the manufacture of munitions, armour plating and the repair of rolling stock and aviation. The May Events, the intervention of the main metallurgical industries by the government of the Republic and the fall of Biscay and Asturias made the situation deteriorate. Between

April and October 1937 activity went down, but metallurgical production again recorded a revival, more moderate this time, at the beginning of 1938. In September 1938, in the middle of the Battle of the Ebro, metal production was 81% of the level of the first half of 1936. Even so, it should be stressed that metal was the exception: the profound depression of the majority of industrial branches was the rule. In 1938, the available estimates suggest that the industrial product per inhabitant of Catalonia was only 60% of that recorded in 1930 (Catalan, 2008).

Agriculture did not suffer so much from the war since, despite the control of prices, demand soared. Export activities continued to be harmed by low demand on the international market, worsened by the loss of customers such as Germany and Italy. Agriculture, however, was able to partially offset the loss of foreign markets by selling to a famished population which was willing to pay, as far as possible, inordinately high prices on the black market. Indeed, if we compare the fall in GDP with that of industrial product, it is clear that the contraction of the latter was higher. According to the estimates available, in 1940 Catalan per capita industrial output was 63% of that of 1930. On the other hand, GDP per inhabitant was 85% of that of 1930 (Alcaide, 2003; Parejo, 2005). Since other activities which integrate GDP suffered from the conflict as much as or more than the manufacturing industry (the cases of construction, potash mining and services), it can be concluded that the lower fall in GDP in relation to industrial product reflects a less unfavourable impact of the war on agriculture.

In any case, what is most surprising is not the size of the fall in Catalan GDP and industrial product during the Civil War, but rather the inability of both macromagnitudes to quickly recover the pre-war level during the post-war period (Barciela, 1981; Carreras, 1984, 1987; Catalan, 1991b; Clavera, 1976; Clavera et al., 1973; Fontana, 1986; García Delgado, 1987; Miranda, 2003; Montserrat & Ros, 1972; Prados de la Escosura, 2003). As suggested in Fig. 7.6, the trend of per capita industrial product in the 1940s or early Franco period was flat. It was not until the 1950s, or Second Francoism, that the recovery appears to have begun. Similarly, if we believe the estimate of Alcaide (2003), per capita GDP in Catalonia in 1950 was still only 84% that of 1930 (Fig. 7.6) (Catalan, 2003). The industrial trend appears to have been even worse. According to the data of Parejo (2005), per capita industrial product in 1950 only attained 66% of the level of 1930. To summarize, in terms of per capita GDP, the Great

Depression in Catalonia was not overcome until well into the 1950s and industry did not fully recover until the end of the decade.

The damage from the Civil War cannot be held responsible for the lack of Catalan recovery in the 1940s (Barciela et al., 2001; Catalan, 1995a; Clavera, 1976). The destruction of buildings during the armed conflict was concentrated in certain regions where the fronts stabilized. In Catalonia, these were the provinces of Lleida and Tarragona, which had little industry, and which had over 6% of buildings destroyed in 1940 (Catalan, 2008, 2012f). On the other hand, Barcelona, which concentrated the majority of the country's industrial capacity, was quickly occupied and had less than 2% of buildings in ruins in the same year. Moreover, countries such as Holland, Italy, France and Austria, which during the Second World War experienced falls in per capita GDP higher than that of Catalonia during the Civil War, recovered much quicker than our Mediterranean region.

Four factors prevented the depression from being overcome in the 1940s: the lack of raw materials, energy restrictions, the fall in labour productivity and the reconstruction model imposed by the winners of the war during the First Francoism. The reconstruction model was not the only cause of the slow recovery, but it contributed to making the bottlenecks arising from the lack of inputs and productive equipment much more intense. The economic management of the early Franco regime was characterized by five features which especially worsened the bottlenecks of the period: extreme market regulation; autarkic industrialization project; support of the Axis during the Second World War; refusal to devalue; and intense political and trade union repression.

The extreme regulation of the markets for goods involved establishing administered prices for raw materials, food and a good number of industrial products (Barciela, 1985, 1986; Barciela et al., 2001; Calvet, 1992; Catalan, 1994; Clavera, 1976; García Delgado, 1985; Miranda, 1998, 2003; Pujol, 1989b). It also entailed the creation of controlling bodies entrusted with distributing the so-called *cupos* of raw materials and with rationing food. It likewise involved submitting investments and imports to a considerably arbitrary regime of licences. The allocations of *cupos* and the granting of licences were dominated by the interests of the military and of bodies created by the new regime. Strong regulation and considerable scarcity led to the generalization of black markets. In these markets you could obtain provisions, paying several times their normal price. The black market made people rich who could enjoy certain impunity to offer goods on these markets (normally people linked to the winning side). On the other hand, it created great differences in the availability of inputs for companies. Furthermore, the controlling bodies did not even attain the objectives that they had set themselves. One example is the iron ingot distributed among the main foundries of Barcelona province in 1949. In that year there was one company (a well-known manufacturer of radiators and sanitaryware) which obtained 130% of the *cupo* of iron ingot that had been assigned to it, while there were 19 others which received less than 60% of their quota. The official price of the ingot was then 1.65 pesetas per kilo, but if acquired on the black market it was necessary to pay four pesetas. By diverting ingots to the black market the capital could be multiplied by 2.4. The main beneficiaries therefore became rich through speculation with raw materials and other black market goods instead of depending on an improvement in quality and cost control in the production process.

The autarkic industrialization programme was a top priority of Francisco Franco and of one of the key men from the early days of his regime: Juan Antonio Suanzes (Catalan, 1989a; García Delgado, 1987; Gómez Mendoza, 1994, 2000; Martín Aceña & Comín, 1991; San Román, 1999; Viñas et al., 1979). The latter began to design his autarky plan in El Ferrol in 1937. Subsequently, he promoted it actively, first as Industry Minister of the Franco regime from 1938 in Burgos, and then as the first president of the National Institute of Industry (INI), from 1941 in Madrid. The autarky foresaw prioritizing domestic production in all the industries related to the war, including obtaining liquid fuel. The INI did indeed devote one-third of its budget in the 1940s to the attempt to synthesize oil from oil shale like the Nazi IG Farben had done. Spanish synthetic oil was just a dream, but the company Empresa Nacional Calvo Sotelo, created by the INI to obtain it, engulfed huge quantities of currency, materials, energy and machinery, which would have been of better use allocated to more conventional branches of industrial activity, such as the production of electric energy. Indeed, the freezing of electricity tariffs, in a context of scarcity of fuels such as oil and coal, caused a rapid growth of demand for electricity during the World War (Barciela et al., 2001; Catalan, 1995a; Miranda, 1998; Ribas, 1978; Sudrià, 1987c, 1995). However, among the first companies controlled by the INI, those conceived exclusively to produce electricity were missing. Before mid-1944, the public holding company prioritized stakes in companies devoted to manufacturing liquid fuel (the aforementioned

Calvo Sotelo), shipping and shipbuilding (Elcano), telecommunications in Morocco (Torres Quevedo), aluminium (ENDASA), air transport (Iberia) and radio equipment (Marconi). ENDESA (1944) and ENHER (1946), conceived to produce electricity, were only created when demand exceeded supply and it was necessary to impose cuts to the supply of power.

In fact, the creation of ENDESA and ENHER was very late. In 1944, there had already been significant electricity restrictions (equivalent to 8% of demand) and, in 1945, they represented an absolute maximum (approximately 28%). Had these companies been created earlier or if the prices had been revised, encouraging a faster increase in the installed power, the restrictions would not have been so intense. They lasted until the mid-1950s and especially harmed Catalan industry. The early Franco regime, as it had done previously due to the scarcity of cotton, ended up having to create an unemployment benefit due to the lack of electricity. During the period with the greatest intensity of restrictions, between August 1945 and December 1950, and according to the Ministry of Labour itself, 61% of the total amount of benefits paid due to lack of electricity in Spain was absorbed by Barcelona province.

In a comparable manner, the autarkic trend of industrial policy accentuated the huge scarcity of automobiles until the mid-1950s (Carreras & Estapé, 2002; Catalan, 1995a, 2006b, 2012c; Nadal, 2010; Nadal & Tafunell, 1992; San Román, 1995, 1999; Solé, 1994; Tappi, 2008). Both General Motors and FIAT presented projects to build automobile assembly plants in Barcelona in 1939, which were rejected by the regime. Ford Motor Ibérica was only granted licences to import parts little by little until the Americans decided to sell their stake to a Spanish group in 1954. The INI put pressure on Hispano-Suiza to hand over its plant in La Sagrera and, when it finally achieved this in 1946 and ENASA was established, the public holding company gave priority to the construction of a truck factory in Madrid. Successive projects presented by Banco Urquijo to build the passenger car factory with a FIAT licence in Barcelona were hindered until 1948. Consequently, the registration of automobiles remained very low during the 1940s and early 50s. The new registrations of passenger cars in Catalonia did not achieve the per capita volume of 1929 until 1956 (Fig. 7.7).

Franco's support of the Axis was undeniable during the majority of the Second World War and took place through numerous channels (Barciela et al., 2001; Catalan, 2012a; García Pérez, 1994; Leitz, 1996; Viñas,

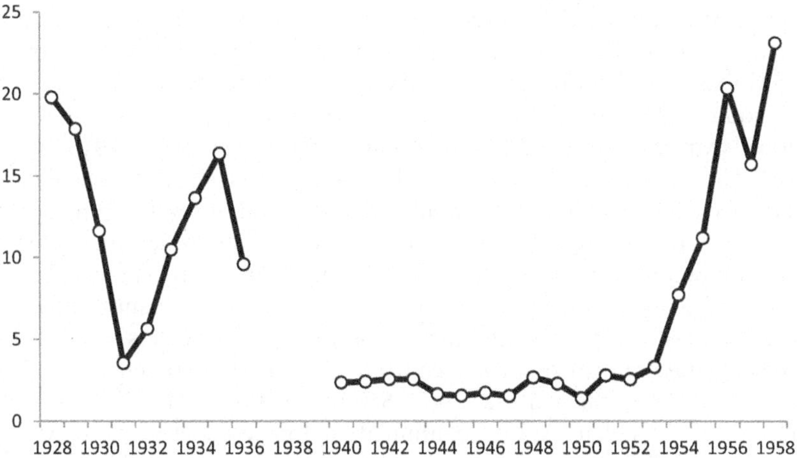

Fig. 7.7 Registration of passenger cars in Catalonia per 10,000 inhabitants, 1928–1958 (*Source* Own elaboration by the author with Catalan [2012f, p. 236])

1984). The refuelling of German submarines was particularly significant, as was the despatch of the Blue Division to the Soviet front and the use of most of the export income obtained by Spain during the conflict (above all through the sale of wolfram) to quickly repay the debt contracted by Franco's side during the Civil War. Unlike Italy, Germany intended to collect the war debt quickly during the World War and in practice achieved this. Thus, on the one hand, this involved sacrificing the imports of inputs needed for reconstruction. Also, in the short term, it meant that the Allies prevented shipments to Spain of basic supplies, such as oil, generating subsequent bottlenecks. In the medium term, Spanish support of the Axis implied exclusion of the Franco government from the Allied aid programmes and, in particular, from the European Recovery Program, announced by the American Secretary of State, George Marshall, in 1947. Although the Marshall Plan aid implied payments by the end receivers, it helped them to access strategic inputs such as fuel or fertilizers and also supplied equipment to modernize factories, hydroelectric power plants and the transport system.

The huge scarcity of raw materials, which contributed to prolonging the depression, could have been mitigated with more imports. However, in a framework of scarce foreign currency and a lack of foreign aid, this previously required the expansion of exports or the obtaining of credit. Franco went so far as to receive the American ambassador with portraits of Mussolini and Hitler and to tell him that he did not need credit from his country. Moreover, exports were less and less competitive in the traditional markets due to the high Spanish inflation of the 1940s, arising from large budget deficits, covered by issuing pesetas. The public deficit recorded an astronomical maximum in 1944, with a level of almost 9% of GDP and an annual inflation rate of 15%.[12] In order to maintain the competitiveness of exports, the exchange rate of the peseta would have had to be gradually devalued at the rate at which Spanish inflation exceeded that of its main commercial partners. Nevertheless, the official exchange rate remained unchanged from 1941, at 10.95 pesetas per dollar (Aixalá, 1999; Catalan, 1992, 2003; Serrano, 2000b; Viñas et al., 1979). The result was that exports continued to lose competitiveness. Maintaining the fiction of a strong peseta was an obsession for Franco, who associated the depreciation of the currency with the fall of the Primo de Rivera dictatorship. He was also influenced by the memory of the *bataglia* of Mussolini's lira and Hitler's refusal to devalue the Reichsmark.

Once the World War ended, Spanish exports lost competitiveness even faster, due to the high inflation rate and to maintaining an invariable official exchange rate of 10.95 pesetas to the dollar, while the majority of economies adopted new rates. This situation meant that in the free market of New York, the exchange rate of the Spanish currency ended up being 34 pesetas per dollar in 1948. That is to say, with one dollar purchased at the official rate in Spain and resold on the free market in New York, you could triple the capital. This gain was even higher than the one that we analysed on speculating with iron ingots. Meanwhile, the volume of Spanish exports remained below 50% of the 1929 level.

Finally, the intense repression unleashed by the winners of the war also contributed to preventing a fast emergence from the crisis (Catalan, 1993; Deu, 2005; Fontana & Nadal, 1976; Maluquer de Motes, 1987; Molinero & Ysàs, 1985; Vilar, 2004, 2009). The workers were not the only ones to suffer from this, although they were those who experienced it with the greatest intensity. In 1939, it was decreed that nominal salaries should return to the level of 1936, but prices did not. This meant that, with the occupation of Catalonia, real salaries in the textile industry were less than half of those before the war.[13] The law on Political Responsibilities and the ban on class-based trade unions prevented the rapid reorganization of the workers' movement and meant that, in the inflationary context of the Second World War, there was a subsequent fall in real salaries, until they bottomed out in 1943.

The better situation at the end of the world war favoured a start in the recovery of real wages. However, the high inflation and bottlenecks, in a framework of a lack of labour freedom, meant that real wages in the textile industry went down again in 1946 and 1947. In 1950, the real salary of a working-class family from Sabadell was still more than a third below the level of 1936.

The early Franco regime therefore represented a permanent reduction in real salaries in Catalan industry (and, in general, in the rest of Spain). In the short term, the permanent decline of salaries reduced the demand for consumer goods and curbed the recovery of most of the activity in which Catalonia was specialized. In the longer term, it caused an intense reduction in labour productivity, on implying the malnutrition of the labour force and favouring the use of productive techniques using little mechanization (Fig. 7.8).

Fig. 7.8 Real wages in the textil industry of Catalonia, 1929–1957 (Numbers Index 1929 = 100) (*Source* Compiled by the author with Maluquer de Motes and Llonch [2005, p. 1224], Maluquer de Motes [2005, p. 1291] and Catalan [1993, pp. 134–135]. See note 13)

The biggest depression of the Catalan economy did not bottom out until the end of the 1940s, when certain both endogenous and exogenous buffers of the crisis began to come into effect (Barciela et al., 2001; Calvet, 1992; Catalan, 1995a, 1995b, 2002b, 2012f; Deu, 2005; Fontana & Nadal, 1976 & García Delgado, 1990a; Nadal et al., 1988; Puig, 2003; Serrano, 2000b; Solé, 2007). The former included the slow shift of the regime's economic policy and the reduction of raw materials and energy bottlenecks, which made possible the reappraisal of the Second Industrial Revolution.

When, at the end of the World War, the defeat of the Axis and the impoverishment that autarky caused began to be perceived, the policy of the early Franco regime began to change its course. The priorities of industrial policy were reoriented towards activities which could generate more externalities and favour the dissemination of the second technological revolution. In Catalonia, the INI ended up promoting the creation of ENHER and SEAT, which achieved considerable prominence in the production of electricity and automobiles from the mid-1950s. The creation of the National Health Service expanded the demand for drugs, which was, partly, supplied by Catalan laboratories. The adoption of a system of multiple exchange rates for the peseta, at the end of 1948, implied a hidden devaluation. Between 1949 and 1953, interventions were also reduced in the industrial markets, official prices were eliminated and food rationing ended up being suppressed. This reduced speculative behaviour, although without eliminating it completely, since the black market remained, for example with foreign exchange, raw materials and licences. Finally, real salaries began to rise again at the end of the 1940s.

The exogenous factors which contributed to the emergence of the depression include, especially, the outbreak of the Korean War, the rapprochement between the United States and the Franco regime and the growing arrival of European tourists. The former temporarily improved the Spanish balance of trade and favoured the importing of fertilizer and raw materials to manufacture them, while permitting a substantial increase in agricultural output. The gestation of the alliance between Franco and Eisenhower, recognized in the 1953 Pact of Madrid, implied access to Atlantic credits and aid. Between 1947 and 1955, the arrival of tourists increased tenfold, representing a corresponding increase in the entry of foreign currency.

In Catalonia, the great depression of the 1930s was not fully overcome until the second half of the 1950s. Like the other long-lasting crises, it had longer term consequences for Catalan development. Despite the fact that the trend of real salaries was moderately upward throughout the 1950s, the level attained in the middle of the decade was still far from before the war: only around two-thirds of the same. This means that the emergence from the depression during the second Franco period occurred with a permanent cut in real salaries for Catalan industry. The long-lasting cut in the cost of the labour force was not just in relation to the Republican era but also, even, in respect of that of the Primo dictatorship. This means that, when it came to choosing techniques, it was relatively cheaper to use those which employed more labour and less machines. The production systems were therefore less mechanized and labour productivity advanced less than in countries with comparable levels of development.

7.3 The Slump of Late Francoism and Transition to Democracy, 1974–1986

After the growth *miracle* of the 1960s (*developmental Francoism*) regime, the Catalan economy again entered a crisis period starting from the end of 1973 (Catalan, 1999, 2013; García Delgado, 1990b; Muns, 1986; Parellada, 1990; Sardá, 1983; Sudrià, 2013a; Serrano, 2011; Solà et al., 2012). The crisis ended up becoming a true depression (bringing the unemployment rate to previously unheard-of levels, above 20% of the working population). It lasted until 1986, Spain's first year in the European Economic Community. The origins of this depression were the sudden increase in the price of oil, the weakness of the Spanish government during the last years of the Franco regime and the transition to democracy, and certain hindrances inherited from the old regime.

Like the previous international depressions, there was an exogenous trigger for the recession. In this case, it was the sudden increase in the price of oil, as a result of the Yom Kippur War. The price of the barrel shot up from $3 to 12 between the end of 1973 and the end of 1974 (Foley & Nassim, 1976; Naredo, 1979; Sudrià, 1987a, 1987b, 2013a). The Western model of development during the Second Industrial Revolution had been based on the cheap consumption of hydrocarbons which did not have a short-term replacement. Their abrupt price rise was transferred to the prices of products and caused an acceleration in inflation. Workers pushed nominal salaries upwards to avoid losing purchasing power and profit rates declined due to the combined increase of energy and salary costs (Armstrong et al., 1991; Brenner, 2006; Eichengreen, 2007; Lamard & Stoskopf, 2009; Rowthorn, 1980; Trevithick, 1977). The fall in profit rates affected investment, causing the contraction of output and loss of employment. In the case of Catalonia, the registration of automobiles per capita already reflected the crisis starting in 1974 and continued to fall during the year of the dictator's death.

A second oil shock, as a result of the triumph of the Islamic Revolution in Iran, caused comparable effects in industrialized economies. Registration of passenger cars in Catalonia fell again at the end of the 70s and remained at a low level at the beginning of the following decade (Fig. 7.9).

The inflationary spiral required strong governments or dominant social partners willing to come to agreements to prevent it from becoming more severe. On the contrary, between 1972 and 1986, Spain had six prime ministers and many changes in the ministries of Finance, Economy and Industry and in the presidency of the INI. This instability prevented tight measures from being taken to curb inflation, especially before the

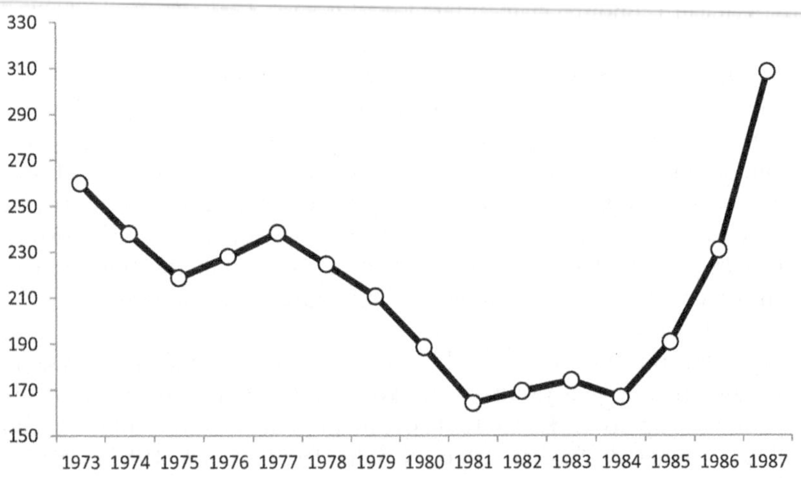

Fig. 7.9 Registration of passenger cars in Catalonia per 10,000 habitants, 1973–1987 (*Source* Compiled by the author with the registration of vehicles from the Dirección General de Tráfico, Estadística de Transporte, several years and population from Fundación BBV [1999, pp. 284–285])

first democratic election of June 1977 (Argandoña & García Durán, 1992; Baiges et al., 1987; Carreras & Tafunell, 2021; Catalan, 2013; Mochón et al., 1988; Rojo, 1987; Sudrià, 2013a). Although, at that time, the Spanish governments were not the only ones to avoid applying resolutely restrictive policies to curb inflation, in the end, the costs in terms of the fall in product (and in employment) were higher the longer it took to confront the rise in prices. Thus, for example, countries that succeeded in controlling inflation during the mid-1970s, such as Switzerland and Germany, suffered less from the depression in the medium and long term than inflationary countries, such as the United Kingdom and Italy (Albert, 1991; Eichengreen, 2007; Katzenstein, 1985; Pekkarinen et al., 1992; Rowthorn, 1980; Woodward, 1999).

The burden from the Franco period did not help an agreement to be reached before the change of regime. The lack of trade union freedom in a framework of a progressive weakening of the dictatorship favoured the mobilization of the workers who demanded higher salaries, better working conditions and recognition of the class-based trade unions and political freedoms. Thus, until the Moncloa Pacts were signed, in the autumn of 1977, salaries appeared to be out of control and, consequently, there were less expectations than in other countries (Albarracín, 1987; Balfour, 1994; Catalan, 1991a; Etxezarreta, 1979; Sanromà, 1990; Trullén, 1990).

This not only implied a drop in investment but also an increasing indebtedness by firms, which had dire consequences when the real cost of money began to rise. Given the difficulties to dismiss employees that the regime had established to offset the lack of trade union freedom, a company that was too indebted found it difficult to reduce the workforce and thus the risk of insolvency rose. Finally, an additional hindrance of the Franco regime which did not help to confront the crisis was the low level of Research and Development in Spain. It was very far from that of the peripheral countries with comparable income, such as Italy and Ireland, and only similar to that of Portugal and Greece, which had recently shared dictatorial regimes.

The depression had four aggravating factors: the rapid increase in salary costs until the end of the 70s; the violent tightening of monetary policy after the first democratic election; the sudden liberalization of strategic branches such as automobiles and banking; and the preference for speculative behaviour by important figures from the world of finance, construction and industry. We have already analyzed the first factor. In a situation with an increase in energy costs, a too-fast rise in nominal salaries caused a decline in investment and corporate debt. According to the data collected by the Research Service of the Banco de Bilbao Vizcaya, the cost of labour in Catalan industry (excluding construction) went from absorbing 46% to 54% of added value between 1971 and 1979. Such an intense and rapid process of redistribution of income curbed investment and harmed production (and employment) in the short and medium terms.

The centre-right UCD government which emerged from the results of the June 1977 election, with Enrique Fuentes Quintana as Economic Vice President, had to confront an annual inflation rate of almost 30%. It did so by agreeing on salary moderation with the opposition in the so-called Moncloa Pacts (Carreras & Tafunell, 2021; Catalan, 2013; Espina et al., 1987; Estefanía, 1987; Fina & Toharia, 1987; Roca, 1991, 1994, 1996; Tamames, 1995; Toharia, 1998; Trullén, 1993; Sevilla, 1985). However, the anti-inflation policy also involved a severe and sudden tightening of credit. Thus, during 1978, the real short-term interest rate increased by almost nine percentage points. Consequently, per capita industrial product bottomed out during that year. Real interest rates continued to rise until 1983 when suspensions of payments also reached their maximum level in Catalonia (valued in constant pesetas). At that time, unemployment exceeded the threshold of 22% of the working population (Fig. 7.10).

From 1972, the late Franco period gradually abandoned the protectionist policy that had characterized the regime. The governments of the transition to democracy continued in this direction, increasing the investment licences and reducing import quotas and tariffs, with a view to joining the EEC. This policy, in times of crisis, made the depression even tougher in activities which were then important for the Catalan productive fabric, such as the manufacture of passenger cars, industrial vehicles, motorcycles, machinery and electric appliances. The most significant case was that of SEAT (Catalan, 2010, 2011; Pérez Sanchó, 2003; Tolliday, 2003). At the end of the Franco regime, while the return of Ford to the Catalan Countries was approved, SEAT was forced to acquire the company AUTHI from Navarre, at a time of surplus capacity in the sector. Moreover, Ford's Almussafes plant specialized in a model, the Fiesta, which was the development of the product with most sales of SEAT at the time, the 127. Finally, contravening what had been agreed for the purchase of AUTHI, the government of Adolfo Suárez approved

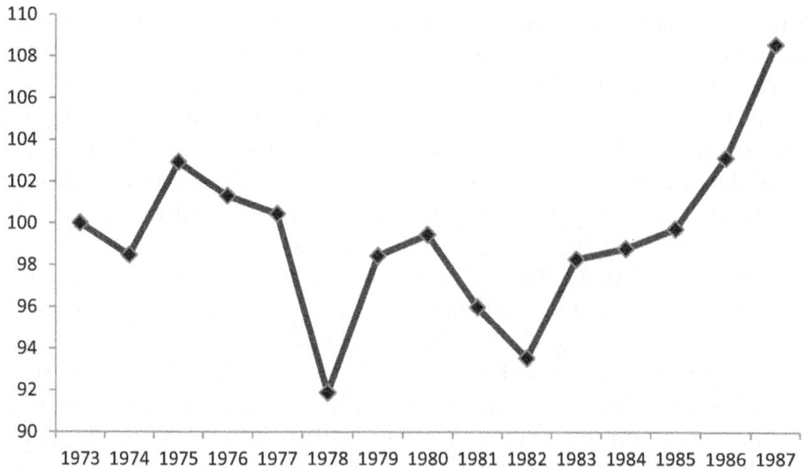

Fig. 7.10 Per capita industrial product of Catalonia, 1973–1987 (Numbers Index 1973 = 100) (*Source* Compiled by the author with the industrial production index of Parejo [2005, pp. 135–136] and the population of Fundación BBV [1999, pp. 284–285])

the establishment in Figueruelas (Zaragoza) of the subsidiary of General Motors, Opel. Overall, this ended up ruining SEAT. FIAT, the most important shareholder of SEAT together with INI, decided to abandon the Barcelona's cars producer. After a short phase of complete public ownership, the PSOE gave up the idea of maintaining an independent automotive brand and ended up handing it over to Volkswagen (Catalan, 2012b; González de la Fe 2003; Llorente, 1997; Recio & Roca, 1998; Solé, 1994).

For its part, the liberalization of the financial sector contributed to provoking the most important banking crisis recorded in Catalonia since the collapse of Banco de Barcelona. During the Franco regime, there had not been any important banking crises. Before 1959, insolvencies were avoided due to considerable post-war regulation, by means of the so-called banking *status quo*, which restricted the creation of new banks. Later, the 1962 reforms endeavoured to specialize banking in accordance with the international evolution of the 30s: commercial banks, devoted to discounting bills, which offered very little remuneration on current accounts and sight deposits; and industrial or investment banks, which attracted long-term saving, with instruments such as certificates of deposit and bond issues, and which offered higher interest rates (Cabana, 2000; Pons, 2002; Poveda, 2001; Pueyo, 2003).

Starting from 1974, the possibility of issuing certificates of deposit was extended to all financial institutions and the more than two-year deposit rates were liberalized. For its part, the 1977 government also left all the Banco de España's rates free, except for the rediscount rate. At the beginning of 1981, the last cabinet of Suárez completed the process, liberalizing six-month deposit rates and that of credit transactions and legalizing credits with variable interest rates.

The liberalization of the banking market eliminated the advantages of industrial banks and intensified the fight to attract liabilities. This policy caused huge increases in costs for the banking institutions and had a very negative effect on the weakest. The savings banks continued to be significantly regulated and, consequently, did not experience any crisis. On the other hand, however, during the depression study, the following banks went bankrupt: Banco Condal, Banco Comercial de Cataluña, Banco de Huesca, Banco Atlántico, Banco Unión, Banco Catalán de Desarrollo, Banca Mas Sardá, Banco de los Pirineos and the joint Banca Catalana—Banco Industrial Cataluña. This latter group brought together, in addition to its own brands, Banco Industrial del Mediterráneo, Banco de Crédito e Inversiones, Banco de Gerona, Banco de Asturias and Banco de Alicante (Barratech, 1985; Cabana, 1989a, 2000; Llarch, 1999). The insolvency of the Banca Catalana group, in 1982, coincided with the worst moment of the depression, according to the per capita GDP data of the Catalan statistical office, IDESCAT (Fig. 7.11). The main owner of the Banca Catalana group was Jordi Pujol, financier and future President of the Generalitat of Catalonia.

The regional government, which was dissolved by Franco in 1939, was re-established in 1978. The reappraisal of the Catalan Generalitat was the only institution of the Second Republic, which after being suppressed, enjoyed a second opportunity under the restored monarchy of King Juan Carlos I.

In any case, although the financial liberalization described contributed to the bankruptcy of the aforementioned institutions, part of the failure can also be explained by the high risks incurred by the administrators of the banking institutions themselves (Baiges et al., 1984; Catalan, 2013; Cuervo, 1983, 1987). They opted for too fast growth and a costly race to open branches. They infringed the legislation in force, paying higher

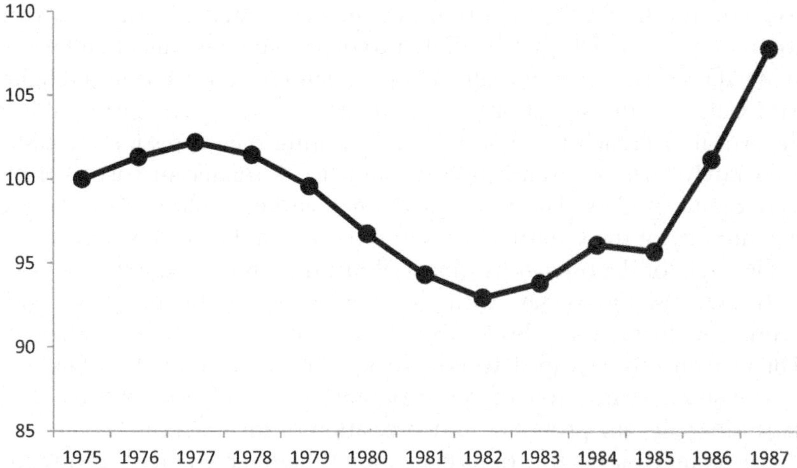

Fig. 7.11 Per capita real GDP of Catalonia, 1975–1987 (Numbers Index 1975 = 100) (*Source* Compiled with the per capita GDP of IDESCAT, included in Solà et al. [2012, p. 302])

interest rates. They quickly swallowed up other institutions and prioritized an increase in market share over an analysis of profitability. The privileged agreements with business groups prevailed over a thorough assessment of the guarantees provided for the credits. Rather than opting for certain strategic lines of specialization, the failed institutions tended to operate in the great majority of industrial sectors. Finally, projects with an indisputable speculative profile, such as real-estate developments or ski resorts, damaged the assets of the banks.

We do not only find the speculative behaviour in the banking institutions which grew rapidly from the 1960s. Construction was a privileged object of enrichment and speculation during the development period of the Franco regime, nourished by the lack of planning and the ease of infringing urban development regulations. When the price of money shot up, at the end of the 70s, numerous dwellings and developments remained unsold and some developers and construction firms were insolvent. As an indicator of the construction crisis, cement sales in Catalonia went from 3403 tonnes in 1977 to just 1795 tonnes in 1985: a fall of almost 50%!

Finally, a concern to place capital safe and sound from the risks of political change predominated among important segments of the business community. During the transition to democracy, capital flight was a very common practice, which contributed to depressing investment and worsening the crisis. As an indicator of this phenomenon, we can highlight, with Galabert, the arrival of tourists in Andorra (Galabert, 2012). While the arrival of French tourists in Andorra during the depression increased moderately, that of Spanish tourists shot up. A significant part of them were capital evaders. The above-mentioned author confirms that, despite the intensity of the Catalan depression, the 70s and early 80s were a true golden age for deposits in the financial institutions of Andorra.

In any case, as we saw with the previous crises, in the 1974–1986 depression there were also factors which contributed to mitigating it. Three main forces helped to counteract the intensity of the crisis: the progressive tertiarization of the economy; the tendency towards fiscal expansion; and the pronounced depreciation of the peseta.

The compensating role of tertiarization is highlighted on observing the significant increase in the weight of the sector (Sanromà, 1999; Therborn, 1986). In 1971, the services sector represented 40.2% of Catalan employment and, on the other hand, in 1987 this speciality had already attained a 54.8% share. During the crisis, it had become the leading productive sector in the volume of employment, dislodging industry. The three most important activities on the first of these dates were, in this order, the textile industry, leather and footwear; commercial services; and agriculture and fishing. On the other hand, in 1987, the first two branches of employment had become commerce and public services (with an important weight for education and health). The clothing industries had gone down to third position (Fundación BBV, 1999).

The struggles to recover their own institutions and the extension of the welfare state contributed notably to the strengthening of tertiarization. The Generalitat, re-established in 1978, became responsible for the generation of 8.4% of GDP ten years later (Bosch & Costa, 1990). Moreover, the provincial councils and, especially, town councils, strengthened by the struggles of the transition to democracy, together generated an additional 5.3% of GDP. In short, the extension of the Catalan public sector contributed to mitigating the depression, expanding the effort made by the Spanish government on expenses such as health, education and public works.

On the other hand, despite the fiscal reform of Francisco Fernández Ordóñez, the weight of the Spanish public deficit more than tripled between 1979 and 1984. It went from around 1.8–6.4% of GDP between these two dates.[14] The above figures suggest that the budgetary policy was notably expansive, adapting to the Keynesian orientation, which recommends increasing the deficit at times of crisis (Catalan, 2013; González Calvet, 1991a, 1991b, 1994; Serrano & Costas, 1990; Sudrià 2013a). It was not until 1985, when the worst moment of the depression had already passed, that the public deficit began to go down. In the last year of the depression, 1986, the imbalance in the Spanish public accounts still represented around 4.6% of GDP, a remarkable proportion. This means that the emergence from the crisis took place with a Keynesian policy.

Another Keynesian component of the economic policy of the transition to democracy was the repeated recourse to the devaluation of the peseta. The peseta was devalued in February 1976 at a time when José Miguel Villar Mir was the Finance Minister of the government of Carlos Arias Navarro, the first of the restored monarchy (Catalan, 1999; Serrano, 2000a). The Spanish currency was again devalued in July 1977, with Fuentes Quintana as Adolfo Suárez's Superminister of the Economy. It experienced a further devaluation when Miguel Boyer took possession as Finance Minister in the first cabinet of Felipe González in December 1982. The peseta continued to depreciate against the dollar until the beginning of 1985. Between February 1976 and 1985, the exchange rate of the Spanish currency went from 60 to 190 pesetas per dollar. The peseta therefore lost 68% of its previous value in relation to the United States currency. Such a formidable depreciation helped exports and curbed imports, constituting a protectionist counterpart to the liberalizing policies of the transition to democracy. It became a key mechanism to the emergence of the depression.

Tertiarization, fiscal expansion and the devaluations of the peseta were the three main elements mitigating the crisis from the mid-1970s. In the last stretch of the depression, in the mid-1980s, certain elements of a more exogenous nature were added to these factors. The decline in the price of oil, European recovery and Spain joining the EEC helped to change expectations. Indeed, registrations of passenger cars, industrial product and GDP all indicated the beginnings of a very clear new cycle of euphoria, starting from 1987.

The depression under study had two very important long-term consequences: an improvement in the living conditions of the majority of wage earners and the establishment of a relatively decentralized democratic state, which in Catalonia materialized in the recovery and strengthening of its own institutions. The figures available indicate that the struggles of the end of the Franco regime and of the transition to democracy ended with a notable increase in real salaries until 1981.[15] For example, in the case of the textile, footwear and leather industry, the real salary could have increased by around 55% between 1973 and 1987. In the automotive industry, which already paid much higher salaries at the time of emergence, the increase in remuneration was even more intense, approaching 60%. As suggested in Fig. 7.12, the moderation policies initiated with the Moncloa Pacts curbed the rate of growth of real salaries, but did not at all overturn the conquests already achieved.

The other remarkable long-term consequence was that of the increase in public expenditure on education, health and infrastructures, which traditionally had not corresponded to the economic weight of Catalonia. Tertiarization, fiscal expansion and the welfare policies of the Catalan and Spanish governments contributed to moderating some of the historical remoras in the long-term process of economic development.

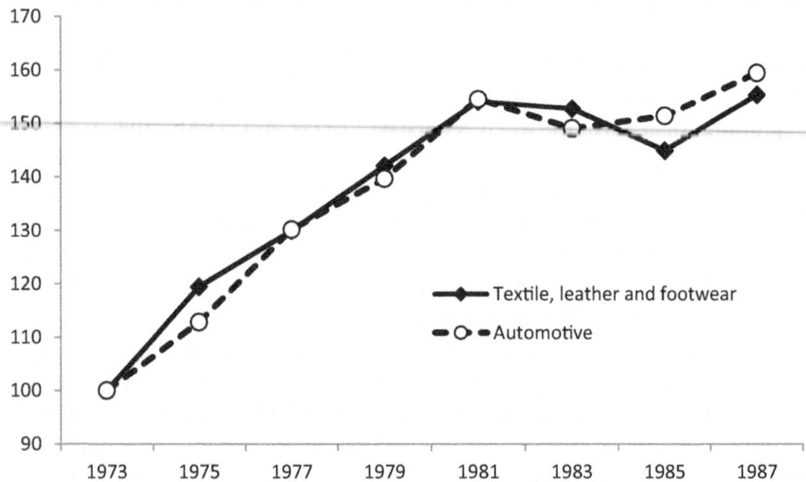

Fig. 7.12 Real wages in the textile, leather and footwear and automotive industries in Catalonia, 1973–1987 (Numbers Index 1973 = 100) (*Source* Compiled by the author based on Fundación BBV [1999])

7.4 The Great Depression of the Euro, 2008–2016

The euro's Great Depression was originally caused by the speculative excesses of the decades at the turn of the century, which ended up causing a huge housing and financial bubble (Akerlof & Shiller, 2009; Bernanke, 2013; Eichengreen, 2015; Kindleberger, 1978; Lapavitsas et al., 2012; Minsky, 1977; Naredo, 1996; Rogoff & Reinhart, 2009; Varoufakis, 2011). The excessive speculation arose from the combined effect of the growing deregulation of financial markets, the rapid industrialization of China and the adoption of the single currency in the majority of the European Union. These three factors favoured, in many Western economies, especially in Catalonia, a rapid process of mounting private debt, which was not very visible for some years, due to the huge revaluation experienced by real-estate assets. When, however, in around 2007, dwellings could no longer find a buyer, their prices went down and the indebted families and institutions which had financed them became insolvent.

The deregulation of the capital market in the West gradually gained strength with the neoliberal shift in economic management, promoted with an iron fist in Margaret Thatcher's England starting from 1979 and, less openly, when the Single European Act came into force in 1987, on the rest of the continent (Brenner, 2006; Eichengreen, 2015; Fontana, 2011; Krugman, 1990, 1994; Stiglitz, 2002, 2003). In Japan, financial deregulation, in addition to the agreement to revalue the yen forced by the Ronald Reagan administration in 1985, caused a speculative bubble which, when it burst, condemned this Asian country to more than two decades of low growth (Koo, 2009, 2013; Krugman, 2009).

In the United States, financial deregulation clashed with the retaining wall of the Glass-Steagall Act, the last vestige of interventionist policies which allowed the Great Depression of the 1930s to be overcome. The Glass-Steagall Act had created the deposit insurance, while separating commercial from investment or business banking. From 1933, the former specialized in deposits and discounted commercial bills, leaving the subscription and placement of securities and the more speculative financial activities for the latter. During 1933, the development of the banking regulation, associated with the act, represented a ban on remuneration for sight deposits and the imposition of ceilings on the interest rates of term and savings accounts. This considerable intervention of the financial sector led to several decades of stability in the sector.

The situation began to change in 1980, with the passing of the Depository Institutions Deregulation and Monetary Control Act. With this legislative change, America began a gradual but continuous process of dismantling the regulation imposed on the financial sector as a result of the Great Depression of the 1930s. This process culminated in 1999 when, in order to please Citibank, which wanted to merge with a company devoted to investment banking, the Bill Clinton administration agreed to remove the restrictions which still remained on commercial banking operations (Eichengreen 2015; Krugman, 2012).

A financial innovation, securitization, likewise helped all kinds of institutions to grant mortgages to people with a low ability to purchase accommodation. Securitization helped banks to place these high-risk, or sub-prime mortgages with their clients, based on fragmenting them and selling them transformed into supposedly safe assets, with the complicity of the rating agencies (Eichengreen, 2015; Kobrak & Wilkins, 2011; Kobrak & Wilkins ed., 2014; Marichal, 2010; Otte, 2010; Roubini & Mihm, 2010; Skidelsky, 2009). Finally, the reduction in interest rates approved by Alan Greenspan in 2001, in order to offset the fall in *.com* securities on the stock exchange, contributed to inflating the real-estate bubble in the United States and, subsequently, in other Western economies (Bernanke, 2013; Krugman, 2009; Ragot, 2013).

In Spain, the savings banks had been considerably regulated since they were created in the nineteenth century, which explains why they did not suffer from the crises that we have analysed above. In 1988, the process of liberalization of the sector began with the approval of the suppression of the rule which prevented the opening of branches outside the region of origin. This measure favoured the uprooting of the savings banks, stimulating a race between the institutions to open branches in new territories. Starting from 1990, the restrictions on the allowances received by the members of the boards of directors were eliminated. Until then, they had been limited given the social bias of the institutions. From the end of the twentieth century, the savings banks concentrated on increasing shares of their assets in mortgage loans, while abandoning their territories of origin, closing traditional services such as libraries, reducing their financing of industry and spoiling their senior managers by increasing their salaries, pensions and incentives. Some financed 100% of the estimated value of properties plus the deed and tax expenses, when the Banco de España requested that this percentage should not exceed 80% (Benaul et al.,

2008; Cabana, 2012; Cals, 2005; Comín, 2002; Martín Aceña et al., 2013; Serra Ramoneda, 2011; Vives, 2001).

The savings banks were not the only financial institutions to abuse housing credit during the first decade of the twenty-first century, and not all exceeded the limits on awarding mortgages. When, however, during the summer of 2010, the first stress test was performed on the balance sheets of financial institutions, the low solvency of many savings banks such as Caixa de Catalunya was discovered. This institution, then headed by Narcís Serra, former vice-president of Felipe González's government, was the second biggest savings bank in Catalonia. It lagged behind most of Spanish financial institutions in the stress tests, which measured the weight of own resources in relation to assets weighted by risk. The ratios of other Catalan savings banks, such as the Terrassa, Sabadell, Tarragona, Penedès, Laietana or Girona, were not good either.

The industrialization of Asia, especially China, also played a role in the gestation of the real-estate bubble in the West (Arrighi, 2007; Bregolat, 2007; Bustelo, 2004; Chang, 2010; Cohen & Bradford De Long, 2010; David et al., 2013; Nesi, 2010; Sachs, 2005). In the Catalan case, the real-estate boom of the beginning of the twenty-first century was fed by the abundant credit granted by savings banks and other financial institutions. However, the former concentrated an increasing share of their assets in mortgages because the price of land and accommodation achieved annual increases of between 10 and 20% (Naredo, 2009; Naredo & Montiel, 2011; Puig, 2011). Meanwhile, the manufacturing industry had gradually reduced its prices as a result of the growing arrival of Chinese imports. China had drastically reduced the foreign prices of its products since Deng Xiaoping began the reforms at the end of the 1970s. One key explanatory element, although not unique, of this process was the tremendous devaluation of the yuan, which took place at the end of the twentieth century. From an exchange rate of $1.6 in 1978, it had been devalued to $8 in 2000. China moreover joined the World Trade Organization in 2001, which implied the dismantling of some of the last quotas that the West maintained on the entry of its products. As a result of all this, the commercial imbalance with China did not stop increasing.

The decline of European industry in the face of Chinese products was shared by most countries, especially those with high degrees of specialization in traditional consumer goods industries. The per capita industrial product, which had gradually increased between 1996 and 1999, did not stop declining from the beginning of the twenty-first century (Catalan,

2012e; Catalan & Sánchez, 2013). In 2007, on the eve of the outbreak of what we have called the Great Recession, it was around 10% below the level of the end of the second millennium (Fig. 7.13). While the manufacturing industry had stopped growing in the initial years of the new millennium, the property increased its value each year. Consequently, credit flowed towards real-estate owning.

The adoption of the euro was also among the significant causes of the Great Depression of the twenty-first century in the peripheral economies of Europe, those which have become known as the PIIGS or GIPSI. Although these acronyms are used for nation-state economies, the Catalan economy followed the same pattern. The adoption of the single currency, between 1999 and 2002, implied an abandonment of monetary sovereignty, reduced fiscal sovereignty, prevented the use of devaluation and, therefore, jeopardized the operation of what had been essential buffers in the previous depressions (Abreu et al., 2013; Barbera & Feltri, 2014; Boyer, 2013; Catalan, 2002a, 2021; Dornbusch, 1996; Eichengreen, 2015; Fitoussi, 1995; Fitoussi & Saraceno, 2013; Gasparoti & Kullas, 2019; Krugman, 2013; Lapavitsas et al., 2012; Louçã, 2012;

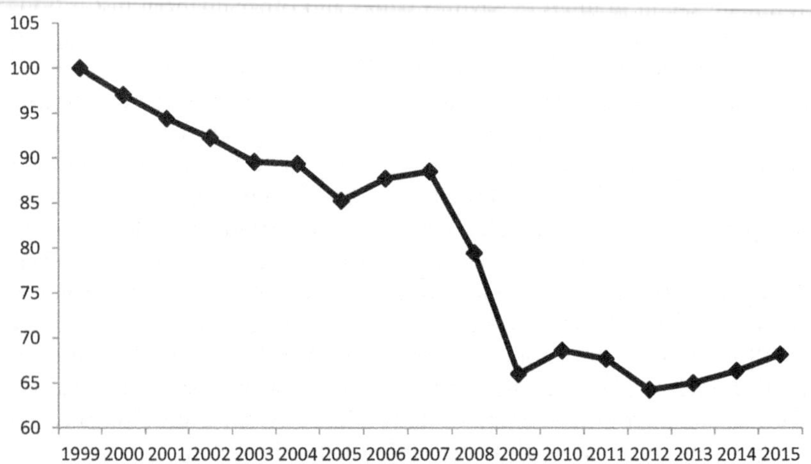

Fig. 7.13 Per capita industrial product of Catalonia, 1999–2015 (Index Numbers 1999 = 100) (*Source* Compiled by the author with the industrial product indices of the INE and the population of IDESCAT)

Mitchell, 2015; Plihon & Rey, 2012; Varoufakis, 2017; Vasapollo et al., 2014).

Initially, the adoption of the euro represented a considerable reduction in interest rates in the peripheral countries, in the years both prior to and subsequent to its effective circulation. The notable reduction in the cost of credits stimulated the demand of families, contributing to inflating the bubble. The single currency also generated erroneous expectations and led banks from countries in the industrial heart of Europe, especially Germany and France, to lend massively to countries on the periphery of the continent. In the case of our savings banks, they even borrowed money of European origin and then lent it to their clients captivated by the possibility of purchasing accommodation.

Very convincing evidence of the responsibility of the euro in the gestation of the crisis is that four European states which belonged to the European Union and its single market, but which did not participate in the single currency were saved from a bubble comparable to the one suffered by their neighbours during the first decade of the twenty-first century. This was the case of Sweden, Poland, the Czech Republic and Hungary. All four continued to converge during the twenty-first century and none of them suffered from a depression comparable to that of Mediterranean Europe (Catalan, 2021).

Three especially significant factors aggravated the depression: the high migratory flow experienced by Catalonia until 2008; the mistaken economic policy during the management of the crisis; and the close complicity between the financial and political elites. Starting with the first of these factors, the Catalan population went from 6.1 million to 7.4 million in the ten years between 1998 and 2008. This strong growth was based on immigration, which was very exceptional for an economy with an old industrialization and at a time when mature industrial countries, particularly Germany, were substantially restricting the arrival of foreign workers. Many years ago, Simon Kuznets identified the existence of a close correlation between the intensity of the migratory flow and the expansion of construction (Catalan, 2012d, 2021; Kuznets, 1965). The arrival of immigrants triggered the demand for accommodation and favoured an increase in prices. The Catalan case was not an exception. Immigrants pushed up the prices of the cheapest property, which their owners sold in order to move to better-off areas, where the prices of accommodation also shot up. The savings banks nourished the expectations of the newcomers, granting easy credit to those with a salary.

However, when the crisis broke out, these immigrants were also the first to lose their job and become insolvent. Since 2008, unpaid loans gradually increased and an important part of them corresponded to immigrants and people naturalized in the last few years.

There were four main mistakes in the management of the crisis. First, the budgetary policies of the government of President José Luis Rodríguez Zapatero and of the Generalitat of José Montilla were exaggeratedly expansive, given the lack of Spanish monetary sovereignty and the limited Catalan fiscal sovereignty. Second, the policy of bank mergers and privatization of the savings banks, promoted by the Banco de España, was obviously a serious mistake. Third, the policy implemented by the Troika and, in particular, the management of Jean-Claude Trichet at the head of the European Central Bank, suffered from an excessively anti-inflation bias. Finally, starting from the spring 2010, a savage adjustment of social expenditure which benefited the holders of debt and banks, was imposed on Spain, Catalonia and on other PIIGS, sacrificing the recovery of the rest of the productive activities and transforming the Great Recession into a true Great Depression. All of these mistakes and the complicity between the financial and political elites favoured a brutal increase in public debt, converting the insolvency of the private agents into a public finance crisis.

Rodríguez Zapatero's socialist government responded to the crisis with extremely improvised measures, such as generalized tax deductions, maternity benefits and the E Plan (Maluquer de Motes, 2013; Serrano, 2011). These measures were in addition to the exaggerated high-speed expansion programmes, subsidies for the producers of electricity, and the need to pay benefits to an unemployed figure which was increasing rapidly at the same time as the construction of housing fell and the manufacturing industry collapsed. In Catalonia, the Finance Minister of the Generalitat, Antoni Castells, also opted to maintain considerable fiscal expansion.

The Spanish Finance Minister, Pedro Solbes, began to have doubts and was replaced by Elena Salgado, who continued to ignore the fact that the Madrid government could not obtain privileged financing from the Banco de España in the event of recording an excessive public deficit. The tripartite government of Catalonia disregarded the limited tax sovereignty of the institution, maybe overestimating the possibilities opened up by the new Autonomy Law which Rodríguez Zapatero had falsely promised to support. The truth was that the deficit of the public administrations ended up reaching an unheard-of 11% of GDP at the end of 2009. Such a huge deficit had never before been recorded in times of peace, not even in Franco's inflationary Spain during the Second World War, when the almost unlimited credit of the Banco de España could be used. During the spring of 2010, in the midst of the Greek debt crisis, the speculators took a position against the debt securities of the so-called PIIGS and the holders of Spanish bonds became alarmed (Otte, 2010).[16] The premiums paid on the public debt shot up. The Ecofin meeting in May demanded a change of policy from Spain. Premier Zapatero also received calls from China and the United States. Finally, he decided on a 180-degree shift in his policy. He backed dramatic cuts in expenditure and approved a salary reduction for public workers. The only previous cut in nominal salaries in the whole of the twentieth century was in 1939, at the end of the civil war and following Franco's victory. In 2010 Catalonia, the regional Minister Castells was also forced to curb expenditure, resort to debt issues and pay succulent interest to their owners and to the financial institutions which acted as intermediaries.

Miguel Ángel Fernández Ordóñez, Governor of the Banco de España, promoted the privatization of the savings banks in response to the crisis, although it appears that there were previous projects pointing in this direction (Cabana, 2012; Serra Ramoneda, 2011). The immediate instrument of privatization was the sale of preferential shares, which the bank managers placed among their clients, often with deceitful promises. In some cases, such as that of Caixa Catalunya, the preferential share issue was carried out from the Cayman Islands tax haven. The small savings banks were moreover obliged to increase their size through a process of mergers, seeking a supposed (and by no means proven) guarantee of better management.

Caixa Sabadell, Caixa de Terrassa and Caixa Manlleu created Unnim Bank, which required injections of public capital for a value of €6bn and ended up being owned by the BBVA. The savings banks of Tarragona and Manresa chose to merge with that of Catalunya, creating the Catalunya Caixa group, which in the spring of 2014 had cost €12bn in public aid and still had to find a private buyer. Caixa Laietana decided to merge with the Caja Madrid group which, transformed into Bankia, was the star of one of the biggest bailouts in the history of Spain, with injections of almost €22bn.[17] Caixa de Girona was taken over by Caixa de Pensions which, now transformed into CaixaBank, is the only heir, although distorted, of the Catalan financial model of the twentieth century. The bailout of savings banks and some banks required a European credit line of up to €100bn, of which the Spanish government officially used some

€40bn. For its part, the Court of Auditors recognized that the bailout of savings banks and banks cost Spanish taxpayers at least €108bn.

Even though the European Central Bank (ECB) brought interest rates down to minimum levels in order to reduce the price of credit in the euro zone, its President, Jean-Claude Trichet, refused to intervene by purchasing the debt of the peripheral countries when the risk premiums shot up in the spring of 2010 (Boyer, 2013; Comín, 2013a; Fitoussi & Saraceno, 2013; Fontana, 2011; Roca, 2012). Unlike the policy of the Federal Reserve with Ben Bernanke (2013), or the more recent Japanese Abenomics, the BCE was exaggeratedly reluctant to purchase public debt, since it had been conceived in the image of the German Bundesbank. Trichet preferred to inject liquidity into the private financial institutions, many of which were directly to blame for the crisis, rather than into the asphyxiated governments. The former obtained credit at extremely low rates, while the latter, asphyxiated, remained in the hands of the speculators. Moreover, Trichet too upset with inflation decided to raise the interest rate of the ECB. In the summer of 2011, the French Governor of the European Central Bank finally demanded from Zapatero a reform of the labour market, to make it more flexible and decoupling of salaries from inflation.

The Chancellor Angela Merkel subsequently suggested the need for the constitutions of European countries to include the principle of budgetary stability and the absolute priority of servicing debt. The Partido Popular (conservatives) and the PSOE (socialists), which usually oppose to the reform of the Spanish Constitution to introduce the right to self-determination for the non-Castilian nationalities, quickly agreed to amend it in the direction demanded by the German Chancellor. Indeed, the Troika, an expression that refers to the joint action of the ECB, the European Commission and the IMF, agreed to demand tough adjustments from the countries which required their aid. Consequently, the new Partido Popular government, headed by President Mariano Rajoy, promoted a policy of reducing redundancy costs, a temporary cut in public worker's pay, a sharp increase in VAT and administrative recentralization. During the Bankia (former Caja Madrid) crisis, the Rajoy government obtained the aforementioned lifeline of credit for a value of €100bn. However, the guarantee, instead of being European, fell on the Spanish taxpayer. The consequence was that, according to EUROSTAT, Spanish public deficit rebounded to 10.6% of GDP in 2012, as an effect of the support for the financial institutions.

At the same time as deciding to save financial interests, brutal cuts were imposed on social expenditure which gave rise to a second recession in countries of peripheral Europe such as Catalonia, which unequivocally suffered from the existence of a Great Depression (Catalan, 2012e; Catalan & Sánchez, 2013; Maluquer de Motes, 2013): after a certain pause in the fall of real activity during 2010, the three-year period from 2011 to 2013 again experienced a marked decline in GDP (Fig. 7.14). Later, the IMF ended up renouncing some of these measures, pointing out that the speed of the adjustment had been exaggerated and had had negative effects on economic recovery. Other institutions (and important local economists) who had enthusiastically supported these policies also gradually distanced themselves from them.

In Catalonia, the finances inherited by the regional government of Artur Mas were almost in a situation of suspension of payments, due to the fall in income, the excess current expenditure and the increase in debt during the period of the tripartite government. The new regional Finance Minister, Andreu Mas-Colell, chose to endeavour to reassure the financial markets, based on showing firmness with the cuts to the civil service. The budget expenditure that Generalitat of Catalonia allocated

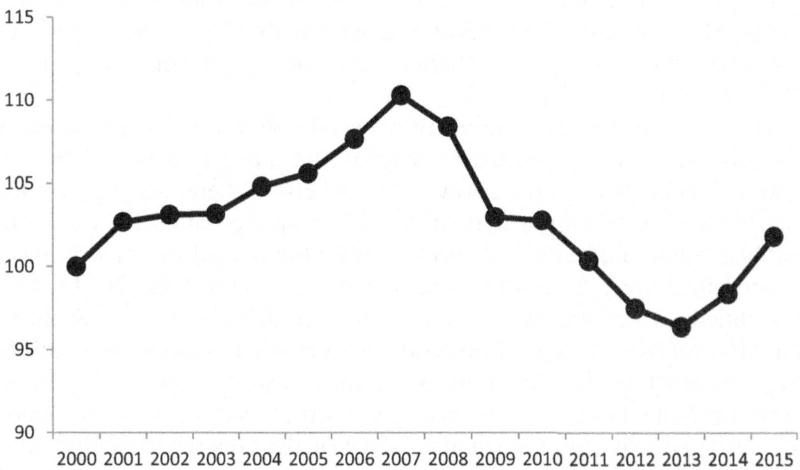

Fig. 7.14 Per capita real GDP Catalonia, 2000–2015 (Index Number 2000 = 100) (*Source* Compiled by the author with the volume index of GDP linked to market prices of the INE [base year 2008] and the population of IDESCAT)

to education, health, research and infrastructures suffered from remarkable cuts during the first half of the second decade of the new century. Moreover, the Catalan government undertook a wave of privatizations, caused by the mounting cost of servicing its debt, and Catalonia became a Spanish autonomous community in which the real wages of public servants recorded the most enduring cuts (Carreras et al., 2018).

Finally, another aggravating factor of the crisis was the close links established between political and financial elites and the big construction companies (Naredo & Montiel, 2011; Puig, 2011; Recio, 2010; Santos, 2013). Real-estate speculation, instead of being controlled by political leaders, was exacerbated by them, through deductions on the purchase of housing and reclassifications of land and properties protected by the planning rules in force (Naredo, 1996). Thus, the great majority of savings banks, where the politicians had increasing representation, speculated more than the banks themselves. Caixa de Pensions (later Caixa Bank), where the management remained in more professional hands, was able to avoid the general insolvency, despite the fact that it benefited from indirect subsidies (such as the bailout of the insolvent motorways of Madrid, in which its subsidiary Abertis had a stake). On the contrary, the savings banks of the Basque Country, where there was strong political representation, but which did not abandon the traditional model of links with the territory of origin and industry, tolerated the depression better and survived united under the umbrella of Kutxabank (Martín Aceña et al., 2013; Serra Ramoneda, 2011).

One indicator of the complicity between political and financial elites and big construction companies may be the intensity achieved by the informal economy. I am unaware of whether there are figures for Catalonia but we do know that, at the most critical point of the real-estate bubble, between 25 and 27% of the €500 notes issued by the European Central Bank were circulating in Spain (Mclean, 2006; Puig, 2011). This percentage, which was not related to the economic weight of Spain in the Monetary Union, corroborates the importance of transactions outside the law, which peaked in 2006. Since then, Spanish demand for €500 notes gradually became more moderate, as the prices of land and buildings deflated. The most qualitative signs of the complicity of the elites include evidence of construction companies financing political parties and of the intermediation of politicians, which appear in the proceedings of the Palau, Pretoria, Gurtel and Bárcenas corruption cases.

In this crisis, traditional buffers of depressions such as devaluation or the adoption of expansive fiscal and monetary policies operated with the limitations arising from the surrender of macroeconomic sovereignty involved in adopting the euro, already indicated. In the specific case of the exchange rate, the depreciation experienced was relatively moderate, because of the prevention by the ECB in front of excessively inflationary policies. Overall, the euro only depreciated by 16% in relation to the dollar between 2008 and 2012, a proportion too weak to constitute a sufficient stimulus for net exports from the peripheral countries in difficulty. On the other hand, the latter could not devalue in relation to their main partners and, therefore, had to continue to suffer from the loss of competitiveness in relation to countries from the industrial heart of Europe and, especially, with regard to Germany.

Fiscal policy was a buffer until 2009, preventing major contractions of demand. However, the option for a tough adjustment starting from May 2010 converted fiscal policy into a deadweight for recovery. The consensus in favour of cuts in social expenditure, which was shared from that date by the administrations of Madrid and Barcelona, contributed to causing a second fall in activity and to transforming the Great Recession into a Great Depression. Given the extremely bad results and following the U-turn of the IMF, which starting from 2013 began to criticize the intensity of the budgetary adjustment, a fiscal policy started to ease, although more in Madrid than in Barcelona.

On the other hand, some sectorial promotion programmes began to have positive effects in the last months of 2013. This was the case of the PIVE plan of subsidies for the purchase of automobiles (Fig. 7.15). It is well-known that the automotive industry is the one with the most carry-over effects to other activities. General Motors was thus bailed out at the beginning of the depression with the federal budget and Angela Merkel herself was willing to subsidize the purchase of Opel by German suppliers, should this European division have split from the parent company (Otte, 2010). In the Catalan case, the registration of passenger cars indicated that recovery began in 2013 and continued to record an improvement until well into 2016.

Nevertheless, monetary policy was the main antidote used throughout the depression, positioning and maintaining interest rates at historical minimums, and even at negative rates (Bernanke, 2013; Ragot, 2013). However, as I have already indicated, the anti-inflationary obsession of Mario Draghi's predecessor at the head of the ECB contributed to

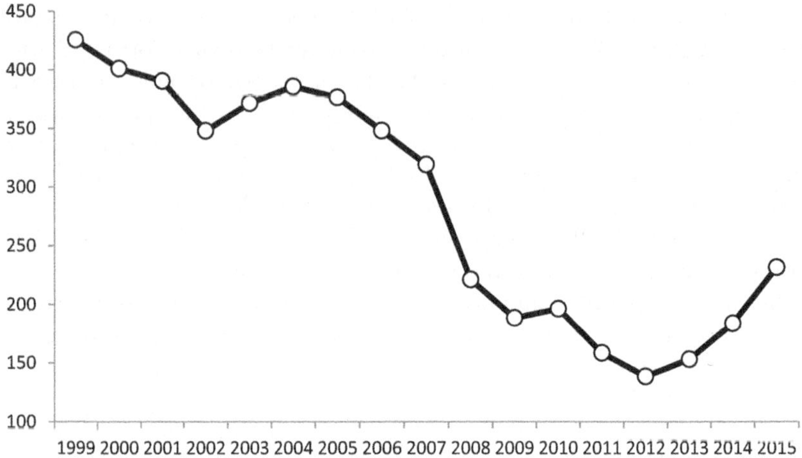

Fig. 7.15 Registration of passenger cars in Catalonia per 10,000 inhabitants, 1999–2015 (*Source* Compiled by the author with the registration of the INE and population of IDESCAT)

gestating the second recession. On refusing to purchase public debt from the governments with the greatest financial difficulties, he placed them in the hands of speculators. The risk premiums shot up and the debt service requirements rose, reinforcing the insolvency of the PIIGS or GIPSI. Draghi, former Vice-Chairman of Goldman Sachs, on the other hand, adopted a more pragmatic position at the head of the bank with headquarters in Frankfurt and began to turn the situation around when, in the summer of 2012, he announced that he was ready to do whatever it took to preserve the euro. Starting from that moment, the risk premiums began to go down, reflecting a change in the expectations of the speculators. The announcement by the Italian President of the ECB and his subsequent operations purchasing various kinds of bonds can be interpreted as a change of course in favour of monetary expansion, which acted as a protective net to prevent a subsequent fall in the peripheral economies, including the Catalan economy.

The previous series indicate that the Great Depression of the twenty-first century bottomed out around 2012. Since then, the variables chosen began to improve (as did employment). However, the long-term consequences of this great depression continue to be of concern. The growing tension between Catalonia and Spain could be considered as a political result of the depression although due to a lack of space, we will leave this outside the present analysis and we'll retake the topic in Chapter 8. On an economic level, three long-term effects of the depression appear to be consolidated as structural characteristics of the Catalan economy of the time: disproportionately high public debts; a weakening of income and rights of workers; and the loss of power in the public sphere in favour of the market.

The shock adjustment undertaken from mid 2010 and the preference of the elites to give priority to saving the financial institutions and the interests of the holders of the debt, not only worsened the depression. They moreover caused a rapid rise in the debt levels of the public administrations. In Spain as a whole, public debt went from representing 36% of GDP in 2008 to 62% in 2010. Between then and the end of 2013, it rose to 92%.[18] Spain became engulfed in the so-called debt trap.

Catalonia does not appear to be in a much better financial situation, given its traditional insufficiency of fiscal resources and the severity of the depression. The weight of public debt in Catalonia almost doubled in three years, going from 18 to 30% of GDP between 2010 and 2013. With the current debt volumes and the moderate growth of productive activity, it is necessary to continue to be indebted just to confront the servicing of the loans. The country shares with a large part of the PIIGS or GIPSI economies what is known as the debt trap. Despite the recovery initiated in around 2013, the weight of debt has not stopped increasing. At the level of the Catalan administration, public debt exceeded 35% of GDP in 2015. For the whole of the Spanish administration, it nearly reached the threshold of 100% of GDP!

Another inheritance of depression is a decline in living conditions for the majority of the population and, especially, employees. Although there may be a discussion about the level, it is difficult to deny that the policies chosen since 2010 have caused real salaries to fall. This is not just the case of public administration workers, who were the preferred scapegoat of the regional Minister Mas-Colell. Other categories of wage earners began to experience significant salary cuts and a pronounced worsening of work conditions. This was especially due to the labour reform approved by Premier Mariano Rajoy, which drastically lowered the cost of laying off employees from 40 to 20 days per year worked. Unlike the depressions of the Great War and of the Transition to democracy, which ended with a permanent improvement in real wages, it appears that this depression will end with a pattern closer to that of the early Franco period: a reduction in labours income and an impoverishment of the workers. Also like that depression, it may entail a delay in the growth of labour productivity in many industries and a relatively poor level of mechanization.

Finally, the crisis appears to be tilting the balance in favour of the markets and to the detriment of the public spheres of production and consumption. Above we analysed the process of privatization of the savings banks, which put an end to the financial model of twentieth-century Catalonia. Moreover, public investment was frozen and the process of privatization, more or less concealed, also made significant progress in domains such as public utilities, health and education.

7.5 Concluding Remarks

Over the last 100 years before the arrival of the Covid-19 pandemics, Catalonia experienced four major depressions: the one which began at the end of the Great War and lasted until the beginning of Primo de Rivera dictatorship (1919–1923); that of the 1930s, which was not fully overcome until the *Second Francoism* (1929–1955); that of the *Late-Francoism* and the transition to democracy (1974–1986); and the Great Depression of the euro (2008–2016). In each crisis there were exogenous causes, of an international nature, which contributed to triggering them: the euphoria of the First World War, the New York stock market bubble prior to the 1929 crash, the rise in the price of oil at the beginning of the 1970s and the real-estate mania of the early twenty-first century. The endogenous causes include a common feature of the four great depressions studied: the speculative excesses of the country's leading financial institutions at times prior to the bursting of the bubble, what John Maynard Keynes would qualify as the over-optimistic expectations of the animal spirits. These excesses led them to insolvency and contributed to the worsening of the depression. The collapse of Banco de Barcelona (1920), Banco de Cataluña (1931), Banca Catalana (1982) and Caixa de Catalunya/Catalunya Bank (2012) were particularly significant. In the four cases mentioned (the most important, but not the only ones), the managers of the insolvent institutions were closely linked to the political elites of the time. The excessive link between public and private interests of the country's financial fabric was negative, since it encouraged the taking of exaggerated risks instead of curbing them. It moreover meant that the function of lender of last resort of the Banco de España was exercised with significant limitations.

There were also important mistakes in economic policy among the endogenous factors which contributed to transforming the crises into great depressions. The most significant case was the adoption of an autarkic model of reconstruction at the end of the Civil War. This model, inspired by the policies of Nazi Germany and Mussolini's Italy in the 1930s, was utterly misconceived for a country with limited natural resources and technologies and which was emerging from a war.

Having allowed the remarkable acceleration of inflation until 1977, it can also be considered to be an important mistake of the late Franco period. The same can be said for the sudden liberalization of the financial and automotive sectors in the middle of the profound crisis of the transition to democracy.

Finally, the adoption of the euro likewise appears in an important position among the endogenous causes of the first Great Depression of the twenty-first century, having encouraged indebtedness before the outbreak of the crisis, and favoured speculation with the debt securities of the peripheral countries during the crisis. The euro moreover prevented the significant depreciation of the currency, which had played a key role in the emergence from the previous profound crises analysed. The path chosen of cutting public expenditure in research, education, health and infrastructures does not appear to be appropriate either, while the debt increased with the bailout of financial institutions and business friends. In the countries of Mediterranean capitalism, this policy converted the so-called Great Recession into a true Great Depression.

The comparative analysis of depressions suggests that there is no single guideline for political emergence from the crisis. The first two were overcome in the framework of a dictatorial regime, while during the third one democratic institutions were taking root. The toughness of the confrontation between the institutional representatives of Catalonia and Spain during the second decade of the twenty-first century can be considered as a result of the intensity of the depression. The crisis left the path open for different types of political solutions. A single result of the depression should not be expected in the sphere of the conflict between capital and labour either. The crisis of the 20s ended with a considerable improvement in real salaries and living conditions of the workers. On the other hand, the depression of 1929–1955 led to a permanent deterioration of the purchasing power of workers and an extension of working hours. The transition to democracy was a second case of overcoming the crisis with a substantial improvement in the living conditions of the majority of the population. The Great Depression of the euro, on the other hand, was overcome in favour of capital and against labour.

Appendix

See Table 7.1.

Notes

1. It should be noted, however, that the moment of full recovery indicated by per capita industrial product, 1928, seems too far-fetched.
2. A significant testimony of how the excess financial speculation ended up harming the rest of productive activity is that of Pedro Gual Villalbí (1930), when he clarifies the reason for his business failure: "The suspension of payments of Banco de B had a huge resonance due to the sum of interests that were involved; so much that, as a consequence, some other banking institutions collapsed and several commercial establishments, including mine, were directly ruined" (p. 223).
3. Among the qualitative evidence, we return to Gual Villalbí (1930), who added "...the consequences of the crisis worsened and reached their climax at the beginnigs of 1921 and continued during several months" (p. 218).
4. Calculated with settled budget balance estimations of Francisco Comín (Comín & Díaz, 2005, p. 951, series 2791) and GDP at current market prices estimations of Leandro Prados (Carreras et al., 2005, p. 1339, series 4744).
5. The peseta rates have been collected by Pablo Martín Aceña in the collective work edited by Albert Carreras and Xavier Tafunell (Martín Aceña & Pons, 2005, pp. 704–706).
6. *Butlletí Mensual d'Estadística*, collected by Bricall (1970, p. 24).
7. The part of the book corresponding to the great depression of the 1930s has been reprinted with the following title: *The Great Contraction 1929–1933* (Friedman & Schwartz, 2008, pp. 7–247).
8. Calculated with Maddison (1995).
9. The percentage has been recalculated with Comín and Díaz (2005, p. 951) and Carreras et al. (2005, p. 1339).
10. *Butlletí Mensual d'Estadística* (several years).
11. Calculated with Bricall (1970, p. 79).

Table 7.1 Registration of passenger cars in Catalonia per 10,000 inhabitants

1913	6.0	1948	2.7	1983	174.1
1914	6.0	1949	2.3	1984	166.7
1915	6.6	1950	1.4	1985	190.7
1916	7.1	1951	2.8	1986	230.8
1917	7.4	1952	2.6	1987	308.4
1918		1953	3.3	1988	354.0
1919		1954	7.7	1989	377.5
1920	7.5	1955	11.2	1990	306.3
1921	4.3	1956	20.4	1991	264.0
1922	6.1	1957	15.7	1992	285.8
1923	9.4	1958	23.1	1993	215.6
1924	11.4	1959	26.1	1994	259.7
1925	11.1	1960	30.7	1995	242.3
1926	13.8	1961	45.5	1996	266.7
1927	13.1	1962	52.3	1997	314.8
1928	19.8	1963	55.3	1998	374.6
1929	17.9	1964	78.0	1999	425.5
1930	11.6	1965	90.1	2000	401.2
1931	3.6	1966	132.9	2001	390.6
1932	5.7	1967	142.3	2002	348.2
1933	10.5	1968	141.7	2003	371.8
1934	13.6	1969	169.4	2004	386.0
1935	16.4	1970	184.7	2005	376.7
1936	9.6	1971	194.2	2006	348.5
1937		1972	222.9	2007	319.5
1938		1973	259.9	2008	221.3
1939		1974	238.0	2009	188.4
1940	2.4	1975	218.7	2010	196.4
1941	2.4	1976	227.9	2011	158.7
1942	2.6	1977	238.3	2012	138.5
1943	2.6	1978	224.6	2013	153.3
1944	1.7	1979	210.6	2014	183.9
1945	1.6	1980	188.5	2015	231.7
1946	1.7	1981	164.1		
1947	1.5	1982	169.4		

Source Compiled by the author. See sources of Figs. 7.4, 7.7, 7.9 and 7.15

12. Calculated with Comín and Díaz (2005, p. 951) and Carreras et al. (2005, p. 1339).
13. Here we estimate the real textile salary linking the salaries of industrial Spain to the evolution of the purchasing power of the salary of a working-class family from Sabadell, calculated by the Chamber of Commerce of this city. The series of nominal salaries for Spain come from Maluquer de Motes and Llonch (2005, p. 1224). We deflate them with the price index of Maluquer de Motes (4654), presented by Maluquer de Motes (2005, p. 1291). As we do not have the salary for 1936 industrial Spain, we suppose that it is the same as for 1935. We also suppose that the real salary in industrial Spain was identical to that of the working-class family of Sabadell, provided to us by the Chamber of Sabadell and included in Catalan (1993, pp. 134–135). See also Molinero and Ysàs (1985, pp. 192–202), Deu (2005, pp. 162–176) and Vilar (2009, pp. 81–154).
14. Calculated with Comín and Díaz (2005, p. 951) and Carreras et al. (2005, p. 1340).
15. I have estimated real salaries for the textile, leather and footwear industry (textiles in the graph) and for transportation material (automobiles) based on the labour cost supplied by Fundación BBV (1999, pp. 130–133). The nominal costs have been deflated with the price index implicit in the gross value added of Catalonia which appears in Fundación BBV (1999, pp. 316–317). Subsequently, they have been divided by the number of wage earners in the respective industry, which is presented in Fundación BBV (1999, pp. 186–189). Finally, they have been converted into index numbers with basis at the initial time.
16. Despite the size of the deficit, it should be highlighted that the United States rode out the Great Recession with a deficit of a comparable size (Bernanke, 2013; Duca, 2015). A deficit above 10% of GDP was also recorded there and, therefore, the intensity of the imbalance reinforces the responsibility of the euro in the depth and duration of the crisis experienced by the so-called GIPSI: it was not so much the level of deficit which overwhelmed the speculation against the debt of the Mediterranean economies as the certainty of the markets that Europe and its central bank would not actively intervene to help the peripheral countries.
17. Bankia shared the podium with Caja de Ahorros del Mediterráneo and Banco de Valencia, which absorbed, respectively, some €25bn and €18bn of public money, according to the Court of Auditors.
18. The figures can be consulted in EUROSTAT.

References

Abelló, T., & Gabriel, P. (1995). L'enfortiment de l'obrerisme. In B. de Riquer (ed.), *Història, política, societat i cultura dels Països Catalans. Volum 8. L'època dels nous moviments socials 1900–1930* (pp. 182–187). Enciclopèdia Catalana.

Abreu, A., Mendes, H., Rodrigues, J., Gusmao, J. G., Serra, N., & Alves, P. D. (2013). *A crise, a Troika e as alternativas urgentes*. Tinta-da-China.

Aixalá, J. (1999). *La peseta y los precios. Un análisis de largo plazo (1868–1985)*. P.U.Z.

Akerlof, G. R., & Shiller, R. J. (2009). *Animal Spirits*. Gestión 2000.

Albarracín, J. (1987). *La onda larga del capitalismo español*. Economistas Libros.

Albert, M. (1991). *Capitalisme contre capitalisme*. Le Seuil.

Alcaide, J. (2003). *Evolución económica de las regiones y provincias españolas en el siglo XX*. Fundación BBVA.

Alcaide, J. (dir.). (2007). *Evolución de la población española en el siglo XX por provincias y comunidades autónomas. Volumen II*. Fundació BBVA.

Aldcroft, D. H. (1977). *From Versailles to Wall Street, 1919–1929*. Allen Lane.

Aldcroft, D. H. (1997). *Studies in the Interwar European Economy*. Ashgate.

Allen, G. C. (1946). *A Short Economic History of Modern Japan, 1867–1937*. G. Allen & Unwin.

Anuario Estadístico de la ciudad de Barcelona. (1917). Impr. de Henrich y cia.

Ardit, M., Balcells, A., & Sales, N. (1980). *Història dels Països Catalans. De 1714 a 1975*. EDHASA.

Argandoña, A., & García Durán, J. A. (1992). *Macroeconomía española. Hechos e ideas*. McGraw-Hill.

Armstrong, P., Glyn, A., & Harrison, J. (1991). *Capitalism Since 1945*. Basil Blackwell.

Arrighi, G. (2007). *Adam Smith in Beijing: Lineages of the Twenty-first Century*. Verso.

Baiges, F., González, E., & Reixach, J. (1984). *Banca Catalana. Más que un banco, más que una crisis*. Plaza & Janés.

Baiges, J., Molinas, C., & Sebastián, M. (1987). *La economía española 1964–1985: datos, fuentes y análisis*. Instituto de Estudios Fiscales.

Balfour, N. (1994). *La dictadura, los trabajadores y la ciudad. El movimiento obrero en el área metropolitana de Barcelona (1939–1988)*. Alfons El Magnànim.

Balcells, A. (1971). *Crisis económica y agitación social en Cataluña (1930–1936)*. Ariel.

Balcells, A. (1977). *Cataluña Contemporánea II (1900–1936)*. Siglo XXI.

Balcells, A. (2013). La crisi econòmica dels anys trenta del segle XX. *Butlletí de la Societat Catalana d'Estudis Històrics, 24*, 349–365.

Balcells, A. (2014). *La Mancomunitat de Catalunya, 1914–1925: el primer pas vers l'autogovern des de la desfeta de 1714*. Diputació de Barcelona.

Balcells, A., Pujol, E., & Sabater, J. (1996). *La Mancomunitat de Catalunya i l'autonomia*. Proa.
Barbera, A., & Feltri, S. (2014). *La lunga notte dell'euro*. Rizzoli.
Barciela, C. (1981). *La financiación del Servicio Nacional del Trigo 1937–1971*. Banco de España.
Barciela, C. (1985). Las investigaciones sobre el mercado negro de productos agrarios en la posguerra: situación actual y perspectivas. *Revista de Historia Económica, 3*(3), 513–517.
Barciela, C. (1986). Introducción. In R. Garrabou, C. Barciela, & J. I. Jiménez Blanco (Eds.), *Historia agraria de la España contemporánea. 3. El fin de la agricultura tradicional (1900–1960)* (pp. 383–454). Crítica.
Barciela, C., López, I., Melgarejo, J., & Miranda, J. A. (2001). *La España de Franco (1939–1975)*. Síntesis.
Barkai, A. (1988). *Nazi Economics*. Berg.
Barratech, F. (1985). *Banca Catalana (1959–1984)*. Planeta.
Beltran, L., & Sardá, J. (1933). *Els problemes de la banca catalana*. Institut d'Investigacions Econòmiques.
Ben-Ami, S. (1983). *Fascism from Above: Dictatorship of Primo de Rivera in Spain, 1923–1930*. Oxford University Press.
Benaul, J. M., Garrido, A., & Sudrià, C. (2008). *Caixa Sabadell. Finances i acció social 1859–2009*. Obra Social Caixa Sabadell.
Bernanke, B. (2013). *The Federal Reserve and the Financial Crisis*. Princeton University Press.
Bernecker, W. L. (1978). *Anarchismus und bürgerkrieg: zur geschichte der sozialen revolution in Spanien 1936–1939*. Hoffmann und Campe.
Blasco, Y. (2007). En el origen de la modernización de las finanzas españolas: el Banco de Barcelona, 1944–1920. *Revista de Historia de la Economía y la Empresa, 1*, 35–58.
Blasco-Martel, Y., & Sudrià, C. (2016). *El Banco de Barcelona 1874–2020. Decadencia y quiebra*. Marcial Pons.
Bonamusa, F. (2004). Economia, finances i col·lectivitzacions industrials. In J. Solé Sabaté (Ed.), *La guerra civil a Catalunya (1936–1939), Volum 2. Una revolució en plena guerra* (pp. 54–92). Edicions 62.
Bosch, N., & Costa, M. (1990). El sector público autonómico y local. In M. Parellada (Ed.), *Estructura económica de Cataluña* (pp. 429–450). Espasa Calpe.
Boyer, R. (2013). The Euro Crisis: Undetected by Conventional Economics, Favoured by Nationally Focused Polity. *Cambridge Journal of Economics, 37*, 533–569.
Bregolat, E. (2007). *La segunda revolución china*. Destino.
Brenner, R. (2006). *The Economics of Global Turbulence: The Advanced Capitalist Economies from Long Boom to Long Downturn, 1945–2005*. Verso.

Bricall, J. M. (1970). *Política econòmica de la Generalitat (1936–1939). Volum primer: Evolució de les formes de la producció industrial.* Edicions 62.
Bricall, J. M. (1979). *Política econòmica de la Generalitat. Volum segon: El sistema financer.* Edicions 62.
Bricall, J. M. (1985). La economía española (1936–1939). In M. Tuñón de Lara (Ed.), *La guerra civil española. 50 años después* (pp. 359–417). Labor.
Bricall, J. M. (2008). Política industrial de la República española (1936–1939). In E. Fuentes Quintana & F. Comín (Eds.), *Economía y economistas españoles en la guerra civil. I. El contexto política e Internacional. Las economías españolas y las políticas españolas* (pp. 503–555). Galaxia Gutenberg.
Butlletí Mensual d'Estadística. (1932–37). Servei Central d'Estadistica
Bustelo, P. (2004). La Xina. In P. Bustelo, C. García, & I. Olivié (Eds.), *Economia contemporània de l'Àsia Oriental* (pp. 118–153). UOC.
Cabana, F. (1965). *La banca a Catalunya.* Edicions 62.
Cabana, F. (1972). *Bancs i banquers a Catalunya.* Edicions 62.
Cabana, F. (1978). *Història del Banc de Barcelona (1844–1920).* Edicions 62.
Cabana, F. (1989a). *Banca Catalana Diari Personal.* Tibidabo.
Cabana, F. (1989b). L'hegemonia de la banca forastera. In J. Nadal, J. Maluquer de Motes, C. Sudrià, & F. Cabana (Eds.), *Història econòmica de la Catalunya contemporània, s. XX, 6. Indústria, finances i turisme* (pp. 242–311). Enciclopèdia Catalana.
Cabana, F. (2000). *Caixes i Bancs de Catalunya. Bancs de Catalunya II.* Enciclopèdia Catalana.
Cabana, F. (2007). *La fallida del Banc de Barcelona (1920).* Pòrtic.
Cabana, F. (2012). *El crepuscle de les caixes.* Dèria.
Cals, J. (2005). *El éxito de las Cajas de Ahorros.* Ariel.
Calvet, J. (1992). *La indústria tèxtil llanera a Espanya, 1939–1959.* Col·legi de Doctors en Filosofia i Lletres i en Ciències.
Calvo, A. (1988). Estructura industrial i sistema productiu a Catalunya durant la Primera Guerra Mundial. *Recerques, 20*, 11–43.
Calvo, A., & Sagnes, J. (1995). Indústria i electricitat. In B. de Riquer (Ed.), *Història, política, societat i cultura dels Països Catalans. Volum 8. L'època dels nous moviments socials 1900–1930* (pp. 124–141). Enciclopèdia Catalana.
Calvo Sotelo, J. (1974). *Mis servicios al estado: seis años de gestión.* Instituto de Estudios de Administración. Original edition: (1931). Imprenta clásica española.
Carreras, A. (1984). La producción industrial española, 1842–1981: construcción de un índice anual. *Revista de Historia Económica, 1*, 127–157.
Carreras, A. (1985). La producción industrial catalana y vasca, 1844–1935. Elementos para una comparación. In M. González-Portilla, J. Maluquer de Motes, & B. de Riquer (Eds.), *Industrialización y nacionalismo* (pp. 197–209). Universitat Autònoma de Barcelona

Carreras, A. (1987). La industria: atraso y modernización. In J. Nadal, A. Carreras, & C. Sudrià (Eds.), *La economía española en el siglo XX* (pp. 280–312). Ariel.

Carreras, A., & Estapé, S. (2002). The Spanish Motor Industry, 1930–1975. In M. Lynskey & S. Yonekura (Eds.), *Entrepreneurship and Organization* (pp. 123–150). Oxford University Press.

Carreras, A., & Tafunell, X. (2021). *Between Empire and Globalisation: An Economic History of Modern Spain*. Palgrave.

Carreras, A., & Yáñez, C. (1992). El puerto en la era industrial: una síntesis histórica. In J. Clavera, A. Carreras, J. M. Delgado, & C. Yáñez (Eds.), *Economía e historia del puerto de Barcelona. Tres estudios* (pp. 81–157). Civitas.

Carreras, A., Mas-Colell, A., & Planas, I. (2018). *Turbulències i tribulacions. Els anys de les retallades*. Edicions 62.

Carreras, A., Prados, L., & Rosés, J. R. (2005). Renta y riqueza. In A. Carreras & X. Tafunell (Eds.), *Estadísticas Históricas de España. Siglos XIX-XX. Volumen III* (pp. 1297–1376). Fundación BBVA.

Casassas, J., & Roig, J. M. (1995). Sota el signe de la Mancomunitat. In B. de Riquer (Ed.), *Història, política, societat i cultura dels Països Catalans. Volum 8. L'època dels nous moviments socials 1900–1930* (pp. 264–279). Enciclopèdia Catalana.

Castells, A. (1993). *Les col·lectivitzacions a Barcelona 1936–1939*. Hacer.

Catalan, J. (1989a). Autarquía y desarrollo de la industria de fábrica durante la Segunda Guerra Mundial. Un enfoque comparativo. In J. L. García Delgado (Ed.), *El primer franquismo. España durante la segunda guerra mundial* (pp. 35–88). Siglo XXI.

Catalan, J. (1989b). En el cincuenta aniversario de la II Guerra Mundial: un fracaso de la economía española. *Revista de Economía, 3*, 87–92.

Catalan, J. (1991a). Del "milagro" a la crisis: la herencia económica del franquismo. In M. Etxezarreta (Ed.), *La reestructuración del capitalismo en España, 1970–1990* (pp. 95–132). FUHEM-Icària.

Catalan, J. (1991b). Los años cuarenta en la periferia de Europa: la economía española en perspectiva comparada. In J. L. Casas (Ed.), *La postguerra española y la segunda guerra mundial* (pp. 59–96). Diputación de Córdoba.

Catalan, J. (1992). Reconstrucción, política económica y desarrollo industrial: tres economías del sur de Europa, 1944–53. In L. Prados de la Escosura & V. Zamagni (Eds.), *El desarrollo económico en la Europa del Sur: España e Italia en perspectiva histórica* (pp. 359–395). Alianza.

Catalan, J. (1993). Economía e industria: La ruptura de posguerra en perspectiva comparada. *Revista de Historia Industrial, 4*, 111–143.

Catalan, J. (1994). Industrialización difusa y desarrollo económico: el retroceso de 1939–58. In J. Nadal & J. Catalan (Eds.), *La cara oculta de la industrialización española* (pp. 369–397). Alianza.

Catalan, J. (1995a). *La economía española y la Segunda Guerra Mundial*. Ariel.

Catalan, J. (1995b). Sector exterior y crecimiento industrial. España y Europa, 1939–1959. *Revista de Historia Industrial, 8*, 99–146.

Catalan, J. (1999). Spain, 1939–96. In M. S. Schulze (Ed.), *Western Europe: Economic and Social Change* (pp. 353–371). Longman.

Catalan, J. (2002a). Costes y beneficios del euro en la Europa periférica: España versus Suecia. *Gaceta Numismática, 145*(2002), 17–33.

Catalan, J. (2002b). Franquismo y autarquía, 1939–1959: enfoques de historia económica. *Ayer, 46*, 264–283.

Catalan, J. (2003). La reconstrucción franquista y la experiencia de la Europa occidental, 1934–1959. In C. Barciela (Ed.), *Autarquía y mercado negro. El fracaso económico del primer franquismo, 1939–1959* (pp. 123–168). Crítica.

Catalan, J. (2006a). Guerra e industria en las dos Españas. In P. Martín Aceña & E. Martínez (Eds.), *La economía de la guerra civil* (pp. 161–227). Marcial Pons.

Catalan, J. (2006b). La SEAT del desarrollo, 1948–1972. *Revista de Historia Industrial, 30*, 143–193.

Catalan, J. (2008). Fabricar para la guerra, padecer por el frente: la coyuntura industrial del conflicto armado español. In E. Fuentes Quintana & F. Comín (Eds.), *Economía y economistas españoles en la guerra civil. I. El contexto política e Internacional. Las economías españolas y las políticas españolas* (pp. 557–599). Galaxia Gutenberg.

Catalan, J. (2010). Strategic Policy Revisited: The Origins of Mass Production in the Motor Industry of Argentina, Korea and Spain, 1945–87. *Business History, 52*(2), 207–230.

Catalan, J. (2011). Los "cuatro franquismos" económicos, 1939–77: de la involución autárquica a la conquista de las libertades. In S. Cruz & J. Ponce (Eds.), *El mundo del trabajo en la conquista de las libertades* (pp. 55–114). Universidad de Jaén.

Catalan, J. (2012a). Francoist Spain under Nazi Economic Hegemony, 1936–1945. In C. Buccheim & M. Boldorf (Eds.), *Europäische Volkswirtschaften unter deutscher Hegemonie 1938–1945* (pp. 229–265). Oldendburg Verlag.

Catalan, J. (2012b). La SEAT del Ibiza, 1981–2010: fuerza de una marca, resistencia de un distrito. In J. Catalan, J. A. Miranda, & R. Ramon Muñoz (Eds.), *Distritos y clusters en la Europa del Sur* (pp. 259–316). Lid.

Catalan, J. (2012c). La SEAT i la represa del districte de l'automoció de Barcelona. In S. Balfour (Ed.), *Barcelona malgrat el franquisme* (pp. 27–72). MUHBA.

Catalan, J. (2012d). La trampa del euro: del declive industrial a la debacle financiera. *Revista de Estudios. Fundación 1º de Mayo, 40*, 22–29.
Catalan, J. (2012e). Orígenes de la Gran Depresión del siglo XXI: un enfoque de historia industrial. *Revista de Economía Crítica, 13*, 84–90.
Catalan, J. (2012f). Reculada i clímax de la industrialització 1936–1975. In J. Nadal, J. M. Benaul, & C. Sudrià (Eds.), *Atles de la industrialització de Catalunya, 1750–2010* (pp. 180–296). Vicens Vives.
Catalan, J. (2013). La depressió del darrer franquisme i la transició democràtica (1973–1986). *Butlletí de la Societat Catalana d'Estudis Històrics, 24*, 367–401.
Catalan, J. (2021). *Mediterranean Capitalism and the Euro, 1999-2019: The Long March to Debt, Depression and Divergence* (Unpublished paper). Universitat de Barcelona.
Catalan, J., & Sánchez, A. (2013). "Cinco cisnes negros". Grandes depresiones en la industrialización moderna y contemporánea, 1500–2012. In F. Comín & M. Hernández (Eds.), *Crisis económicas en España 1300–2012* (pp. 83–112). Alianza.
Chang, H. J. (2010). *23 Things They Don't Tell You About Capitalism*. Penguin Books.
Clavera, J. (1976). Industrialització i canvi de cojuntura a la Catalunya de la postguerra. *Recerques, 6*, 205–221.
Clavera, J., Esteban, J., Monés, M. A., Montserrat, A., & Ros, J. (1973). *Capitalismo español: de la autarquía a la estabilización (1939–1959). Tomo I (1939–1950)*. Cuadernos para el Diálogo.
Cohen, S., & Bradford De Long, J. (2010). *The End of Influence. What Happens When Other Countries Have the Money*. Basic Books.
Comín, F. (1987). La economía española en el período de entreguerras (1919–1935). In J. Nadal, A. Carreras, & C. Sudrià (Eds.), *La economía española en el siglo XX* (pp. 105–149). Ariel.
Comín, F. (1989). *Hacienda y economía en la España contemporánea (1800–1936), Volumen II*. Instituto de Estudios Fiscales.
Comín, F. (2002). Spanish Savings Banks and the Competitive Cooperation Model (1998-2002). *Revista de Historia Económica/Journal of Iberian and Latin American Economic History, 2*(4), 199–229.
Comin, F. (2013a). Apuros, ahorros, arreglos y bancarrotas. Las crisis de la deuda pública, 1504–2012. In F. Comín & M. Hernández (Eds.), *Crisis económicas en España 1300–2012* (pp. 169–202). Alianza.
Comín, F. (2013b). La gran depresión internacional y la Segunda República. In E. Llopis & J. Maluquer de Motes (Eds.), *España en crisis* (pp. 133–164). Pasado y Presente.

Comín, F., & Díaz, D. (2005). Sector público administrativo y estado del bienestar. In A. Carreras & X. Tafunell (Eds.), *Estadísticas Históricas de España. Siglos XIX-XX. Volumen II* (pp. 873–966). Fundación BBVA.

Comín, F., & Martín Aceña, P. (1984). La política monetaria y fiscal durante la dictadura y la segunda república. *Papeles de Economía Española, 20*, 236–261.

Cuervo, A. (Ed.). (1983). *Crisis bancarias. Soluciones comparadas.* UIMP-Asociación Española de Banca Privada.

Cuervo, A. (1987). *La crisis bancaria en España 1977–1985.* Ariel.

Cuevas, J. (2013). De la burbuja ferroviaria a la tecnológica. In P. Martín-Aceña, E. Martínez, & M. A. Pons (Eds.), *Las crisis financieras en la España contemporánea, 1850–2012* (pp. 159–196). Crítica.

David, H., Dorn, D., & Hanson, G. H. (2013). The China Syndrome: Local Labor Market Effects on Import Competition in the United States. *American Economic Review, 103*(6), 2, 121–168.

De Madariaga, J. (2004). Les indústries de guerra. In J. Solé Sabaté (Ed.), *La guerra civil a Catalunya (1936–1939), Volum 2. Una revolució en plena guerra* (pp. 89–93). Edicions 62.

De Madariaga, J. (2008). *Tarradellas y la industria de guerra de Cataluña (1936–1939).* Milenio.

Deu, E. (1988). Els beneficis industrials durant la Primera Guerra Mundial: el cas de la indústria llanera de Sabadell. *Recerques, 20*, 45–60.

Deu, E. (1990). *La indústria tèxtil de Sabadell, 1896–1925.* Col·legi Oficial de Doctors i Llicenciats en Filosofia i Lletres i en Ciències de Catalunya.

Deu, E. (2005). *La indústria metal·lúrgica i de construccions mecàniques a Sabadell.* Centre Metal·lúrgic.

Dirección General de Tráfico (various years). *Estadística de Transporte.* Madrid.

Dornbusch, R. (1996). Euro fantasies. *Foreign Affairs, 75*(5), 110–124.

Duca, J. V. (2015). *The Great Depression Versus the Great Recession in the US: How Fiscal, Monetary, and Financial Policies Compare.* Paper presented to the International Conference on Large Scale Crises: 1929 vs 2008. Ancona.

Eichengreen, B. (1995). *Golden Fetters.* Oxford University Press.

Eichengreen, B. (2004). The British Economy Between the Wars. In R. Floud & P. Johnson (Eds.), *The Cambridge Economic History of Modern Britain. Volume II. Economic Maturity, 1860–1939* (pp. 314–343). Cambridge University Press.

Eichengreen, B. (2007). *The European Economy Since 1945.* Princeton.

Eichengreen, B. (2015). *Hall of Mirrors.* Oxford University Press.

Eichengreen, B., & O'Rourke, K. (2009). A Tale of Two Depressions. *VOX. CEPR Policy Portal.* https://voxeu.org/article/tale-two-depressions-what-do-new-data-tell-us-february-2010-update#apr609. Accessed 11 March 2019.

Engelhard, P. (2012). Making Room for Beetle. *Automotive History Review, 54*, 14–21.

Enrech, C. (2005). *Indústria i ofici*. Publicacions UAB.

Espina, A., Fina, L., & Sáez, F. (Eds.). (1987). *Estudios de economía del trabajo en España. II Salarios y política de rentas*. Ministerio de Trabajo y Seguridad Social.

Estefanía, J. (1987). Los pactos sociales en el decenio democrático. In J. A Fernández-Villa (Ed.), *Mineros, sindicalismo y política* (pp. 205–240). Fundación José Barreiro.

Etxezarreta, M. (1979). *La economía española (1970–1979)*. El Viejo Topo.

Fàbrega, A. (2009). *Cum Grano Salis. La sal i la potassa a Súria 1885–1982*. Ajuntament de Súria.

Fina, L., & Toharia, L. (1987). *Las causas del paro en España. Un punto de vista estructural*. IESA.

Fitoussi, J.-P. (1995). *Le débat interdit. Monnaie, Europe, Pauvreté*. Arléa.

Fitoussi, J.-P., & Saraceno, F. (2013). European Economic Governance: The Berlin-Washington Consensus. *Cambridge Journal of Economics, 37*, 479–496.

Foley, G., & Nassim, C. (1976). *The Energy Question*. Penguin.

Fontana, J. (1986). Reflexiones sobre la naturaleza y las consecuencias del franquismo. In J. Fontana (Ed.), *España bajo el franquismo* (pp. 8–38). Crítica.

Fontana, J. (2011). *Por el bien del imperio*. Pasado & Presente.

Fontana, J., & Nadal, J. (1976). España 1914–1970. In C. M. Cipolla (Ed.), *Historia económica de Europa (6). Economías contemporáneas 2* (pp. 95–163). Ariel.

Fontana, J. M. (1953). *Sobre Economía Textil. Historia-Estructura-Dinámica*. Talleres Gráficos Hija de J. Ferrer Coll.

Friedman, M., & Schwartz, A. (1963). *A Monetary History of the United States*. Princeton University Press.

Friedman, M., & Schwartz, A. (2008). *The Great Contraction 1929–1933*. Princeton University Press.

Fundación BBV. (1999). *Renta nacional de España y su distribución provincial. Serie homogénea. Años 1955 a 1993 y avances 1994 a 1997. Tomo I*. Documenta.

Gabriel, P. (1988). Sous i cost de la vida a Catalunya a l'entorn dels anys de la Primera Guerra Mundial. *Recerques, 20*, 61–91.

Galabert, M. (2012). Un cas d'èxit als Pirineus: el desenvolupament econòmic d'Andorra, 1866–2007. *Recerques, 64*, 57–88.

Galbraith, J. K. (1954). *The Great Crash, 1929*. Houghton Mifflin.

García Delgado, J. L. (1980). La política económica española de 1930: el "error Argüelles." *Papeles de Economía Española, 1*, 43–47.

García Delgado, J. L. (1985). Notas sobre el intervencionismo económico del primer franquismo. *Revista de Historia Económica, 3*(1), 135–145.

García Delgado, J. L. (1987). La industrialización y el desarrollo económico de España durante el franquismo. In J. Nadal, A. Carreras, & C. Sudrià (Eds.), *La economía española en el siglo XX* (pp. 164–189). Ariel.

García Delgado, J. L. (1990a). Crecimiento económico y cambio estructural (1951–1975). In P. Martín Aceña & F. Comín (Eds.), *Empresa pública e industrialización en España* (pp. 137–160). Alianza.

García Delgado, J. L. (Ed.). (1990b). *Economía española de la transición y la democracia, 1973–1986*. CIS.

García Pérez, R. (1994). *Franquismo y Tercer Reich*. Centro de Estudios Constitucionales.

Gasparoti, A., & Kullas, M. (2019). *20 Years of the Euro: Winners and Losers*. Freiburg, Centre for European Policy.

Glynn, S., & Booth, A. (1992). The Emergence of Mass Unemployment: Some Questions of Precision. *Economic History Review, 45*, 731–738.

Gómez Mendoza, A. (1994). *El "Gibraltar económico": Franco y Riotinto, 1936–1954*. Civitas.

Gómez Mendoza, A. (Ed.). (2000). *De Mitos y Milagros. El Instituto Nacional de Autarquía (1941–1963)*. Monografías de Historia Industrial.

González Calvet, J. (1991a). Crisis, Transición y Estancamiento. La Política Económica Española, 1973–82. In M. Etxezarreta (Ed.), *La reestructuración del capitalismo en España, 1970–1990* (pp. 133–175). FUHEM-Icària.

González Calvet, J. (1991b). Transformación del sector público e intervención en la economía. In M. Etxezarreta (Ed.), *La reestructuración del capitalismo en España, 1970–1990* (pp. 177–237). FUHEM-Icària.

González Calvet, J. (1994). Prestaciones sociales, eficiencia y equidad. In J. Albarracín (Ed.), *La larga noche neoliberal* (pp. 223–269). Icaria.

González de la Fe, P. (2003). SEAT en la encrucijada (1972–2002). In J. L. Garcia Ruiz (Ed.), *Sobre ruedas* (pp. 95–126). Síntesis.

Gual Villalbí, P. (1930). *Memorias de un industrial de nuestro tiempo*. Sociedad General de Publicaciones.

Hernández Andreu, J. (1986). *España y la crisis de 1929*. Espasa-Calpe.

Hortalà, J. (2007). Índice histórico de renta variable de la Bolsa de Barcelona: 1846–2006. In M. L. Cabañes (Ed.), *Abstracción y realidad en la economía. Ensayos en homenaje al profesor Alejandro Lorca Corrons* (pp. 69–99). Minerva.

James, H. (1986). *The German Slump: Politics and Economics, 1924–1936*. Clarendon Press.

James, H. (2001). *The End of Globalization: Lessons from the Great Depression*. Harvard University Press.

James, H. (2009). *The Creation and Destruction of Value*. Harvard University Press.

Katzenstein, P. (1985). *Small States in World Markets: Industrial Policy in Europe*. Cornell University Press.
Kindleberger, C. P. (1973). *The World in Depression 1929–1939*. University of California Press.
Kindleberger, C. P. (1978). *Manias, Panics and Crashes*. Macmillan.
Kobrak, C., & Wilkins, M. (2011). The "2008 Crisis" in an Economic History Perspective: Looking at the Twentieth Century. *Business History, 53*(2), 175–192.
Kobrak, C., & Wilkins, M. (Eds.). (2014). *History and Financial Crisis*. Routledge.
Koo, R. C. (2009). *The Holy Grail of Macroeconomics*. Wiley.
Koo, R. C. (2013). Balance Sheet Recessions and the Global Economic Crisis. In H. Flassbeck, P. Davidson, J. K. Galbraith, R. Koo, J. Ghosh (Eds.), *Economic Reform Now: A Global Manifesto to Rescue Our Sinking Economies* (pp. 85–131). Palgrave Macmillan.
Krugman, P. (1990). *The Age of Diminished Expectations: U.S. Economic Policy in the 1990s*. MIT Press.
Krugman, P. (1994). *Peddling Prosperity: Economic Sense and Nonsense in an Age of Diminished Expectations*. Norton.
Krugman, P. (2009). *The Return of Depression Economics and the Crisis of 2008*. Norton.
Krugman, P. (2012). *End This Depression Now!* Norton.
Krugman, P. (2013). Revenge of the Optimum Currency Area. *NBER Macroeconomics Annual, 27*, 439–448.
Kuznets, S. (1965). *Economic Growth and Structure: Selected Essays*. Norton.
La Maquinista Terrestre y Marítima [LMTYM]. (1980). *La Maquinista Terrestre y Marítima S. A. 125 Aniversario 1855–1980*. Din.
Lamard, P., & Stoskopf, N. (Eds.). (2009). *1974–1984 Une décennie de désindustrialisation?* Picard.
Lapavitsas, C., Kaltenbrunner, A., Labrinidis, G., Lindo, D., Meadway, J., & Michell, J. (2012). *Crisis in the Eurozone*. Verso.
Leitz, C. (1996). *Economic Relations Between Nazi Germany and Franco's Spain 1936–1945*. Oxford University Press.
Lewis, A. W. (1949). *Economic Survey 1919–1939*. George Allen and Unwin.
Llarch, E. (1999). Bancs i caixes. In B. de Riquer (Ed.), *Història, política, societat i cultura dels Països Catalans. Volum 12. Autogovern i reptes de la fi de segle 1890–1997* (p. 174). Enciclopèdia Catalana.
Llorente, F. (1997). Las estrategias de los fabricantes de automóviles. El caso de SEAT, 1980–1995. In J. Roca (Ed.), *La formació del cinturó industrial de Barcelona* (pp. 275–289). Proa.
Lo Cascio, P. (2013). *La guerra civile spagnola*. Carocci.
Louçã, F. (2012). *A Dividadura. Portugal na crise do euro*. Bertrand.

Maddison, A. (1995). *Monitoring the World Economy 1820–1992*. OECD.

Maluquer de Motes, J. (1987). Salarios y renta nacional. In J. A Fernández-Villa (Ed.), *Mineros, sindicalismo y política* (pp. 187–203). Fundación José Barreiro.

Maluquer de Motes, J. (1989). Precios, salarios y beneficios. La distribución funcional de la renta. In A. Carreras (Ed.), *Estadísticas históricas de España. Siglos XIX-XX* (pp. 495–532). Banco Exterior.

Maluquer de Motes, J. (1994). El índice de la producción industrial de Cataluña. Una nueva estimación (1817–1935). *Revista de Historia Industrial, 5*, 45–71.

Maluquer de Motes, J. (2005). Consumo y precios. In A. Carreras & X. Tafunell (Eds.), *Estadísticas Históricas de España. Siglos XIX-XX. Volumen III* (pp. 1247–1296). Fundación BBVA.

Maluquer de Motes, J. (2013). España en el país de las maravillas. La nueva gran depresión de la economía española. In E. Llopis & J. Maluquer de Motes (Eds.), *España en crisis* (pp. 221–245). Pasado y Presente.

Maluquer de Motes, J., & Llonch, M. (2005). Trabajo y relaciones laborales. In A. Carreras & X. Tafunell (Eds.), *Estadísticas Históricas de España. Siglos XIX-XX. Volumen III* (pp. 1155–1245). Fundación BBVA.

Manera, C. (Ed.). (2002). *Las islas del calzado*. Lleonard Muntaner.

Marichal, C. (2010). *Nueva historia de las grandes crisis financieras. Una perspectiva global, 1873–2008*. Debate.

Marseille, J. (1984). *Empire colonial et capitalisme français*. Albin Michel.

Martín Aceña, P. (2000). La pesseta entre dues guerres i una crisi, 1919–1936. In J. L. García Delgado & J. M. Serrano (Eds.), *Del ral a l'euro* (pp. 67–85). Caixa de Pensions.

Martín Aceña, P., & Comín, F. (1991). *INI. 50 años de industrialización española*. Espasa Calpe.

Martín Aceña, P., & Pons, M. A. (2005). Sistema monetario y financiero. In A. Carreras & X. Tafunell (Eds.), *Estadísticas Históricas de España. Siglos XIX-XX. Volumen II* (pp. 645–706). Fundación BBVA.

Martín Aceña, P., Martínez, E., & Pons, M. A. (2013). Siglo XXI: Recesión y crisis financiera. In P. Martín-Aceña, E. Martínez, & M. A. Pons (Eds.), *Las crisis financieras en la España contemporánea, 1850–2012* (pp. 241–294). Crítica.

Massana, C. (1981). Vagues, cicles i política (1900–1936). *Recerques, 11*, 81–101.

Mclean, R. (2006, April 19). One in Four Euro 500 Bills are in Spain. Why? Crime Might be the Answer. *The New York Times*.

Minsky, H. P. (1975). *John Maynard Keynes*. Columbia University Press.

Minsky, H. P. (1977). The Financial Instability Hypothesis: An Interpretation of Keynes and an Alternative to "Standard" Theory. *Nebraska Journal of Economics and Business, 16*(1), 5–16.

Miranda, J. A. (1992). Els orígens del model industrial valencià. Elx 1850–1930. *Recerques, 25*, 159–173.

Miranda, J. A. (1994). La industria del calzado española en la posguerra: los efectos del intervencionismo en una industria de bienes de consumo. *Revista de Historia Económica, 12*(2), 317–339.

Miranda, J. A. (1998). *La industria del calzado en España (1860–1959)*. Institut de Cultura Juan Gil-Albert.

Miranda, J. A. (2003). El fracaso de la industrialización autárquica. In C. Barciela (Ed.), *Autarquía y mercado negro. El fracaso económico del primer franquismo, 1939–1959* (pp. 95–121). Crítica.

Mitchell, W. (2015). *Eurozone Dystopia: Groupthink and Denial on a Grand Scale*. Edward Elgar.

Mochón, F., Ancochea, G., & Ávila, A. J. (1988). *Economía española 1964–1987*. McGraw-Hill.

Molinero, C., & Ysàs, P. (1985). *"Patria, justicia y pan". Nivell de vida i condicions de treball a Catalunya 1939–1951*. La Magrana.

Montserrat, A., & Ros, J. (1972). Entorn del retard en el recobrament dels nivells macroeconòmics de pre-guerra a l'Espanya dels 1950. *Recerques, 2*, 231–246.

Muns, J. (1986). *Historia de las relaciones entre España y el Fondo Monetario Internacional 1958–1982*. Alianza.

Muñoz, J. (1988). *El fracaso de la burguesía financiera catalana. La crisis del Banco de Barcelona*. Endymion.

Nadal, J. (1985). *Catalunya, la fàbrica d'Espanya*. Ajuntament de Barcelona.

Nadal, J. (2010). Discurs d'acceptació del títol de doctor honoris causa. In *Cerimònia Acadèmica d'investidura com a doctor Honoris Causa del professor Jordi Nadal*. Universitat Pompeu Fabra.

Nadal, J., & Sudrià, C. (1981). *Història de la Caixa de Pensions*. Caixa de Pensions.

Nadal, J., & Tafunell, X. (1992). *Sant Martí de Provençals, pulmó industrial de Barcelona (1847–1992)*. Columna.

Nadal, J., Benaul, J. M., & Sudrià, C. (2012). La formació d'una societat industrial, 1833–1935. In J. Nadal, J. M. Benaul, & C. Sudrià (Eds.), *Atles de la industrialització de Catalunya, 1750–2010* (pp. 140–142). Vicens Vives.

Nadal, J., Carreras, A., & Martín Aceña, P. (Eds.). (1988). *España, 200 años de tecnología*. Ministerio de Industria.

Naredo, J. M. (1979). Energía y crisis de civilización. *Cuadernos de Ruedo Ibérico, 63–66*, 39–70.

Naredo, J. M. (1996). *La burbuja inmobiliario-financiera en la coyuntura económica reciente (1985–1995)*. Siglo XXI.

Naredo, J. M. (2009). La cara oculta de la crisis. El fin del boom inmobiliario y sus consecuencias. *Revista de Economía Crítica, 7*, 118–133.

Naredo, J. M., & Montiel, A. (2011). *El modelo inmobiliario español y su culminación en el caso valenciano*. Icaria.

Nesi, E. (2010). *Storia della mia gente. La rabia e l'amore della mia cita da industriale di provincia*. Bompiani.

Noakes, J., & Pridham, G. (1984). *Nazism 1919–1945. 2: State, Economy and Society 1933–1939*. Exeter University Press.

Otaegui, M. (1986). Censo de Comités paritarios de Guipúzcoa y Vizcaya. In J. L. García Delgado (Ed.), *La crisis de la Restauración. España, entre la primera guerra mundial y la II República* (pp. 291–313). Siglo XXI.

Otte, M. (2010). *Die Krise hält sich nicht an Regeln*. Econ.

Overy, R. J. (1982). *The Nazi Economic Recovery 1932–1938*. Cambridge University Press.

Overy, J. (1994). *War, Economy and the Third Reich*. Oxford University Press.

Palacio, J. I. (1986). Crisis política y crisis institucional: la experiencia del Instituto de Reformas Sociales en el período 1914–1924. In J. L. García Delgado (Ed.), *La crisis de la Restauración. España, entre la primera guerra mundial y la II República* (pp. 271–289). Siglo XXI.

Palafox, J. (1976). Contradicciones del capitalismo español durante la depresión económica de los años treinta. *Información Comercial Española, 514*, 110–118.

Palafox, J. (1991). *Atraso económico y democracia*. Crítica.

Parejo, A. (2004). La industrialización de las regiones españolas durante la primera y la segunda revolución tecnológica. Andalucía, Cataluña, País Vasco (1830–1975). *Revista de Historia Económica, 13*(3), 668–705.

Parejo, A. (2005). *Estadísticas históricas sobre el sector industrial minero y energético en Andalucía. Siglo XX*. Instituto de Estadística de Andalucía.

Pekkarinen, J., Pohjola, M., & Rowthorn, B. (Eds.). (1992). *Social Corporatism: A Superior Economic System?* Clarendon Press.

Parellada, M. (Ed.). (1990). *Estructura económica de Cataluña*. Espasa Calpe.

Pérez Baró, A. (1970). *Trenta mesos de col·lectivisme a Catalunya*. Ariel.

Pérez Sanchó, M. (2003). La industria del automóvil en la Comunidad Valenciana: el caso de Ford España. In J. L. Garcia Ruiz (Ed.), *Sobre ruedas* (pp. 126–166). Síntesis.

Planas, J., & Valls, F. (2011). *Cacics i rabassaires*. Eumo.

Plihon, D., & Rey, N. (2012). España, doce años de ceguera. In H. Sterdyniak, D. Plihon, & B. Coriat (Eds.), *Economistas aterrados. Europa al borde del abismo* (pp. 121–140). Barataria.

Pons, M. A. (2002). *Regulating Spanish Banking, 1939–1975*. Ashagate.

Poveda, R. (2001). La regulación y supervisión bancarias en los últimos cuarenta años. In J. L. Malo de Molina & P. Martín Aceña (Eds.), *Un siglo de historia del sistema financiero español* (pp. 243–294). Alianza.

Prados de la Escosura, L. (2003). *El progreso económico de España (1850–2000)*. Fundación BBVA.

Prat, M., & Molina, O. (2014). State Corporatism and Democratic Industrial Relations in Spain 1926–1935: A Reappraisal. *Labor History, 55*(2), 1–19.

Pueyo, J. (2003). Oligopolio y competencia en la banca española del siglo XX: concentración económica y movilidad intra-industrial. *Revista de Historia Económica, 1*, 147–198.

Puig, A. (2011). El modelo productivo español en el período expansivo de 1997–2007: insostenibilidad y ausencia de políticas de cambio. *Revista de Economía Crítica, 12*, 64–81.

Puig, N. (2003). *Bayer, Cepsa, Repsol, Puig, Schering y La Seda. Constructores de la Química Española*. Lid.

Pujol, J. (1984). Les crisis de malvenda del sector vitivinícola català entre 1880 i 1936. *Recerques, 15*, 57–78.

Pujol, J. (1989a). L'agricultura. 1. Modernització i especialització 1914–1936. In J. Nadal, J. Maluquer de Motes, C. Sudrià, & F. Cabana (Eds.), *Història econòmica de la Catalunya contemporània 5. S. XX. Població, agricultura i energia* (pp. 131–155). Enciclopèdia Catalana.

Pujol, J. (1989b). L'agricultura. 2. La reculada durant l'autarquia, 1936–1955. In J. Nadal, J. Maluquer de Motes, C. Sudrià, & F. Cabana (Eds.), *Història econòmica de la Catalunya contemporània 5. S. XX. Població, agricultura i energia* (pp. 155–169). Enciclopèdia Catalana.

Ragot, X. (2013). Les banques centrales dans la tempête. In P. Askenazi & D. Cohen (Dirs.), *5 crises. 11 nouvelles questions d'économie contemporaine* (pp. 371–422). Albin Michel.

Ramon Muñoz, R. (2003). El comercio exterior del aceite de oliva en Italia y España, 1850–1936. In C. Barciela & A. Di Vittorio (Eds.), *Las industrias alimentarias en Italia y España durante los siglos XIX y XX* (pp. 497–555). Publicacions de la Universitat d'Alacant.

Ramon Muñoz, R. (2010). Product Differentiation and Entry Barriers: Mediterranean Export Firms in the American Markets for Olive Oil Prior to World War II. *Business History, 52*(3), 390–416.

Ramon Muñoz, R. (2011). La industria catalana del aceite de oliva: exportaciones, localización y empresas, 1861–1921. In J. Catalan, J. A. Miranda, & R. Ramon-Muñoz (Eds.), *Distritos y clusters en la Europa del Sur* (pp. 57–80). Lid.

Recio, A. (2010). Capitalismo español: la inevitable crisis de un modelo insostenible. *Revista de Economía Crítica, 9*, 198–222.

Recio, A., & Roca, J. (1998). The Spanish Socialists in Power: Thirteen Years of Economic Policy. *Oxford Review of Economic Policy, 14*(1), 139–158.

Riba, J. (2003). *Història de l'explotació dels lignits del districte de Calaf*. Eumo.

Ribas, A. (1978). *L'economia catalana sota el franquisme (1939–1953)*. Edicions 62.

Risques, M., Bengoechea, S., Tavera, S., & Roig, J. M. (1995). Unes relacions determinades per la violència. In B. de Riquer (Ed.), *Història, Política, Societat i Cultura dels Països Catalans. Volum 8. L'època dels nous moviments socials 1900–1930* (pp. 202–221). Enciclopèdia Catalana.

Roca, F. (1979). *Política econòmica i territori a Catalunya 1901–1939*. Ketres.

Roca, J. (1991). *Pacte social i política de rendes*. Capellades.

Roca, J. (1994). Evolución de los salarios y evolución del "discurso oficial" sobre los salarios. In J. Albarracín, D. Anisi, F. Esteve, J. González, J. F. Martín Seco, P. Montes et al. (Eds.), *La larga noche neoliberal* (pp. 197–222). Icaria.

Roca, J. (1996). Reflexiones sobre el desempleo masivo: análisis y políticas. In O. Juan, J. Roca, & L. Toharia (Eds.), *El desempleo en España. Tres ensayos críticos* (pp. 63–102). Ediciones de Castilla-La Mancha.

Roca, J. (2012). La crisis económica y las respuestas políticas. *Revista de Economía Crítica, 13*, 91–96.

Rogoff, K. S., & Reinhart, C. M. (2009). *This Time Is Different: Eight Centuries of Financial Folly*. Princeton University Press.

Rojo, A. (1987). La crisis de la economía española, 1973–1984. In J. Nadal, A. Carreras, & C. Sudrià (Eds.), *La economía española en el siglo XX* (pp. 190–200). Ariel.

Roldán, S., & García Delgado, J. L. (1973). *La formación de la sociedad capitalista en España 1914–1920*. 2 volumes. CECA.

Roubini, N., & Mihm, S. (2010). *Crisis Economics: A Crash Course in the Future of Finance*. The Penguin Press.

Rowthorn, B. (1980). *Capitalism, Conflict and Inflation*. Lawrence and Wishart.

Royes, A. (1999). *El Banc de Terrassa en el marc de la decadència bancària catalana, 1881–1824*. Proa.

Sachs, J. (2005). *The End of Poverty: Economic Possibilities for Our Time*. Penguin Books.

Sáenz de Buruaga, G. (1961). La exportación de vinos de Rioja. *Información Comercial Española, 339*, 238–259.

San Román, E. (1995). El nacimiento de la SEAT: autarquía e intervención del INI. *Revista de Historia Industrial, 7*(1995), 141–165.

San Román, E. (1999). *Ejército e industria: El nacimiento del INI*. Crítica.

Sanromà, E. (1990). Mercado de trabajo y distribución de la renta. In M. Parellada (Ed.), *Estructura económica de Cataluña* (pp. 85–111). Espasa Calpe.

Sanromà, E. (1999). Les mutacions en el mercat de treball i el problema de l'atur. In B. de Riquer (Ed.), *Història, política, societat i cultura dels Països Catalans. Volum 12. Autogovern i reptes de la fi de segle 1890–1997* (pp. 182–199). Enciclopèdia Catalana.

Sardá, J. (Ed.). (1983). *L'economia de Catalunya, d'avui i de demà*. Banco de Bilbao.
Sardá, J. (1987). El Banco de España, 1931–1962. In R. Fernández Ortega (Ed.), *Escritos (1948–1980). Juan Sardá Dexeus* (pp. 285–342). Banco de España.
Sauvy, A., & Hirsch, A. (1984). *Histoire économique de la France entre les deux guerres*. Economica.
Scherner, J. (2010). Nazi Germany's Preparation for War: Evidence from Revised Industrial Investment Series. *European Review of Economic History, 14*(3), 433–468.
Santos, I. (2013). *La élite del poder económico en España*. Maia.
Serra Ramoneda, A. (2011). *Els errors de les caixes*. Viena edicions.
Serrano, J. M. (1986). La política arancelaria española al término de la Primera Guerra Mundial: proteccionismo, arancel Cambó y tratados comerciales. In J. L. García Delgado (Ed.), *La crisis de la Restauración. España, entre la primera guerra mundial y la II República* (pp. 199–223). Siglo XXI.
Serrano, J. M. (2000a). Tècnica sense disciplina durant els anys de flotació, 1974–1989. In J. L. García Delgado & J. M. Serrano (Eds.), *Del ral a l'euro* (pp. 150–189). Caixa de Pensions.
Serrano, J. M. (2000b). Veinte años de soledad. La autarquía de la peseta, 1939–1959. In J. L. García Delgado & J. M. Serrano (Eds.), *Del ral a l'euro* (pp. 107–124). Caixa de Pensions.
Serrano, J. M. (2011). *De la crisis económica en España y sus remedios*. Prensas Universitarias de Zaragoza.
Serrano, J. M., & Costas, A. (1990). La reforma institucional en la economía de la transición. In J. L. García Delgado (Ed.), *Economía española de la transición y la democracia, 1973–1986* (pp. 502–525). CIS.
Sevilla, J. (1985). *Economía política de la crisis española*. Crítica.
Skidelsky, R. (2009). *Keynes, the Return of the Master*. Allen Lane.
Solà, J., Sáez, X., & Termes, M. (2012). Entre dues crisis: desindustrialització i globalització. In J. Nadal, J. M. Benaul, & C. Sudrià (Eds.), *Atles de la industrialització de Catalunya, 1750–2010* (pp. 295–445). Vicens Vives.
Solé, A. (2007). La indústria farmacèutica catalana durant el franquisme: el cas d'Uriach. *Recerques, 54*, 93–114.
Solé, E. (1994). *SEAT (1950–1993)*. La Tempestad.
Soler, V. (1984). *Guerra i expansió industrial: País Valencià (1914–1923)*. Alfons el Magnànim.
Soto, A. (1989). *El trabajo industrial en la España contemporánea (1874-1936)* (pp. 519–581). Anthropos.
Stiglitz, J. E. (2002). *Globalization and Its Discontents*. Norton.
Stiglitz, J. E. (2003). *The Roaring Nineties: Seeds of Destruction*. Norton.

Sudrià, C. (1987a). El dilema energètic en el creixement econòmic català. *Revista Econòmica de Catalunya, 4*, 88–100.

Sudrià, C. (1987b). Un factor determinante: la energía. In J. Nadal, A. Carreras, & C. Sudrià (Eds.), *La economía española en el siglo XX* (pp. 313–363). Ariel.

Sudrià, C. (1987c). Segunda Parte: 1936 a 1961. In S. Coll & C. Sudrià (Eds.), *El carbón en España, 1770–1961. Una historia económica*. Paracuellos del Jarama.

Sudrià, C. (1990). Los beneficios de España durante la gran guerra. Una aproximación a la balanza de pagos española, 1914–1920. *Revista de Historia Económica, 8*(2), 363–396.

Sudrià, C. (1995). Energy as a Limiting Factor to Growth. In P. Martín Aceña & J. Simpson (Eds.), *The Economic Development of Spain since 1870* (pp. 268–309). Edward Elgar.

Sudrià, C. (2007). La banca catalana en los años de entreguerres y el debate sobre la decadència. Una revisión. *Revista de Historia de la Economía y la Empresa, 1*, 269–287.

Sudrià, C. (2013a). Atraso económico y transición política (1975–1985). In E. Llopis & J. Maluquer de Motes (Eds.), *España en crisis* (pp. 193–219). Pasado y Presente.

Sudrià, C. (2013b). Les crisis bancàries a Espanya: una perspectiva històrica. *Revista Econòmica de Catalunya, 67*, 59–61.

Tamames, R. (1995). *La economía española 1975–1995*. Temas de Hoy.

Tappi, A. (2008). *Una impresa italiana nella Spagna di Franco*. CRACE.

Tarradellas, J. (2007). *La indústria de Guerra a Catalunya (1936–1939)*. Pagès.

Tedde, P. (1984). El Banco de España en la Segunda República. *Papeles de Economía Española, 20*, 262–265.

Temin, P. (1989). *Lessons from the Great Depression*. The MIT Press.

Temin, P. (1990). Socialism and Wages in the Recovery from the Great Depression in the United States and Germany. *Journal of Economic History, 50*(2), 297–307.

Termes, J. (1987). *De la revolució de setembre a la fi de la guerra civil (1868–1936)*. Edicions 62.

Therborn, G. (1986). *Why Some Peoples Are More Unemployed Than Others*. Verso.

Toharia, L. (Ed.). (1998). *El mercado de trabajo en España*. McGraw Hill.

Tolliday, S. (2003). The Origins of Ford Europe: From Multidomestic to Transnational Corporation, 1903–1976. In H. Bonin, Y. Lung, & S. Tolliday (Eds.), *Ford, 1903–2003: The European History* (Vol. I, pp. 153–242). P.L.A.G.E.

Tooze, A. (2007). *Ökonomie der Zerstörung- Die Geschchite der Wirtschaftt im Nationalsozialismus*. Siedler.

Tortella, G. (1994). *El desarrollo económico de la España contemporánea*. Siglo XXI.
Tortella, G., & Jiménez, J. C. (1986). *Historia del Banco de Crédito Industrial*. Alianza.
Tortella, G., & Palafox, J. (1982). Banca e industria en España, 1918–1936. *Investigaciones Económicas, 20*, 33–64.
Trevithick, J. A. (1977). *Inflation*. Penguin.
Trullén, J. (1990). Características generales del modelo de crecimiento a partir del decenio de 1960. In M. Parellada (Ed.), *Estructura económica de Cataluña* (pp. 41–52). Espasa Calpe.
Trullén, J. (1993). *Fundamentos económicos de la transición política española. La política de los Acuerdos de la Moncloa*. Ministerio de Trabajo y Seguridad Social.
Valls, F. (2003). La indústria del cava. De la substitució d'importacions a la conquista del mercat internacional. In J. Colomé (Ed.), *De l'aiguardent al cava. El procés d'especialització vitivinícola a les comarques del Penedès-Garraf*. Ramon Nadal.
Valls, F. (2011). El cava catalán ¿éxito de la empresa o del distrito? In J. Catalan, J. A. Miranda, & R. Ramon-Muñoz (Eds.), *Distritos y clusters en la Europa del Sur* (pp. 101–121). Lid.
Varoufakis, Y. (2011). *The Global Minotaur: America, the True Origins of the Financial Crisis and the Future of the World Economy*. Zed Books.
Varoufakis, Y. (2017). *Adults in the Room*. The Bodley Head.
Vasapollo, L., Martufi, R., & Arriola, J. (2014). *El despertar de los cerdos*. Maia.
Velarde, J. (1968). *Política económica de la dictadura*. Guadiana.
Vilar, M. (2004). La ruptura postbélica a través del comportamiento de los salarios industriales: nueva evidencia cuantitativa (1908–1963). *Revista de Historia Industrial, 25*, 81–126.
Vilar, M. (2009). *Los salarios del miedo*. Fundación 10 de Marzo.
Viñas, A. (1984). *Guerra, dinero y dictadura*. Crítica.
Viñas, A., Viñuela, J., Eguidazu, F., Fernández Pulgar, C., & Florensa, S. (1979). *Política comercial exterior en España (1931–1975)* (2 vols.). Banco Exterior.
Vives, X. (2001). La industria financiera española en el inicio del siglo XXI: situación y retos de futuro. In J. L. Malo de Molina & P. Martín Aceña (Eds.), *Un siglo de historia del sistema financiero español* (pp. 415–456). Alianza.
Woodward, N. (1999). The Search for Economic Stability: Western Europe since 1973. In M. S. Schulze (Ed.), *Western Europe: Economic and Social Change* (pp. 63–80). Longman.

CHAPTER 8

Conclusions: Five Mediterranean Lessons from Catalonia—Diversity, Exchange, Development, Crises and Resilience

Jordi Catalan Vidal

Since the Bronze Age to the nineteenth century, the costs of transportation by sea had been much lower than by land. The diversity of endowments along the Mediterranean Basin favoured the emergence of towns which exported manufactures and imported cereals. The expansion of exchange, specially from East to West, favoured the transmission

The author is grateful for the financial support of the Ministry of Science and Innovation of the Spanish Government (MCIN/AEI/10.13039/501100011033), and of the European Regional Development Fund of the European Union (ERDF) (A way of making Europe) through project PGC2018-093896-B-I00, "Mediterranean Capitalism? Successes and Failures of Industrial Development in Spain, 1720–2020." He also thanks to the Generalitat de

J. Catalan Vidal (✉)
University of Barcelona, Barcelona, Spain
e-mail: jordi.catalan@ub.edu

J. Catalan Vidal (ed.), *Crises and Transformation in the Mediterranean World*, Palgrave Studies in Economic History,
https://doi.org/10.1007/978-3-031-24502-2_8

of innovations and higher levels of development and well-being. But this was not a sustained process given that the sea could also favoured invasions by more extractive peoples or the transmission of pandemics and resulting crises.

A particularly intense crisis took place during the Late Bronze Age, even if there is not agreement about its ultimate cause: invasions, climatic shocks or changes in comparative advantage. In any case, the Ancient Mediterranean showed a remarkable resilience and thalassocratic peoples such as Phoenicians and Greeks newly intensified exchanges, transmission of innovations and foundation of colonies all over the Basin. Later, a more extractive power, Rome, conquest the whole Inner Sea. However, Roman legions, infrastructures and coins led to a boom in Mediterranean exchange which peaked between the second century BC and the first century AD.

The golden age of Rome ended during the late second century AD. Recurrent crises derived from pandemics, barbaric invasions, high inflation and internal wars between imperial candidates, led Mediterranean exchanges to squeeze in a rather sustained way until the eighth century AD, in spite of the radical reforms undertaken by emperors Diocletian, Constantine and Justinian. As time went, Late Antiquity opened the door to Feudalism.

The Commercial Revolution can be considered as a resilient response to the great crisis of the Late Antiquity which reached a nadir with the Arab conquests. However, the recovery of trade and the improvement in the levels of well-being did not take place with the same economic foundations as the Later Roman Empire, but rather represented a great transformation of the basin's pillars of development. While feudalism took root in the hinterland of the western Mediterranean, some cities of its coastal area expanded thanks to the revival of exchanges. The resilience based on the diversity of the basin was again revealed.

Catalunya, and the Centre d'Estudis Jordi Nadal of the University of Barcelona, which contributed to support the publication of this chapter in several ways. He also is in debt with Doctor Andreu Ginés who commented me the chapter in detail and helped with the edition. The possible errata are the exclusive responsibility of the author.

Barcelona emulated the thalassocratic vocation of the Italian mercantile republics and dragged the maritime territories of the Crown of Aragon along this path. The commercial orientation of the Iberian coast and the military conquests strengthened the links between Catalonia, Valencia, the Balearic Islands, which since the thirteenth century had been expressed in a shared language, Catalan. These territories did not always form part of a common political unit. However, during the Late Middle Ages, the link created by Catalan as the common language, the thalassocratic mercantile tradition and the shared political history transformed these territories into a cultural unit, comparable to that of other peoples and trading nations of the Basin.

The history of this cultural community was similar to that of the Greeks or Phoenicians of the ancient world. Without the need to be integrated in a unified state, shared the same culture gestated over centuries. In the case of Greece, the sense of community and of a people continued to exist after the fall of Constantinople and until the creation of the Greek state at the beginning of the nineteenth century. In a comparable manner, for centuries, the Italians formed part of a cultural unit divided between different principalities, kingdoms and empires. Even so, they were able to share a common culture from the Middle Ages until the construction of the Kingdom of Italy in the mid-nineteenth century. In an even more dramatic but significant manner, the Hebrew people preserved their cultural identity, despite living in foreign lands for two millennia.

The Industrial Revolution was the most radical transformation in the global model of development which took place since the Neolithic Revolution, and was not originated in the Mediterranean but in Britain during the last decades of the eighteenth century. The great majority of the Mediterranean was left on the sidelines of the First Industrial Revolution which, from England, gradually spread around the neighbour regions of Western Europe during the nineteenth century. The only Mediterranean exceptions were Catalonia, the Genoa-Milan-Turin triangle and Marseille in the North-west corner of the Great Sea, where industrialization took off. The rest of the Mediterranean recorded poor levels of industrialization or even deindustrialization throughout the nineteenth century.

On the other hand, the Second Industrial Revolution favoured generalized resilience of the overall economies of the north Mediterranean in the twentieth century. Catalonia, Valencia and Mallorca stood out among the most industrialized regions of the Mare Nostrum at the beginning of the 1970s. The diffusion of electrification and the combustion engine had favoured the intense catching up of the levels of development with core European regions which had plenty supply of energy in their coal fields. Manufacturing industry and tourism formed the foundations of the economic convergence of the north of the Mediterranean with the countries of north-west Europe.

Industrialization and the exchange of touristic services have also been explored as development strategies in the Southern Mediterranean countries more recently and with less success. It is still a promise of resilient growth for the Southern part of the basin, provided that respect of diversity within their nation-states is guaranteed and regional wars end. However, the intense process of deindustrialization experienced by the Northern neighbours and the poor respect to the rights of the national minorities of some of their governments, such as Spain with the Catalans, doesn't allow to be very optimistic.

8.1 Diversity, Exchange and Development in the Bronze Age

For thousands of years, until the spread of railways, transport by sea was much cheaper than by land. Together with the diversity of ecosystems and forms of social organization throughout the Mediterranean basin, this encouraged exchange. Diversity and trade favoured specialization in accordance with a competitive advantage, the transmission of innovations and ideas, the improvement of production and consumption levels and the set of benefits which, according to Adam Smith, we could associate with the extension of free markets.

The Minoan civilization, based on a constellation of cities, emerged on the island of Crete. They achieved a high level of prosperity. Some specialized in craft activities such as the production of wool textiles. These fabrics were exported to Pharaonic Egypt, in exchange for the wheat necessary to feed the population of an island with limited agricultural resources. Knossos was considered to be the first thalassocracy or sea power in history, according to Herodotus and Thucydides (Abulafia, 2011, 2014; Bairoch, 1985; Bellwood, 2005; Boserup, 1965; Finley, 1963, 1970, 1973; Mollat du Jourdin, 1993; Postrel, 2020).

A similar case could be Ugarit, which had connections with the Egyptian and Hittite empires, trading with both giants. It supplied them with local products, such as cedar wood, textiles and purple from the Levant, and others from Mycenae, Crete or Cyprus, such as ceramics, fabrics and copper objects. It produced wine and olive oil. Its most important exports appear to have been wood and linen and wool textiles (Abulafia, 2011; Bairoch, 1985; Bryce, 2009; García Morá, 2018).

From continental Greece, Mycenae, located inland on the way between Argos and Corynth, succeeded in exporting its ceramics throughout the eastern Mediterranean. It also exported them to Taranto, in southern Italy, and even managed to cross the Alps. Other urban settlements of artisans and traders from the Mycenaean civilization were Pylos, Tiryns and Thebes. These were also merchant cities, which traded across the Great Sea and imported the cereals that their deficient agricultural production conditions required (Abulafia, 2011, 2014; Finley, 1963, 1970, 1973; Sapwforth, 2018).

The Cypriot cities controlled the trade of metals to the Aegean, exporting ingots, swords and other weapons, thanks to the copper ore deposits of the Troodos Mountains. They also traded abroad with their own ceramics made on a potter's wheel and those of Mycenaean cities, supplying different markets from the Aegean to the central Mediterranean and, especially, the Hittite and Egyptian empires (Abulafia, 2011; Bryce, 2009; García Morá, 2018; Sherratt, 2016).

Mythical Troy supplied the Mediterranean with horses and resold ceramics in the north. Its location at the mouth of the Dardanelles allowed it to control trade between the Black Sea and the Aegean. It favoured trade between the nomadic and cattle-raising peoples of the steppes, the artisans of the Greek cities and the farmers of Anatolia (Abulafia, 2011; Akurgal, 1986; Bryce, 2009).

In short, islands, continental ports and locations close to the coasts of mountainous territories unsuitable for agriculture gave rise to cities of merchants and artisans which, through exchange, favoured specialization, the improvement of welfare and the dissemination of innovations. They thus achieved a high level of development during the Late Bronze Age.

These cities then traded with theocratic empires, which were very diverse and more hierarchical social organizations. At their head there was the Pharaoh or Emperor, flanked by warriors, and the temples, run by priests. The majority of the population was made up of farmers and shepherds. War had led to the subjugation of neighbouring cultures and slave labour, the construction of impressive religious and funerary monuments and major hydraulic works. They produced an agricultural surplus which was traded for manufactured goods or raw materials with some of the above commercial and artisan cities. The exchange, based on diversity, was of benefit to both sides and, consequently, the eastern Mediterranean created a shared network of prosperity even before the second millennium before Christ (Bryce, 2009; Hudson, 2010; Manning, 2018).

8.2 The Crisis of the Late Bronze Age

However, the Mediterranean, as well as bringing prosperity through exchange, also favoured pillage, invasions and the transmission of infections by sea. The diversity of levels of welfare among civilizations could impel other peoples to take the accumulated profit by force, especially at times of bad harvests and shortage, when famine encouraged population movements. Piracy and plundering from the sea increased. It appears that an important episode of structural crisis and profound transformation in the development of the eastern Mediterranean took place during the second millennium before Christ.

Between 1663 and 1616 BC Santorini volcano erupted, causing significant climate change in the Aegean. It has been associated with earthquakes, tsunamis, ash falls, drought and famine, which affected the islands of the Aegean and, in particular, Crete. In around 1425 BC, Knossos was completely destroyed and was not rebuilt. It is not at all clear whether its demise was due to physical phenomena or to the arrival of invaders from the sea. Whatever the case the Achaeans, identified with the *Ekwesh* of the Egyptians or the *Ahhiyawa* of the Hittites, ended up settling there. The Minoan civilization evaporated, and the hieroglyphic language of the island ended up being replaced with the so-called Linear B script typical of the Greeks (Black, 2020; Bryce, 2009; Finley, 1970; Manning, 2018; Spawforth, 2018).

The hypothesis that the attacks by those generally called Sea Peoples intensified during the time of the Pharaohs Akhenaton and Ramesses II appears to be even more likely. According to Egyptian chronicles, the latter had to confront the *Lukka* and the *Sherden* in 1295 and 1277 BC, respectively.

It also appears that the sudden end of cities like Mycenae and Pylos occurred in around 1200. It is not at all clear whether the invaders were the Achaeans themselves or other Indo-European peoples from the Carpathian Mountains and the Danube, as was believed for a long time. However, it appears to have been at that time when the change occurred from burial to cremation and the spread of urnfields, typical of Indo-European populations.

Imperial records have allowed us to more accurately date the aggressions by invaders and pirates who confronted Ramesses in the Nile Delta and the land of Canaan in 1178. These invasions led to the collapse of the Hittite Empire. Egyptian sources talk about a coalition of attackers with a great diversity of peoples which they associated with the sea: *Peleset, Sherden, Wheshesh* and other. It appears that the *Peleset* or Philistines, having plundered Cyprus, put an end to Ugarit and settled in the region of Canaan. Their origin could have been Greek since, in Cyprus as well, the original hieroglyphic writing was replaced with Linear B script with Greek roots.

While Ramesses III had to agree to the loss of his Asian territory in favour of the Philistines, the Pharaoh succeeded in repelling the rest of the peoples. It appears that the *Sherden* ended up settling in Sardinia. Byblos, Sidon and Tyre also survived the attacks by the Sea Peoples and the collapse of the Hittite Empire, promoting their commercial and industrial orientation.

It is difficult to establish with certainty the forces which pushed such different groups of peoples to attack Knossos, Mycenae, Cyprus, Ugarit, the mythical Troy and the Hittite and Egyptian empires. In any case, this favoured the first great structural depression of the Mediterranean, after a period of development of trade in the Levant. One of the elements most debated has been of a technological nature: the spread of iron allowed a much greater offensive capacity than bronze (Finley, 1970). In recent times, climatic changes which might derive in drought and famine are more popular explanations (Manning, 2018).

On the other hand, a few authors have defended the thesis that part of the change could be due to autonomous transformations of the trading dynamics, or even, a first period of proto-globalization. Cyprus merchants would have been trading with bronze manufactures, ceramics and even iron, around 1150 and might have ruined previous producers such as Mycenae or Pylos (Sherratt, 2016).

It is possible that there was a certain Malthusian pressure on resources, favoured by environmental changes, which made life on the steppes difficult and impelled some peoples towards Anatolia and to cross the sea. Indeed, Herodotus spoke of maritime emigration from parts of Lydia, driven by famine. Likewise, some have included the increase in slavery due to debts arising from the impoverishment of peasants among the causes of the movement of peoples during the Late Bronze Age (Bryce, 2009; García Morá, 2018). Others have insisted on the destructive effects of eruptions and earthquakes, which could be associated with climate change (Manning, 2018).

In any case, the attacks by peoples from the sea and the great crisis of the twelfth century BC clearly illustrate the dilemma in the development of the Mediterranean. Diversity and exchange favoured specialization, transforming living conditions and, consequently, encouraging a higher level of development and well-being in trading and artisan centres and agricultural and stockbreeding empires. However, whether out of greed or need, the disparity of living conditions attracted other peoples, which the sea aided in their arrival and attempted conquest.

8.3 Resilient Thalassocracies

At any rate, the resilience of the Mediterranean was clear during the first millennium before Christ. To the south of Canaan, manufacturing and trade revived in cities such as Byblos, Sidon and, above all, Tyre. Their traders, called ***phoenikios*** (reds) by the Greeks, strengthened their exports of fabrics dyed with purple, jewels, ceramic pieces, perfumes and weapons to the furthest shores (Abulafia, 2011; Aubet, 1993; Aubet & Sanmartí, 1996; Bairoch, 1985; Bryce, 2009; Quinn, 2018; Sherratt, 2016).

It is documented that, in exchange for its exports, Tyre imported wheat and olive oil from a neighbouring kingdom of shepherds and farmers who venerated a single god and which at the time was governed by King Solomon during the tenth century before Christ. With the death of this king, who was considered to be fair, in 921 BC, the cultural unity of the Hebrew people continued, but its political organization was fragmented into two states: Israel and Judah. The former maintained its independence until 746, when it was conquered by the Assyrian Empire (Bryce, 2009).

Meanwhile, the Phoenician ships sailed the seas and exchanged their manufactured goods for wheat from Africa and Anatolia and silver from the Pangaion Hills to the north of the Aegean, the Cyclades and even from distant Tartessos. They also traded in slaves, helping to complete what Marx would call their primitive accumulation of capital. To favour their commercial penetration, they likewise founded cities such as Kition,

Carthage, Leptis, Malaka and Gades along the southern islands and coasts of the sea and even beyond the Pillars of Hercules (Abulafia, 2011; Aubet, 1993; Aubet & Sanmartí, 1996; Bairoch, 1985; Bryce, 2009; Quinn, 2018; Sherratt, 2016; Woolmer, 2017).

Phoenician trade helped to spread the consumption of purple-dyed fabrics, papyrus, perfumes, metal jewels and ceramics, wine and olive oil throughout the Mediterranean, while improving the levels of consumption and well-being. They moreover leveraged a key innovation for the development of the basin: their alphabet was the origin of the Greek alphabet, in places like Euboea, Rhodes and Crete, in around the eighth century. The Phoenicians probably represented the clearest case of the lack of a unified state and organization in relatively free and independent city-states of traders and artisans (Aubet & Sanmartí, 1996; Montanelli, 1959; Quinn, 2018; Sherratt, 2016; Woolmer, 2017).

The Greek cities also maintained a highly decentralized organization, although they ended up recording episodes of unequivocal imperialist ambition, which led them to fight among themselves and attack their neighbours. The unity of Hellas was more cultural than political (Abulafia, 2011; Finley, 1970; Spawforth, 2018).

The limited capacity to feed a growing population in Attica, the Peloponnese, Thessaly or the islands not only favoured the resumption of trade in manufactured goods (especially ceramics) but also, in around 1050 BC, encouraged the colonization of the coast of Anatolia and the establishment or revival of cities such as Miletus, Izmir, Phocaea and Ephesus. These Ionian cities discovered coins thanks to their contact with Lydia, which began to issue them in the seventh century BC. Coins spread among the major trading cities of Hellas, such as Samos, which exported wine, and Corinth and Athens, which exported ceramics. Mediterranean philosophy and scientific experimentation arose in the Ionian cities and democracy began in Corinth, Athens and Sparta. From there coins, manufactured goods and humanist and scientific knowledge gradually spread throughout the basin.

In Athens, the creation of the assembly of citizens at the end of the sixth century was linked to the prohibition of slavery due to the debts of the small farmers. This demonstrates that excessive debt was a significant problem for the first Mediterranean communities, which the proto-democracies had to confront in order to correct the inequalities that free trade tended to create (Anderson, 1979; Montanelli, 1959; Spawforth, 2018).

Expansion towards the west led the Greeks to settle in the Bay of Naples in around 750 BC. The Corinthians founded Syracuse in 733 and the Hellenic presence gradually took root in the east of Sicily. Settlers from the island of Thera reached what is now Libya, establishing Cyrene. The Phocaeans founded the future Marseille in around 600 BC and then, from there, they sailed further west and south and founded Emporion.

The Mediterranean expansion of both the Phoenicians and the Greeks fits in well with the idea of thalassocracies or maritime and commercial powers, rather than empires based on pure military strength and extractive exploitation (Abulafia, 2014; Acemoglou & Robinson, 2012; Landes, 1998; Mollat du Jourdin, 1993; Vilar, 1974b). Encouraging exchange with the local population fostered the transformation of the Mediterranean, improving the levels of well-being and transferring knowledge throughout the basin. In the case on which we focus, the Iberians, like so many other peoples of the Mare Nostrum, learnt from the Phoenicians casting metal and growing olive trees and vines. The Hellenes transferred knowledge on how to mint coins and use the alphabet. These innovations allowed a significantly higher stage of development to be achieved for all the Iberian tribes which peopled the western coast of the sea (Asensio & Jornet, 2019; Aubet, 1993; Aubet & Sanmartí, 1996; Bosch i Gimpera, 1932; Feliu, 2012; Ferrer & Moncunill, 2019; Grau, 2021; Lazuela-Fox, 2017; Maluquer de Motes, 1987; Ripollès, 2012; Tarradell, 1962).

The Greek cities freed themselves from the kings, limited the power of the nobility, created political representation mechanisms and tested significant precedents of republican governments. By the fifth century, the consolidation of mechanisms of representation and the sustained increase of exchange in Athens encouraged the diffusion of coinage and taxation. The availability of silver deposits in Laurion also contributed to the minting of coins with higher metal weight, as the tetradrachma which tended to substitute the drachma and didrachma in more ambitious commercial deals (Davies, 2007; Iriarte, 2018; Lyttkens, 2013).

Greek polis was not, however, free from annexationist temptations and violent military conflicts. The war between the leagues of cities led by Athens and Sparta decimated the Peloponnese and Attica in the fifth century. Its almost 30-year duration caused a great crisis in the standard of living of the Delos and Sparta coalitions. The war was also the vehicle for infection by one of the first epidemics documented in history. Three waves of plague occurred in 430, 429 and 426, respectively. It would appear that the plague reached Athens from Piraeus. The ships which sailed the

Mediterranean accommodated small passengers, which ended up causing a notable reduction in the population of the Attic cities (Anderson, 1979; Finley, 1963, 1970; Spawforth, 2018).

During the fourth century before Christ, the population of shepherds and warriors of Macedonia defeated the big Greek cities. Alexander's conquests allowed him to build an empire on three continents, even reaching the Indus. On his death in 323, the empire broke up, but its generals founded royal lineages which maintained power in Greece, Syria and Egypt, until they were removed by Rome.

Another commercial power which became an annexationist empire was Carthage. This colony, founded at the end of the ninth century by the Phoenicians of Tyre, gradually capitalized on the growing pressure of the Assyrian and Babylonian empires on the lands of Canaan. Nebuchadnezzar II ended up occupying the Kingdom of Judah, destroying the temple of Jerusalem and deporting the Hebrew people to Babylonia in 586 BC. He then besieged Tyre and ended up subjecting it to vassalage from 572. From then on, Carthage replaced Tyre as the main Phoenician metropolis in the Mediterranean.

Carthage gradually established settlements in the Balearics, the south of Iberia, Malta, the west of Sicily, Sardinia and Corsica. It traded olive oil, wine, ceramics and jewels in exchange for metals. As a canonical thalassocracy, it tended to transform from a commercial power into a military occupation. However, after decades of conflict with the Greeks from Syracuse, the Punics ended up losing their battle with Rome, a city which had driven out the last king in 509 BC (Abulafia, 2011, 2014; Aubet, 1993; Aubet & Sanmartí, 1996; Bryce, 2009; Mc Evedy, 2011).

8.4 Empire, Exchange and Development Under Rome

For half a millennium Rome was an aristocratic republic which gradually subjected neighbouring populations, such as Sabines, Latins, Etruscans, Samnites and the citizens of Magna Graecia. Between 264 and 146, Carthage and Rome fought successive wars for hegemony in the Mediterranean, with a favourable result for the latter which, in addition to the Punic possessions, succeeded in conquering Macedonia and Corinth. Starting from 146 the power of Rome spread to the east and west, and north and south, of the Mediterranean. It obtained fabulous spoils, numerous slaves and substantial compensation from the defeated (Bang, 2008; Beard, 2016; De Martino, 1980; Kay, 2014; Lo Cascio, 2007).

If we consider that data of shipwrecks are acceptable indicators of Mediterranean trade, the exchanges in the basin gradually grew with a sustained trend from the eighth century BC (see Fig. 1.1. in Chapter 1). This suggests that the resilience of maritime exchange throughout the basin continued under Rome. Trade encouraged a process of specialization which favoured economic development and lasted for centuries (Maddison, 2007; Parker, 1992; Temin, 2017).

A significant increase in this trade volume indicator took place in the second century BC (when it multiplied by 2.4), associated with the conversion of the Great Sea into the Mare Nostrum. The fabulous minting of silver deniers and other Roman coins provided a sound method of payment for trade throughout the basin. On the other hand, the triremes and the ports and roads built by Rome stimulated specialization and trade throughout the Mediterranean. This led to the appearance of large estates, which worked with slave labour and supplied cereals, wine and olive oil to feed the big cities of the basin and, in particular, the capital of the empire. Trade also increased in manufactured goods, such as ceramics, glass, textiles, perfumes, jewels or garum. The campaigns to free the sea from pirates reduced the risk of navigation and favoured a subsequent extension of exchange until it reached its climax (Abulafia, 2011; Beard, 2016; Black, 2020; Brunt, 1971; Hopkins, 1980; Kay, 2014; Maddison, 2007; Montanelli, 1957; Temin, 2017).

The effects of the civil wars of the first century BC were not sufficiently big to reverse this process and trade, measured by the number of shipwrecks, continued to increase. Augustus, despite putting an end to the republic, never wanted to be crowned king. He continued to fight the pirates with a firm hand and, with more peace and infrastructures, increasing specialization reinforced the development of the basin (Comín, 2011; Kay, 2014; Lo Cascio, 2007; Parker, 1992; Temin, 2017; Turching & Nefedov, 2009).

Overall, between 149 BC and 164 AD, the hegemony of Rome led to a golden age in trade throughout the Mediterranean. The basin tended to achieve a previously unknown level of development and per capita income. My conclusion therefore coincides with the opinion of classical historians, such as Gibbon or Rostovtzeff, and the quantitative estimates of more contemporary economic historians, such as De Martino 1980, Lo Cascio,

Maddison, Kay, Temin and Harper (De Martino, 1980; Gibbon, 1776–1778; Harper, 2017; Kay, 2014; Lo Cascio, 2007; Maddison, 2007; Rostovtzeff, 1926; Temin, 2017).

This progress was obviously not for those who had known freedom and became slaves or for the small farmers who could not resist the competition of the big estates working with forced labour. It should not therefore be overlooked that, in the three centuries of the golden age of Rome, the remarkable standards of development and well-being were compatible with high levels of internal inequality (which were probably not found among the barbarian peoples who lived outside the empire's borders).

In the case of particular interest to us, the control of Rome left a series of new cities in the lands of the Iberians, linked by the Via Augusta and equipped with infrastructures such as ports, aqueducts, baths and sewers, which improved the living conditions of the inhabitants, very often retired legionaries. Hispania Tarraconensis, one of the most backward areas of the sea, was linked to foreign trade as an exporter of wine, garum, other foodstuffs and a few manufactured products. Latin gradually replaced the Iberian language, Greek and Punic (Comas, 1997; Maluquer de Motes, 1987; Nolla, 1996; Prevosti & Guitart, 2011).

8.5 The Long Decline of Mediterranean Exchange

The second major crisis analyzed in this book began in the second century AD and did not bottom out until the eighth century, when the number of shipwrecks in the Mediterranean recorded a minimum, this probably also being the case for the volume of trade and level of development (Parker, 1992). This depression did not result in a return to the previous point of equilibrium but rather a deep transformation of the Mediterranean world during Late Antiquity, while opening the doors to the Middle Ages, as analyzed by Professor Salrach in Chapter 2 (Salrach, 1987; Wickham, 1984, 2005, 2016).

Rome demonstrated a certain resilience at some moments of this great crisis (second, fourth and sixth centuries) and in some territories (Byzantium) but, overall, in the western Mediterranean the involution was clear until the eighth century. The collapse of the Western Roman Empire gave way to a new mosaic of peoples, states and empires which, once again, renewed and strengthened the characteristic diversity of the sea.

There is a quite remarkable range of interrelated causes of the great depression which put an end to the levels of development achieved during the golden age of Rome (Anderson, 1979; Beard, 2016; Bernardi, 1970; Buenacasa, 2013; De Martino, 1980; De Palol, 1996; Depeyrot, 1991; Espluga, 1998; Gibbon, 1776–1788; Harper, 2017; Lo Cascio, 2007; Rostovtzeff, 1926; Salrach, 1987; Spawforth, 2018; Wickham, 1984, 2005, 2016). It should be stressed that since 165 AD included the epidemic, possibly of smallpox, which decimated maybe a fifth of the population and negatively affected the defensive capacity of the legions. The attacks and looting by the barbarians gradually became more frequent, as did the confrontations among the candidates for the imperial tiara. The end of the Roman Climatic Optimum, which made living conditions on the steppes tougher, helped push back successive waves of barbarian peoples towards the Mediterranean. Pandemics became more frequent and it was increasingly difficult to recruit legionaries, with fewer men and without the booty that the previous victories had provided.

A new epidemic of Dantesque proportions occurred starting from 252. This possible pandemic, caused by a virus of Ethiopian origin, similar to Ebola, again spread quickly by sea to the main emporiums of the Mediterranean. It is estimated that Alexandria, the second biggest city of the basin, may have lost 60% of its population.

During the previous century the legions were still well paid, resorting to moderate devaluations (of around 20%) during the reigns of Marcus Aurelius, Septimius Severus and Caracalla. However, between 253 and 284 a large number of emperors and candidates confronted each other and resorted to reductions in the metal content of the *denarius* and its successors, until silver was almost completely removed, unleashing inflation. The attacks by the Visigoths, Ostrogoths, Franks, Alemanni, Suebi, Alans, Heruli, Scythians, Persians and Moors weakened the empire and impoverished it. Its cities had to build walls and, even so, could not prevent the loss of population. Trade became riskier and transactions and the level of development gradually declined.

The responses to the tremendous contraction of the third century, cushioned the fall a little, without being able to reverse the trend of depression. Furthermore, the solutions adopted from the end of that century and during the fourth century profoundly transformed the economy and the social and political relations of the empire, sowing the seed of mediaeval development (Bloch, 1947; De Martino, 1980; McCormick, 2001; Salrach, 1987; Wickham, 1984, 2005, 2016).

Diocletian failed in his attempt to control prices by administrative means, in the persecution of the Christians, and in bringing political stability to the empire with the tetrarchy system. On the other hand, his fiscal reform, based on taxation of land and men (*iugatio* and *capitatio*) and the imperial cadastre allowed sufficient resources to be generated to strengthen the legions, obtain some success in the fight against the barbarians and extend the life of the empire. The fiscal reform also allowed the renewed minting of precious metals and prevented the excesses in the debasement of the currency. The replacement of Rome with another four capitals (Nicomedia, Milan, Sirmium and Treverorum), closer to the border conflicts, temporarily helped to improve security (Depeyrot, 1991; Salrach, 1987, 1997; Wickham, 1984, 2005, 2016).

The mortality caused by the epidemics of the second and third centuries gradually diminished the number of slaves on offer and increased their price. Furthermore, the reduction in the empire's offensive capacity progressively reduced the contingents of prisoners of war who could be sold as serfs, subsequently aggravating the shortage and increasing the relative price of slaves. Faced with the worsening shortage and increase in the price of slave labour, the big estates reacted by establishing tenant settlers on their properties, who could be retired legionaries, former peasants or freed ex-serfs (De Martino, 1980; Espluga, 1998; Harper, 2017; Salrach, 1987, 1997).

In 332, Constantine banned the abandonment of the land by free peasants. This precedent of mediaeval servitude confirms that the scarcity of peasant labour was a recurrent characteristic in the economy of the Later Roman Empire. The emperor himself also restricted the mobility of industrial workers and grouped them in hereditary guilds (Bonnassie, 1985; De Martino, 1980).

Constantine placed gold at the heart of the Roman monetary system and created the *solidus*. This gold coin became the main unit of account and was used to pay the legions and collect tax. It was likewise used as a safe deposit for the more well-off layers of society, while the poor used the copper *nummus*. The prices indexed in *nummus* continued to run wild, while they tended to stabilize in gold (Depeyrot, 1991).

The lack of gold currency, with which taxes were paid, led settlers and peasants to link themselves to certain big owners, who benefited from the practice of *autopragia*, which allowed landowners to collect the tax from settlers and peasants and transfer it directly to the state. This possibility reinforced the tendency towards patronage, which was typical in ancient Rome and became consolidated in that period of insecurity and difficulties of the poorest peasants to generate sufficient resources to bear the high fiscal pressure. Clientelism, which already had precedents in ancient Rome, emerged as one of the most characteristic systems of the Mediterranean universe. The big landowners gradually took on functions which were previously public, maintaining security with their own troops and, occasionally, private prisons (Beard, 2016; De Martino, 1980; McCormick, 2001).

The Edict of Milan, which guaranteed freedom of religion, represented a decisive step in favour of Christianity, which gradually gained strength among the imperial elite until it became the state religion. The belief in a single God became a new force legitimizing the power of the emperor in the face of the diversity of beliefs which for centuries had been associated with polytheism. Aurelian had tried it before, promoting the worship of the sun and identifying himself as its priest on Earth. However, the final victory of monotheism was associated with the split emerging from Judaism, especially from when Theodosius the Great made it the official religion and banned pagan cults.

While Constantine and Theodosius promoted Christianity, the emperors gradually disregarded the former *caput mundi*. The former created the New Rome in Byzantium. Theodosius died in Milan, without ever having set foot in ancient Rome. On his death in 395, the empire was divided into two parts, with respective capitals in Constantinople and Milan. While the Mediterranean appeared to be united in the Christian faith, the political diversity of the region emerged with the East–West duality. The Christian faith itself tended to be fragmented into numerous interpretations which gave rise to different churches. The Arian faith was an important belief among those which spread among the barbarian peoples (Gibbon, 1776–1788).

The apparent resilience of the fourth century was interrupted during the next century in the Western Empire, due to the renewed push by the barbarians who again attacked the Mediterranean. Rome was plundered for the first time by the Visigoths in 410. Gaul was occupied by Attila's Huns, although they were defeated in the Catalaunian Plains in 451. Leo I succeeded in stopping the advance of the Huns in Italy, but the Vandals attacked from Africa and again plundered the *caput mundi* in 455. Finally, 16 years later, the Herulian Odoacer deposed the emperor of the West, Romulus Augustus.

The Visigoths founded the Kingdom of Toulouse in 410. They then crossed the Pyrenees, occupying Hispania Tarraconensis and, for a short while, Barcelona became the seat of its court. For most of the century, the Tarraconensis was governed from Toulouse, capital of the Visigoths, who ruled as *foederati* of Rome. In 507, the Franks drove them out and they emigrated east and south. Provence, Galla Narbonensis, Hispania Tarraconensis and Hispania Carthaginensis remained under Visigoth rule, in an alliance with the Ostrogoth Theodoric, who had assassinated Odoacer and ruled in Ravenna since 493. Between 507 and 549, the Visigoth court resided between Narbonne and Barcelona, and continued to be a tributary of the Ostrogoths, established in Italy (De Palol, 1996; Járrega, 2013; Salrach, 1987).

Justinian, emperor of the East, succeeded in recovering a large part of the territories of the West on expelling the Vandals from north Africa and conquering Italy, the islands of the western Mediterranean and the south of Hispania. The legal records of 527 likewise indicate a certain strengthening of the imperial regulatory framework. However, another epidemic, probably of Black Death, reached Constantinople in 542 and in less than a year infected the main cities of the Mediterranean. The epidemic put an end to the resilience shown by the empire under Justinian. The new fall in population led to generalized deflation and increased the difficulties to recruit legionaries. To pay them, the emperor had to increase the fiscal pressure on the surviving population, reaching one of the most asphyxiating levels of the entire Roman age (Felice, 2015; Harper, 2017; McCormick, 2015, 2016).

In 568, the Lombards took a large part of the Po Valley under imperial control and established their capital in Pavia. They then advanced towards the south of the peninsula, while the imperial troops resisted close to Ravenna. In Hispania, the Visigoths drove the Byzantines out of the south. After trying different capitals, the Visigoth Kingdom ended up governing from Toledo.

Now even weaker, the decimated legions countered the offensive by a people of shepherds and warriors from Arabia, who advanced under the aegis of another monotheistic faith, Islam. After the 636 Battle of the Yarmuk, the emperor Heraclius withdrew his legions and Jerusalem and Alexandria fell. In just a few decades, the Arabs conquered the whole of north Africa. They crossed into Europe in 711 at Gibraltar. They conquered the kingdom of the Visigoths, crossed the Pyrenees, occupied Narbonne and were only stopped by Charles Martel's Franks at Poitiers in

732. His descendants pushed back the Arabs and defeated the Lombards. His grandson, Charlemagne, was crowned emperor of the West in Rome in 800. His empire extended from Aachen to Pisa and Barcelona.

If, as we believe, the number of shipwrecked vessels in the Mediterranean is a good indicator of the volume of trade in the basin, the worst century of the entire period between the seventh century BC and the fifteenth century AD was the eighth century (see Fig. 1.1. in Chapter 1). The invasion of Hispania and Gaul by the Arabs therefore coincided with an absolute minimum, in more than a millennium, in the level of development recorded in the Mare Nostrum. An additional indicator of the involution recorded in the north-western Mediterranean at that time is that the circulation of gold almost completely collapsed in that territory (Abulafia, 2011; Cipolla, 1975; Le Goff, 2010; Parker, 1992; Pirenne, 1973).

8.6 Renewed Diversity: The Case of the Catalan Counties

The Franks conquered Barcelona in 801 and converted it into the capital of its county. They created a series of counties on both sides of the Pyrenees, which served as a retaining wall against Al-Andalus. The names of these counties corroborate the diversity and resilience characteristic of the Mediterranean: some invoked the names of former tribes of the Iberians, such as Cerdanya (*ceretani*), Berga (*bergistani*), Osona (*ausetani*); and others reflected the legacy of the cities created by Greek (Empúries) and Roman (Roussillon, Barcelona and Girona) colonization (Asensio & Jornet, 2019; Aubet & Sanmartí, 1996; Bolós & Hurtado, 2009; Bosch i Gimpera, 1932; D'Abadal, 1969; De Palol, 1996; Ferrer & Moncunill, 2019; Grau, 2021; Lazuela-Fox, 2017; Maluquer de Motes, 1987; Salrach, 1987, 2006, 2020; Sanmartí, 1996; Tarradell, 1962; Vilar, 1962).

From among all the legacies, that of Rome was the most present in the Pyrenean counties looking towards the Mediterranean. On the one hand, Latin remained the official language of written documents and the one that was spoken, as a dialect, by the majority of the population. Most county capitals were cities with Roman origins or with a large Roman settlement. The counties ruled in partnership with the Roman Church, to which they transferred land and granted an important role in the formation of the elites. In addition, the Carolingians recovered an old tax as the tithe in order to strengthen their links with the Church.

In addition to the dominant Roman influence, the counties of the Gothic March or Hispanic March inherited from the Franks the monetary system based on the denier (*denarius*) and its multiples, the shilling (*solidus*) and the pound (*libbra*). This monetary system was also inspired by Rome, despite the fact that the lack of gold in the Carolingian Empire led to it being based only on silver. Only the denier was minted, while the shillings and pounds were exclusively multiples, used as units of account. The territories of the counties continued to count in deniers, shillings and pounds until the nineteenth century, unlike the majority of the Iberian Peninsula which did not adopt the Carolingian system (Bloch, 1954; Cipolla, 1975; Crusafont, 1989, 1996, 2015; Vilar, 1962).

The social organization of the counties was likewise inherited from the Carolingians. The counts were initially civil servants appointed by the empire, supported by a series of assistants such as vicarious, bailiffs or castellans.

Although servile workers continued to exist, the peasants who, following Germanic tradition, settled in areas of risk and cultivated the land for 30 years, retained ownership of the same. Free peasants coexisted with colons and slaves. As Professor Salrach underlines in Chapter 2, the Carolingians restored the Roman notion of public power in key aspects as the army, land, taxation and justice.

However, the civil servant elites soon ended up transferring their positions to their successors and became ennobled gentlemen: viscounts, barons or lords. On the other hand, the peasants had to seek a protector, as feudal violence significantly increased in around the years 950–1050. The lords very often forced peasant submission in exchange for protection.

One way to limit the excess of violence by the nobles was the creation of the Peace and Truce of God assemblies, which began to proliferate in the eleventh century in cities of the counties such as Toulouges, Vic, Barcelona, Girona and Elne. These meetings included ecclesiastics, nobles and cities and were the precedent of the mediaeval courts. The first written text in Catalan which is preserved is also from the eleventh century. It refers to a vassalage pact signed in the county of Pallars (Bonnassie, 1990; D'Abadal, 1969; Fontana, 2014; Salrach, 1987, 1997; Sobrequés, 2007).

From the beginning Barcelona exercised a certain hegemony among the Pyrenean counties of the Franks. Count Wilfred the Hairy, who came from a lineage from Carcassonne, already succeeded in bringing various counties under his control and transmitting them to his successors. The result was that the heirs of the same family were at the head of the county of Barcelona for more than half a millennium, from 878 to 1410 (Bolós & Hurtado, 2009; Bonnassie, 1990; D'Abadal, 1969; Salrach, 1987, 2006; Salrach & Duran, 1982).

Several Spanish historians, of whom Gabriel Tortella is perhaps the most characteristic example, have sought to show that Catalonia has never been independent and was always linked to Spain (Tortella, 2018). The historical truth is that before Roman rule, the peninsula included many different peoples such as Iberians, Turdetans, Celts, Celtiberians and Vascones and there was not a Spanish state. Such a state did not exist under the Roman Empire either, since the latter governed its different provinces from the *caput mundi*. It cannot even be considered that the Visigoths formed a single Spanish kingdom since, as we have seen, they had several capitals on both sides of the Pyrenees. Arabic rule lasted less than a century in the lands located between Barcelona and Roussillon. Also, during the ninth and tenth centuries, the counties of the Hispanic March belonged to the Carolingian Empire and to the Kingdom of the Franks.

From the end of the 10th and in the following centuries, we do find evidence of an emerging state which was governed from Barcelona and without links to Spain. The historical reality is that, in 985, Al-Mansur looted Barcelona. The count at the time, Borrell II, did not receive military support from the Frankish king Hugh Capet as was compulsory under the vassalage pact. The count of Barcelona therefore stopped attending the Frankish court to pay tribute to Capet and, therefore, began to act as an independent state (Bonnassie, 1990; D'Abadal, 1969; Fontana, 2014; Sobrequés, 2007; Vilar, 1962).

His descendant Ramon Berenguer I, count of Barcelona, Girona and Osona, began to refer to himself as the prince of the principality during the 1064 court. The contemporary sources of Al-Andalus indicate that the king (*màlik*) of the Franks (*ifrànj*) lived in Barcelona. The followers of Islam, although formally mistaken, recognized the effective sovereignty that the count of Barcelona enjoyed (Balañá, 2002).

In the following century, another proof of external recognition of de facto independence should be underlined. For the first time, the Pisan sailors talked about their arrival in a land called *Catalania*, which included the counties of Barcelona, Osona, Girona and Empúries. One of the first commercial republics of the Mediterranean therefore corroborated the emerging sovereignty of this group of counties (Udina, 2000).

Between 801 and 1156, these counties were a borderland with the caliphate of Cordoba, first, and then with the taifa kingdoms and emirates into which it divided. The feudalism established within the counties was based on the exploitation of peasant labour, with conditions that varied greatly, going from servitude to emphyteusis, but which, as already mentioned, worsened with the unbridled violence in around the year 1000 (Bonnassie, 1990; D'Abadal, 1969; Salrach 1987, 1997; Salrach & Duran, 1982). As the county of Barcelona slowly wrestled land from the followers of Islam, the former Franks benefited from some of the innovations applied by the Arab-Berbers, especially those concerning vegetable garden crops, canals, waterwheels, mills, paper, the astrolabe, new textile techniques and the dissemination of the number 0 and the decimal system (Balañá, 2002; Barceló et al., 1996; Batet, 2001; Riera, 2006; Vernet, 1978). The Christian monasteries, which grew quickly, helped to spread some of these innovations (Van Zanden, 2009). The counties also included important Jewish communities, which stood out as artisans, financiers and even a few mathematicians (Forcano, 2014). The interaction favoured a slow progression in trade and the level of development, after the nadir of the eighth century.

8.7 Mediterranean Resilience Between Feudalism and the Commercial Revolution

During the twelfth century the power of the aristocracy increased and the public sphere weakened still more in key aspects as taxation, the army and justice, which tended to by captured by local knights and castle guardians (*castlans*), in what some authors like to characterize as feudal revolution, as Professor Salrach does in Chapter 2. The Catalan feudal state codified a legal system (*Usatges de Barcelona*) which confirmed the deep inequality between lords and peasants. The troops of the milites rapidly expanded and castles proliferated, forcing peasant vassalage and obtaining all kind of tributes of them. The Count of Barcelona had promoted the territorial organization based on royal agents (*veguers* and *battles*) which were responsible for justice and tax collection. But in many cases, the same agents abused from the violence against peasants.

In 1117, count Ramon Berenguer III conquered the former Tarraco and his son married Petronilla of Aragon, so that the lineage of Barcelona could finally wear the royal crown. The last Muslim stronghold to the north of the River Ebro was conquered by Ramon Berenguer IV in 1156. This count already began to refer to himself as Prince of Catalonia. His son, Alfons I the Troubadour, held the titles King of Aragon and Count of Barcelona and Provence (Bisson, 1986, 2009; Salrach, 1987; Sobrequés, 2007).

The strengthening of the ties with the territories of the Mediterranean coast where the Occitan language was spoken was a priority for the first counts of Barcelona. Some wrote in this language, very close to written Catalan. Catalans and Provençals were considered a single nation in Jerusalem in 1187 (Le Roy Ladurie, 1962; Martel, 2019; Vilar, 1962).

King Peter I the Catholic died defending his Languedocian vassals, who had been indulgent with Cathar heresy. The 1213 Battle of Muret ended in favour of the troops of Simon de Montfort, who had the support of the Pope and of the King of France. The defeat put an end to Catalan expansion to the north and helped reorientate the Mediterranean strategy of the counts of Barcelona.

We can consider that King James I, with the conquest of Mallorca (1229) and Valencia (1238), boosted the transformation of the Kingdom of Aragon into a thalassocracy led by Barcelona. Starting from 1253, King James began to appoint consuls in important cities of the Mare Nostrum. The majority were concentrated in Languedoc, Provence and Italy. However, he also appointed them in important locations of north Africa, Muslim Spain, the Byzantine Empire and the Mediterranean Levant. From the beginning of the century, the Catalans promoted trade in spices with the eastern Mediterranean. In 1266, King James granted the city of Barcelona the privilege of appointing the commercial representatives of the Crown of Aragon in the eastern ports, with the name of consul of the Catalans. With this decision, the king recognized Barcelona's role as a spearhead for the commercial expansion of the Crown of Aragon. The same monarch created the Consell de Cent which, in a similar manner to the Italian republics, represented the interests of traders, the liberal professions and artisans and chose the government of Barcelona (Abulafia, 2011, 2014; Batlle, 1988; Bisson, 1986; Dufourcq, 1969; Mollat du Jourdin, 1993; Smith, 1940; Vilar, 1962).

The Barcelona merchants had begun to look for spices in Alexandria at the end of the twelfth century. As well as consuming them domestically, with time they re-exported them around the Mediterranean. They went as far as the counties of Toulouse and Savoy, while they imported wheat from Languedoc and Provence. During the thirteenth century they acquired slaves, gold and coral in north Africa and they also sold spices, as well as Catalan drapery and iron. They also imported slaves from Genoa, in addition to Phocaean alum, in exchange for wool from Valencia and Aragon, which was also acquired by Pisans and Florentines (Abulafia, 2011, 2014; Batlle, 1988; Bisson, 1986; Coulon, 2013; Crusafont, 1996, 2015; Cuadrada, 2001; Dufourcq, 1969; Kocka, 2013; Mollat du Jourdin, 1993; Vilar, 1962).

Penetration in Sicily (1282) and Sardinia (1326) favoured the subsequent importation of cereals and exportation of Catalan textiles. At the beginning of the fourteenth century, the Barcelona merchants imported spices from Rhodes, Alexandria, Beirut and Cyprus and resold Languedocian and Flemish textiles there, in addition to the so-called *draps de la terra*. The textiles exported from Barcelona were manufactured in locations as distant as Perpignan and Valencia, Berga and Lleida.

With the increase in trade led by the Barcelona merchants and the conversion of the Crown of Aragon into a thalassocracy, we can consider that Catalonia, Valencia and Mallorca joined the Commercial Revolution, which the Italian cities had led for some centuries. After the nadir of the eighth century, and in accordance with the shipwreck indicator, after a parenthesis of almost 800 years foreign trade in the Mediterranean had begun to grow (see Fig. 1.2 in Chapter 1). This initial recovery of Mediterranean trade continued in a sustained manner until the beginnings of the fourteenth century. The change of trend in the volume of trade during the eleventh-thirteenth centuries can be attributed to what has been called the Commercial Revolution (Abulafia, 2011; Benvenuti, 1989; Crowley, 2011; Crusafont, 1996, 2015; De Roover, 1942; Lopez, 1976; Malanima, 2018; Miskimin, 1975; Parker, 1992; Tilly, 1990).

It again demonstrates the capacity for resilience of the Mare Nostrum, which once again experienced a period of development and improvement in the levels of production and well-being. However, it should be added that the recovery of the Mediterranean exchange coincided with a significant improvement of climate conditions, which has been known as the Mediaeval Warm Period.

The Commercial Revolution can be considered as a resilient response to the great crisis which put an end to the Roman Empire, put to rest once and for all with the Arab conquests. In any case, the recovery of trade and the improvement in the levels of well-being did not take place with the same economic foundations as the Later Roman Empire, but rather represented a great transformation of the basin's pillars of development. While feudalism took root in the hinterland of the western Mediterranean, some cities of its coastal area revived thanks to mercantile capitalism. In short, the diversity of the basin was once again revealed.

Initially, in the tenth-eleventh centuries, the revival of maritime trade was led by cities which combined activities of military aggression or piracy with the promotion of trade. Some were favoured by the campaigns of cross-aggression that the feudal Christians undertook against the Islamic world. Paradigmatic examples of this type of development include the Italian cities of Venice, Amalfi, Pisa and Genoa. It should be noted that none of these cities was a big capital and extractive centre of antiquity like Rome, Constantinople and Athens.

On the other hand, although the followers of Islam also participated in the recovery of Mediterranean trade, the dynamism of their exchanges with the sea's northern shore was limited due to the ban on their merchants settling in the ports of infidels and even of trading with non-believers. When traders from Muslim cities became important in Mediterranean trade, they were often Jews who had settled in those territories, as occurred with the Hebrew communities of Cairo and Islamic Mallorca (Abulafia, 2011).

From the twelfth–thriteenth centuries, and until the arrival of the Black Death, the Commercial Revolution took off even more and the accumulation of commercial and manufacturing profit consolidated the leadership of Venice, Genoa and Florence (Benvenutti, 1989; De Roover, 1942; Dini, 1995; Felloni & Laura, 2004; Goldthwaite, 2009; Kocka, 2013; Lopez, 1976; Malanima, 2018; Mollat du Jourdin, 1993). These three republics from the north of Italy were close to or exceeded 100,000 inhabitants in 1347, being among the 10 most populated cities of the basin. Their commercial success allowed them to accumulate precious metals, once again mint silver coins with high content and launch gold pieces with their emblems in the fourteenth century, six centuries after the Carolingians adopted monometallism based on silver (Bloch, 1954; Catalan, 2020; Cipolla, 1975; Crusafont, 1989, 1996, 2015; Le Goff, 2010; Vilar, 1962). It should also be underlined that, despite the renewed resilience of Mediterranean trade, promoted by these cities in northern Italy, their trading activity continued to be frequently combined with maritime pillage, military aggression and the slave trade, additional sources of profit and accumulation of capital for the thalassocratic republics.

Table 8.1 stresses the great transformation of the Mediterranean, according with the changes in the population of a significant number of cities in the basin (never more than 200 kilometres from the sea). It should be advised that the dates are approximate and there are major shortcomings in the sample, such as Alexandria, Smirna, Ragusa or Jerusalem. The exclusion is not voluntary, but rather only the cities for which it was possible to find estimates for all the years of the comparison were included.

In around the year 1000 the top of the main cities of the Mediterranean was formed by the Islamic metropolises (Palermo and Cairo) and big cities, often capitals, of the Ancient World (Constantinople, Rome, Naples and Milan). Both groups were major centres of consumption, where extractive elites resided who, through the fiscal system, obtained their income from huge agricultural hinterlands (Acemoglou & Robinson, 2012; Epstein, 1992; Landes, 1998; Tilly, 1990; Wickham, 1984, 2005).

At the beginning of the eleventh century, the main outsider in the vertex of the ranking was Venice, which was in fourth position among the cities considered but did not correspond to any of the above categories. As already indicated, it was a republican city-state which had grown above all as a fulcrum of trade in the eastern and western Mediterranean.

Three centuries later, at the vertex of the most populated cities of the Mare Nostrum, the big cities of the Islamic world and the capitals of the Antiquity continued to appear. However, at the end of the thirteenth century, other leading figures from the Commercial Revolution already accompanied Venice. In Italy, both Genoa and Florence had experienced a huge leap in the ranking of the most populated cities, confirming their important role in the resilience of Mediterranean trade from the Latin peninsula. In the south of France, Marseille and Montpellier recorded significant progress.

In the case on which we are focusing, the clear improvement in the rankings of Table 8.1. should be observed for Barcelona and Valencia, confirming the remarkable role played by both populations on the Iberian coast in the Commercial Revolution. It should moreover be noted that

Table 8.1 Population ranking of important Mediterranean cities, 1000 vs. 1300. Thousands of inhabitants

		1000			*1300*
1	PALERMO	350	1	CAIRO	400
2	CONSTANTINOPLE	300	2	CONSTANTINOPLE	150
3	CAIRO	135	3	GRANADA	150
4	VENICE	45	4	VENICE	110
5	THESSALONIKI	40	5	GENOA	100
6	ROME	35	6	MILAN	100
7	NAPLES	30	7	FLORENCE	95
8	MILAN	30	8	NAPLES	60
9	ALMERIA	27	9	PALERMO	51
10	GRANADA	26	10	THESSALONIKI	50
11	**MALLORCA**	**25**	**11**	**BARCELONA**	**48**
12	CARCASSONNE	20	**12**	**VALENCIA**	**44**
13	VERONA	20	13	MALAGA	40
14	MALAGA	17	14	PISA	38
15	ATHENS	15	15	MONTPELLIER	35
16	GENOA	15	16	PADUA	35
17	**VALENCIA**	**15**	17	MARSEILLE	31
18	FLORENCE	13	18	ROME	30
19	MANTUA	12	19	MANTUA	30
20	NARBONNE	12	20	NARBONNE	30
21	PADUA	10	21	VERONA	30
22	PISA	9	22	ATHENS	25
23	MARSEILLE	9	23	ALMERIA	18
24	**BARCELONA**	**5**	**24**	**MALLORCA**	**17**
25	MONTPELLIER	1	25	CARCASSONNE	15

Source Compiled by author with Bairoch et al. (1988) and others
The three bold cities are Barcelona, Valencia and Ciutat de Mallorca, which are the main towns of the Catalan-speaking countries, the preferential object of the book

the former was the city which recorded the biggest leap between the two rankings considered. The relative improvement of Barcelona was, indeed, the most marked between the years 1000 and 1300. Although the population data for both Barcelona and the rest of the cities are very speculative, the spectacular improvement of Barcelona confirms its noteworthy participation in the Commercial Revolution and its role as a driving force at the heart of the Crown of Aragon (Abulafia, 2014; Bisson, 1986; Coulon, 2013; Dufourcq, 1969; Molat du Jourdin, 1993; North & Thomas, 1973; Vilar, 1962).

Indeed, as maintained in Chapter 3, Barcelona emulated the thalassocratic vocation of the Italian mercantile republics and dragged the maritime territories of the Crown of Aragon along this path. Authors such as Pierre Vilar and Josep Fontana considered Catalonia to be one of the first nation-states of Europe, highlighting its consolidated political structure and the existence of representative courts (Fontana, 2014; Vilar, 1962). Others, more focused on analyzing the evolution of trade, like Dufourq, Bisson, Molat, Coulon and Abulafia, characterized late mediaeval Barcelona, its hinterland Catalonia and even the whole of the Crown of Aragon as a true thalassocracy (Abulafia, 2014; Bisson, 1986; Coulon, 2013; Dufourcq, 1969; Molat du Jourdin, 1993).

The emergence of a nation-state favoured the spread of written Catalan, as an administrative, religious and literary language. The commercial orientation of the Iberian coast and the military conquests strengthened the links between Barcelona, Valencia, Mallorca and Roussillon, which since the thirteenth century had been expressed in a shared language, Catalan (Batlle, 1988; Belenguer, 1996; Salrach, 2006; Salrach & Duran, 1982; Sobrequés, 2007; Soto, 2001; Vilar, 1962). These territories did not always form part of the same political unit, and therefore the latter two became the Kingdom of Mallorca on the death of James I, Roussillon was annexed by France in the 1659 Treaty of the Pyrenees and the Crown of Aragon was dissolved by the Bourbon Philip V at the beginning of the eighteenth century.

Whether or not they belonged to the same state, the territories of the Principality of Catalonia, Roussillon, the Kingdom of Valencia and the Balearic Islands always maintained intense exchange among them. Moreover, since the Late Middle Ages, the link created by Catalan as the common language, the thalassocratic mercantile tradition and the shared political history within the confederal framework of the Crown of Aragon, transformed their people into a cultural unit, comparable to that of other peoples and trading nations of the basin. We therefore believe that it makes complete sense to use the term Catalan Countries to refer to the whole.

The history of this cultural community was therefore similar to that of the Greeks or Phoenicians of the ancient world. As we have seen, both these peoples, without the need to be integrated in a unified state, shared the same culture gestated over centuries. In the case of Greece, the sense of community and of a people continued to exist after the fall of Constantinople, under the Ottoman empire, and until the creation of the

Greek state at the beginning of the nineteenth century. In a comparable manner, for centuries the Italians formed part of a cultural unit divided between different empires. Even so, they were able to share a common culture from the Middle Ages until the construction of the Kingdom of Italy in the mid-nineteenth century. In an even more dramatic but significant manner, the Hebrew people preserved their cultural identity, despite living in foreign lands for two millennia. Their identity, strongly based on religion, allowed them to survive despite repeated attempts by the gentiles to annihilate them, until the establishment of the state of Israel in 1948.

8.8 The Great Late Mediaeval Depression

The pattern of development of the Mare Nostrum experienced a severe shock in the fourteenth century. Indeed, the Mediterranean shipwreck indicator recorded a 70% contraction in relation to the previous century, indicating a tremendous crisis in trading levels (see Fig. 1.2 in Chapter 1). During the 1300s, there was a series of bad harvests, associated with the end of the Mediaeval Warm Period, and the intensification of military conflicts such as the outbreak of the Hundred Years' War in France and the beginning of the conquest of the Balkans by the Ottomans. However, the main factor in the depression of that century was the transmission of the Black Death which, like other epidemics, arrived across the Mare Nostrum and, in this case, achieved Dantesque proportions: it cost the life of around 50% of the population of the basin! (Abulafia, 2011; Allen, 2019; Benedictow, 2004; Bois, 2000; Campbell, 2016; Cipolla, 1962; Epstein, 1991, 2000; Furió, 2017; Le Roy Ladurie, 1967; Lo Cascio & Malanima, 2005; Lopez, 1976; Malanima, 2010, 2018; Miskimin, 1975; North & Thomas, 1973; Vilar, 1962).

Catalonia and the maritime territories of the Crown of Aragon were paradigmatic examples of how the pandemic achieved a previously unknown speed of infection and levels of mortality. During the first outbreak of infection, a third of the population of Catalonia may have died and, including the subsequent waves, the reduction in the population of the Catalan Countries may have been more than half (Benedictow, 2004; Cuadrada, 2012; Nadal, 1992a).

Nowadays, we now know that the cause of the epidemic was the bacteria *Y pestis*. Infection was from the bites of fleas, living on the black rat, which transmitted it, and from the spasms of those infected. The Genoese caught the disease in their fight against the Tartars in Caffa.

The Genoese ships took it to Constantinople and then spread it around the Mediterranean. The disease reached Mallorca, via Sardinia, in March 1348, and Perpignan, via Narbonne, in the following month. From the Balearics, the epidemic was exported to Barcelona and Valencia, where it arrived in May 1348. In Catalonia the slump lasted until 1376.

This extreme mortality led to a contraction in demand, a fall in agricultural and industrial production and an erosion of the income of landowners. The nobility became impoverished and the king himself, a big feudal landowner, experienced growing financial difficulties. The indebtedness of the nobility tended to increase. The average long-distance maritime foreign trade in Barcelona declined by two thirds and bottomed out in 1366 (Batlle, 1988; Catalan, 2020; Coulon, 2013; Feliu, 2016a; Vilar, 1962).

Debtors and religious extremists blamed the Jews for poisoning the water and took advantage of the situation to seek a scapegoat. The Jewish quarters of Barcelona and of Morverdre (present day Sagunt) were plundered in 1348, and during the 1370 outbreak, the attacks on Hebrew properties spread to Mallorca, Perpignan and Valencia (Batlle, 1988; Feliu, 2016a; Forcano, 2014; Vilar, 1962).

The Crown of Aragon moreover had to confront the uprising in Sardinia in 1354 and the prolonged war against Castile in 1356–1357. A wave of bank failures took place in 1359. There was also an exceptional outbreak of famine in the three years from 1374 to 1376.

However, despite having suffered from the most tragic epidemic in history, the Catalan Countries showed notable resilience during that tremendous depression of the central part of the fourteenth century. One of the most noteworthy elements in favour of recovery was the increase experienced in real wages, as a result of the reduction in labour supply. Agricultural yields also improved, since the surviving peasants could plough better land. In short, the part of the working population which did not die could feed itself better and ended up increasing the demand for agricultural and manufactured goods.

The remarkable resilience was, however, also the result of significant institutional innovations of the time. The fiscal difficulties of the Crown led it to make concessions. King Peter the Ceremonious accepted the creation of a permanent representation of the Courts, which was in charge of collecting taxes and which worked when the parliament was not in session. This *Diputació del General* or *Generalitat* could convene the

Courts when it deemed this to be necessary and, thanks to this prerogative, could act as the supervisory institution of the monarchy and seed of democratic government. It was responsible for collecting two new taxes on, respectively, the production of woollen fabrics (*dret de bolla*) and foreign trade (*dret d'entrades i eixides*). The creation of these two taxes confirms that manufacturing and foreign trade were significant sources of value creation in the country at the time. They moreover contributed to improving the state fiscal capacity, along the lines of modern states. King Peter the Ceremonious also converted the duty to march with the Princeps to defend the country against a foreign invasion (*Princeps namque*), which was included into a money payment or direct tax for financing the war (Bisson, 1986; Fontana, 2014; Sánchez Martínez, 1995, 2003; Usher, 1943; Vilar, 1962).

Some decades later, another very significant innovation was the creation of the first European public bank, with the establishment of the Taula de Canvi de Barcelona in 1401. Other cities from the Mediterranean territories of the Crown imitated Barcelona and created their own public banks. This was the case, in this order and among others, of Perpignan, Valencia, Vic, Tarragona and Girona (Feliu, 2000, 2016a, 2016b; Usher, 1943; Vicens, 1958, 1959; Vilar, 1962).

The majority of quantitative variables available agree on indicating the robust resilience of Barcelona and Catalonia during the last third of the fourteenth century. Not only did long-distance foreign trade, compiled by Professor Coulon, tend to recover, but moreover it achieved its absolute maximum around 1403 (Catalan, 2020; Coulon 2013). The taxes on entering Barcelona and the overall tax collection of the city also recorded vigorous growth in the last third of the 1300s, although there were further financial panics and shameful attacks on the Jewish quarters (Broussolle, 1955; Ortí, 2000, 2018).

If we analyze the situation from a comparative perspective, despite the brutal shock of the Black Death, Barcelona and Valencia maintained their relative position in the rankings of Mediterranean cities between 1300 and 1400 (Compare Tables 8.1 and 8.2). The relative resilience of the Principality of Catalonia and the Kingdom of Valencia contributed decisively to promoting the development of the rest of the Crown of Aragon.

The fiscal and political representation system tested in Catalonia, with the creation of the Generalitat, spread to the rest of the crown territories. Thanks to tax collection, we know that in the 1380s Catalonia represented

Table 8.2 Population ranking of important Mediterranean cities, 1400 vs. 1500. Thousands of inhabitants

		1400			*1500*
1	CAIRO	360	1	CAIRO	400
2	GRANADA	100	2	CONSTANTINOPLE	200
3	GENOA	100	3	NAPLES	125
4	VENICE	100	4	VENICE	100
5	MILAN	90	5	MILAN	100
6	CONSTANTINOPLE	75	6	GRANADA	70
7	FLORENCE	55	7	GENOA	58
8	NAPLES	45	8	FLORENCE	55
9	THESSALONIKI	42	9	PALERMO	55
10	MALAGA	40	10	ROME	55
11	**BARCELONA**	**38**	11	VERONA	50
12	**VALENCIA**	**36**	12	MARSEILLE	45
13	VERONA	35	**13**	**VALENCIA**	**42**
14	ATHENS	35	14	MALAGA	42
15	PADUA	34	15	ALMERIA	30
16	ROME	33	16	PADUA	29
17	PALERMO	27	17	CARCASSONNE	25
18	ALMERIA	25	18	MANTUA	25
19	MANTUA	25	**19**	**BARCELONA**	**20**
20	PISA	23	20	THESSALONIKI	19
21	MARSEILLE	21	**21**	**MALLORCA**	**13**
22	CARCASSONNE	18	22	PISA	10
23	MONTPELLIER	17	23	ATHENS	10
24	**MALLORCA**	**9**	24	MONTPELLIER	6
25	NARBONNE	2	25	NARBONNE	5

Source Compiled by author with Bairoch et al. (1988) and others.
The three bold cities are Barcelona, Valencia and Ciutat de Mallorca, which are the main towns of the Catalan-speaking countries, the preferential object of the book

50% of the indirect tax income obtained by the monarchy in Iberian territories, and the Kingdom of Valencia represented another 33% (Chismol, 2019). Together, they generated 83% of the monarchy's indirect income in Iberia and, therefore, were the two main axes that drove the Crown of Aragon. They both resisted the shock of the fourteenth century well and showed notable resilience.

On the contrary, it was not possible to completely overcome the great depression of the fifteenth century, especially in Catalonia. This was not the only case. As Table 8.2 shows, a significant number of other cities which had dominated the Commercial Revolution lost positions in the population rankings of the Mediterranean between 1400 and 1500: Genoa, Florence, Pisa and even Valencia, among others. Indeed, the number of shipwrecks presented by Parker, which we incorporated in Chapter 1, indicates that the level of trade in the Mediterranean did not return to the maximum of the thirteenth century during the fifteenth (Fig. 1.2).

Trade with Alexandria was jeopardized by the policy of the Mamluks banning sales of spices to foreign merchants in the 1420s. For their part, the Ottomans gradually took territory from Byzantium, until it ended up conquering the capital in 1453. Their control of the silver mines of Serbia and Bosnia was a further hindrance to maritime trade. Harvests were harmed by another period of solar cooling, known as the Spörer Minimum. The wars between European states did not stop and, together with famines, favoured infection by new outbreaks of plague. Although they never reached the brutal intensity of 1347, between that date and 1534 there were 17 outbreaks of plague in Europe (Bois, 2000; Campbell, 2016; Catalan, 2020; Cuadrada, 2012; De Roover, 1962, 1942; Feliu, 2000, 2016a; Furió, 2013, 2017; Malanima, 2010, 2018; Mazower, 2005; Miskimin, 1975).

If the previously mentioned factors can explain the relative decline of important cities which led to the Commercial Revolution of the Mediterranean during the fifteenth century, the specific case of Barcelona and of the Catalan Countries as a whole was much more dramatic. The great depression of the Late Middle Ages lasted more than a century, from 1404 to 1528 (Catalan, 2020; Ortí, 2000, 2018).

The crisis began with bank failures due to excess debt and the closing of the Egyptian market to Catalan fabrics by the Mamluk sultan (Coulon, 2013; Feliu, 2016a). The situation became much more complicated because of the conflict between the nobility and the servile peasants (*remences*) (Batlle, 1988; Freedman, 1991; Salrach, 1989; Salrach & Duran, 1982; Vicens, 1958a; Vilar, 1962). The remensa peasants gradually became closer to the kings, who always needed money for their military campaigns and, in particular, to Alfonso the Magnanimous, who was in great need due to the exorbitant cost of the Naples campaign. This monarch was the second of the new family lineage, the Trastámara, which reigned in the Crown of Aragon after the last king of the House of Barcelona died without a recognized heir. Alfonso is represented with the grandeur of a new Roman emperor on the bas-reliefs sculpted on the

Castel Nuovo of Naples and, like so many monarchs from the Great Sea, dreamed with reestablishing the Latin empire. The second Trastámara invested a huge quantity of resources to increase his Italian domains. He ended up succeeding in 1422, with the conquest of the ancient Neapolis. He transferred his court there and never returned to Barcelona or Valencia (Belenguer, 2019; Vicens, 1958a).

However, the funding of the Neapolitan policy gradually worsened the debt problems of the cities of the Crown of Aragon, which had been significant since the fourteenth century. The biggest cities tried to solve these problems with the creation of public banks at the beginning of the following century. Smaller Catalan towns, however, such as Cardona and Cervera, had to suspend payments from the beginning of the fifteenth century (Galera, 2019; Verdés, 2019).

There was also high debt in Mallorca, which concentrated the fiscal pressure on the population outside the city and on artisans. Both groups rose up in 1451 in the so-called revolt of the *forans* (outsiders). They were defeated thanks to the Neapolitan mercenaries sent by the Magnanimous. They executed the leaders and imposed heavy indemnities on the rebel settlements of the island (Belenguer, 2019; Jover, 1996; Salrach & Duran, 1982).

The Magnanimous died in 1458, but then there were two groups openly opposed in the Principality, and they ended up causing a dramatic civil war in Catalonia during the reign of John II, Alfonso's brother and heir to Aragon. On the one hand, there was the Diputació del General (dominated by the military and ecclesiastical arms of the Courts) and the Consell de Cent (under the control of the party of the citizens' oligarchy, the Biga); and on the other hand there was King John, the remensas and the Busca (party of the Barcelona artisans, unhappy with the manufacturing crisis and indebted, who imposed a radical devaluation). The war lasted from 1462 to 1472 and continued in Roussillon for some time after that. The final victory was for by King John, who had married his son Ferdinand to Isabella of Castile (Vicens, 1958a; Vilar, 1962; Sobrequés, 2007; Sobrequés & Sobrequés, 1973).

The civil war not only represented a worsening of the commercial crisis suffered by Barcelona but also entailed a catastrophe for Catalonia from which it would take a long time to emerge. The known fiscal data for cities from the interior of the country in the fourteenth century (Cardona and Cervera) show that these towns did not recover pre-war levels of tax collection in what remained of the century. The same happened with the tariffs on the entry of goods into Barcelona by land (*lleuda de Mediona*), as presented by Ortí. Furthermore, the long-distance maritime foreign trade data compiled by Professor Del Treppo suggest that the certain resilience shown after the devaluation of the denier in 1454 and of the florin in 1456 was aborted by the civil war and that after the conflict there was no recovery in what was left of the century (Catalan, 2020; Del Treppo, 1972; Galera, 2019; Ortí, 2000, 2018; Verdés, 2019).

In the 1475 Concord of Segovia, Isabella and Ferdinand agreed to enjoy the same power in each of their respective kingdoms of Castile and Aragon. John II died in 1479 and his son took over the Crown of Aragon as Ferdinand II, while sharing power in Castile with his wife. As Count of Barcelona, and after a new peasant uprising against feudalism, he made decisions which favoured the Catalan countryside in the long term, such as the so-called 1486 Decision of Guadalupe or the provision on *masos rònecs*. The former declared the abolition of servitude and other feudal benefits, in exchange for monetary compensation of the monarchy and the lords, through the payment of an initial lump sum of more a moderate annual amount. In exchange, the former remensas obtained the right to retain, bequeath and even mortgage the land on which they worked. The second provision allowed peasants to work on the *masos rònecs* (lands which had been previously abandoned), in exchange for further monetary compensation. These measures implied the abolition of the toughest features of feudalism in Catalonia. For some classical economic historians, such as Professors Vicens Vives and Brenner, this laid the foundations for the favourable development of the country on creating a prosperous class of quasi-landowning peasants (Brenner, 1978; Vicens, 1958a). Other historians, like Serra and Salrach, were not as optimistic, indicating that the peasants who benefited from the measures only represented part of the workers of the land (Salrach, 1989; Serra, 1980).

On the other hand, Ferdinand II and his wife Isabella, known as the Catholic Monarchs, implemented a xenophobic policy which had very negative consequences for the technical and scientific development and the general economic progress of their kingdoms. In Catalonia, they imposed the Castilian Inquisition, implacable in its pursuit of converted Jews, starting from 1487. The deputies of the Generalitat and the councillors of Barcelona, who were indignant, refused to receive the new inquisitor on his arrival in the Principality, but could not prevent the succession of trials. By 1498, more than 3000 people had been sentenced to death by the Inquisition in Catalonia. Even John II's former treasurer and his wife were burnt at the stake in 1505 (Abulafia, 2011; Catalan, 2020; Forcano, 2014).

Isabella of Castile and Ferdinand of Aragon also signed the deplorable decrees to expel Jews from their kingdoms. In 1483, they were expatriated from Castilian Andalusia. Moreover, in the Palace of the Alhambra in Granada, when they had just conquered the Muslim kingdom in 1492, they signed the edicts which forced Hebrews to choose between conversion and expulsion. The Jews of Catalonia, Valencia and Mallorca, many of them artisans, traders and bankers, departed for Italy and the Ottoman Empire. In Rome, some were welcomed by the Valencian Pope Alexander VI Borgia. Sultan Bayezid II, who provided them with shelter in Constantinople and Thessaloniki, said of the Catholic King: "*Why do you call that Ferdinand wise, when he has impoverished his country to enrich mine?*" (Forcano, 2014). The so-called Catholic Monarchs, on imposing the Castilian Inquisition in the Crown of Aragon and expelling the Hebrews from their kingdoms, embarked upon a deplorable policy of persecution of religious diversity in the Mediterranean, which became characteristic of modern Spain.

The Kingdom of Valencia appears to have experienced a more enlightened 1400s than Catalonia and Mallorca (Belenguer, 1976, 1996, 2019; Furió, 2013, 2017; Iradiel, 2017; Llibrer, 2014). Valencia constructed its merchant loggia and developed its own legislation of Sea Consulates. It exported ceramics, cereals, wool, cereals, sugar and slaves and experienced some progress in drapery. However, it did not improve its position in the ranking of Mediterranean towns Moreover, the fifteenth century Valencian better performance than the rest of Catalan Countries did not prevent the revolt of the brotherhoods (*Germanies*) in 1520 against the grandson of the Catholic Monarchs, Charles V of Habsburg.

8.9 The Mare Nostrum, from Centre to Periphery

Charles of Habsburg ended up with an immense empire which was not just Mediterranean but also European and American. From his father he inherited Flanders, Luxemburg and the Franche-Comté. From his paternal grandfather, Maximilian, he received the states of the House of Austria and the right to be chosen as Emperor of Germany. From his grandfather Ferdinand he obtained Aragon, Naples, Sardinia and Sicily. From Castile, in addition to its Iberian possessions and some towns of the Maghreb, he obtained huge territories on the American continent, which provided him with increasing quantities of financial resources (especially silver). These new revenues were used to become the hegemonic military force of Christian Europe and the Mediterranean (Dantí, 2018, 2021; Feliu, 1991; Hamilton, 1934; Mauro & Parker, 1977; Salrach & Duran, 1982; Vicens, 1959).

Charles reigned since the death of Ferdinand in 1516 and became German emperor in 1519. However, in Valencia the Germanies revolted already in 1520, fact which can indicate a worsening of living conditions among significant strata of the population, and in particular among the wool carders, drapers and silk artisans, that were over-represented among the rebels. The guild members demanded more political representation, occupied the palaces of feudal lords and burnt scriptures. They were finally defeated in Xàtiva and Alzira in 1522. Meanwhile, the brotherhoods of Mallorca rose up, emulating those of Valencia, demanding a reduction in rent and taxes and resisting until 1523. The defeat involved the signing of death penalties and new compensation payments for the revolting guilds and towns. The general pardon did not arrive until 1528. During this long period of regression, the Catalan Countries which had been sovereign kingdoms gradually became peripheral possessions of the Habsburg Empire (Belenguer, 1997; Duran, 1982; García Carcel, 1981; Iradiel, 1989; Jover, 1996; Llibrer, 2014; Navarro, 1999; Pérez, 2017; Salrach & Duran, 1982).

On the Old Continent, the emperor repeatedly confronted France, taking the Duchy of Milan in 1521 and defeating and capturing Francis I in the Battle of Pavia four years later. Despite declaring himself a paladin of Catholicism, Charles V's troops looted Rome in 1527. Even so, three years later he was crowned Emperor of the Holy Roman Empire and King of Italy in Bologna by Pope Clement VII.

The Habsburg's imperialism increasingly leant towards religious intransigence, insisting on the path against ideological diversity on which his grandparents Isabella of Castile and Ferdinand of Aragon had embarked. In 1523, Charles V forbade the dissemination of the works of Martin Luther. In the next decade he confronted the German princes who had embraced the Reformation and joined the Schmalkaldic League. In 1546, he publicized the first list of books that it was forbidden to read and supported the sessions of the Council of Trent, which laid the foundations for the Catholic Counter-Reformation.

In the Mediterranean he fought against Islam and succeeded in annexing Tunis in 1527. The Ottomans had conquered Cairo in 1517 and were advancing by sea and land in the Mare Nostrum. Suleiman I conquered Buda in 1526 and occupied Hungary, but was repelled in his attempt to conquer Vienna. The emperor offered Malta to the Order of Knights of the Hospital of Saint John, who had lost Rhodes, to help attack the Turks (Norwich, 2006). The Ottoman invasion of the island in 1565 was prevented by the Knights Hospitaller, but the Turks did not fail in Tripoli. The confrontation between the Habsburgs and their allies, Venice and the Pope, on the one hand, and the Ottomans, on the other, provoked growing polarization in the Mediterranean, which tended to reduce diversity and penalize trade.

The huge cost of Habsburg imperialist policy could be financed thanks to the loans granted to the emperor by Genoese and German bankers (Carande, 1949). The guarantee which allowed the growing debt to be financed was the precious metals that Castile sought and obtained in America. According to Pierre Vilar and David Landes, the colonization of the New World was more a feudal undertaking in search of booty than a commercial empire (Landes, 1998; Vilar, 1974a, 1974b). According to Tilly, and Acemoglou and Robinson, we could talk about an extremely coercive and extractive empire (Acemoglou & Robinson, 2012; Tilly, 1990). This empire was lucky to find huge silver deposits in Potosí and Zacatecas to finance its ambitious expansionist policy.

Castile exploited the American continent under a strictly mercantilist regime, round-trip trade being necessary in fleets which departed from and arrived in Seville (with a stop in Cadiz). The merchants of Barcelona, upon asking the emperor in 1522 to be able to directly trade with the New World, obtained a negative response, it being alleged that it was a Castilian monopoly. All the metals which reached Seville were stored in the Torre del Oro and the emperor obtained an eighth of them. The arrivals of silver increased in a sustained manner in the sixteenth century and, paradoxically, encouraged Habsburg indebtedness. The reserves of the American treasury, which were regularly increasing, embarked on the journey by land from Seville to Laredo, to be shipped to Antwerp. Later, when Flandes revolted against the Hispanic monarchy, the preferred way was land transport to Barcelona. From there they were re-embarked to Genoa, where they served the debt of local bankers or continued by land across the Alps to Augsburg. Genovese and German financers prospered.

Charles granted Genoa free trade with Napols and Sicily in 1536. This caused tremendous discontent among Catalan drapers and merchants, which had to compete harder against a traditional rival, both as exporter of woollens and importer of cereals. The relationships between the Principality and the Habsburg worsened (Fontana, 2014).

In 1556 Charles abdicated in favour of his son Phillip and assigned the Holy Roman Empire to his brother Ferdinand. Philip II accentuated the imperialist and xenophobic policies in all the kingdoms that he inherited, increasingly basing his power on the Crown of Castile's financial resources and men (Braudel, 1949; Comín, 2013; Hamilton, 1934; 1949; Mauro & Parker, 1977; Nadal, 2001; Vicens, 1959; Yun, 2002). In 1560, Madrid became the permanent capital of his court.

The monarch enthusiastically supported the agreements of the Council of Trent and the repression undertaken by the Inquisition. The 1564 list of the *Index Librorum Prohibitorum* of Trent confirmed the policy of persecution of free thinking and intensified the repression against religious or intellectual dissidence in an alliance with the Papacy of Rome. The Inquisition was responsible for persecuting those who disseminated the works included in the index. It would end up by including works ranging from Epicurus to Copernicus, and from Descartes to Newton. The tremendous divide between Protestant and Catholic Europe would have dramatic long-term consequences for the levels of literacy and book production in the Mediterranean world (Flora, 1973; Kamen, 1993; Tortella, 1994; Van Zanden, 2009).

Moreover, Castile attacked the islands where Magellan died in the first circumnavigation of the Earth. It succeeded in annexing them and, from then on, the Philippines were known with the name of the Spanish monarch. It is calculated that around a third of the population of the archipelago died during the life of Philip II.

The Habsburg Netherlands revolted in 1556. Calvinist heresy had spread rapidly there. The Duke of Alba was sent as a military governor, and sowed terror with his repressive policies against protestants and those in favour of independence. The Castilians ended up looting Antwerp in 1576. They could not, however, prevent the emancipation of the territories of the north of Flanders, which became independent as the Dutch Republic from 1581.

King Sebastian of Portugal died during the 1578 invasion of Morocco. Taking advantage of the situation, Castile attacked its peninsular neighbour and took control of another empire with possessions to the west (Madeira, the Azores and Brazil), south (a series of African factories) and east (from Goa to Malacca and Macao).

England became an increasingly dangerous adversary, against which Philip II spared no effort. With the support of Sixtus V, who declared the invasion of Great Britain to be a crusade, the Castilian monarch attempted an initial attack in 1588, but his armada was defeated. Another attempt in 1597 also failed.

Although there were further victories in Malta (1565) and Lepanto (1571), in the Mediterranean the war against the Turks could not prevent subsequent Ottoman advances, such as the final conquest of Cyprus (1571) and that of Tunis (1574). The growing polarization not only hindered trade in the basin and reduced diversity. The coasts of the western Mediterranean also became very insecure, due to periodic attacks from the sea, which led people to abandon the coastline. In the Catalan Countries the most dramatic episode was the attack and destruction of the Menorcan city of Ciutadella in 1558 (Casasnovas, 2006; Salrach & Duran, 1982).

Castile continued its expansion in America. In the south it obtained the Strait of Magellan while in the north it reached California and Florida. According to Maddison, the population of Latin America decreased from 17.5 million in 1500 to just 8.6 million in one century (Maddison, 2007). The demographic impact was therefore at least comparable to that of the Black Death, although in a context of military aggression and destruction of ecosystems and pre-Columbian societies. The conquerors disembarked their germs, such as smallpox, flu and the plague, against which the indigenous population was not immunized. The conquerors moreover imposed feudal institutions of a clearly extractive nature, such as the *encomienda* and the *mita*. The lives of the indigenous population were cut short by epidemics and their poor adaptation to work in the mines and on the plantations, which favoured repopulation with African slaves. The first 125,000 slaves disembarked in the sixteenth century to work in Castilian and Portuguese territories (Acemoglou & Robinson, 2012; Crosby, 1986; Diamond, 1997; Landes, 1998; McNeill & McNeill, 2003; Vilar, 1974a, 1974b).

The arrivals of gold in Seville reached their peak from 1551 to 1560 with a total of 46 tonnes. However, those of silver continued to increase in a sustained manner from 303 tonnes in the aforementioned decade to 2708 tonnes from 1591 to 1600. This huge treasure helped to finance the cost of building Philip II's exorbitant extractive empire on which, according to the monarch himself, the sun never set. Multiplying the Castilian monetary base did, however, lead to continuous inflation, which we know as the price revolution. Much higher differential inflation transformed Castile into a tremendous rentier economy, which consumes rather than produce and a significant importer of manufactured products from the rest of Europe and the world (Braudel, 1949; Feliu, 1991; Hamilton, 1934; Nadal, 2001; Vicens, 1959).

Moreover, the treasure of the Indies favoured indebtedness on a greater scale with Philip II than in the time of his father. The debts contracted were so exorbitant that on three occasions the monarch had to declare the suspension of payments: in 1557, 1575 and 1596. These insolvencies gave rise to loan renegotiation processes and forced the monarchy to seek complementary revenues (Comín, 2013; Mauro & Parker, 1977; Reinhart & Rogoff, 2009).

The Catalans, who had obtained the Habsburg rejection of their desire to participate in the colonization of the Indies and who had representative courts and a constitutional tradition, opposed the increase in fiscal pressure that Philip II demanded. Thus, when in 1571 the Pope granted the Catholic monarch the biggest tithe of each parish (the *excusado*) in order to build galleys against the Turks, the Catalan Courts were the only ones to oppose this measure. Furthermore, the 1588 Courts published the Constitutions of the Principality. Among other legislative powers, the Constitutions required the approval of the Courts to validate new taxes and to send troops from the country to fight outside the Principality. After a long century of peace, the institutions of Catalonia again openly disagreed with the monarch's demands (Elliott, 1963, 2018; Fontana, 2014; Nadal-Farreras, 1983; Sales, 1989; Salrach & Duran, 1982; Serra, 1991, 2015).

To summarize, Habsburg imperialism was of an extractive rather than commercial type. Being based more on direct exploitation than on exchange, it did not adapt to the thalassocratic orientation of the Crown of Aragon's maritime front. Furthermore, the permanent confrontation with the Turks greatly hindered trade, and made the coasts less safe. Indeed, the cities that had led the Commercial Revolution in the Late Middle Ages did not make noticeable progress in the seventeenth century.

Constantinople again became the largest city of the Mediterranean basin in the sixteenth century, confirming its control of an immense and growing agricultural hinterland thanks to a tax system based on taxing land. Rome, another great extractive capital, also improved its relative position as a city of the Mare Nostrum between 1500 and 1600, because of the strengthening of the temporary power of the Papacy with the Counter-Reformation (see Tables 8.2 and 8.3).

On the contrary, Florence and Genoa declined in the Mediterranean population ranking during the sixteenth century (Crowley, 2011; Felloni, 1970; Malanima, 2010, 2018). Even Marseille, a commercial city of the north-western Mediterranean which benefited from the more condescending policy of the Valois with the Turks, also lost positions in the commercial ranking of 1600 compared with 1500 (Braudel, 1949). The big commercial cities of the basin were not only adversely affected by the

Table 8.3 Population ranking of important Mediterranean cities, 1600 vs. 1700 Thousands of inhabitants

		1600			*1700*
1	CONSTANTINOPLE	700	1	CONSTANTINOPLE	700
2	CAIRO	200	2	CAIRO	350
3	NAPLES	275	3	NAPLES	300
4	VENICE	151	4	VENICE	138
5	MILAN	120	5	ROME	135
6	PALERMO	105	6	MILAN	125
7	ROME	100	7	PALERMO	100
8	FLORENCE	76	8	MARSEILLE	90
9	GRANADA	69	9	FLORENCE	72
10	**VALENCIA**	**65**	10	GRANADA	70
11	GENOA	63	11	GENOA	65
12	THESSALONIKI	50	**12**	**VALENCIA**	**50**
13	VERONA	45	13	THESSALONIKI	40
14	MARSEILLE	45	14	VERONA	35
15	PADUA	33	**15**	**BARCELONA**	**34**
16	ATHENS	33	16	PADUA	37
17	**BARCELONA**	**32**	17	MALAGA	30
18	MANTUA	30	18	CARCASSONNE	27
19	CARCASSONNE	30	**19**	**MALLORCA**	**24**
20	**MALLORCA**	**17**	20	MONTPELLIER	23
21	MONTPELLIER	15	21	MANTUA	22
22	PISA	13	22	ATHENS	13
23	MALAGA	11	23	PISA	11
24	ALMERIA	7	24	ALMERIA	10
25	NARBONNE	5	25	NARBONNE	8

Source Compiled by author with Bairoch et al. (1988) and others
The three bold cities are Barcelona, Valencia and Ciutat de Mallorca, which are the main towns of the Catalan-speaking countries, the preferential object of the book

polarization provoked by the war between the Habsburg and Ottoman empires. The opening of a new spice trade route through the Cape of Good Hope by the Portuguese also decisively harmed one of the traditional businesses of the Mare Nostrum's big mercantile cities. The business of sugar and slavery moved also to the Atlantic (Armenteros, 2012; Crowley, 2011).

Barcelona and Valencia experienced a slight improvement in this recessive trade context (García Espuche, 1998). Catalonia, Valencia and Mallorca benefited from having recorded lower inflation than Castile, as can be gathered from the price indices compiled by Hamilton and Feliu (Hamilton, 1949; Feliu, 1991). Lower differential inflation offered the opportunity to export certain goods to Castile, Portugal and their colonies. Thanks to Professor Dantí, we know that between 1575 and 1620 there was a significant increase in the departures of ships from the ports of Catalonia (especially Barcelona, but also Portvendres, Mataró, Arenys and Tarragona) (Dantí, 2018, 2021). Seventeen per cent of the journeys were to peninsular ports from outside the Crown of Aragon—Cadiz, Seville and Lisbon—where they embarked goods for America. Even so, trade with the Mediterranean was still absolutely dominant: 63% of journeys by Catalan ships were to Italy.

The port of Alacant was important in the Kingdom of Valencia, becoming the point of departure for Castilian wool. Professor Torró, who has studied the collection of the *dret de bolla* tax in Alcoi, indicated the existence of a peak in the woollen fabrics sector in this Valencian town in 1571 (Torró, 2020). Likewise, fabric-producing towns from the inland mountains of Catalonia began a period of expansion of the putting-out system in those years, while endeavouring to reduce the costs of the Barcelona manufacturing industry (Torras, 1981, 2018, 2021). The Principality also benefited from the possibility of cheap transport to Castile in the return journeys of the animals that had taken the silver to be embarked for Genoa. Another expanding manufacturing activity during the century in Barcelona was the production of ceramics—shown by the number of potters on the city's census—as demonstrated by García-Osés (García-Osés, 2018).

In any case, the growing polarization between the Turkish and Spanish empires, on curbing Mediterranean exchange, did not encourage the long-term development of the basin. Although it had improved its position on the Mediterranean ranking in relation to 1500, in 1600 Barcelona was still very far from its relative position of 200 years earlier (Compare

Tables 8.2 and 8.3). The resilience of Catalonia in the sixteenth century was very moderate, even more so in the agricultural hinterland than in the capital of the county. The ranking of cities indicates that, in Mallorca and Valencia, resilience under the Habsburgs was a little more important, despite the defeat of the brotherhoods, on also suffering from lower inflation than the Crown of Castile.

The Kingdom of Valencia benefited temporarily from the immigration of the descendants of Moors from Granada (moriscos), who suffered from an initial expulsion as a result of the Rebellion of the Alpujarras from 1568 to 1570. Some of them dominated the silk textile art, in addition to being familiar with cultivating mulberries. These newcomers from the south increased the population of Moorish origins of Valencia, which was already a significant part of the agricultural labour in both rainfed and irrigated cultivation, where they were characterized by promoting irrigation works such as the construction of canals and waterwheels (Esquilache, 2021; Nadal, 1971).

However, the notable resilience of Valencia in the sixteenth century was brought to a sudden standstill by another xenophobic decision by the Hispanic monarchy against diversity. In 1609, Philip III decreed the expulsion of the moriscos who still lived in his kingdoms. In the case of Valencia, the impact of what Geoffrey Parker called a true *ethnic cleansing of Spain* was exorbitant and tragic (Parker, 2001). Professor Nadal estimated that around 118,000 moriscos expelled from Valencia represented a huge 26% of the 450,000 inhabitants that the kingdom had at the time! (Nadal, 1971).

The subject is dealt with in Chapter 4 of this volume by Professor Manuel Ardit, one of the leading specialists on the topic, sadly in a posthumously published study (Ardit, 1987, 2004). His estimation of the population losses because of the expulsion is slightly higher than Nadal, around 135,000 people. Moreover, the details of tithes of the archbishopric of Valencia, collected by Ardit, indicate an astronomical 40% fall in Valencian agricultural production between the decades 1601–1610 and 1641–1650! The expulsion of the moriscos was not the only cause since, as we will see, this was also a time of minimal solar radiation and, consequently, of bad harvests.

As Geoffrey Parker emphasized, in the seventeenth century the sun had entered a new phase of lower activity, pointed out contemporarily by the Jesuit Giovanni Battista Riccioli on noting the reduction in sunspots (Parker, 2001). We now know that solar radiation was decreasing and moving towards the so-called Maunder Minimum, which began in the 1640s and continued until the beginning of the eighteenth century. In around 1640, the volcanic activity of the Earth intensified and, according to the thinning of preserved tree rings, temperatures went down and the years of drought increased. The harvests took longer to mature and were poor. The height of the highest lands cultivated in the Alps again went down. What has been called the European Little Ice Age began.

In Catalonia, as we will see, the 1640s coincided with the revolt against Castilian domination. Thanks to the works of Professor Eva Serra, we know that the tithes of cereals and legumes harvested in the regions around Barcelona declined from the end of the sixteenth century in a very considerable manner (Serra, 1986). Catalonia, like the Kingdom of Valencia, and a good part of the Mediterranean and Europe, underwent a profound agricultural crisis in the seventeenth century. However, the comparison with Valencia, presented here posthumously by Professor Ardit, is very significant since there were few moriscos in the Principality of Catalonia and, consequently, the expulsions in the latter case were negligible (0.8% of the population).

If, as we have said, there was a 40% decline in the tithes of the archbishopric of Valencia between 1601–1610 and 1641–1650, in Girona they only fell by 20%. Despite the fact that the proportion is also very high in the north of the Catalan Countries, it only represents half of the contraction in the south. In the Pyrenean territories adjacent to Seu d'Urgell, the revenues of the lords were even similar from 1641 to 1650 to what they were from 1601 to 1610. Consequently, the great depression of the seventeenth century was much more intense in the Kingdom of Valencia than in neighbouring Catalonia (Ardit, 1987, 2004; Casey, 1979, 2005).

The expulsion of the moriscos did not only provoke the collapse of Valencian agricultural production. The departure of cultivators of the land also contributed to the fall in revenues of the lords. Consequently, the Valencian nobles first became indebted and, then, ended up going bankrupt. The consumption of manufactured products also went down and the crisis broadened, even affecting artisans. Thanks to Professor Torró, we know that the production of woollen fabrics from Alcoi was already declining from 1561 to 1570, but the lowest point of the whole of the seventeenth century was during the decade following the expulsion of the moriscos, from 1611 to 1620. At that time the production of fabrics declined by 29% compared with the previous decade. The level of production of Alcoi from 1601 to 1610 was not achieved again until 1651–1660, that is to say half a century later! (Torró, 2020).

Our rankings of Mediterranean cities confirm the fall back of Valencia (see Table 8.3). Again borrowing Professor Parker's expression, the ethnic cleansing promoted by the Hispanic monarchy was in all likelihood the main cause of the fall that Valencia experienced between 1600 and 1700 (from 10 to 12th position). This decline contrasts with the rise of Barcelona in the same period (from 17 to 15th place), despite having suffered from the differential event of the Reapers' War, which we analyze below, and having shared other contractive shocks during the century.

The depression was much more intense in the Kingdom of Valencia, but Catalonia and the Balearic Islands, like the majority of Europe and the Mediterranean, also experienced a situation of great depression during a substantial part of the 1600s (Catalan & Sánchez, 2013; Elliott, 1963, 2018; Nadal-Farreras, 1983; Parker, 2001; Sales, 1989; Serra, 1986). One of the causes was the return of bubonic plague which the rats in the bilges of the ships, and the soldiers who went to war and then returned, again transported around the Mare Nostrum (Felloni, 1970; Nadal, 1971; Parker, 2001). After the relative peace of the central part of the sixteenth century, Barcelona recorded a virulent outbreak of plague from 1589 to 1592, setting the tone for the following century. This wave successively infected Tarragona and Perpignan.

In 1629, the Great Plague of Milan was spread by the German and French armies which crossed the Alps. It caused mortality of almost 50% in the capital of Lombardy and, from there, it spread to many cities of northern Italy. It likewise infected Provence and Languedoc and then moved towards Roussillon, Barcelona, Sitges and Valencia (Nadal, 1971).

The outbreak of bubonic plague from 1647 to 1652 appears to have entered Valencia on a vessel from Algiers, where the disease, as in most of north Africa, had tended to become endemic. From Valencia it infected Alacant in 1647. It reached Tortosa via a sick soldier in 1650. In the same year it infected Tarragona. From Barcelona it went to Mallorca in 1652. Very often human movement associated with war continued to act as an important element spreading the epidemic.

On the other hand, in the seventeenth century the Habsburgs from Madrid continued with the financial problems of their predecessors. Initially, they only participated cautiously in the Thirty Years' War, which confronted powers and religious confessions between 1618 and 1648.

Even so, Philip III helped the empire, sending the Army of Flanders to invade the Palatinate.

The arrivals of American silver had begun to decline with the new century, progressively falling from 2708 tonnes in the decade from 1591 to 1600 to just 443 tonnes from 1651 to 1660. To try to increase his revenues Philip III, who only reigned between 1598 and 1621, imposed a 30% tariff on all products entering Sicily, including those from Catalonia. This island was the main Italian market for Catalan merchants and, therefore, the measure was very unpopular in Barcelona. It did not, however, prevent the monarch from suspending payments again in 1607 and having to start to renegotiate his debts. Before he died he tried to collect a fifth of the municipal revenues of Catalonia but, like his father, he encountered the refusal of the Courts of the Principality (Elliott, 1963, 2018; Fontana, 2014; Hamilton, 1934, 1949; Morineau, 1976; Nadal-Farreras, 1983; Salrach & Duran, 1982; Serra, 1991, 2015).

Philip II's grandson, Philip IV, wore the crown from 1621 to 1665, and superated his grandfather with, at least, four successive suspensions of payments in 1627, 1647, 1652 and 1662 (Comín, 2013; Mauro & Parker, 1977; Reinhart & Rogoff, 2009). His minister, Count-Duke of Olivares, tried to set up the so-called Union of Arms in 1626. The project consisted of recruiting a body of soldiers theoretically made up of the different kingdoms of the Hispanic monarchy. The respective quotas required from each of them would have been as follows: Castile and the Indies, 44,000 men; Catalonia, Portugal and Naples, 16,000 men each; Flanders, 12,000 men; Milan, 8000 men; Aragon, Valencia, Mallorca/Sardinia and Sicily, 6000 men, respectively. We can use the quotas as an indicator of the economic capacity of each territory.

In those years in Catalonia it was not only the inhabitants of the coasts who were discontent with the repeated attacks by Turkish and Maghrebi pirates. Banditry had become another torment in the interior of the country, without a solution being seen (Nadal-Farreras, 1983; Sales 1989; Salrach & Duran, 1982; Torres, 2007). The Catalan constitutions required the approval of the Courts for any tax and military operation that was not the strict defence of the territory. In a context of great inland instability, the Union of Arms project, which was interpreted as an effort to finance new imperial adventures abroad, was overturned by the Courts.

In 1635, Louis XIII declared war on Philip IV and the French and Castilian tercios confronted each other beyond the Pyrenees. Palafrugell was pillaged by Philip IV's troops and the Catalans were obliged to give shelter to the soldiers. In 1639, Salses was occupied by the French. In 1640 Catalan reapers revolted against the high cost of housing the Spanish soldiers and their misdemeanours (Elliott, 1963, 2018; Nadal-Farreras, 1983; Salrach & Duran, 1982; Serra, 1991, 2015). The viceroy was assassinated. The emissaries of the Diputació del General made a pact with Richelieu to proclaim a republic under the protection of the King of France. According to Serra, the models of the Catalans were Genoa and the Dutch Republic (Serra, 2015). The Catalan Republic was short-lived and the Generalitat, later, offered the crown to Louis XIII, which was proclaimed Count of Barcelona. Meanwhile the rebellion of Catalonia spread to Portugal.

Portugal achieved independence with the support of England and France. The latter, however, after a bloody war in Catalonia which lasted during 1640–1652, ended up reaching an agreement with Castile. In the 1659 Treaty of the Pyrenees Louis XIV, who had abandoned the Catalans, annexed the county of Roussillon and the rest of the adjacent territories. Catalonia lost its second most populated city, Perpignan, and a large part of the deposits of Pyrenean iron ore which fed its forges to obtain the metal.

8.10 Atlantic Exchange as a New Development Opportunity

The conflicts between Castile and France continued intermittently during the reign of Charles II (1665–1700). However, unlike what happened after the civil war in the fifteenth century, Catalonia demonstrated notable resilience in the last section of the seventeenth century. This time the reorientation of trade towards the Atlantic favoured the transformation of the Catalan development model and prepared its industrial renaissance (Camprubí, 2021; Catalan, 2019; Dantí, 2018, 2021; Fontana, 1955, 2014; Marfany, 2012; Nadal, 1992a; Torras, 1981, 2018, 2021; Valls, 2004; Vilar, 1962).

During the seventeenth century, the Netherlands and England became major maritime commercial powers, with a thalassocratic vocation. Their repeated ocean trips in search of spices, calicoes and other exotic products stimulated demand for eau-de-vie, which was added to the water to prevent it from becoming rotten during the long periods of navigation. Traditionally, this spirit was obtained on the Atlantic maritime coast of

France. However, Louis XIV's confrontations with his neighbours led the Dutch and British traders to seek alternative supplies further south.

Catalonia and, to a lesser extent, the Kingdom of Valencia, began to supply eau-de-vie to Holland and England. Distilling eau-de-vie was free in the Crown of Aragon, while it was regulated in Castile. This, together with the lower rainfall than in Atlantic Europe, led to the cultivation of vines close to the Mediterranean coast and the appearance of small distilleries to transform wine into eau-de-vie, the so-called *fassines*. The epicentre of the process was the Catalan town of Reus, just a few kilometres from Salou, where the barrels of distilled liquor were embarked for the Netherlands, the United Kingdom and other countries of Atlantic Europe (Fontana, 1955; Torras, 1984, 2021; Valls, 2004; Vilar, 1962). In exchange, the Catalans imported cod, cereals and the so-called new draperies, lighter and cheaper than those traditionally produced in the Mediterranean. This forced the woollen textile industry of Barcelona to continue to restructure, favouring the transfer of production phases to mid-mountain areas of inland Catalonia (Marfany, 2012; Torras, 1981, 2018). There, as underlined by Torras, the putting-out system of drapery work had a lower opportunity cost (Torras, 1981, 2018).

The Atlantic's high demand for eau-de-vie favoured increasing income growth for the coastal towns of the Catalan south, thanks to the mutual advantage generated by the trade. A new model of development began to be set up, radically transforming the Iberian Mediterranean regions. Despite the oscillations in the process, analyzed in Chapter 5 by Francesc Valls and Àlex Sánchez, Catalonia's new pattern of development lasted until the end of the eighteenth century.

Pierre Vilar and Josep Fontana were pioneers in underlining the importance of the change experienced by Catalonia in the last third of the seventeenth century (Fontana, 1955; Vilar, 1962). Fontana demonstrated that the importations from the north of Europe in the port of Barcelona went from a total of just 9% in 1665 to 29% in 1696 and, on the contrary, those of the Mediterranean countries from outside the Iberian Peninsula declined from 45% to just 18% between the same dates. Barcelona's trade with America also gained strength, going from just 6% of Barcelona's imports in 1665 to a notable 21% in 1696. Imports of sugar stood out among the colonial products.

The new model of development based on the exchange between Catalonia and the Atlantic, which could already be glimpsed in the late seventeenth century, was the centre of research interest of the also unfortunate Francesc Valls, who presents one of his last studies here. Following in the footsteps of the previous authors and of other masters such as Jaume Torras, Valls showed that, from the end of the seventeenth century and for the majority of the 18th, a growing number of Catalan territories specialized in viticulture and thus participated in the improvement in revenues favoured by Atlantic trade (Fontana, 1988; Torras, 1984, 2021; Valls, 2004; Vilar, 1962). The growing exports also favoured demand for cereals, wine, olive oil, woollens, printed calicoes, paper, leather or iron in inland Catalonia and established an expansion such as the one that Adam Smith had in mind, based on specialization in accordance with diversity and comparative advantage.

The comparison of Barcelona's position in the 1600 and 1700 rankings, reproduced in Table 8.3, confirms the analysis of the above authors. Despite the disaster of the Reapers' War and the fact that the Treaty of the Pyrenees amputated North Catalonia, Barcelona demonstrated notable resilience in the seventeenth century with expanding industries such as distilleries, ceramics or books-printing (Camprubí, 2021; Dantí, 2018, 2021; García Espuche, 2005; García-Osés, 2018; Nadal, 1992a; Vilar, 1962). It relatively improved unlike what happened with Genoa, Florence and Valencia. The former leaders of the Commercial Revolution in the Mediterranean lost business due to Dutch and British control of the Atlantic spice trade routes (Cipolla, 1970; Felloni, 1970; Malanima, 2010, 2018). Valencia, as we have seen, suffered particularly from the economic collapse arising from the expulsion of the moriscos and, in 1693, recorded another uprising of the brotherhoods, during which the peasants again revolted against their harsh living conditions and heavy feudal charges (Ardit, 1987, 2004; Casey, 1979, 2005; Duran, 1982; Salrach & Duran, 1982).

Charles II died in 1700 without any direct descendants. He bequeathed the crown to Philip V of Bourbon, Louis XIV's grandson. Austria, England, the Netherlands, Portugal and Savoy did not accept the decision and declared war on Castile, at the time aligned with France. Austria's allies supported the pretender Archduke Charles of Habsburg. The kingdoms of Aragon were not initially involved in the contest. However, Philip V banned trade with England and Holland, which had been important commercial partners of the Catalans for already 30 years. Consequently, Catalonia entered the war in support of Charles of Austria starting from 1705. The Archduke disembarked in Altea, where it was proclaimed King by the Valencians, and, later, in Barcelona, where swore allegiance to the Catalan constitutions. The rest of the Crown of Aragon also ended up mobilizing on the side of the Habsburg candidate (Nadal-Farreras, 1983; Salrach & Duran, 1982; Sobrequés, 2007).

Despite the fact that initially the evolution of the war was in favour of the Archduke's supporters, in 1707 the Valencians were defeated in Almansa. Valencian towns such as Xàtiva were set on fire by the occupiers. The main powers considered the conflict to have ended with the 1713 Peace of Utrecht, which involved Castile ceding Gibraltar and Menorca to Great Britain, the strongholds of the north of Flanders to the Dutch Republic and Nice and Sicily to Savoy. Shortly afterwards, in the Treaties of Rastatt and Baden, Austria obtained the majority of Flanders, Luxembourg, Naples, Milan and Sardinia. Abandoned by the allies, the inhabitants of Catalonia and the Balearics resisted until 1714 and 1715, respectively (Albareda & Esculies, 2013; Sobrequés, 2007).

The Bourbon repression was very intense. The Crown of Aragon was dissolved and all the kingdoms lost their Courts and constitutions. Castilian was imposed as the official language of the Catalan Countries. Part of Barcelona was taken to build a military fortress. Its university was closed, as was that of almost all Catalan cities. A new direct tax, the *cadastre*, was also imposed on Catalonia but, despite its punitive nature, it had the advantage of taxing land ownership in particular. The *talla* tax was imposed in Mallorca, and the equivalent in Valencia. However, in this aspect Bourbon absolutism was very incomplete. Direct taxation was only introduced in the former territories of the Crown of Aragon. On the other hand, the attempts to introduce the cadastre in Castile failed throughout the rest of the eighteenth century, due to the opposition of the noble big landowners, who traditionally controlled the kingdom (Albareda & Escullies 2013; Ardit et al., 1980; Ferrer & Albareda, 1995).

In Chapter 6, Sánchez and Valls identify the period of war from 1706 to 1715 as the most intense and prolonged episode of crisis in Catalonia in the eighteenth century. However, despite the undeniable harshness of the repression which followed defeat, the resilience of this Mediterranean region after the War of Spanish Succession was even greater than that analyzed in the period subsequent to the Treaty of the Pyrenees.

The model of development based on the expansion of Catalan exchange with the Atlantic regained strength throughout the eighteenth century. This favoured huge economic prosperity, despite political defeat. Eau-de-vie exports recorded a very expansive path until the 1790s. The export revenues were spent on locally produced goods, favouring an intense process of productive specialization in inland Catalonia:cereals on the plains of the west (around Lleida), drapery in the hills of the centre-north (from Igualada to Berga and Pugicerdà), vines and spirits in the south-east (with Reus as epicentre), printed calicoes and cotton manufactures in Barcelona, Reus, Vic, Olot, and Manresa, and other manufactured goods in specialized districts such as Les Garrigues and Tortosa (olive oil), Capellades and La Riba (paper), Ripoll (iron), Igualada and Vic (leather), Sant Feliu de Guíxols and Arenys (ships) and Empordà (cork). Catalan manufactured goods were moreover stimulated by the abolition of customs duties with the former Crown of Castile, where woollens, calicoes and paper began to be sold on a mass scale. Finally, it should be remarked that the transformation of cotton and linen in which Barcelona became specialized was, paradoxically, favoured by the mercantilist policy of Philip V, who banned the importation of printed calicoes and other fabrics in 1718 and 1728 (Carreras, 2019; Catalan, 2019; Delgado, 1992, 1995; Ferrer, 1987, 2008, 2021; Fontana, 1988; Grau & López, 1974; Gutiérrez, 1999; Marfany, 2012; Pascual et al., 2022; Sánchez, 1989, 2000, 2012, 2013; Solà, 2004; Thomson, 1993; Torras, 1981, 1984, 2018, 2021; Valls, 2004; Vilar, 1962).

In the 1730s, there were already records of the development of the manual cotton fabric printing industry in Barcelona (Grau & López, 1974; Sánchez, 1989). Subsequently, the fibre began to be woven, with cotton thread imported through Malta. Thanks to Àlex Sánchez, we know that in 1768 the former capital of the county had about 30 calicoes factories, which operated with over 1000 looms and employed 4000 people (Sánchez, 1989, 2000, 2012, 2013).

The monopoly of trade with America, which had benefited Seville with the Habsburgs, and Cadiz with the first Bourbons, gradually became more flexible in the reign of Charles III, who held the crown of Spain between 1759 and 1788. In 1765, he authorized direct trade of nine peninsular ports with five American islands. Barcelona was one of these ports and this favoured imports of Caribbean sugar and exports of linen textiles printed in the city's factories (imported raw from Silesia) and of local calicoes. In 1770, Carles III eliminated the exemption for the importing of thread from Malta and this encouraged the Barcelona manufacturers to undertake autochthonous spinning. Increasing quantities of raw American cotton, which came from the Antilles, began to be processed in Barcelona. In 1778, this policy was extended, authorizing direct trade of 13 peninsular ports with 22 on the American continent.

Catalonia experienced formidable growth thanks to the development model of the 1700s, based on the expansion of exchange which was both external (towards Atlantic Europe, Spain and America) and internal (favoured by progressive regional specialization linked to Mediterranean diversity). In 1793, eau-de-vie, wine and pure agricultural products such as hazelnuts continued to be exported to north Europe. Fabrics, cotton calicoes, paper and iron were sold to Spain. Printed linen, spirits, olive oil and paper went to America. All these goods, derived from diversity and comparative advantage, were traded in the shops of the main regional capitals of the Principality (Catalan, 2019; Delgado, 1992, 1995; Ferrer, 1987, 2008, 2021; Fontana, 1988; Gutiérrez, 1999; Marfany, 2012; Pollard, 1981; Sánchez, 1989, 2000, 2012, 2013; Solà, 2004; Thomson, 1993; Torras, 1981, 1984, 2018, 2021; Valls, 2004; Vilar, 1962).

Thanks to the work of Sánchez and Solà we know that, from the 1780s, the first spinning jennies began to be imported to Catalonia, with dozens of spindles for spinning cotton (Sánchez, 1989, 2000, 2012, 2013; Solà, 2004). Martínez Galarraga and Prat, following Bob Allen's interpretation about the training force of the British Industrial, argued that relatively high real wages fostered Catalan mechanization (Allen, 2019; Martinez Galarraga & Prat, 2016).

From 1788 to 1820, a period in which slave trafficking was legal, Fradera documented the active presence of Catalan merchants in the slave trade in the Antilles (Fradera, 1987). The triangular business was strengthened with the exporting of manufactured goods and slaves to America, and the importing of sugar and raw cotton to Catalonia.

In 1787, Catalonia stood out as the leading industrial region of Bourbon Spain, with over 26,000 workers employed in manufacturing activity. It was followed by Andalusia which, despite having enjoyed the commercial monopoly of Seville and Cadiz, only had 15,000 people employed in industrial tasks. Bourbon Spain's third biggest industrial region was Valencia, with around 8000 workers in manufacturing activities (Fontana, 1988; Sánchez, 2012; Vilar, 1962).

As a result of the change of development model which began at the end of the last third of the 1600s, by 1800 Barcelona stood out as one of the top 10 Mediterranean cities in our ranking. Between 1700 and 1800, it went from 15 to 9th position in the cities of our sample, ordered in accordance with their population (Compare Tables 8.3 and 8.4).

Table 8.4 Population ranking of important Mediterranean cities, 1800 and 1850. Thousands of inhabitants

		1800			*1850*
1	CONSTANTINOPLE	570	1	CONSTANTINOPLE	785
2	NAPLES	430	2	NAPLES	409
3	CAIRO	211	3	CAIRO	267
4	ROME	153	**4**	**BARCELONA**	**220**
5	PALERMO	139	5	MILAN	209
6	VENICE	138	6	MARSEILLE	195
7	MILAN	135	7	ROME	175
8	MARSEILLE	101	8	PALERMO	168
9	**BARCELONA**	**100**	9	GENOA	128
10	GENOA	90	10	VENICE	127
11	FLORENCE	81	11	FLORENCE	94
12	**VALENCIA**	**80**	12	MALAGA	93
13	THESSALONIKI	70	**13**	**VALENCIA**	**87**
14	GRANADA	70	14	THESSALONIKI	70
15	VERONA	51	15	GRANADA	62
16	MALAGA	49	16	VERONA	51
17	CARCASSONNE	35	17	PADUA	47
18	PADUA	33	18	MONTPELLIER	45
19	MONTPELLIER	33	19	CARCASSONNE	45
20	**MALLORCA**	**29**	**20**	**MALLORCA**	**40**
21	MANTUA	25	21	PISA	34
22	PISA	23	22	ATHENS	30
23	ATHENS	12	23	MANTUA	30
24	ALMERIA	7	24	ALMERIA	23
25	NARBONNE	9	25	NARBONNE	13

The three bold cities are Barcelona, Valencia and Ciutat de Mallorca, which are the main towns of the Catalan-speaking countries, the preferential object of the book
Source Compiled by author with Bairoch et al. (1988) and others

We did not find any increase in the Mediterranean between 1700 and 1800 comparable to that of Barcelona. Genoa improved a little and was, therefore, the most similar to Barcelona among the Italian cities which were leaders of the Commercial Revolution. On the contrary, Venice and Florence declined, remaining on the margin of progress in manufacturing (Felice, 2015; Felloni, 1977; Malanima, 2010).

Still in Italy, Naples also increased, becoming the second most populated city in the Mediterranean basin by 1800. However, its rise was not so much the result of a new development model based on exchange or manufacturing production as the consequence of having recovered its status as a state capital. On becoming the seat of the Bourbon court of the Kingdom of the Two Sicilies, it strengthened its role as an important centre for the consumption of the surpluses generated in its big agricultural hinterland. On the contrary, Palermo, now subordinate to the capital of continental Italy, declined.

The big Islamic metropolises also lost importance: Constantinople in absolute terms, despite remaining in first position on the ranking, and Cairo, which went from second to third place in the most populated cities. The limits of economic development in Islamic countries began to become significant during the eighteenth century. The Ottoman Empire reached its maximum territorial size in the sixteenth-seventeenth centuries, but its decadence began when the military annexation machinery weakened.

Turkish society was based on four strata: soldiers, bureaucrats, men of religion and peasants (Lewis, 1970). As time went, the Jenissars lost its character of elite corps, derived from the feature of being former Christians separated from their original families (Schevil, 1991). Top bureaucracy was linked too much to the Harem, and the sale of public offices became usual and corrupt (Schevil, 1991). Islam's polygamy tended to fragment and increase the tendency to fight for the inheritance of descendants (Issawi, 1995; Maddison, 2007). Women extreme submission led to very low levels of literacy (Issawi, 1982, 1995). A large deal of the *ulemas* tended to oppose any innovation which seemed to depart too much of the teachings of Al Koran (Schevill, 1991). On the other hand, trade and manufacturing were frowned upon and often left in the hands of the non-Islamic minorities, such as Greeks, Jews, Armenians or Syrian Christians (Issawi, 1982, 1995).

Moreover, the displacement of the major trading routes towards the Atlantic moreover weakened the role as intermediaries of the merchants who transported goods across the Red Sea, the interior of Asia and north Africa. The plague had also become endemic in the region (Maddison, 2007). Islam paid a high price for forbidding its merchants from establishing their residence in the land of the infidels. They not only sacrificed the improvements in well-being associated with exchange, but also became increasingly isolated from technical and scientific innovations, which spread quickly around modern Europe. In Constantinople, the use of the printing press to reproduce Arabic scripts was only authorized in 1727 (Issawi, 1982, 1995). Islamic Africa had to wait another century, until 1820 when, under Mohammed Ali's rupturist regime and in a situation which favoured industrialization, it set up its first printing press for books (Batou, 1991; Landes, 1969, 1998; Maddison, 2007).

To return to the Catalan Countries, eighteenth-century Mallorca followed a very stable path, based on agricultural growth and some wine and spirit exports when trade with America was liberalized (Manera, 1986). According to Ardit, Balcells and Sales, neighbouring Menorca made notable progress during the period of British rule. Its population doubled as a result of specialization in livestock and viticulture, which were promoted by the English, and thanks to the security of foreign trade associated with the protection of the British Navy (Ardit et al., 1980; Casasnovas, 2006).

Valencia, despite experiencing notable agricultural growth in the eighteenth century, did not achieve industrial growth comparable with Catalonia, and went down in the ranking of Mediterranean cities. However, some of the industrial districts of Valencia recorded remarkable progress: according to Professor Torró's estimation, production of fabrics in Alcoi increased in a sustained manner throughout the 1700s (Torró, 2020).

8.11 The Challenge of the First Industrial Revolution

Although between 1716 and 1792, Catalonia successfully transformed its development model and intensified the exchange with the Atlantic, the subsequent multitude of crises required a new reorientation of the long-term growth pattern. The War of the Convention (1793–1795), the Anglo-Spanish War (1804–1809) and the Napoleonic occupation (1804–1814) dismantled the foreign trade model. The independence process of the colonies of continental America (1816–1825) and the ban on trade with them was a final, irreversible blow to the previous exchange and development model (Delgado, 1992; Fontana, 1971, 1988; Fradera, 1987; Sánchez, 2000, 2012, 2013; Solà, 2004; Valls, 2004).

The Spanish monarchy, which had the good fortune to see how the arrival of American silver rose again in the eighteenth century, had extraordinary war-related expenses and declining resources with the change of century. Ferdinand VII, Charles III's absolutist grandson, reigned in Spain after the constitutional experiences of the Napoleonic period. He repudiated the debt contracted by the Courts of Cadiz in

1814 and reversed the liberal reforms. However, none of the attempts to restructure the debt and the finances undertaken by his ministers in 1817, 1823, 1825 and 1828 was able to prevent what Professor Fontana rightly called the bankruptcy of the absolute monarchy (Comín, 1988, 2013; Fontana, 1971, 1988). The loss of the colonies in continental America brought the flow of American silver to a standstill and required a complete change of direction.

In the short intervals of enlightened and constitutional governments, the Spanish liberals endeavoured to reduce the debt, establishing the confiscation of mortmain land, usually held by ecclesiastic institutions. Those opposed to these reforms rose up against Isabella II, who Ferdinand designated as his heiress on his death in 1833. The absolutist forces supported Ferdinand's brother, Charles, and a civil war broke out which, despite its duration (1833–1840), helped to consolidate the liberal regime in Spain first through the regent mother, Maria Cristina, and then the queen herself, starting from 1843.

As shown by Sánchez and Valls in Chapter 5, the worst crisis of this long period of depression was the time of the Napoleonic invasion. The Catalan textile industry suffered in particular due to the arrival of French and British fabrics and printed calicoes. However, eau-de-vie exports had been suffering since the resumption of the wars with England. Subsequently, the loss of the American colonies represented the collapse of the market for printed linen, spirits and paper. The Catalan Countries recorded a tremendous fall in production and amazing deflation. The end of the arrival of silver led to even more deflation (Catalan & Sánchez, 2013; Delgado, 1992; Fontana, 1971, 1988; Marfany, 2012; Nadal, 1975, 1992b; Pascual, 1990; Sánchez, 1989, 2000, 2013; Thomson, 1993; Valls, 2004).

In such a depressive context, the response of Catalan industry was exceptionally resilient (Carreras & Yañez, 1992; Nadal, 1975, 1985, 1992b; Nadal et al., 2003; Pascual, 1990; Pla, 2014; Sánchez, 1989, 2000, 2013; Solà, 2004). Despite the brutal crisis, the Catalan version of spinning jennies, called *bergadana*, spread. By 1800, cities such as Barcelona, Reus, Vic and Olot each had over 10,000 manual spindles installed. The first hydraulic waterframes were installed in Manresa in 1802. Six years later, Barcelona and Manresa had incorporated the first mule-jennies, driven by animal or hydraulic force, with over 4000 spinning spindles each.

Investment contracted during the period from 1805 to 1829, but the previous maximums almost doubled in the 1830s. Despite the Carlist uprising in the mountains, in 1833 Barcelona opened the first factory with a steam machine. Unfortunately, it was not saved from Luddite flames in the 1835 revolutionary uprising.

The most radical Barcelona liberals of the 1835 revolt formed the *Junta Superior Governativa del Principat de Catalunya*. This organization decided to mint its own coins, create a provisional study with the records of the confiscated convents and demand the reopening of the University of Barcelona, closed for more than a century. It also proposed the restoration of the Crown of Aragon to the corresponding junta of Valencia. The sending of troops headed by General Espoz y Mina led to the dissolution of the Barcelona Junta, but the episode shows that a century after the War of Succession, the memory of the institutions dissolved by Philip V was still very much alive among Catalan liberals (Ardit et al., 1980; Sobrequés, 2007).

Despite the political reversal, the economic transformation continued in the subsequent decades, especially thanks to the cotton sector. Steam machines proliferated. Continuous machines began to spread in the 1840s and self-acting machines from the 1850s. Manual looms were also replaced with mechanical looms in these two decades. *Perrotines* and stamping cylinders were as well adopted to print the cloths. In short, the First Industrial Revolution spread in Catalonia. These innovations allowed the price of printed calicoes to go from 100 in 1831–1835 to 42 in 1856–1860 (Carreras, 1985, 1990a, 2019; Carreras & Yánez, 1992; Catalan, 2019; Nadal, 1975, 1985, 1992b; Nadal et al., 2003, 2012; Pascual, 1990; Pla, 2014; Prat, 2003; Solà, 2004; Vicens, 1958b).

In a framework of high tariff protection, on this occasion the resilience of the Catalan economy looked towards conquering the Spanish market. Thanks to Lemeunier and Pérez Picazo, we know that, during 1814–1820, only 25% of the textiles consumed in the Castilian region of Murcia were of Catalan origin, the remainder being English (26%), French (25%) and from the rest of Spain (24%). However, in 1840–1850, the importance of Catalan textiles in the shops of Murcia was already 69%, while those of all other origins had declined (Pérez Picazo & Lemeunier, 1984).

The impact of the First Industrial Revolution can again be seen in Barcelona's rise among the big cities of the Mediterranean between 1800 and 1850 (Table 8.4). Over this period, it became bigger than Palermo, Rome, Milan, Venice and Marseille, being positioned for the first time among the four top cities of the basin. It should moreover be noted that, during this period, in Italy only Milan and Genoa improved, vertices of the so-called Italian *Triangolo Industriale* (Cafagna, 1989; Doria, 1998; Felice, 2015; Fenoaltea, 2011; Zamagni, 1993). Marseille also made substantial progress (Raveux, 1998). Barcelona, Genoa and Marseille were among the few cities of the basin which shared the honour of having been leaders of both the Late Mediaeval Commercial Revolution and the First Industrial Revolution of the 1800s. Valencia and Mallorca, which experienced a nineteenth-century development model more based on agriculture in this period, went down on the ranking (Manera, 1986, 2002; Millan, 1990; Palafox, 1987, 2001).

8.12 Nations Versus Empires, Empires Versus Nations

Together with the formidable transition in Catalonia's economic development model in the first half of the nineteenth century, we can also talk about political resilience in the Mediterranean. During the last decades of the previous century and the first decades of the 19th, the Greek merchants, operating at the heart of the Ottoman Empire, promoted maritime trade between the east and the west. Their clear commercial orientation helped them to introduce textiles and other European manufactured goods and to export raw materials from the empire. The accumulation of profit was accompanied by the spread of Greek nationalism and the assertion of the orthodox Christianism, protected by Moscow. After the fall of Napoleon, the British obtained sovereignty over some Ionian Islands. In 1821, a Greek army invaded Moldavia and the Peloponnese revolted against the Ottomans. England, Russia and France provided political and military support for the re-creation of the independent Greek state, which approved its first constitution in 1822. Athens replaced Nafplio as the capital of the new country. In 1864, England ceded its islands and two years later Crete drove out the Ottomans. Four centuries after the fall of Constantinople and despite Turkish efforts to prevent it, Greece became consolidated as one more state within Mediterranean political diversity (Beaton, 2021; Clogg, 1992; Gallant, 2001; Mazower, 2021).

Italians also felt the need to drive out the foreign lineages and powers that had occupied them for centuries. From 1848 to 1849, the Kingdom of Piedmont attacked Austria which, in addition to Lombardy, had controlled Venice since the Congress of Vienna. The first attempt was unsuccessful. On the second occasion, it had the support of France under Napoleon III and the 1859 war ended with the conquest of Lombardy. Garibaldi's redshirts disembarked in Sicily in 1860, took Palermo, and then attacked the continent. They drove out the Bourbons and, in 1861, proclaimed the Kingdom of Italy, only the Papal States and Austrian Venice remaining outside. The latter was incorporated in 1866 after another war with the Habsburgs. The annexation of most of the remaining Papal States was agreed in the 1870 treaty.

The same powers which to the north of the basin supported the nations who were fighting against the empires which controlled the Mediterranean began to show their imperialist ambitions in the south. They took advantage of the fact that Islam was increasingly behind technologically due to its lack of presence in the western ports and markets. In particular, the Ottoman empire, which had been a remarkable exporter of cotton yarn, carpets and other textile goods, revealed itself unable to compete with the combined effect of the technologies of the industrial revolution and its declining size. It experienced a dramatic deindustrialization process throughout the nineteenth century (Issawi, 1981, 1982, 1995; Keyder, 1991; Pamuk, 1987, 2006; Pamuk & Williamson, 2010).

Napoleon had already tried to occupy Egypt from 1789 to 1805. France attacked again, invading Algeria from 1830 and establishing a colonial regime, based on expropriation of the land from the Ottomans and the establishment of French cultivators (Marseille, 1984; McDougall, 2017). The United Kingdom forced a tariff agreement with Mohamed Ali's independent Egypt in 1838, which implied low tariff duties for the African country (Batou, 1991; Issawi, 1981, 1982; Landes, 1958, 1998; Maddison, 2007). It also intervened militarily in Lebanon in 1840 to curb Egyptian expansion. During the process of negotiation of the 1878 Treaty of Berlin, the United Kingdom obtained Cyprus from the Ottomans.

Some of the new states of the Mediterranean were subject to important insolvencies in the 1800s. Greece repeatedly suspended payments of its foreign debt: in 1826, 1843, 1860 and 1893 (Clogg, 1992; Reinhart & Rogoff, 2009; Schönhärl, 2021). Tunisia went bankrupt in 1867, as did Egypt in 1875 (Brown, 2008; Issawi, 1981, 1982; Landes, 1958, 1998). In this they were not very different from the former Mediterranean empires, since liberal Spain was insolvent in 1834, 1851, 1867, 1872 and 1882, while the Ottoman Empire went bankrupt in 1876 (Comín, 1988, 2013; Pamuk, 1987; Reinhart & Rogoff, 2009; Tunçer, 2014).

Egypt's bankruptcy led Isma'il Pasha to sell his stake of the Suez Canal to Britain in 1875. Since then, both France and Britain were the main shareholders of the company. Both countries intervened in the Egyptian government. Since 1882, and after bombing Alexandria, Great Britain invaded Egypt and took control of the whole country.

By its part, France established the protectorate of Tunisia in 1881. The occupation of the African Mediterranean was to be complete with the distribution of Morocco between France (1905) and Spain (1909) and the annexation of Libya by Italy in 1911. In short, the powers of the north aimed to limit the diversity of the Mediterranean, as the Ottoman Empire had done for centuries (Batou, 1991; Issawi, 1981, 1982; Landes, 1958, 1998; Maddison, 2007; Marseille, 1984; Pamuk, 1987).

In the Balkans, the Ottoman and Austrian empires tried to resist the pressure of their nationalities to recover full sovereignty. Nevertheless, Montenegro succeeded in been recognized as an independent nation-state after the Congress of Berlin in 1878 (though Britain got the control of Cyprus). Greece obtained Thessalia in 1881. As a result of the two Balkan Wars during 1912–1913, Albania was recognized as Principality and Greece recovered Crete and Macedonia. In the latter region, which had Thelassoniki as its main port, an incipient process of industrial spurt based on woollen fabrics had been taking place during the late decades of the nineteenth century within the Ottoman empire (Lapavitsas & Cakiroglu, 2019). Although independent Greece did not reach outstanding levels of industrialization, its long-term merchant tradition helped to transform the country into a Mediterranean leader in shipping (Harlaftis, 2019).

8.13 The Financial Instability of Nineteenth-Century Capitalism

Returning to Catalonia, in the first half of the nineteenth century the country also recorded notable expansion of the naval construction industry, while navigation was still with sails and wooden vessels. On the contrary, due to the lack of coal, it was not able to develop a modern naval construction or steel industry during the second half of the 1800s. As coal was scarce and had a low calorific value, during the second half of the century Catalan manufacturing specialized in less energy-intensive activities, such as the food industries, leather transformation, woollen textiles, the publishing industry and some branches of chemistry. Its importance in the creation of the railway network, inaugurated in the peninsula with the line from Barcelona to Mataró in 1848, moreover favoured the appearance of some railway machinery and equipment constructors (Carreras, 1990a; Carreras & Tafunell, 2021; Catalan, 2019; Maluquer de Motes, 1994; Nadal, 1975, 1985, 1992b; Nadal et al., 2012; Pascual, 1990, 1999, 2015; Pascual et al., 2022; Sudrià, 1987; Vicens, 1958b).

It was precisely the exorbitant expectations created by the railway which gave rise to an intense crisis in 1866, which Professor Pere Pascual analyzes in Chapter 6 of this volume. Another, longer-lasting, crisis was the one that arose from the bursting of the bubble of the so-called gold rush in 1882. This was the result of the excessive printing of notes, after the concession of the issuing monopoly to the Banco de España from March 1874 (Carreras & Tafunell, 2021; Catalan & Sánchez, 2013; Pascual, 1990, 1999, 2015; Prados de la Escosura, 2003, 2017).

Spain was experiencing the extremely short First Republic (February 1873–December 1874), which, exceptionally, had two out of four Catalan presidents: Estanilao Figueras and Francesc Pi i Margall. They had to confront another Carlist uprising, the proclamation of the Catalan State by their fellows in Barcelona in March 1873 and a federal insurrectionary outbreak in other peninsular industrial cities, such as Alcoi or Cartagena. The Banco de España's issuing monopoly was granted by General Serrano's government, which arose from the attack on congress by General Pavia and the Civil Guard. For their part, and in an attempt to win over the Catalans, the Carlists proclaimed the reestablishment of the Diputació del General in October 1874. Finally, in December, General Arsenio Martínez Campos rose up in favour of the Bourbon Restoration in the figure of Isabella's son, Alfonso XII.

There was no going back on the Banco de España's issuing monopoly. The laxity in granting credit to the government led first to a period of easy money and the appearance of new banks. One of the results of too much issuing of paper money is that Spain could not join the gold standard (Roldan, 2017). In this, the Spanish experience was not very different to the Italian, Greek and other Balkanic neighbours (Catalan et al., 2001; Dritsas, 1999; Morys, 2016; Roldan, 2022; Tattara, 2003).

In the case of Catalonia, the bubble was moreover fed by the exceptional exports of wine to France, while the world's leading consumer suffered from the phylloxera plague. Wine exports to France from Valencia and Mallorca were also exceptionally good (Colomé et al., 2022;

Manera & Parejo, 2012; Palafox, 1987, 2001; Pan Montojo, 1994; Pascual, 1990).

This insect, a parasite of the vine, did not, however, stop at the Pyrenees. Barcelona, Lleida, Valencia and Tarragona were the four provinces of Spain with the largest surface area of cultivated vineyards. The spread of the epidemic by this insect led to the collapse of wine production. The crisis arising from the mortality of the vines was added to the contractive impact of the financial bubble bursting. The ruin of the cultivators accentuated emigration to the industrial centres (Colomé, 2012; Colomé et al., 2022; Garrabou, 1975; Garrabou et al., 1992; Manera & Parejo, 2012; Palafox, 1987, 2001; Pan Montojo, 1994; Catalan & Sánchez, 2013).

In Valencia and the areas where irrigation was possible, the collapse of the wine industry led to the planting of orange trees (Abad, 1984; Palafox, 1987, 2001). Growth of this export crop improved peasant income from the end of the nineteenth century and favoured the appearance of certain externalities in labour-intensive industries such as footwear, wood processing, paper, ceramics and mechanical construction workshops (Bernabé, 1976; Gomis, 1990; Lluch, 1976; Martínez Galárraga, 2009; Millan, 1990; Miranda, 1992; Nadal, 1987, 1994). Alcoi experienced hard times to compete with agglomeration economies in Sabadell and Terrassa's woollen industries and Capellades and Basque paper producers but still showed a significant resilience as industrial district in both specialities (Aracil & Garcia Bonafé, 1974; Benaul, 1994; Camps, 1995; Cuevas, 2001; Cuevas & Torró, 2002; Gutiérrez, 1994, 2011).

The Balearic Islands followed a development pattern not very different from the Valencian one, but at a lower scale. It also specialized in food processing and in highly intensive manufacturing industries such as footwear (Casasnovas, 2006; Manera, 2002; Manera & Molina, 2022; Manera & Parejo, 2012). As a whole, the Catalan Countries developed a constellation of industrial districts in labor-intensive industries which had many features in common with Italian and French industrial districts (Bernabé, 1976; Boix & Galetto, 2008; Catalan & Ramon-Muñoz, 2013; Cuevas & Torró, 2002; Gutiérrez, 1994, 1999, 2011; Le Bot & Perrin, 2011; Llonch, 2007, 2011; Lluch, 1976; Manera, 2002; Manera & Molina, 2022; Millan, 1990; Miranda, 1992, 2011; Molina, 2003; Molina, 2008; Nadal, 1987, 1994; Ramon-Muñoz, 2000, 2011, 2020).

8.14 Acceleration of Development During the Second Industrial Revolution

The Second Industrial Revolution departed in Catalonia (and Spain) with the illumination of the Barcelona Rambla in 1875 by Francesc Dalmau. The first automobile patented and built in the peninsula was by the Barcelona citizen Francesc Bonet in 1889. The pioneering initiatives of Dalmau, Xifrà and Muntadas in the fields of electrification and the production of motors and lightbulbs attracted the attention of big international groups such as Pearson, Siemens and Philips, which set up in Catalonia even before the Great War. As regards the automobile, local initiatives such as Hispano-Suiza and Elizalde ended up attracting the Ford assembly plant to Barcelona in 1923 (a previous attempt in Cadiz having failed). Other local firms producing all kind of metallic products rapidly earned size: La Maquinista (engines), Girona (wagons), Torras (steel), Roca (radiators), Serra (textile machinery) or Riviere (wire). The early years of the twentieth century also saw Catalan production of sulphuric acid and superphosphates (Cros), caustic soda (Electroquímica de Flix), anilines (Fabricación Nacional de Colorantes) and calcium carbide (Fabricación Española de Carburos Metálicos) (Carreras, 1990a, 1990b, 2019; Catalan, 1995, 2013, 2019; Maluquer de Motes, 1994; Nadal, 2020; Nadal et al., 2012; Puig, 2003; Villar, 2022).

In around 1910, the Catalan Countries as a whole employed 28% of the active population in secondary activities (industry and construction), as can be seen in Table 8.5. The proportion was slightly lower than that of France (33%) and similar to that of Italy (27%). This indicator of the level of industrialization was much less significant in the rest of the Mediterranean economies, with available data, such as Greece (16%), Spain (15%) or Egypt (11%).

The success of the First Industrial Revolution and the drive of the Second favoured the appearance of autochthonous political parties in Catalonia, which demanded the granting of regional autonomy in the framework of the Spanish monarchy under Alfonso XIII. This monarch from the House of Bourbon replaced his mother, regent since Alfonso XII's death, and reigned between 1909 and 1931.

The long-awaited decentralization was introduced in 1914. The *Mancomunitat* of Catalonia (a Devolution institution which federated some services of the provinces of Barcelona, Tarragona, Girona and Lleida) operated successfully until 1925. The institution made a great

Table 8.5 Proportion of active population employed in the secondary sector (industry and construction) in Mediterranean countries (%)

	1910		*1930*		*1950*	
France	33	1911	33	1931	36	1954
Catalan Countries	28		46		42	
Italy	27	1911	31	1931	32	1951
Israel					32	1948
Spain	15		26		25	
Greece	16	1920	16	1928	19	1951
Egypt	11	1907	9	1927	12	1947
Turkey			8	1935	7	
Morocco					9	1952
Algeria					6	1948

Source Compiled by the author with Mitchell (2003) and (2007) and Spanish Population Censuses

effort to build roads, the telephone service, technical schools and libraries (Ardit et al., 1980; Balcells, 2014; Sobrequés, 2007; Termes, 1987). However, it was dissolved by General Miguel Primo de Rivera following a coup d'état in 1923. As occurred in the previous year in Italy with Mussolini, the leader of the coup had the king's support. A dictatorship was established which, in the Spanish case, was led by Primo de Rivera until 1930.

Despite again losing its own regional institutions, Catalonia continued to grow and diversify very quickly during the 1920s. The First World War ended with a (short) crisis, analyzed in Chapter 7. However, the conflict greatly favoured long-term factory interests. It boosted exports of cotton textiles, woollen fabrics, footwear and other manufactured products. It encouraged import substitution of equipment and chemical and pharmaceutical products. It also favoured the energy transition from the use of coal to hydroelectricity. Catalonia, which had a large potential deposit of energy in its mountains, especially the Pyrenees, accelerated its electrification. Finally, at the end of the conflict, the trade union offensive which began with the Barcelona Traction strike achieved the 48-hour working week. Consequently, real wages experienced a significant increase, recovering the purchasing power lost with wartime inflation (Carreras, 1990a, 1990b; Catalan, 1995, 2013, 2019; Diez Minguela et al., 2019; Maluquer de Motes, 1994; Nadal, 1985; Nadal et al., 2012; Sudrià, 1987).

For the above reasons, and despite the dictatorship, Catalan industry continued to grow and diversify acutely until the eve of the Spanish Civil War, which broke out in 1936. At that time Catalonia produced 86% of Spanish cotton textile output, 83% of wool and 87% of rayon. It was also responsible for 50% of Spanish leather production and 29% of paper. It likewise undertook 35% of metallurgical transformation, being the leader in the construction of automobiles, machinery, wire and electrical equipment. It moreover contributed 50% of consumer chemicals: paint, perfumery and pharmaceutical products. It likewise stood out in the production of flour, olive oil and the Catalan version of champagne (cava). Barcelona also shared leadership in the Spanish publishing industry with Madrid (Carreras 1990; Catalan, 2013; Catalan & Gil-Mugarza, 2014; Colomé et al., 2022; Gutiérrez, 1994; Nadal, 1985; Pascual et al., 2022; Puig, 2003; Ramon-Muñoz, 2011; Valls, 2011).

The Valencian and Balearic industries also experienced intense growth and structural transformation thanks to the fact that electrification favoured the competitivness of labour-intense manufacturing production. The 1920s were very good for Valencian exports of citrus fruit. This favoured the growth of its wood processing, paper and fertilizer industry. Southern districts such as Elx and Elda developed the footwear industry. Naval construction also progressed thanks to the Unión Naval de Levante (Catalan, 1995; Martínez Galárraga, 2009; Miranda, 1992; Nadal, 1987; Soler, 1984). In the Balearic Islands, the expansion of the food industry likewise occurred, together with the consolidation of footwear districts in Inca and Menorca (Casasnovas, 2006; Manera, 2002; Manera & Molina, 2022; Manera & Parejo, 2012; Molina, 2003).

Overall, as shown in Table 8.5, the Catalan Countries achieved an exceptional level of industrial development in 1930, with a formidable 46% of active workers devoted to secondary employment (industry and construction). The rate even exceeded that of France (33% in 1931), which can be understood if we bear in mind that the branches of specialization of Catalonia, Valencia and Mallorca were very labour-intensive. The rate of the Catalan Countries was far ahead of that of Italy (31% in 1931) and that of Spain (26%) which, although more slowly, had progressed in the early decades of the twentieth century. This was not the case in Greece (16% in 1928) and even less in the southern Mediterranean, specialized in supplying agricultural products after experiencing severe de-industrialitzation during the nineteenth century: we do not have data for all countries, but both Egypt and Turkey had figures below 10%

for industrial employment (Hansen, 1997; Issawi, 1981, 1982; Keyder, 1987; Pamuk, 2006; Pamuk & Williamson, 2010).

The Republic of Turkey had risen up from the ashes of the Ottoman Empire under the leadership of Mustafa Kemal (Göçek, 2011; Keyder, 1987). Along the way, there was one last stab at imperial xenophobia, on leading an episode of ethnic cleansing from 1915 to 1923 which overshadowed that of the Spanish monarchs in the early modern period: Armenian Genocide. We can interpret this holocaust as a new chapter of the empires against the diversity of the Mediterranean, involving around one and a half million deaths and another million deported.

However, overall, the Great War weakened the empires, leading to the emergence of about a decene of new nation-states in Europe. The old, sleeping colossus of the Mediterranean, Egypt, moreover retrieved its independence in 1922, freeing itself from British tutelage. The struggle between imperialism and diversity began to favour the latter.

8.15 The Worst Crisis of the Twentieth Century

In Spain, the republican parties won the municipal election in April 1931 in the main peninsular cities. In the morning of 14 April, the Basque town Eibar was the first to proclaim the Second Spanish Republic. During the morning the councillors elected in Valencia (led by PURA, Autonomist Republican Union Party) likewise proclaimed the Second Republic. In Barcelona, at the beginning of the afternoon, there was an initial attempt to follow along these lines by Lluís Companys, from ERC (Republican Left of Catalonia). Shortly afterwards Francesc Macià, the head of ERC, which was the winning force in the municipal election within the region, proclaimed the Catalan Republic with the desire to join a Confederation of Iberian Peoples (Ardit et al., 1980; Balcells, 2014; Sobrequés, 2007; Termes, 1987).

At eight o'clock at night, Alfonso XIII took the train to Cartagena, where he embarked for Marseille, while the Provisional Government of the Second Spanish Republic was formed in Madrid. Macià began a process of negotiation with the representatives of this new government, which chose Niceto Alcalá Zamora as its president. The negotiations gave rise to a pact, by means of which Macià backed down, exchanging the Catalan Republic for the Generalitat of Catalonia. This name evoked that of the mediaeval institution emanating from the Courts, which controlled the finances of the king for almost four centuries in the years between

1359 and 1714. The pact between the Second Spanish Republic and the Generalitat led to the approval of the 1932 Statute of Autonomy of Catalonia, which regulated the powers of the new regional autonomous government. The second statute of autonomy, that of Euskadi, was not approved until October 1936, when the Spanish military had already been revolting for four months. Meanwhile, Lluís Companys proclaimed the Catalan State within the Spanish Federal Republic and ended up being imprisoned in October 1934. He was not freed until the triumph of the Front of the Left and the Popular Front in February 1936. However, part of the Spanish army rose up against decentralization and the agricultural and military reforms that the governments of the Second Republic had begun to implement.

In Catalonia, where anarcho-syndicalism was predominant, the workers' committees took over the factories and attempted to collectivize them, giving rise to a bottom-up revolutionary process. The Generalitat, through regional Minister Josep Tarradellas, tried to redirect the process and approved a decree on collectivizations and workers' control, which gave rise to an experience of decentralized socialism during the first year of the war (Bricall, 1970, 1979; Catalan, 2012a, 2012b; Deu, 2020; De Madariaga, 2008; Termes, 1987).

When the military uprising broke out, almost all the territories of the Catalan Countries remained loyal to the Republic. The only exceptions were the islands of Mallorca and Ibiza. The former was used as an aeronautical base for the planes of Mussolini who, together with Hitler, was the main support of the rebels. Valencia (1936–1938) and Barcelona (1938–1939) acted as successive capitals of the Republic and were bombed by the fascist CR-32 and Savoia, which attacked from Mallorca. The massive Italian and Nazi military support allowed General Francisco Franco, the leader of the rebels, to proclaim final victory in the war on 1 April 1939.

The depression of the 1930s was relatively moderate in Catalonia during the period from 1930 to 1935. Catalan specialization in the production of consumer manufactured goods such as textiles, food, leather, perfumes, pharmaceutical products, some metal manufactured products and books was favoured in the republican context of rising wages. The situation was worse in Valencia and the Balearics, more dependent on exports of agricultural products to the international market. They suffered especially from the reduction in international trade in goods such as citrus fruit and wine. On the contrary, the shoemaking industry resisted well in the Spanish market.

During the 1936–1939 war, industrial production collapsed in Catalonia, in particular that of textile and chemical products. Pro-Franco regime and conservative authors tended to blame the perverse effects of the revolution and collectivizations for the indisputable decline in production. The truth was that the continued decline in textile and chemical production was especially due to the uninterrupted reduction in trade with Spain occupied by Franco. In the metallurgical industry, where there was more demand due to the war, the industrial collapse was not as important or continuous. The same occurred with the small coal mining industry that existed in Catalonia. In Valencia, industry was stimulated by the demand for military uniforms and footwear, and by the transfer of some factories previously located in the centre. The industry of Mallorca, on Franco's side, also prospered (Abad, 1984; Bricall, 1970, 1979; Catalan, 2012b; De Madariaga, 2008; Deu, 2020; Girona & Navarro, 2009).

The most disruptive aspect for the Catalan Countries as a whole was that there was no recovery from the crisis in the 1940s. The lack of resilience for more than a decade was due to the policies adopted by General Franco's governments, from the time of the Civil War until 1948. The economy of the Catalan Countries did not recover its levels of industrialization and per capita GDP until the mid-1950s (Carreras, 1990a, 1990b, 2019; Catalan, 1995, 2012b; Fabra, 2000; Manera & Parejo, 2012; Palafox, 2001).

As explained in Chapter 7, the policy of autarky in the early Franco regime was completely negative for the development model of the Catalan Countries, an economy oriented during the twentieth century towards trade with Spain and the rest of the world. Franco imitated the policies that had been applied by Fascist Italy and the Third Reich since the 1930s, in a very different economic context, that of reconstruction. He fixed prices and intervened in the distribution of raw materials, giving priority to the assignment to military ministries and the public companies which belonged to Instituto Nacional de Industria (INI), a public holding imitating the Italian IRI. Price controls and central allocation of raw materials led to the emergence of black markets and a shortage of essential inputs for Catalan industry, such as cotton, scrap metal or phosphates. The freezing of electricity prices led to periodic power cuts which, in Catalonia, lasted until 1955. The ban on free trade unions and the establishment of a single Vertical Union for workers contributed to a severe loss of purchasing power (Carreras & Tafunell, 2021; Catalan, 1995, 2010, 2012a, 2012b; Clavera, 1976).

Political parties were also forbidden. Prisons were full with former Republican politicians and members of the class-unions. The Generalitat was supressed. The repression was so hard that his last president, Lluís Companys, was arrested by Nazi agents during his exile in France and delivered to Franco, who, after a military trail was shot in 1940.

Unlike the countries where fascism was defeated during the Second World War, the decline in the income of workers in the Catalan Countries and in the rest of Spain was permanent: real wages lost over 30% of purchasing power between 1939 and 1955. The size of the reduction caused a drop in demand for consumer manufactured goods, such as textiles, footwear and paper, three Catalan, Valencian and Balearic specialities. Furthermore, and despite unbridled inflation, Franco decided to maintain an unchanged fixed exchange rate between 1941 and 1948 (11 pesetas per dollar). This caused a continuous loss of competitiveness of exports from the Catalan Countries. The problem was particularly dramatic for trade in citrus fruit, a strong Valencian specialization (Catalan, 1995, 2010, 2012a, 2012b; Fabra, 2000; Ginés, 2010; Manera, 2002; Manera & Molina, 2022; Manera & Parejo, 2012; Palafox, 2001).

Overall, the Catalan Countries recorded a huge depression during the period from 1929 to 1955, the longest crisis of the twentieth century (Carreras, 1990a, 1990b, 2019; Carreras & Tafunell, 2021; Carreras & Yañez, 1992; Catalan, 1995, 2012b; Catalan & Sánchez, 2013; Fabra, 2000; Ginés, 2010; Palafox, 2001; Prados de la Escosura, 2003, 2017; Prados de la Escosura & Zamagni, 1992). Their per capita GDP was stagnant between these two dates that is for a period of 25 years. The Second World War also curbed the industrialization of the countries which experienced it in their territory. However, despite having registered greater destruction during World War Two than Spain during the Civil War, neither France, nor Italy, nor even Post-Civil war Greece suffered from such a great involution. In around 1950, the three economies mentioned recorded levels of industrial activity greater than those of 1930 (see Table 8.5). On the contrary, Spain declined slightly, from 26 to 25% of the active population employed in industry during the 20 years following 1930. In the Catalan Countries, the fall back was much more severe: from 46% of workers employed in secondary sector to 42% in 1950. There was involution, instead of resilience, during this dramatic episode of the second third of the twentieth century!

In the rest of the Mediterranean, the Second World War again weakened the empires and promoted the diversity of nations and free peoples. Syria and Lebanon became independent in 1946. Israel, as compensation for the most dramatic holocaust in history unleashed by the Third Reich against the Hebrew people, became a new independent state in 1948. Unfortunately, the neighbouring Arabs did not recognize the state of Israel's right to exist and tried to occupy it from the beginning. Nevertheless, diversity again won over standardization (Shapira, 2012; Stein, 2009).

8.16 The Climax of the Second Industrial Revolution

In Spain, the peseta was significantly devalued in that year by adopting a system of (more depreciated) multiple exchange rates. Also in 1948, the government authorized the creation of the automobile company SEAT, after a decade of opposition from Madrid to the different proposals by FIAT, which would transfer its technology. The INI moreover embarked on important investments, such as the Empresa Nacional Hidroeléctrica Ribagorzana, which, in just a few years, increased electricity supply. The price controls of many raw materials and foodstuffs were likewise eliminated in the period from 1949 to 1953 and their rationing was abolished. All of this, added to a new external environment arising from the Korean War and the arrival of American aid, led to a dramatic improvement in the availability of raw materials and energy. Consequently, the Second Industrial Revolution resumed in the Catalan Countries starting from the mid-1950s (Catalan, 1999, 2010).

During the period from 1955 to 1973, the Catalan Countries recorded the highest rates of growth of their history thanks to industrial progress brought about by the culmination of the Second Industrial Revolution. When the problems of lack of foreign exchange reoccurred in 1957, 1959 and 1967, the peseta was again devalued and accelerated growth continued. The growth of this indisputable golden age of economic development was moreover stimulated by the boom in mass tourism. Increased income and motorization in Western Europe were the cause (Carreras, 1990b; Carreras & Tafunell, 2021; Catalan, 1999, 2012b; Manera & Parejo, 2012; Soler, 1990).

Catalonia became consolidated as the leading Spanish industrial centre in the manufacture of passenger cars, motorcycles, consumer electronics, electric machinery, textile machinery, ethylene, artificial fibres, pharmaceutical products, perfumes and detergents and processed plastic products (Carreras, 1990a, 2019; Catalan, 2012b, 2013, 2019; Nadal, 2020; Puig, 2003). It moreover maintained leadership in industries such as the production of several textile and paper specialities, cava or books (Catalan & Gil-Mugarza, 2014; Catalan & Ramon-Muñoz, 2013; Colomé et al., 2022; Llonch, 2007, 2011; Ramon-Muñoz, 2011; Valls, 2011). Valencia consolidated its position as the main region producing footwear, ceramics, toys, wood and furniture (Gomis, 1990; Miranda, 2011; Palafox, 2001; Soler, 1990). The Balearics were second in footwear and outstood as producer of artificial jewellery (Casasnovas, 2006; Manera, 2002; Manera & Molina, 2022). Overall, they were very labour-intensive industries, which marketed their goods in the rest of Spain and Europe and, in some cases, the United States. The three regions also became privileged destinations for European tourists (Segreto et al., 2009).

As a result of the consolidation of this development model, which had significantly losen strength in the previous period, secondary activity in the Catalan Countries went from 42% in 1950 to 49% in 1970 (compare Tables 8.5 and 8.6). On this latter date, the proportion was even much higher than that of France (40% in 1968) and Italy (42% in 1971). It was also considerably higher than that of Spain (37%), Israel (31%, in 1972) and Greece (26% in 1971).

In any case, overall the 1950s, 1960s and early 1970s were a true *golden age* in growth and industrialization in most of the economies of the north Mediterranean (Abramovitz, 1986; Crafts, 1999; Eichengreen, 2007; Fontana, 2011; Freeman & Louçã, 2001; Maddison, 1995; Pollard, 1981; Temin, 2002). This group of countries likewise benefited from the emergence of mass tourism, which covered the Mediterranean coasts with hotels, campsites and other types of accommodation. Exchange with north Europe began to be reoriented from goods towards services (Carreras & Tafunell, 2021; Dritsas, 2014; Freris, 1986; Rowthorn & Wells, 1986; Segreto et al., 2009; Solà et al., 2012; Zamagni, 1999).

Table 8.6 Proportion of active population in the secondary sector (industry and construction) in Mediterranean countries (%)

	1970		*2000*		*2020*
France	40	1968	25	2004	20
Catalan Countries	49		37		23
Italy	42	1971	32		26
Israel	31	1972	23	2003	17
Spain	37		30	2001	20
Greece	26	1971	36		15
Egypt	18	1976	20		28
Turkey	12		23	2004	26
Morocco	29	1982	20	2003	22
Algeria	21	1977	26	2004	31

Source Compiled by the author with Mitchell (2003) and (2007), United Nations (2021) and Spanish Population Censuses

8.17 A New Drive to Mediterranean Diversity

The political diversity of the basin took another decisive step with the independence of the African countries of the Mediterranean. Libya achieved sovereignty in 1951. Morocco and Tunisia recovered their independence in 1956. Also, despite the fact that French imperialism resisted more, unleashed considerable repression and that there was an armed uprising by the National Liberation Front, it could not avoid the proclamation of independence of its oldest colony. Algeria recovered full sovereignty in 1962 (McDougall, 2017).

It was not just, however, the political diversity of the basin that increased, but also its economic diversity. The majority of the countries of the north continued to be mixed economies. Since 1947 and under the Soviet Union's pressure, state socialism was adopted in most of the Balkan countries. The most extreme case was Enver Hoxha's Albania, which adopted a tough model of a centrally planned economy (Fevziu, 2016). More innovative was the self-management socialism experience of Marshal Tito's Yugoslavia (Berend, 1996; Mazower, 2000).

There were also various models in south-east Mediterranean. While Hassan II's Morocco chose capitalism with touches of mixed economy, Nasser's Egypt, the Syria of the Ba'ath Party and Boumedian's Algeria were inspired by the Soviet model (Hansen, 1997; McDougall, 2017). Israel innovated with the kibbutz, but with time openly supported the mixed economy model with an extremely high weight of military public expenditure (Shapira, 2012; Stein, 2009; Zeira, 2021). Unfortunately, the dominant political trend was to one strong man systems: single-party regimes or authoritarian monarchies and republics (Hansen, 1997; Issawi, 1982, 1995; Keyder, 1987; Lugan, 2000; Owen & Pamuk, 1998; Perrault, 1992; Tuquoi, 2001). Israel was the most significant exception.

Something that the north and south of the Mediterranean shared during the period of accelerated growth known as the golden age was the commitment to industrialization as a means of development (Berta, 2001; Carreras, 1990b; Carreras & Tafunell, 2021; Catalan, 1999, 2015; Doria, 1998; Felice, 2015; Freris, 1986; Petri, 2002; Zamagni, 1993, 1999). Turkey, which explicitly adopted import-substitution policies expanded its secondary sector from 7% in 1950 to 12% in 1970. Egypt increased its secondary activity from 12% in 1947 to 18% in 1976. Algeria went from just 6% in 1950 to 21% in 1977. Morocco increased from 9% in 1952 to 29% in 1982. The advance in industrialization meant that per capita income tended to progress faster than before independence. But the performance was better in the countries which did not distort excessively exchange incentives by trying to bring too far the imitation of central planned economies. Therefore, during the golden age, Israel, Turkey, Tunis, Morocco and even Palestine tended to close the gap with the world's leading economy, the United States, as well. It was not the case with Egypt, Syria or Algeria (Maddison, 2007; Pamuk, 2006).

The intense economic development experienced by Spain from 1955 to 1973 was not accompanied by political change. Franco's dictatorship lasted until the general's death in 1975. His successor as head of state, Juan Carlos I of Bourbon (Alfonso XIII's grandson), promoted the transition towards a democracy in the form of a constitutional monarchy.

Catalonia, together with the Basque Country, led the fight against the Franco dictatorship. A huge majority of Catalan parliamentarians elected in the first democratic election of June 1977 supported the three most important demands of the political opposition: freedom, amnesty and statute of autonomy. The Spanish prime minister at the time, the centrist ex-Franco supporter Adolfo Suárez, decided to restore the Generalitat of Catalonia in the figure of its exiled president, the republican Josep Tarradellas. The latter returned to Barcelona in October with mass support. From that moment, Catalonia recovered its autonomous government, the Generalitat of the former Principality being the only institution from the period of the Second Spanish Republic that was recognized by the new constitutional monarchy (Ardit et al., 1980; Sobrequés, 2007).

The 1978 Constitution ratified the decentralization of Spain, opening the door to the creation of new autonomous communities. In the Catalan Countries, the other respective autonomous governments chose the names *Generalitat Valenciana* (the institution of 1418) and *Govern Balear* (created in 1983). Like Catalonia, they had their own statutes and legislative assemblies (Flor, 2017; Serra-Busquets, 2017).

8.18 From Stagflation to Deindustrialization

Like in the 1930s, the recovery of democracy and autonomy coincided with a new period of economic crisis, which began with the multiplication of oil prices during the 1973 Yom Kippur War. Inflation accelerated until 1977 and, to curb it, a monetary adjustment was necessary which led to the bankruptcy of many industrial companies. The crisis lasted until mid-1980s and two forces acted as elements of resilience: the sustained increase in public expenditure on items such as education, healthcare and infrastructures, which had been abnormally low during Franco's dictatorship; and a series of devaluations, which favoured the resilience of foreign exchange, harmed by the differential inflation rate and lack of competitiveness (Carreras & Tafunell, 2021; Catalan, 1999, 2017; Clavera, 1992; Muns, 1986; Prados de la Escosura, 2003, 2017; Roca, 1991; Sobrequés, 2017; Trullén, 1993).

The Catalan Countries shared a high technological dependence in confront of the US and core European countries, similar to others Mediterranean regions. Until the 1970s the majority of the industrial growth had been achieved on the basis of renting foreign licences or imitating foreign processes and products. France and Italy were in a much better position, since for some time they had had companies with a certain leadership in the European context and, as republican democracies, they had made a much greater research, development and innovation effort than the Spanish and Greek dictatorships (Catalan, 1999, 2010; Freris, 1986). Their industrial sector was moreover strengthened by higher levels of competition, as original signatories to the treaties of Paris (1951) and Rome (1957), which contributed to a common market of industrial goods in the framework of the European Economic Community (Eichengreen, 2007; Zamagni, 1993, 1999). Moreover, France and, above all, Italy weree significantly favoured by the postwar undervaluation of their national currencies (Boltho, 1996; Di Nino et al., 2013; Toniolo, 2013).

Greece and Spain (together with Portugal) decided to continue along this path. They succeeded in being accepted in the EEC in 1981 and 1985, respectively. From then on, they took advantage of the beneficial increase in exchange with Europe (Carreras & Tafunell, 2021; Freris, 1986; Prados de la Escosura, 2003, 2017). This was also the case of Italy, where devaluations and the increase in public expenditure had also played a key role in its long-term pattern of development, and which experienced notable resilience of the 1980s (Boltho, 1996; Di Nino et al., 2013; Toniolo, 2013; Zamagni, 1999). Even France had also benefited from significant devaluations during the golden age. During the 1980s, and in a short lapse of time, François Mitterrand's France went from increasing state intervention and resorting to devaluations, to becoming a champion of deregulation of the capital market and the European monetary unification (Boltho, 1996; Guyomarch, 1999).

The conditions to form part of the Monetary Union established in the Maastricht Treaty negotiations were difficult to achieve for Mediterranean countries, especially exchange rate stability in the framework of the European Monetary System. Despite the fact that Italy and Spain had undertaken not to devalue, currencies such as the lira and the peseta could not fulfil their commitments during the 1992 Monetary Storm. They tried to by raising their interest rates and this provoked a new crisis (Eichengreen, 2007).

It was only possible to overcome the new crisis of the economies of the north Mediterranean through several devaluations and the expansion of the EMS fluctuation band. Once again resilience in the Mediterranean was linked to currency depreciation (Catalan, 1999, 2017).

The second half of the 1990s was another period of expansion in the north of the Mediterranean, thanks to the aforementioned exchange-rate corrections and the expansive effects of the dissemination of the innovations of the Third Technological Revolution. Technologies linked to information processing and transmission, such as the Internet and mobile telephony, conceived in the United States, began to spread to the rest of the world. They favoured a new wave of expansion during the last five years of the twentieth century, which also reached the economies of the north Mediterranean (Freeman & Louçã, 2001).

From the 1970s, employment in services grew faster than industry in very industrialized regions of the Mediterranean such as France, the Industrial Triangle of Italy, Israel and the Catalan Countries. This phenomenon, known as deindustrialization, initially arose from the faster pace of growth in labour productivity in manufacturing compared to services (Amatori et al., 1999; Catalan, 2019, 2021; Colli & Rinaldi, 2017; Dei Ottati, 2018; Rowthorn & Wells, 1986; Solà et al., 2012). In the 1980s, relative industrial employment also began to decline in the more backward regions of Italy and Spain (see Table 8.6).

On the contrary, industrial development continued to be strong in a large number of economies of the east and south of the Mediterranean during the last decades of the twentieth century. In Greece, the active population employed in the secondary sector increased from 26 to 36% between 1971 and 2000. In Turkey, the respective progression was from 12 to 23% between 1970 and 2004. In Egypt, the proportion of the active population in industry and construction increased from 18% in 1976 to 20% in 2000. In Algeria, it went from 21% in 1977 to 26% in 2004. On the contrary, Lebanon, which had been a small oasis of development in the Middle East, became engrossed in a tremendous civil war. In addition to the confrontation between Christian, Muslim and secular factions, Syria, Israel and Palestinian volunteers intervened in the conflict. The war lasted from 1975 to 1990. It caused 150,000 deaths and a million people left for exile.

The 1990s were years in which the experiences of state socialism and the planned economy were abandoned. Albania began to decisively and peacefully distance itself from the model from 1992, but with a significant migratory exodus (Berend, 1996; Glenny, 2012; Mazower, 2000).

The end of Yugoslav self-management socialism was more tragic (Berend, 1996; Glenny, 2012; Grmek et al., 1993; Mazower, 2000). Serbian imperialism did not accept the peaceful self-determination of the former republics that coexisted as the state of the South Slavs from 1918. First it made the Yugoslav army attack Slovenia, when it declared its independence after a referendum in which 89% of residents voted in favour. In the same year, 1991, after a more tragic confrontation, Croatia gained independence. Much more bloody were the wars in Bosnia, which declared its independence in the following year. During Bosnia's armed conflicts with Croatia and with the remaining Yugoslavia, the Mediterranean again experienced a tragic attack on its diversity which lasted until 1995. The Muslim Bosnians suffered especially, being massacred by the Serbs. Despite the assassination of over 100,000 people, Serbian imperialism was unable to prevent the independence of Bosnia-Herzegovina. It was also unable to stop that of other territories which subsequently abandoned the failed Yugoslav state: North Macedonia, Montenegro, and even Kosovo. The diversity of the Mediterranean once again triumphed over imperialist unitarianism.

During the nineteenth and most of the twentieth century, the countries of the north and east of the Mediterranean were areas with net emigration. Until the 1950s, the main destination was America, a less populated continent, with a great deal of land and resources which offered the peasants of southern Europe and the Levant a better future. During the golden age after the Second World War, the main migratory flows were redirected towards the industrial heartland of Europe: Germany, northern France Switzerland, Benelux and England. The Italian *Triangolo Industriale* and the Catalan Countries likewise received numerous emigrant workers from the south of their respective peninsulas.

However, from the end of the twentieth and during the twenty-first century the countries of the north of the Mediterranean became net recipients of immigration, receiving growing flows of residents from eastern Europe, Latin America, Asia and Africa. The improvement in the development and level of well-being of the north Mediterranean during the second half of the twentieth century, on the one hand, and the economic divergence recorded in a good part of the above regions, on the other hand, made southern Europe a coveted destination.

The massive arrivals of immigrants, especially in Spain and Greece, led to a dramatic increase in demand for accommodation and fuelled a construction and finance bubble. This property bubble was encouraged by low-interest rates and the arrival of capital from northern Europe, associated with the adoption of the European single currency. Greece and Italy moreover became indebted to continue financing their public sectors. Overall, the Mediterranean economies of the euro area reached dangerous levels of indebtedness, while their manufacturing industries suffered from growing competition from Asian imports (Catalan, 2021).

When China joined the World Trade Organization in 2001, with a highly depreciated exchange rate of the yuan, it flooded the world with manufactured products. The Catalan Countries, like Italy, the rest of Spain and Greece, suffered particularly from Chinese competition. They were specialized in the production of consumer goods such as textiles, footwear, toys, wood, domestic appliances, automobiles and motorcycles, sectors in which China and other Confucian economies such as Japan and South Korea were much more competitive. Consequently, the industrial crisis of the economies of southern Europe began before the 2008 Great Recession broke out in the United States (Arrighi, 2007; Colli & Rinaldi, 2017; Dei Ottati, 2018; Felice, 2015, 2017; Toniolo, 2013).

8.19 The Euro's Crisis

The Mediterranean countries of the euro area did not only lose an increasing amount of competitiveness in relation to the Far East. They also accumulated an increasingly high deficit with the industrial heartland of Europe, especially Germany (Boyer 2013; Eichengreen, 2015; Lapavitsas et al., 2012; Varoufakis, 2011, 2017). In the previous crises, the main instrument that contributed to Mediterranean resilience had been currency depreciation. The euro prevented competitiveness from being improved in relation to the more developed Europe through devaluation (Dornbusch, 1996). Furthermore, the monetary policy of the ECB under Jean Claude Trichet was much more restrictive than that of Ben Bernanke at the Federal Reserve, causing individual debt crises which led to the bailout of Greece, Portugal, Spain and Cyprus. In exchange for refinancing them, the European Commission, the IMF and the ECB demanded very tough adjustments, which caused the collapse of all of the Mediterranean economies of the euro area (Boyer, 2013; Carreras et al., 2018; Catalan, 2021; Eichengreen, 2015; Lapavitsas et al., 2012; Toniolo, 2013; Varoufakis, 2017). Consequently, GDP fell in all these countries, including Italy, and the industrial crisis was further aggravated. The Covid-19 pandemic led to another recession. According to the OECD, in 2020 Italy, Greece and Spain had a real per capita GDP lower than that of 2008.

If we observe the behaviour of the secondary sector in the north of the Mediterranean in Table 8.6, the deindustrialization which had already begun in the twentieth century accelerated acutely in the first 20 years of the 21st. In France, between 2004 and 2020, the secondary activity rate fell by 5 percentage points to 20%. Italy went down by 6 points to 26% between 2001 and 2020. It also declined by 6 points in Israel between 2003 and 2020, to 17%. In Spain, the contraction was of 10 points between 2001 and 2020, to 20%.

Greece, with another tremendous construction bubble and the Troika treatment, declined 21 points from 36% in 2000 to just 15% in 2020, the most dramatic fall. However, in the Catalan Countries, the industrial collapse was also amazing and brutal. Secondary activity fell by a huge 14 points, going from 37% of employees in 2000 to just 23% in 2020!

Neither the Napoleonic invasion nor the depression of the early years of the Franco regime involved such weak resilience of industry in the Catalan Countries. Social discontent was increasing in Catalonia, which transferred between 6 and 10% of GDP to the rest of Spain each year through the tax system and public expenditure (Bosch & Espasa, 2017; Carreras, 2019; Carreras et al., 2018; Catalan, 2017, 2019; Omnium Cultural, 1998; Pons & Tremosa, 2005). A society which, for centuries, had seen how its level of development and well-being tended to progress, now found itself in a situation without resilience or prospects.

The socialist Pasqual Maragall, president of the Generalitat of Catalonia, had a new Statute of Autonomy drafted in order to improve the financing conditions of the regional government, in the aforementioned context of an accelerated increase in population and social welfare needs. Seventy-four per cent of voters endorsed this new Statute in the referendum held in 2006. In the previous election campaign, the future premier of the Spanish government and also socialist, José Luis Rodríguez Zapatero, had guaranteed his full support for the law which was passed in the Catalan parliament. However, when the Statute reached the Madrid parliament it was brutally cut back by the socialist majority in Congress. The breach of this political agreement in a context of a tremendous industrial crisis led to growing discontent in Catalan society and an exceptional increase in the supporters of independence.

In 2014, the president of the Generalitat of Catalonia, Artur Mas, a centre-right politician, organized a consultation which encountered the opposition of Mariano Rajoy, then the conservative premier of the Spanish government. Eighty-four per cent of voters supported Catalonia becoming an independent state. A new referendum was organized in October 2017, with the active opposition of the Spanish government, which forbade it and unsuccessfully attempted to confiscate the ballot boxes. The Spanish police brutally hit some electors who were waiting to vote and confiscated ballot boxes. Despite this, the brutal repression of the Spanish police sent by Rajoy did not prevent 2.3 million Catalans from voting. Ninety per cent of voters endorsed independence. It should be stressed that the attitude of the voters was completely peaceful, while the Spanish police violently repressed the citizens who wanted to vote.

Given the overwhelming result of the referendum, in its session on 27 October 2017 the Catalan parliament proclaimed the establishment of the Catalan Republic as an independent state. The president of the Generalitat, Carles Puigdemont, went into exile a few days later and the members of the government who remained in Catalonia and some leaders of social movements were imprisoned. The Generalitat was intervened by the government of President Mariano Rajoy (Puigdemont, 2018).

In the elections to the Catalan parliament in both December 2017 and February 2021, the pro-independence forces again achieved an absolute majority of parliamentarians and formed a government. The new president invested in 2021, Pere Aragonés, belonged to ERC, the same party as Macià. He succeeded in having some of the political prisoners pardoned by the government of the socialist Pedro Sánchez. However, Spain persistently denied the Catalan people the possibility of freely exercising the right to self-determination.

8.20 Resilient Mediterranean Diversity

Since 1600, Catalonia has openly tried to sever links with the Madrid monarchy at least once each century: 1640, 1705, 1835, 1873, 1931 and 2017. The first revolts (1640 and 1705) were armed uprisings. Fortunately, the more recent ones (1835, 1873, 1931 and 2017) were peaceful rupturist attempts which sought to re-establish the Crown of Aragon (1835) or proclaim the Catalan Republic (1873, 1931 and 2017). At present, this persistent long-term disagreement with the history of Spain has led the majority parties of the Catalan parliament to insistently demand a referendum agreed with Madrid, in order to exercise the right to self-determination, comparable to those agreed by Canada with Québec and the United Kingdom with Scotland. The final result is uncertain since Catalonia, as a plural and diverse Mediterranean society, has been a place of refuge for numerous migratory waves of varied origin and these citizens are not historically linked to Catalan culture. Even so, and despite rhetorical declarations, Spain has shown itself to be intransigent and to prefer repression to agreement.

Valencia, the Balearic Islands and French Roussillon, despite forming part of the same cultural unit, have not had such a conflictive contemporary relationship with Spain or France. In these three territories, there is only minority support for independence. This corroborates the fact that, like in ancient Greece, in the Phoenician world, in the Italy of the Renaissance, the Arab world, contemporary Latin America or the Germany-Austria nexus, cultural unit does not necessarily imply a common political project. It is also obvious that the Catalan Countries are an example of diversity within diversity. Some may feel at ease in their current nation-state and others want to form another. What does not make sense is to want to impose a national identity on those who do not feel it, as Spain is doing with Catalonia.

Books such as the one by Professor Tortella are the intellectual alibi of those who do not want to accept the historical diversity of Catalan economic development that this book has endeavoured to analyze (Tortella, 2018). Our study has tried to demonstrate that Catalonia was formed as a people by the cross-fertilization of Iberian, Greek, Phoenician, Roman, Gothic, Arab-Berber and Frankish cultural heritages. Furthermore, there was a decisive moment in the formation of its identity, this being the leadership achieved in trade with other peoples of the Mediterranean during the Late Mediaeval Commercial Revolution. The counties of North Catalonia, Valencia and Mallorca also participated in this model of development.

The orientation towards foreign trade of late mediaeval Catalonia was associated with the construction of a Mediterranean empire with a strong thalassocratic bias. In this respect, it again resembled the ancient Greeks and Phoenicians. The Crown of Aragon, led by Barcelona, undeniably exercised military imperialism in the late mediaeval Mediterranean, but this was always accompanied by a desire to achieve commercial penetration which, by increasing trade, tended to favour shared development and an improvement in the levels of well-being in the colonized territories of the basin. Here, it was significantly different from the previous and subsequent extractive-type empires, which above all sought to annex land, collect taxes or access deposits of precious metals.

Even the Roman Empire, the most successful of the Mediterranean, was originally an extractive state. However, it would probably not have been able to last for so many centuries if it had not had the capacity, through the boom in exchange, to favour the joint development of the metropolis and the provinces, reaching a true golden age of Mediterranean trade between 149 BC and 164 AD. Furthermore, it would not have been able to persuade the western Mediterranean peoples to gradually abandon their local languages and accept Latin as the main vehicle of first written and then oral communication just through repression.

Arab imperialism was more extractive and unstable, its expansion coinciding with minimum trade in the Mediterranean in the seventh century. This does not mean that there was no development, since the

Arabs innovated in agricultural products and techniques and, through this channel, encouraged conversion to Islam and the dissemination of their language among the conquered populations. They also helped to improve the West's accounting and navigation techniques. However, the fact that Islam forbade the residence by Muslims in the countries of infidels distanced them from the stimuli of European technical and scientific knowledge.

On the contrary, Venice, Genoa, Florence, Marseille and Barcelona had *fonduks* in Muslim countries and could accumulate substantial profit on exchanging spices for manufactured products or slaves. The merchants from these cities combined extractive activities such as piracy with more strictly commercial enterprises, becoming new examples of thalassocratic societies. They were leaders of the Commercial Revolution, which can be considered as an example of the resilience of Mediterranean trade after centuries of crisis.

However, the emergence from the crisis of the ancient world did not imply its restoration; rather, the resilience was associated with a Mediterranean development model with a great deal more political diversity. The long struggle between the Holy Roman Empire and the emerging Italian cities resulted in greater diversity. In Italy, the number of sovereigns was incomparably higher than during the early Roman Empire: kingdoms in Naples and Sicily, republics in Venice and Genoa, and a theocratic state in Rome, among other. While in the times of Augustus there were only four sovereign states or free peoples in the Mediterranean, by 1400 there were that least 30 (Table 8.7).

At the end of the Middle Ages, the Ottomans, an extractive empire, which above all wished to obtain territories and taxes, ended up devouring Byzantium. In the sixteenth century they were at the gates of Vienna and defeated the Mamluks in north Africa. One of the main shows of resistance that they encountered was from the Habsburgs who, strengthened by the huge American treasure of Castile, became paladins in the struggle against the religious and ethnic diversity of the Mediterranean. Despite belonging to this other extractive empire, Catalonia was not at ease with the situation and its parliament repeatedly pronounced against financing the costs of this empire. In the War of the Spanish Succession it was allied with England and Holland, emerging empires which fitted in better with the Catalan thalassocratic vocation than those of Castile and France, which were more clearly extractive.

Table 8.7 The persistence of diversity: sovereign states and peoples of the Mediterranean, first-twenty-first centuries

Year 6	*Year 732*	*Year 1000*	*Year 1400*	*Year 1714*	*Year 1914*	*Year 2020*
Rome	Umayyad	Byzantium	Mamluks	Ottomans	France	France
Lycia	Byzantium	Holy Emp	Ottomans	France	G. Britain	Italy
Thrace	Franks	Fatimids	France	Spain	Austria	Spain
Mauritania	Italy	Cordoba	Aragon	Habsburg	Ottomans	Turkey
	Spoleto	France	Castile	Savoy	Italy	Egypt
	Benevento	Bulgaria	Hungary	Venice	Spain	Algeria
	Croats	Burgundy	Venice	Genoa	Greece	Morocco
	Serbs	Serbia	Genoa	Papal St	Bulgaria	Libya
	Liburnians	Croatia	Milan	Morocco	Cyprus	Syria
	Mauri	Zachlumia	Naples	Tuscany	Albania	Greece
		Venice	Papal St	Modena	Montenegro	Israel
		Sardinia	Florence	Montenegro	Vatican	Palestine
		Zanata	Bosnia	Ragusa	Monaco	Lebanon
		Aleppo	Provence	Malta		Tunisia
		Sicily	Granada	Lucca		Cyprus
		Barcelona	Marinids	Elba		Albania
		Salerno	Zayyanids	G. Britain		Croatia
		Benevento	Hafsids			Slovenia
		Capua	Cyprus			Bosnia-H
		Naples	Athens			Montenegro
		Amalfi	Arta			Malta
		Zirids	Bosnia			Gibraltar
			Rhodes			Monaco
			Epirus			Vatican
			Ragusa			Macedonia
			Cephalonia			Kosovo

(continued)

Table 8.7 (continued)

Year 6	*Year 732*	*Year 1000*	*Year 1400*	*Year 1714*	*Year 1914*	*Year 2020*
			Siena			Serbia
			Lucca			
			Habsburg			
			Piombino			
			Monaco			
			Savona			
			Zeta			
			Mat			
			Croja			
			Lesbos			
			Valona			
			Karaman			
			Ramadanids			
			Sicily			

Sources Own elaboration with Duby, 2001 and *Euratlas Historical Maps, Sovereign States*

The extractive empires governed from Constantinople and Madrid curbed the economic development of their territories of origin while limiting the diversity and potential of the Mediterranean. Catalonia, on the other hand, politically defeated at mid-seventeenth century and, again, at the beginning of the eighteenth century, successfully reoriented its model of development towards Atlantic exchange. The resilience of Catalonia was based on the promotion of trade with the north of Europe and the West Indies, as emphasized by Fontana, Vilar, Torras and Valls, among others (Fontana, 1955, 1988, 2014; Torras, 1984, 2018, 2021; Valls, 2004; Vilar, 1962). The Catalans within the Spanish Empire acted like the Greeks, Armenians and Jews in the Ottoman Empire—as promoters of exchange. Furthermore, like some cities from northern Italy from the end of the 18th and during the nineteenth century, they began to imitate the English and mechanize textile production. Printed calicoes and mechanization of cotton spinning led a new boom in exchange, now with the Spanish market, well studied by Nadal and Sánchez (Nadal, 1975, 1992b; Nadal et al., 2003, 2012; Sánchez, 1989, 2000, 2013).

While, in the eighteenth and nineteenth centuries, the extractive empires of the Sublime Porte and Madrid were already in decline, those of England and France gained strength (Abulafia, 2014; Acemoglou & Robinson, 2012; Allen, 2019; Alvarez del Nogal & Prados de la Escosura, 2007; Carreras & Tafunell, 2021; Fradera, 2018; Marseille, 1984; Pamuk, 1987; Pollard, 1981). Great Britain, the most thalassocratic power, began with small bases, like Gibraltar and Menorca. Revolutionary France was extremely ambitious and much more extractive. Napoleon tried to occupy Egypt, Italy, Spain and ruled on the Ionian islands. He failed, but opened the doors to further British occupations in Malta and the Greek islands. From 1830, the French extractive empire set foot in Algeria, triggering the race for Africa. Although the progressive weakening of the Ottoman Empire favoured the creation of a group of new Balkan states, starting with Greece, in 1914 the political diversity of the Mediterranean was again at a historic valley. The whole of the eastern and southern Mediterranean was in the hands of a few states from the north (Table 8.7).

In terms of economic development, the great majority of the Mediterranean was left on the sidelines of the First Industrial Revolution which, from England, gradually spread around the regions of north-west Europe. The exceptions were Catalonia in Spain, the Genoa-Milan-Turin triangle in Italy, Marseille in France, and, perhaps, Macedonia in the Ottoman empire. The maritime front of these territories had led them all to lead the

Late Mediaeval Commercial Revolution and the First Industrial Revolution of the 1800s. However, the rest of the Mediterranean recorded lower levels of industrialization or even deindustrialization, and, consequently, the gap of well-being in relation to the countries of western Europe in the nineteenth century, in other words divergence, sustainably increased.

On the other hand, the Second Industrial Revolution favoured generalized resilience of the overall economies of the north Mediterranean in the twentieth century (Carreras, 1990b, 2019; Carreras & Tafunell, 2021; Chandler, 1990; Chandler et al., 1997; Freeman & Louçã, 2001; Landes, 1969; Maddison, 1995, 2007; Pollard, 1981; Prados de la Escosura, 2003, 2017; Prados de la Escosura & Zamagni, 1992; Rosés & Wolf, 2019; Zamagni, 1999). The spread of electricity, the combustion engine and the new chemical and pharmaceutical products, encouraged all Mediterranean countries to develop their manufacturing industries and achieve record levels of well-being, in particular during the so-called golden age from 1953 to 1973. Furthermore, during this period they began to benefit from a new model of specialization based on exchange: they became suppliers of tourist services for the workers of north Europe, who likewise benefited from the prosperity which followed the Second World War (Dritsas, 2014; Segreto et al., 2009). Manufacturing industry and tourism formed the foundations of the economic convergence of the north of the Mediterranean with the countries of north-west Europe.

Although the trend in the twentieth century was of improved economic development and generalized resilience in the north of the Mediterranean, the states of the region fought each other in two world wars and several of them experienced authoritarian regimes. The weakening of the empires gave rise to new states which mobilized peoples previously subjected by the colonial powers. Once again, Mediterranean diversity was strengthened in the face of standardizing trends. However, many of the new African and Middle Eastern states suffered from authoritarian tendencies comparable with those experienced by their neighbours in Mediterranean Europe.

The intransigence of Serbian imperialism resulted in a new armed conflict in the Balkans, in an attempt to prevent the peaceful self-determination of the peoples who had formed Yugoslavia until 1991. However, despite a series of avoidable wars and deaths, diversity ended up imposing itself on the desire to subjugate peoples against their will. At the end of the twentieth century, the number of sovereign states in the Mediterranean basin had almost doubled in relation to 1914 (Table 8.7).

The Arab Spring of the twenty-first century did, transitorily, away with some of the authoritarian regimes of the south-east Mediterranean, but did not succeed in strengthening the economic development processes. In some cases, it led to traumatic wars, fuelled by foreign intervention and radical Islamism, as in the cases of Libya and Syria. Indeed, the attempts to transform the authoritarian regimes led to new rounds of economic crisis and armed conflict.

The resilience of the south-east Mediterranean will only be ensured if we are capable of guaranteeing economic development and respect for political diversity. The promotion of industrialization in labour-intensive manufacturing and exchange with the west must make possible to improve levels of well-being and to curb the tendency to emigrate. The exploitation of the abundant solar energy reservoir must favour new patterns of less extractive energy exchange than the traditional hydrocarbon and minerals exports. Moreover, the exchange of tourist services must help development to an extent comparable to that which occurred in the countries of the European Mediterranean in the second half of the twentieth century.

The economies of the north Mediterranean, without completely giving up the traditional exports of manufactured goods and tourist services, must explore new trading patterns with higher added value to tackle competition from the Far East. One important Mediterranean example is the state of Israel which, throughout its contemporary history, has stood out thanks to innovation, from the drip irrigation system to the pen drive and information transmission technologies. Israel is currently the Mediterranean economy which tends to led the generation of patents per capita and a paradigmatic case of long-term resilience, development and diversity (Senor & Singer, 2009).

Diversity is certainly the most important of all the lessons from the crises and transformation of the Mediterranean. The wars in Syria and Libya must end, with respect for all sides. Israel must allow the strengthening of the Palestinian state. The Arab countries must accept the existence of Israel. Morocco must allow the people of Western Sahara to decide on their future in the self-determination referendum that the United Nations General Assembly approved in 1979. Turkey must release the Kurdish militants imprisoned for years and endeavour to find a solution for the Kurdish people radically different to the one applied to the Armenians. Spain must allow Catalonia to freely exercise the right to self-determination. Furthermore, all the peoples on the shores of the Mare Nostrum should try to transform their development model on the basis of using renewable energies and techniques which are less aggressive to their ecosystems. This is the only way to ultimately guarantee the preservation of the diversity of the Great Sea.

References

Abad, V. (1984). *Historia de la naranja, 1781–1939*. CGEFC.

Abramovitz, M. (1986). Catching Up, Forging Ahead, and Falling Behind. *The Journal of Economic History, 46*(2), 385–406.

Abulafia, D. (2011). *The Great Sea*. Penguin.

Abulafia, D. (2014). Thalassocracies. In P. Horden & S. Kinoshita (Eds.), *A Companion to Mediterranean History* (pp. 139–153). Willey Blackwell.

Acemoglu, D., & Robinson, J. (2012). *Why Nations Fail: The Origins of Power, Prosperity, and Poverty*. Crown.

Akurgal, E. (1986). *Civilisations et Sites Antiques de Turquie*. Haset Kitabevi.

Albareda, J., & Esculies, J. (2013). *La guerra de 1714*. Pòrtic.

Allen, R. C. (2019). *The British Industrial Revolution in Global Perspective*. Cambridge University Press.

Alvarez del Nogal, C., & Prados de la Escosura, L. (2007). The Decline of Spain: Conjectural Estimates (1500–1850). *European Review of Economic History, II*, 319–366.

Amatori, F., Colli, A., & Crepas, N. (Eds.). (1999). *Deindustrialization and Reindustrialization in 20th Century Europe*. Franco Angeli.

Anderson, P. (1979). *Passages from Antiquity to Feudalism*. New Left Books.

Aracil, R., & Garcia-Bonafé, M. (1974). Els inicis de la industrialització a Alcoi. *Recerques, 1974*, 23–45.

Ardit, M. (1987). Expulsió dels moriscos i creixement agrari al País Valencià. *Afers, 5–6*, 273–316.

Ardit, M. (2004). *Creixement econòmic i conflicte social: la foia de Llombai entre els segles XIII i XIX*. Afers.

Ardit, M., Balcells, A., & Sales N. (1980). *Història dels Països Catalans. De 1714 a 1975*. EDHASA.

Armenteros, I. (2012). *Cataluña en la era de las navegaciones. La participación catalana en la primera economía atlántica (c. 1470–1550)*. Milenio.

Arrighi, G. (2007). *Adam Smith in Beijing*. Verso.

Asensio, D., & Jornet, R. (2019). Territoris polítics i territoris ètnics a la Catalunya interior i Baix Aragó en època ibèrica. In M. C. Belarte, J. Noguera, R. Plana-Mallart, & J. Sanmartí (Eds.), Urbanization in Iberia and Mediterranean Gaul in the First Millennium BC, *Treballs d'Arqueologia de la Mediterrània Antiga* (Vol. 7, pp. 179–196). ICAC.

Aubet, M. E. (1993). *The Phoenicians and the West: Politics, Colonies and Trade*. Cambridge U.P.

Aubet, M. E., & Sanmartí, E. (1996). La incorporació a les civitlitzacions mediterrànies. In E. Junyent (Ed.), *Història, Societat i Cultura dels Països Catalans. 1. Els temps prehistòrics fins al segle V* (pp. 220–261). Enciclopèdia Catalana.

Bairoch, P. (1985). *De Jéricho à Mexico.* Gallimard.

Bairoch, P., Batou, J., & Chèvre, P. (1988). *La Population des villes européennes, 800–1850.* Droz.

Balañá, P. (2002). *L'Islam a Catalunya (segles VIII–XII).* Rafael Dalmau.

Balcells, A. (2014). *La Mancomunitat de Catalunya, 1914–1925. El primer pas vers l'autogovern des de la desfeta de 1714.* Diputació de Barcelona.

Bang, P. (2008). *The Roman Baazar. A Comparative Study of Trade and Markets in a Tributary Empire.* Cambridge University Press.

Barceló, M., Kirchner, H., & Navarro, C. (1996). *El agua que no duerme. Fundamentos de la arquitectura hidráulica andalusí.* Legado Andalusí.

Batet, C. (2001). Els usos feudals de l'aigua a la Vall del Corb. *Recerques, 43*, 105–128.

Batlle, C. (1988). *L'expansió baixmedieval (segles XIII–XV).* Edicions 62.

Batou, J. (1991). Muhammad-Ali's Egypt, 1808–1848: A Command Economy in the 19th Century? In J. Batou (Ed.), *Between Development and Underdevelopment: The Precoucious Attempts at Industrialization of the Periphery, 1800–1870* (pp. 181–218). Droz.

Beard, M. (2016). *SPQR: A History of Ancient Rome.* Profile.

Beaton, R. (2021). *The Greek Revolution of 1821 and its Global Significance.* AIORA Press.

Belenguer, E. (1976). *València en la crisi del segle XV*. Edicions 62.

Belenguer, E. (1996). Temps d'expansió i temps de crisi. In E. Belenguer & C. Cuadrada (Eds.), *Història. Política, societat i cultura dels Països Catalans. 3. La forja dels Països Catalans. Segles XIII–XV* (pp. 15–74). Enciclopèdia Catalana.

Belenguer, E. (1997). La Primera Germania. In E. Serra & X. Torres (Eds.), *Història. Política, societat i cultura dels Països Catalans. 4. Crisi institucional i canvi social* (pp. 335–337). Enciclopèdia Catalana.

Belenguer, E. (2019). *Los Trastámara.* Pasado y Presente.

Bellwood, P. (2005). *First Farmers: The Origins of Agricultural Societies.* Blackwell.

Beloch, J. (1937–1961). *Bevölkerungsgeschichte Italiens* (3 Vols.). De Gruyter.

Benaul, J. M. (1994). Especialización y adaptación al mercado en la industria textil lanera. In J. Nadal & J. Catalan (Eds.), *La cara oculta de la industrialización española* (pp. 191–223). Alianza.

Benedictow, O. J. (2004). *The Black Death, 1346–1353: The Complete History.* Boydell.

Benvenuti, G. (1989). *Le Reppubliche Marinare. Amalfi, Pisa, Genova, Venezia*. Newton & Compton.
Berend, I. T. (1996). *Central and Eastern Europe, 1944–1993*. Cambridge University Press.
Bernabé, J. M. (1976). Canvis tecnològics i estructures industrials: el calçat a la Vall del Vinalopó. *Recerques, 6*, 159–182.
Bernardi, A. (1970). The Economic Problems of the Roman Empire. In C. M. Cipolla (Ed.), *The Economic Decadence of Empires* (pp. 16–83). Methuen & Co.
Berta, G. (2001). *L'Italia delle fabbriche*. Il Mulino.
Bisson, T. N. (1986). *The Medieval Crown of Aragon: A Short History*. Oxford University Press.
Bisson, T. N. (2009). *The Crisis of the Twelfth Century*. Princeton University Press.
Black, J. (2020). *A Brief History of the Mediterranean*. Robinson.
Bloch, M. (1947). Comment et pourquoi finit l'esclavage antique. *Annales*. 2on année (1), 30–44.
Bloch, M. (1954). *Esquisse d'une histoire monétaire de l'Europe*. Armand Colin.
Bois, G. (2000). *La grande dépression médiévale, XIVe-XVe siècles. Le précédent d'une crise systémique*. Presses Universitaires de France.
Boix, R., & Galetto, V. (2008). Marshallian Industrial Districts in Spain. *Scienze Regionali/Italian Journal of Regional Science, 7*(3), 29–52.
Bolòs, J., & Hurtado, V. (2009). *Atles dels Comtats de Rosselló, Conflent, Vallespir i Fenollet (759–991)*. Rafael Dalmau.
Boltho, A. (1996). Convergence, competitiveness and the exchange rate. In N. Crafts & G. Toniolo (Eds.), *Economic Growth in Europe since 1945* (pp. 107–130). Cambridge University Press.
Bonnassie, P. (1985). Survie et extinction du régime esclavagiste dans l'Occident du haut moyen âge (IVe-Xie s.). *Cahiers de Civilisation Médievale, XXVIII*(4), 307–343.
Bonnassie, P. (1990). *La Catalogne au tournant de l'an mil*. Albin Michel.
Bosch i Gimpera, P. (1932). *Etnologia de la Península Ibèrica*. Alpha.
Bosch, N., & Espasa, M. (2017). Catalan Grievances: Do Fiscal Flows Matter? *Journal of Economic Policy, XXXIII*(3), 345–374.
Boserup, E. (1965). *The Conditions of Agricultural Growth: The Economics of Agrarian Change Under Population Pressure*. Allen & Unwin.
Boyer, R. (2013). The Euro Crisis: Undetected by Conventional Economics, Favoured by Nationally Focused Polity. *Cambridge Journal of Economics, 37*, 533–569.
Braudel, F. (1949). *La Méditerranée et le monde méditarrenéen à l'époque de Philippe II*. Armand Colin.

Brenner, R. (1978). Agrarian Class Structure and Economic Development in Pre-industrial Europe. *Past and Present, 70*, 30–75.
Bricall, J. M. (1970–1979). *Política econòmica de la Generalitat (1936–1939)* (2 Vols.). Edicions 62.
Broussolle, J. (1955). Les impositions municipales de Barcelone de 1328 à 1462. *Estudios de Historia Moderna, 5*, 1–164.
Brown, L. C. (2008). *The Tunisia of Ahmad Bey 1837–1855*. Princeton University Press.
Brunt, P. (1971). *Italian Manpower, 225BC-AD14*. Clarendon.
Bryce, T. (2009). *The Routledge Handbook of the Peoples and Places of Ancient Western Asia*. Routledge.
Buenacasa, C. (2013). La crisi del segle III, preludi de la fi del món antic. *Butlletí de la Societat Catalana d'Estudis Històrics, XXIV*, 191–218.
Cafagna, L. (1989). *Dualismo e sviluppo nella storia d'Italia*. Marsilio.
Campbell, B. (2016). *The Great Transition*. Cambridge University Press.
Camprubí, X. (2021). La importació i exportació de llibres a la Barcelona moderna: un balanç fet a partir del dret de periatge (1693–1699). In J. Dantí (Ed.), *Història connectada entre Catalunya i la Mediterrània (segles XVI–XVIII)* (pp. 153–204). Rafael Dalmau.
Camps, E. (1995). *La formación del mercado de trabajo en la Cataluña del siglo XIX*. Ministerio de Trabajo.
Carande, R. (1949). *Carlos V y sus banqueros*. Sociedad de Estudios y Publicaciones.
Carreras, A. (1985). La producción industrial catalana y vasca, 1844–1935. Elementos para una comparación. In M. González-Portilla, J. Maluquer de Motes, & B. de Riquer (Eds.), *Industrialización y nacionalismo* (pp. 197–209). Universitat Autònoma de Barcelona.
Carreras, A. (1990a). Cataluña, primera región industrial de España. In J. Nadal & A. Carreras (Eds.), *Pautas regionales de la industrialización española (siglos XIX y XX)* (pp. 259–295). Ariel.
Carreras, A. (1990b). *Industrialización española. Estudios de historia cuantitativa*. Espasa Calpe.
Carreras, A. (2019). *L'economia catalana: una visió plurisecular*. Institut d'Estudis Catalans.
Carreras, A., Mas-Colell, A., & Planas, I. (2018). *Turbulències i tribulacions. Els anys de les retallades*. Edicions 62.
Carreras, A., & Tafunell, X. (2021). *Between Empire and Globalisation: An Economic History of Modern Spain*. Palgrave.
Carreras, A., & Yáñez, C. (1992). El puerto en la era industrial: una síntesis histórica. In J. Clavera, A. Carreras, J. M. Delgado, & C. Yáñez (Eds.), *Economía e historia del puerto de Barcelona. Tres esutudios* (pp. 81–157). Civitas.

Casasnovas, M. A. (2006). *Història econòmica de Menorca. La transformació d'una economia insular (1300–2000)*. Moll.
Casey, J. (1979). *The Kingdom of Valencia in the Seventeenth Century*. Cambridge University Press.
Casey, J. (2005). *La terra i els homes. El País Valencià a l'època dels Àustria*. Afers.
Catalan, J. (1995). *La economía española y la Segunda Guerra Mundial*. Ariel.
Catalan, J. (1999). Spain, 1939–1996. In M. S. Schulze (Ed.). *Western Europe. Economic and Social Change since 1945* (pp. 353–371). Longman.
Catalan, J. (2010). Los cuatro franquismos económicos 1939–77: de la involución autárquica a la conquista de las libertades. In S. Cruz & J. Ponce (Eds.), *El mundo del trabajo en la conquista de las libertades* (pp. 55–114). Universidad de Jaén.
Catalan, J. (2012a). *Francoist* Spain under Nazi Economic Hegemony, 1936–1945. In C. Buchheim & M. Boldorf (Eds.), *Europäische Volkswirtschaften unter deutscher Hegemonie 1938–1945* (pp. 229–265). Oldendburg Verlag.
Catalan, J. (2012b). Reculada i clímax de la industrialització, 1936–1975. In J. Nadal, J. M. Benaul, & C. Sudrià (Eds.), *Atles de la industrialització de Catalunya 1750–2010* (pp. 179–293). Vicens Vives.
Catalan, J. (2013). The Barcelona Cluster. Hub Firms and Business Cycles in Spain's Automotive District, 1889–2012. *Automotive History Review, 55*, 12–23.
Catalan, J. (2015). *El Gran Viaje. Sesenta Años de Industria en España, 1955–2015*. Escuela de Organización Industrial.
Catalan, J. (2017). Una economia entre crisi i represa, 1975–2015: del clímax industrial a la tercera revolució tecnològica. In J. Sobrequés (Ed.), *A 40 anys de la mort de Franco (1975–2015)* (pp. 179–210). Centre d'Història Contemporània de Catalunya.
Catalan, J. (2019). La política industrial y la industrialización de Cataluña, 1685–2018. In J. L. García Ruiz (Ed.), *La política industrial en España* (pp. 157–198). Paraninfo.
Catalan, J. (2020). Del crecimiento con crisis a la crisis de crecimiento, 1315–1516. La gran depresión bajomedieval y la economía catalana. *Revista de Historia Industrial, 80*, 13–83.
Catalan, J. (2021). *Mediterranean Capitalism and the Euro, 1999–2019: The Long March to Debt, Depression and Divergence*. Unpublished paper, Universitat de Barcelona.
Catalan, J., & Gil-Mugarza, G. (2014). Les clusters de l'édition de Barcelone et de Madrid et leur cycle de vie depuis 1898. *Entreprises et Territoires, 74*, 53–70.

Catalan, J., & Ramon-Muñoz, R. (2013). Marshall in Iberia. Industrial Districts and Leading Firms in the Creation of Competitive Advantage in Fashion Products. *Enterprise and Society, 14*(2), 327–359.
Catalan, J., & Sánchez, A. (2013). Cinco Cisnes Negros: Grandes depresiones en la industrialización moderna y contemporánea, 1500–2012. In F. Comín & M. Hernández (Eds.), *Crisis económicas en España 1300–2012* (pp. 83–112). Alianza.
Catalan, J., Sudrià, C., & Tirado, D. (2001). Peseta y Protección: el debate historiográfico. In C. Sudrià & D. Tirado (Eds.), *Peseta y protección* (pp. 11–42). Univesitat de Barcelona.
Chandler, A. D. (1990). *Scale and Scope: The Dynamics of Industrial Capitalism*. Belknap Press.
Chandler, A. D., Amatori, F., & Hikino, T. (Eds.). (1997). *Big Business and the Wealth of Nations*. Cambridge University Press.
Chismol, G. (2019). Una aproximació a la conjuntura econòmica de les finances reials de Pere El Cerimoniós a partir de la seua tresoreria. In L. Tudela & P. Cateura (Eds.), *La crisi baixmedieval a la Corona d'Aragó (1350–1450)* (pp. 199–212). Illa.
Cipolla, C. M. (1962). *The Economic History of World Population*. Penguin.
Cipolla, C. M. (1970). The Economic Decline of Italy. In C. M. Cipolla (Ed.), *The Economic Decadence of Empires* (pp. 196–214). Methuen & Co.
Cipolla, C. M. (1975). *Le aventure della lira* (pp. 196–2014). Il Mulino.
Clavera, J. (1976). Industrialització i canvi de cojuntura a la Catalunya de la postguerra. *Recerques, 6*, 205–221.
Clavera, J. (1992). Los últimos treinta años. El significado de la actual plataforma marítima barcelonesa (1961–1990). In J. Clavera, A. Carreras, J. M. Delgado, & C. Yáñez (Eds.), *Economía e historia del puerto de Barcelona. Tres esutudios* (pp. 159–237). Civitas.
Clogg, R. (1992). *A Concise History of Greece*. Cambridge University Press.
Colli, A., & Rinaldi, A. (2017). Istituzioni, política e struttura industriale. In P. di Martino & M. Vasta (Eds.), *Ricchi per caso* (pp. 183–230). Il Mulino.
Colomé, J. (2012). Las consecuencias demográficas de la crisis filoxérica en la región vitícola del Penedés (Cataluña). *Historia Agraria, 57*, 47–77.
Colomé, J., Planas, J., & Soler, R. (Eds.). (2022). *Vinyes, aiguardents i caves. La comercialització de la producció vinícola catalana (segles XVIII–XXI)*. Universitat Rovira i Virgili.
Comas, M. (1997). *Les marques d'àmfora*. IEC-Museu de Badalona.
Comín, F. (1988). *Hacienda y economía en la España contemporánea, 1800–1936*. Instituto de Estudios Fiscales.
Comín, F. (2011). *Historia económica mundial. De los orígenes a la actualidad*. Alianza.

Comín, F. (2013). Apuros, ahogos, arreglos y bancarrotas. Las crisis de la deuda pública, 1504–2012. In F. Comín & M. Hernández (Eds.), *Crisis económicas en España 1200–2012* (pp. 169–201). Alianza.

Coulon, D. (2013). *Barcelona i el gran comerç d'Orient a l'edat mitjana*. Base.

Crafts, N. R. O. (1999). The Great Boom: 1950–1973. In M. S. Schulze (Ed.), *Western Europe. Economic and Social Change since 1945* (pp. 42–62). Longman.

Crosby, A. W. (1986). *Ecological Imperialism: The Biological Expansion of Europe*. Cambridge University Press.

Crowley, R. (2011). *City of Fortune*. Faber and Faber.

Crusafont, M. (1989). *Barcelona i la moneda catalana*. Caixa de Pensions.

Crusafont, M. (1996). *Història de la moneda catalana*. Crítica.

Crusafont, M. (2015). *Història de la moneda de la Corona Catalano-aragonesa medieval*. Societat d'Estudis Numismàtics, IEC.

Cuadrada, C. (2001). *La Mediterrània, cruïlla de mercaders (segles XIII–XV)*. Rafael Dalmau.

Cuadrada, C. (2012). *El llibre de la pesta*. Rafael Dalmau.

Cuevas, J. (2001). Fabricants, comerciants i banquers: la formació de l'empresariat industrial d'Alcoi el segle XIX. *Recerques, 41*, 77–108.

Cuevas, J., & Torró, L. (2002). Pels camins de la "via valenciana": la indústria en el segle de la revolució. *Recerques, 44*, 21–60.

D'Abadal, R. (1969–1970). *Dels Visigots als Catalans* (2 Vols.). Edicions 62.

Dantí, J. (2018). El comerç catalá al Mediterrani als segles XVI i XVII. Continuïtat i articulació del territori. In J. Dantí (Ed.), *Relacions mediterrànies a la Catalunya moderna* (pp. 14–45). Rafael Dalmau.

Dantí, J. (2021). Catalunya i les relacions mediterrànies 1660–1702. In J. Dantí (Ed.), *Història connectada entre Catalunya i la Mediterrània (segles XVI–XVIII)* (pp. 15–52). Rafael Dalmau.

Davies, J. K. (2007). Classical Greece: Production. In W. Scheidel, I. Morris, & R. Saler (Eds.), *The Cambridge Economic History of the Greco-Roman World* (pp. 333–361). Cambridge U.P.

De Madariaga, J. (2008). *Tarradellas y la industria de guerra (1936–1939)*. Milenio.

De Martino, F. (1980). *Storia economica di Roma antica* (2 Vols.). La Nuova Italia.

De Palol, P. (1996). La baixa romanitat i l'etapa visigòtica. In E. Junyent (Ed.), *Història, Societat i Cultura dels Països Catalans. 1. Els temps prehistòrics fins al segle V* (pp. 380–403). Enciclopèdia Catalana.

De Roover, R. (1942). The Comercial Revolution of the Thirteenth Century. *Bulletin of the Business Historical Society, XVI*, 34–39.

De Roover, R. (1962). *The Rise and Decline of the Medici Bank, 1397–1494*. Mass Harvard University Press.

Dei Ottati, G. (2018). Marshallian Industrial Districts in Italy: The End of a Model or the Adaptation to the Global Economy. *Cambridge Journal of Economics, 42*, 259–284.

Del Treppo, M. (1972). *I mercanti catalani e l'espansione della corona d'Aragona nel secolo XV*. Arte Tipografica.

Delgado, J. M. (1995). La indústria naviliera. In B. de Riquer (Ed.), *Història, Política, Societat i Cultura dels Països Catalans. 5. Desfeta política i embranzida econòmica. Segle XVIII* (pp. 298–299). Enciclopèdia Catalana.

Delgado, J. M. (1992). El puerto de Barcelona en la época preindustrial. In J. Clavera, A. Carreras, J. M. Delgado, & C. Yáñez (Eds.), *Economía e historia del puerto de Barcelona. Tres estudios* (pp. 17–79). Civitas.

Depeyrot, G. (1991). *Crises et inflation entre Antiquité et Moyen Âge*. Armand Colin.

Deu, E. (2020). *L'economia de Guerra a Sabadell, 1936–1939*. Abadia de Montserrat.

Di Nino, V., Eichegreen, B., & Sbracia, M. (2013). Tasso di cambio reale, commercio internazionale e crescita. In G. Toniolo (Ed.), *L'Italia e l'economia mondiale* (pp. 487–523). Marsilio.

Diamond, J. (1997). *Guns, Germs and Steel: The Fates of Human Societies*. W. W. Northon.

Diez Minguela, A., Martinez-Galarraga, J., & Tirado Fabregat, D. (2019). *Regional Inequality in Spain: 1860–2015*. Palgrave.

Dini, B. (1995). *Saggi su una economia-mondo. Firenze e Italia fra Mediterraneo ed Europa (secc. XIII–XVI)*. Pacini.

Doria, M. (1998). *L'imprenditoria industriale in Italia dall'unità al "Miracolo economico."* Giappichelli.

Dornbusch, R. (1996). Euro Fantasies. *Foreign Affairs, 75*(5), 110–124.

Dritsas, M. (1999). Monetary Modernisation in Greece: Bimetallism or the Gold Standard (1833–1920). *Journal of European Economic History, 28*, 9–48.

Dritsas, M. (Ed.). (2014). *Tourism and Crisis in Europe XIX–XXI centuries*. Kerkyra.

Duby, G. (2001). *Atlas historique mondiale*. Larousse.

Dufourcq, C. (1969). *L'expansió catalana a la Mediterrània occidental*. Vicens Vives.

Duran, E. (1982). *Les Germanies als Països Catalans*. Curial.

Eichengreen, B. (2007). *The European Economy since 1945. Coordinated Capitalism and Beyond*. Princeton University Press.

Eichengreen, B. (2015). *Hall of Mirrors*. Oxford University Press.

Elliott, J. H. (1963). *The Revolt of Catalans: A Study in the Decline of Spain (1598–1640)*. Cambridge University Press.

Elliott, J. H. (2018). *Scotts and Catalans: Union and Disunion*. Yale University Press.

Epstein, S. R. (1991). Cities, Regions and the Late Medieval Crisis: Sicily and Tuscany Compared. *Past and Present, 130*, 3–50.
Epstein, S. R. (1992). *An Island for Itself: Economic Development and Social Change in Late Medieval Sicily*. Cambridge University Press.
Epstein, S. R. (2000). *Freedom and Growth: The Rise of States and Markets in Europe, 1350–1750*. Routledge.
Espluga, X. (1998). La decadència de l'esclavisme. Un mite historiogràfic que s'esvaeix. *Butlletí de la Societat Catalana d'Estudis Històrics, IX*, 9–22.
Esquilache, F. (2021). Serching for the Origin: A New Interpretation for the Horta of Valencia in the Time of Al-Andalus. In H. Kirchner & F. Sabaté (Eds.). *Agricultural Landscapes of Al-Andalus, and the Aftermath of the Feudal Conquest* (pp. 127–152). Brepols.
Fabra, M. A. (2000). *El País Valencià (1939–1959): autarquia i industrialització*. Universitat de València.
Felice, E. (2015). *Accesa e declino*. Il Mulino.
Felice, E. (2017). Dalla convergenza al declino: l'economia italitana dall'Unità a oggi. In P. di Martino & M. Vasta (Eds.), *Ricchi per caso* (pp. 23–73). Il Mulino.
Feliu, G. (1991). *Precios y salarios en la Cataluña moderna* (2 Vols.). Banco de España.
Feliu, G. (2000). Moneda y Banca en Cataluña en el siglo XV. In A. M. Bernal (Ed.), *Dinero, moneda y crédito en la monarquía hispánica* (pp. 121–131). Marcial Pons.
Feliu, G. (2012). *Història econòmica de Catalunya*. Base.
Feliu, G. (2016a). Finances, Currency and Taxation in the 14th and 15th Centuries. *Catalan Historical Review, 9*, 25–44.
Feliu, G. (2016b). *Els primers llibres de la Taula de Canvi de Barcelona* (2 Vols.). Fundació Noguera.
Felloni, G. (1970). Italy. In C. Wilson & G. Parker (Eds.), *An Introduction to the Sources of European Economic History 1500–1800* (pp. 1–36). Weidenfeld and Nicolson.
Felloni, G., & Laura, G. (2004). *Genoa and the History of Finance: A Series of Firsts?* Genoa.
Fenoaltea, S. (2011). *The Reinterpretation of Italian Economic History*. Cambridge University Press.
Ferrer, J., & Moncunill, N. (2019). Paleohispanic Writing Systems: Classification, Origin and Development. In J. Velaza & A. G. Sinner (Eds.), *Paleohispanic Languages and Epigraphies* (pp. 78–108). Oxford University Press.
Ferrer, L. (1987). *Pagesos, rabassaires i industrials a la Catalunya Central (segles XVIII–XIX)*. Abadia de Montserrat.
Ferrer, L. (2008). La diversitat de l'activitat de l'activitat econòmica a la Catalunya moderna: més enllà de la renda feudal. *Pedralbes, 28*, 725–764.

Ferrer, L. (2021). La transició demogràfica primerenca de Catalunya: natalitat, mortalitat i migracions (segles XVIII i XIX). *Recerques, 78*, 27–96.

Ferrer, L., & Albareda, J. (1995). La fiscalitat. In B. de Riquer (Ed.), *Història, Política, Societat i Cultura dels Països Catalans. Desfeta política i embranzida econòmica. Segle XVIII* (pp. 206–220). Enciclopèdia Catalana, Barcelona.

Fevziu, B. (2016). *Enver Hoxha: The Iron Fist of Albania*. Tauris & Co.

Finley, M. I. (1963). *The Ancient Greeks*. Chatto & Windus.

Finley, M. I. (1970). *Early Greece: The Bronze and Archaic Ages*. Norton.

Finley, M. I. (1973). *The Ancient Economy*. University of California Press.

Flor, V. (2017). L'oportunitat perduda (1975–2015). In J. Sobrequés (Ed.), *A 40 anys de la mort de Franco (1975–2015)* (pp. 115–149). Centre d'Història Contemporània de Catalunya.

Flora, P. (1973). Historical Process of Social Mobilization: Urbanization and Literacy 1850–1965. In S. N. Eisenstadt & S. Rokkan (Eds.). *Building States and Nations*. Sage.

Fontana, J. (1955). Sobre el comercio exterior de Barcelona en la segunda mitad del siglo XVII. Notas para una intrepretación de la coyuntura catalana. *Estudios de Historia Moderna, 5*, 197–220.

Fontana, J. (1971). *La quiebra de la monarquía absoluta, 1814–1820*. Ariel.

Fontana, J. (1988). *La fi de l'Antic Règim i la industrialització 1787–1868*. Edicions 62.

Fontana, J. (2011). *Por el bien del imperio*. Pasado y Presente.

Fontana, J. (2014). *La formació d'una identitat. Una història de Catalunya*. Eumo.

Forcano, M. (2014). *Els jueus catalans*. Angle.

Fradera, J. M. (1987). *Indústria i mercat. Les bases comercials de la industrialització catalana moderna (1814–1845)*. Critica.

Fradera, J. M. (2018). *The Imperial Nation: Citizens and Subjects in the British, French, Spanish, and American Empires*. Princeton University Press.

Freedman, P. H. (1991). *The Origins of Peasant Servitude in Medieval Catalonia*. Cambridge University Press.

Freeman, C., & Louçã, F. (2001). *As Time Goes By*. Oxford University Press.

Freris, A. (1986). *The Greek Economy in the Twentieth Century*. St. Martin's Press.

Furió, A. (2013). La primera gran depresión europea (siglos XIV–XV). In E. Llopis & J. MaluquerJ (Eds.), *España en crisis* (pp. 17–58). Pasado y Presente.

Furió, A. (2017). La gran depressió baixmedieval. Una mirada des dels Països Catalans. *Recerques, 72–73*, 45–103.

Galera, A. (2019). La crisi en el cas del comtat de Cardona segons els indicadors fiscals municipals: evolucio de les imposicions a la vila de Cardona i els seus arrendaments entre 1420 i 1478. In L. Tudela & P. Cateura (Eds.), *La crisi baixmedieval a la Corona d'Aragó (1350–1450* (pp. 143–160). Illa.

Gallant, T. W. (2001). *Modern Greece*. Arnold.
García Carcel, R. (1981). *Las Germanías de Valencia*. Península.
García Espuche, A. (1998). *Un siglo decisivo. Barcelona y Cataluña (1550–1640)*. Alianza.
García Espuche, A. (2005). *Barcelona entre dues guerres: economia i vida quotidiana: 1652–1714*. Eumo.
García Morá, F. (2018). *Atlas de Historia Antigua. Volumen I: El Próximo Oriente Antiguo*. Síntesis.
García-Osés, I. (2018). Barcelona i Florència, dos centres de producció i distribució de ceràmica, segles XVI–XVII. In J. Dantí (Ed.), *Relacions mediterrànies a la Catalunya moderna* (pp. 47–78). Rafael Dalmau.
Garrabou, R. (1975). La crisi agrària espanyola de finals del segle XIX: una etapa del desenvolupament del capitalisme. *Recerques, 5*, 163–216.
Garrabou, R., Pujol, J., & Colomé, J. (1992). La crisi finisecular i la recomposició del món rural a Catalunya. *Recerques, 26*, 107–132.
Gibbon, E. (1776–1788). *The History of the Decline and Fall of the Roman Empire* (6 Vols.). Strahan & Cadell.
Ginés, A. (2010). *La instauració del franquisme al País Valencià*. PUV.
Girona, A., & Navarro, J. (2009). *Fa setanta anys. La Guerra Civil al País Valencià (1936–1939)*. PUV.
Glenny, M. (2012). *The Balkans. Nationalism, War, and the Great Powers, 1804–2011*. Penguin.
Goldthwaite, R. A. (2009). *The Building of Renaissance Florence: An Economic and Social History*. Johns Hopkins University Press.
Göçek, F. (2011). *The Transformation of Modern Turkey: Redefining State and Society from the Ottoman Empire to the Modern Era*. Tauris.
Gomis, J. M. (1990). *Evolució històrica del taulellet*. Diputació de Castelló.
Grau, I. (2021). L'àrea central d'Ibèria. In MAC, *L'enigma iber* (pp. 69–81). Barcelona: Museu d'Arqueologia de Catalunya.
Grau, R., & López, M. (1974). Empresari i capitalista a la manufactura catalana del segle xviii. Introducció a l'estudi de les fabriques d'indianes. *Recerques, 4*, 19–57.
Grmek, M., Gjidara, M., & Simal, N. (1993). *Le nettoyage ethnique. Documents historiques sur un idéologie serbe*. Fayard.
Gutiérrez, M. (1994). Tradición y cambio tecnológico. La industria papelera española, 1750–1936. In J. Nadal & J. Catalan (Eds.), *La cara oculta de la industrialización española* (pp. 341–368). Alianza.
Gutiérrez, M. (1999). *Full a full*. Abadia de Montserrat.
Gutiérrez, M. (2011). Papel de fumar y mercado exterior: la historia de un éxito. Los casos de Capellades y Alcoi, 1800–1936. In J. Catalan, J. A. Miranda, & R. Ramon (Eds.), *Distritos y clusters en la Europa del Sur* (pp. 37–56). LID.

Guyomarch, A. (1999). France. In M. S. Sculze (Ed.), *Western Europe. Economic and Social Change since 1945* (pp. 285–302). Longman.

Hamilton, E. J. (1934). *American Treasure and the Price Revolution in Spain, 1501–1650*. Octagon Books.

Hamilton, E. J. (1949). *War and Prices in Spain, 1651–1800*. Harvard University Press.

Hansen, B. (1997). *Political Economy of Poverty, Equity, and Growth: Egypt and Turkey*. World Bank-Oxford University Press.

Harlaftis, G. (2019). *Creating Global Shipping*. Cambridge University Press.

Harper, K. (2017). *The Fate of Rome*. Princeton University Press.

Hopkins, K. (1980). Taxes and Trade in the Roman Empire (200BC–400AD). *Journal of Roman Studies, 70*, 101–102.

Hudson, M. (2010). Entrepreneurs: From the Near East Takeoff to the Roman Collapse. In D. Landes, J. Mokyr, & W. Baumol (Eds.), *The Invention of Enterprise* (pp. 8–39). Princeton University Press.

Iradiel, P. (1989). L'evolució econòmica (segle XV). In E. Belenguer (Ed.) *De la Conquesta a la Federació Hispànica. Història del País Valencià. Vol. 2* (pp. 267–324). Edicions 62.

Iradiel, P. (2017). *El Mediterráneo medieval y Valencia*. PUV.

Iriarte, U. (2018). La moneda en Atenas durante la tiranía de los Pisistrátidas. *Antesteria, 7*, 103–120.

Issawi, C. (1981). Egypt, Iran and Turkey, 1800–1970. In P. Bairoch & M. Levy Leboier (Eds.), *Disparities in Economic Development since the Industrial Revolution* (pp. 227–252). St. Martin's Press.

Issawi, C. (1982). *An Economic History of the Middle East and North Africa*. Columbia University Press.

Issawi, C. (1995). The Balkan and the Middle East: Economic and Social Development in the Ottoman Successor States. In B. Etemad, J. Batou, & D. Thomas (Eds.), *Pour une histoire économique et sociale international. Mélanges offerts à Paul Bairoch* (pp. 193–203). Editions Passé Présent.

Járrega, R. (2013). Crisi i canvis estructurals a la Hispània oriental entre l'Alt Imperi Romà i l'Antiquitat Tardana. *Butlletí de la Societat Catalana d'Estudis Històrics, XXIV*, 219–266.

Jover, G. (1996). Endeutament, desigualtat econòmica i despossessió pagesa. El cas de la parròquia de Petra, 1443–1524 (Mallorca). *Recerques, 33*, 9–32.

Kamen, H. (1993). *The Phoenix and the Flame: Catalonia under the Counter Reformation*. Yale University Press.

Kay, P. (2014). *Rome's Economic Revolution*. Oxford University Press.

Keyder, Ç. (1987). *State and Class in Turkey*. Verso.

Keyder, Ç. (1991). Creation and Destruction of Forms of Manufacturing: The Ottoman Example. In J. Batou (Ed.), *Between Development and Underdevelopment: The Precoucious Attempts at Industrialization of the Periphery, 1800–1870* (pp. 157–180). Droz.

Kocka, J. (2013). *Geschichte des Kapitalismus*. Beck.

Landes, D. (1958). *Bankers and Pashas: International Finance and Economic Imperialism in Egypt*. Heinemann.

Landes, D. (1969). *The Unbound Prometheus: Technological Change and Industrial Development in Western Europe from 1750 to the Present*. Cambridge University Press.

Landes, D. (1998). *The Wealth and Poverty of Nations: Why Some Are So Rich and Some So Poor*. Norton.

Lapavitsas, C., & Cakiroglu, P. (2019). *Capitalism in the Ottoman Balkans*. Tauris.

Lapavitsas, C., Kaltenbrunner, A., Labrinidis, G., Lindo, D., Meadway, J., & Michell, J. (2012). *Crisis in the Eurozone*. Verso.

Lazuela-Fox, C. (2017). *La forja genètica d'Europa; una nova visió del passat de les poblacions humanes*. Universitat de Barcelona.

Le Goff, J. (2010). *Le Moyen Âge et l'argent*. Perrin.

Le Roy Ladurie, E. (1962). *Histoire du Languedoc*. PUF.

Le Roy Ladurie, E. (1967). *Histoire du climat depuis l'an mil*. Flammarion.

Le Bot, F., & Perrin, C. (Eds.). (2011). *Les chemins de l'industrialisation en Espagne et en France. Les PME et le développement des territoires (XVIIIè–XXIè siècles)*. Peter Lang.

Lewis, B. (1970). Some Reflections on the Decay of the Ottoman Empire. In C. M. Cipolla (Ed.), *The Economic Decadence of Empires* (pp. 215–234). Methuen & Co.

Llibrer, J. A. (2014). *Industria textil y crecimiento regional: la Vall d'Albaida y el Comtat en el siglo XV*. Universitat de València.

Llonch, M. (2007). *Tejiendo en red. La industria del género de punto en Cataluña (1891–1936)*. Publicaciones RHI.

Llonch, M. (2011). La competitividad internacional de los distritos industriales valencianos: un análisis desde la historia económica. In J. Catalan, J. A. Miranda, & R. Ramon (Eds.), *Distritos y clusters en la Europa del Sur* (pp. 185–212). LID.

Lluch, E. (1976). *La via valenciana*. Eliseu Climent.

Lo Cascio, E. (2007). Crescita e declino. L'economia romana in prospettiva storica. *Rivista di Storia Economica, 23*(3), 269–282.

Lo Cascio, E., & Malanima, P. (2005). Cycles and Stability: Italian Population before Demographic Transition (225 BC–AD 1900). *Rivista di Storia Economica, 21*(3), 197–232.

Lopez, R. S. (1976). *The Commercial Revolution of the Middle Ages, 950–1350*. Cambridge University Press.
Lugan, B. (2000). *Histoire du Marroc*. Perrin.
Lyttkens, C. H. (2013). *Economic Analysis of Institutional Change in Ancient Greece: Politics, Taxation and Rational Behaviour*. Routledge.
Maddison, A. (1995). *Monitoring the World Economy 1820–1992*. OECD.
Maddison, A. (2007). *Contours of the World Economy, 1–2030 AD: Essays in Macroeconomic History*. Oxford U.P.
Malanima, P. (2010). The Long Decline of a Leading Economy: GDP in Central and Northern Italy, 1300–1913. *European Review of Economic History, 15*, 169–219.
Malanima, P. (2018). Italy in the Renaissance: A Leading Economy in the European Context, 1350–1550. *Economic History Review, 71*(1), 3–30.
Maluquer de Motes, J. (1987). *Prehistòria i edat antiga fins al segle III*. Edicions 62.
Maluquer de Motes, J. (1994). El índice de la producción industrial de Cataluña. Una nueva estimación (1817–1935). *Revista de Historia Industrial, 5*, 45–71.
Manera, C. (1986). Les relacions comercials entre Mallorca i les colònies americanes (1778–1820). *Recerques, 18*, 187–201.
Manera, C. (Ed.). (2002). *Las islas del calzado. Historia económica del sector en Baleares (1200–2000)*. Lleonard Muntaner.
Manera, C., & Molina, R. (Eds.). (2022). *Industrialització històrica i nova indústria a les Balears (1850–2022)*. Lleonard Muntaner.
Manera, C., & Parejo, A. (2012). El índice de producción industrial de las Islas Baleares, 1850–2007. *Revista de Historia Industrial, 50*, 17–47.
Manning, J. G. (2018). *The Open Sea*. Princeton University Press.
Marfany, J. (2012). *Land, Proto-Industry and Population in Catalonia, c. 1680–1829*. Routledge.
Marseille, J. (1984). *Empire colonial et capitalisme français. Histoire d'un divorce*. Albin Michel.
Martel, P. (2019). *Histoire de l'Occitanie*. Yoran.
Martínez Galárraga, J. (2009). *La producción industrial en el País Valenciano (1861–1920). Tirando del "hilo industrial"*. Milenio.
Martinez Galarraga, J., & Prat, M. (2016). Wages, prices, and technology in early Catalan industrialization. *The Economic History Review, 69*(2), 548–574.
Mauro, F., & Parker, G. (1977). Spain. In C. Wilson & G. Parker (Eds.), *An Introduction to the Sources of European Economic History 1500–1800* (pp. 37–62). Weidenfeld and Nicolson.
Mazower, M. (2000). *The Balkans: A Short History*. Modern Library.
Mazower, M. (2005). *Salonica. City of Ghosts: Christians, Muslims and Jewish, 1450–1950*. Knopf.
Mazower, M. (2021). *The Greek Revolution*. Allen Lane.

McCormick, M. (2001). *Origins of the European Economy*. Press Syndicate of the University of Cambridge.

McCormick, M. (2015). Tracking Mass Death during the Fall of Rome's Empire (I): A First Inventory of Mass Grave. *Journal of Roman Archeology, 28*, 325–357.

McCormick, M. (2016). Tracking Mass Death during the Fall of Rome's Empire (II): A First Inventory of Mass Grave. *Journal of Roman Archeology, 29*, 1004–1007.

McDougall, J. (2017). *A History of Algeria*. Cambridge University Press.

McEvedy, C. (2011). *Cities of the Classical World*. Allen Lane.

McNeill, R., & McNeill, W. M. (2003). *The Human Web: A Bird's-Eye View of World History*. Norton.

Millan, J. (1990). L'economia i la societat valencianes, 1830–1914. Les transformacions d'un capitalisme perifèric. In P. Ruiz Torres (Ed.), *Història del País Valencià. V. Època contemporània* (pp. 29–76). Edicions 62.

Miranda, J. A. (1992). Els orígens del model industrial valencià. Elx, 1850–1930. *Recerques, 25*, 159–173.

Miranda, J. A. (2011). La competitividad internacional de los distritos industriales valencianos: un análisis desde la historia económica. In J. Catalan, J. A. Miranda, & R. Ramon (Eds.), *Distritos y clusters en la Europa del Sur* (pp. 185–211). LID.

Miskimin, H. A. (1975). *The Economy of Early Renaissance Europe, 1300–1460*. Cambridge University Press.

Mitchell, B. R. (2003). *International Historical Statistics. Europe 1750–2000* (6th ed.). Macmillan.

Mitchell, B. R. (2007). *International Historical Statistics: Africa, Asia & Oceania, 1750–2005* (5th ed.). Macmillan.

Molina, X. (2008). Los distritos industriales en la Europa Mediterránea: las diferencias entre Italia y España. *Mediterráneo Económico, 13*, 183–201.

Molina, R., (2003). *Treball intensiu, treballadors polivalents. Treball, salaris i cost de la vida, Mallorca 1860–1936*. Govern Balear.

Mollat du Jourdin, M. (1993). *Europe and the Sea*. Blackwell.

Montanelli, I. (1957). *Storia di Roma*. Longanesi.

Montanelli, I. (1959). *Storia dei Grecci*. Rizzoli.

Morineau, M. (1976). Des métaux précieux americains au XVIIe et XVIIIe siècles et leur influence. *Bulletin de la Société d'Histoire Moderne*, 17–33.

Morys, M. (2016). *Financial Supervision to Fight Fiscal Dominance? The Gold Standard in Greece and South-East Europe Between Economic and Political Objectives and Fiscal Reality, 1841–1939*. Discussion Papers 16/05, Department of Economics, University of York.

Muns, J. (1986). *Historia de las relaciones entre España y el Fondo Monetario Internacional 1958–1982*. Alianza.

Nadal, J. (1971). *La población española* (2nd ed.). Ariel.
Nadal, J. (1975). *El fracaso de la revolución industrial en España, 1814–1913*. Ariel.
Nadal, J. (1985). *Catalunya, la fàbrica d'Espanya: Un segle d'industrialització catalana, 1833–1936*. Ajuntament de Barcelona.
Nadal, J. (1987). El desenvolupament de l'economia valenciana a la segona meitat del segle XIX: una via exclusivament agrària? *Recerques, 19*, 115–132.
Nadal, J. (1992a). *Bautismos, desposorios y entierros*. Ariel.
Nadal, J. (1992b). *Moler, tejer y fundir. Estudios de historia industrial*. Ariel.
Nadal, J. (1994). La transición del zapato manual al zapato "mecánico" en España. In J. Nadal & J. Catalan (Eds.), *La cara oculta de la industrialización española* (pp. 321–339). Alianza.
Nadal, J. (2001). *España en su cénit (1561–1598)*. Crítica.
Nadal, J. (2020). *La Hispano Suiza*. Pasado y Presente.
Nadal, J., Benaul, J. M., & Valdaliso, J. M. (2003). Las industrias de la Primera Revolución Industrial. In J. Nadal (Dir.), *Atlas de la industrialización de España 1750–2000* (pp. 131–175). Fundación BBVA-Crítica.
Nadal, J., Benaul, J. M., & Sudrià, C. (2012). La formació d'una societat industrial, 1833–1935. In J. Nadal, J. M. Benaul, & C. Sudrià (Eds.), *Atles de la industrialització de Catalunya 1750–2010* (pp. 55–177). Vicens Vives.
Nadal i Farreras, J. (1983). Catalunya sota els Àustries. In J. Nadal i Farreras, & P. Wolff (Eds.), *Història de Catalunya* (pp. 355–384). Oikos Tau.
Navarro, G. (1999). *Los orígenes de la sedería valenciana. Siglos XV–XVII*. Ajuntament de València.
Nolla, J. M. (1996). Organització i explotació del territori sota l'Imperi. In E. Junyent (Ed.), *Història, Societat i Cultura dels Països Catalans. 1. Els temps prehistòrics fins al segle V* (pp. 302–315). Enciclopèdia Catalana.
North, D., & Thomas, R. (1973). *The Rise of the Western World*. Cambridge University Press.
Norwich, J. J. (2006). *The Middle Sea: A History of the Mediterranean*. Chatto & Windus.
Omnium Cultural. (1998). *Catalunya i Espanya: una relació fiscal a revisar*. Proa.
Ortí, P. (2000). *Renda i fiscalitat en una ciutat medieval: Barcelona, segles XII–XIV*. CSIC.
Ortí, P. (2018). Noves dades seriades per a noves hipòtesis sobre la crisi baixmedieval a Catalunya. In J. Morelló, P. Ortí, & P. Verdés (Eds.), *Renda feudal i fiscalitat a la Catalunya baixmedieval* (pp. 463–484). CSIC.
Owen, R., & Pamuk, S. (1998). *A History of the Middle East Economies in the Twentieth Century*. Tauris.

Palafox, J. (1987). Exports, Internal Demand, and Economic Growth in Valencia. In N. Sánchez-Albornoz (Ed.), *The Economic Modernization of Spain* (pp. 1830–1930). New York University Press.

Palafox, J. (2001). La tardía industrialización de la economia valenciana. In L. Germán, E. Llopis, J. Maluquer, & S. Zapata (Eds.), *Historia económica regional de España, siglos XIX y XX* (pp. 390–412). Crítica.

Palairet, M. (1997). *The Balkan Economies, c. 1800–1914, Evolution without Development*. Cambridge University Press.

Pamuk, S. (1987). *The Ottoman Empire and European Capitalism, 1820–1913.* Cambridge University Press.

Pamuk, S. (2006). Estimating Economics Growth in the Middle East since 1820. *Journal of Economic History, 66*, 807–828.

Pamuk, S., & Williamson, J. G. (2010). Ottoman Deindustrialization, 1800–1913: Assesing the Magnitude, Impact, and Response. *The Economic History Review, 64*, 159–184.

Pan Montojo, J. (1994). *La bodega del mundo.* Alianza.

Parker, A. J. (1992). *Ancient Shipwrecks of the Mediterranean and the Roman Provinces.* British Archeological Reports.

Parker, G. (2001). *Europe in Crisis: 1598–1648* (2nd ed.). Blackwell.

Pascual, P. (1990). *Agricultura i industrialització a la Catalunya del segle XIX.* Crítica.

Pascual, P. (1999). *Los caminos de la era industrial.* Edicions UB.

Pascual, P. (2015). *El ferrocarril a Catalunya (1848–1935). Una història de la seva explotació* (2 Vols.). Eumo.

Pascual, P., Estrada G., Riba J., Farreras G. (2022). *El rec d'Igualada.* CECI.

Pérez, P. (2017). *Las germanías de Valencia en miniatura y al fresco.* Tirant.

Pérez Picazo, M. T., & Lemeunier, G. (1984). *El proceso de modernización econòmica de la región murciana (siglos XVI–XIX).* ERM.

Perrault, G. (1992). *Notre Ami Le Roi.* Gallimard.

Petri, R. (2002). *Storia economica d'Italia. Dalla Grande guerra al miracolo economico (1918–1963).* Il Mulino.

Pirenne, H. (1973). *Mahomet et Charlemagne.* Presses Universitaires de France.

Pla, L. (2014). *Els Girona. La Gran Burgesia Catalana del Segle XIX.* Fundació Noguera.

Pollard, S. (1981). *Peaceful Conquest: The Industrialization of Europe, 1760–1970.* Oxford University Press.

Pons, J., & Tremosa, R. (2005). *L'espoli fiscal: una asfixia premeditada.* Eliseu Climent.

Postrel, V. (2020). *The Fabrics of Civilization: How Textiles Made the World.* Basic Books.

Prados de la Escosura, L. (2003). *El progreso económico de España (1850–2000).* Fundación BBVA.

Prados de la Escosura, L. (2017). *Spanish Economic Growth, 1850–2017*. Palgrave.

Prados de la Escosura, L., & Zamagni, V. (Eds.). (1992). *El desarrollo económico en la Europa del sur: España e Italia en perspectiva histórica*. Madrid.

Prat, M. (2003). Fabricar i comerciar a mitjan del segle XIX: els casos dels Muntadas i els Batllori. *Recerques, 47–48*, 29–50.

Prevosti, M., & Guitart, J. (Eds.). (2011). *Ager Tarraconensis 2. El poblament/ The Population (PAT 2)*. Institut Català d'Arquelogia Clàssica.

Puig, N. (2003). *Bayer, CEPSA, REPSOL, Puig, Schering y la Seda. Constructores de la química española*. LID.

Puigdemont, C. (2018). *La crisi catalana*. La Campana.

Quinn, J. (2018). *In Search of the Phoenicians*. Princeton University Press.

Ramon-Muñoz, R. (2000). Specialization in the International Market for Olive Oil Before World War II. In S. Pamuk & J. G. Williamson (Eds.), *The Mediterranean Response to Globalization Before 1950* (pp. 159–198). Routledge.

Ramon-Muñoz, R. (2011). La industria catalana del aceite de oliva: exportacioes, localización y empresas, 1861–1921. In J. Catalan, J. A. Miranda, & R. Ramon (Eds.), *Distritos y clusters en la Europa del Sur* (pp. 57–80). LID.

Ramon-Muñoz, R. (2020). The Expansion of Branding in International Marketing: The Case of Olive Oil, 1870s–1930s. *Business History, 62*(1), 98–122.

Raveux, O. (1998). *Marseille, ville des métaux et de la vapeur au XIXe siècle*. CNRS.

Reinhart, C. M., & Rogoff, K. (2009). *This Time Is Different*. Princeton University Press.

Riera, A. (2006). Els orígens de la manufactura tèxtil medieval a la Corona catalanoaragonesa (c. 1150–1298). In R. Narbona (Ed.), *XVIII Congrés d'Història de la Coronad'Aragó* (pp. 821–901). Universitat de València.

Ripollès, P. P. (2012). The Ancient Coinages of the Iberian Peninsula. In W. E. Metcalf (Ed.), *The Oxford Handbook of Greek and Roman Coinages* (pp. 356–374). Cambridge. Cambridge University Press.

Roca, J. (1991). *Pacte social i política de rendes*. Eumo.

Roldan, A. (2017). Costes y beneficios de la no entrada de España al patrón oro (1874–1914): una revisión. *Investigaciones de Historia Económica, 13*, 69–80.

Roldan, A. (2022). The Golden Fetters in the Mediterranean Periphery. How Spain and Italy Overcame Business Cycles Between 1870 and 1913. *Economics, 16*(1), 170–193.

Rostovtzeff, M. (1926). *The Social and Economic History of the Roman Empire*. Clarendon Press.

Rosés, J. R., & Wolf, N. (2019). *The Economic Development of Europe's Regions*. Routledge.

Rowthorn, R., & Wells, J. R. (1986). *De-industrialisation and Foreign Trade: Britain's Decline in a Global Perspective*. Cambridge University Press.
Sales, N. (1989). *Els Segles de la Decadència. Segles XVI–XVII*. Edicons 62.
Salrach, J. M. (1987). *El procés de feudalització (segles III-XII)*. Edicions 62.
Salrach, J. M. (1989). *La pesta negra i els orígens del problema remença*, Anuario de Estudios Medievales, A 24, Barcelona.
Salrach, J. M. (1997). *La formación del campesinado en el Occidente antiguo y medieval*. Síntesis.
Salrach, J. M. (2006). *La formació dels Països Catalans*. UOC.
Salrach, J. M. (2020). Ramon d'Abadal i els orígens històrics de Catalunya. *Butlletí de la Societat Catalana d'Estudis Històrics, XXXI*, 63–78.
Salrach, J. M., & Duran E. (1982). *Història dels Països Catalans. Dels orígens a 1714* (2 Vols.). EDHASA.
Sànchez, A. (1989). L'estructura comercial d'una fàbrica d'indianes barcelonina: Joan Rull i Cia. (1790–1821). *Recerques, 22*, 9–24.
Sánchez, A. (2000). Crisis econòmica y respuesta empresarial. Los inicios del sistema fabril en la industria algodonera catalana 1797–1839. *Revista de Historia Económica, 18*(3), 485–523.
Sánchez, A. (2012). Els orígens de la industrialització, 1750–1832. In J. Nadal, J. M. Benaul, & C. Sudrià (Eds.), *Atles de la industrialització de Catalunya 1750–2010* (pp. 11–53). Vicens Vives.
Sánchez, A. (2013). *Indianes, 1736–1847. Els orígens de la Barcelona industrial*. MUHBA.
Sánchez Martínez, M. (1995). *El naixement de la fiscalitat d'Estat a Catalunya (segles XII–XIV)*. Eumo.
Sánchez Martínez, M. (2003). *Pagar al rei en la Corona de Aragón durante el siglo XIV*. CSIC.
Sanmartí, E. (1996). El plom grec d'Empúries. In E. Junyent (Ed.), *Història, Societat i Cultura dels Països Catalans. 1. Els temps prehistòrics fins al segle V* (pp. 226–227). Enciclopèdia Catalana.
Schevill, F. (1991). *A History of the Balkans*. Dorset Press.
Schönhärl, K. (2021). *European Invesment in Greece in the 19th Century*. Routledge.
Segreto, L., Manera, C., & Pohl, M. (Eds.). (2009). *Europe at the Seaside: The Economic History of Mass Tourism in the Mediterranean*. Berghahn.
Senor, D., & Singer, P. (2009). *Start-Up Nation: The Story of Israel's Economic Miracle*. Twelve.
Serra, E. (1980). El règim feudal català abans i desprès de la sentència arbitral de Guadalupe. *Recerques, 10*, 17–32.
Serra, E. (1986). Per una cronologia i interpretació de la crisi del segle XVII. In R. Garrabou (Ed.), *Terra, treball i propietat* (pp. 214–246). Crítica.

Serra, E. (1991). 1640: Una revolució política. Les implicacions de les institucions. In E. Serra (Ed.), *La revolució catalana de 1640* (pp. 1–65). Crítica.
Serra, E. (2015). *La potencialitat democrática de la Catalunya histórica*. Ajuntament de Barcelona.
Serra-Busquets, S. (2017). Una mirada històrica a les Illes Balears. In J. Sobrequés (Ed.), *A 40 anys de la mort de Franco (1975–2015)* (pp. 151–163). Centre d'Història Contemporània de Catalunya.
Sherratt, S. (2016). *Ensayos sobre economía e ideología en el Mediterráneo antiguo*. Edicions Bellaterra.
Shapira, A. (2012). *Israel: A History*. Brandeis University Press.
Smith, R. S. (1940). *The Spanish Guild Merchant: A History of the Consulado, 1250–1700*. Duke University Press.
Sobrequés, J. (2007). *History of Catalonia*. Base.
Sobrequés, J. (2017). Presentació. In J. Sobrequés (Ed.), *A 40 anys de la mort de Franco (1975–2015)* (pp. 9–12). Centre d'Història Contemporània de Catalunya.
Sobrequés, J., & Sobrequés, S. (1973). *La guerra civil catalana del segle XV* (2 Vols.). Edicions 62.
Solà A. (2004). *Aigua, indústria i fabricants a Manresa (1759–1860)*. Col·legi d'Enginyers.
Solà, J., Sáez, X., & Termes, M. (2012). Entre dues crisis: Desindustrialització i globalització, 1976–2010. In J. Nadal, J. M. Benaul, & C. Sudrià (Eds.), *Atles de la industrialització de Catalunya 1750–2010* (pp. 297–453). Vicens Vives.
Soler, V. (1984). *Guerra i expansió industrial: País Valencià (1914–1923)*. Alfons el Magnànim.
Soler, V. (1990). L'arrencada industrial (1960–1975). In P. Ruiz Torres (Ed.), *Història del País Valencià. V. Època contemporània* (pp. 353–382). Edicions 62.
Soto, R. (2001). Fronteres i colònies medievals: el regne de Mallorques. *Recerques, 43*, 77–104.
Spawforth, T. (2018). *The Story of Greece and Rome*. Yale University Press.
Stein, L. (2009). *The Making of Modern Israel, 1948–1967*. Cambridge University Press.
Sudrià, C. (1987). El dilema energètic en el creixement econòmic català. *Revista Econòmica de Catalunya, 4*, 88–100.
Tarradell, M. (1962). *Les arrels de Catalunya*. Vicens Vives.
Tattara, G. (2003). Paper Money but a Gold Debt: Italy on the Gold Standard. *Explorations in Economic History, 40*(2), 122–142.
Temin, P. (2002). The Golden Age of European growth reconsidered. *European Review of Economic History, 6*, 3–22.

Temin, P. (2017). *The Roman Market Economy*. Princeton University Press.
Termes, J. (1987). *De la Revolució de Setembre a la fi de la Guerra Civil 1868–1936*. Edicions 62.
Thomson, J. (1993). *A Distinctive Industrialization: Cotton in Barcelona, 1728–1832*. Cambridge University Press.
Tilly, C. (1990). *Coercion, Capital and European States A.D. 990–1990*. Basil Blackwell.
Toniolo, G. (2013). La crescita economica italiana, 1861–2011. In G. Toniolo (Ed.), *L'Italia e l'economia mondiale* (pp. 5–51). Marsilio.
Torras, J. (1981). Estructura de la indústria pre-capitalista. La Draperia. *Recerques, 11*, 7–28.
Torras, J. (1984). Especializacion agricola e industria rural en Cataluña en el siglo XVIII. *Revista De Historia Económica, 11*(3), 113–128.
Torras, J. (2018). *Fabricantes sin fàbrica*. Crítica.
Torras, J. (2021). *Canvis i conflictes en el món rural català (segles XVIII–XIX)*. Documenta Universitària.
Torres, X. (2007). *Cavallers i bandolers. Nyerros i cadells a la ciutat i vegueria de Vic (1580–615)*. Eumo.
Torró, L. (2020). Economic Crises and Industrialisation in Southern Europe: The Valencian cloth-Making Town of Alcoi (1600–1800). *Revista de Historia Industrial, 80*, 85–117.
Tortella, G. (1994). Patterns of Economic Retardation and Recovery in South-Western Europe in the Nineteenth and Twentieth Centuries. *Economic History Review, XLVII*, 1–21.
Tortella, G. (2018). *Catalonia in Spain: History and Myth*. Palgrave Macmillan.
Trullén, J. (1993). *Fundamentos económicos de la transición política española. La política de los Acuerdos de la Moncloa*. Ministerio de Trabajo y Seguridad Social.
Tuquoi, J. (2001). *Le dernier roi. Crépuscule d'une dynastie*. Grasset & Frasquelle.
Tunçer, A. C. (2014). *Sovereign debt and international financial control: The Middle East and the Balkans, 1870–1914*. Palgrave Mcmillan.
Turching, P., & Nefedov, S. A. (2009). *Secular Cycles*. Princeton University Press.
Udina, F. (2000). *El nom de Catalunya* (Revised). Rafael Dalmau.
Usher, A. P. (1943). *The Early History of Deposit Banking in Mediterranean Europe*. Harvard University Press.
United Nations. (2021). *Statistical Yearbook*. UN.
Valls, F. (2004). *La Catalunya atlàntica*. Eumo.
Valls, F. (2011). El cava catalán ¿éxito de la empresa o del distrito? In J. Catalan, J. A. Miranda, & R. Ramon (Eds.), *Distritos y clusters en la Europa del Sur* (pp. 101–121). LID.
Van Zanden, J. L. (2009). *The Long Road to the Industrial Revolution*. Leiden.

Varoufakis, Y. (2011). *The Global Minotaur*. Zeed Books.

Varoufakis, Y. (2017). *Adults in the Room*. The Bodley Head.

Verdés, P. (2019). L'evolucio dels ingressos fiscals del municipi de Cervera (1331–1516): Un indicador de la conjuntura economica? In L. Tudela & P. Cateura (Eds.), *La crisi baixmedieval a la Corona d'Aragó (1350–1450)* (pp. 121–141). Illa.

Vernet, J. (1978). *La cultura hispanoárabe en Oriente y Occidente*. Ariel.

Vicens, J. (1958a). *Els Trastàmares. Segle XV*. Vicens Vives.

Vicens, J. (1958b). *Industrials i Polítics (Segle XIX)*. Vicens Vives.

Vicens, J. (with J. Nadal) (1959). *Manual de Historia Económica de España*. Teide.

Vilar, P. (1962). *La Catalogne dans l'Espagne moderne. Recherches sur les fondaments économiques des structures nationales*. SEVPEN.

Vilar, P. (1974a). *Or et monnaie dans l'histoire, 1450–1920*. Flammarion.

Vilar, P. (1974b). The age of Don Quixote. In P. Earle (Ed.), *Essays in European Economic History 1500–1800* (pp. 100–112). Clarendon Press.

Villar, C. (2022). Treballar "a les llaunes": Polítiques de contractació, condicions laborals i gènere a la indústria metal·lúrgica de Barcelona. *Recerques, 80*, 55–82.

Wickham, C. (1984). The other transition: From Ancient World to Feudalism. *Past & Present, 103*, 3–36.

Wickham, C. (2005). *Framing the Early Middle Ages: Europe and the Mediterranean 400–800*. Oxford University Press.

Wickham, C. (2016). *Medieval Europe*. Yale University Press.

Woolmer, M. (2017). *A Short History of the Phoenicians*. Tauris.

Yun, B. (2002). Las raíces del atraso económico español: crisis y decadencia (1590–1714). In F. Comín, M. Hernando, & E. Llopis (Eds.), *Historia económica de España. Siglos X–XX* (pp. 85–119). Crítica.

Zamagni, V. (1993). *Dalla periferia al centro. La seconda rinascita economica dell'Italia, 1861–1990*. Il Mulino.

Zamagni, V. (1999). Italy. In M. S. Schulze (Ed.), *Western Europe. Economic and Social Change since 1945*(pp. 319–335). Longman.

Zeira, J. (2021). *The Israel Economy: A Story of Success and Costs*. Princeton University Press.

Index

J. Catalan Vidal (ed.), *Crises and Transformation in the Mediterranean World*, Palgrave Studies in Economic History,
https://doi.org/10.1007/978-3-031-24502-2

B

E

G

H

J

N

O

P

The manufacturer's authorised representative in the EU is Springer Nature Customer Service Centre GmbH, Europaplatz 3, 69115 Heidelberg, Germany. If you have any concerns regarding our products, please contact ProductSafety@springernature.com

Printed and bound by CPI Group (UK) Ltd, Croydon, CR0 4YY
28/09/2026
02224060-0011